THE SPRING WILL BE OURS

The Spring Will

Be Ours

Lawrence W. Tyree Library
Santa Fe Community College
3000 NW 83rd Street
Gainesville, Florida 32606

Poland and the Poles
from Occupation
to Freedom

Andrzej Paczkowski

Translated by Jane Cave

THE PENNSYLVANIA STATE UNIVERSITY PRESS

UNIVERSITY PARK, PENNSYLVANIA

First published in Poland as *Pół wieku dziejów Polski, 1939–1989.*
Copyright © 1995 by Wydawnictwo Naukowe PWN Sp. z o.o., Warszawa.
Copyright © 1998 by Wydawnictwo Naukowe PWN S.A., Warszawa.
Published by arrangement with Polish Scientific Publishers PWN.

Publication of this translation has been funded by the Adam Mickiewicz Institute—the Polish Literary Fund

©POLAND

It is the policy of The Pennsylvania State University Press to use acid-free paper. Publications on uncoated stock satisfy the minimum requirements of American National Standard for Information Sciences—Permanence of Paper for Printed Library Materials, ANSI Z39.48-1992.

The Pennsylvania State University Press is a member of the Association of American University Presses.

Library of Congress Cataloging-in-Publication Data

Paczkowski, Andrzej, 1938–
Pół wieku dziejów Polski. English
The spring will be ours :
Poland and the Poles from occupation to freedom /
Andrzej Paczkowski ; translated by Jane Cave.
p.   cm.
Includes bibliographical references and index.

ISBN 0-271-02308-2 (cloth : alk. paper)

1. Poland—Politics and government—1945–1980.
2. Poland—Politics and government—1980–1989.
I. Title.

JN6760.P33 P313 2003
943.805-dc22   2003022446

English translation copyright © 2003
THE PENNSYLVANIA STATE UNIVERSITY
All rights reserved

Printed in the United States of America
Published by The Pennsylvania State University Press, University Park, PA 16802-1003

Contents

Preface to the American Edition

WITHOUT MUCH DIFFICULTY one can find countries and nations that managed to stay out of trouble while traversing the twentieth century. Revolutions and social upheavals passed them by, no international armed conflict took place on their territory, civil rights were respected, living conditions improved, and new technologies rapidly made their way into the everyday lives of at least the majority of their citizens. Some of these countries, like New Zealand, were situated far from the epicenter of disturbances and wars; others, like Switzerland, managed to protect themselves from the storms of history even though terrible human tragedies were occurring close by. Such countries and nations are, however, far outnumbered by those that struggled, often constantly, with severe internal conflicts, fought in bloody wars, or were attacked by their neighbors and deprived of their sovereignty.

One of the countries subjected to such painful trials and tribulations was Poland. This in itself is no reason to pay it particular attention, since any attempt to establish a ranking in terms of casualties, to calculate who endured the greatest wrongs or suffered the greatest losses, is without intellectual significance, although it has considerable importance in national mythology and relations between nations. It seems to me that an outside observer will find the history of Poland and the Poles of interest, not because of the casualties, although there were many, but because on several occasions in the twentieth century this relatively small country influenced developments on a broader, global scale. This was the case in 1920, when Poland, newly reborn after more than a century of continuous occupation, fought off an offensive mounted by the Red Army, thus preventing the Bolshevik revolution from spreading to Western Europe. The revolution's destructive potential was thereby reduced, although not destroyed, as the Soviet Union's neighbors were made all too painfully aware in 1939–40. This was the case in 1939, when Poland became the first country to reject Hitler's dictatorship and take up the challenge to wage war against Nazi Germany, at that time the most bloodthirsty country in Europe, thus providing an example of how, if all other means fail, a country must take up arms to defend its independence. This was also the case in 1989, when internal social conflict in Poland set in motion a process that began to transform the system. This had a domino effect across the whole Soviet bloc; attempts to reform real socialism were abandoned, the entire system was discarded, and the Soviet Union itself collapsed.

Of course, I am not trying to argue that Poland was the sole causal factor, but only that its role was significant because it obliged other countries to take action that had far-reaching consequences. In the first case, it caused the Bolshevik revolution to remain confined within the boundaries of a smaller Russian empire, a factor that undoubtedly influenced the shape of the Soviet system. In the second case, it prompted the formation of the anti-Nazi coalition that finally defeated Hitler. In the third case, it showed that it was possible to dismantle the communist system peacefully and thus encouraged its communist neighbors to make similar efforts. The history of Poland is therefore interesting not just in itself but also because the events that took place in the country had an impact on other countries, even those that were much more powerful.

In his book, *The Age of Extremes,* the noted British Marxist historian Eric Hobsbawm introduced the notion of "the short twentieth century." This covers the years 1914–91, in other words the period from the eruption of World War I to the collapse of the Soviet Union. This approach works well in terms of world history, although individual countries may have different chronological boundaries. In the case of Poland, Hobsbawm's boundaries fit fairly well: the outbreak of World War I and its subsequent course were indeed decisive in the rebirth of the Polish state, and the fall of the communist system in Poland preceded the collapse of the Soviet Union by only two years. One could even argue that Poland did not finally bid farewell to communism until the disappearance of the Soviet Union, which after 1989 was the only force capable of reinstalling the system in Poland, just as it had engineered its creation in 1944–45. My ambitions are, however, far more modest than those of the author of *The Age of Extremes.* Not only because this book deals with the history of Poland, and world history appears only in the distant background, but also in the sense that it focuses on the second half of the short twentieth century, from the outbreak of World War II to the fall of communism. I am interested in two main questions: How was a system as universal as communism introduced and made to function in a country that Lenin saw as the implacable foe of the Bolshevik revolution? And:

How did a nation that had for years equated anticommunism and anti-Sovietism with the interests of both itself and the state adapt to this system?

The main part of the book begins with the outbreak of World War II, since it was at that point—or more precisely, on 23 August 1939, when the Soviet Union and the Third Reich signed what became known as the Ribbentrop-Molotov pact—that there began a sequence of events that led to fundamental changes in the affairs of Poland. As a result of Moscow's shifting alliances (initially with Germany, and then, from mid-1940, with Britain and the United States) and the military campaign that ended with the triumphal entry of the Red Army into Berlin, Poland was changed completely. It was not just that the borders had moved or that the Holocaust and the subsequent resettlement of millions had altered the national composition of the population; Poland became part of the Soviet "internal empire" and was forced to adopt the Soviet political system. It would therefore be difficult to understand what happened after the end of the war without taking a look at what happened during the war, with the proviso that I believe the attitudes of the population and the behavior of the Polish political elite, as well as the position of the Soviet Union and the Third Reich in relation to Poland and its inhabitants, to be more important than military events. The main part of the book—which takes the form of a traditional chronological narrative—ends in 1989, when futile attempts to reform the communist system gave way to its total transformation.

This book draws on a substantial body of literature, although not every period has been equally well researched. Not surprisingly, a far greater number of monographs and memoirs have been written and far more documents have been published about the war years and the immediate postwar period than about later years. I have benefited from the work of so many Polish and foreign historians that it would be impossible to mention even the most important publications. I would, however, like to note that the work of Professor Krystyna Kersten (including her book, *The Establishment of Communist Rule in Poland, 1943–48,* which has been published in the United States) has been a major source of intellectual inspiration, as have the numerous conversations and discussions that we have had together. The work of Zbigniew Brzezinski was of special importance in understanding the international context, both his early book, *The Soviet Bloc,* and his more recent work, *The Grand Failure.*

Regardless of the enormous debt I owe to authors on whose work I draw, much of the information—especially concerning the years 1944–45 and 1980–89—comes from my own archival research. This research has largely focused on Polish archives, particularly documents issued by the top decision-making bodies of the communist party. I have also examined documents issued by the security apparatus, by the military authorities, and by the government and its agencies, and I have been able to examine documents collected by some communist party dignitaries. I have also had the opportunity to search the Russian archives. My research on the last ten years of communist rule benefited enormously from two international conferences devoted to the oral history of the period, which I organized together with American colleagues at the National Security Archives in Washington, D.C. These focused, respectively, on the period 1980–82 and 1986–89, and participants included many of the people who played a major role in the events of those years. I have also drawn on what is called "personal knowledge." It so happens that I am more or less the same age as the events described in this book, and there came a point—1956, to be exact—when I became a conscious and direct observer. Of course, such a situation involves the risk of losing one's objectivity, but it also makes it easier to understand attitudes and behavior and, most of all, to develop a feel for the overall climate of a period, which is hard to recreate on the basis of documents alone.

The original Polish edition covered the years 1939–89. For this American edition I have, at the request of the publisher, somewhat expanded the chronological framework. I was persuaded by the argument that, without some information about the prewar period, the non-Polish reader would find it difficult to understand some of the events that took place in later years, I have therefore added a short introduction, "Twenty Years of Independence." Given the interest in the changes that have taken place since the fall of communism, I also agreed to add an account of developments since 1989 and to try to present the legacy of the *ancien regime*. This is the subject of the last section of the book, "Poland After Communism." This edition also contains a new bibliographical appendix. Instead of providing references to Polish-language works inaccessible to the non-Polish reader, the bibliography now covers basic works that have appeared in English, which should be useful to anyone who wants to read further on the subject or compare the argument set out here with another perspective. Since my competence in the English language is somewhat limited, Dr. Padraic Kenney of the University of Colorado at Boulder, a distinguished student of Polish affairs, kindly agreed to compile the bibliography, for which he has my deepest thanks. I have also added an appendix containing short biographical notes about the most important people in the world of Polish politics, most of whom do not feature in American or British encyclopedias.

I have no intention of ignoring the custom—which, to tell the truth, has only recently arrived in Poland—of thanking the people who helped to make this book possible. Thanks are due, first of all, to those who were instrumental in relation to the original edition: Professor Jan Kofman, editor in chief at the PWN publishers in Warsaw, who convinced me that I would "cope" with the subject and urged me to write; Professor Wojciech Roszkowski at the Institute of Political Studies in Warsaw, the author of an overview of recent Polish history that was published before mine, who thus provided me with an additional incentive that was obviously unintentional on his part but nonetheless effective; and Adam Michnik, who twenty-five years ago persuaded me to abandon my research on Polish history during the period 1918–39 and focus instead on communist Poland on the grounds not only that it was an interesting subject but also that one had to counteract the lies of the authoritarian regime; he thereby issued an intellectual, ethical, and political challenge that I could not refuse. The idea of publishing this book in the United States originated with my young colleague Tomasz Tabako in Chicago, but it would not have appeared without the kindly recommendation of several American historians (whose identity I know not) familiar with the Polish original. My greatest thanks go, of course, to my editor, Peter Potter, who was not discouraged by early difficulties in raising the necessary funding, and to my translator, Jane Cave, who has coped splendidly with my sometimes complex style of writing.

Glossary of Abbreviations

AK	Armia Krajowa	Home Army
CKON	Centralny Komitet Organizacji Niepodległościowych	Central Committee of Organizations Fighting for Independence
CRZZ	Centralna Rada Związków Zawodowych	Central Trade Union Council
DiP	Doświadczenia i Przyszłośc	Experience and the Future
KIK	Klub Inteligencji Katolickiej	Club of Catholic Intelligentsia
KKP	Krajowa Komisja Porozumiewawcza	National Coordinating Commission
KOP	Korpus Ochrony Pogranicza	Border Defense Corps
KOR	Komitet Obrony Robotników	Workers' Defense Committee
KPN	Konfederacja Polski Niepodległej	Confederation for an Independent Poland
KPP	Komunistyzczna Partia Polski	Communist Party of Poland
KRN	Krajowa Rada Narodowa	National Council for the Homeland
KRP	Krajowa Reprezentacja Polityczna	Homeland Political Representation
KWK	Kierownictwo Walki Konspiracyjnej	Directorate for Conspiratorial Struggle
MBP	Ministerstwo Bezpieczeństwa Publicznego	Ministry of Public Security
MKS	Międzyzakładowy Komitet Założycielski	Inter-Factory Founding Committee
MO	Milicja Obywatelska	Citizens' Militia
NOWa	Niezależna Oficyjna Wydawnicza	Independent Publishing House
NPR	Narodowa Partia Robotnicza	National Workers' Party
NSZ	Narodowe Siły Zbrojne	National Armed Forces
NZS	Niezależny Związek Studentów	Independent Students' Union
ONR	Obóz Narodowo-Radykalny	National-Radical Camp
OP	Organizacja Polska	Polish Organization
OPW	Obóz Polski Walczącej	Fighting Poland Camp

OPZZ	Ogólnopolskie Porozumienie Związków Zawodowych	All-Poland Trade Union Agreement
ORMO	Ochotnicza Rezerwa Milicji Obywatelskiej	Citizens' Militia Volunteer Reserve
PKPG	Państwowa Komisjia Planowania Gospodarczego	State Economic Planning Commission
PKWN	Polski Komitet Wyzwolenia Narodowego	Polish Committee for National Liberation
POP	Podstawowa Organizacja Partyjna	Primary Party Organization
PPN	Polskie Porozumienie Niepodległościowe	Polish Independence Compact
PPP	Polska Partia Pracy	Polish Labor Party
PPR	Polska Partia Robotnicza	Polish Workers' Party
PPS	Polska Partia Socjalistyczna	Polish Socialist Party
PRON	Patriotyczny Ruch Ocalenia Narodowego	Patriotic Movement for National Rebirth
PS	Polscy Socjaliści	Polish Socialists
PSL	Polskie Stronnictwo Ludowe	Polish Peasant Party
PZPR	Polska Zjednoczona Partia Robotnicza	Polish United Workers' Party
RJN	Rada Jedności Narodowej	Council of National Unity
ROMO	Ruchome Odwody Milicji Obywatelskiej	Citizens' Militia Mobile Units
ROPCiO	Ruch Obrony Praw Człowieka i Obywatela	Movement in Defense of Human and Civil Rights
RSA	Ruch Społeczeństwa Alternatywnego	Movement for a Social Alternative
SB	Służba Bezpieczeństwa	Security Service
SD	Stronnictwo Demokratyczne	Democratic Party
SdRP	Socjaldemokracja Rzeczpospolitej Polskiej	Social Democratic Party of the Republic of Poland
SKS	Studencki Komitet Solidarności	Student Solidarity Committee
SL	Stronnictwo Ludowe	Peasant Party
SLD	Sojuz Lewicy Demokratycznej	Democratic Left Alliance
SN	Stronnictwo Narodowe	National Party
SZP	Służba Zwycięstwu Polski	Polish Victory Service
TKK	Tymczasowa Komisja Koordynacyjna	Interim Coordinating Commission
TKN	Towarzystwo Kursów Naukowych	Society for Academic Courses

UB	Urząd Bezbieczeństwa	Office of Security
WiN	Wolnośc i Niepodległośc	Freedom and Independence Group
WiP	Wolnośc i Pokój	Freedom and Peace
WRN	Wolność-Równośc-Niepodległośc	Freedom-Equality-Independ ence
WRON	Wojskowa Rada Ocalenia Narodowego	Military Council of National Salvation
ZBoWiD	Związek Bojowników o Wolność i Demokrację	Union of Fighters for Freedom and Democracy
ZMP	Związek Młodzieży Polskiej	Union of Polish Youth
ZMS	Związek Młodzieży Socjalistycznej	Union of Socialist Youth
ZMW	Związek Młodzieży Wiejskiej	Union of Rural Youth
ZOB	Żydowska Organizacja Bojowa	Jewish Fighting Organization
ZOMO	Zmechanizowane Odwody Milicji Obywatelskiej	Citizens' Militia Mechanized Units
ZSL	Zjednoczone Stronnictwo Ludowe	United Peasants' Party
ZSP	Związek Studentów Polskich	Union of Polish Students
ZWZ	Związek Walki Zbrojnej	Union for Armed Struggle

Twenty Years of Independence

THE MAIN POLITICAL FORCES

For two hundred years, until the mid-seventeenth century, the Poland that dominated the eastern part of Europe was one of the powers of the Continent. The country suffered, however, from numerous internal weaknesses; modernization lagged behind, and a succession of wars had inflicted considerable damage. During the eighteenth century three neighboring states—Russia, Prussia, and Austria—developed into absolutist powers that exerted constant pressure on Poland. In 1795 they finished dividing the country between them, and Poland disappeared from the world map. This happened despite feverish efforts to reform the state (which included the adoption of the Constitution of 3 May 1791, the first constitution passed in Europe) and despite the armed struggle of 1794 led by Tadeusz Kościuszko, known for his role in the American Revolution. The Poles subsequently made numerous attempts to regain their independence, and each time they were defeated. They lost even during the years 1807–12, when they tried to take advantage of Napoleon's expansionist policies, becoming his most loyal ally, and during the years 1830–31 and 1863–64, when they waged a lonely insurgent struggle against Russia, which had seized the largest part of the Polish state. They also lost when they took action in tandem with revolutionary movements in Prussia and Austria (1848) and in Russia (1905).

From the end of the eighteenth century the problem of how "to fight one's way to independence" dominated Polish political thinking and shaped the main ideological divisions. It became one of the basic components of Polish culture and helped to create a national mythology that glorified struggle, self-sacrifice, and death in the cause of the homeland. This way of viewing the world and Poland's fate was reinforced by the romantic era, which prized the dramatic act of the lonely individual. For some romantics, Poland itself came to personify such an individual; it was seen as "the Christ of Nations," from whose suffering a new and better world would arise, one in which all nations would be equal and free. There was no shortage of alternative visions. Some people thought that uprisings brought nothing but

1

BORDERS OF THE THREE PARTITIONING POWERS AND THE NEW POLAND

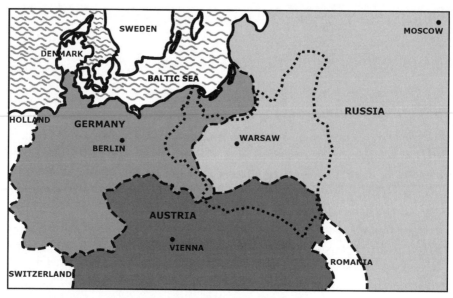

▬ ▬ ▬ ▪ **BORDERS OF GERMANY, AUSTRIA, AND RUSSIA, CA. 1914**

▪▪▪▪▪▪▪ **BORDERS OF THE NEW POLAND, CA. 1921**

In 1795, Poland disappeared from the world map as Russia, Germany, and Austria divided the country among them. This map shows the boundaries of the partitioning countries as of 1914 and the new Poland that emerged after World War I.

bloodshed and that Poland's situation worsened after each successive defeat. They argued that the nation's survival would be better served by cultivating religious belief and the mother tongue, and, in particular, by modernizing society and ensuring economic progress. This tendency became especially strong after the defeat of the 1863 uprising and had ties to European positivism and scientism. Others thought that Poland should merge into the monarchies that had divided the country and, in exchange for supporting them, obtain partial autonomy. There were also some people who argued that only a worldwide revolution of the dispossessed would bring general liberation. But many Poles, of course, focused on their immediate concerns and did not think in terms of the nation. Poland remained a society based on estates, and only a narrow stratum drawn from the *szlachta*—nobility, landowners, and gentry—and the intelligentsia was active in public life. The majority of the population paid little attention to political questions, and the partitioning powers even managed on several occasions to turn the Polish peasantry against the insurgents, the great majority of whom were members of the *szlachta* or intelligentsia of *szlachta* origins.

The situation began to change during the last decades of the nineteenth century, when, in Poland as elsewhere, modern political tendencies and parties began to form, and rapid economic and social change drew an increasing number of people into public life. While Poland was in many ways similar to other countries, the Polish political landscape also had its own specific characteristics. One major difference was the fact that Poland was divided into three regions subordinate to three different countries, each region differing from the others in terms of political and economic conditions. The opportunities for political activity in liberal Prussia, which was undergoing rapid modernization but was also strongly anti-Polish and xenophobic, were different from those in backward Austria, whose rulers were engaged in a process of liberalization and aiming to create a multination state. The situation was different again in authoritarian and centralized Russia, which was without a parliament or political parties until 1905. As a result, political organizations were fragmented; for example, three separate socialist parties existed, one of which—in Russian Poland—was illegal. In Austrian Poland there emerged a relatively strong peasant party that for many years had no equivalent in the rest of Poland. The nationalist party had a single clandestine central body but in each part of the country it was active under a different name and pursued slightly different policies. Each part of the country had a different currency, different banks, a different level of economic development, a different structure of property ownership, different relations between the various ethnic groups, and—in Russian Poland—even different weights and measures, including a different railroad gauge. Also important was the fact that in all three cases Polish territory lay on the periphery, forming a border area in which the central authorities were more concerned with constructing fortifications than with developing industry.

In each part of Poland, however, the key issue was the same: the lack of an independent state. The question of whether to attempt to revive the Polish state and, if so, how this could best be achieved was the subject of bitter disputes of a kind unknown in democratic republics such as France, in democratic and liberal monarchies such as Great Britain, or in constitutional monarchies such as Italy. From this point of view Polish political groups at the beginning of the twentieth century and during World War I can in general terms (which inevitably involve simplification) be divided into the independence movement, the nationalist movement, and a number of lesser ideological-political groups.

Members of the independence movement believed that it would be impossible to create a sovereign state without the use of armed force and that the conflicts emerging among the partitioning powers—between Russia on one side and Germany and Austria on the other—would result in a war that would create conditions for a national uprising. Poland's most famous romantic poet, Adam Mickiewicz, had already prayed for "a war of the peoples" that would create an opportunity for Poland to regain independence. This political tendency was led by Józef Piłsudski, one of the founders of the Polish Socialist Party (PPS), which began functioning in Russian Poland in 1892 after being established by émigrés in Paris. Although Piłsudski was a socialist, he believed that regaining independence was more important than social revolution. For the PPS, the main enemy was tsarist Russia, and the party carried out its first broad-based actions (including terrorist attacks) during the revolution in Russia, which spread to what had formerly been Polish territory. Piłsudski tried to turn the revolution into a national uprising in which workers were supposed to play the major role. The failure of the revolution in Russia crushed all hope that such a struggle could bring success, but it did not mean that the notion of military action was abandoned. The independence movement included socialist parties in all three parts of the country, as well as smaller left-wing and centrist groupings that had emerged out of the nationalist party. It was active in all parts of Poland, albeit to varying degrees—weakest in Prussia, strongest in Austria.

The one country in which Poles enjoyed genuine autonomy and had significant political influence was Austria, so it was only there that preparations could be made to create a Polish army. Piłsudski thus offered to assist the Austrian general staff in the approaching war with Russia. His offer was accepted. Some politicians associated with Piłsudski, especially the conservatives, thought the best possible solution would be to transform the dual Austro-Hungarian monarchy into a triple, Austro-Hungarian-Polish, monarchy and that the best opportunity for such an outcome would be provided if the Polish territory seized by Russia could be annexed to Austrian Poland.

As soon as World War I broke out, Piłsudski and the Austrians formed the Polish Legions, a force that was attached to the Austrian Army. They took part in the fighting along the eastern front but their attempt to instigate a mass uprising in Russian Poland during the early days of the war was unsuccessful. Most of the population remained passive, partly out of fear of taking a personal risk and partly because of the strong influence of the nationalist movement, which advocated a completely different approach. The Legions numbered roughly twenty-five thousand volunteer soldiers, and were thus of little military significance when viewed against the overall scale of what became known as the Great War. They did, though, possess their own uniforms, banners, and decorations, and commands were issued in Polish. They also created a strong esprit de corps, as the legionaries had a strong sense of mission and saw themselves as a kind of collective romantic hero, whose self-sacrifice would bring Poland's dreamed-for independence. Their very name evoked the legions that the Poles had established to fight alongside Napoleon's army. As their leader, Józef Piłsudski became the center of carefully nurtured cult, a fact that acquired tremendous importance at a later date. While Germany and Austria were happy to exploit the anti-Russian sentiments harbored by many Poles, they had no intention of carrying out Piłsudski's plan or the plan of those who advocated the creation of an independent Polish state after Russia had been driven out of central Poland in 1915. Local self-government was introduced, and it was now permissible to speak Polish in schools and administrative offices, but Berlin and Vienna were in no hurry to merge Polish territory into a single unit or to grant the Poles sovereignty over even a tiny corner of it. They were, of course, lavish with their promises, and they even established some ersatz institutions of state power: first, a Provisional Council of State, then a Regency Council and, beneath it, a government with extremely limited powers. In the summer of 1917, after the tsar had been overthrown and the United States had entered the war, thus tipping the balance in favor of the Entente, Piłsudski renounced all further loyalty to Austria and Germany. He was arrested and imprisoned in the fortress at Magdeburg, near Berlin, and on his orders the Polish Military Organization (POW) was formed, an illegal organization that was intended to be a continuation of the now disbanded Legions. Piłsudski thereby demonstrated that his previous alliance with Austria and Germany had been purely tactical and that he remained determined to fight for Polish independence.

The second major political tendency to emerge at the end of the nineteenth century (in 1894, to be exact) was the nationalist movement, which also advocated independence for Poland but believed all attempts to confront the partitioning powers with armed force were doomed to failure. Supporters of this tendency argued, instead, that the struggle for independence required that national consciousness be instilled and steadily reinforced among the peasantry, petite bourgeoisie, and working class. They advanced the notion of national solidarity and attached great significance to Catholicism as a defining characteristic of Polish national identity in opposition to the Protestantism of Prussia and the Orthodoxy of Russia. They opposed any cooperation with revolutionary movements in the partitioning countries, both because they were generally opposed to revolution based on class struggle and because they believed that such a revolution conflicted with Poland's national interest. The nationalist movement had deep roots in Prussian Poland, where the economic dynamism and nationalism of the Germans were especially evident, but the German *Drang nach Osten* was feared by Poles in all parts of the country. The nationalist movement was, then, largely anti-German, which naturally tempered its anti-Russian elements. The movement was also influential in Russian Poland, although until 1905 it could not function there openly. Eventually, the nationalist movement came to regard the Jews, too, as an enemy, and its use of anti-Semitic propaganda increased its popularity among the petite bourgeoisie, who saw the Jews as their chief competitors. Because of its proclaimed solidarism— both social and national—and its attachment to religion, the nationalist movement attracted many conservatively inclined landowners, Catholic priests, and members of the tiny Polish bourgeoisie. It possessed a clandestine central organization, known as the National League, separate political parties in each region of the country, and an influential youth organization (Zet). The parties founded by the League referred to themselves as national democrats, and they became known collectively as the "Endecja." Also close to the League were the Christian-democratic parties and trade unions that were emerging at this time. The League was led by Roman Dmowski, more of an ideologue and political thinker than a charismatic leader. The nationalist movement was more cohesive than the independence movement, which was essentially a loose conglomeration of different groups and parties.

Events in Russia during 1905–7 had a decisive influence on the final shape of the nationalist movement. The Endecja adamantly opposed the PPS's attempt to transform the revolution into a national uprising, and the dispute was such that armed gangs from the two sides clashed with each other. Dmowski believed that Russia's evolution toward liberalism would make it possible to broaden the autonomy of Polish territory and that Russia's economic and technological backwardness meant that, in the long run, it posed less of a threat than Germany, which was rapidly modernizing. He thus advocated Polish participation in the newly created quasi-democratic institutions, such as the parliament (Duma). In the emerging conflict between Germany and Austria on the one hand and the Triple Entente of Russia, France, and England on the other, Dmowski supported Russia and hence the Entente. When the nationalists adopted a pro-Russian line, abandoning their slogans calling for independence in favor of a program calling for autonomy within a tsarist state, several groups and organizations—including Zet and the National Workers' Union—defected to the independence movement. Although Endecja influence was thereby weakened among the intelligentsia, which was attached to the romantic myth of armed struggle for independence, it remained strong among the social strata that provided the movement with most of its support.

After the outbreak of war Dmowski increased his efforts to persuade Russia to declare that one of its goals was to unify Polish territory, and he assumed that Russia's democratic partners in the Entente would accelerate the liberalization of the tsarist state. When Russian forces were beaten back from central Poland, most of the Endecja leaders left for Russia, while Dmowski went to Western Europe to lobby on behalf of Poland. After the overthrow of the tsar and the creation of the democratic Russian Republic, he intensified his efforts, with considerable success: in June 1917 a Polish army was formed in France; the Polish National Committee, set up by the Endecja, established contacts with a number of political leaders and diplomats, and in the fall of 1917 was recognized by the Entente as Poland's official representative. The committee's representative in the United States was the famous pianist, Ignacy Paderewski, who had some influence in the White House. One point of the peace program that President Woodrow Wilson presented to Congress on 8 January 1918 concerned the establishment of an independent Polish state.

While the nationalist and independence movements were forming, other political groupings also emerged and entered into various kinds of relationships with the two main tendencies. Political parties representing conservative landowning interests were influential in all the areas where large landed estates were to be found. Such parties were especially influential in Austria, where Polish conservatives frequently held high government office. They had little impact, however, on the broader society. The situation was quite different in the case of the peasant parties, which gradually expanded their influence in rural areas—and peasants made up the majority of the population—but had no influence among the elites. The strongest peasant party, known as the Polish Peasant Party (PSL), emerged in Austrian Poland as early as 1895. There were also some tiny liberal-democratic parties, supported by the intelligentsia, and some Christian-democratic parties, which were heavily influenced by the clergy. Associations and organizations of the kind we refer to as civil society developed rapidly—cooperatives, business and professional associations, learned societies, savings and loan associations, sports and tourism clubs.

Given that this book is concerned with the fragment of Polish history lasting from 1939 to 1989, we must make separate mention of the revolutionary movement based on orthodox Marxism, since the party that emerged from that movement became the dominant political force in Poland after World War II. Its adherents, initially few in number, believed that Poland's independence was a secondary issue and that the struggle for independence simply served to mask the class contradictions that were the real motive force of history. In 1893 there emerged a party calling itself the Social Democracy of the Kingdom of Poland and Lithuania (SDKPiL), which functioned in Russian Poland and cooperated closely with the Bolsheviks, Lenin's faction of the Russian Social-Democratic Party. Some of its ideologues, such as Rosa Luxemburg, not only denied the need to struggle for Poland's independence but also argued that, given worldwide tendencies toward economic integration, the notion of national sovereignty was a pernicious utopia. During the years 1905–7, when the SDKPiL became a significant political force, some PPS members also came to believe that priority should be given to social (proletarian) revolution; they opposed Piłsudski's policies and created a separate party called the PPS—Left (PPS—Lewica). After the collapse of the revolution both these parties lost influence and gradually drew closer together, a process that was particularly evident in Russia in 1917, when they both voiced support for the Bolsheviks. Several SDKPiL members played a major role in the October Revolution, among them Feliks Dzerzhinsky (Dzierżyński), who came from a similar social background (*szlachta*) and the same region of Poland as Piłsudski. In 1918 these two parties held a joint conference in Warsaw, where they merged to form the Polish Communist Party (KPP).

All in all, from the 1890s to the end of World War I, despite the fact that no Polish state existed, a political scene emerged that was similar to those existing in the democratic or liberal countries of Europe: from advocates of worldwide political revolution (the KPP) to left-wing groups (such as the

PPS) and centrist parties (the PSL), to right-wing (Endecja) and conservative tendencies. There was a large political elite and some well-known leaders. From this point of view, Poland was prepared for independence, but it lacked the military strength to overcome the partitioning powers. The appropriate moment finally came in the fall of 1918, when, as a result of their defeat in war, first Austro-Hungary and then Germany found itself engulfed by revolution. In Russia civil war had already been raging for a year. Something like a geopolitical vacuum was created. Poland now had an exceptional opportunity, but to exploit it fully the Poles would have to fight for several years to obtain advantageous borders. And they also had to wage an internal struggle over the nature of the state and who would lead it.

THE STRUGGLE OVER TERRITORY

The armed struggle over the shape of Poland's frontiers lasted until 1921. In relative terms, the borders with Lithuania and Czechoslovakia were established with the least military effort, but in both cases one of the two sides was dissatisfied with the outcome. Lithuania objected to Vilnius being included in Polish territory, while Poland laid claim to the part of Silesia around Cieszyn (the so-called Trans-Olza region) that was now part of Czechoslovakia. There was no armed confrontation with Austria, which collapsed completely in the course of just a few weeks in the fall of 1918. Nor was there a problem with the German forces that had occupied the territory of Russian Poland—they agreed to withdraw without fighting. But in December 1918 an anti-German uprising exploded in Poznań, leading to a six-month struggle over the western frontier and access to the Baltic. Polish units quickly occupied most of the area of Prussian Poland inhabited by Poles, but the situation was not finally settled until the Polish-German border was determined at the Versailles Peace Conference (attended by President Wilson). The decisions of the great powers were especially important in the case of access to the Baltic, but they did not satisfy the Poles, since Gdańsk, the largest port in the region, was designated a Free City under the direct administration of the newly created League of Nations and thus did not form part of Poland's sovereign territory. The Germans accepted this situation only because they had no choice. Another bone of contention was the fact that Polish territory (what the Germans called the Polish corridor) separated East Prussia from the rest of Germany. In an effort to ensure that the economically valuable region of Silesia was incorporated into Poland, the Poles organized three uprisings—in 1919, 1920, and 1921. Finally, in

9

1922, the Entente agreed to divide the region in a manner that left roughly half a million Poles on German territory and a quarter of a million Germans in Poland.

In chronological terms, the first war was not with the Germans but with the Ukrainians, who made up the majority of the population in Eastern Galicia, which formed part of Austrian Poland. The Polish-Ukrainian conflict reached back hundreds of years. It was not only an ethnic and religious conflict but also a social one, as almost all the landowners were Polish and the great majority of the peasants were Ukrainian. Most Poles favored the rebirth of the state within its pre-partition borders, which extended far to the east. Piłsudski dreamed of drawing all the nations situated between Germany and Russia into an enormous federation in which Poland, by virtue of its size, would be the leader, while Dmowski wanted to see a unitary Polish state, in which other Slav peoples would become assimilated. The Ukrainians, however, had been going through a national revival since the mid-nineteenth century and believed that the independent Ukrainian state then being formed should include all the land currently inhabited by them, including the areas that had belonged to Kievan Rus only until the twelfth century. Conflict was unavoidable. It erupted in November 1918, when Austria collapsed and the Ukrainians attempted to make Lvov—a city in which the majority of inhabitants were Poles—the capital of the Western Ukrainian People's Republic. The fighting lasted more than six months and ended in complete victory for the Polish forces. This bloody confrontation served to deepen the chasm between Poles and Ukrainians, who felt humiliated by their defeat.

Poland's eastern frontier, including the frontier in areas inhabited by Ukrainians, was actually determined by the outcome of the Polish-Soviet war, the greatest challenge to the reborn state. The first clashes between Polish and Bolshevik forces took place in January 1919. The Poles enjoyed a string of successes in battle, seizing control of Vilnius and Minsk, with some assistance from Latvia, which was also fighting against Bolshevik Russia. Piłsudski, who was president (literally, "head of state") and commander in chief, could not, however, bring himself to join forces with General Denikin, who in the summer of 1919 appeared to be defeating the Red Army. At that time the Poles were more afraid of the White Russians, who had not recognized Poland's independence, than of the Bolsheviks, whose days seemed to be numbered. Only when the main White Russian forces had been defeated by the Bolsheviks did Poland conclude a treaty of alliance with the Ukrainian Republic, headed by Semyon Petlura. Under the terms of the treaty, the Ukraine ceded eastern Galicia and Volhynia to Poland, and Poland pledged to launch an offensive against Bolshevik Russia, liberating the entire Ukraine. Following a lightning attack, Polish forces, aided by Petlura's troops, entered Kiev in May 1920. Their success was, however, short-lived, partly because of the attitude of many Ukrainians, who remembered the recent war with Poland and did not support Petlura's policy. At the same time, the Bolsheviks had decided to try to carry the revolution to Western Europe and were preparing a massive offensive. They introduced conscription and tried to induce tsarist officers to join the Red Army; Trotsky's advisers even included the former commander in chief of the tsar's forces, General Aleksei Brusilov. Fearing that they would be encircled, the Poles withdrew from Kiev. They did so at the very last minute, when the Russian offensive under the command of Mikhail Tukhachevsky got under way on 4 July 1920. The Polish retreat was conducted in conditions approaching panic.

Within a month the Red Army had penetrated deep into Polish territory. The Russians set up their own, Soviet, power structure, and on 1 August in Białystok they established the Polish Provisional Revolutionary Committee, a makeshift institution of state power that was headed by well-known Polish communists. The West European left was hostile toward Poland, which it viewed as a "counterrevolutionary state," and a number of strikes—including strikes by dockworkers—shut down deliveries of weapons and ammunition. In Poland, however, the sight of the Red Army on the banks of the Vistula galvanized the population and led to a political consolidation, from which only the communists dissented. As a result, Polish forces succeeded in halting the Russians on the outskirts of Warsaw, and on 16 August they launched a counteroffensive that ended in complete victory—in less than two months Polish forces were once again in Minsk and had reached the former Austro-Russian border. Both sides were, however, completely exhausted, and a cease-fire was signed on 12 October. Five months later, on 18 March 1921, in Riga, the Latvian capital, they signed a peace treaty, which determined the border between the two countries and provided for the establishment of diplomatic relations. Paradoxically, then, Poland was both the first country to clash militarily with Bolshevik Russia and the first to country to recognize *de jure* its existence. Under the terms of the treaty Poland recognized Soviet Russia's right to central and eastern Ukraine, and disarmed and interned Petlura's army as well as the tiny Belorussian contin-

POLAND AND ITS NEIGHBORS, 1918–1939

BALTIC SEA

LATVIA

LITHUANIA

GERMANY

GDANSK

GERMANY
(EAST PRUSSIA)

VILNIUS

PRUSSIA
(PART)

USSR

POZNAN

RUSSIA
(PART)

WARSAW

KATOWICE

AUSTRIA
(PART)

KRAKOW

LVIV

CZECHOSLOVAKIA

HUNGARY

ROMANIA

—————— POLISH FRONTIERS

.... FORMER FRONTIERS OF PARTITION
(1815)

— · — — FRONTIERS BETWEEN NEIGHBORS

▪ MAIN CITIES

THE STRUGGLE FOR POLAND, 1918–1921

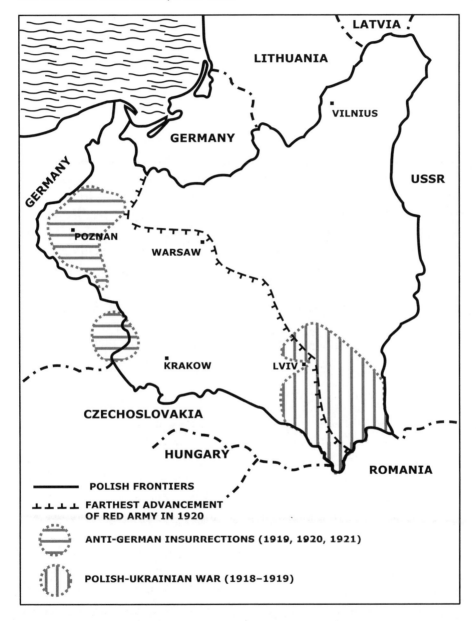

LATVIA

LITHUANIA

VILNIUS

GERMANY

GERMANY

USSR

POZNAN

WARSAW

KRAKOW

LVIV

CZECHOSLOVAKIA

HUNGARY

ROMANIA

——— POLISH FRONTIERS

⊥⊥⊥⊥ FARTHEST ADVANCEMENT
OF RED ARMY IN 1920

ANTI-GERMAN INSURRECTIONS (1919, 1920, 1921)

POLISH-UKRAINIAN WAR (1918–1919)

gent that had fought alongside the Poles. Thus Piłsudski's notion of a grand federation evaporated under the pressure of events.

For nearly three years—from 1 November 1918, when the Polish-Ukrainian war broke out, to 5 July 1921, when a cease-fire was signed following the third Silesian uprising—Poland was engaged in exhausting struggles to determine the shape of its territory. It emerged finally as a state with a surface area of 389,000 square kilometers and a population of 27.2 million (as a result of the high birthrate, the population had risen to 35 million by 1939). In terms of both area and population, Poland ranked sixth among the countries of Europe. It was thus a medium-sized country, but among the "Versailles states," that is to say, those countries that had been formed or had acquired a new territorial identity after World War I, Poland was both the largest and the most populous. For this reason, and because of the memories it nurtured concerning its former glory, it was also the most ambitious. There was widespread feeling that Poland was—or rather, ought to be—the leader of the entire region. One must, however, agree with the view that the countries of Versailles were "an unstable collection of weak states, divided by historic and irredentist animosities," and that "the power vacuum" that emerged in the region as a result of wars and revolution "invited foreign manipulation and influence. Predominantly conservative regimes dreaded the new Bolshevik virus and succeeded in repelling it, but the renascent Germany's economic and military power proved irresistible."[1]

INDEPENDENT POLAND: PROBLEM NUMBER ONE—THE ECONOMY

Poland's weakness was evident to outside observers and to a large part of the country's political elite. Shortly after the wars and the uprisings had come to an end, many Poles began to feel that they were under threat. This feeling was initially stifled by the awareness that the country's greatest enemies—Russia (now communist) and Germany—were living through a lean period and licking their wounds. Nevertheless, people were already asking themselves: How long can this state of affairs last? What will happen when these countries once again become militarily powerful? The chief "Polish problem" remained, then, essentially the same as it had been since the end of the eighteenth century: in the event that Russia and Germany resumed their places on the international stage, it was highly likely that they would

1. Bennet Kovrig, *Of Walls and Bridges: The United States and Eastern Europe* (New York, 1991), 6.

query Poland's territorial integrity—meaning, of course, its independence. Many factors contributed to Poland's being weaker than the Poles would have liked and weaker than it needed to be to ensure its own security. At the time, political conflicts and personal rivalries between party leaders were singled out as a leading cause of weakness. With the benefit of hindsight, however, other factors appear more important. Two were crucial: the state of the economy and divisions between the various nationalities.

Poland was a relatively poor and largely agricultural country (the peasantry made up 65 percent of the population). A large part of agriculture was extremely backward, and landholdings were dispersed. Only in the west were larger owner-operated farms to be found, while the central and eastern regions were dominated by *szlachta* estates, in which modern management methods had made few inroads. In terms of industry, the most highly developed region was again the west, including Upper Silesia, an industrial center on a European scale. Also significant were the industrial centers of Warsaw, the Dąbrowski Basin, and the Kraków Basin; the oil fields around Lvov; and the textile industry in Łódź, exaggeratedly referred to as "the Polish Manchester." After years of war and wasteful exploitation, the country was devastated: industrial output in 1919 was less than one-third of the prewar level; roughly 30 percent of the country's physical assets had been destroyed. The country had virtually no capital, and throughout the interwar period one of the greatest issues facing the Polish government was the need to obtain—and repay—foreign loans. The influx of private capital was often of a speculative nature; during the period 1929–33, for example, roughly 2.5 billion dollars left the country in the form of interest payments and dividends—an amount equal to the state's annual budget at that time.

The lack of financial resources resulted in large part from the disruption of economic ties and the loss of markets and access to cheap raw materials. Previously, each part of the country had been linked with the economy of its partitioning power: agriculture in the western regions flourished as the supplier of food to Berlin, one of the largest and richest cities in Europe; the textile workers of Łódź dominated the limitless Russian market all the way to Vladivostok; oil from Galicia was guaranteed a market across the entire Austro-Hungarian empire. All this had come to an end: Russia descended into chaos and then proceeded to build a powerful, but autarchic, economy; Germany, once the country's largest trading partner, had its own problems, partly because of the need to pay war reparations; and the Austrian market simply ceased to exist after the collapse of the monarchy and

15

was subdivided into three smaller markets with reduced absorptive capacity. The vortex of revolution and civil war in Russia destroyed many Polish fortunes, landholdings, and bank accounts; nearly half a million Poles—wealthy managers and merchants, or highly valued (and highly paid) experts—returned from Russia to face unemployment. During the early postwar years many social groups suffered enormous losses as a result of hyperinflation: in 1923, in the course of a single month, the exchange rate of the dollar—the main currency used for trading purposes—increased more than fivefold. Out of fear of its enemies to the east and the west, Poland was obliged to maintain a sizable army. This was a point on which all parties agreed, but the effort placed yet another burden on the economy.

It was a costly and time-consuming process to unify the economy, to create a single market and financial system (a new currency, the złoty, was introduced 1924), a single communications network, administrative structure, and legal system. For example, a uniform penal code was not introduced until 1932, leaving the three codes of the partitioning powers in force for more than ten years. Although the feeble domestic market and impoverished population yielded only a trickle of tax revenue, the state felt obliged to provide assistance to the economy. It was largely thanks to such assistance—akin to Roosevelt's New Deal but on a much larger scale—that economic reconstruction and development took place. It was a slow process, and successes were achieved with only the greatest difficulty, but still, during the 1930s signs of modernization were clearly visible: the tiny fishing village of Gdynia was transformed into an ultramodern port, which during 1937–39 handled more cargo that any other port on the Baltic; several hydroelectric power stations were constructed in the south of the country, and a number of factories in the chemical, metal, and defense industries were built to high technical standards; an enormous number of public buildings were erected (museums, theaters, universities, schools, post offices, stadiums, railroad stations, and so on), and new railroad lines were established. Just how slow this progress was, however, is attested to by the fact that only in 1938 did industrial output reach the level of 1913. Periods of rapid growth were few and relatively short-lived (1921–22, 1926–28, 1935–38). Other countries, such as Czechoslovakia, Lithuania, Latvia, Estonia, and Finland, had similar problems in creating new domestic markets and economic systems.

Agriculture, with its many structural problems, was in dire straits and suffered most from the Great Depression that began on faraway Wall Street and about which the Polish peasants had, of course, not the slightest idea. As a result of overall backwardness and the effects of the crisis, many peasants—especially in eastern and southern Poland—lived outside the market framework, consuming most of what they produced and selling the tiny surplus for a few miserable pennies in the local markets. While industry had already emerged from the crisis in 1933, the countryside did not revive until two years later. The minuscule purchasing power of the peasantry had a negative effect on the development of industry and contributed to the retention of archaic trading customs in rural areas. In many regions the only forms of contact with the national economy were small-town fairs, which many peasants could reach only by walking long distances, and the small traders who went from village to village peddling their wares. Only slowly did the age-old division between smallholders and landless peasants on the one hand and wealthy landowners on the other begin to disappear. In 1919 and 1920 parliament passed a law on agrarian reform, limiting the size of landholdings, but neither the state nor the peasantry had the resources needed to purchase land. The result was a rapid increase in the number of what were referred to as "surplus people" in rural areas. Young people who went to seek their fortune in the cities had a far greater chance of reinforcing the ranks of the unemployed than of finding even short-term employment. One of the most important channels of reducing overpopulation—emigration to America—was blocked by Washington's new immigration policy. All this resulted in an unstable social situation; on several occasions the country was rocked by a wave of strikes, which—as in the fall of 1923 and the spring of 1936—turned into riots that the police suppressed with the use of firearms. During the period 1934–37 peasants also staged a number of strikes involving the boycott of local markets. The largest such strike, in 1937, lasted ten days, and several dozen people were killed by the police.

In this respect, however, Poland was no different from other European countries. Even countries that were relatively much wealthier than Poland, such as Great Britain, France, and Germany, were frequently shaken by strikes. Although poor, Poland was not, then, "the pariah of Europe": per capita national income was the same as in Spain or Portugal and much higher than in the Balkans. In spite of all its economic problems—both structural and short-term (such as inflation or the Great Depression)—thanks to its considerable size and relatively large population, Poland was a country that had to be reckoned with in Europe. Or in any event, one that could not be ignored: either as a producer (of coal, for example) or as a potential consumer. Poland was also an active consumer and producer in the field of culture, in terms of both high-quality artistic endeavor (for example, Władysław Reymont received the Nobel Prize for Literature in 1924) and popular culture: a large number of newspapers and periodicals were published, films were produced, thousands of people turned out to watch football matches, and Poland won several Olympic medals. Poland also "exported" scientists and artists. Some Polish products were renowned, and Poles had particular cause for pride in the successes of the country's pilots, who flew planes that were produced in Poland. Nevertheless, this did not create a real power, despite the numerous statements the country's rulers made to that effect in the 1930s in the attempt to convince their citizens that Poland was a strong state.

PROBLEM NUMBER TWO—RELATIONS BETWEEN NATIONALITIES

Another factor that weakened the country was its national composition. Like the majority of Versailles countries, Poland was made up of several nationalities. Ethnic Poles accounted for approximately 65 percent of the population; the largest non-Polish groups were Ukrainians (roughly 15 percent), Jews (nearly 10 percent), Belorussians (about 5 percent), and Germans (about 4 percent). The geographical distribution of the national minorities was of great significance. Large concentrations of Germans were to be found in Silesia and Pomerania, areas adjoining Germany. In many eastern parts of the country the minorities were actually in the majority. In the province of Volhynia, for example, Poles made up less than 25 percent of the population, Jews accounted for 5 percent, while 70 percent were Ukrainians; Belorussians made up a similar majority in Polesie. The Jewish population was far more dispersed, living mostly in the towns and cities of central and eastern Poland. As a result, Jews made up roughly one-third of the inhabitants of Warsaw, and in several other large towns—such as Łódź or Vilnius—40–50 percent. Many small towns were actually Jewish settlements (*shtetl*), and in some cases fewer than 10–20 percent of the inhabitants were Poles. Ethnic divisions were overlaid by social differences. The overwhelming majority of Belorussians and Ukrainians were peasants, who for centuries had regarded Polish landowners with hatred, and the large landholdings that were divided up in the regions where they lived were largely assigned—with government assistance—to Polish soldiers who had distinguished themselves in the war of 1920. The Germans were generally wealthier than their Polish neighbors, and this was true of both farmers in Pomerania and skilled workers in Silesia. Jews dominated many professions, which aroused envy among the Poles, while many of them made a living from trade in rural areas and were thus perceived by Polish and Ukrainian peasants as "bloodsuckers." Ethnic differences were reinforced by religious differences: the great majority of Poles were Catholics; the Germans were usually Protestants; the Jews, of course, followed Judaism; and the Belorussians and some of the Ukrainians were Orthodox, although most of the latter were Uniates. During the nineteenth century some assimilation of Polish language and culture did take place. This process was most advanced among the Jews living in the larger towns of Russian and Austrian Poland (in Prussian Poland, the Jews assimilated German culture). However, the overwhelming majority of the national minorities lived within their own cultures and did not speak Polish. To the majority of Jews, it was simply an alien culture; to the Germans it was "inferior" to their own; and to the Ukrainians it was the culture of an occupying power. It is striking that Nobel laureate Isaac Bashevis Singer, a Jewish writer born in Poland, has written numerous stories set in Poland but Poles rarely appear in these tales and usually do so only as figures in ethnic conflicts. There was some common ground: roughly 10 percent of Jews declared Polish to be their mother tongue, numerous Jewish newspapers and books were published in Polish, the Polish boxing champion, Rotholc, was a Jew, and the Polish national chess team was made up of Jews; Wilimowski, a German from Silesia, was one of the stars of Polish football. A considerable proportion of the Polish intellectual and cultural elite—poets, actors, theater and film directors—consisted of assimilated Jews. They frequently came under attack from Polish nationalists, but the majority of Jews also viewed them as alien. During the 1930s a process of assimilation was evident among young people who studied the Polish language and Polish history in school or served in the Polish armed forces. Nevertheless, the dominant feeling was one of difference, strangeness, and often—enmity. This was true not only of minority attitudes toward Poles but also of Polish attitudes toward the minorities.

National differences are not necessarily a source of weakness, of course. Poland's culture and economy flourished in the fifteenth and sixteenth centuries thanks in part to such figures as the great astronomer, Nicolaus Copernicus, a German from Toruń, who studied in Kraków and was a member of the Polish clergy, and Wit Stwosz (Veit Stoß), who was born in Nuremberg but lived in Poland, where he carved the altar in Kraków's Mariacki Church, the greatest Polish work of art of that period. German merchants from Polish Gdańsk exported grain and timber to Western Europe, thereby providing a living to the Polish *szlachta*. Many of the latter were actually of Lithuanian or Russian origin, and one of Poland's greatest poets, Mikolaj Rej, was a Protestant. During the interwar years, more than a hundred years after the fall of the multination *szlachta* republic, after years of intensive russification and germanization, in a new geopolitical situation, things were different. The presence of unassimilated minorities, frequently hostile to Poland and the Poles, had a negative influence, both internally and externally.

In domestic politics, it led to the development of radical nationalist tendencies, which in turn led to the deepening of political and ideological divisions in the country. Radical nationalism was to be found not only among Poles, but also among Ukrainians and Germans. It even existed among Jews, in the form of the party of the so-called revisionist Zionists, but they did not attack the Polish state. An organization that did have antistate aims was the Ukrainian Military Organization, a clandestine terrorist organization that was more active than the legal Ukrainian political parties, which had set themselves the goal of gradually and peacefully winning national autonomy within the Polish state, along the lines envisaged by Dmowski during the period 1905–15. The proliferation of nationalisms injected a strong element of violence into political life. A telling example is the case of the first Polish president, Gabriel Narutowicz, who was murdered by a Polish fanatic in December 1922 after right-wing extremists accused him of having come to power only with the help of parliamentary deputies representing the national minorities. Ukrainian terrorists carried out numerous assassination attempts. Some of these were unsuccessful, as in the case of President Stanisław Wojciechowski in 1924; others were successful, as in the case of the minister of internal affairs, Bronisław Pieracki, murdered ten years later. In retaliation, the police conducted a brutal pacification of the villages where the bandits had taken refuge; often such operations were carried out on the basis of nothing more than suspicion or denunciation. Not only homes and businesses were destroyed, but also churches; and mass arrests were carried out. As a result, Ukrainians were the largest single group among political prisoners during the whole interwar period, outnumbered only by communists of various nationalities.

The onset of the Depression brought with it an increase in anti-Semitism, an age-old phenomenon—as it was throughout Europe—and one that had acquired drastic forms during the Polish-Ukrainian and Polish-Bolshevik wars. Although no large-scale pogroms took place after 1920, during the 1930s there were more than a dozen acts of aggression involving crowds of people, and a far larger number on a smaller scale. Their victims were usually Jewish shopkeepers in small towns, who were attacked by their local Polish competitors and peasants from the surrounding villages. In some cases people were killed, but in the best-known pogrom, which took place in 1936 in the town of Przytyk, one of the three people killed was a Polish woman. In another incident, police shot and killed four people while dispersing the crowd. One major change in comparison with previous periods was the growth in anti-Semitism among the intelligentsia. For example, despite opposition from left-wing students and faculty, several universities introduced what became known as "bench ghettos" (Jewish students had to sit separately from the Poles), there were demands for the enforcement of a *numerus clausus* to limit the percentage of Jewish students to the percentage of Jews in the population as a whole, and there were even demands for the complete exclusion of Jews from the universities. Nationalist gangs attacked Jewish students and their defenders on the left. The representatives of some professions, notably lawyers and physicians, demanded legal limits on the number of Jews entering the profession. The state authorities never went that far. Nevertheless, in the second half of the 1930s some members of the ruling group suggested organizing the large-scale migration of Jews (to Madagascar, for example) and proposed restrictions on Jewish religious practices (ritual slaughter); in 1936 Prime Minister Felicjan Składkowski became famous for his remark concerning Jewish trade: "A boycott? Most certainly." In his defense we can only add that the alternative to a boycott was pogroms. The authorities supported Jewish emigration, but on the basis of an agreement with Zionist organizations. As a result, at the end of the 1930s roughly 40 percent of the Jews in Palestine came from Poland. Some of them made the journey feeling they were going to the Promised Land rather than fleeing danger; others left for both reasons.

Anti-Semitic tendencies were reinforced by much of the Polish press, which continued to feature a cartoon stereotype that first appeared during the war of 1920: the Bolshevik Jew, a giant with a knife between his teeth, joins forces with the Russian, a bloodthirsty bear, to attack Poland, an innocent woman trying to protect her young children. Another favorite motif was a caricature of Leon Trotsky with exaggerated Semitic features and Lenin as a "slant-eyed Asiatic." Although the nationalist parties were generally anti-German, from 1933 onwards they were happy to point to the "de-Judaization" of Germany and took from Nazi propaganda the caricature of the Jewish plutocrat and the image of the disease-bearing insect.

Polish-Belorussian and Polish-German relations were less tense, although they periodically flared up. The Poles never really rid themselves of their fear of Germany, a fear mixed with hatred, and the brutal and perfidious Teutonic Knight was often cited as the typical German. The Germans living in Poland had no difficulty understanding the anti-Polish message contained in the contemptuous and disdainful remarks made by many German politicians—or their reminders that Poland was just a "seasonal state."

The country's non-Polish inhabitants had the same civil rights as the Poles, and could take part in elections to parliament and local self-government bodies (the Jews even had their own communal assemblies). The national minorities had their own political parties, trade unions, cooperatives, banks, newspapers, and sports clubs. There was, then, no discrimination *de jure,* but regardless of which particular party was in power, discrimination existed de facto. Ukrainians, Belorussians, and Germans were most affected, Jews less so. This discrimination was not drastic, but the national minorities found it painful and irksome. It was virtually impossible for a non-Pole to become a state official or a judge, to get a job with the police, the post office, or the railroads. They were not admitted to officer training schools or to elite military units, such as the air force or navy. The few Jews who became high-ranking officers (up to the level of general) and state officials owed their careers to the fact that they had served in Piłsudski's Legions, which were predominantly left-wing in their politics. A few Georgians who had previously served in the Russian army served temporarily in the Polish army (among them the father of the future Chairman of the Joint Chiefs of Staff, General John Shalikashvili, who was born in Warsaw), but no Polish citizen of Ukrainian nationality achieved a similar status. With the exception of communists and socialists, non-Poles did not belong to Polish political parties, and the parties of the national minorities did not form parliamentary coalitions with the Polish parties. Most of the time, in fact, they had no desire to do so.

Despite all this, it cannot be said that Poland was any worse than other European countries with a multinational citizenry. In democratic Czechoslovakia, Ukrainians, Hungarians, and Poles had absolutely no chance of reaching high office; even the Slovaks complained about Czech dominance, and some of them wanted to break away from the republic. In those days standards concerning treatment of minorities were different from those of today (in the United States, gentlemen's clubs would not admit Jews or Catholics, and the same was true of Harvard). One way or another, national conflicts had a devastating effect on Polish political life and undoubtedly had a destabilizing influence on the state.

One further aspect of these conflicts is relevant to an understanding of the Poles' attitude toward communism and socialism. The majority of people among the national minorities who were dissatisfied with their lot swelled the ranks of nationalist groups, but there were some who opted instead for the communist movement. The movement espoused not only social equality, which would already have been enough to ensure support, but also internationalism, a slogan that the Soviet party seemed to be putting into practice, given the high positions achieved by russified members of other national groups—Jews (Trotsky), Poles (Dzerzhinsky), and Georgians (Stalin). From the moment the revolutionary movement appeared on Polish soil, it attracted national minorities, particularly Jews from the intelligentsia and the middle class. Just like everywhere else in Europe.

The situation changed after 1918, when communism began making inroads among Ukrainians and Belorussians. The KPP was transformed into a kind of federation that included two autonomous sections, the Communist Party of Western Ukraine and the Communist Party of Western Belorussia. It is estimated that ethnic Poles made up roughly 33 percent of KPP membership, Jews—about 25 percent, and Ukrainians and Belorussians—40 percent. Of course, there were considerable regional variations: in the eastern provinces the party was largely made up of Jews and Ukrainians or Belorussians, in the central regions—Jews and Poles (the party had very few members in the western provinces). Regardless of the fact that Jewish or Ukrainian communists were regarded—as were their Polish comrades—as "outcasts" by the majority of the national group to which they belonged, many Poles came to believe that the KPP was not only anti-Polish but also non-Polish. Right-wing groups seized on this point repeatedly in their propaganda, as did some groups in the political center. This made it easier for the public to accept the fact that the KPP had been banned, even though the reason for banning was that the communists had called for the overthrow of the "reactionary" Polish state.

Despite the severity of these conflicts—especially between Poles and Jews and Poles and Ukrainians—they did not by themselves threaten the security and territorial integrity of the state. The threat largely came from

Poland's neighbors: both the Soviet Union and Germany (first the Weimar Republic, then the Third Reich) tried to make use of the national minorities to intervene in Poland's internal affairs, and essentially to prize away part of its territory. The Soviet Union was especially active in this regard in 1924. In the eastern provinces, inhabited largely by Belorussians, subversive units made their way across the border to carry out attacks on landed estates, local officials, and even small towns. This activity was halted by the specially created Border Guard that was stationed along the entire length of the Polish-Soviet border. Moscow did not try anything like this subsequently, but there was always a state of tension along the border. The Soviets operated through the KPP, which, as a section of the Comintern, was wholly subordinate to Moscow. Some spying also took place, and in 1939 the Soviets organized subversive operations that were intended to assist the Red Army's invasion of Poland. Germany did not use the Germans living in Poland to engage in any overtly seditious activity, although during 1938–39 subversive groups were organized and espionage increased. The Germans' chief weapon in their efforts to weaken Poland was the Ukrainian radical nationalist movement, whose headquarters were located in Berlin. There terrorists received training and were provided with safe haven. Pro-German sentiments among the Ukrainians were relatively strong, and Berlin promised—directly or indirectly—to establish an independent Ukrainian state on territory then belonging to Poland and the Soviet Union.

On an international scale, more significant than subversive activity was the constant pressure on Poland, which Soviet and German propaganda depicted as a country that oppressed its national minorities. By the mid-1930s both countries had again become major powers and each of them was ready to defend its "kinsmen": Moscow—the Ukrainians and Belorussians, Berlin—the Germans. This made it easier to conceal aggressive intentions, although it is certain that most Ukrainians were not longing to be part of the Soviet empire (especially once they had information about the great famine in the Ukraine). Nor did anyone ask whether all the Germans wanted to become citizens of the totalitarian Third Reich. While it cannot be said that information about the disadvantaged position of Poland's national minorities was actually inaccurate, it was frequently exaggerated in order to provide a pretext for aggression. On occasion, Jewish groups also joined in the propaganda campaign against Poland. The fact that after 1933 these attacks coincided with the Nazi's anti-Polish campaign was a bitter paradox. Bitter for both Jews and Poles.

DOMESTIC POLITICS

Despite the major political changes that took place in Poland after 1918, the main ideological groupings that had been formed before World War I survived unchanged. As a result, the main political conflict continued to be that between the independence movement led by Piłsudski, subsequently known as the "legionaries" or "Piłsudski-ites," and the Endecja, led by Dmowski until his death in 1939. Nevertheless, during the crucial years 1918–20 these two camps managed—while maintaining their ideological disputes and sometimes violent political clashes—to arrive at a consensus on the most important issues and even at a division of roles. As head of state, Piłsudski assumed command of the armed forces and responsibility for the situation at home. Dmowski became Poland's chief representative at the Versailles Conference and defended the state's interests in the diplomatic arena. In November 1918 Piłsudski appointed a left-wing government, but faced with a difficult internal situation, he decided in January 1919 that he needed to reach agreement with his opponents and assigned the post of prime minister to Paderewski, who was politically close to Dmowski. One of the main tasks of this government was to hold parliamentary elections; these took place on 19 January and resulted in the Endecja holding the largest number of seats. The parliament passed the so-called Small Constitution (intended to be temporary), which stabilized the position of the highest state authorities, and also confirmed Piłsudski in his position as head of state and commander in chief, giving him extremely broad powers. In 1920, when the country's very existence was threatened by the Red Army, a coalition government was formed under the leadership of Wincenty Witos, head of the largest peasant party and considered a politician of the center-right; his deputy, on the other hand, was a socialist, Ignacy Daszyński. The government, referred to as the Government of National Salvation, also included members of the Endecja. Nevertheless, once the threat had passed, the two camps resumed their all-out political struggle and never again cooperated with each other. Even in 1939, in the face of war, the Piłsudski-ites—by that time ruling without Piłsudski, who died in May 1935—disdainfully rejected the opposition's proposal to create a coalition government. This had no bearing on the outbreak of war or the course that it took, but it was evidence of the changes that had taken place in Poland and the depth of political divisions.

Generally speaking, the interwar years can be divided into several periods, although the most important turning point is undoubtedly that of May

1926, when Piłsudski—with the support of the socialists and the entire left (including the communists)—carried out a coup d'état. While the country was still fighting to establish its borders (1918–21), political life was lively, developments followed one another rapidly, and debates were heated, but it was external events that were most important during this period. The next period, which opened with the passage of the Constitution of 17 March 1921, is usually referred to as the period of "Sejmocracy." The constitution favored the legislature over the executive, and, at the same time, numerous political groups were emerging onto the political stage. As a result, successive governments lacked a stable parliamentary majority, and Sejm deputies were the dominant force in shaping one government after another. The moment of truth came in November 1922, when for the first time elections were held across the country to both the Sejm and the Senate; together they were to elect the president, which involved abolishing the position of head of state. Piłsudski was dissatisfied with the much reduced role of the presidency under the new constitution and announced that he would not be a candidate for the office. The election campaign was marked by sharp disputes, and the outcome was unexpected: no single party had enough seats to form a government alone. The Endecja list obtained 28 percent of the seats, several quarreling centrist parties jointly had 30 percent, and the left had 22 percent. The greatest surprise was the success of the national minorities, who fielded a joint list; despite the fact that most Ukrainians boycotted the elections, the list obtained 20 percent of the seats and thus became a force to be courted by all sides.

The most important point about the elections was, however, that they brought home the fact that Piłsudski, the dominant political figure of his time, a charismatic leader with a strong authoritarian bent, did not have his own political party. The only party that claimed close association with him did not obtain a single seat. He could, of course, count on the support of the PPS and the smaller left-wing parties, but this was not enough to allow him to play the role that he had envisaged. The Piłsudski-ites began to question the value of parliamentary democracy, and since they held senior positions in the armed forces and the state administration, their opinions could not be ignored. The murder of Narutowicz brought with it a sharp escalation of political conflict; as a last resort, a nonparty government was formed under General Władysław Sikorski, who speedily gained control of the situation, but the event deepened the gulf between the left and the right and Piłsudski. A succession of center-right governments carried out the administrative, financial, and economic unification of the country, but this was accompanied by severe social conflicts, partly the result of hyperinflation. A major factor in political life was the instability of the center parties, without which no government could be formed. Numerous splits in these parties resulted in frequent changes of government, and government weakness brought with it, as is often the case, corruption. This made it easier for the Piłsudskiites to criticize democracy and argue the need to "cleanse" or "purify" the state. (Their use of the old-fashioned word *usanować* resulted in the group thereafter being known as the Sanacja.) In the spring of 1926, when the Endecja and centrist parties formed yet another government, headed by Wincenty Witos, Piłsudski's supporters stepped up their attacks.

This time it was no longer just a matter of words. Piłsudski, in retirement since 1923, had for several months been preparing his return to political life, and the formation of the new government provided his supporters and the entire left with the pretext they needed to act. On 12 May 1926, several thousand soldiers, under Piłsudski's command, marched from their barracks near Warsaw to the capital, where no more than a few hundred soldiers were stationed. After three days of skirmishes, in which 400 people were killed, the president and the government resigned in order to spare the country a full-scale civil war. At Piłsudski's suggestion, the marshal of the Sejm, Maciej Rataj, appointed as prime minister Kazimierz Bartel, a professor at Lvov Polytechnic. The Sejm and the Senate accepted the fait accompli, and with the votes of the left and the center, Piłsudski was elected president. To everyone's surprise, however, he turned down the post, saying that by its vote parliament had legalized the coup and that he wished for nothing more. He did, though, have a candidate for the post in the person of Ignacy Mościcki, another professor and even less well known than the prime minister. On 1 June Mościcki was elected president.

The period of "Sejmocracy" thus came to an end, although Piłsudski was often obliged to take account of the balance of forces in parliament, as the left-wing parties gradually deserted him to join the opposition. The elections that took place in March 1928 had little effect on the situation. These had been delayed for several months in order to give Piłsudski and his supporters time to organize a political party. They put together a conglomeration of various political tendencies, ranging from a group of socialists who had left the PPS to conservatives, and they called it the Non-Party Bloc for Cooperation with the Government (BBWR), a name that reflected Piłsudski's dislike of traditional political parties. Although the Endecja suffered a huge defeat (obtaining only 8 percent of seats in the Sejm), as did the centrist parties (roughly 12 percent), and while the BBWR was the largest party (with 27 percent of seats), it did not have enough seats to form a government on its own. For the next two years, therefore, Piłsudski exploited a number of legal loopholes. He frequently changed prime ministers, sometimes heading the government himself. Sometimes he threatened Sejm deputies and sometimes he made them promises. In one way or another he finally removed all opponents from the state administration and self-government agencies, from the boards of state enterprises and banks, from the police and the officer corps. To a large extent the BBWR became a ruling party that attracted careerists rather than an organization with a firm ideological basis. In 1930, when the hitherto divided opposition began to form a coalition under the name of the Union in Defense of Law and the People's Freedom (known as the "Centrolew"), Piłsudski decided it was time for the final offensive. At the end of August 1930 the president dissolved parliament. Shortly afterwards, twenty former Sejm deputies were arrested and consigned to the military prison at Brześć, on the River Bug; among them was Witos, three times prime minister. A number of less well known activists were arrested across the country. The crackdown was especially severe in the eastern provinces: several dozen Ukrainian deputies were arrested, and armed clashes and a brutal pacification campaign cost the lives of more than a dozen people.

For all intents and purposes the opposition was paralyzed, and the next elections were characterized by numerous cases of fraud; in some cases votes cast for the Centrolew were declared invalid. In these conditions, the BBWR won 56 percent of seats in the Sejm. This was enough to form a government but not enough to change the constitution. Unless, of course, the government could use its powers to take advantage of a number of loopholes to introduce changes. This turned out to be the case, and in April 1935 a new constitution was finally approved by parliament. This took place just a few weeks before the death of Piłsudski, who had been ailing for some time; it goes without saying that the changes had his complete approval. What became known as the April Constitution sanctioned the authoritarian nature of the state. The president acquired enormous powers, plainly towering over not only the government but also parliament (among other things, he appointed one-third of the senators and had the power to dissolve parliament at will, to call it into session, and to defer sessions). He had the power to issue decrees with the force of law and to conclude and ratify international treaties without their being approved by the Sejm. According to one article of the constitution, the president was responsible "to God and history," not the nation. The age at which people became eligible to vote was raised to twenty-four, and the new electoral law avoided all mention of political parties as society's basic representatives. In protest, the opposition boycotted the next elections in September 1935.

After 1930—and essentially after the May coup—Poland came less and less to resemble a democratic state, although it was not a dictatorship like the Third Reich or fascist Italy: opposition political parties continued to exist and their newspapers continued to appear; independent trade unions and associations functioned, and there was considerable freedom of speech. Nevertheless, a single group exerted such a grip on power that it became impossible to bring about a change in leadership. One of the chief requirements of democracy was thus unfulfilled. Although efforts were made to observe the law, political opponents were subjected to brutal treatment. For example, in 1934 the government introduced regulations allowing people to be imprisoned without first having been sentenced by a court of law, simply on the basis of an administrative order. The people detained in this way were confined, under harsh conditions, at a camp in Bereza Kartuska. Eleven of the politicians arrested in 1930 were sentenced to prison, but a number of them—including Witos and Herman Lieberman, a socialist—managed to leave the country. Also in emigration was the Christian-democrat politician, Wojciech Korfanty, the popular leader of the Silesian uprisings of 1919–20 and another politician who had been prosecuted.

Because of their roots in the Legions, military personnel played a major role in the state, often occupying positions in the government and administration; in 1936 the president referred to Piłsudski's successor to the highest position in the army as "the second most important person in the state." Of course, when Piłsudski was alive, it was he and not the president who was the most important person in the state. After his death, disputes erupted within the Sanacja. The BBWR was dissolved and replaced in 1937 by the Camp of National Unity, whose program was both more authoritarian and more nationalistic. Despite personal conflicts among some of the more liberal Piłsudski-ites, and despite deepening social and political conflicts, the Sanacja retained sufficient cohesion to remain in power. A ruling triumvirate emerged, its members consisting of President Mościcki, who had been reelected in 1933; Edward Rydz-Śmigły, who took over the position of General Inspector of the Armed Forces, the highest position in the military, and who was appointed marshal in 1936; and Józef Beck, minister of foreign affairs since 1932. Economic policy, a major issue in light of the high level of state ownership in industry and banking, was in the hands of Eugeniusz Kwiatkowski, a talented manager, who was close to the president and held the position of deputy prime minister. All in all, then, the Sanacja was unified and self-confident. Its leaders, who were also the leaders of the state, were convinced that Poland, too, was unified and strong.

One reason why the Sanacja believed it was in a position to govern indefinitely was the fact that the opposition remained fragmented. The parties were simply too diverse. In addition, political attitudes had become so polarized that a rapprochement between nationalists and socialists was out of the question, and the centrist parties even began to distance themselves from the Endecja. Nevertheless, some consolidation took place. The most important such development was the 1931 merger of the three peasant parties into a single Peasant Party (SL), in which a younger generation of activists, people such as Stanisław Mikolajczyk and Stanisław Mierzwa, came to play a more prominent role, although the party's unquestioned leader was Witos, the "king of the peasants." In 1937 several groups joined together to form the Labor Party (SP). It was headed by Karol Popiel, and included among its supporters General Sikorski, who had been ousted from the army following the May coup. In 1936 a number of politicians in exile agreed to cooperate with each other in the political arena. The group included Witos, Lieberman, Korfanty, and Sikorski, a frequent visitor to France, where he was much admired. This agreement was forged under the patronage of Paderewski, who had been living abroad since 1924, and the group became known as the Morges Front, after the town in Switzerland where his house was located. The Peasant Party was particularly active, organizing many mass demonstrations and the peasant strike of 1937. The Labor Party was much weaker, but had some influence among the middle and working classes. The PPS was both active and influential, but after the death of Daszyński the absence of a leader capable of bridging the differences between its right and left wings reduced the party's effectiveness. The left wing was interested in cooperating with the communists, who since 1935—when the Comintern launched its policy of popular fronts—had been trying to play a role in legal political life and rid themselves of the accusation that they were agents of a hostile power. This cooperation was beginning to bear fruit for the communists when the party was dissolved by the Comintern in 1938, as part of Stalin's Great Purge. All the most important leaders, who were in

Moscow, were shot. Paradoxically, the only leaders to be saved were those then sitting in Polish prisons.

On the surface, the biggest loser of the May coup—leaving aside Polish democracy itself—was Roman Dmowski. The Endecja, which in 1929 renamed itself the National Party (SN), never regained the influence it had had before 1926. In addition, an extremely active and radical group led by Bolesław Piasecki broke away in 1934 to form what was essentially a fascist organization, the National Radical Camp (ONR). The National Party was not a weak organization; it had a large membership, published several newspapers, and had a clear-cut—and increasingly radical—political line, but the temptations of sharing in power or at least establishing better relations with the ruling camp were too strong for the nationalists' traditional social base, the landowners and bourgeoisie, and the wealthier middle class and civil servants. Even the Catholic clergy no longer supported the SN as solidly as before. The party was also weakened by the fact that the aging and ailing Dmowski had no successor capable of leading the party. I said above that the Endecja was the biggest loser "on the surface," because while the party itself no longer played the role that it did in earlier times, the nationalism that it espoused took root in a variety of social groups, including some that had hitherto been immune. Even the Sanacja became infected, although Piłsudski himself always thought first in terms of the state, not the nation. Nationalism was nourished by social attitudes but attitudes were themselves shaped by the extremist propaganda and aggressive actions of a few small but determined political groups. Many of them made a major impression on the public, as was the case in 1936 when a gang of hoodlums occupied the tiny town of Myślenice, in symbolic tribute to Mussolini's "March on Rome." While it remained anti-German and anti-Ukrainian, the National Party became increasingly anti-Semitic in its focus. Perhaps because this particular enemy was weaker than the others.

Although the opposition was unable to oust the Sanacja from power, it had considerable influence in society, especially during the years 1936–39, after Piłsudski's death. While it was clear who governed Poland, it was hard to say who ruled the hearts and minds of its citizens.

DIPLOMACY AND WAR

Poland's situation was by no means secure, although for many years its two great neighbors and enemies were seriously weakened and completely absorbed in domestic issues. Bad relations with Lithuania and Czechoslovakia were of less consequence. Lithuania laid claim to Vilnius, despite the fact that only a tiny percentage of its inhabitants were Lithuanians, and for most of the interwar period Poland had no diplomatic relations with Kaunas. Only in the spring of 1938, during the turmoil brought about by the *Anschluß* of Austria, did Poland insist on an exchange of ambassadors. This normalized the situation, but there was no question of an alliance between the two countries. Relations with Czechoslovakia were somewhat better but far from friendly. Poland objected to Czechoslovakia's acquisition in 1919 of the Trans-Olza, a region in which the majority of inhabitants were Polish. In the fall of 1938, following the agreement reached in Munich with Great Britain, France, and Italy, the Third Reich seized part of the Czech lands. Polish forces took the opportunity to occupy the Trans-Olza, which was then incorporated into Poland. This step did nothing to improve Poland's international standing and was of little strategic significance in the event of a German attack. Czechoslovakia did not share Poland's fears regarding potential aggression on the part of Moscow and viewed with suspicion Poland's ambition to lead East-Central Europe. It tried to assume leadership of the anti-Hungarian alliance known as the Little Entente, and viewed as hostile to its interests the good relations between Poland and Hungary. Prague supported the moderate Ukrainian nationalists, and for a period of time even provided a home for the émigré government of the People's Republic of Western Ukraine, clearly an unfriendly gesture in relation to Poland. The fact that Piłsudski and Thomas Masaryk, each of whom dominated the politics of his own country, had such different personalities and visions of the world also played a role in the relationship between Warsaw and Prague. Poland enjoyed relatively good relations with Latvia, a small and militarily weak country with which it shared a border. Latvia was in no position, however, to provide support and in any case tended to gravitate toward the other countries of the eastern Baltic (Finland, Estonia, and Lithuania). Poland's warmest diplomatic relations were with Romania, with which it signed a treaty in 1921 concerning mutual assistance in the event of a Soviet attack, but the country was internally too weak to be a full-fledged partner.

Although it might have seemed that the West European powers would be interested in ensuring a strong and stable Poland, this was not in fact the case. This was largely the result of the position adopted by Great Britain; its traditional interest in maintaining equilibrium in Europe led it to be concerned about the position of Germany, and during the crucial years 1919–20 it was surprisingly hostile to Poland's involvement in the war with Soviet

Russia. It was the British foreign secretary, George Curzon, who proposed in 1919 that Poland's territory extend as far as a line (referred to as the Curzon Line) that roughly corresponded to Russia's western border at the time of the 1795 partition. In 1920, when Tukhachevsky was mounting his fiercest offensive, Prime Minister Lloyd George endorsed the idea. Fortunately, Polish forces won the war, but if peace had been achieved earlier on terms proposed by the British, the Polish-Soviet border would have been situated barely a hundred kilometers east of Warsaw and the country's territory would have been 40 percent smaller. In later years, too, London treated Poland with a certain amount of disdain, and it was only when Hitler's increasing aggression persuaded Britain to abandon the policy of appeasement that the British recognized Poland's significance in the effort to restrain the Third Reich. In the spring of 1939 Poland received Britain's formal guarantee of assistance in the event of a German attack, but the treaty on mutual assistance was not signed until 24 August, less than a week before Germany invaded.

France, despite the *entente cordiale* between the two countries, always displayed a certain amount of reserve toward Britain and adopted a policy that was more favorable to Poland. It was the only country that supported Poland in the war with Soviet Russia, and the French military mission—in which Lieutenant Charles de Gaulle served—was instrumental in preparing the counteroffensive of 1920. In 1921 Piłsudski visited France and signed a declaration of friendship and a treaty of alliance together with a military agreement. However, the so-called Rhine Treaty signed in Locarno in 1925, which involved a multilateral commitment (on the part of Great Britain, Italy, and Poland, among others) to defend France from German attack but committed only France to the defense of Poland's western border, was interpreted in Warsaw as giving the Germans a free rein to their east. Over the next few years Paris and London signed numerous multilateral agreements, as though it was paper and not force that was going to determine whether there was war or peace. It was only with the change in German policy and the remilitarization of the Rhineland in 1936 that relations with Poland became closer. In May 1939 Poland and France signed a secret protocol that committed France to launch a major offensive within fifteen days of a German attack on Poland. This agreement constituted a major supplement to the agreement of 1921, which had effectively been dormant for many years. A more important factor, however, was the existence in France of influential groups whose views were either pro-German or radically pacifist. The famous article, "Mourir pour Dantzig?" (Should we die for Danzig?), reflected not only the views of the author, Marcel Deat, who had made the journey from communism to fascism, but the views of a broad section of the public—even those of the chief of the general staff and many other officers and politicians.

During the 1920s Poland made numerous efforts to improve relations with France and Great Britain (and also with Italy), but these were largely unsuccessful. These relations were especially important to Poland as a rapprochement was taking place between Weimar Germany and the Soviet Union, both of which had a negative attitude toward the Treaty of Versailles. Their first agreement was signed in Rapallo in 1922; this was followed in 1926 by a treaty signed in Berlin, in which both sides pledged friendship and neutrality in the event of disputes with third parties. In observing the treaty, Moscow paved the way for Germany to disregard the military restrictions imposed at Versailles: Germany was able to train tank officers and airmen in the Soviet Union in exchange for information on technological innovations. No one doubted that at least one of the main aims of the agreement was to encircle Poland. Piłsudski was one those Polish politicians who most feared such an eventuality, but at the same time he did not trust the West European powers and trusted only in his own strength. He referred to relations with Britain and France as illusory, "exotic" alliances. He therefore initiated what became known as "the policy of equal distance" (to Berlin and to Moscow). Under Piłsudski's direct supervision Beck took advantage of a cooling in Soviet-German relations to negotiate a Polish-Soviet nonaggression pact, signed in Moscow on 25 July 1932 (in 1934 it was extended for a further ten years) and a joint Polish-German declaration, signed in Berlin on 26 January 1934, in which both sides pledged themselves not to attack the other. "Poland is now sitting on two stools," Piłsudski used to say in private, but he usually added: "This situation can't last for very long. We have to know which one we will fall off first, and when."[2] He was right in his prediction that the situation would not last long, but he was wrong about one thing: Poland fell off both stools at once.

The tragic chain of events began to unfold in the fall of 1938, when Hitler, flush with his "victory" over Czechoslovakia, selected Poland as the next victim of his "peaceful conquests." In October the foreign minister of the Third Reich, Joachim von Ribbentrop, presented the Polish ambassador

2. Wojciech Roszkowski, *Historia Polski, 1914–1999* (Warsaw, 2000), 79.

in Berlin with the suggestion that the two countries form a common front against the Soviet Union. This was intended to sweeten the pill of Germany's planned annexation of the Free City of Gdańsk and the construction through Polish Pomerania of a highway and railroad line between Germany and East Prussia. Hitler was not really counting on a positive response and shortly after he had occupied Prague (on 15 March 1939), he ordered his military commanders to begin preparations, code-named *Fall Weiß*, for the invasion of Poland. Stalin, who had just completed the bloodiest phase of the purges, came to the conclusion that Europe was about to become embroiled in armed conflict and decided that the Soviet Union could turn the situation to its advantage. The Comintern believed that the coming "imperialist" war would most probably end in the same way as the previous one—in a series of revolutionary upsurges. Except that this time they would have the support of the Homeland of the World Proletariat and would thus be victorious. In any event, when Hitler rescinded the nonaggression treaty with Poland on 28 April 1939, Moscow began to play a double game, simultaneously engaging in secret talks with Berlin while engaged in official negotiations with Britain and France, which were seeking to persuade Moscow to oppose the Third Reich. The Western powers were inclined to accept the conditions set out by the newly appointed Soviet foreign minister, Vyacheslav Molotov. However, the two countries most directly affected could not agree: Poland and Romania feared that the Soviet proposal to have the Red Army march through their territory could result in a situation more akin to foreign occupation than to military assistance. At this time, Berlin hastened—secretly, of course—to present Moscow with a proposal whereby the two sides would divide Poland between them, would divide the whole of Eastern Europe, from Finland to Romania, into two separate zones of influence, and Germany would act as a mediator in the protracted armed conflict between the Soviet Union and Japan. On 23 August Ribbentrop and Molotov—the well-known photograph of the occasion shows Stalin standing modestly in the background—signed in Moscow a nonaggression pact containing a secret protocol that provided for the complete partition of Poland and the "transfer" of neighboring territory—Lithuania to the German zone of influence, and Finland, Estonia, Latvia, and Bessarabia (now Moldova) to the Soviet zone. This protocol was one of the Soviet Union's most closely guarded secrets at the time of its signing, and it remained so: not until 1990 did Moscow officially acknowledge its existence.

As a result, Poland found itself between the hammer and the anvil. The only—and essentially theoretical—chance of salvation lay in becoming an ally, which really meant a satellite, of one of the two totalitarian powers. However, Poland had no desire to join forces with either Hitler or Stalin. Neither the romantic uprisings of the nineteenth century nor the bitter struggles of 1918–20 had taken place so that Poland could once again become a vassal. At that time a tragic quip was in circulation: "What is the right answer to the question, Who is Poland's worst enemy, the Soviet Union or Germany? The Germans will take our body, and the Soviets will take our soul." Indeed, there was no good solution for Poland.

CHAPTER 1

Captivity and Struggle

Germany attacked early in the morning of Friday, 1 September 1939. After a number of short border skirmishes, the overwhelming force of the Third Reich delivered a series of lightning blows. On 6 September the Polish commander in chief ordered his forces to withdraw beyond the Vistula and San Rivers, while top government officials had already started leaving the capital on 5 September. Two days later, all central government institutions found themselves east of the River Bug. The commander in chief and his staff were in the Brest fortress, the government—in Łuck, and the president—in Ołyka. On 12 September the president met with the prime minister, the minister of foreign affairs, and the commander in chief, and they decided to prepare for a final counteroffensive at the junction of the Stryj and Dniester rivers, in the hope of seeking support from allied Romania or neutral Hungary. In the event, the Poznań and Pomorze army units were able to halt the German offensive in the central sector for only a short time (the battle of the River Bzura, 9–16 September).

Poland's allies, Great Britain and France, declared war on Germany on 3 September, but the allies' Supreme Military Council, meeting on the same day as the meeting at Ołyka, decided not to attack at that point. Germany's advanced armored units had already broken through defenses in the southern and central sectors along the Vistula, and in the north they had crossed the Narew and were approaching the outskirts of the capital. Polish armed units were fighting in isolation, and the civilian population, mercilessly attacked by German aircraft, was engaged in a massive evacuation toward the east. By 15 September, the state authorities found themselves in a region close to the border with Romania, but efforts to bring about an orderly retreat of the forces fighting between the Vistula and the Bug were unsuccessful.

Meanwhile, Poland's eastern neighbor began preparing to invade, in line with the secret clause of the "Non-Aggression Pact" signed by the Soviet Union and the Third Reich on 23 August 1939 (the Ribbentrop-Molotov

Pact). On 4 September a partial mobilization was ordered, and 11 September saw the creation of the Belorussian and Ukrainian Fronts, which reached fighting strength within a few days. Joseph Stalin was under pressure from the Germans, who were unsure how Poland's allies would react, were anxious for immediate military results, and preferred not to be seen as the sole aggressor; he only took the final decision regarding the date of the invasion on 15 September, when he agreed to a cease-fire with Japan.

At 3 A.M. on Sunday, 17 September, the Soviet authorities attempted to deliver to Poland's ambassador in Moscow a note informing him that "all treaties between Poland and the USSR are no longer valid," and two hours later Red Army units began crossing the Polish border. In a "general directive" issued at 4 P.M., the commander in chief ordered Polish units to combat Soviet forces "only in the event that they attack," and to fall back toward Romania and Hungary. During the night of 17–18 September, nearly all the Republic's highest government officials crossed the Romanian border. While they expected Romania to honor both the Polish-Romanian treaty of friendship and the commonly accepted principles of international law, the Romanian government was under strong pressure from the Germans. Faced with passivity on the part of France and Great Britain, the Romanians not only interned the Polish officials but separated them into small groups, holding them in a number of places, for the most part some distance from Bucharest.

In two subsequent battles at Tomaszów Lubelski (18–20 and 23 September), the remnants of the armed forces on the central and northern fronts were crushed. The besieged capital defended itself without any hope of outside help. Units of the Border Defense Corps were too few and too widely scattered to be capable of resisting the Red Army forces, nearly half-a-million strong, and were unable to protect the Polish army units withdrawing to the south. The Polish state now faced the threat of not only total military defeat, but also the loss of legal and constitutional continuity. Almost its entire territory was controlled by an enemy alliance, and its constitutional authorities had been incapacitated by an erstwhile ally. The situation was further complicated by the deep divisions between the followers of Józef Piłsudski, who had ruled Poland continuously since May 1926, and opposition political groupings, including the Polish Socialist Party (PPS) on the left, the Peasant Party (SL) in the center, and the National Party (SN) on the right. Neither the threat of war nor the outbreak of hostilities could induce the ruling group to respond positively to proposals to reach agreement and form a coalition government. Most probably this did not affect the course of military events, but it constituted an additional factor undermining the government 's authority.

Opposition groups did not openly criticize the government, but some of them soon began to consider the possibility of a change in the ruling group. As early as 3 September, General Władysław Sikorski met with activists of the Peasant Party. By mid-September he had become a candidate for the highest state office. A former colleague of Józef Piłsudski, Sikorski was a distinguished veteran of the war of 1919–20 and had served as prime minister from 1922 to 1923; following the May coup of 1926 he was ousted from the army and became associated with the centrist opposition group, the Morges Front; he was well known in Europe as a military theorist, and especially esteemed in France. Without having been assigned a post in the government, General Sikorski left Warsaw at the same time as the civil and military authorities, arriving in Romania on 18 September. There he not only gained the support and goodwill of the French ambassador to Poland, who had also fled to Bucharest with the rest of the diplomatic corps, but he also found supporters among the staff of the Polish embassy. Opposition politicians gathered in the Romanian capital, although many of those who commanded the greatest public respect were missing; some (such as the socialist Mieczysław Niedziałkowski and Peasant Party activist Maciej Rataj) remained under siege in Warsaw, while others (such as Wincenty Witos) hesitated to leave the country.

The government of the Republic tried in vain to free itself from the "Romanian trap," and in light of the total military collapse, considered it vital to maintain continuity in state institutions. Thus on 22 September, when the French ambassador left Bucharest—accompanied by General Sikorski—he was carrying two sealed envelopes given to him by Polish president Ignacy Mościcki. One of these was addressed to the Polish ambassador in Paris, the second to his counterpart in Rome, General Bolesław Wieniawa-Długoszewski. This second letter appointed General Wieniawa, "the most faithful of the faithful" subordinates of Marshal Piłsudski, vice president of the Polish Republic. The French government, however, declared that, "to its deep regret, it can see no possibility of recognizing any government" that the vice president designate might appoint. After a series of heated discussions in Paris among the ever-growing number of Polish politicians of various stripes who were gathering there, General Wieniawa relayed to Romania his decision to resign. Three ambassadors—Julian Łukasiewicz from Paris,

Edward Raczyński from London, and General Wieniawa—decided on 28 September to support the candidacy of Władysław Raczkiewicz, currently speaker of the Sejm, formerly minister of internal affairs in many governments and provincial administrator, and someone who for some time had not been directly involved in the political feuding. His candidacy was supported by the group around General Sikorski, and thus by the French also. On 29 September President Mościcki put his signature to a document announcing his own resignation and the appointment of Radkiewicz. Prime Minister Felicjan Sławoj-Składkowski also announced the resignation of the entire government. The following day the new president was ceremoniously sworn in. After a brief hesitation, he entrusted General Sikorski with the task of forming a new government. Sikorski's cabinet, sworn in on 1 October, was a coalition of the kind needed to effect a "gentle" transfer of power. In this way, thanks to the authoritarian Constitution of 1935, whose article 24 allowed for the president to appoint his successor without requiring the decision to be ratified by any other body, the formal legal continuity of the state was preserved.

During the night of 26–27 September, thus at a time when both the president and the prime minister, as well as the commander in chief, still formally held office and Warsaw was on the verge of capitulation, the commander of the forces defending the capital, General Juliusz Rommel, relayed to General Michał Karaszewicz-Tokarzewski the order issued by Marshal Edward Rydz-Śmigły granting him the authority to form an underground military organization. This decision was recognized by both the Commissioner for the Civil Defense of Warsaw, Stefan Starzyński, and by leading opposition politicians present in the city. Before any Wehrmacht units entered Warsaw, Tokarzewski established the Polish Victory Service (SZP), with the approval of the Polish government.

Although crushed by two incomparably stronger enemies, the Polish state—understood as a set of institutions functioning on the basis of the Constitution of the Republic—affirmed its continuity relatively quickly, thanks to the far-reaching agreement reached by the country's major political forces.

THE POLICY OF THE OCCUPYING POWERS

An additional factor that made it essential to ensure the continuity of state institutions and maintain their constitutional legitimacy and international recognition was that both the aggressors had agreed, in the pact of 23 August, that "in the course of subsequent events," they would discuss the eventuality "of retaining a separate Polish state." It seems that the Third Reich was particularly interested in creating some kind of satellite state structure (*Reststaat*), since Hitler still counted on coming to an agreement with France and—first and foremost—Great Britain. Such an eventuality was also taken into account in Moscow, although it is hard to envisage what kind of Soviet-German condominium might have emerged. In any event, in the joint communiqué signed by the Third Reich and the USSR the day after Soviet forces marched into Poland, both governments proclaimed that their goals included "the restoration of peace and order in Poland" and "assisting the Polish population to rebuild conditions allowing for its political existence." Similarly, the communiqué of 22 September, published the following day, with its reference to a "demarcation line" rather than a "border" could be seen as suggesting that such a plan was under consideration. Only on 25 September did Stalin state clearly, in a conversation with the German ambassador, that "he considered it an error to retain an independent, rump Polish state."

The "Agreement on Borders and Friendship," signed during the night of 28–29 September in Moscow, assumed that the boundary established by the two aggressors was "final" and that responsibility for "the necessary state system" would be assumed on each side by the government of the Reich and the USSR respectively. Stalin proposed an amendment to the "secret clause" of the August pact that would "give back" to Germany Polish territory up to the Bug (rather than the Vistula) in exchange for Lithuania being transferred to "the Soviet sphere of influence." In this he was undoubtedly motivated by the desire to rid himself of territory whose population was overwhelmingly Polish and hence a major political problem. Nevertheless, in the first half of September both Germany (in the so-called Moltke Plan) and the USSR took initial steps to carry out the provisions of the Ribbentrop-Molotov Pact. The agreement signed on 28 September, in accordance with Stalin's proposal, established a boundary line along the San, Bug, Narew, and Pisa rivers, although isolated Polish units continued to resist occupation (the crew of the Hel capitulated on 2 October, and a larger unit, the Polesie Operational Group under General Franciszek Kleeberg, surrendered on 6 October). Poland's total defeat was obvious before this, and both aggressors celebrated their victory for the first time on 23 September with a joint parade in Brest. Stalin in particular had many reasons to be satisfied: he had enlarged Soviet territory at little cost, achieving domination over the Baltic states and the western part of Romania (which he would soon "consume" by incorporation), and leading the Red Army to the banks of the River Bug, to the very gates of Central Europe. In addition, the Western powers continued to display—to put it mildly—extreme restraint in the face of his attack on Poland. The British government acknowledged (after some discussion) that it was not "bound by any treaty to take part in a war against the USSR" and publicly expressed "the deepest reservations" regarding such a step. France adopted an identical position. Both countries admitted clearly that faced with war against the Third Reich and the probability that it would engage in further acts of aggression in Europe, it was not in their interest to increase tensions with the Soviet Union. Since neither Britain nor France had taken any military action against the Germans, the two totalitarian states considered they were free to deal as they liked with the territory they had divided between themselves.

The two powers did not coordinate subsequent actions relating to Polish territory nor did they bother to inform each other about such actions. They each adopted different policies in relation to the "state system," partly as a result of differences in their long-term goals and political systems, and partly because Germany occupied by far the largest part of the territory that was ethnically Polish.

The Soviet Union's first moves involved steps toward seizing control over Lithuania. In order to facilitate the early stages of this takeover, the Soviet leadership reached an agreement with Lithuania (signed on 10 October), whereby it transferred to Kaunas part of the former Polish-Lithuanian border area, together with Vilnius, which the Lithuanians regarded as their historic capital. In exchange, Lithuania agreed to allow Red Army units to be stationed on its territory. In Poland's remaining eastern provinces, a short and violent propaganda campaign was followed, on 22 October, by elections held in an atmosphere of brutal pressure. This totalitarian-style voting gave birth, in Białystok, to the People's Assembly of Western Belorussia, and, in Lvov, to the People's Assembly of Western Ukraine. These bodies then requested that the Supreme Soviet of the USSR allow them to be incorporated into, respectively, the Belorussian and Ukrainian Soviet Socialist Republics. On 1 November the Supreme Soviet granted the request of the Białystok deputies and a day later reached a similar decision regarding the request from Lvov. Poland's eastern provinces were thus simply incorporated into the USSR and became—from Moscow's point of view—an integral part of its territory. Soviet administrative and political structures were quickly developed, and in a decree of 29 November the Presidium of the Supreme Soviet granted all permanent residents of these provinces Soviet citizenship. With this came the obligation to serve in the Red Army. All in all, Stalin incorporated nearly one half of the territory of the Second Republic, an area inhabited by roughly 14.3 million people (excluding those who had fled there from western and central Poland). Estimates suggest that more than half of these were Ukrainians and Belorussians.

Hitler imposed his "state system" on Polish territory somewhat more quickly than Stalin, since he saw no need to mimic democracy in the Soviet fashion. On 8 October he issued a decree annexing to the territory of the Third Reich the regions of Pomerania, Wielkopolska, and Silesia. By the end of November a similar fate had befallen the region around Łódź, northern Mazowsze, Suwałki, and the so-called Kraków Basin. This annexed territory, covering approximately ninety thousand square kilometers, had a population of roughly ten million.

A separate decree of 12 October (published two weeks later) established on the remaining Polish lands the Government-General for the Occupied Polish Territories (after the defeat of France, the reference to Poland was dropped, so that no trace remained of their former national status). The Government-General (GG) was divided into four districts, its "capital" was Kraków, and the governor wielded power from Wawel Castle. This part of former Poland, an area of approximately ninety-eight thousand square kilometers, had a population of over twelve million, which increased rapidly when, from early October, the German authorities began the massive expulsion of Poles and Jews from the directly annexed territories.

Thus, just a few weeks after the end of the September campaign, the former territory of the Second Republic was under the control of four different regimes imposed by the occupying forces: a small part had been absorbed by Lithuania; three further parts, more or less similar in size and population, had been incorporated into the Soviet Union, annexed by the Third Reich, or brought under the rule of the newly established occupying structures of the Government-General. Although Stalin and Hitler assured each other in their agreement of 28 August that the "system" they had introduced would provide a "firm foundation for the progressive development of friendly relations" between their nations, this provision of the fourth partition of Poland was broken in less than two years.

PARTITION OF POLAND, SEPTEMBER 1939–JUNE 1940

(1) ANNEXED BY GERMANY

(2) GOVERNMENT-GENERAL

(3) VILNIUS REGION CONTROLLED BY LITHUANIA,
OCTOBER 1939–JUNE 1940

(4) ANNEXED BY USSR   (RIBBENTROP-MOLOTOV PACT)

SOVIET OCCUPATION POLICY

While the two occupying powers had quite different long-term goals, simi-
larities could be found in the way they treated the inhabitants of the territory they had seized. Stalin undoubtedly viewed the incorporation of
Poland's eastern borderlands into the Soviet Union as a step in the direction
of implementing the plan for world revolution, which also happened to further the imperialist interests of the Soviet state. The immediate goal was to
incorporate the newly captured provinces into the USSR by, among other

things, imposing Soviet administrative structures, legal institutions, and regulations, including those relating to property and economic management. By decreeing the borderlands part of Belorussia and Ukraine, the Soviet Union cleared the way for their "belorussification" and "ukrainianization" rather than their "russification," but the main aim was their sovietization. The nationalization of industry, poorly developed in the region, was accompanied by the "socialization" of trade and the transformation of large landholdings into state farms. All Polish, Belorussian, Ukrainian, and Jewish organizations—political, social, economic, and cultural—were shut down. Newspapers and periodicals were closed, regardless of their political affiliation or the ethnicity of the publishers. The activities of the clergy and religious organizations—whether Catholic, Orthodox, or Jewish—were restricted. The entire fabric of social and public life was destroyed and replaced by Soviet-style institutions and organizations.

The Poles, who were seen as constituting the main obstacle to systemic change, were not the only victims, but they were undoubtedly the chief victims in this rapid process of unification. While fighting was still taking place, the political officers of the Red Army called for "a settling of accounts" with the "Belopoles" and the "Polish lords." While such calls belonged to the standard revolutionary repertoire of class warfare, they were closely intertwined with aggression toward all Poles, clearly expressed in propaganda equating the Polish population with the class enemy and appealing to "our oppressed Ukrainian and Belorussian brothers." When Soviet forces were entering Poland and while the new authorities were being installed, several thousand people, including many civilians, fell victim to execution, lynching, and numerous other acts of violence. Voluntary militia groups were established in the majority of small towns and villages, their members recruited largely from the Belorussian, Ukrainian, and Jewish populations. They initially assisted front-line units maintain order and subsequently worked with the People's Commissariat for Internal Affairs (NKVD), whose staff was almost entirely drawn from the far reaches of the USSR. Similarly, a large proportion of responsible positions in the administration, the economy, education, and culture were filled by people newly arrived from Kiev, Minsk, or even Moscow, rather than by local people "liberated from Polish domination." Such restrictions also applied to communists, who carried the stigma of the 1938 dissolution of the Polish Communist Party, and especially to the Poles and Jews who had fled eastward from the approaching front and the numerous fugitives from German occupation.

The external appearance of the captured territory changed rapidly, becoming similar to that of the whole USSR: streets and squares, and even cinemas and theaters, were given new names drawn from the revolutionary or even "progressive" repertoire (in this, priority was given to local, but not Polish, traditions); goods disappeared from the stores in a flash, and customers waited in long lines of a kind not seen since the end of the previous war (shortages were aggravated by the massive purchase of all kinds of goods by the newcomers from the USSR); propaganda billboards and banners became a permanent feature of the landscape in cities and towns; in Lvov, the largest—and essentially sole—cultural center, both universities underwent "ukrainianization," although Poles continued to teach there, among them fugitives from the Government-General, such as the writer, Tadeusz Boy-Żeleński. Churches—both Catholic and Orthodox—and synagogues were gradually turned into warehouses or, in some cases, "museums of atheism"; Soviet teaching programs and Soviet customs were introduced into the schools; new newspapers appeared, the Polish-language paper bearing the characteristic title *Czerwony Sztandar* (Red Banner); the repertory of cinemas and theaters underwent a great change, and in the case of the latter, so did the audience—the most visible sign of the cultural revolution initiated by the new authorities.

Among the main national groups who inhabited the captured provinces there was no shortage of people willing to participate in these changes. Some took part for ideological reasons; these were not only communists but also (at least, as far as the Poles were concerned) some left-leaning intellectuals without any particular party affiliation. Others joined in out of the desire to conform or from simple careerism. Many members of the former national minorities who took part were motivated by resentment of, and hostility to, Poland, where they had felt themselves (with good reason) to be second-class citizens. Those who collaborated with the new authorities even included people who had until recently belonged to nationalist organizations, although the majority of these did not collaborate but tried to engage in underground activity. In January 1941, forty members of Stepan Bandera's Organization of Ukrainian Nationalists (OUN) were sentenced to death in a grand show trial.

From 1938 on, the NKVD, under the new leadership of Lavrenty Beria, somewhat moderated the terror in the USSR itself, but this was not the case in the freshly incorporated territories. In the fall of 1939 they were swept by a massive wave of arrests, whose victims included political, social, and economic activists from a variety of backgrounds, government officials, retired military personnel, priests, and—in January 1940—even some procommunist writers. Prison cells were also filled with people who had been caught trying to flee the country, most often on the Romanian or Hungarian border. November saw the first arrests of those engaged in the growing underground resistance movement. Many of these arrests were the result of denunciation, the activity of agents and informers, and, in the case of those trying to flee, provocation. The notorious special courts of the Soviet Union handed down stiff sentences, many of them imposed in absentia. In March 1940 the Politburo of the Communist Party of the Soviet Union (CPSU) took the decision to execute eleven thousand out of nineteen thousand prisoners. There was no mercy for "speculators," most of whom were simply ordinary people trying to put together supplies that would see them through a hard winter under occupation.

In order for the terror to be effective, however, it had to be applied on a mass scale: in the first half of 1940, whole families and entire social groups were deported—at least 330,000 people, according to secret NKVD data. In February, the victims included Polish settlers, virtually the whole staff of the forestry service, and state administration employees; in April—the families of prisoners of war and of those who had been arrested or sentenced; in June—fugitives from central and western Poland (most of them Jews). The deportees were transported in appalling conditions to Kazakhstan, to the Urals, and to western Siberia, where they were given the same status as Soviet "special migrants," people sentenced to deportation not by the courts but by Special Boards of the NKVD. This meant that they were not only deprived of all rights but left without work or a means of livelihood. Their condition did not attract particular attention, since these regions had been settled in similar fashion for over ten years, largely by the victims of collectivization.

More than 200,000 prisoners of war also suffered a cruel fate. In April 1940, after a few hundred had been selected and moved to a separate camp (Griazowiec), all remaining officers, both professionals and reservists, including soldiers of the Border Defense Corps and State Police officials, were murdered on the order of the CPSU Politburo. Altogether some fifteen thousand people who had been detained in camps in Kozielsk, Starobielsk, and Ostaszków were killed, among them teachers, doctors, scientists, lawyers, and engineers. By Christmas 1939 chaplains and clergy of all denominations had already disappeared from the camps. Only a few soldiers and NCOs were freed or handed over to the Germans; some remained in the labor camps scattered over Ukraine and Belorussia while others were transported to the camps in Komi, in the northern Urals, or to the depths of Siberia. Sizable groups were dispatched to the regions from which no one returns, Kolyma and Chukotka. After being incorporated into the Soviet Union, the Baltic states were also "purged," but the big wave of deportations took place just before the outbreak of war between Germany and the Soviet Union, in May-June 1941, when about ninety thousand people were forcibly removed from the former Polish provinces.

If we include smaller waves of transports, at least 400,000 people were deported; of these, two-thirds were Poles and 20 percent were Jews. Several tens of thousands—excluding prisoners of war—were detained in camps and prisons. These (former) Polish citizens who were dispatched to Siberia and elsewhere against their will included young people liable to be called up for military service; these draftees (as many as 200,000, according to some estimates) were usually assigned to "construction battalions" or "mobilized" as manual workers. In less than two years, as many as one million people were deprived of their freedom in one way or another; of these, a substantial proportion (20–25 percent, according to some estimates) were murdered or died as a result of extremely harsh living conditions. By the time war broke out between Germany and the Soviet Union, when retreating NKVD units murdered several thousand prisoners, the eastern provinces of the Polish Republic had been soaked in blood and literally decimated.

Stalin's policy toward the region was not, however, simply to unleash a reign of terror. The terror was not an end in itself but an integral part of the system. People who more or less willingly took part in sovietization were generally not threatened and could even count on receiving—in line with Soviet customs and possibilities—various privileges and perquisites. After the fall of France, the central authorities in Moscow were clearly interested in constructing some kind of "Polish alternative." The 9,500 soldiers and policemen captured in Lithuania did not meet the same fate as those who had been murdered just two months previously. On 25 November 1940 a ceremonial gathering of Soviet Slavic specialists celebrated the eighty-fifth anniversary of the death of Adam Mickiewicz. While it is true that three former prime ministers of the Polish Republic (Leon Kozłowski, Aleksander Prystor, and Leopold Skulski) found themselves in prison, a fourth, Kazimierz Bartel, who continued to teach at Lvov Polytechnic, was summoned to

Moscow on several occasions. One can assume that the discussions ranged beyond issues related to his specialty, descriptive geometry. Early in the fall of 1940 Beria ordered that a select group of Polish officers (among them Colonel Zygmunt Berling, who had been relieved of his command shortly before the outbreak of war) be taken to Malachówka in order to begin preparations for the creation of an army. At the beginning of June 1941, the highest Soviet authorities decided to create an armed division made up of "people of Polish nationality."

Around this time, a group of Polish communists was assigned to the Comintern school and told to come up with proposals for the future of their country. In January 1941 they published the first issue of a monthly journal, *Nowe Horyzonty* (New Horizons). Its editor in chief was Wanda Wasilewska, the daughter of one of Józef Piłsudski's close associates, who had joined the Soviet Communist Party in December 1940. From March 1941, a growing number of former members of the Polish Communist Party were politically rehabilitated and accepted as members of the Soviet party. The NKVD began recruiting Poles willing to gather intelligence in the areas occupied by Germany.

It is difficult to assess the effectiveness of the sovietization campaign. If we believe the accounts of eyewitnesses such as Józef Mackiewicz, many people adapted to the new reality, and the number of people willing to cooperate actively, even to denounce others, was large enough to meet the needs of the authorities. In October 1939 a frightened population turned out en masse to vote, although it is reasonable to suppose that the high turnout resulted from the illusions nurtured by the non-Polish inhabitants regarding a system that so strongly proclaimed its internationalism. The enormous difficulties encountered by those who were trying to organize resistance suggest not only extensive penetration by the NKVD but also widespread reserve toward such efforts in the Polish community. The resistance in Lvov experienced particular difficulties, but in the Białystok region organized resistance remained sporadic until the second half of 1941. A substantial number of people continued to be active in cultural and scientific life, and the *Dekalog Polaka*, a set of unofficial guidelines on how to conduct oneself when dealing with the occupying forces, widely distributed in the Government-General, was not published in the Soviet zone.

Nevertheless, groups of partisans continued to be active long after the death of the famous Major Hubal, and the spring of 1940 brought them new recruits in the form of young men avoiding military service. In the early

49

summer of 1941, when all the borderlands found themselves under German occupation, the resistance movement developed rapidly, not only among the Poles but also among the Ukrainians, whose efforts to resist Soviet occupation had been weak and had met with severe persecution. In both Belorussia and Lithuania, political activists emerged. It is probably true to say that in the years 1939–41, terror was more important than persuasion in determining the behavior of the population of the borderlands, irrespective of nationality.

THE CASE OF THE VILNIUS REGION

The fate of the population of Vilnius and the surrounding region was quite different, but only for a period of a little under nine months. The Lithuanian army and administration did not take control of the region until 27 October 1939, which gave the NKVD more than a month to carry out numerous arrests and to seize a large amount of property. This served to heighten the sense of relief when the new authorities took over. The Kaunas government was decidedly hostile toward Poles (and Jews), but it did not resort to terror of the kind inflicted by the NKVD. Polish soldiers and officers were interned, and their living conditions were harsh, but they were not threatened with extermination. Vilnius underwent a rapid process of "lithuanization," but the young republic had neither the strength nor the means to undertake radical measures. The university was "de-polonized," many state and community officials lost their jobs, a large proportion of the Polish inhabitants were deprived of their civil rights, and extremist groups of Lithuanian nationalists attempted to intimidate the Polish and Jewish population with the aid of armed bands that roamed the streets with impunity. Many Lithuanian priests were also ill disposed toward the Poles and gave vent to their feelings. These conflicts persisted despite a resurgence of activity on the part of supporters of Polish-Lithuanian understanding, traditionally numerous in the region, and who received permission to publish a newspaper, *Gazeta Codzienna* (Daily Gazette). For many Polish groups—especially the intelligentsia and fugitives from German and Soviet occupation—this degradation was painful, but Lithuania's relative prosperity meant that the standard of living was considerably higher than in the Government-General or Białystok and Lvov, and as for the level of personal security, there was no comparison. While most Poles considered themselves to be living under occupation, the real danger arrived with the Red Army, which invaded Lithuania on 15 June 1940.

THE OCCUPATION POLICY OF THE THIRD REICH

While Moscow's policy toward all the incorporated provinces of the Polish Republic was more or less uniform, the Third Reich had more complex and longer-range plans for the territory it had seized. Those regions that had been directly annexed and were intended to remain so even in the event of an agreement with France and Great Britain were to undergo complete and rapid germanization. This meant that the inhabitants of the annexed territories were the first to experience Nazi terror.

The terror began at the same time that the battlefront was moving eastward and reached its peak during the first few weeks following annexation. Specially trained units carried out a campaign, code-named *Unternehmen Tannenberg,* as a result of which sixteen thousand people were either killed on the spot or incarcerated. The chief targets were the intelligentsia, social activists, and wealthy property owners. These social groups—as well as all Jews—formed the majority of those who were deported. By the spring of 1940, around 400,000 people, most of them from Pomerania and Wielkopolska, had been dispatched to the Government-General. Before deportation they were stripped of all possessions, although such action only became "legal" in a decree dated 17 September 1940, nearly a year after such deportations began.

The wave of expropriation and expulsion continued for much longer, a large proportion of deportees being sent as forced labor to the Reich. Many peasants had their land confiscated and were left to work as daylaborers for German settlers, who gradually arrived not so much from the Reich itself as from German communities in Latvia, Estonia, and Transylvania. All Polish institutions and organizations, including businesses, as well as educational institutions at all levels, were liquidated. At the same time, Poles were denied the right to worship in their own language: 461 of the 681 priests in the Poznań diocese were sent to concentration camps, and nearly all the others were deported to the Government-General; of the eight hundred churches in and around Warta, the Germans left Poles with only thirty (and Germans with fifteen).

One departure from the policy of germanization by uprooting Poles was the campaign, undertaken after the outbreak of war with the Soviet Union, to register people as German nationals (*Volksdeutsche*). According to some estimates, as many as two million Poles registered, some of them voluntarily, others under pressure. Some of these people were candidates for germanization, others were destined to become cannon fodder for the

Wehrmacht. A similar scheme involved the kidnapping of Polish children who had the appropriate "racial characteristics." Czesław Madajczyk has estimated that between 150,000 and 200,000 children (but not all of them from territory annexed to the Reich) were germanized in this way.[1] German policy in the annexed territories varied somewhat from one region to another: Poles faced the harshest terror in Pomerania, the terror in Silesia was relatively milder, and in northern Mazuria (annexed to East Prussia), conditions were more like those in the Government-General.

The population of the regions within the boundaries of the Government-General was overwhelmingly Polish, with Jews to be found in the towns and smaller urban settlements and some Ukrainians in the southeast. These people were to be gradually germanized. While the details of this process were left somewhat vague, the main aim was clear: to transform the Poles into a class of slave-laborers whose numbers would be determined by "demand" and to exterminate and/or deport the "surplus" to the eastern regions of the future Great Reich. The Germans also planned to colonize whole regions by creating "islands" from which they would remove the Polish population (one such attempt was made, unsuccessfully, in the region around Zamojsk). During the war, however, the General Plan for the East had to be put on hold.

If we exclude (but why should we?) the murders carried out at the front, systematic, physical terror began shortly after the establishment of a civilian administration and the creation of the Government-General. The first blow was of a symbolic kind: on 6 November, 183 faculty members in Kraków's colleges and university (including 34 members of the Polish Academy of Learning) were arrested and sent to concentration camps. The Polish intelligentsia had become public enemy number one. Another act of terror, intended to intimidate the population, was carried out on 27 December in Wawer, near Warsaw, where 106 Poles were rounded up on the streets and shot in revenge for the killing of two German soldiers. Late in the spring of 1940, the Nazis carried out a sweeping campaign known as the Extraordinary Pacification Campaign (*Ausserordentliche Befriedungsaktion*), during which they arrested 3,500 political and social activists, most of whom were executed over the next few weeks (among those murdered were Maciej

---

1. Czesław Madajczyk, *Faszyzm i okupaja, 1938–1945*, vol. 1 (Poznań, 1983), 244. According to other Polish historians, the number of children subjected to germanization did not exceed fifty thousand.

Rataj and Mieczysław Niedziałkowski). We cannot exclude the possibility that this campaign was coordinated with Stalin's decision to execute Polish officers in the Soviet Union, most of them reservists.

Campaigns of this kind, carried out over the whole territory of the Government-General or undertaken at the lowest levels of the complex machinery of police terror directed against the civilian population, were a constant feature of the occupation. All non-German inhabitants of the Government-General were subject to summary courts, established on 31 October 1939. On 1 January 1942, a "special criminal law" (*Polenstrafrecht*) came into effect, its provisions covering not only the local population but also Poles who had been deported to the Reich as forced laborers. On 21 June 1943, the territory of the Government-General was designated a "region threatened by bandits" (*Bandenkampfgebiete*), which signified not so much a change in legal principles as an increase in police terror. It was in the Government-General that the Germans built a vast network of concentration camps (in May 1940 work began on the construction of the camp at Auschwitz), which was needed to deal with the infinite number of candidates for incarceration. Yet another form of terror were the raids in which people were seized on the street and then dispatched to a camp, deported to Germany as forced labor, or summarily executed in reprisal for some action on the part of the resistance.

Germany's policy toward the Polish population became harsher when its forces began the push to the east. The attack on the USSR was also the signal to begin realizing imperial ambitions on a world scale. In 1942 alone, seventeen thousand Poles were executed, and in the fall of that year the "Zamojsk experiment" got under way, with the expulsion of 150,000 people from the region. The machinery of death was set in motion and did not slow down even after the German defeat at Stalingrad (February 1943), when some attempts were made to implement the "new approach" demanded by Goebbels. Between October 1943 and July 1944, eight thousand people were executed in Warsaw alone. Every year, more than 100,000 people were dispatched to prisons and concentration camps. From March 1943 onward, any Pole sentenced to more than six months' imprisonment, anyone convicted of a misdemeanor or petty theft, could be sent to the death camps.

In contrast to the annexed territories, the Germans allowed some Polish institutions in the Government-General to continue functioning under their direct supervision. Secondary schools and all institutions of higher education were closed down, but elementary schools continued to operate, as did some vocational schools. Local administration was generally in the hands of Poles, although the authorities made constant efforts to restrict its sphere of competence and to bring in Germans or *Volksdeutsche*. Polish courts continued to function, except that they now dealt only with civil cases and only if they did not involve Germans. The Germans also used former police officers and commanders to staff the newly established Polish Police (commonly referred to as the "blue police"), which had between eleven and twelve thousand employees.

Some commercial enterprises also continued to operate, including the Społem network of retail cooperatives and the PKO savings bank. The Polish Red Cross was allowed to function, as was the Main Welfare Council, a charitable organization. Poles continued to hold executive positions in the postal service, the railroads, and tax offices. The Government-General issued its own postage stamps, including one depicting Wawel Castle, where the governor, Hans Frank, had set up office. Partly in order to facilitate the economic exploitation of the territory, the Government-General issued new banknotes. These were denominated in złoties and bore the name of the Issuing Bank of Poland. All property of the Polish state was confiscated, while medium- and large-scale property holdings were placed under German trusteeship. Land holdings remained undisturbed, except that farm production was dictated by the needs of the Third Reich, which imposed a system of compulsory deliveries, and many estates were managed by German trustees.

As early as the fall of 1939, the Germans made work compulsory for all inhabitants of the Government-General between the ages of fourteen and sixty. The purpose of this order was to ensure a steady supply of labor to the Reich. Although there were constant calls for volunteers, the overwhelming majority of those who went to work in Germany were forced to do so, often because they had been rounded up in a street raid. In 1939, several tens of thousands of people were forcibly transported to Germany and the annexed territories; in the years 1940–41, nearly 500,000 people were sent to join them. In the spring of 1940, a large proportion of the nearly 400,000 private soldiers and NCOs held prisoner of war were drafted as forced labor; by the summer of 1944, 1.3 million Poles were engaged in forced—or rather, slave—labor.

Following the outbreak of war with the USSR, the Germans annexed Eastern Galicia (together with Lvov), turning it into a fifth district of the

Government-General and introducing all the principles and methods used elsewhere in the territory—but in an even more extreme form. The brutality of the first weeks of German occupation far surpassed anything encountered during the early period of the Government-General. While Kraków's professors had "only" been sentenced to Sachsenhausen concentration camp, their counterparts in Lvov were subjected to a bloody massacre carried out by one of the "action groups" (*Einsatzgruppen*) that the Nazis set up to terrorize the population behind the front. The Białystok region met a somewhat different fate; it was subordinated to the administration of East Prussia. The areas around Wołyn, Nowogród, and Vilnius also remained outside the Government-General, and were divided among various occupying bodies.

The Nazi takeover of territory previously occupied by the Soviet Union rendered the situation of the Polish population immensely more complicated. While Soviet totalitarianism had seen the Poles as the most dangerous enemy in the provinces it had seized from the Republic, it was not a nationalist regime in the traditional sense of the term; Ukrainian, Belorussian, and Lithuanian advocates of independence also suffered repression. The Germans were far from satisfying even the most modest aspirations of these nationalities, but they implemented a policy of a well-controlled "free play of forces" among the nationalities inhabiting Poland's eastern borderlands. They fostered, more or less discretely, the natural anti-Polish sentiments of the other nationalities, and from the very beginning of the occupation encouraged the creation of various kinds of paramilitary, or even outright military, and police formations. Apart from indigenous communists (who were often simply people who had cooperated with the Soviet authorities) and the future Soviet partisans, the Germans identified Poles and Jews as their chief enemies. The main wave of aggression toward the Polish population began in the second half of 1942, culminating in the slaughter of several tens of thousands of people in Wołyn in 1943. But from the very beginning, in both Galicia and in the Vilnius region the Poles faced not one but essentially two enemies.

Thus, after 22 June 1941, all the territory of the Second Republic was under the control of a variety of German occupying agencies. The Government-General occupied 39 percent of the area; approximately 30 percent had been directly annexed by the Third Reich, and the rest—leaving aside a tiny area assigned to Slovakia—was administered by two Commissariats,

PARTITION OF POLAND, JUNE 1941– MARCH 1944

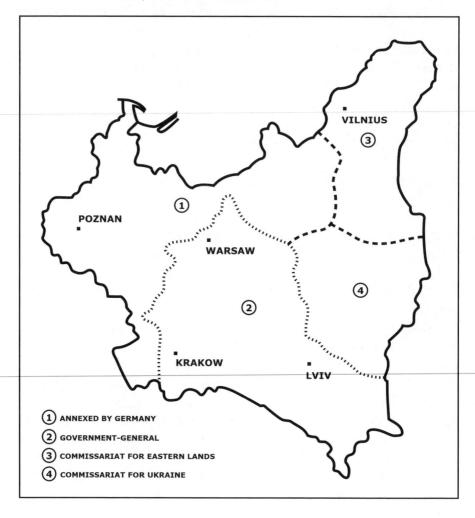

one for Ukraine and one for the so-called Eastern Lands. Nevertheless, everywhere the fate of the Polish population was the same. And everywhere it provoked the same reaction.

Poland's Jews, the largest diaspora in Europe, suffered a far more tragic fate than others. Racism formed the core of the Nazi worldview, and anti-Semitism was its central component. In some cases, usually on the grounds of short-term expediency, Hitler managed to rein in or apply selectively his anti-Slavism (for example, in dealing with Slovenia and Croatia), but in his anti-Semitism he took no heed of tactics or political pragmatism. At the very beginning of their occupation of Poland, the Germans introduced a series of special regulations. These ranged from obliging all Jews to wear a blue or yellow Star of David on their clothing, to forcibly resettling Jews in newly established "Jewish areas" (ghettos) and confiscating all property, to closing off the ghettos and condemning their inhabitants to death by starvation.

In March 1941, Jews—and gypsies, who were also forbidden to move around the country and confined in special camps—were deprived of all legal rights and protections; from October of that year, the death sentence could be imposed not only on anyone who left the ghetto without permission but also on anyone who assisted or sheltered such a person. In the ghettos, the mortality rate reached 20 percent, and more than half the inhabitants found themselves on the verge of death by starvation. Infectious diseases were rampant. Hundreds of thousands of people were dispatched to concentration camps.

After the outbreak of war between Germany and the Soviet Union, preparations for the "final solution"—the enigmatic and bureaucratic term for the operation to murder all the Jews—accelerated. In the fall of 1941, the Germans began construction of extermination centers, among them Majdanek, Chełmno, Bełżec, Treblinka, and Sobibór, and they began experimenting with gas chambers in Auschwitz. Following the liquidation of the smaller ghettos in the Government-General and the "Jewish districts" in the Warta region and the transfer of their population to the larger ghettos of central Poland in January 1942, there began, in the spring of 1942, the final, apocalyptic chapter in the history of Polish (and European) Jewry. Hundred of thousands of people, including many from the West European countries occupied by Germany, were transported to extermination camps and killed in gas chambers; their bodies were subsequently burned in specially constructed crematoria or in monstrous pyres. In the eastern occupied territories, the Germans made greater use than elsewhere of "traditional" methods of extermination, executing people by firing squad in the street, in their homes, or in the camps.

The liquidation of the Warsaw ghetto and its population of more than half a million began in July 1942. Desperate uprisings erupted in some ghettos (for example, the Bialystok uprising of November 1942), the most famous being the Warsaw ghetto uprising in April–May 1943. According to current estimates, approximately half a million Polish Jews died in the ghettos and camps, and a further 2.2 million were killed, not including the thousands who perished or were murdered in the Soviet Union. They accounted for about 90 percent of Poland's Jewish population, of whom about 100,000 people survived, either in hiding or in labor camps, while two or three times that many survived in the USSR. About one million Soviet Jews also died, as did a further two million in the rest of Europe. The Nazis carried out their genocidal campaign with strict precision, often assisted by collaborationist governments or like-minded police or military gangs, and always ignoring all economic and military calculations. The implementation of the racist idea turned out to be the main raison d'état of the Third Reich.

However, when not hindered by aberrant political opinions, Hitler was perfectly capable of engaging in political calculation; this could be seen not only during the years 1933–39, when he exploited all the weaknesses of the Western powers, the conflicts between various countries and national groups (in the Danube basin, for example), and Stalin's revolutionary-imperial ambitions, but also after the outbreak of war. He routed the French army and humiliated Paris, but he allowed the formation there of a satellite government; he agreed to the creation of a collaborationist Croatian state; after occupying Denmark, he left in place the very government on which he had declared war; and in Holland he left the local administration, as well as business and professional organizations, undisturbed. There is no doubt that, in the case of countries considered "racially related" or identical to Germans, this policy had a basis in ideology and formed part of the overall program of the Third Reich. But collaboration and the creation of puppet governments were not confined to the "Nordic" countries, and the Nazi elite contained many people who advocated a more traditional imperialist policy, one that would, for example, exploit ethnic conflicts within the USSR or the anticommunism to be found among the Russians.

While some nuances could be discerned in German policy toward Poland, these more often resulted from a divergence in short-term interests (and ambitions) on the part of different sections of the occupying apparatus than from any differences in overall approach. No administrative agency of the Third Reich suggested to any of the more important political groups in Poland that they collaborate with the occupying forces, nor did the Polish elite come forward with any proposal to cooperate at the political level, and the few such suggestions that came from isolated individuals would seem to confirm this rule. Hitler had no interest in having Poland and the Poles collaborate. Because Poland produced neither a collaborationist government nor any military or paramilitary groups willing to collaborate, and because no Polish Waffen SS units were formed, although more than 200,000 volunteers signed up for such units elsewhere in Europe, it is widely assumed that the Poles—with a few individual exceptions—engaged in determined and unyielding resistance to German occupation.

The situation here really was quite different from that in the regions under Soviet occupation. While it is true that no Polish administrative or paragovernmental structures were created, a considerable number of people cooperated, for ideological reasons, with the Soviet authorities and even tried to engage in political activity, which became somewhat more feasible after 1940. However we assess the results of Stalin's anti-Polish policies, they were based on class rather than nationality or race (at least, during this period).

In the Government-General, and even more so in the territories directly annexed to the Reich, there was no room for maneuver, not even for those, such as the extremist groups of the National-Radical Camp, whose ideology was close to fascism. The attitude of Polish society toward this occupying force was thus essentially much more uniform than that of any other European country occupied by the Nazis. This did not mean, of course, that every Pole "reached for his (or her) weapon" or took an active part in the resistance. Naturally enough, most people, cautious and fearful, sought to adapt somehow, and the most common ways in which they evaded the obligations imposed by the occupying forces were based more on prosaic motives of economic and physical survival than on patriotic ideals.

It is hard to categorize as sabotage such activities as concealing crops and inventory, black market trading, smuggling, employment off the books, and widespread theft—either in the workplace or during transportation—even though they were detrimental to the occupying powers. And they were perceived as such: a large number of those who were arrested, sentenced, and sent to concentration camps, or even executed in the street, had been seized while engaged in just this sort of "economic crime." It is hard to tell whether the scale of the "underground economy" was greater in Poland than in other occupied countries. It certainly existed everywhere, even in the Reich itself, but it could not have existed on such a scale without widespread corruption on the part of the occupying administration, something that the resistance movement also used to its advantage.

It was difficult to be involved in the economy—whether legal, semilegal, or black-market—or in the local administration and business organizations that functioned in the Government-General without cooperating with the occupying forces, which in every instance held complete power over all subordinate institutions and would-be contractors seeking to realize their own ends. Such cooperation was widespread, but even when people engaged in such activity without the agreement, direct or indirect, of the underground resistance, they did not go on to collaborate with the German authorities—in other words, they did not actively and deliberately participate in the subjugation of the Polish population.

Nevertheless, the boundary was not always clear, and the very fact that a person was willing to take a position (that of *wójt*, or village elder, for example) that involved implementing instructions issued by the Germans—such as registering all those eligible for forced labor or ensuring compulsory deliveries—could be seen as going beyond unavoidable or even necessary cooperation. One institution that found itself on this boundary was the "blue police," whose duties included not only such neutral activities as apprehending thieves, breaking up brawls, or maintaining public order, but also taking part (albeit in a subordinate role) in roundups, pacification actions, and in the search for Jews. While a number of police officials cooperated with the underground—according to some estimates, in 1944 this was true of 10 percent of policemen and 20 percent of officers—the general population tended to view the police as an entirely collaborationist institution.

Public opinion also regarded prostitutes whose clients were Germans to be engaged in a form of collaboration, and indeed this was true of all contacts with the Germans, even those that did not go beyond cooperation at the level of the black market and other forms of speculation, behavior that may have been reprehensible, but did not endanger the rest of the population. It is virtually impossible to estimate the scope of such behavior. One indirect indicator is the fact that the resistance leadership established special Adjudication Commissions, which handed down sentences of infamy, reprimands, fines, and even flogging. It would appear that spontaneous actions such as boycotts, beatings, and even executions were more common than sentences handed down by the commissions. Denunciation was one form of collaboration in the Government-General that was by all accounts widespread, as was information-gathering on behalf of the various occupying agencies—the Gestapo, Abwehr, security services, and police. So far, it has not been possible to compile sufficient reliable data concerning the scale of the network of agents established by the Germans, but Włodzimierz Borodziej estimates that "nearly one-third of those under suspicion or arrested found their way into the Gestapo files on the basis of information provided by informers."[2] In many cases, the discovery and liquidation of resistance groups, including groups in the top leadership, resulted from information provided by secret agents. Between January 1943 and June 1944, underground courts sentenced to death around two thousand informers and agents. It should be noted that this form of collaboration, which posed such a threat to the resistance, was rarely motivated by ideology or politics. Most often, the motive was the expectation of financial gain, ensuring the safety of oneself or one's family, or the desire for revenge.

There was relatively little *overt* collaboration involving activity condemned by the resistance (and undoubtedly by the broad public), such as working for the Polish-language press established by the Germans (as did Feliks Burdecki and Jan Emil Skiwski) or appearing in films and propaganda spectacles (as did Bogusław Samborski and Igo Sym). Such cases are still awaiting serious research, but it would seem that "economic" motives outweighed political considerations. A number of such collaborators were recruited from among the Volksdeutsche, members of the former German minority, who placed national loyalty ahead of loyalty to the Polish state, which carried such risks during the occupation. A special case was the collaboration of a group led by a well-known figure in the Podhale region, Wacław Kreptowski, who accepted the Germans' proposal to function as the "führer" of the mountain dwellers around Zakopane.

There were also cases—although exceedingly rare—of a kind of military collaboration, without necessarily any political subtext. In the western territories especially, during 1943–44 partisan units and occupying forces occasionally established a local "cease fire." The best-known such case— and one that had a clear ideological basis—was the agreement between the Świętokrzyska Brigade of the National Armed Forces (NSZ) and German units on a joint withdrawal to the west in the face of advancing Soviet forces.

Neither the Polish population nor any political grouping responded when, in 1943, German propaganda raised the slogan of the "defense of Europe" against the Bolshevik invader. An appeal for volunteers in the summer of 1944 drew only a few hundred people, most of them delinquents and people from the social margins, and the Germans were unable to form a Polish legion. There is, of course, no way of knowing how the population

2. Włodzimierz Borodziej, *Terror i polityka. Policja niemiecka i polski ruch oporu w Generalnej Guberni, 1939–1944* (Warsaw, 1985), 85.

and the political elites would have behaved had the Germans come forward with broader proposals for collaboration or had taken up any of the few offers (that of Władysław Studnicki, for example) that were forthcoming from the Polish side. Such temptations did not, however, exist.

One unintended but unavoidable consequence of the war and occupation was widespread demoralization, including a sharp increase in banditry, a phenomenon that was fought by both the occupying authorities and the resistance (in 1943 alone, the resistance tried and executed some 700 bandits). One of the most despicable activities brought by the war was the blackmail of Jews hiding from the Nazis. Alongside the German's secret agents, who more or less systematically infiltrated various groups and betrayed the Jews they found for a given payment, a horde of individual blackmailers, sometimes working in gangs, "hunted" for Jews of their own accord and without any arrangement with the Germans. This latter group did not act out of ideological or racial motives, although one should not underestimate the role of the widespread and deeply entrenched anti-Semitism to be found in some social groups. It is unlikely that we shall ever know exactly how many Jews were the victims of denunciation or blackmail (the blackmailers frequently handed their victims over to the Germans immediately after taking all their remaining possessions). Neither the numerous appeals and commands issued by the resistance leadership nor the execution of the most dangerous individuals had much effect. War and occupation led to a clearly visible intensification of nationalism, but while the Germans succeeded in exploiting conflicts between the nationalities inhabiting the Second Republic, their efforts to drive a wedge between the Poles themselves—by propagandizing, for example, the notion of a mountain Volk, or urging the Kashubians of Pomerania to turn against their fellow Poles—ended in total fiasco.

Although we should not minimize either the moral dimension or the practical outcomes of the activities of secret agents, informers, and blackmailers, these people constituted a marginal group, albeit a dangerous one and one that, even if small, was still too large. They were one element in a broad field of demoralization consisting of activities that did not extend to treason or participation in Nazi genocide. The draconian nature of the occupation, the constant presence of death, the unending threat associated with the unprecedented impoverishment of many social groups, the acute shortages, and the corruption of the occupying forces themselves—all this resulted in the proliferation of egotism and cynicism; people became callous in the face of others' misfortune, indifferent to the breakdown in moral norms, and inured to brutality.

Despite all this, the Polish population displayed—in my opinion—considerable resistance to what Jan Strzelecki called the Era of the Gas Ovens.[3] The more institutionalized forms of this resistance will be examined below, but here it should be noted that an organized resistance movement would not have been possible without the enormous protection provided by people who had nothing to with the resistance but were prepared to accept its slogans and to render spontaneous assistance to those from the underground. The majority of those who did not capitulate were simply people who remained faithful to the eternal values that demand that we offer aid to those in need and who remained loyal to their own circle, to their own conception of their country, in its immediate and more distant forms. And also to the Polish state. Moreover, there was never a shortage of political, intellectual, and, above all, spiritual authorities who day after day sustained this resistance, resistance that could, after all, be expressed in ways other than armed struggle or underground activity. The mass terror and unprecedented brutality of the occupying power were unable to counteract the factors that helped to integrate society and strengthen attitudes of national solidarity. These same factors, although provoked by a different enemy, also played a role in the territory seized by the Soviet Union.

THE BEGINNINGS OF THE UNDERGROUND STATE

From October 1939 on, the Polish authorities in exile, together with Polish exiles and émigrés, were engaged in unceasing efforts—both political and military—to defend Poland's raison d'état. At the same time, the country that had been crushed by the invaders was engaged in its own efforts to create an underground state and to defend national dignity and identity. It was also preparing for the day of liberation.

During the first few months of partition and occupation following the September defeat, an estimated 150 resistance groups and organizations emerged. According to Tomasz Strzembosz, there were "thousands of small, completely informal groups made up of a dozen or so people who came together to undertake a specific action or simply in order to exchange views."[4] These tiny groups usually—and sooner rather than later—

3. Jan Strzelecki, *Próba świadectwa* (Warsaw, 1971), 16.
4. Tomasz Strzembosz, *Refleksje o Polsce i Podziemiu, 1939–1945* (Warsaw, 1990), 23.

established contact with existing organizations or else formed the nuclei of new ones. Strzembosz not only points to the state of almost feverish activity but also emphasizes the essential, formative role in the Polish resistance played by small groups held together by ties of collegiality or outright friendship and based on a "community of experience and interests." This appears to have been a factor of major significance, but perhaps more psychological than political. We should also take note of a characteristic but by no means unique feature of resistance that helps to explain some of its mechanisms: by its very nature resistance is an activity best carried out in small groups. Even the largest organizations were made up of groups with no more than three or five members, and conspirators knew only a relatively small number of their closest colleagues or associates. The leadership bodies of various underground organizations formally adopted many orders and decisions by circulating proposals in writing for the approval of their members. Commanders did not conduct inspections of their units, nor even, very often, of their complete staff. Political leaders had no opportunity to meet with supporters of their party. Soldiers and party members did not even know the names of all their commanders or leaders, and they usually knew their immediate superiors only by sight and by their pseudonym or false surname. In these circumstances, loyalty and trust were far more important than during times of normal, open, political activity.

The resistance also created, especially during the early phase of the occupation, conditions allowing the emergence of spontaneous local initiatives within a particular area or social group. It encouraged the decentralization and even "decomposition" of existing political parties and social organizations, and the emergence of new leaders and, of course, commanders. Even those groups considered marginal in relation to the main political groups, could, if they had bold and enterprising activists, make as much noise (by publishing newspapers, pamphlets, and leaflets) as the traditional, established political organizations.

While some political groups had for some time been warning of the threat of war, essentially no one was prepared for such a turn of events, and the rapidity with which the front collapsed and a large number of political and military leaders left the country made it even more difficult to adapt to the unexpected situation. The first actions undertaken by the occupying powers were also unexpected, largely because of their unprecedented brutality. The essence and methods of totalitarianism—and both these occupations, despite the differences between them, were carried out by totalitarian states—were unfamiliar and unimagined, even though people knew a fair amount about both the Nazi state and Stalin's Bolshevism. The state authorities had prepared neither a coherent response nor an appropriate intelligence network. Both the General Staff Operational Group for Subversion, established in 1923, and the so-called Committee of Seven (K7), established in 1934 to coordinate the activities of the Intelligence Department of the General Staff and the Ministry of Foreign Affairs, had made preparations for activity in enemy territory. Only after war broke out did they hastily make plans for activity on enemy-occupied Polish territory.

The military defeat and the departure of the state leadership and many members of the high command at a time when the country was still fighting, even if hopelessly, had major political and psychological repercussions in terms of the mood and behavior of the population. Vehement and often extremely emotional accusations were directed at the government and its supporters and the whole "post-May system." The ruling group, until recently a major social force, suddenly found itself in a state of political collapse, where it remained until the end of the war and the occupation. Both within the country and among the émigré community, groups that before September had been in opposition to the government now took steps to remove to the sidelines all members of the previous ruling group. The shifts in moods and opinions brought about a differentiation and a kind of "decentralization" of underground political—and military—life.

The first resistance organizations emerged before the formation of the Polish Victory Service (SZP), mentioned above. In Stanisławów, to the east of Warsaw, Lieutenant-Colonel Jan Mazurkiewicz established on 17 September (i.e., before occupation), the Civil Emergency Service, whose members were drawn from an existing subversive network and which subsequently became known as the Secret Military Organization. On 19 September the Silesia group was formed in Kraków and went on to publish the first clandestine newspaper, *Polska żyje* (Poland Lives). Several days later, also in occupied Kraków, the Union of the White Eagle, subsequently known as the Organization of the White Eagle, was formed from an existing subversive network and groups belonging to the Federation of Riflemen's Clubs. On 29 September in Warsaw, when the German army was just entering the city, members of the Association of Silesian Insurgents created the Association of National Insurgents. At the end of September members of several nationalist political parties formed the Homeland (Ojczyzna) organization in Poznań. During October a number of organizations began to emerge, among them: the Headquarters of the Defenders of Poland (KOP), created at the order of and financed by a disbanded unit of the Border Defense Corps led by General Wilhelm Orlick-Ruckman; Warszawianka, led by Jan Hopper; the Union of Defenders of the Republic, under the command of Tadeusz Żenczykowski; the Musketeers, led by Stefan Witkowski; the Sword and Plow organization, led by Father Leon Paplau; the Wilki Military Organization, under Lieutenant Józef Bruckner; the Secret Polish Army of Lieutenant-Colonel Jan Włodarkiewicz; the Polish Peasant Freedom Action; and the Armed Liberation Command.

Also during October the leaders of virtually all the main political parties decided to begin clandestine activity—the National Party on 13 October, the Polish Socialist Party (under the name Freedom—Equality—Independence [WRN], adopted after the party had officially dissolved itself) on 16 October. They were followed by the Democratic Party (SD), the Labor Party (SP), the two wings of the National Radical Camp—ONR-ABC, which took the name of its journal, *Szaniec* (Bulwark), and ONR-Falanga , under the name Pobudka (Reveille). In mid-February 1940 the Peasant Party (now known as the Peasant Resistance Movement [Roch]), became the last to decide formally to engage in clandestine activity, although it had been active since the very beginning of the resistance.

Some social organizations also began clandestine activity. In addition to the Federation of Riflemen's Clubs and the Association of Silesian Insurgents, other active organizations included the Union of Rural Youth (ZMW Siew), which now called itself the Peasant Organization for Freedom (code name Racławice), and the Firefighters' Resistance Movement, known as Skala. Some of the political parties active in the underground formed their own military organizations. The National Party formed its National Military Organization in October, the PPS established its People's Guard in November, and the Szaniec group created its military wing, the Salamander Union, at the same time as it began underground activity. There were also cases where the military unit was formed before the civilian: in December 1939, for example, the Secret Polish Army established a political organization, Znak (Signal).

Conditions in the underground made it possible—or easier—to institutionalize some of the political differences within various political parties. The National Party lost not only the Homeland group in Poznań but also a group led by Karol Stojanowski known as the National People's Fighting Organization. The left wing of the PPS did not join the WRN, forming instead a group that took the name of its journal, *Barykada Wolności* (Freedom's Barricade), under the leadership of Stanisław Dubois. The leader of the ONR-Falanga, Bolesław Piasecki, took no part in establishing the Pobudka organization, setting up his own group, which came to dominate a coalition of right-wing groups known as the National Confederation.

All these organizations and groups—military, political, and politico-military—indicate how ideologically diverse and geographically dispersed were the beginnings of the resistance. Yet more organizations emerged during the spring of 1940, some of them the result of fusion, others the result of secession and splits. Some, but by no means all, of the last occurred when the occupying powers liquidated an organization's leadership, necessitating its replacement by a new organization, often with a completely different political program. Very often, especially in the case of groups or organizations starting from scratch and without any roots in the surrounding community or political infrastructure, membership in one organization or another was largely a matter of chance: the need for secrecy both created strong bonds of personal loyalty and also made it difficult for an underground activist to contact a group whose political views would more closely match his or her own. In fact, the most important thing for most activists was to take part in resistance activity of some kind or another, not to express their political opinions. Thus the KOP, established by a group of military officers, eventually came to cooperate with the communists. A similar political route was taken by part of the National Defense Guard, established in September 1939 under the command of Colonel Julian Skokowski.

As noted above, the aftereffects of the "September shock" contributed directly to this diversity. The fact that General Michał Karaszewicz-Tokarzewski formed the Polish Victory Service on the orders of Marshal Rydz-Śmigły not only deterred many people from volunteering for service but also led other political groups to look for ways in which they could consolidate their forces. These efforts proceeded even though Tokarzewski, considered a "liberal Piłsudski-ite" before the war, a theosophist and cultured person, succeeded in obtaining the cooperation of the main parties of the pre-September opposition. By 10 October, shortly before his departure on a tour of inspection of the southern and eastern regions of what would become the Government-General, a number of political leaders agreed to establish the Main Political Council, their intention being that it would constitute an integral part of an overall structure resembling the Polish Military Organization of World War I. Among those who established the Council were representatives of the Socialist Party (Mieczysław Niedziałkowski and Zygmunt Zaremba), the Peasant Party (Maciej Rataj, Stefan Korboński), the Democratic Party (Mieczysław Michałowicz), as well as Leon Nowodworski from the National Party. The Council was intended to be an advisory body within the Polish Victory Service, and its chairman (Niedziałkowski) was to fulfill the function of Commissioner for Civilian Affairs and second deputy commander of the SZP.

At first glance it seems surprising that the politicians agreed to a subordinate role in relation to the military commanders, but they formed the Main Political Council while still in a state of shock over the battle for Warsaw and at a time when they considered the situation to be temporary. It is clear from the above that not all political groupings were involved in the creation of the council. Leaving aside the former "government camp," which found itself in a state of crisis exacerbated by the departure from the country of most of its leaders, the National Party disassociated itself from Nowodworski, the Labor Party did not participate in the discussions, and this was true also of the two ONR groups and the right-wing National Workers' Party (NPR). Also absent was the Morges Front, an informal but nevertheless influential grouping, especially after General Sikorski became prime minister. Also missing, obviously, were representatives of various social organizations, some of them extremely powerful, and some of which had recently decided to engage in underground activity. Undoubtedly, participation in the negotiations was also determined by the fact that all these discussions were conducted in secrecy, that communication was difficult, and that many people were moving around—some returning from the east, others making for the south in the hope of crossing into Hungary or Romania—while still others were in hiding.

One of the most important attempts at consolidation, apart from the political parties associated with the Victory Service, was undertaken as early as October by Ryszard Świętochowski, a well-known journalist associated with the Morges Front and the peasant movement. He established the Central Committee of Organizations Fighting for Independence (CKON), which was joined by some of the traditional parties (the SP, NPR, ONR-ABC), some social organizations (ZMW Siew), and some of the newly created resistance groups (the Musketeers, the Secret Polish Army, the National Defense Guard, and the Union for Armed Action). Świętochowski was aided not only by the fact that he was known to be politically close to Sikorski but by the fact that the Polish leaders in Paris favored an approach to resistance activity that completely ignored political parties. He obtained the informal but unequivocal support of the prime minister, which found expression in, among other things, financial support in the form of funds transferred via courier. In light of the fact that the Victory Service was only in its early stages, Świętochowski refused to acknowledge either its claim regarding the exclusive right to organize an underground army or its authority over political parties.

The prime minister needed his own source of political support, because of the restricted membership of the Main Political Council and the Sanacja associations of the SZP, and because the absence of rapid and systematic communications between Poland and the émigré community led to increased confusion. After Świętochowski was arrested in Slovakia in April 1940 while on his way to Paris, his committee disappeared, but a large proportion of its member-organizations established the Coordinating Committee of Organizations Fighting for Independence, which had about twenty-five member groups in June 1940. In September of that year other former members of CKON set up the National Confederation, which was subsequently taken over by Bolesław Piasecki, after most of its member-organizations had left. In October 1942 a dozen or so smaller organizations—including some that had once belonged to CKON—established the Social Self-Defense Organization, this time without any ambition to compete with the large political parties, but undoubtedly with the sense that they had been pushed to the sidelines of the resistance movement.

Colonel Stefan Rowecki, appointed chief of staff and first deputy commander of the Victory Service, turned out to be a most energetic figure and played a major role in establishing the military structures of the underground state. At the beginning of December, work had already begun on creating seven military-district commands, a staff headquarters, and a courier network. Meanwhile, in Paris the Committee of Ministers for the Homeland drew up its own proposals for a resistance movement and established the Association of Armed Struggle (ZWZ), with General Kazimierz Sosnkowski as its commander. On 4 December 1939 Sosnkowski issued Directive No. 1 stipulating that the ZWZ was to be made up of six districts directly subordinate to the commander. The ZWZ was to be a purely military organization, an integral part of the Polish armed forces, and its organizers envisaged no role in it for representatives of political parties. Rowecki was appointed commander of the First District (Warsaw), and Tokarzewski was named commander of the Third (Lvov).

This directive, which reached Warsaw a month after it had been signed, caused considerable confusion and consternation. Nevertheless, the Victory Service leadership began its implementation, taking advantage of the fact that Sosnkowski had authorized Colonel Rowecki (to whom the directive was addressed) to display "flexibility." The political intentions of the creators of the ZWZ were quite clear: the leaders of the Polish Republic in exile were to exercise sole central authority. In advocating such an arrangement, the prime minister was influenced by his distrust of the officers who would be leading the resistance and his fear that a powerful group with political ambitions might emerge among them.

General Sosnkowski soon realized that the ZWZ as initially envisaged could not be made to work. In a second directive, dated 16 January 1940, he ordered the creation of separate commands for the German and Soviet zones, appointing Rowecki commander of the former and Tokarzewski commander of the latter. This more or less corresponded with the intentions of the two creators of the Victory Service, although they argued that Sosnkowski should appoint a deputy inside the country and give him considerable authority. This Sosnkowski agreed to do after the collapse of France had drastically altered the situation. On 18 June, just a few days before his evacuation to England, Sosnkowski appointed Rowecki, already promoted to the rank of general, his deputy. On 30 June, already in London, he appointed him commander of the ZWZ, extending Rowecki's authority over the whole of Poland, and created a new unit within the office of the commander in chief, the Independent Department for the Homeland (Department IV), to maintain contacts with the ZWZ command. In this way, there emerged the basic framework of the main component of the Polish underground state—the underground army. While the ZWZ was the largest military organization, it was not the only one, and a dozen or so underground organizations had yet to be brought under its command. At the same time, there was as yet no overall concept of the role to be played by the forces of the resistance in the overall military strategy of the Allies. These were the tasks awaiting the forty-five-year-old Rowecki, who now called himself General Grot and whose real name was known only to a few.

As far as military structures were concerned, the dissolution of the Victory Service involved a fairly straightforward process of reorganization, but Directive No. 1 had never envisaged any political representation or civilian component. It had proposed that delegates be appointed but had defined neither their status nor the way in which they were to be selected. For its part, the ZWZ leadership in Poland wanted to retain the arrangements set out in the Victory Service statute and approved by several political parties. However, even those parties that had been cooperating with General Tokarzewski from the very beginning were not enthusiastic about being limited to an advisory role. They were thus even more ill disposed to the government's position, which they saw as relegating them to the sidelines of political life.

The parties grouped around the emerging ZWZ belonged to the prewar opposition and had already had enough of the struggle against "partisan politics" that had been waged since 1926. The fact that Sikorski supported Świętochowski's initiative strengthened their conviction regarding the need to form a coalition and maintain contacts with the official military resistance. The arrest of Niedziałkowski and Rataj, the first politicians to cooperate with the commanders of the Victory Service, reinforced this belief. In February 1940 there took place a series of meetings, whose participants included the ZWZ leadership, which resulted in the creation, on 26 February, of the Political Consultative Committee (PKP). The committee was made up of representatives of the three largest prewar opposition parties: PPS-WRN (Kazimierz Pużak), SL-Roch (Stefan Korboński), and the National Party (Aleksander Dąbski). Close cooperation with the ZWZ and acknowledgment of its commanders' professional competence did not mean that committee members had complete political confidence in the military leaders, even though many of them had been directly involved in political activity before the war. The politicians were, no doubt, also mindful of the fact that formal command of the ZWZ rested with the Piłsudski-ite General Sosnkowski.

Cooperation with the parties of the former opposition suited Colonel Rowecki, since it undermined criticism, voiced at home and in exile, regarding the Sanacja sympathies of the military forces he was assembling. At the same time, a certain sense of community among those "at home" versus those "in exile" was created, a completely natural development in the circumstances. This did not signify, of course, a lack of loyalty toward the constitutional authorities, although all the parties of the Consultative Committee were opposed to the Constitution of 1935. The ZWZ's attempts to achieve autonomy largely grew out of technical considerations (effectiveness of leadership, communications, and so on). The chief concern of the politicians was to become a partner of the government, whose main base of support was, after all, in Poland. The arrest of Świętochowski, the founder of CKON; the PKP's good—if not always conflict-free—cooperation with Rowecki, in which the leading role was played by Pużak; and above all, the collapse of France forced the government to change its attitude toward the Consultative Committee. On 18 June now-General Rowecki not only received news of his nomination as Sosnkowski's deputy but was informed that the PKP would henceforth be considered the country's official political representative.

It was at this extremely difficult time for the Polish population, that Colonel Jan Skorobohaty-Jakubowski arrived in Warsaw with the information that he had been nominated as the government's delegate to the homeland and was equipped with the powers of plenipotentiary to organize and lead the entire nonmilitary resistance movement. The collapse of France, however, undermined the authority of the émigré government, especially that of the prime minister, and simultaneously strengthened the position of the military and political leadership within Poland. On 28 June, at a meeting with General Rowecki and Skorobohaty-Jakubowski, the Consultative Committee decided that this group, with exactly this membership, would be known as the Collective Delegatura and would "carry out its activities over the entire territory of the Republic in the name of the government of the Polish Republic." As a gesture of goodwill toward Sikorski, the group co-opted to the PKP Franciszek Kwieciński, a member of the Labor Party, the party closest and most loyal to him. The formation of such an agency signified the creation of a unified, central authority for the resistance, a development that had the potential to reduce the role of the state authorities residing in London to that of representative functions, foreign relations, and command of a small number of armed forces.

General Sikorski managed, nevertheless, to overcome this crisis, strengthening his position vis-à-vis his most vociferous opponents, who themselves had no interest in expanding the competence of an agency created by those political parties against which they had engaged in such bitter struggle for so many years. Hence the government refused to recognize the Collective Delegatura, while its member-parties, known as the "big four," did not wish, and were in no position, to enter into open conflict with it. The Collective Delegatura was dissolved, and the PKP thereby reconstituted itself, while reserving the right to nominate candidates to be the government's delegate, who would thus be obliged to take the views of the Consultative Committee into account. Despite reservations on the part of the representatives of the Socialist and Peasant Parties, the PKP was informed on 3 December 1940 that Cyryl Ratajski, the former president of Poznań and Labor Party activist, had been nominated the government's delegate.

In this way, a year after a start was made on organizing the structure of the underground state, its framework assumed final form, consisting of three separate but interconnected components: military (the Association for Armed Struggle), administrative (the Delegatura—the government delegate and his staff), and political (the Political Consultative Committee). Apart from the delegate's office, their underground structure was already well developed.

IN EXILE

The Polish government-in-exile was, undoubtedly, one of the country's most authoritative institutions, but one that had few opportunities to influence the Polish population directly. It was formed, as noted earlier, on the basis of a far-reaching agreement among the main political parties, whose representatives found themselves in allied France and who made their way to Britain after France fell to Germany. The most notable example of this fragile compromise was the composition of General Sikorski's first cabinet, whose members included politicians from the prewar opposition (Stanisław Stroński as deputy prime minister, Jan Stańczyk, General Józef Haller, Marian Seyda, Aleksander Ładoś, and, from December on, Stanisław Kot) and from the ranks of prominent Piłsudski-ites (August Zaleski, Adam Koc, and General Kazimierz Sosnkowski).

While General Sikorski was a politician who espoused democratic values, he concentrated considerable power into his own hands. Following the resignation of Marshal Rydz-Śmigły, Sikorski took over (on 7 November) the position of commander in chief, which he merged with that of minister for military affairs. His deputies in the ministry (General Marian Kukiel and Ljdoi Modclski) weic officcio completely loyal to him and long antagonis tic to Piłsudski's followers. He rid himself quite rapidly of several inconvenient politicians: as early as November 1939 he dismissed Łukasiewicz from his post as ambassador to France, and Adam Koc left the government in December. On 10 October a special commission was established under the chairmanship of General Haller "to determine the causes of the recent events in Poland," a move clearly directed against the former power elite and intended to discredit it completely. Another commission "to investigate the September campaign" was formed in the summer of 1940. In the end, though, as Eugeniusz Duraczyński points out, General Sikorski "did not allow an overall settling of accounts . . . , considering that an appropriate moment for this would arise when the country had been liberated from its invaders."[5]

Although many leading politicians, and even career officers, were subjected to various petty annoyances, this does not mean that all the prime minister's opponents were at his mercy. Despite strong pressure from Sikorski, President Raczkiewicz designated General Sosnkowski his own successor, and appointed as minister of foreign affairs—one of the most important government posts for a government in emigration—the former head of the ministry during 1926–32, August Zaleski. Nor could Sikorski engage in any major shifts of personnel in the armed forces, which was only natural, given the professional nature of this service and the ongoing war. The approach to the organization of the underground forces in Poland adopted in November 1939 suited the politicians opposed to the prime minister, as did the fact that both the Committee of Ministers for the Homeland (established on 8 November) and the Association for Armed Struggle were headed by General Sosnkowski, Sikorski's chief rival.

The whole opposition—and even some of those belonging to the "post-May" camp—were sharply critical of the 1935 constitution, but it was clear to everyone that in the current situation, upholding the constitution and acting according to the letter of its provisions was a major factor in securing the external legitimacy of the Polish state and a deterrent to all those who might wish to present themselves as the government or quasi-national representatives of the nation, including those who might do so with the encouragement of the occupying powers. Nevertheless, the former opposition feared the enormous power that the constitution conferred on the president of the Republic and demanded that President Raczkiewicz accept certain restrictions on his powers. After understandable resistance the president agreed, issuing a declaration (announced over the radio on 30 November and subsequently published in *Monitor Polski*) in which he stated that in exercising his constitutional powers to engage in "independent activity," he would act "in close cooperation with the chairman of the Council of Ministers." He also declared that any eventual successor to the presidency would also be bound by these restrictions. While this so-called Paris agreement never became law in the literal sense of the word, it constituted a major

5. Eugeniusz Duraczyński, *Rząd polski na uchodźstwie 1939–1945* (Warsaw, 1993), 51.

element in the compromise reached between the political parties in exile. The fact that the president's declaration referred to the prime minister rather than the whole Council of Ministers clearly strengthened Sikorski's position—and in relation to not only the president but also his colleagues in his own cabinet.

During November and December 1939 several further politico-legal measures were undertaken. On 2 November the president dissolved the Sejm and Senate, and on 1 December signed an order calling for new elections to take place two months "after the cessation of *force majeur*" (i.e., the war and occupation). In a decree issued a week later, he established the National Council, which was to act as an advisory body to the president and the government. The council had no decision-making powers and was intended to provide the government with political support. This was evident from its membership: the nominal chairman was former prime minister Ignacy Paderewski, respected and still quite popular but now seriously ill; his deputy was Stanisław Mikołajczyk, the highest-ranking member of the opposition Peasant Party abroad, who was now beginning a brilliant political career. The nucleus of the National Council—like that of the government— was made up of leading politicians from the prewar opposition, but apart from Herman Lieberman (PPS), Tadeusz Bielecki (SN), and Stanisław Mackiewicz, there were no other well-known figures. The council's twenty-one members also included a representative of Poland's Jews, Sejm deputy Ignacy Szwarcbart. This formal structure—president, commander in chief, Council of Ministers, and National Council—lasted for the whole war despite several serious cabinet crises, which arose largely from the rivalry between the former government camp and the former opposition, and from deepening differences over foreign policy, essentially policy toward the Soviet Union.

The constitutional legitimacy of the Polish government-in-exile made it easier for Poland's allies and neutral governments to recognize the new government. Diplomatic relations with all the country's former partners— with the obvious exceptions of the Third Reich and the USSR—were maintained, despite pressures brought to bear on some of them by Germany. This situation changed only as a result of military developments, but despite Germany's hopes, only the satellite countries demanded, after considerable resistance, that Poland's embassies be closed down—Romania, in November 1940; Hungary, in December; Bulgaria, in March 1941; and Finland, in June. Japan also broke off diplomatic relations (in October 1941), and following Italy's attack on France in June 1940, the Polish government recalled its ambassador to Rome. Of course, countries that lost their independence or established quisling governments ceased to be political partners of Poland, but the government maintained diplomatic relations with other governments in exile, whose number grew considerably during 1940–41. General Sikorski even tried to play the role of "dean" among such governments or less formal émigré bodies, but this obviously had little significance in light of the scale of the conflict, which during the second half of 1941, became a world war in the full sense of the term. Nevertheless, the authority of the Polish state, both abroad and at home, was enhanced by the presence of its representatives in so many countries.

Of crucial significance for Poland, of course, were relations with its allies, France and Great Britain. From the outside these relations appeared to be "frank and cordial," to use diplomatic jargon, but they were not relations among equals. The very fact that in September 1939 France and Britain, despite their promises, maintained an Olympian composure in the face of German aggression, suggested that Poland should temper its expectations and clearly indicated that its Western allies did not intend to abandon their well-established practice of acting only in their own interests. What was disturbing was not only their complete military passivity (maliciously but accurately referred to as *drôle de guerre*) or their slowness in creating conditions for the formation of a Polish army—a new military agreement with Britain was signed on 18 November and with France, not until 4 January 1940—but also the fact that they simply ignored the issue of the eastern provinces incorporated into the Soviet Union. That this attitude indicated some shrewdness on the part of the allies, which had not lost their belief in the fragility of the German-Soviet alliance, was little comfort to Poland or the Polish government, which found itself in a difficult situation.

During the first few months no one in the Polish émigré community suspected that one of these allies would prove to be incapable, militarily and psychologically, of resisting German attack. The Polish government, and especially General Sikorski, considered the formation of an army to be an urgent task. Polish embassies in Budapest, Bucharest, Belgrade, and Rome (especially the first two) were almost exclusively concerned with moving military personnel to France, and by the middle of June 1940, forty-three thousand soldiers and officers—about 60 percent of all those who had succeeded in crossing into Romania and Hungary—had been evacuated. Attempts were also made to organize conscription among the Polish community in France, which numbered more than half a million, but these efforts met with only limited success. By May 1940, a substantial force of about eighty thousand soldiers and officers had been assembled, albeit with considerable variations in the level of training. The Podhale Brigade was the first to achieve battle readiness; it was intended that the unit take part in the Finnish-Soviet war, but the Allied Expeditionary Force was not ready in time (Finland declared defeat on 12 March 1940), and the Poles instead took part in the short-lived fighting over Narvik (from 8 May on).

On 10 May 1940, when the French campaign was just beginning, two Polish divisions and several smaller units (numbering about forty thousand altogether) were in a state of battle readiness. They did not, however, constitute a unified grouping but fought alongside the French, whose morale was far from that needed to mount effective resistance. Sikorski tried to act as battlefield commander, but this effort was obviously unrealistic and served only to increase the already considerable confusion brought about by the German attack. After four weeks the campaign was over, and even more important, the French government decided to capitulate and seek a compromise with Hitler. Only those Polish units, numbering some twenty-seven thousand enlisted men and officers, that had not taken part in the campaign succeeded in making their way to Britain. The evacuation began on 19 June, the day after Sikorski paid a lightning visit to London. Two days later Raczkiewicz arrived to make his home in the United Kingdom, which since 10 May had been under the leadership of Winston Churchill, who rejected the possibility of any compromise with Nazi Germany. From that time on, London was the capital of Poland in exile.

The collapse of France was of momentous significance for the future course of events, not only on a global scale, reinforcing Germany's sense of its own power, but also at the level of the issues confronting Poland's exiled government, military forces, and political elites. For the politicians and military personnel from the former ruling group, the French defeat provided a psychological breath of fresh air, putting their own defeat of the previous September in perspective. At the same time, Sikorski's oft-repeated expressions of confidence in France, especially its military leaders, were used against him. The result was a major crisis, in which additional ammunition was provided by a recent, and somewhat unfortunate, memorandum from the prime minister, dealing with the possibility of forming military units in the Soviet Union.

On 18 July President Raczkiewicz dismissed Sikorski from his position as prime minister, but under pressure from several military officials (which was in breach of the law) and thanks to the intervention of General Sosnkowski, a compromise was reached, allowing Sikorski to retain both of his key posts. This actually strengthened his position, especially in view of the fact that in the new situation, direct command of all resistance military activity was now in the hands of General Rowecki—something the resistance had already been calling for—which deprived General Sosnkowski of his most important function. Even before this, Sikorski and his supporters—especially Stanisław Kot, an agile politician and a sworn enemy of the Piłsudski-ites—had managed to divide "homeland affairs" into military and political issues.

Despite the compromise outcome, the July events in London did not so much resolve the conflict as simply stifle it. They also enhanced the stature of those politicians who had supported Sikorski, particularly Stanisław Mikołajczyk and Karol Popiel. The prime minister tried to shape his cabinet as he thought fit and sought to concentrate all decisions about ministerial appointments in his hands. Not surprisingly, the political parties argued that they had the right to nominate candidates for office in any government that called itself a Government of National Unity. Some differences of opinion also emerged between the prime minister and some members of the National Council, who sought to broaden the scope of the council's competence by, among other things, asking questions of the government, and debating the budget and the reports presented by the prime minister and members of the cabinet.

These differences and conflicts were not allowed to hinder joint efforts to rebuild the armed forces. In August, twenty-six thousand men, including seven thousand officers, were under arms, and a further 4,400—members of the Carpathian Brigade, which would later distinguish itself at Tobruk—were on their way from the French protectorate of Syria to British-ruled Palestine. Given the millions of people involved in the war, this was an insignificant force, but at this point Britain was isolated and its forces were relatively weak. Poland possessed an additional trump card in the fact that the French campaign was followed by the Battle of Britain, in which 151 Polish pilots made up 10 percent of those who fought in the skies on the side of the Allies (which included fourteen French pilots). In mid-July 1940 preparations were already under way for the formation of the first Polish squadron, known as RAF Squadron 302 or the Poznań Squadron; this was followed, two weeks later, by the formation of the celebrated Squadron 303, otherwise known as the Warsaw-Tadeusz Kościuszko Squadron.

The Polish government, and particularly the prime minister, sought to play an active part in international politics. One of the most important of such initiatives was the agreement reached with Czechoslovak political leaders in exile. On 11 November 1940, the anniversary of the end of World War I, the two sides signed a declaration pledging close cooperation. The declaration also outlined a proposal for a future framework for the region as a whole in the form of a loose confederation designed to protect Central Europe from both Western and Eastern powers. Discussions and debates took place at various levels, even though from the very beginning there were major differences of opinion arising from the conflict over the Trans-Olza, which had flared up again in 1938, as well as differences in attitude toward the Soviet Union. Poland also needed such contacts to counteract continuing criticism regarding its role in the subordination of its southern neighbor to the Third Reich (critics usually forgot to mention the role of France and Great Britain). Both Sikorski and those most closely associated with him on this issue (including Ambassador Edward Raczyński) genuinely attributed great importance to the creation of a bloc of friendly states in Central Europe.

General Sikorski also visited, in April 1941, Canada and the United States in order to urge members of the Polish communities in both countries to join the Polish Armed Forces, an effort that proved a complete fiasco, since only one thousand volunteers signed up. He also hoped to establish closer contacts with U.S. president Franklin Roosevelt, an advocate of U.S. involvement in the conflict in Europe. Three weeks before Sikorski's departure, Congress passed the Lend-Lease Act, authorizing the president to sell and lend military equipment to countries considered significant in the defense of the United States. This act would soon prove a vital factor in the war machine and a major element in Allied cooperation.

One of the key problems preoccupying the Polish government-in-exile was how to maintain contact with the country, especially after the fall of 1940, when it was no longer possible to use the embassies in Bucharest and Budapest. Radio contact with the embassies had been established in February 1940, and on 5 April the government received via Budapest its first communiqué from Poland. After moving to London the government quickly reestablished contact with the country, and soon (from 18 September on)

79

had direct contact with Warsaw. According to Józef Garliński, before the collapse of France the government had already sent twenty-three emissaries to Poland and received fourteen.[6] Close contacts existed between the section of the commander in chief's staff in charge of communications with military units in Poland and Britain's Special Operations Executive, an intelligence and counterintelligence unit established in July 1940. These contacts did not play a major role in the conflict taking place in Poland, since the British focused their activity on areas traditionally of interest to them in Europe. In addition to their immediate neighbors across the English Channel, they were most concerned with the eastern Mediterranean, including the Balkans. Britain valued Poland as a military ally, particularly as it had no others, but Poland did not lie within the sphere of its immediate interests. While the French seemed to have a better understanding of Poland's concerns, they were no longer in a position to play a role in the ongoing conflict.

Many political leaders counted on the collapse of the Soviet-German alliance—and there is much to suggest that Sikorski was among them—and from the spring of 1941 tensions between Moscow and Berlin were clearly increasing, partly as a result of the German invasion of Yugoslavia. Despite a growing number of intelligence reports concerning the buildup of German forces along the Soviet border, the attack launched on 22 July 1941 along the whole length of the border came as a surprise. It even surprised Stalin, who was totally unprepared for such an eventuality. The attack certainly surprised the Polish government in London, where no one had taken seriously such a possibility, and where, in any event, no preparations had been made for such a development or for Poland to react to it. The outbreak of hostilities between Nazi Germany and the Soviet Union did not affect Poland's goals, which remained, as before, to rebuild an independent state, to expand its borders to the west and north, and to form a close coalition of Central European states. It did, however, affect—and in a fundamental manner—the conditions under which Poland was to pursue these goals and the possibilities for achieving them.

First to speak was Churchill, who realized that Hitler's decision to attack created an opportunity to put an end to the ceaseless expansion of the Third Reich and to break its power once and for all. On the very day that hostilities broke out, he gave a speech in which he declared that His Majesty's Government would "accord Russia and the Russian people all the assis-

6. Józef Garliński, *Polska w Drugiej Wojnie Światowej* (London, 1982), 131.

tance that we are capable of." He laid down no conditions and—as far as we know—did not meet with the Soviet ambassador before addressing the public.

The next day Sikorski took to the airwaves. Recognizing that "the turn of events is highly advantageous for Poland," he declared that Russia ought to declare the pacts of August and September 1939 null and void, which would "return us logically to the position we were in as a result of the Treaty of Riga." He also called for the release of hundreds of thousands of prisoners and "a quarter million prisoners of war." On 4 July, when German forces were advancing unchecked to the east, Polish-Soviet talks, with the participation of the British, got under way in London.

Despite the setbacks on the front, Ambassador Ivan Maiski showed no tendency to compromise on two major issues: the call for an unequivocal declaration that the Treaty of Riga retained its legal force and the demand that all Polish citizens and prisoners of war be unconditionally released. He suggested, on the other hand, the possibility that Moscow might establish a "Polish National Committee," a suggestion that sounded very much like blackmail. As noted above, Stalin had already ordered the creation of a Polish military force under Colonel Berling, although the Polish community in London was not aware of this.

A subsequent round of negotiations (on 5, 11, and 17 July) failed to produce a compromise that would satisfy the Poles. For their part, the British—and Churchill personally—urged Sikorski to conclude the discussions as quickly as possible. On 25 July, at a meeting of the Council of Ministers, the prime minister declared, "There is not, and there cannot be, any hope of obtaining, today or tomorrow, the Soviets' agreement to change the wording of the treaty." He pointed out that if the council rejected the agreement, Poland was in danger of losing British support, and he urged its acceptance.

Three members of the government (Marian Seyda, General Sosnkowski, and August Zaleski), who had earlier declared that in light of the desperate situation of the Red Army it would be more prudent to wait than to agree too hastily to the proposed agreement, voted against acceptance and tendered their resignations. The remaining five supported the prime minister. On 29 July President Raczkiewicz refused to authorize General Sikorski to sign the agreement. The prime minister, however, dug in his heels, and the next day the treaty was concluded. The signing ceremony took place at the Foreign Office headquarters and was attended by Churchill and British foreign secretary Anthony Eden. During the exchange of notes between

Britain and Poland and during Eden's speech to the House of Commons later that day, the British did not go beyond the wording of the treaty and offered no guarantees as to Poland's future borders.

Not only did the treaty fail to guarantee the restoration of the eastern frontier as it had been before the Soviet invasion of Poland, but it also contained—in a secret protocol—a clause concerning an amnesty for Polish citizens, a clause that could be construed as acknowledging their guilt, which was to be magnanimously expunged from the record. The treaty provoked a political crisis with far greater repercussions than that of a year earlier. The severity of the crisis resulted from, among other things, the fact that the split did not run along traditional lines: this time, General Sikorski's opponents included some members of the prewar opposition, on both the right (even Marian Seyda) and the left (among them, Adam Ciołkosz). Given the lack of channels allowing speedy communication in 1940, neither the ZWZ nor the underground political parties were able to inform London of their attitude toward developments there. At the same time, while General Sikorski did receive some support from Warsaw for his actions, it was far from enthusiastic, and, more important, the PPS-WRN leadership expressed reservations. Nevertheless, Sikorski was able to remain prime minister thanks to strong support from the émigré leaders of the Peasant, Labor, and Socialist Parties and the unambiguous backing of the British—and of Churchill himself, who was, after all, the great hero of the war.

The government ceased, however, to be a government of "national unity": the National Party withdrew, and the Piłsudski-ites were no longer represented. General Sosnkowski became a victim of the crisis when he was formally dismissed from his position as commander of the ZWZ. Given that General Rowecki had been given essentially the same function in June 1940, Sosnkowski's dismissal was more symbolic than real, but it nevertheless suggested that he had not only lost Sikorski's confidence but had earned his enmity. Although Sikorski emerged victorious from this battle, the real victor was Peasant Party leader Stanisław Mikołajczyk, to whom the prime minister owed a great deal during these few weeks. Mikołajczyk was appointed minister of internal affairs (a major political position that essentially involved oversight of everything going on in Poland), as well as deputy prime minister and Sikorski's de facto second in command. He was the first member of the generation that had entered public life after Poland's reemergence as an independent country to achieve such high government office.

The crisis of July–August 1941 reinforced the deep divisions within the émigré elite, divisions that deepened further with the passage of time and as events unfolded. These conflicts were based both on political differences dating back to the prewar era and the different visions of the country's future derived from them and on personal conflicts and ambitions. They also contained elements of a long-standing Polish dilemma, often referred to as the dispute or struggle between "realists" and "idealists," or "romantics" and "positivists," which gave depth to the conflicts, magnified the differences, and made it difficult to achieve a compromise. These divisions were by no means confined to "the London Poles," but ran through the whole society, and the level of tension, both political and emotional, only increased as the war began to die down. Meanwhile, those Poles who found themselves far from occupied Poland began to turn their attention to the hundreds of thousands of Polish deportees, prisoners of war, and prisoners—and to the question of how to turn them into an army.

THE UNDERGROUND STATE: THE ARMY

The largest role in the underground state was played by the military, although the process of merging into a unified whole numerous groups and organizations as well as the military units formed by various political parties proceeded slowly and was, in essence, never completed. At the beginning of 1940 the PPS-WRN transferred its military units to the ZWZ, which also absorbed the Organization of the White Eagle. This was a good start, but for a long time it was the only success of Rowecki and the organization that he headed, an organization that was supposed to transcend party divisions to become the sole military structure operating within Poland and an integral part of the Polish Armed Forces.

The many parties and groups remaining outside the "big four" were not the only ones in no hurry to subordinate themselves to the ZWZ command. The National Party also declined to hand over control of its National Military Organization, and in August 1940 the SL-Roch began to organize its own Peasant Battalions, indicating the party's lack of confidence in the ZWZ command and its belief that it would prove impossible to liquidate all the "political armies." A breakthrough came in February 1942, when the commander in chief decreed that the ZWZ would henceforth be known as the Home Army (AK), and further progress was made after 15 August of that year, when he ordered all military units to subordinate themselves to the Home Army. Some organizations split over the issue of joining the AK; the best-known example involved the National Military Organization, which split when a large number of its units refused to subordinate themselves to AK command. The "mutineers" joined forces with the Salamander Union of the Szaniec group (formerly the ONR-ABC) to establish, on 20 August 1942, the National Armed Forces (NSZ), part of which finally merged with the AK in March 1944. The SL-Roch also resisted joining the Home Army, and when a further directive was issued ordering the merger of military units, transferred only its "tactical units."

Nevertheless, the enormous effort invested by the staff officers at AK command, by Rowecki and his deputy, General Tadeusz Bór-Komorowski, and by several political leaders, yielded visible results. The underground military underwent a major expansion and became, to the extent that conditions allowed, far more coordinated and unified: in the fall of 1941, some 40,000 officers and enlisted men had been sworn into the ZWZ; by the summer of 1942—more than 140,000; by March 1943—roughly 185,000; and a year later, when universal conscription was introduced, more than 300,000 people, in various formations, were under AK command. This was not, however, a regular army. In late 1943 and early 1944, there were some 270 fighting units (partisan and ad hoc detachments and diversionary patrols) made up of no more than seven thousand soldiers and officers—only two percent of the Home Army's total forces at that time. Most of the "political armies" that had merged with the AK remained under the command of their previous leaders and were guaranteed the right to maintain communications with their parent organizations.

Most of the clandestine fighters had no regular training in partisan warfare, guerrilla tactics, or street fighting (General Rowecki was a specialist in this area). The same was true of a substantial proportion of commanding officers, and the 316 special agents trained in guerrilla tactics who were parachuted into the country after mid-February 1941 were too few in number to do all that was needed. The AK forces were poorly armed: at the beginning of 1944 they had only 53,000 firearms at their disposal, of which 33 percent were handguns, and only 6 percent were machine guns. Many of these weapons dated from the September campaign and were in need of repair. The Allies dropped only an insignificant number of weapons, initially (1941–42) because of considerable technical difficulties, and subsequently (from 1943 on) because Polish territory was viewed as a theater of operations of the Red Army, which had no interest in arming the partisan movement against which it was to fight. Taken as a whole, the Home Army was akin to a popular movement and in no condition to play an independent role on the modern-day field of battle.

The underground army acquired this precise form partly because of the fait accompli presented by the creation, in the early stages of the resistance, of "political armies" on a mass scale (the Peasant Brigades numbered more than 100,000 sworn members, and the National Military Organization claimed to have "up to 100,000") and partly because of the doctrine adopted by the ZWZ-AK command and the London-based commander in chief. At the time when the Polish Victory Service and the ZWZ were being established, it was widely believed that the war would be over quite quickly (hardly anyone believed that the Allies would maintain their passive stance later than the early summer of 1940). Nevertheless, military leaders, both in Poland and at ZWZ headquarters in Paris, and government officials were opposed to any spontaneous initiatives aimed at "continuing the Polish campaign." Such initiatives were undertaken in the German zone—by the famous Autonomous Detachment of the Polish Army led by Major Henryk Dobrzański (code name Hubal)—and in the Soviet zone, where partisan detachments emerged out of regular units of the Polish Army in the fall of 1939 and remained active until at least the summer of 1940. They included a group led by cavalry officer Jerzy Dąmbrowski, well known for his exploits behind enemy lines during the war against Russia in 1919–20.

The doctrine adopted by the ZWZ presupposed that the aim of the organization was to prepare for an uprising that would erupt at the moment when regular units of the Polish Army crossed into Poland. The main task, then, was to organize a staff and to muster a cadre of officers and NCOs to command the units that were to be reconstituted at the appropriate moment in order to take part in regular fighting. Thus from the very beginning of its existence, the ZWZ was involved in complex long-term planning that was rendered more complex by the changing global situation. A year later, on 5 February 1941, when General Rowecki put his name to the operational plan for the uprising, he doubtless anticipated that some of the potential scenarios it contained would soon lose their relevance. This is exactly what happened after 22 July, when war broke out between Germany and the Soviet Union, and Poland signed a treaty with the latter. A subsequent version of the plan was signed in September 1942, when the last detachments of General Jarosław Anders's army left the USSR, and the collapse of the Polish-Soviet treaty was already a foregone conclusion, a development that would affect the possibilities for carrying out the uprising.

The final outcome of this work, which had to take account of the new developments that were so unfavorable to Poland, was the plan for Operation Tempest (Burza), set out in an order issued by the AK commander on 20 November 1943. This operation was begun in February 1944 (with the mobilization in Volhynia) and ended with the Warsaw uprising. The idea of a popular uprising was the most important issue for the ZWZ-AK as a whole and for its role within the Polish Armed Forces, even though the timing of such an uprising and the conditions in which it would take place were constantly changing. Roughly 100,000 soldiers (excluding the Warsaw insurgents) took part in Operation Tempest, which was more or less the number envisaged in plans for the first stage.

This mobilization involved more than sixty partisan detachments created during the course of 1943. Beginning on 15 October of that year, they were given the names of former regiments of the Polish Army, a move that was intended to signify that they were regular army units. From early 1944, mobilization—actual or planned—involved the establishment of division-level units. These units did not, of course, have a full complement of personnel, but most of them were capable of conducting sabotage and guerrilla operations to the extent that their equipment and training would allow. The AK never achieved the level of military readiness that its founders had hoped for at the end of 1939. There were no other forces with which it could engage in joint action, and in May-June 1944 the Wehrmacht rearguard alone had about 270,000 soldiers supported by a far greater number of the so-called Osttruppen, recruited largely from among Soviet prisoners of war. Nevertheless, the AK carried out the main task entrusted to it: as the front moved westwards, it engaged in a mass mobilization and began to fight the enemy as it retreated.

Although this mass armed uprising was intended to be the crowning achievement of the underground army, it soon became obvious that preparations for this event should not be allowed to crowd out all other forms of activity. After all, the enemy was on Polish territory, and when it became clear that he had no intention of leaving any time soon, it became necessary to devise various forms of day-to-day warfare. Hence staff work aimed at preparing units for the battlefield was accompanied by training in guerrilla tactics, self-defense, retaliatory strikes, intelligence gathering, and—extremely important—propaganda and information campaigns intended to maintain the spirit of resistance among the population. In light of the doctrine that Poland had two enemies, the tactics to be used were those of limited struggle and they were to be carried out by units with the appropriate training and equipment, operating in accordance with a set of coordinated plans.

The first unit intended to carry out—or rather prepare for—this day-to-day warfare was the Retaliatory Union, set up on 20 April 1940. This was followed by the formation, in November 1940, of the Small Sabotage Organization (code name Wawer). Nevertheless, because of difficulties in preparations and the course taken by the war itself, the Home Army's plans for running combat were not fully realized until 1942. The first half of 1941 was a particularly difficult period, since the Government-General became the site of enormous troop concentrations in advance of the German attack on the Soviet Union. Neither the ZWZ command in Poland nor the government in London was willing to risk the losses among the conspirators—and the civilian population—that could occur in the event of a premature or ill-prepared operation. In June 1940, faced with the collapse of France, General Sosnkowski had already issued an order prohibiting armed combat unless "necessary for the security of the organization."

The situation changed after 22 June 1941, when the Germans began using Polish territory as a supply base for the eastern front. In the fall of that year, elite guerrilla detachments were formed; under the code name Fan (Wachlarz), they conducted operations in the region to the east of the former Polish border. In May 1942 the Organizations for Special Combat Operations were formed, and in the fall, the Retaliatory Union was rapidly expanded to form the Diversionary Directorate, known as Kedyw, whose first commander was Colonel August Fieldorf. Kedyw had units in every military district. Overall guerrilla and retaliatory operations were coordinated by a group of officers from the AK central command, known as the Directorate of Conspiratorial Struggle (KWK), which also had direct responsibility for some units of the Office of Information and Propaganda and for counterintelligence. The KWK was headed by the AK commander. In this way, staff departments at AK headquarters and in the districts were divided into those that dealt mainly with preparing for an uprising and those that focused on day-to-day combat. General Rowecki had also intended the KWK to coordinate all underground activity in Poland: "All private resources and initiatives should be subordinated to it," he wrote in a dispatch to London. This task proved, however, impossible to carry out, although the scope of such coordination increased somewhat when, in July 1943, the Directorate of Underground Struggle was formed. Together with the former KWK, its members also included the head (Stefan Korboński) of the Directorate of Civilian Struggle, itself part of the Delegatura, and a number of smaller resistance organizations worked closely with it. Self-defense was another area in which progress was made: the development of counterintelligence was accompanied by an increasingly effective struggle against informers (including those who betrayed Jews), who were brought before underground tribunals, first established in the spring of 1940 and later transformed into Special Military Courts. It is estimated that AK execution squads carried out about 2,500 death sentences handed down by these courts.

A full account of the whole spectrum of diversionary activity, sabotage, and guerrilla fighting carried out by all underground armed organizations still remains to be written. Little is known about operations conducted in the Soviet zone, and there are no comprehensive accounts of the activities of such major groups as the National People's Fighting Organization and the National Armed Forces. What information is available comes largely from underground sources, and most of it has yet to be analyzed in conjunction with data gathered by agencies of the occupying powers. According to official publications based on information provided by the Polish Armed Forces, dealing only with the activity of the ZWZ-AK and only during the period from January 1941 to the end of June 1944, various ZWZ-AK units derailed 732 transport trains, and damaged or destroyed about 26,000 railroad wagons and steam engines, more than 4,000 military vehicles, and nearly 3,000 pieces of factory machinery. They carried out around 5,700 attacks on Germans. According to information gathered by the Wehrmacht, covering the activity of all underground organizations during the period from July 1942 to July 1944, a total of about 110,000 attacks of various kinds were carried out on the territory of the Government-General. These included roughly 1,500 attacks on railroad transports and a similar number involving road transport, the destruction of 135 bridges, and 4,500 attacks on soldiers and police officials.

A further indication of the scale of underground activity is provided by the losses suffered by the resistance. They were extremely high. According to data collected by the Polish Armed Forces, by July 1944—namely, before Operation Tempest and the Warsaw uprising—the various units of the ZWZ-AK had lost about 62,000 soldiers, or close to 20 percent of their maximum enrollment. Severe losses were also suffered by the Peasant Battalions, the People's Guard–People's Army, and the National Armed Forces. If we assume that the percentage of losses was similar in all underground organizations, this would mean that, up to July 1944, at least 90,000–100,000 resistance members died—not all of them with a gun in his or her hand. While any attempt at comparison seems unfruitful, we can point out that these losses were much greater than those suffered by the 700,000-strong Polish Army during the September campaign, and many times greater than the losses suffered by all regular armed forces fighting under Polish colors during 1940–44.

THE UNDERGROUND STATE: THE DELEGATURA

Alongside the Home Army, the second pillar of the underground state was the civilian administration, established, from the top down, by the government delegate, who set up central administrative units, or departments, while at the same time appointing regional government delegates to operate in the field. By July 1944, fifteen departments, equivalent to ministries, had been created. One department was concerned with the day-to-day business of the delegate, and several others were responsible for broad-based conspiratorial activity. These included the Department of Education and Culture, which organized, coordinated, and provided financial assistance to a far-reaching network that offered elementary, secondary, and higher education to hundreds of thousands of children and young people. The Department of Information and Propaganda published the government's official paper, *Rzeczpospolita Polska* (The Polish Republic), and managed its press agency, Kraj (Homeland). The Department of Labor and Social Security was mainly concerned with providing assistance to the families of people who had been taken prisoner or killed. The Delegatura also oversaw the activity of the Council to Assist the Jews, known as Żegota.

Most of the Delegatura's central agencies produced studies on how their equivalent government agency would function in an independent Poland: they prepared economic and social analyses, drafted legislative and administrative proposals, and trained personnel for public administration. The Department of Internal Affairs not only organized fifteen regional offices, covering the entire territory of the Republic, but also began to establish a future state police force, known in the underground as the State Security Corps, which to begin functioning the moment the uprising erupted. Another important agency, although one that did not engage in any ongoing organizational activity, was the Bureau of New Territories, which was concerned with planning Poland's takeover of Eastern Prussia, Western Pomerania, and the region around Opole, in Silesia. The Bureau trained several thousand people who were familiar with the regions and who would be charged with establishing a new administration. An extremely important part of the Delegatura's activity was maintaining radio contact with the Polish government in London. This provided not only a channel for the transmission of opinion and current information but also a basis for the Polish-language radio station, *Świt* (Dawn), which was located in Britain but pretended to be transmitting programs from inside Poland.

While the underground military remained, despite various pressures, beyond the direct influence of political parties, the Delegatura could not possibly function as a "purely administrative" agency. The parties belonging to the Political Consultative Committee ensured that they had an influence over appointments to the posts of delegate and regional delegate, a process that involved some fairly subtle negotiations among the "big four," in which the Labor Party found itself in the most advantageous situation because, although relatively weak, it was situated in the center and was thus "palatable" to the other parties; the Peasant Party also achieved a strong bargaining position. After a long-drawn-out dispute between political leaders in Poland and the government-in-exile, the prime minister finally gave in, dismissing Ratajski and appointing as delegate a moderate member of the Peasant Party, Jan Piekałkiewicz. After his arrest (on 19 February 1943), he was succeeded by Labor Party member Jan Jankowski. At this time, the sphere of competence of the delegate and his office was clearly spelled out in a presidential decree (issued on 1 August 1942), and the agency evolved toward becoming a part of the London-based Council of Ministers functioning in Poland, a state of affairs that received confirmation in a decree issued on 26 April 1944 establishing the Homeland Council of Ministers. The council's members consisted of the delegate, who had the rank of deputy prime minister, and representatives of three other political parties (Adam Bień from the Peasant Party, Stanisław Jasiukowicz from the National Party, and Antoni Pajdak from the Polish Socialist Party). The central and regional state administrative apparatus consisted at this time of several thousand sworn officials.

THE UNDERGROUND STATE: POLITICIANS AND POLITICS

Political representation constituted the third component of the underground state. The Political Consultative Committee fulfilled this role, de facto, from June 1940 on, but this state of affairs did not achieve de jure force until the decree of 1 August 1942, which accorded the Consultative

Committee a consultative role and—more important—an advisory role in relation to the government delegate. The "big four" tenaciously and successfully defended their position, although they were far from being monolithic.

The Socialist and Peasant Parties immediately began close cooperation and even attempted to draft a joint political program. This effort was, however, unsuccessful, and in 1941 the PPS-WRN issued its own "Program for a People's Poland." The main source of conflict between the SL-Roch and the PPS-WRN was—apart from their natural political ambitions—their differing attitudes toward General Sikorski's "eastern policy." The socialists (and the majority of PPS members in emigration) were opposed to the Polish-Soviet treaty of 1941 on the grounds that it sanctioned the incorporation of Poland's eastern provinces into the Soviet Union. As a result, Kazimierz Pużak resigned from the Consultative Committee, and for a year-and-a-half his position was occupied by delegates of the Polish Socialists (PS), a party that had split from the PPS in 1939 and was now increasingly moving toward the left, toward cooperation with the communists. Close cooperation between the PPS and SL-Roch, particularly during the early period of the resistance, was based in part on their common antipathy toward the National Party and their fear that the army would be dominated by members of the former governing group. They also had a similar approach to Poland's future political system (a parliamentary system and far-reaching social and economic reforms) as well as similar views on Poland's place in Europe (a confederation of Central European states).

The National Party presented a radically different vision of what was often called the "Third Republic," one based on the slogan of a Catholic State for the Polish Nation. This program contained fairly strong authoritarian elements, rejected equal rights for national minorities, and called on Poland to play a central role in shaping the future of Central and Eastern Europe. Some members of the National Party favored a coup d'état, or unilateral seizure of power, but by 1942 the dominant view within the organization was that cooperation and compromise with other political parties were necessary. both during the war and during postwar reconstruction.

A presidential decree of 21 March 1943 renamed the Consultative Committee the Homeland Political Representation (KRP), but made no change in its membership. On 15 August, the anniversary of the 1920 Battle of Warsaw, the four political parties issued a declaration, announcing their agreement to continue their coalition until elections to constitutional bodies could be held and urging their émigré counterparts to maintain a similar coalition. The document emphasized that the eastern provinces were an integral part of Poland and set out demands for changes to the country's northern and western frontiers. It proclaimed the need to carry out social (and especially agrarian) reforms in an independent Poland, guaranteed the rights of national minorities, promised the introduction of a parliamentary system, and called for the establishment of a confederation of Central and Eastern European states, based on the closest possible cooperation between the Polish and Czech governments. The signatories also announced that work was in progress to establish a body to be called the Council of National Unity, which would function as a clandestine parliament. This declaration demonstrated the success of the Peasant and Socialist Parties, but most of all, the success of the notion of consultation and cooperation among the country's leading political forces. In numerous statements, the KRP endorsed the position of the government-in-exile regarding Soviet territorial claims, argued on behalf of improved relations with Ukraine, and rallied support for the government's representatives in Poland. The KRP thus provided a source of political support to both the delegate and the government-in-exile as well as, indirectly, the Home Army.

In keeping with the evolution of "official" clandestine structures and their growth in stature, on 9 January 1944 the KRP was replaced by the Council of National Unity (RJN), a move intended to signify a broadening of the range of political forces exerting a direct influence over the Delegatura and its agencies and the AK. The council's members included, alongside the "big four," representatives of the Catholic clergy (but no formal representative of the Catholic Church), the Homeland and Racławice groups, and the Democratic Association. Members of the former KRP, however, had three representatives on the council, while the newcomers had only one each. Essentially, then, the change was largely cosmetic, although the formal role of the new body was much broader than that of its predecessor. On 15 March the council published a lengthy declaration titled, "Why the Polish Nation Is Fighting," which expanded on the declaration of 15 August 1943 and constituted the fullest exposition to date of all that the main clandestine parties had agreed among themselves. The signatories were still, however, the same political parties; to the very end the "big four" retained a de facto political monopoly and constituted a kind of clandestine political elite.

At the same time, political life was becoming increasingly diverse, something that was also true of the political parties and groups that recognized the London government's agencies in Poland. The National Confederation, led by Bolesław Piasecki was particularly active. There was a succession of moves to the left as various groups and parties tried to distance themselves from the "big four" and the Delegatura. In mid-1942, Piłsudski-ite circles, hitherto crushed by their responsibility for the September debacle and the flight of their leaders, began to revive. In August the Fighting Poland Camp (OPW) was formed under the auspices of Marshal Rydz-Śmigły (in hiding since his escape from Romania, but soon to return to Poland), and was followed in October by the Convention of Organizations Fighting for Independence, established in opposition to the OPW and headed by Zygmunt Hempel. None of these groupings was admitted to the Council of National Unity, and although this exclusiveness was partly justified in light of the need to maintain secrecy, it weakened the authority of the council and that of the Delegatura.

Complete coordination was rendered impossible by the very nature of clandestine activity. In addition, with the passage of time, two parallel processes became ever more pronounced: the ZWZ-AK and Delegatura became stronger, expanding to embrace new areas of activity and ever larger numbers of people; simultaneously, other organizations continued to function and grow outside the framework of the underground state. The most important changes in these other structures took place during 1942–43.

The refusal on the part of some sections of the National Military Organization to merge with the AK and the subsequent creation of the National Armed Forces greatly strengthened the extreme nationalist wing of the resistance. The Polish Organization (OP), a conspiratorial group dating back to before the war, provided the core of this grouping. In 1940 the OP established the Salamander Union and the Szaniec group, which had a separate section named the Civilian Commissariat; from the very beginning these organizations constituted a source of opposition to the ZWZ and the Consultative Committee. Over time the OP groups expanded, developing their own security service, Special Action, and even their own judicial apparatus. Following the creation of the National Armed Forces, the groups belonging to the OP tended to separate themselves even further from the "official" resistance. The OP joined forces with a section of the National Party that was ill disposed, and even hostile, to the government delegate and the Consultative Committee and had split from the party in the summer of 1942 to create the Provisional Governing Commission of the National Party. Members included former party activists who had broken away in 1939 to form the National People's Fighting Organization, as well as newcomers. After lengthy negotiations, the Polish Organization and the Provisional Commission set up the Provisional National Political Council, which assumed control of the National Armed Forces and turned the Civilian Commissariat into the Nation's Civilian Service, which grew to have nineteen departments, equivalent to government ministries, and a network of regional agencies. According to Zbigniew Siemaszko, this agency "absorbed several thousand specialists."[7] The formation of the Provisional Council and the NSZ was sharply attacked by the leadership of the underground state. The government delegate, among others, issued a condemnatory statement that appeared under the title "Troublemakers" in the official publication of the AK command, *Biuletyn Informacyjny.* The NSZ and its supporters responded with a press campaign that left readers in no doubt as to their attitude toward the underground state. The NSZ itself grew rapidly and claimed in the fall of 1943 to have 72,000 soldiers; however, fewer than 1,000 were officers, so compared to the AK, the NSZ was more like a levy en masse.

The radical nationalists differed from the "big four" parties not only in their vision of the future Poland, which they envisaged as a state with totalitarian features, but also in their view of the international situation, a difference that became particularly pronounced after the Battle of Stalingrad and Moscow's decision to sever relations with the Polish government. The leadership of the NSZ—and presumably the overwhelming majority of its soldiers—considered that, in light of the ever greater prospect of Nazi Germany's defeat, Poland's greatest enemy was now the USSR. This view had implications not only for the NSZ's political program but also for its activities in the field: the group decided that one of its main tasks, if not its most important task, was to combat communist partisans and the growing number of Soviet guerrilla groups now on Polish territory. Following this line, Special Action units became involved in a number of local skirmishes, the best-known of which involved the execution on 9 August 1943 of twenty-six members of a People's Guard unit captured near Borów and four peasants who had been helping them. This operation was roundly condemned by the AK command, but the NSZ did not change its approach. Another example of the organization's political profile was its plan to concentrate troops ahead of the approaching front and then—unlike the plan for Operation Tempest—to withdraw to the immediate rear of the German army and

7. Zbigniew Siemaszko, *Narodowe Siły Zbrojne* (London, 1982), 131.

enter territory "occupied by the Western allies." Such a strategy had many advocates among both the leadership of the underground state and émigré politicians and military personnel, but they were either in a minority or had no direct influence over government policy. While AK counterintelligence units did keep a watch on communist groups, and the Delegatura set up an Anticommunist Committee, known as Antyk, no central agency proposed armed struggle against the People's Guard.

Despite renewed discussions about a possible merger, the National Armed Forces were clearly separate from the basic structures of the underground state. A fresh order to merge, issued by the Home Army commander on 31 March 1944, did not resolve the conflict. The leaders of the Polish Organization, fearing loss of control over their combat units and seeing no possibility of controlling the AK if they were to join forces, largely succeeded in blocking the merger. As a result, most of the NSZ units that had formerly belonged to the Salamander Union refused to subordinate themselves to the AK. The Provisional Council was replaced by a new body, the Political Council of the NSZ, whose members were drawn exclusively from the Polish Organization.

From the point of view of long-term impact, the most important—and initially underrated—clandestine organization was to be found at the opposite end of the political spectrum from the NSZ: on 5 January 1942, members of the communist Initiative Group, educated and trained in the Soviet Union and parachuted into Poland, established the Polish Workers' Party (PPR).

Polish communists, paralyzed since the dissolution in 1938 of the Polish Communist Party and relegated to the sidelines of political life in the wake of the Ribbentrop-Molotov Pact and the Soviet invasion of 27 September 1939, began in the summer of 1940 to establish a number of small, local organizations. Most of these groups adhered to the old Communist Party line on the question of Poland's sovereignty, expressed in such slogans as "Long live the Polish Soviet Republic!" and in the names adopted by some groups—the Association of Friends of the USSR, for example, or the Revolutionary Workers' and Peasants' Council. The outbreak of war between Germany and the Soviet Union infused new life into these groups and in October 1941 several of them united to form the Union of Struggle for Liberation.

At the same time, the Polish group attending the Comintern school in the Soviet Union was preparing to reactivate the Communist Party, something that was unfeasible as long as the Berlin-Moscow alliance remained in force. This group was reinforced by combat veterans of the Spanish Civil War, who were smuggled out of France by the NKVD and Soviet military intelligence. After 22 June 1941 the pace of work quickened and in August the first team of the so-called Initiative Group was ready to be parachuted into Poland. These plans were thwarted when the plane carrying the group over the front lines crashed, and it was not until December 1941–January 1942 that ten members of the group finally made their way to Poland.

They included Marceli Nowotko, who would become general secretary of the future Central Committee, and Bolesław Mołojec, slated to be commander of the communists' military units, a veteran of the Dąbrowski Brigade, which had fought in Spain. In a relatively short time they turned the network of groups and former Communist Party activists into a small but dynamic clandestine party. The party's members also included communists who had remained in Poland during the German invasion, either of their own accord or as part of the Soviet intelligence network. Thus the PPR leadership came to include, among others, Władysław Gomułka, Franciszek Jóźwiak, and (in 1943) Bolesław Bierut.

Like all the communist parties in occupied Europe, the PPR launched a political program drawn up by the Comintern and akin to that of the prewar Popular Front period and called for immediate armed struggle. The party also created a military organization, the People's Guard. The PPR maintained contacts (the details of which have still not been revealed) with the Soviet intelligence network, which, some sources indicate, "transferred" to the party a number of people, including Michał Żymierski, a former member of Piłsudski's legions and a one-time general in the Polish Army who had been demoted and sentenced to prison in 1927. In 1944, under the pseudonym of Rola, he became the formal commander of the communist partisans.

At the end of 1942, after less than a year in existence, the PPR lost both its leaders. In circumstances that remain obscure to this day, Nowotko was shot. Most of the party's top leadership believed this action to have been instigated by Mołojec, who was subsequently killed on the orders of the Central Committee. Given the numerous ambiguities in the short history of the clandestine PPR, it is difficult to say whether these events were the result of internal party struggles or personal conflicts among its leaders, or whether they derived from conflicts among the various Soviet intelligence agencies active in Poland. A year later, in the fall of 1943, Nowotko's successor, Paweł Finder, who had also come from the Soviet Union, was ambushed and killed. His place was taken by Władysław Gomułka, who had been active inside Poland since the end of 1941.

Regardless of these events, the Polish Workers' Party was, in relation to its size, extremely active and conducted a lively propaganda campaign, urging a broadening of sabotage and guerrilla combat, action that party members themselves were more than ready to take. Engaging in a propaganda struggle against "the forces of reaction" and attacking the AK for "standing still with their weapons at the ready," the PPR—in keeping with Comintern policy advocating the creation of National Fronts—aimed to become part of the underground state. In February 1943 the party initiated a series of meetings with representatives of the AK command and the Delegatura. The communists refused, however, to swear that they were not affiliated with any foreign agency (meaning the Comintern), nor would they condemn the Ribbentrop-Molotov Pact and its consequences. Negotiations came to an abrupt halt, as they no doubt would have done anyway, once the Katyn massacre came to light.

In the spring of 1943 Stalin began unambiguous and overt preparations to influence directly the future course of Poland's internal affairs: in May the Kościuszko Division was formed, and in June the Union of Polish Patriots held its First Congress. At the same time, the PPR went on the political offensive. The party intensified its propaganda campaign and began an energetic search for allies among left-leaning activists in the peasant and socialist movements. In the late fall of 1943 the party began forming its own quasi-governmental structure. At a meeting on 31 December 1943–41 January 1944, the communists set up the National Council of the Homeland (KRN), which presented itself as the sole authentic and legal representative of the Polish people. A similar initiative, which had the blessing of the Comintern and Stalin, was taken by their comrades in the Soviet Union who, at the end of 1943, decided to create the Polish National Committee. Their preparations advanced to the point where they had decided appointments to top ministerial positions and drafted a political program, but information concerning the formation of the KRN brought an end to these plans. Nevertheless, as Zbigniew Kumoś notes, they created, on Stalin's orders, "a reserve cadre and a command center" in the form of the Central Bureau of Polish Communists in the USSR, an embryonic political party.[8] The Bureau

8. Zbigniew Kumoś, *Zhiązek Patriotów Polskich. Założenia programmowo-ideowe* (Warsaw, 1983), 144.

took over political supervision of the Union of Polish Patriots and Polish forces in the Soviet Union.

The Polish Workers' Party was aided, first and foremost, by members of the socialist left, who in the fall of 1939 had come into conflict with the leadership of the PPS-WRN and found themselves outside the party. In September 1940 they created an organization called the Polish Socialists (PS) under the leadership of Adam Próchnik. The role of the PS grew immeasurably when the PPS-WRN, in protest against the Sikorski-Maiski agreement, resigned from the Political Consultative Committee, and Pużak's place was taken by Próchnik. This state of affairs lasted until March 1943, causing numerous conflicts within the Polish Socialists which led eventually to an outright split: some members joined the PPS-WRN, while the majority created the Polish Workers' Socialist Party, whose program was close to that of the communists. The peasant movement, where some evolution toward the left might have been expected, proved to be more cohesive than the socialists and only a few small groups were inclined to cooperate with the communists. The PPR was thus obliged to rely on communist peasant activists. Not until in February 1944 did they form the People's Will Peasant Party (SL Wola Ludu), a party dependent on the PPR for every aspect of its functioning, including conspiratorial know-how.

In the spring of 1944 the communist partisans clearly intensified their activity. This was partly the result of new people being parachuted into the territory of the Government-General (the first groups landed on 4 and 24 April) and the creation (on 5 May) of a separate Polish Partisan Command based near Równo, which had already been liberated by the Red Army. This unit, like its Ukrainian, Belorussian, and Lithuanian counterparts, had under its command a battalion of about 1,500 storm troopers assigned to them from General Berling's army, but only a small proportion of the soldiers with appropriate training were parachuted into the country. Nevertheless, the People's Army already numbered some twenty thousand people, organized in more than 100 partisan units. This was a considerable force, especially given that it was concentrated along the axis of the Soviet offensive planned for the summer.

The establishment of the PPR and its underground armed forces, as well as the formation of the KRN, greatly complicated Poland's internal situation. Above all, these organizations, especially the KRN, provided Stalin with a convenient weapon in his struggle with the Polish leadership, allowing him to blackmail the government-in-exile and bring pressure to bear on Britain and the United States.

During 1943 there finally emerged two groups aspiring to seize power and not recognizing the underground state: on the one hand, the NSZ and its political superstructure, on the other hand, the communists. Nevertheless, the "big four" parties, the Delegatura, and the Home Army command shared a great deal of common ground with the NSZ and its supporters. The same could be said of the National Confederation, led by Bolesław Piasecki, which was part of the AK, or the National Party, which frequently sparred with the socialists and Peasant Party members but still belonged to the Political Consultative Committee and took part in the work of the Delegatura. All these institutions shared a commitment to an independent Polish state and its territorial integrity, although they differed on the nature of its political system.

Both because of its ideological traditions and because of its relationship with a hostile power whose every move it obediently and openly endorsed, the Polish Workers' Party was separated from the remainder of the resistance by a deepening chasm, which could not be bridged by the small and ever less independent socialist left or by assorted people without moral authority who declared themselves to be "democrats," "cooperative activists," or "radical peasant activists." Although the NSZ enjoyed less public support than did either the peasant movement or the National Party, it was certainly far greater than that enjoyed by the PPR. But the communists' political strength increased as advanced armored units of the Red Army crossed into Poland.

Given the draconian conditions of occupation, the political life of the resistance was highly diverse and—paradoxically—quite unfettered. The AK commander might condemn the anticommunist excesses of the NSZ, but neither he nor the government delegate was in a position to bring the perpetrators before a court. The Communist Party, illegal for the entire twenty years of the interwar period, was now an equal member of the resistance. No district administrator could officially question the contents of an article in the press, no matter how critical it might be of the government or even the president. The extreme situation in which everyone found him or herself also unleashed the most radical and fanciful political proposals (and there had been no shortage of these before the war). Political struggle frequently transcended the framework of even the sharpest polemics and conflicts, escalating to a physical settling of accounts with one's enemies. The murders that took place in Borów have often been termed the beginnings of a civil war. There were numerous, less spectacular instances of this kind—for example the leadership of the People's Army mistakenly betrayed to the Germans a print shop belonging to the PPR rather than one belonging to the AK. There were also reprisals, and the "liquidation of enemies" did not spare people with left-wing views who were associated with the AK command.

It can be said, however, that a considerable number of the disputes and conflicts constituted a kind of "underground within the underground," the details of which never reached the broader public or even a large number of those actively involved in sabotage or armed resistance. The shape of underground Poland—both that created by the supporters of the government-in-exile and by those outside it—was determined by the struggle against the occupying powers, military and civilian. Most spectacular were the great "railroad operations," such as Wieniec (Wreath) (7–8 October 1942) and Wieniec II (on New Year's Eve that same year) which involved blowing up trains and railroad equipment. Excitement was aroused by attacks on leading members of the repressive apparatus, regardless of whether they were successful (among others, the attack on SS-Gruppenführer Kruger, General Kutscher, and the high-ranking police officer, Koppe), and by the freeing of prisoners, as during the most famous of such operations, at the Warsaw Arsenal. From the summer of 1943 on various kinds of partisan units intensified their activity, and during the mobilization associated with the approach of the front, serious fighting broke out around Lublin against regular German units that were "clearing the ground" in advance of the front. Guerrilla activity and sabotage not only constituted Poland's contribution to the military efforts of the anti-German coalition, but was also a major factor shaping social attitudes, strengthening passive resistance, and influencing the state's authority and the degree of loyalty to it. These effects were taken into account by the founders of the ZWZ, and were especially valued by General Rowecki.

"External" evidence of the scope of organized resistance was provided by the clandestine press, which had existed since the very beginning of the occupation. Initially most underground publications were primitively reproduced newssheets, but over time some publications acquired printing presses capable of a more sophisticated output. In 1939 more than thirty publications appeared, in 1940—no fewer than 250, in 1941—about 320, in

1942—close to 400, in 1943—more than 500, and in 1944—around 600. Altogether, at least 1,500 different titles were published. The majority appeared in the German zone, but illegal newspapers were also published during 1939–41 in Soviet-occupied territory. The largest publisher was the ZWZ-AK and its supporters, which brought out at least 250 titles, nearly one in six of all underground papers. Given the modest reading habits of the rural population, the number of publications—170—issued by the peasant movement was something of a phenomenon. The PPS-WRN and other socialist groups published more than 100 periodicals, and nationalist groups, broadly defined, produced at least 120. The communists gave the press a prominent role in their activity and produced a total of about 200 publications.

Very often, underground activity began with the decision to publish a paper, and a group was formed in the course of gathering information (most of it taken from radio broadcasts), printing, and distribution. By far the majority of underground publications contained both information and propaganda, but every larger political group aimed to publish its own programmatic-ideological periodical, while the military produced numerous technical publications. There was also a handful of cultural, satirical, and children's publications, and scouting organizations published about fifty titles. Information services also operated, and there were publications for French prisoners of war and for the British. The AK command set up a special subversive propaganda group that produced German-language publications for soldiers of the Wehrmacht. The ghettos, especially the Warsaw ghetto, also had their own publications, about fifty all told, most of them in Polish.

Almost every underground organization had its own press service, usually linked to its propaganda department. The largest of these was the AK Information and Propaganda Bureau, dating back to the time of the Polish Victory Service, which published the most popular weekly, the *Biuletyn Informacyjny,* established in 1939 by Aleksander Kamiński. By the beginning of 1943 the bulletin had a print run of more than twenty thousand; a year later, the number of copies printed had risen to forty thousand. The gathering of information, its subsequent editing, and the printing (or copying) and distribution of the underground press involved tens of thousands of people, undoubtedly a larger army than that which was engaged in armed combat or sabotage. Editors, printers, and distributors were in as much danger of losing their lives as those who fought with a gun in their hands.

The underground press was intended to provide an antidote to the Pol-

ish-language publications produced by the occupying forces. The "oppositional" aspect of the illegal press was less visible in the Soviet zone, where
both the sovietized Polish press and underground publications were relatively few. In the Government-General, on the other hand, the German authorities placed great emphasis on their Polish-language press. Although
only a few dozen publications—popularly known as *gadzinówki* ("reptilian
press")—appeared during more than five years of German occupation, they
included a dozen or so dailies with a joint print run in 1942 of 400,000. In
terms of circulation *Nowy Kurier Warszawski* (New Warsaw Courier) held
the record, with a print run of 200,000, equal to that of many prewar dailies.
Despite repeated appeals, the underground did not succeed in persuading
the public to boycott the German press.

The clandestine press created a protective zone around the organized
resistance movement, although it is impossible to say just how great its
readership was. It also fulfilled a vital role within the resistance itself as the
main—and often only—forum for the exchange of views, discussion, and
political disputes. The resistance movement was, then, unusually complex
and internally diverse. Alongside large organizations, there were groups
with only a few dozen members; political views spanned the full range, including Trotskyites; and active groups included those that were purely military, political parties with their own military units, and others that confined
themselves to propaganda and political activity. Much of the sabotage and
propaganda activity, such as painting slogans on walls or distributing
leaflets, was carried out by individuals who never belonged to any organization. It is estimated that about half a million people took part in organized
resistance of various kinds and that a far greater number of people engaged
in activity on their own or provided ad hoc support to members of the resistance.

The resistance reached everywhere: intelligence and assistance units
existed in the prisons; organized groups were to be found in the concentration camps, in prisoner-of-war camps, and among forced laborers; the resistance penetrated the blue police, as well as administrative agencies. All
social groups and strata were involved in underground activity, although
conditions were most propitious in large towns. In some cases, virtually all
the members of a particular group were active in the resistance, as was the
case with the scouting movement, which provided thousands of combatants
and was responsible for most of the acts of small-scale sabotage. Cultural
activity was an essential element in the resistance, although one that was

by definition carried out by an elite: volumes of poetry appeared in print, and clandestine theatrical events and concerts were organized. Many Poles lived double lives, and their illegal lives were the more important—whether they were cadets at a clandestine military college, poets who recited their verses, teachers in clandestine classrooms, newspaper distributors, or people who "only" let their apartments be used to pass on messages.

POLES AND NATIONAL MINORITIES

For the most part, the Polish resistance movement was a monoethnic enterprise, although there were some notable exceptions. A number of factors contributed to this situation: the clandestine nature of underground activity; age-old resentments and persisting stereotypes; the dominant, or most visible, attitudes of the various national minorities; and German policy, and—to some extent in the eastern provinces—Soviet policy also.

Until the outbreak of war between Germany and the Soviet Union, the resistance on Soviet-occupied territory basically had no contacts with the Ukrainian independence movement, which was then rather weak. After June 1941, contacts between Polish and Soviet partisans were based, at best, on mutual toleration, and combat between the two was far more common than cooperation. Essentially, Poles and Ukrainians—and to a lesser extent, Poles and Lithuanians—were fighting a "second war," a war that the Germans tried to control and one in which the Soviet partisans constituted a yet another side. Only the Belorussians, lacking their own resistance movement, eagerly joined forces with the Home Army.

Polish-Ukrainian relations were of greatest strategic significance, and not only from the Polish point of view, but neither side was inclined to make contact. The issue became especially urgent at the end of 1942, when an increasing number of Ukrainians began taking an active part in the anti-German resistance, and the Soviet Union was becoming increasingly vocal in advancing its claims to Poland's eastern lands. The first official Polish declaration (a resolution passed by the government-in-exile on 31 March 1943) did not go beyond recognizing the equal rights of all the nationalities residing in Poland, a stand that could not have satisfied the Ukrainian independence fighters. Despite the efforts of some émigré politicians, the Ukrainians were not invited—as the Jews had been—to send a representative to the National Council. In the summer of 1943, Ukrainian nationalists began the bloody campaign to "cleanse" Volhynia and eastern Galicia of Poles, and the appeal "To the Ukrainian People" issued by the KRP fell on deaf ears.

The Jewish resistance, functioning in the most extreme circumstances, did have ties, albeit weak ties, with the Polish underground. The resistance grew out of the tiny Jewish Military Union, founded in Warsaw in December 1939. In 1940 some Jewish political parties and social organizations (largely youth organizations) were able to renew activity, among them the Bund, Hechaluc, Poalej Syon, the Zionists, and Cukunft. As more became known about the terrible fate of the people confined to the ghettos, Jewish groups began to give greater priority to military training and showed a greater willingness to cooperate with each other. In November 1942 six political parties came together to form the Jewish National Committee, which together with the Bund set up the Coordinating Commission. This was followed by the creation, in December 1942, of the Jewish Fighting Organization (ŻOB), which built on the combat groups established by Hechaluc the previous summer. From its very beginning, the Jewish Military Union maintained contacts with the Polish underground, partly because its founders included a number of professional army officers. The AK commander recognized the ŻOB as an associated paramilitary organization, but could offer it only the most meager assistance. The People's Guard also had contact with the resistance in the Warsaw ghetto.

The Warsaw ghetto uprising, the largest but by no means the only armed uprising among the Jews, was not part of the plan for a popular uprising drawn up by the Home Army. Its organizers were not counting on success, but saw the uprising as an expression of national dignity—an act that was all the more vital to the despairing younger generation in light of the fact that millions of their people were going to hideous deaths without a word of protest and amidst widespread indifference on the part of the surrounding Poles, who were focused on their own fate and were to a considerable extent ill disposed or even hostile to the Jews. Fighting broke out on 19 April 1943, when German soldiers began "clearing" the ghetto. The ŻOB forces were led by Mordechaj Anielewicz, and the main detachment of the Military Union, by Dawid Apfelbaum. A few groups from Kedyw, the Socialist Fighting Organization, and the People's Guard tried to help the insurgents, but none of those who fought was counting on victory. Their aim was an honorable death.

The fighting raged for a month, and the turning point came when the Germans discovered the bunker that housed the ŻOB commanders, all of whom committed suicide. A few combatants managed to escape from the ghetto; some of them formed partisan detachments, while others joined Polish units; the Icak Cukierman ŻOB Detachment subsequently fought in the Warsaw uprising. The ghetto uprising evoked no reaction on the part of the Allies, despite the appeals of the government-in-exile and the desperate act of Szmul Zygielbojm, a member of the National Council in London who committed suicide on 13 May in the hope of arousing world opinion. In fact, the same was true of the entire process set in motion to exterminate the Jews, even though the Polish authorities provided relevant information on numerous occasions to the leaders of the Western democracies.

While war and occupation drastically and tragically altered the relations between the different nationalities in Poland, they did nothing to alter the attitudes of these nationalities toward each other. It is likely that they intensified previously existing conflicts and animosities and that they even produced new ones, whether because of the slaughter in the east or the bitterness of the Jews, who felt hopelessly isolated all through the years of the Holocaust. This deepening chasm could not be bridged by ephemeral attempts at Polish-Ukrainian negotiations, which were doomed to failure, nor by the fact that thousands of Poles were killed for having assisted or sheltered Jews who had escaped from the ghettos. Although the main problem that Jews encountered in their relations with Poles was the widespread indifference of the latter toward the Holocaust, it was the numerous acts of aggressive hostility that left the deepest imprint on Jewish memory. The precise numbers remain unknown, but undoubtedly thousands of Jews were handed over to the Germans, and similar numbers were murdered by Poles themselves, whether out of "pure" hatred or out of the desire to seize Jewish assets. When war broke out between Germany and the Soviet Union, and Wehrmacht forces marched into Polish territory, numerous pogroms of the Jewish population took place. These were encouraged by the German military police, and special groups of Gestapo were dispatched to the region to initiate such attacks. The most brutal pogroms, and the largest, took place at the beginning of July 1941, in three small towns east of Warsaw— Jedwabne, Radziłów, and Wąsacz—where more than one thousand Jews were murdered, most of them burned alive. These murders were accompanied by massive looting and plunder of Jewish property. In this regard, Poland was no exception in occupied Europe or in the rest of the world at war: differences between Slovaks and Czechs deepened; Croats butchered hundreds of thousands of Serbs; French police hunted down Jews, who were then murdered not only by Germans but also by Hungarian fascists; the fratricidal struggle between General Mihajlovic's Chetniks and Tito's

Partisans intensified; and in 1943–44 Italian partisans took their revenge for the years spent under Mussolini's regime. The world was teeming with people hungry for power, collaborators large and small, informants and assistants to the Nazi executioners. Such was the Age of the Gas Ovens.

POLAND AND THE USSR: FROM THE KREMLIN TO KATYN

On 14 August 1941 a military agreement modeled on previous agreements with France and Great Britain was signed in Moscow. The Polish Army in the USSR was to be commanded by General Władysław Anders, imprisoned since the fall of 1939 in the Lubyanka. An energetic and imaginative officer, Anders had fought bravely during the September campaign and also had the virtue—in the eyes of General Sikorski, at least—of having taken the side of the legal government during the May coup. Given the number of soldiers rounded up in September 1939 and the number of Poles assigned to the Red Army and construction brigades, it was likely that an army of at least 200,000, with an almost complete officer corps, could be recruited within the USSR. However, the agreement initially provided food rations for only thirty thousand, and recruitment proceeded at a much slower pace than expected.

To a certain extent, this resulted from what might—with difficulty—be called objective circumstances: the majority of Poles who were of an age suitable for military service were to be found along the Pechora, in the Urals, and in Siberia, and it was impossible to arrange their rapid transportation to the regions where units were being assembled. Soviet officials, however, erected a number of obstacles, sometimes deliberately, sometimes less so: in many camps and construction brigades, Poles were not told that an army was being formed, or various obstacles were placed in the way of their departure. Far more important, though, was the fact that a considerable number of prisoners of war had died or disappeared, and nearly all Polish officers had been murdered. When asked about the fate of Polish prisoners of war, Soviet officials were evasive or else declared that they were holding only twenty thousand such prisoners, which more or less corresponded to the situation as of July 1941. Those who had survived were unable to provide any information other than to confirm that in the spring of 1940 whole groups had been taken away from the officers' camps and that rank-and-file soldiers had been detained in terrible conditions. The search continued, but by the spring of 1942 it was clear that the missing officers would never be found.

To the Poles it was obvious that their concerns could not be limited to military issues. There was also the matter of the hundreds of thousands of "special migrants," most of them women and children. Concern for their welfare was essentially the province of the civilian service, the embassy and its regional outposts, but the areas in which units were being assembled were bound to attract other deportees and, in addition, offered greater chances than other places of surviving yet another winter. It was also Sikorski's intention to evacuate some of these soldiers to strengthen the Polish Armed Forces in the West, a move eagerly awaited by the British, who were deeply disturbed by the military situation in North Africa and the Middle East.

Negotiations at the highest level were needed, and on 30 November Sikorski flew to Kuibyshev, where the Polish embassy, along with other embassies, was now located. Before any meeting took place, the Soviet government sent a clear signal regarding its intentions by declaring that it considered only Polish nationals to be Polish citizens. The purpose of this decision was twofold: to prevent the recruitment of Jews, Belorussians, and Ukrainians to the Polish Army and to remove them from the oversight of the Polish embassy, and, above all, to affirm Soviet sovereignty over the eastern provinces seized in 1939. Two days later, on 3 December, the first negotiating session took place, to be followed, the next day, by a banquet and the signing of a joint declaration. It was agreed that the Polish forces would consist of six divisions, that the assembly point would be moved further to the south (to Uzbekistan and Kirghizia), and that the USSR would provide a loan of a hundred million rubles to aid the civilian population. Stalin also agreed to the evacuation of twenty-five thousand Polish soldiers to the Middle East. The fate of the missing Polish officers remained unclarified and the status of Polish citizens of non-Polish origin remained unchanged. Most important, Stalin completely ignored Polish efforts to raise the issue of Poland's borders. He did not, however, conceal from his British allies the fact that he had no intention of abandoning the territory he had seized in 1939, information that they failed to pass along to Sikorski. When Anthony Eden recounted to the Polish prime minister the discussions he had held in Moscow, he made no mention of the Soviet Union's position regarding the territorial integrity of its Polish ally.

Following his unfruitful discussions in the Soviet capital, Sikorski went to visit the assembling forces, at which point, the war, already bloody and difficult enough, took a further leap across the world stage. On 7 December

Japan attacked the U.S. Pacific Fleet in Pearl Harbor, and four days later Hitler signed his own death sentence when he declared war on the greatest economic power in the world, the United States. At that moment, what had hitherto been essentially a European conflict became a global one. These events rapidly gave birth to a new division of power in the world, one that would for decades to come shape the course of events from the Arctic to the Antarctic. Doubtless, few observers at the time realized that this was happening. For the majority, including the Poles, the direct involvement of the United States in the war signified, first and foremost, that the anti-Nazi alliance now had an immeasurably greater chance of victory. Polish political leaders, or at least the prime minister and his supporters, also believed that "the world's largest democracy," and President Roosevelt in particular, would intercede on behalf of all just causes.

Although Polish-Soviet relations were far from cordial and there was every indication that improving them would be no easy task, the fact that during 1942 they steadily worsened was cause for growing concern. It also gave rise to further tensions among the Poles themselves. General Anders undoubtedly expressed the fear and animosity of a large proportion—if not the outright majority—of his troops, when he refused to allow individual units to be sent into battle if they were inadequately trained and if they were made up of people who not long ago had been fainting from hunger and who remained susceptible to diseases arising from poverty and imprisonment. The soldiers, who were recruited largely from among inhabitants of the territory seized by the USSR, also lived in a state of constant fear and anxiety regarding their families, who were barely surviving in appalling conditions, not all of them receiving help from the embassy. The idea of evacuating the army gained, then, in popularity, but would not have won acceptance among the troops unless they had been allowed to take with them the civilian population, both their own families and the families of those Poles who had died or disappeared.

These tendencies meshed—although not always consciously—with the opinions of those who nurtured the far-reaching and age-old distrust of Russia, regarded with suspicion any alliance with the Soviet Union, and were thus critical of General Sikorski's policy. The prime minister himself was inclined, it would seem, to continue his existing strategy. Although opposed to the reckless shedding of Polish blood, he believed that mounting a strong force on the eastern front and a military presence alongside Allied forces engaged in active combat (in the Mediterranean and Western Europe) would greatly strengthen Poland's hand in its international dealings. Thus he supported the idea of a partial evacuation and on 10 March 1942 gave his assent to the proposal that all soldiers in excess of the number receiving Soviet food rations (at that time forty-four thousand) should be evacuated to Iran. The first transports got under way on 24 March, and by 3 April more than twenty-four thousand soldiers (without weapons) and ten thousand civilians, among them three thousand children, had left Krasnodar. More than forty thousand soldiers remained in the Soviet Union. Neither they nor their commander wished to stay. The British, who were experiencing a series of defeats at the hands of Rommel's Afrika Korps (Tobruk fell on 21 June 1942), had a vital interest in the relocation of these troops.

The Kremlin leadership believed that, from the political point of view, the absence of Polish troops on the eastern front would be more advantageous to the Soviet Union in that it would solve the problem of the unwanted ally and thus free it of any obligations toward Poland. During 10–31 August, a second phase of evacuation took place, in which nearly seventy thousand people, including about twenty-five thousand civilians, left the USSR. Despite clear resistance from Soviet officials, several thousand Polish Jews also managed to leave. All told, about 110,000 of the roughly one million people who had been deported, imprisoned, or assigned to various Soviet agencies, military and civilian, now found themselves outside the Soviet Union. According to the calculations of the Polish embassy, a further 680,000 Poles remained in the country. It was they who became the first victims of the deepening chill in Polish-Soviet relations, when in the second half of 1942 the administrative authorities and the NKVD restricted the activities of the several hundred Polish welfare agencies, arresting a considerable number of their personnel and preventing supplies from reaching them. They also put a stop to all further recruitment to the army and closed down the recruiting stations.

General Sikorski tried without success to persuade the British leadership of the need to support the Poles in their conflicts with the Kremlin. Discussions with Roosevelt in Washington in March 1942 were similarly unsuccessful. German forces had reached the Volga and the Caucasus, the fate of not just the eastern front but the entire war hung in the balance, and the Allies had no intention of doing anything that might undermine the alliance with Stalin. Polish proposals to open a second front in the Balkans and suggestions concerning a federal structure for East-Central Europe were forwarded by the Americans to the British, but the latter now clearly acknowledged the primacy of the USSR in the region and were more concerned—understandably—about their own interests in the Middle East and Asia than about the fate of Poland. Of far greater importance was the outcome of the Battle of Stalingrad, then under way: if Germany succeeded in breaking through the front, there was a very real danger not only that it would seize control of the Caucasus and cut off access to oil supplies in Iran and Iraq but also that the Red Army would collapse completely and the Soviet Union would be eliminated from the war. This vision had haunted General Anders for some time and was one of the reasons why he led his troops out of the Soviet Union. Stalin was happy to make frequent reference to the "flight" of the Poles, and the British considered them unrealistic: "General Sikorski,' said Eden, "is more sensible than most Poles but despite this, he has not learned a great deal."

Soviet policy created a succession of *faits accomplis,* which the Poles were powerless to prevent, despite the travels of the prime minister, despite the appointment of Tadeusz Romer, a professional diplomat, as ambassador in place of Stanisław Kot, whom the Soviets had treated in the most hostile manner, and despite the fact that the Red Army was in an extremely difficult situation. On 19 January 1943 the Soviet authorities announced that they now considered all inhabitants of the territory annexed in 1939, including Poles, to be Soviet citizens. This not only meant that they would be deprived of—the increasingly illusory—assistance from the embassy, but also confirmed yet again that Moscow considered the borders set out in the Soviet-German "friendship" treaty to be inviolable. After a short period of formal correctness in the late summer and fall of 1941, Polish-Soviet relations were approaching a critical point. In March 1943 Mikołaczyk wrote in a dispatch to his colleagues in the clandestine peasant movement that a complete breakdown in diplomatic relations "cannot be excluded . . . and may occur in the nearest future."

This became fact a few weeks later. On 13 April Berlin radio announced that a mass grave containing the remains of Polish officers formerly detained in the prisoner of war camp in Kozielsk had been discovered in Katyn, near Smolensk. Initial disbelief quickly turned to shock. On 15 April General Anders sent a cable to London asking that the government demand a response from the Soviet authorities and recalling that in 1941 Polish officials had spent months in the unsuccessful attempt to find these prisoners of war and to obtain information as to their fate. The same day, Radio Moscow broadcast a communiqué accusing the Germans of having carried out the

Katyn massacre, despite the fact that the decision to execute had been taken by both Stalin and Molotov personally—and they had affixed their signatures to this decision, set out in a document drawn up by Beria. On 16 April the Polish Ministry of National Defense issued a communiqué declaring the need for the matter to be investigated "by an appropriate international agency," and the government-in-exile called on the International Red Cross in Geneva to carry out such an investigation. The same day, the German Red Cross issued a similar appeal to Geneva.

The Western Allies, especially Churchill, did not hesitate to bring pressure to bear on the Poles, with the aim of persuading them to moderate their demands and not to bring the matter before an international forum. But even General Sikorski, so often inclined to give way under pressure from Britain, did not consider it possible either to renounce further action or to accept the Kremlin's position. He was supported in this by the dispatches he was receiving from Poland, which on the basis of information from reliable witnesses confirmed the veracity of the German communiqué. In an official statement, the government-in-exile denied Germany the right "to derive arguments in its own defense from a crime of which they accuse others," but did not rescind its appeal to the International Red Cross. Soviet propaganda sounded the alarm by arguing that Poland's position demonstrated the influence of "pro-Nazi elements" in Sikorski's government. In keeping with Kremlin custom, during the night of 24–25 April Molotov summoned the Polish ambassador and read to him a lengthy note that ended with the declaration that it had been decided to "break off" relations with Poland. Despite cables sent by Churchill and Roosevelt, the "cunning Georgian" did not change his mind. On 5 May Ambassador Romer left the Soviet Union.

IN THE SHADOW OF TEHRAN

Although the timing of the decision was dictated by the terrible discovery made by the Germans, Stalin immediately seized the opportunity to dot the final "i" in his policy toward Poland. Although the group of officers who had earlier been sent to Małachowka was transferred to General Anders after the signing of the Sikorski-Maiski agreement, and Polish communists who in July 1941 in Gomel called for the formation of partisan units "in all corners of Poland" received no support from Moscow, the Soviet Union took steps in the fall of 1941 to create its own source of support among the Poles by setting up a Polish-language radio station (named after Tadeusz Kościuszko). In May 1942 the journal *Nowe Widnokręgi* (New Horizons) began to appear again, and at the end of the second wave of evacuation, the commander of the embarkation base in Kislovodsk, Lieutenant-Colonel Zygmunt Berling, obeyed NKVD orders to desert his troops and remain in the Soviet Union. In December he resurfaced in Moscow, where he presented a memorandum, written to order, proposing the formation of a Polish army. It was addressed to Vsevelod Merkulov, Beria's closest associate and head of the People's Commissariat for State Security. It was no accident that precisely this agency of the Soviet apparatus instigated the proposal and supervised its implementation.

While every weapon was valuable in this war, this business was political rather than military. At the same time, other preparations were being made from a different direction, the Comintern. On 1 March 1943 the organizing committee of the Union of Polish Patriots was formed in Moscow. It was headed by Wanda Wasilewska, well known for her political activity in Lvov, since August 1941 a colonel in the Red Army, and the wife of Alexander Kornichuk, the deputy minister of foreign affairs of the USSR. In the first issue of its journal, *Wolna Polska* (Free Poland), published a week later, the union acknowledged the Soviet Union's right to the eastern borderlands. During the two weeks following the rupture in relations with Poland, the union leadership met several times with a General Zhukov of the NKVD, former plenipotentiary for the formation of a Polish army. On 8 May a communiqué was issued announcing the formation of the Tadeusz Kościuszko Infantry Division, and on 9–10 May the Union of Polish Patriots held its first congress in Moscow.

Stalin issued Poland—and the Poles—a clear challenge. It was also a signal to the Western Allies that the Soviet Union intended to shape the situation in Europe in accordance with its own interests. This signal was intensified with the creation in August 1943 of the Free Germany Committee, whose members included both communists and military officers selected from among prisoners of war, an indication that Soviet aspirations extended far to the west of the Curzon Line. All of this, in conjunction with the euphoria induced by the great victory at Stalingrad and the capture of Field Marshal von Paulus's entire army, and given the Americans' engagement in the Pacific and the absence of a second front in Europe, created an ominous question mark concerning the future of Poland, although it could still be supposed that this was "only" a question of territorial concessions. Poland's agreement to give up its eastern provinces would undoubtedly have reduced the tension, but such a decision was in practice impossible, since it would not only have undermined the raison d'état of a sovereign state, a partner in the anti-Hitler coalition, but would also have signified that Poland was weak and small and hence susceptible to further pressure from its neighbor to the east.

Neither at home nor abroad was there a responsible political or military leader who could—or would want to—raise the question, let alone actually propose such a decision. Nevertheless, the mutual distrust of the various sides to this internal Polish dispute increased, a process that was aided by the fact that both General Anders and the majority of the troops under his command in the Middle East supported those politicians who were critical of the prime minister. General Sikorski traveled to the Middle East in the hope of bringing to an end the conflict between himself as commander in chief and the commander and soldiers of Poland's largest combat force— and also with an eye to the anticipated invasion of southern Europe (the German forces in Africa finally capitulated on 12 May 1943). On 27 May he held his first meeting with General Anders and spent the period 1–17 June inspecting the troops assembled in Iraq. Without much difficulty they agreed on the measures needed to establish the Second Corps; the meetings with the military commanders went well, and the personal contact between the two generals clearly eased the tension between them, although Sikorski did not conceal the fact that he still counted on Stalin to show some flexibility and on the Allies to exert some pressure on the Soviet Union.

He was not to see the outcome of his discussions with Anders, who went on to win the legendary battle of Monte Cassino: returning to London late on the evening of 4 July 1943, Sikorski's plane plunged into the sea shortly after leaving the British base in Gibraltar. The crash killed Sikorski, his daughter Zofia, his chief of staff and chief of operations, the British government liaison officer, and several other members of Sikorski's entourage. The only survivor was the injured chief pilot, Eduard Prchal, a Czech. Despite numerous attempts to establish the cause of the accident and a search for possible saboteurs, the precise cause of the accident remains unclear to this day. Nor has anyone found conclusive evidence that it was the result of an attack.

Whatever the cause—accident or sabotage—the death of General Sikorski was a severe blow to Poland. He enjoyed considerable prestige abroad, bolstered in no small part by the independence of mind he displayed before the war. For Poles at home, and even for the troops abroad who were critical of his policies, he was a symbol of Polish resistance and endurance. He was more closely associated than was the president with Fighting Poland. His sudden departure opened the door to internal political strife, which complicated the situation at an already critical moment, when Stalin had severed diplomatic relations and the Kremlin had made clear its intentions regarding the future of the Polish state. There is little point in speculating as to how Polish issues might have played out in the international arena had Sikorski not been killed, since we cannot know how he might have behaved in specific situations or even what political line he might have followed, but we can say unequivocally that in the domestic arena his death had a clear-cut and almost immediate impact.

On 5 July, after news of the Gibraltar tragedy had reached London, Sikorski's position was taken over, with the knowledge and agreement of the president, by Stanisław Mikołaczyk, hitherto deputy prime minister. Sikorski's political opponents considered that this presented a good opportunity to bring about some major changes in both personnel and policy. Some of the changes were obvious: although Mikołaczyk had taken part in the Wielkopolska uprising and the 1920 campaign, he had not risen above the rank of lance corporal and could not, therefore, occupy the position of commander in chief. In their first discussion on the subject, President Raczkiewicz told Mikołaczyk that he intended to appoint General Sosnkowski to the post. The peasant movement leader objected vigorously and obtained the support of the rest of the cabinet, while the British did not hesitate to inform the president that they had reservations concerning his candidate. The result was open conflict and a crisis that was resolved only with the greatest difficulty and thanks to the mediation of the socialists and the intervention of the British.

Mikołaczyk, a decided advocate of continuing the line followed by Sikorski, was charged with forming a government, while General Sosnkowski was appointed commander in chief, a position whose sphere of competence had been somewhat curtailed more than a year earlier. It would be difficult, however, to describe this as a serious political compromise of the kind that Sikorski had been able to impose by virtue of his authority. The commander in chief, a large proportion of military commanders, and numerous political opponents were openly hostile to, and even contemptuous of, the new head of the government. This conflict, which was clearly visible even in times of relative domestic peace, escalated into an open struggle that became increasingly bitter over time and was conducted with ever-greater ruthlessness. Above all, a kind of self-perpetuating mechanism came into play whereby opposing views, interests, and ambitions grew ever further apart, with the result that an ever-widening chasm separated the views of the various sides, while the situation on the ground demanded convergence and agreement on the course of action to be taken.

Although the anticipated invasion of the Continent did indeed begin (in Sicily) on 10 July, the most important military event of 1943 in Europe was the Red Army's defeat of the largest German armored offensive of the war. On 4 August Soviet armored units successfully completed their counterattack at Kursk. Two weeks later Churchill and Roosevelt met in Quebec to agree on the American plan for the invasion of Europe. It was decided that it would take place along the Atlantic coast. This concurrence of events was essentially coincidental—the American command had long settled on this variant—but the implications for Poland were considerable: unless an unforeseen catastrophe befell Soviet forces, the Red Army would march into Polish territory before the Western Allies.

This scenario was adopted despite reservations on the part of the British. It was in line with the long-term plans of the U.S. president, whose vision of the postwar world was based on cooperation among four powers (the United States, the USSR, Great Britain, and China), with the economically most powerful country, the United States, taking the lead. In the huge struggles taking place on the Russian plain and in the Pacific, there was no place for smaller states to assert their independence, especially those states that were situated within the immediate sphere of interest of one of the major powers and were, moreover, under enemy occupation. This applied to Poland and to other countries that found themselves at the forefront of Stalin's imperial ambitions. General Sikorski's hopes of reaching an agreement with his eastern neighbor, hopes that were nurtured also by his successor, proved illusory. Nevertheless, the very real fact remained that more than twenty million Poles still occupied the land of their ancestors and would not be able to emigrate.

Mikołaczyk and the clear minority of the émigré population who supported him considered it necessary to pursue any possibility of reaching agreement with Stalin. In this they counted on the support of the British and Americans and did not exclude the possibility of territorial concessions. The majority of the émigré population was in favor of a firm stand on the principles of the Atlantic Charter—adopted by Great Britain and the United States in August 1941—which referred to the inviolability of prewar frontiers. Although this option implied strong criticism of the Western powers, and General Sosnkowski did not rule out the possibility of "a sharp conflict between Poland's raison d'état and that of Britain," its advocates also assumed that these powers would oppose Soviet domination. And would even use force, if necessary. The notion of "two enemies," so obvious before 22 July 1941, was once more on the agenda.

At the same time, Poland's military and political situation became ever more difficult. A week before the conference of foreign ministers of the Big Three, which was to prepare for the first summit conference and was due to take place on 18 October 1943, a division under the command of General Berling (appointed general by a decree of the Supreme Soviet of the USSR) set out to do battle in the Smolensk region. Although the battle at Lenino (12–13 October) was an exceptionally bloody baptism of fire and actually ended in defeat, the main point was the political implications of having at the front Polish troops under the command of communists, something that Molotov was able to use at the foreign ministers' conference. Eden pointed out that other Polish units were preparing for battle, but General Anders's corps did not begin loading supplies and equipment for the landing in Italy until 15 December.

Everyone was aware that time was pressing. On 28 October the commander of the Home Army sent a telegram to London asking for instructions concerning behavior toward the Red Army, which was expected to enter Polish territory within a month or so. He demanded that all decisions on the matter be "politically expedient and historically transparent." Poland's political and military leaders were soon to discover how difficult it is to reconcile political expedience with the judgment of future generations. Exactly one day earlier, Mikołajczyk's cabinet had accepted the instructions drawn up by General Sosnkowski. The document set out a number of options, taking into account the possibility that the USSR and the Third Reich would sign a separate peace agreement or that the Western Allies would march into Poland. In the most likely event—that the Red Army would arrive in Poland and the Soviet government would not recognize the existing Polish authorities—the instructions envisaged that underground forces would engage in anti-German guerrilla actions for demonstration purposes, would remain in hiding from the occupying-liberation forces, and would undertake only defensive actions. These instructions were imbued with anxiety and insecurity.

The debate between the Big Three, and especially the decisions they took during the course of the conference held in Tehran from 28 October to

1 November 1943, could only have deepened this anxiety, although many of the issues discussed remained secret. The British proposal to attack the Germans from Italy and the Adriatic and then to move in the direction of Vienna was rejected. On the last day the participants also agreed that Poland's eastern frontier would more or less follow the line set out in the German-Soviet treaty, that the western frontier would be moved westwards, to the Oder River, and that a large-scale migration of Poles would be necessary—none of which the Poles learned officially until nearly a year later. The position of the government-in-exile, set out in a well-reasoned memorandum drawn up by Mikołaczyk on 16 November, was ignored. The memorandum demanded that the eastern frontier set out in the Treaty of Riga be maintained and that Poland be granted some acquisitions to the north and the west, while stressing that the latter should not be regarded as compensation for ceding territory in the east to the Soviet Union. Poland did not, of course, have a representative at the Tehran talks, not even an expert witness. In this, the country was not alone: General de Gaulle was not invited to Tehran, nor were the Chinese—soon to be recognized as a "great power"—asked to send a representative. From the Polish point of view, this amounted to a dictate. But there was nothing to be done; no gesture or action could change the state of affairs. During the night of 4–5 January 1944, advance troops of the Red Army entered the territory of the Polish Republic for the second time since 17 September 1939 and this time as the enemy of Poland's enemy and the ally of its allies. But was the Soviet Union an enemy or an ally?

These advance forces were not actually the first Soviet units to be active in the region. Since at least 1942, and especially since the spring of 1943, the northeast borderlands had been full of Soviet partisans, coordinated and supplied from behind the front and carrying out both military and political tasks. Nevertheless, the appearance of regular army units created a completely new situation. In view of the unyielding position of the government-in-exile in relation to the eastern frontier and Stalin's growing ambitions, an escalation of the conflict was inevitable. Although Poland's declaration of 6 January was somewhat tempered under pressure from the British, the Soviet declaration of 11 January unequivocally recognized the legality of the "elections" held in 1939. This public exchange of declarations was repeated on 14 and 16 January, with Moscow now accusing the Poles of engaging in an anti-Soviet—and hence pro-German—campaign in relation to the Katyn murders. The USSR demanded changes in the Polish government (the dismissal of the two best-known followers of Sikorski, Kot and Kukiel) as well as the appointment of a new commander in chief.

The Soviet position stiffened as the front moved west, and the Western Allies were not inclined to offer the Polish government wholehearted support. Roosevelt postponed a meeting with Mikołaczyk, and in a speech to parliament on 22 February 1944 Churchill declared that His Majesty's Government regarded Stalin's frontier demands as justified. Poland's room for political maneuver had become reduced to a dangerously narrow margin. And by this point, nothing could be done to change the situation: neither government activity in the international arena nor the implementation of plans for Operation Tempest, which, in accordance with the order of the AK commander issued on 20 November 1943, was to proceed as follows: the underground army would be mobilized, retreating German forces would be attacked, Polish fighters would engage in tactical cooperation with Red Army forces, and representatives of the underground administration would identify themselves to Soviet commanders.

Soviet forces forged ahead to the west, and although the initial experience following their encounter (March 1944) with the Twenty-Seventh Volhynia AK Infantry Division commanded by Major Jan Kiwerski was ambiguous rather than totally negative, the overall situation remained unchanged. At the same time, the Soviet Union was hastily reinforcing the units under the command of General Berling: in the late summer of 1943 it had already been decided to turn them into a corps, and on 16 March 1944 a decree of the Supreme Soviet ordered the formation of the First Polish Army. At the end of April, three of its divisions were transferred to Volhynia, where they joined troops already fighting along the Belorussian front, which was moving in the direction of Warsaw and Berlin. Their commander was General Konstanty Rokossowski, the future marshal of Poland.

During this time, General Anders's troops were also preparing to join the front. Between 11 and 18 May, the Third Carpathian and Fifth Borderland Divisions suffered severe casualties while leading the victorious storming of Monte Cassino, a major factor in breaking the German defense blocking the route to Rome. Also preparing to fight, for the first time since June 1940, was the First Armored Division commanded by Colonel Stanisław Maczek, which landed on the Continent on 1 August, seven weeks after the Normandy landing. During the night of 7–8 June this unit took part in the first skirmishes, and then played a major role in the fighting at Falaise on 15–21 August. Polish air units were constantly in action (during 1944 alone they shot down one hundred Luftwaffe planes and also took part in bombing raids), but given the unprecedented increase in the number of Allied forces, the role of Polish troops in the fighting could not be as significant, as visible, and as effective as during the memorable Battle of Britain in 1940. Two million Allied soldiers and eleven thousand aircraft took part in the invasion of Europe. At this time the Polish Armed Forces had 81,000 troops at the front line (50,000 in the Second Corps), and around 33,000 support troops. Thus although Polish soldiers fought courageously, the scale of Poland's military effort was constantly declining relative to the overall numbers involved in the conflict and had no real influence over the course of the fighting.

The same was true of Polish policy, regardless of the extent to which the leadership was prepared to be flexible. To an ever-increasing extent, Poland came to find itself the object of a game between the great powers, and this at a time when the era of the bipolar world was only just beginning. Among the émigré political elite in London two diametrically opposed views of events, and reactions to them, were clearly represented by the prime minister and the commander in chief. General Sosnkowski believed that the most important thing was to ensure that the underground continue in existence. He was opposed to the underground authorities revealing themselves and to clandestine forces being openly involved in fighting; he even had reservations regarding the participation of Anders's troops in the fighting at Monte Cassino and believed that any discussions with Moscow served only to strengthen Stalin's position.

Mikołajczyk declared that only a flexible approach had any hope of success—even if only partial success. He was already speaking clearly of the need for territorial concessions as the price for internal sovereignty, and was also inclined to favor the notion of a "grand coalition," along the lines of those that were being established in France and Italy, which would give the communists a role in government. He agreed with the policy of the AK command concerning the Red Army. Mikołajczyk was untiring in his efforts to obtain support, both military and above all political, from the Western powers. In this he was so successful that after his visit to the United States in June, Roosevelt managed to persuade the Kremlin to meet with the Polish prime minister. On 23 July, the day after Moscow announced the formation in Lublin of the Polish Committee for National Liberation (PKWN) and published its manifesto, Stalin agreed to meet with Mikołajczyk.

When Mikołajczyk left London on 26 July, the Council of People's Commissars was signing a secret agreement with the PKWN concerning Poland's eastern frontier and a public agreement that placed the area along the front under the jurisdiction of the Soviet military authorities. When he landed in Moscow on 30 July Operation Tempest was in its death throes, crushed by the Red Army: the units fighting for Vilnius (6–13 July), for Lvov (22–25 July), and dozens of towns of varying size east of the Vistula had been disarmed, their commanders arrested, and their soldiers—if they were unwilling to join Berling's troops—had been deported. The uprising in Warsaw was due to start in two days.

If it can be said that anyone who holds in his hands all the trump cards plays a masterful game, then Stalin was certainly masterful in his playing. He kept his visitors from London waiting until 3 August before granting them audience, by which time the front outside Warsaw had come to a halt and it was clear that the insurgents had not—and would not—seize control of the capital. What the Kremlin had to tell the Poles constituted the very worst scenario of all those that Mikołaczyk had envisaged in his exposé to the National Council on 23 June 1944, when he predicted that Stalin, after forcing the Poles to accept changes in their frontier, would move on to blackmail by threatening to form an alternative government and urging the Poles to come to an agreement among themselves. In Poland, the Soviet leader told his guests in the Kremlin: "There cannot be two governments. . . . Under no circumstances will we allow this." At a meeting with a delegation from the PKWN, which he attended despite the position of the Polish government, Mikołajczyk also learned that while they were offering him the position of prime minister, the majority of seats (fourteen out of eighteen) in any new government were to be occupied by "people from Lublin"— exactly the opposite proportions from those that he had envisaged. The people from Lublin also totally downplayed the significance of the uprising taking place in Warsaw, while Stalin declared his desire, without actually committing himself, to assist those fighting for the capital, which was, of course, also one of the most important communications junctions of Central Europe.

Mikołajczyk's policy was simply overwhelmed by Stalin's intransigence. The policy of his opponents became irrelevant, since it depended completely on the Western powers deciding to engage in armed conflict with the Red Army.

Two Polands

By the beginning of August 1944 the Red Army offensive had been under way for five weeks and, taking the shortest route to Berlin, had come to a halt on the banks of the Vistula. From 20 August Stalin focused his efforts on the Balkans, where the Axis powers, severely wounded already, retreated from Romania (23 August) and Bulgaria (9 September). The Soviet advance forces had almost reached the straits that barred the Red Fleet from entering the Mediterranean. Like the troops of Aleksandr II in 1878, the units under the command of Fyodor Tolbukhin did not dig themselves in on the Bosporus—this would not only have violated Turkey's neutrality (although Moscow would undoubtedly have managed to deal with this) but would also have intruded into Britain's sphere of interest.

It was for different reasons that the troops under Konstanty Rokossowski, recently appointed marshal, did not advance as planned to reach the Warsaw district of Praga, on the right bank of the Vistula, by 6 August and did not establish a bridgehead in the city. The German armored counterattack slowed the pace of the offensive, and Soviet command headquarters ordered a halt. Regardless of how justified these military considerations might have been, Stalin was not interested in having the Red Army fight a battle for Warsaw: since the afternoon of 1 September the city had been the site of an uprising that was both the continuation and the culmination of Operation Tempest.

Detachments from the Warsaw AK garrison were hoping to seize control of strategic locations in the city and assist Rokossowski's troops to cross the Vistula. The Homeland Council of Ministers, the Council of National Unity, and the Commander of the AK were to greet them in the name of the Republic. If troops on the Belorussian front continued their offensive, this would assist the Poles fighting in Warsaw and help to achieve both the military and political goals of the government-in-exile and the underground leadership. If the thirty thousand AK soldiers initiated the battle for Warsaw, Stalin would find himself in an exceedingly awkward situation: either he would have to recognize the authority of the resistance leaders or he would have to act as he had done in Vilnius and Lvov when he crushed Operation Tempest. Doubtless this would not be easy, and it would undoubtedly entail serious international repercussions.

For Stalin both outcomes were equally undesirable. So he opted for a third. For six weeks the Red Army made no attempt to strike, not even in those parts of the city on the right bank of the Vistula, abandoning the insurgents to their own devices. Countless attempts by the government-in-exile and the president to obtain material assistance from the Allies were frustrated by the Soviet refusal to allow Allied planes to land at Soviet airfields. This constituted a death sentence for tens of thousands of soldiers and the people of Warsaw.

The front line divided Poland in two. West of the Vistula, German occupation continued with undiminished brutality. To the east, the Red Army reigned supreme, and beyond the Bug, in Poland's eastern provinces, there was a bloody repetition of the events of 1939–41. Jails were filled with AK fighters, political-party activists, members of other conspiratorial groups, and intellectuals. Convoys of deportees and people who had been sentenced to labor camp once more set off for the far reaches of the Soviet Union. No Polish newspapers were published, nor were any nongovernmental organizations revived. Both the Soviet authorities and the Ukrainian partisans pressured the Polish population to migrate west of the Curzon Line. In eastern Galicia and Volhynia, though, the Soviets directed their main efforts against the Ukrainian population. Troops belonging to the Ukrainian partisans fighting for independence, who had not been able to fall back to the west together with the front (as the NSZ Świętokrzyska Brigade was able to do in January 1945), found themselves in a desperate situation and in the winter of 1944 began to engage in fierce fighting. According to official Soviet data, in the course of the pacification carried out in 1944–45, tens of thousands of people were killed and at least 120,000 were deported. While Poles were certainly among the victims, they constituted a minority. Victims of the crackdown in Lithuania mirrored the national composition of the population as a whole and thus contained a greater proportion of Poles. In general, though, the Soviet aim was to have the Poles migrate to the "new Poland." For the Ukrainians and Lithuanians considered "undesirable" in their homeland, there remained only the echelons formed by the convoy troops of the NKVD. The process of sovietization accelerated rapidly, although "the struggle against the kulaks" would not get seriously under way until 1948–49.

To many Poles, regardless of whether they found themselves among those fighting in Warsaw, or in Lublin, Lvov, London, or Chicago, it was manifestly obvious that between the Vistula and the Bug, an embryonic "seventeenth republic," a "Polish Soviet Socialist Republic," was taking shape. There are no grounds to believe that Stalin actually harbored such intentions, even if we regard his public statements concerning a Poland that would be "independent," "democratic," and "strong" as nothing more than mendacious propaganda. Many people, among them Prime Minister Mikołajczyk, also believed that the existence of the PKWN not only signified that Poland was to be made dependent on its giant neighbor but also constituted a first step in the communization of the country's internal life. This belief gave rise to the conviction that the struggle should not be halted. The problem was, however: by what means should it be continued?

Meanwhile the war raged on, and west of the Vistula underground Poland had been in existence for over five years. For two bloody months it took to the streets of Warsaw and ruled over an ever-diminishing remnant of the prewar republic. The decision to launch the uprising in the capital was based on a number of considerations: political—a demonstration of the will to fight the Germans and to demonstrate that the fight was being waged by the legal authorities of a sovereign state; military—the Wehrmacht was in retreat and the recent (20 July) attempt to assassinate Hitler revealed the presence of a determined opposition within the military and seemed to signify that the Third Reich was on the verge of collapse, reminiscent of the course of events on the fall of 1918; and psychological—the Warsaw Home Army, the largest concentration of underground fighters, had for several years been preparing for this moment and wanted to fight, come what may. The creation of the PKWN, the publication of its manifesto, its recognition by the Soviet Union, and the participation of "Berling's army" in the July offensive—as well as the provocative calls for a battle for Warsaw broadcast by Radio Kościuszko—provided additional incentives to fight.

The course of events at the front and the prime minister's visit to Moscow placed the issue at the operational rather than strategic level, although many politicians, both at home and abroad, were skeptical or downright opposed to continuing Operation Tempest, despite the dramatic events in Vilnius. Nevertheless, such people were not to be found among either the civilian or military underground leadership, and Commander in Chief Sosn-kowski, who had voiced major reservations concerning the entire concept of Operation Tempest, was accompanying General Anders's troops in Italy and could not bring himself to inform the president that he opposed the uprising.

For the leaders of the underground state, the problem was not so much the decision itself but the choice of the opportune moment. An uprising begun a day too soon could encounter too much resistance on the part of the Germans, while to begin at the moment when the forces of Marshal Rokossowski and General Berling were crossing the river into Warsaw could mean political disaster. In addition, no one—not General Komorow-ski, not Deputy Prime Minister Jankowski, not Council of Unity Chairman Kazimierz Pużak—was in a position to foresee that the isolated capital would have to engage in such a long-drawn-out battle against such a strong and self-confident opponent.

The decision to begin the uprising was taken between 21 and 31 July, when the underground leadership received information confirming the presence of Soviet troops in Praga. Early on the evening of the thirty-first, the commander and government delegate fixed 1700 hours the next day as the time that fighting was to break out. Although the Germans knew about the Poles' decision, the first phase of the fighting brought some decided— although not decisive—victories for the insurgents. They would certainly have been enough if the front had continued to advance to the west.

SS General Erich von dem Bach-Zalewski assumed command of the German forces in Warsaw. He had considerable experience of fighting against partisan units; and on 5 September his forces, which included Ost-truppen units and a brigade made up of criminals released from prison in order to fight, began to counterattack with an offensive all along the main lines of communications and a push against the Warsaw district of Wola, defended by select, but small, Kedyw units under the command of Lieuten-ant Colonel Jan Mazurkiewicz (code name Radosław). The city's territory on the left bank was divided into segments—the Central District, Żoliborz, Wola, Ochota, and Mokotów. The fall of Wola was followed by that of Ochota, the city's second western district. The uprising could not extend to Praga, as this was the site of the front line. After a month the AK evacuated the Old Town and from 6 September on the constantly growing German forces began a series of victorious battles to gain control over the whole left bank of the Vistula. On 24 September the Germans began the attack on

Mokotów, which fell three days later, and on 29 September they advanced on Żoliborz. Only the Central District continued to defend itself.

Street fighting is one of the most vicious and destructive forms of warfare, and Warsaw was no exception. German units struck, not so much with determination (although they certainly did not want for this) as with unprecedented brutality. In Wola some forty thousand civilians were shot, and a similar number were executed after the capture of the Old Town. Inhabitants were driven from the city, and air attacks were used to terrorize the local population rather than to strike at insurgent positions. During the bombardment, food supplies were drastically reduced, a growing number of districts were deprived of water and electricity, and uncontrollable fires raged across the city.

Life became a nightmare; people no longer expected anyone to come to their aid. Here, nevertheless, was free Poland. Newspapers, including communist papers, were published without restriction, both the local administration and health service functioned, and a radio station was established. The government delegate, the Homeland Council of Ministers, and the Council of National Unity issued declarations and appeals and published the official gazette, *Dziennik Ustaw,* setting out regulations that would govern public life after independence had been regained. Every house and apartment building was a fortress—and not just for those who were fighting. Help between neighbors became one of the prime conditions for physical survival and psychological perseverance: together, people obtained food, extinguished fires, and protected the weakest among them; and together they prayed.

At the beginning of September the Polish authorities considered the conditions for their capitulation that the Germans had proposed on 18 August, but rejected them in light of the changing situation in the east. On 10 September the Red Army renewed its attack on Praga, and Stalin simultaneously granted Allied aircraft permission to land at Soviet airfields. On 16 September units of the Third Division of Berling's army attempted to establish a bridgehead on the left bank of the Vistula but, given that the insurgents had lost control of this area, the maneuver ended in total failure and an extremely large number of casualties. Warsaw's fate was sealed.

The leaders of the uprising finally began negotiations for capitulation that ended on 2 October with them agreeing to an unconditional surrender, but with AK soldiers being accorded prisoner of war status. The surrender document stipulated that all inhabitants would leave the city, effectively sentencing them to homelessness, concentration camp, or forced labor. It also signified that the city was destined for destruction. And so it was; the Polish capital was physically destroyed, block by block.

Beneath the rubble lay the remains of some 180,000 civilian casualties. Approximately eighteen thousand insurgents (40 percent of the total) as well as some 3,500 combatants from the Kościuszko Division had perished in the fighting. The fierceness of the conflict can be seen in the fact that German casualties included approximately ten thousand killed and seven thousand missing (out of a total of fifty thousand involved in the fighting). The Warsaw uprising also played a certain operational role on a broader scale. The fighting drew many German units away from the front and disrupted communications in a major center, which undoubtedly helped the Red Army establish a bridgehead on the left bank of the Vistula, south of the city.

This military defeat, involving an extremely large number of losses and the destruction of Poland's largest city, was not the only outcome of the uprising. The failure of the uprising was also a major political defeat. Most of the best-trained troops at the disposal of the AK central command were either killed in action or captured, and the government-in-exile thereby lost its real power base. The defeat created a general sense of yet another national disaster after the catastrophe of September 1939 and raised again the question of the responsibility to be borne by the country's elites. It diminished the prestige of Poland's allies, who had shown themselves to be powerless (if not heartless), and it destroyed any hope of retaining territorial integrity and state sovereignty. The heroism of the insurgents and the dignity of the civilian population evoked admiration among Poles and foreigners, but feelings of pride only came later, when the struggle of the "unsubdued city" became one of the most resonant symbols of resistance to enemies and adversity of all kinds.

The AK commander, General Tadeusz Bór-Komorowski (appointed commander in chief the day before the capitulation) was taken prisoner, together with his chief of staff, General Tadeusz Pełczyński, the leader of the insurgents, General Antoni Chruściel, and around twelve thousand soldiers and officers. However, nearly all the members of the Council of Ministers and the Council of National Unity, together with senior staff of the Delegatura, were able to escape from the city. General Leopold Okulicki, whom General Komorowski had appointed his deputy before the uprising, also managed to escape, along with his staff officers and probably several thousand AK soldiers. Also at large was General Emil Fieldorf, commander of an organization established in the spring under the name Independence (*Niepodległość*), which was intended to constitute a military-political underground force in the event of Soviet occupation.

The hundreds of thousands of Warsaw inhabitants who were driven from the city without means of livelihood and on the eve of winter suffered the most dramatic fate: transit camps, deportation to forced labor, resettlement in the far-flung corners of a country destroyed by a five-year war. The Main Welfare Council and Polish Red Cross provided what assistance they could; in this they were aided by the agencies of the Delegatura and by the rest of the population of the Government-General, which provided shelter to many who had lost their homes. German propaganda tried to exploit the mood of despair, the fear of a "Bolshevik onslaught," and the weariness of the population by intensifying efforts, under way since 1943, to persuade the Poles of the need for a joint "defense of Europe against Asiatic barbarism." This yielded no perceptible results, although it may perhaps have increased people's suspicion of the Soviet forces arrayed on the far side of the Vistula, but the continuing repression, the numerous arrests, roundups, and executions of people seized on the street intensified their perception of the Germans' exceptional brutality.

Of the units mobilized for Operation Tempest, some ten thousand troops were kept in a state of battle readiness, while the reservists were sent home. (The largest number of troops had been mobilized in the Radom military district and had tried unsuccessfully in mid-August to fight their way to Warsaw.) However, in view of the enormous number of Soviet troops, both at the front and in the rear, any armed action was extremely risky and its participants would in all likelihood be totally annihilated. Partisan and subversive action thus declined (as it also did on the part of the Soviet troops who had been parachuted into the country earlier) and became essentially defensive in nature. On 26 October General Okulicki ordered a halt to Operation Tempest. The staff of the Home Army commander managed to establish contact fairly quickly with district commanders on the west bank of the Vistula, but it was obvious that the AK had lost most of its fighting capability. Rather, the main problem was how to survive until the next offensive, which everyone imagined would take place the following spring. The military leadership remained in close contact with the underground civilian authorities and the Council of National Unity, but all of them were condemned to political passivity.

Nevertheless, Polish forces continued to fight, breaking through the German lines that blocked the route to the northern part of Italy; General Stanisław Maczek's division fought hard in Holland; and General Stanisław Sosabowski's Parachute Division, which had been created with the aim of landing in Poland to aid the planned general uprising, was bloodied during the fighting at Arnhem. Losses were made up by recruiting Polish prisoners of war who had been forced into the Wehrmacht; the Second Army Corps, for example, took twenty thousand such recruits.

The main contentious issue now became that of Poland's international situation, which gave rise to major differences of opinion among leading Polish politicians. Mikołajczyk's August discussions in Moscow had ended in failure, a failure from which various groupings within the émigré community, including the military, drew varying and often diametrically opposite conclusions. The prime minister and a group that was clearly in the minority believed that far-reaching concessions were necessary in order to salvage even limited sovereignty and to create a basis from which to mount social resistance to the anticipated sovietization of the country. To this end, they were prepared to offer territorial concessions by treating the "Riga frontiers" as a demarcation line, while hanging on to Vilnius and Lvov (and in the final analysis only the latter). They were also prepared to offer political concessions by recognizing the communist party and including it as a fifth participant in the governing coalition and by expressing Poland's readiness to establish neighborly relations and to cooperate with the Soviet Union on a wide range of issues.

This last proposition evoked the fewest reservations, but Mikołajczyk's remaining proposals met with open and vociferous opposition when presented to the president, the National Council, and the government, and to the general public in Poland. Opposition was voiced in the press and also made itself heard among the military, mainly in the Second Corps commanded by General Anders. Political tensions were heightened by the lonely struggle being waged by Warsaw and by news about what was happening in the eastern territories and between the Bug and Vistula. The sharpest opposition came from military leaders and those closest to the president, but to all the prime minister's opponents, wherever they stood on the political spectrum, it seemed an appropriate moment to overthrow the government. The atmosphere was given dramatic expression in a statement issued by General Sosnkowski on the anniversary of the outbreak of the war, accusing the Allies of having abandoned Poland in 1939.

Mikołajczyk succeeded, however, in forcing through his position, and on 29 August the cabinet approved the text of a memorandum addressed to the Soviet government. They did not have to wait long for a reply: on 6 September the Soviet news agency TASS issued a communiqué announcing that the memorandum had been forwarded to the PKWN. Stalin rejected all proposals for compromise; he, and only he, was to dictate conditions. And dictate he did. To some people it seemed that there was still some room for maneuver and that Allied support could help bring about if not an honorable compromise—for that it was much too late—at least an acceptable one. To the concessions already offered, others were added: under pressure from the government and the British, the president dismissed General Sosnkowski from his position as commander in chief (he had already lost his post as vice president), replacing him with Tomasz Arciszewski, who had been smuggled out of Poland. It seemed that this really exhausted the concessions that Mikołajczyk's government could make.

Nevertheless, at the insistence of Churchill, who clearly had a guilty conscience regarding the Poles, the prime minister went once more to Moscow. This visit took place after the surrender of the Warsaw insurgents and when the PKWN had been governing Lublin for two months. Stalin was not inclined to consider the slightest compromise, and the same was true of Bierut. After numerous discussions during the period 12–20 October, no agreement had been reached, and Mikołajczyk discovered by chance that the Allies had already agreed during the conference in Tehran to adopt the Curzon Line as Poland's eastern frontier. The course of the Moscow negotiations and the dramatic news coming in from the areas seized by the Red Army strengthened the prime minister's determination and that of his closest associates to return to Poland even if they did so as a junior partner of the communists. When Roosevelt refused to provide any guarantees of support for Poland's efforts to retain Lvov and the Drohobycz oil field, Mikołajczyk realized that the Polish government-in-exile had exhausted all possibilities for action. He found himself in a minority within his own government, and on 24 November he tendered his resignation, an event that many people in the émigré community had long been hoping for.

The new government, formed by the socialist Arciszewski and without the participation of the Peasant Movement, did not find support among the British or Americans. Stalin took advantage of this situation to make his next move: on 5 January 1945 the PKWN transformed itself into the Provisional Government, and the authorities of the old republic were no longer considered a potential partner by the Kremlin. The Red Army would soon launch its final offensive from beyond the Vistula, crushing all remaining possibilities for Polish sovereignty.

THE COMMUNISTS ESTABLISH A BASE CAMP

The land between the Vistula and the Bug now became the site of what Mikołajczyk had long feared: the PKWN, shielded by the Red Army, strengthened its position and established a virtually impregnable bridgehead, a kind of "communist base camp," from which to launch further expansion. PKWN activity took two forms. First, the communists destroyed all underground networks and terrorized the population. Second, they set about creating their own institutions and taking control of those that had existed during the occupation. To this end, they sought out groups and individuals willing to cooperate with them and made efforts to attract those sections of society most susceptible to promises of social revolution.

All this took place in the presence of an army several million strong. Moreover, the task of "clearing the ground" was undertaken by both the Soviet counterintelligence agency, Shmersh, and NKVD units. An NKVD division was established on 15 October, with eleven thousand well-equipped and well-trained soldiers to deal with a relatively small area. These NKVD troops had recently been engaged in combat against the Ukrainian partisans, and as the front moved west, rank-and-file troops were joined by General Ivan Sherov, deputy people's commissar for internal affairs and a well-known specialist in mass campaigns of pacification. NKVD units and rearguard units of the Red Army not only carried out massive raids but also arrested specific individuals, using information compiled by, among others, the subversive groups that had been sent into Poland since 1943. By the end of 1944, the NKVD division referred to above had arrested, on its own, nearly seventeen thousand people. If we include the AK soldiers who had been interned following the crushing of Operation Tempest, by January 1945 several tens of thousands of people had been arrested. Many of them were dispatched to the far reaches of the Soviet Union. According to NKVD data, in the summer of 1945 more than twenty thousand AK soldiers were interned in Soviet camps, and the number of people sentenced to labor camps was certainly not much smaller. Hundreds, if not thousands, of people were murdered outright.

The real rulers in the field were the military commissars of towns and rural districts, who interfered in all the details of public and social life and whose interference was backed by armed force. They also had official support in the form an agreement, dated 26 July, whereby the PKWN gave the Red Army jurisdiction over territory "behind the front." But foreign bayonets, no matter how numerous, were unable to resolve the situation. Neither Stalin nor the Polish communists wanted the existing state of affairs to be perceived as an occupation.

One of the first components of the administrative apparatus to be erected on the territory under Soviet control was the security apparatus. Within the structure of the PKWN, there was a separate Department of Public Security, headed by the prewar communist, Stanisław Radkiewicz. The department was staffed by about two hundred people who had undergone a few months of training at the NKVD training facility in Kuibyshev and by people who had belonged to diversionary and partisan groups and had also received counterintelligence training. Nearly all of them had belonged before the war to the Polish Communist Party or (more often) its youth organization, and most of them had spent time in the construction battalions or in exile, whence they had made their way to the Kościuszko Division. As early as 1943 some troops from this division had been assigned to the Special Storm Battalion, a new unit that was actually subordinated to the Union of Polish Patriots and became the kernel of the forces controlled by Radkiewicz. After hesitating for a few weeks, the communists incorporated into the Security Department the police, or citizens' militia (MO), whose personnel was drawn mainly from the People's Army. At the beginning of October 1944 the department also gained jurisdiction over prisons and internment camps (initially used largely to detain ethnic Germans, who were speedily rounded up). At the end of 1944 the security apparatus—excluding the police, internal troops, and the prison service—employed some 2,500 people.

The PKWN made sure that the activities of the security services were sanctioned by law, although the relevant legal regulations were usually issued with some delay. Most important were the decrees on "the dissolution of secret organizations" (24 August), the punishment of war criminals and "traitors to the Polish nation" (31 August), the military penal code and military courts (23 September), and defense of the state (issued on 30 October but in force retroactively from 15 August). The regulation dealing with "traitors" was used—and would be used for many years to come—in a particularly perfidious manner. In accordance with political requirements the notion of traitor was expanded to include all those who had belonged to the AK or had worked in the Delegatura, people generally deemed to be not only "reactionary" but also "pro-Nazi" or "collaborators."

Despite the statement in the manifesto of 22 July to the effect that social reforms would not conflict with the provisions of the constitution of 1921, the communists quickly abandoned efforts to introduce "peacefully" the most far-reaching of them, the so-called agrarian reform. Ignoring the decree on the implementation of the reform, issued on 6 September 1944, they began the process of land confiscation and allocation, bypassing the agencies that had been established for this very purpose. The decision to do so was clearly a political one, designed to attract support for the new regime among the landless peasantry and those who had only small landholdings. "Land-parceling brigades" set out from the towns; often they were warmly received, but there were occasions when they required military assistance. A large proportion of the peasantry was in dire straits; the countryside that had been ravaged by the war and by the predatory economy imposed by the Germans was now supposed to provide new conscripts and feed an enormous army. Nevertheless, it was precisely in the villages—poor and dilapidated—that the communists found the most support at that time, although, obviously, not all the members of the roughly one hundred thousand families that were allocated land automatically became enthusiastic supporters of the new authorities; it was precisely the villages and the peasantry that constituted a natural base for partisans fighting for independence.

The new order was far less visible in the towns. What few industries there were in the region were taken over, on the grounds that they had been abandoned by the Germans, but most factories and plants were managed by people who had worked there previously. Retail trade remained in private hands, but the role of the Społem cooperative had expanded during the occupation. The overwhelming majority of lower-level administrators and municipal employees returned to (or remained at) work, the courts were run by former judges, and former teachers returned to the newly reopened schools. In the fall, the Catholic University of Lublin reopened its doors, and, as a counterbalance, a new Lublin University was established, staffed for the most part by prewar faculty.

After the nightmare of German occupation and the constant sense that everyone and everything was endangered, many people—probably the majority—perceived the new situation as a return to normalcy. Of course, the region was full of Red Army soldiers, who were often ill-mannered and uncouth, and assaults and rapes were an everyday occurrence; of course, Home Army members were mercilessly hunted down, and the security service was everywhere. Nevertheless, the government-in-exile and the president still existed in London, the Polish Armed Forces were in the West, and Mikołajczyk traveled to Moscow for discussions with Stalin himself. A large proportion of the public calculated that the communists would not succeed in exerting total control over the country. Some people placed their hopes in pressure from the Western Allies; others believed that with the defeat of the Third Reich, the anti-German coalition would fall apart and a new world war would erupt and lead, inevitably, to the victory of democracy over Bolshevism.

But most of those who reasoned thus adapted to the situation and began working in the public institutions, which had to function, come what may. Such work was regarded as akin to activity in the underground and was seen as hastening the restoration of a sovereign Poland. There were instances in which entire lower units of the police were staffed by clandestine groups from the AK or NSZ. Farm workers took over the land allocated during the forcible redistribution, and redistribution was frequently preceded by the outright theft of landholdings. Although the authorities did not make a clear public pronouncement on the issue, workers in many factories began to set up factory councils with the aim of taking over factory management. For many people, the existence of a Polish army played a great role, even though most of its commanders were Red Army officers. The mass mobilization was not proceeding as the authorities had hoped, as many potential conscripts managed to evade service. Nevertheless, the prestige traditionally enjoyed by the military in Poland helped "Berling's army" gain public acceptance, a process that was also helped by the fact that Berling's troops fought on the front line to establish a bridgehead, attempted to enter Warsaw, and on 15 August—the anniversary of the 1920 Battle of Warsaw— took part in a ceremonial commemoration of Soldier's Day that included an open-air mass and military parade.

The public mood was also influenced by the communists' efforts to attract (or at least neutralize) adherents of various political tendencies as well as the cultural elite, a group that had been considered of prime importance from the very beginning. They concentrated their main efforts on those groups in which they had previously sought allies; activists returning from the Soviet Union provided additional assistance.

On 10–11 September 1944 the socialists met in Lublin. Calling their meeting a conference (later referred to as the party's Twenty-Fifth Congress), the Polish Socialist Party formally resumed legal activity. While the resolutions passed by the conference clearly suggested that the socialists had not taken this initiative on their own, the founders of the PPS were genuine—if second-rank—activists, and the party soon had about eight thousand members. The peasant movement gave less than wholehearted support to the "new reality." At a conference held on 17–18 September peasant activists did pass a resolution to reactivate the Peasant Party (SL), but the many political declarations they adopted included a "recommendation" that Mikołajczyk and other émigré Peasant Party activists return to Poland, a demand that Sejm and Senate elections be held immediately after liberation, and a call for a return to the constitution of 1921 and for the observance of "full civil freedoms." The conference even refused to acknowledge that the Curzon Line was the final word on Poland's eastern frontier. A month later the communists managed to oust from the SL leadership the most independent activists (such as Andrzej Witos, a member of the presidium of the Union of Polish Patriots and brother of Wincenty), but they still could not count on the complete loyalty of the party. On 24 September the Democratic Party (SD), which had always had a relatively small membership, resumed activity. In November the leadership of the Polish Workers' Party decided to use a group that had broken away from the Party for a National Upsurge to form the Labor Party (SP), a party that would actually be a tool of the communists. The communists even considered reviving, under their control, the National Party. The peasant youth movement, ZMW Wici, was reactivated, as were the socialist Association of Workers' Universities and its associated youth movement. At the end of November the Central Trade Union Commission was formed, perpetuating the name of one of the largest prewar labor organizations.

Even though these organizations by no means enjoyed widespread support, they provided a certain amount of democratic camouflage, helped to win over some people who had been keeping their distance, and offered an outlet for those who were looking for ways to express their desire to be socially active. All in all during these first months, the further to the left that a particular circle or grouping was on the political spectrum, the easier it was for the communists to find there people willing to cooperate with them; but they also invested considerable effort in gaining control of precisely these circles.

The PPS-WRN continued to function underground, however, and in the countryside the clandestine cells of the Peasant Party were particularly active. Both parties maintained close contacts with other parties, usually with the strongest party in the region, the National Party. They issued joint declarations and appeals, held meetings, kept the underground administration functioning, and published leaflets and a small number of newssheets. Despite a wave of brutal repression, arrests, and deportations, the communists did not succeed in liquidating the military underground and the partisan units. The Home Army reestablished a command headquarters in the Lublin District, which maintained radio contact with London. In the Białystok province, a region with a less clear-cut sense of national identity and one that had been less involved in Operation Tempest, the former command structure, under Colonel Mieczysław Liniarski, was still active. This region contained a particularly large number of units that had withdrawn from the eastern provinces. Local units of the Peasant Battalions also remained intact and underground, and the AK was active in the region around Rzeszów. Some of these underground groups carried out retaliatory attacks on police units, and in some areas they were active in opposing land confiscation and redistribution.

The Home Army and a number of political parties continued to function underground under extremely difficult circumstances in the territory that had been incorporated into the USSR, where the number of people deported to the far corners of Russia reached alarming proportions. In these areas activity was largely confined to propaganda campaigns designed to persuade people of the need to remain on their ancestral land and not to report for resettlement on the far side of the Bug—officially referred to as "repatriation"—a process that had begun shortly after the PKWN had signed the necessary agreements with the Belorussian and Ukrainian Soviet Republics (9 September) and with the Lithuanian Republic (22 November). The underground independence movement, both its military and political wings, gradually recovered from the shock inflicted by the defeat of Operation Tempest and the seizure of power by the new government. However, the presence of the million-strong Red Army and the powerful forces belonging to the NKVD made it impossible to carry out large-scale activity of any kind, even purely political activity. In addition, the sense of national solidarity that had provided the main source of support for the underground during the German occupation began to erode and fragment.

One reason for this was that the communists launched a major offensive on the cultural front. As early as the beginning of August they reactivated the Polish Artists' Union, followed, in September, by the Polish Writers' Union, headed by the well-known avant-garde poet Julian Przyboś. A short time later the Architects' Association and the Composers' Union resumed activity. The communists diligently sought out all the writers and artists of one kind or another who were to be found in the liberated territories and brought them—even by plane—to Lublin, where they soon assembled everyone who had ever had any kind of contact with the Union of Polish Patriots. On 3 September, before the publication of the first issue of the PPR's own newspaper, the first issue of a literary-cultural weekly, *Odrodzenie* (Rebirth), appeared, to be followed in the fall by the first slim volumes of poetry. The Lublin theater season began with the premiere of Stanisław Wyśpiański's *Wyzwolenie* (Liberation), and a series of public lectures was opened by Juliusz Kleiner, a distinguished historian of literature. Just as Soldier's Day had been celebrated, Independence Day, on 11 November, was celebrated with considerable pomp and the occasion was even honored by a telegram of congratulations from Stalin himself.

The fact that all the party leaders who had spent the war in the Soviet Union (the "Muscovites") and most of those who had spent the war in Poland (the "nationalists") were now to be found in the region ruled from Lublin helped the communists take control of the basic instruments of state power. Both Bolesław Bierut, head of the Committee of National Unity, and Władysław Gomułka, PPR general secretary, left Warsaw at the beginning of July and crossed to the right bank of the Vistula, in anticipation of the arrival of the Red Army and Polish forces. They were quickly summoned to Lublin. Although there was plenty of discord within the PPR, some of it based on personal ambition, the pressures of the situation brought people together, and the party leadership became a fairly cohesive political team. Members of the newly created Politburo of the Central Committee included two "nationalists"—Bierut and Gomułka—and three "Muscovites"—Jakub Berman, Hilary Minc, and Aleksander Zawadzki. Also playing a major role were Edward Ochab, Franciszek Jóżwiak, Stanisław Radkiewicz, and Roman Zambrowski, all of them long-standing communists. Among those associated with the Union of Polish Patriots, only Wanda Wasilewska withdrew from political life in Poland, deciding to remain with her husband in the Soviet Union. The communists occupied virtually all the most important positions in the apparatus of the PKWN, and they appointed to the remainder the most amenable activists of the "democratic parties." These included PPS leader Edward Osóbka-Morawski, who was appointed PKWN chairman and subsequently prime minister of the provisional government, Stanisław Szwalbe, also from the PPS, and Wincenty Rzymowski from the SD. General Żymierski was appointed commander in chief of the Polish Army. The communists also took great care in selecting the heads of the local administration and the leadership of the local national councils. They were even more careful when deciding whom to assign to the operational groups designed to seize power in the wake of a general offensive.

At the same time as they were creating new institutions, such as the security service and the national councils, and staffing old ones, the communists were involved in feverish organizational activity to expand the PPR itself, which had been a relatively small party while underground. By December the party had grown to twenty thousand members, among whom there was no shortage of careerists ready to support any ruling party. Essentially, though, the PPR recruited members from among former communists, various left-wing organizations, and, in the countryside, from the communists' underground military units, the People's Army.

At the beginning of October and at the direct instigation of Stalin, who had concluded that the first stage—the establishment of a basic administrative structure and the major instruments of power, and the attraction of supporters—had been completed, the communists began to harden their line. Perhaps the moment was chosen to take advantage of the pessimism that followed the defeat of the Warsaw uprising. Certainly, there was some fear that a possible compromise with Mikołajczyk, however unlikely, would strengthen opposition to the communists. The changes in the implementation of the agrarian reform mentioned above were one of the signs of the new line. First and foremost, however, both the Polish and Soviet security forces intensified their efforts to crush the military and political underground. After several groups of Home Army fighters had deserted from the Polish Army, nearly all soldiers and officers of the Polish Army who had previously served in the AK were interned. This move was accompanied by a heightened propaganda campaign against the Home Army and the government-in-exile. No longer content with slogans referring to "reactionary cliques," the communists now referred to "London" and the underground as "accomplices of Nazi Germany." This campaign yielded some immediate success, although it would soon become clear that destruction of the underground would be a lengthy and far bloodier process than anticipated.

At the beginning of 1945 the Polish Workers' Party was growing in both organization and membership; it controlled the instruments of power that it had established, and it had worked out and tested the basic mechanisms to be used in controlling public life. The party could also point to its first diplomatic achievement—General de Gaulle's agreement (under considerable pressure from Stalin) to send a mission to Poland—although this was probably of greater domestic than international significance. The underground networks created under German occupation were now merely a shadow of the former underground state. The émigré political elites were riven by dissension, and since the formation of Arciszewski's cabinet, the government of the Republic of Poland had lost the trust of its allies.

END GAME

Such, more or less, was the state of the "Polish question" at the moment when, on 12 January 1945, the Red Army launched its winter offensive, a truly lightning operation, especially in the southern and central regions of Poland: on 17 January Warsaw was taken, on 19 January—Kraków and Łódź, and on 30 January Polish troops crossed the former German frontier while Soviet armored units reached the Oder. Before the end of February German forces had been ousted from the whole territory of the Republic, apart from along the coast, where fighting continued until the end of March. Public rejoicing at the disappearance of the hated invader was tempered by fear of the future. The most radical decision was taken by the Świętokrzyska Brigade of the NSZ, which escaped to the west as the German forces retreated, then regrouped on Czech territory and went over to the Americans. General Okulicki did not order a resumption of Operation Tempest, which at that point would have been without either military or political significance. Nevertheless, some AK units attacked retreating German forces, and on several occasions such attacks were carried out jointly with Soviet troops. On 19 January the Home Army commander dissolved the organization, releasing all combatants from the oath they had sworn on taking up arms. There was no question, however, of dissolving the Independence organization.

Many units interpreted the order to dissolve as simply a maneuver designed to provide them with formal protection against charges of belonging to an illegal organization. Some units ignored the order (the whole Białystok District, for example), and all district and local headquarters remained intact. Large underground organizations outside the Home Army, such as the NSZ and the National Military Union, formed in the fall by a breakaway group of AK troops, did not dissolve themselves. The government delegate and the Committee of National Unity also decided to continue clandestine activity.

In the regions liberated from German occupation both the NKVD and Polish security forces immediately began to "clear the ground" with sweeping arrests of AK fighters and people who had worked for clandestine administrative agencies. In many areas all judges and lawyers were arrested, while landowners and intellectuals in the smaller towns were also frequent targets. Soviet intelligence and the People's Army were already quite well informed about developments in the Polish underground. Everywhere they noted that some political activists (largely from the Peasant Party) and the intelligentsia were hesitant about resuming open political activity and applying for work in public institutions. As early as 25 January a member of the Homeland Council of Ministers, Stanisław Jasiukowicz, informed the prime minister that the council "will allow people to occupy any position, except for political positions, as long as they are loyal to us." For his part, General Okulicki noted that "in light of the mood at lower levels . . . we are obliged to be more cautious in issuing orders to boycott the instructions" of the Provisional Government. The dominant mood was clearly one of extreme disquiet—in light of the terror, which many AK commanders considered worse than that of the Germans—combined with an attitude of wait and see. After all, the Western powers still had a say on the Polish question.

The second (and penultimate) meeting between the leaders of the Big Three took place in the Crimea and lasted eight days, from 4 to 11 February. The conference agenda was wide-ranging: the occupation of Germany and war reparations, the establishment of a world organization, the situation in the Far East, the Soviet Union's participation in the war against Japan, and the question of Iran. Churchill, Roosevelt, and Stalin appeared at Yalta accompanied by a staff of political and military advisers and by their ministers of foreign affairs, who were well acquainted with each other as a result of numerous personal meetings. Opinions were sharply divided on many issues, but the discussants tried to find some kind of modus vivendi. In the end, they reached agreement on most of the issues.

The British already sensed that, in view of the might of their two partners, they were doomed to lose their position as a world power. The U.S. president placed most emphasis on his favorite notion of world order maintained by the Great Powers and on achieving the speediest possible end to the war in the Pacific. Stalin's forces were racing into the heart of Europe, they controlled a large part of the Balkans, they ruled over the Baltic, and their highly regarded fighting skills could be invaluable in the conflict with Japan.

The issue that took up most time and proved to be one of the most difficult was the problem of Poland, or strictly speaking, the issue of the government and the border with Germany. To the Western Allies it was obvious that Stalin had acquired decisive influence over the internal affairs of both Poland and the other countries liberated (or being liberated) by the Red Army and that their own possibilities of acting as a countervailing force were slight and were likely to remain so. They—especially Churchill—were also alarmed by the fact that the Soviet Union would soon extend its influence as far west as Vienna and Berlin, that it had strong support in Greece, and that it enjoyed considerable prestige among many in Western Europe and the United States. The British and the Americans considered that in the circumstances they could do little more for Poland than to obtain minimal guarantees regarding its internal sovereignty. Thus despite a number of public statements, their proposals were largely defensive. At the same time, they were opposed to moving Poland's frontiers too far to the west. It became obvious that even if Poland had considerable internal sovereignty, the country would constitute a kind of buffer state (if not a staging post) and that its frontiers would most probably become the borders of an "external empire." It was also assumed in advance that the London government-in-exile would not be a party to any eventual compromise.

With great self-assurance, Stalin and Molotov demolished a succession of proposals advanced by the British and Americans, and the provisions concerning Poland were essentially formulated at the dictate of the Soviet leaders. Perhaps only the enigmatic note on the border question was not to their liking, and they pushed for less ambiguous wording than "a substantial expansion of territory to the north and the west." The provisions dealing with the formation of the government (Provisional Government of National Unity) took the "Lublin government" as their basis, with the addition of "democratic politicians" from within Poland and the émigré community, although Stalin categorically rejected the possibility of any participation by Mikołajczyk. The final composition of the government was to be decided by negotiations among a group of Poles, whose members were to be selected by the three powers. The future government was obligated to hold "free and unfettered elections as soon as possible, allowing for the participation of "all democratic and anti-fascist parties." The final communiqué solemnly confirmed that the eastern border would follow the Curzon Line ("with deviations of from five to eight kilometers to Poland's advantage"). For most Poles at home—and certainly for the whole émigré community—this provision came as a shock. Even for those who had long realized that far-reaching concessions would be required. Poland, the first country to stand up to Hitler's armed aggression, had been abandoned to the mercy of Stalin, who did not enjoy in Poland the same reputation that he did in the West. Quite the opposite.

The government-in-exile immediately issued a public protest against the Yalta communiqué while also appealing for calm among the outraged military. While underground leaders in the Council of National Unity also expressed their opposition to its provisions, they recognized that they were "obliged to adapt to them," which essentially constituted a declaration of readiness to take part in negotiations over the composition of the future government, The PPS-WRN and Peasant Party decided to begin preparations to abandon clandestine activity. The Labor Party was hesitating, and only the National Party, expressing considerable skepticism, decided to await further developments before deciding whether or not to leave the underground.

Negotiations between representatives of the three powers dragged on, however, as they could not agree on who was to take part in the "consultation" over the government. The sticking point was the possible participation of Mikołajczyk and several activists who remained in hiding. To "simplify" the debate Stalin cunningly managed to exclude virtually the entire underground leadership from the future talks: on 27 and 28 March General Okulicki, Delegate Jan Jankowski, members of the Homeland Council of Ministers, and representatives of the political parties making up the Council of National Unity were arrested in Pruszków, after allegedly meeting with a "representative of the First Belorussian Front" (which was a total fabrication). They were flown to Moscow, together with the chairman of the National Party, who had been arrested a few weeks earlier.

The idea of kidnapping underground leaders was more far-reaching than first appeared—on 6 May the TASS news agency announced that these sixteen activists had been arrested and would stand trial on charges of subversive activity behind the Soviet front lines. The arrest of the leaders of the underground state signified that the Kremlin was determined to bypass completely the independence movement; this became even clearer when they began seeking appropriate candidates among left-wing Polish groups in Britain and the United States.

Mikołajczyk, fervently urged on by the British, finally forced himself to issue (on 15 April) a public declaration stating that he recognized the Yalta agreement, thus fulfilling a condition set by Stalin. Toward the end of May, Harry Hopkins, a special envoy of the U.S. president, flew to Moscow in order to finalize the list of those who would select the provisional government.

During this whole period, the communists subjected the Home Army and other underground networks to incessant pressure, including a major propaganda campaign, and they kept up a barrage of hostile propaganda directed at the government-in-exile. Horror at German occupation gradually gave way to fear of the violence unleashed by the new rulers and to a feeling of helplessness in the face of the maneuvering on the part of the Great Powers. The population was also preoccupied with the extremely difficult material situation. While the front had moved on quickly, it had brought a new round of destruction and stripped the country of all remaining food supplies. With the arrival of spring, a real migration got under way: people who had sought refuge from the front returned to their homes after being forced out of the towns; those who had been deported from Wielkopolska started marching westwards; transports of people to be "repatriated" began arriving from beyond the Bug; and from Lower Silesia and Western Pomerania came Polish (and Soviet) forced laborers, prisoners of war, and prisoners. In these extremely harsh conditions, people began to rebuild their dwellings, places of work, and normal, everyday life.

The Provisional Government and the PPR put considerable effort into gaining control of social life and the economy, and alongside unremitting struggle against the underground and threats against individual social groups, they forcefully emphasized their national and decidedly nonrevolutionary calling. They cited the great national traditions, celebrated the holiday of 3 May with great ceremony, proudly announced that Warsaw would resume its place as Poland's capital, and feted well-known artists and intellectuals. They also began maneuvers around the Catholic Church with the aim of neutralizing this great social force. On 24 March, with the approval of Archbishop Sapieha, *Tygodnik Powszechny* (Universal Weekly) began to appear, the first publication independent of the PPR and its allies. Nevertheless, over all this loomed the shadow of Yalta, the arrest of the "sixteen" and many other leading political activists, the pacification and capture of AK members, and the strengthening of the security forces. These events also cast a shadow over the obvious rejoicing at the capitulation of the Third

Reich and satisfaction at the role played by Polish forces in the fighting in Germany and the storming of Berlin. At the end of May a change took place in the PPR's approach, linked no doubt with the fact that final preparations for the Moscow negotiations were now under way. At a meeting of the Central Committee on 21–22 May participants sharply criticized the excesses of the security organs, raised the issue of according greater autonomy to the PPR's allies in the Provisional Government, and decided to moderate policy toward the Home Army. A contributing factor in the changes was, no doubt, the growing resistance. The forests were filled with young people hiding from arrest, and conscripts were continuing to desert the armed forces. The authorities did not know how the population would react in the event that the underground political parties resumed open activity. This also encouraged some Peasant and Socialist Party activists who were cooperating with the communists to emphasize their independence.

The underground authorities tried to find a solution to the complicated situation, and those associated with the Home Army command certainly had no desire to make it worse. The Independence organization was dissolved, and on 7 May the acting commander in chief ordered the creation of the post of Homeland Armed Forces Delegate, appointing to the post Colonel Jan Rzepecki, former head of the Propaganda and Information Department of the AK Central Command. As de facto head of the former AK, Colonel Rzepecki considered one of his major tasks to be the gradual demobilization of the underground forces. Together with the acting government delegate, he issued several appeals calling for an end to armed struggle and a return to "work for the reconstruction of the country." Statements issued by the Council of National Unity also helped defuse the situation. While the council declared on 17 May that "the struggle continues," it called on conspirators to "return to normal life and constructive work." The situation of underground networks was further complicated by internal differences, some of them concerning attitudes toward the government of Tomasz Arciszewski. Such differences of opinion caused the SL-Roch to suspend its membership in the council (on 7 May).

In mid-June Polish public opinion was focused on Moscow, where on 16 June discussions began between a group of independent politicians led by Mikołajczyk and representatives of the Provisional Government, led by Gomułka and Bierut. Three days later, in the Hall of Columns of the House of the Trade Unions (the site of many show trials during the purges), the Military Council of the USSR Supreme Court held its first session in the trial of the Polish leaders arrested in Pruszków. Together, these two events constituted a well-produced spectacle whose ending was already known to its authors in the Kremlin. Mikołajczyk, poorly aided by his colleagues obtained nothing more than the opportunity for an honorable capitulation on his part: several second-rank government portfolios, with the position of deputy prime minister for himself, a place for Witos in the presidium of the National Council of the Homeland, a promise—agreed to but not signed by the Powers—of places for Peasant Party members in the National Council of the Homeland and local national councils, and in government and economic institutions. The PPR leaders were clearly sure of themselves and the outcome of the negotiations. At one point Gomułka simply stated, "Now we have seized power, we shall never surrender it." "You can shout all you want," he said heatedly, "that the blood of the Polish nation is flowing, that the NKVD rules Poland, but you will not force us from our path." The end of the trial of the "sixteen," which resulted in sentences of up to ten years, seemed to exemplify this threat. Although no one was condemned to death, three of those sentenced—General Okulicki, Deputy Prime Minister Jankowski, and Minister Jasiukowicz—were to end their days in Soviet captivity. Representatives of the Big Three confirmed, without much ado, that discussions "among Poles" had fulfilled the provisions of the Yalta agreement. On 28 June Bierut established the Provisional Government of National Unity, which was recognized just one day later by France, eagerly courting Stalin, and on 5 July by the remaining permanent members of the United Nations Security Council: Britain, the United States, and China.

On 1 July, after lengthy discussions, the Council of National Unity published a manifesto addressed to "the Polish Nation and the United Nations," together with a document titled, "The Testament of Fighting Poland." In these documents the council declared its determination to continue the fight for those goals that the nation had set itself in 1939, when it set out to wage a struggle against the invaders, but that now it would engage in a political struggle. The council also presented a list of demands to serve as a rallying cry of further struggle for independence: the departure from Poland of all foreign armies and the NKVD, an end to persecution, the release and return of all Poles deported to Siberia and elsewhere in the Soviet Union, and personal liberty and political freedoms for all the parties of underground Poland. At the same time, the council announced its own dissolution, with a dissenting voice from the National Party, which declared it would continue underground activity. Acting government delegate Jerzy

Braun acknowledged that he would carry out only those duties that resulted from the liquidation of civilian structures, which had in any case been under way for some time. Within the Armed Forces Delegatura the first steps were already being taken to transform the agency into a politico-military organization. At the beginning of August these efforts received the endorsement of the commander in chief, who sent a telegram to Poland saying: "We no longer intend to wage armed struggle as we did under German occupation."

The dissolution of the basic institutions of the underground state and the government-in-exile's loss of recognition on the part of the Great Powers (whose example was soon followed by the majority of other countries) signaled the end of a major chapter in Polish history, a chapter that could be called Independent Poland and Fighting Poland; independent Poland now found itself in exile, while fighting Poland was to be found at home, fighting in various ways and with varying intensity. Nevertheless, a new era was beginning: an era of a Poland deprived of independence and incorporated into a great ideological empire. "Poland shall be free and independent," declared Mikołajczyk in August 1944, "even if we go through difficult times for the next twenty or thirty years." He certainly did not imagine exactly how difficult the times would be. And he did not dare predict that they would last a lot longer. But he was certainly right about some things.

CHAPTER 3

The New Reality

A DIFFERENT COUNTRY

The greatest war in history inflicted dreadful wounds on Poland, wounds that fundamentally changed the country. The area of the state had been reduced by 20 percent; it had lost its eastern provinces (nearly half of its former territory) and had shifted westwards to occupy lands that had been settled and civilized by others. When the postwar population transfers were completed, Poland had about 30 percent fewer inhabitants than it had had in 1939. Its entire territory, both its former provinces and those recently acquired (at that time referred to as the Reclaimed Territories), had been ravaged by war, by the economic exploitation of the occupying powers, and by the depredations of the Red Army when it occupied areas of the Third Reich. Several cities lay in ruins, and about one-quarter of all villages had been destroyed. Several million people had been crippled, infectious diseases were rampant, and an extremely high child mortality rate was further undermining the country's human potential.

Essentially, this was a completely new country. Two great cultural centers, Lvov and Vilnius, were now on the far side of the border, which followed the Curzon Line. Some two million people (including roughly 300,000 who since 1943 had fled the brutal fighting of the Ukrainian Insurgent Army) had lost their "immediate" homeland—the family property, the surroundings, and the landscape that had been a part of their culture. They had also lost many people who had been close to them, relatives and compatriots who had decided to remain on the land of their ancestors. Most of these people were resettled on territory that was unknown to them and whose culture was different from their own. The towns and settlements of Poland's former central and southern provinces had not only been devastated or completely ruined, but had also lost—through the Holocaust—their Jewish population, a neighbor that was generally not much liked but nonetheless a neighbor since time immemorial and one that had its permanent place in the social order. The overpopulated villages of these provinces—and even the war and terror inflicted by the invaders could not eradicate

POLAND AFTER 1945

this problem—set off on a westward march. By the end of 1948 the newly acquired western territories had been settled by roughly 2.7 million people from beyond the Wieprz, the Narew, the Vistula, the Pilica, and the Warta rivers. For these people, the region in which they settled was both new and alien: brick houses in the countryside, paved roads, indoor plumbing, farms of thirty to fifty hectares, and walled settlements. Here they met up with many compatriots from beyond the Bug and in many regions also with Poles who had outlasted centuries of German presence.

Together they created an ersatz version of the former, multination re-public, here and there enlivened by returning émigrés from France and Bel-gium, by Jews who had survived the war by being exiled to Kazakhstan, by

Ukrainians deported from the southeastern provinces in 1947 during Operation Vistula, and finally by those Germans who had been kept in Poland because of their professional skills. The group that made the greatest impact, although it was by no means the largest in terms of numbers, were the people from the borderlands: a "little Lvov" quickly emerged in Wrocław, a part of the Vilnius intelligentsia settled in Pomerania, and former inhabitants of Volhynia settled in Olsztyn. The eastern singsong accent could be heard all over Poland. After four years of resettlement, most of it organized but some of it spontaneous and unauthorized, more than five million people had moved into the region, and they gradually began to create genuine local communities.

Inevitably, this was a process that would take more than one generation, and to a large extent it was impeded by both uncertainty regarding the future of these territories and mistrust of the state authorities, both local and central. This process, especially in its early phase, was by no means free of conflict. Apart from the Germans, the chief victims were the previous inhabitants of the region, the Silesians, Mazovians, and Warmians, who were treated like Germans not only by the "liberating army" but also by a large proportion of their fellow Poles who took up residence among them. The early years were dominated by uncertainty and by fears concerning not only access to goods and services but also the very preservation of life and physical well-being. The destruction of social structures and local networks, of church parishes and other organizations had the effect of disabling the inhabitants of Poland's western and northern regions, rendering them more passive politically and making it easier for them to be manipulated by political blackmail and other forms of pressure.

This kind of intermingling also took place, but on a much smaller scale, in the country's former territories, which also absorbed settlers from the east. After many years citizens of Wielkopolska who had been evicted from their farms returned home, as did former inhabitants of Pomerania; residents of Warsaw, dispersed following the collapse of the uprising, returned to rummage through the rubble of their native city. Flight and deportation, passing fronts, bloody terror, and the Holocaust—all this resulted in whole areas empty of population. Often they were nothing more than a wasteland of ruins.

Although the Western democracies opposed (at least officially) all forms of xenophobia, and the Soviet Union boasted loudly of its internationalism, they readily agreed that the new Polish state ought to be monoethnic and that the Germans should be removed from territory that would no longer lie within Germany's frontiers. In February 1946, at the recommendation of the Allied Control Council, the process of evacuation was begun, a process that was as massive in scale as it was painful and difficult for the Germans involved and one that was marked by numerous excesses and outright plunder. In just under two years, roughly three million people were transported to the west of the River Oder. If we count the two million or so who abandoned their patrimony in the winter of 1945, fleeing ahead of the approaching onslaught, and the several hundred thousand who set off west in the summer of that year without waiting for transport, by 1950 only 200,000–300,000 Germans out of a prewar population of seven million remained on the territory acquired by Poland. A smaller-scale exodus also took place, in different circumstances but still under duress, in the region adjacent to the eastern border. The Poles who had been uprooted were replaced by some 480,000 Ukrainians, 40,000 Belorussians, and 15,000 Lithuanians who "opted," usually under pressure, for the Soviet republics, deserting the settlements their forebears had inhabited for centuries. The Polish state thus became a single-nation state, probably the most uniform state in this part of Europe, and the national minorities, now widely scattered—apart from the Belorussians—were no longer the problem they had been during the Second Republic. Nevertheless, the circumstances in which this state of affairs came about did nothing to diminish mutual animosities and phobias and even gave birth to many new hatreds—on the part of all concerned.

This massive process of displacement and resettlement proceeded at full force during 1945–46, diminishing somewhat during the following year. This unprecedented population movement also included a wave of repatriation. The overwhelming majority of the 600,000 Polish forced laborers who had been transported to Germany and found themselves east of the Oder when Poland was liberated returned home, although some of them returned to discover that what had once been their home was now situated on the far side of the Curzon Line. More than 1.5 million forced laborers, prisoners of war, and concentration camp inmates from all zones of occupied Germany returned to Poland, many of them to settle in the new territory. Also repatriated were some 280,000 of the "special migrants" of 1940–44, half of them Jews and most of them "refugees" who had been deported. Many of those who returned from Siberia did not return to their former homes in the borderlands but were dispersed across the country, while most of the Jews made their way to Lower Silesia. Several hundred thousand soldiers of the

Polish Armed Forces, most of them from the central provinces, also returned home, more often from Britain than from the Second Corps. Around 150,000 people returned from emigration in Western Europe, Belgium, northern France, and Westphalia, as well as Yugoslavia and Romanian Bukovina, some of them born and raised outside Poland.

Although Poland became a national state and nearly a million Silesian Poles, who had never previously lived in a Polish state, found themselves within its borders, this did not mean that the homeland drew everyone to its new territory. Unlike the situation following World War I, the Polish émigré community scarcely reacted. Out of more than half a million Polish émigrés in France, fewer than eighty thousand decided to return. According to official Soviet statistics, in 1950, 1.5 million Poles were living in the Soviet Union, suggesting that a large proportion of the inhabitants of the borderlands had decided to remain or had been refused permission to leave. Many of those who had managed to survive the torment of the camps, prison, and deportation remained in the depths of Russia, kept there by fate or, more often, by the authorities. The Poles in the Soviet Union, wherever they happened to live—whether on the edge of the "inhuman land" or in their old borderland settlements deprived of their intelligentsia, who had been killed or had moved away to the Vistula or the Oder—were treated as second-class citizens and had no possibility for social advancement. They were completely cut off from all contact with Poland.

Most of the civilian émigrés and soldiers belonging to the Polish Armed Forces who were in Western Europe remained there, particularly—but not only—those who originally came from the territory now incorporated into the Soviet Union. Some 300,000 people who at the end of the war found themselves in Nazi Germany or on territory that it had occupied decided against returning home. It is estimated that the number of Polish émigrés grew by at least half a million. Thousands of members of the intelligentsia, whose ranks had been so cruelly thinned by war and terror, remained in the West, as did a large proportion of the intellectual and political elite, as well as what remained of the government of the Second Republic, with its official seals and banners. A large émigré community emerged, probably the largest political diaspora that existed at the time.

The Polish nation came out of the war numerically weakened, in pain from its traumatic experience and unexpected reversals of fortune, with its communities shattered, family members lost and separated, and hundreds of thousands of people orphaned, crippled, and made homeless. A large proportion of the elite and local leaders had been killed; libraries and schools had been burned to the ground; a large number of teachers and clergy had been murdered. After all these dramas and tragedies, a large proportion of the population—perhaps one-third—with great difficulty sought to make a new home for themselves, often hundreds or thousands of kilometers from their former "immediate" homeland, some of them along the Oder, others along the Thames.

But with several years of determined struggle behind it, a large section of this nation that had experienced such brutality was well trained in combat—and armed. It was also armed with the irrefutable conviction that independence is the supreme value and that tradition tells us independence cannot be achieved without sacrifice.

PAWN ON A CHESSBOARD

The end to the fighting in Europe and the construction and use of the atom bomb, which crushed the Japanese will to fight and brought a rapid end to the war in the Pacific, clearly loosened the ties that had bound together the coalition of the Big Three. Their common enemy had been not simply defeated but destroyed. Everything that divided the Western democracies from the Eastern totalitarian empire now moved to the foreground, emphasized by the fact that the rapidly growing might of the Soviet Union suggested the possibility of further conquests in which both military and ideological weapons would play a role. But the course of events altered the balance of forces in the world not only through the defeat of the two major powers that had been the most determined and open in their desire for this war. The German invasion of the Soviet Union in 1941 put an end to the international isolation that had surrounded the country since its very beginnings. In 1939 Hitler had needed the Soviet Union, but after 22 June 1941 it became the physical nucleus of the anti-Nazi coalition. After the Battle of Stalingrad in 1943, a new bipolar world began to emerge, one in which it turned out that Britain had only enough power to defend itself and nothing more. The international stage was now dominated by the world's two most powerful states—one whose power was based on economic might and one whose power was based on military might. The rivalry between them was to shape world events for decades to come. While this state of affairs was not yet clearly defined and acknowledged in 1945, many events were already unfolding in accordance with its logic. Including events that affected Poland.

Although two massive armies, each of them flush with success, confronted each other on either side of a line running from Lübeck to Trieste (as well as in distant Korea, on the thirty-eighth parallel), neither side wanted a rupture serious enough to lead to armed conflict. The scenarios that envisaged precisely such an outcome—and many Poles, not just military or political leaders, dreamed up such scenarios—were written without asking the actors involved if they wished to play the parts being written for them. Neither Washington nor Moscow was inclined to do so, although at that time undoubtedly neither the Kremlin nor the White House thought that the inevitable conflict would be expressed in a series of "shoving matches" rather than in the form of a traditional war—what was already being called World War III.

During the first phase of abandoning the coalition and forming a new front, it seems that both sides ascribed greatest importance to gathering their supporters around them. The two superpowers went about this in quite different ways—at least, in Europe. The Soviet Union constructed a system of vassal states, subordinate to it both militarily and economically and ruled—from Szczecin to Chukhotka—by the same monolithic and monopolistic ideology imposed by a group of Comintern graduates. The United States aimed to guarantee its allies internal stability, the best defense against the temptations of a new social revolution, and it did so chiefly in relation to the economy under the "protective umbrella" of its armed forces.

If the decisions reached at Tehran still left open the possibility that Poland's eastern border might come to form the western frontier of the Soviet empire, a series of subsequent *faits accomplis* that were ratified at the Yalta conference undermined any such hope. The acceptance of Moscow's terms by the Western democracies, their withdrawal of recognition from the London government, and above all, the decisions agreed at the long-running (17 July–3 August) conference in Potsdam, finally put paid to such illusions. The position of the British and Americans was largely unaffected by the changes that had taken place in the leadership of the two countries. Neither Harry Truman, who had become U.S. president following Roosevelt's death, nor Clement Attlee and Ernest Bevin, who had assumed command of the British ship of state in the wake of Churchill's electoral defeat, introduced any overall changes in policy toward the Soviet colossus. Nevertheless, various details in Roosevelt's policy, considered too "soft" by his successor, were eliminated, so that by the summer of 1945 policy toward the Soviet Union was dominated by mistrust and a sense of threat. There gradually emerged a new political line, subsequently known as containment, that aimed at preventing any further territorial expansion on the part of the Soviet Union. Events taking place in Poland and elsewhere in the region were one of the chief reasons for these changes, but their impact on the issue of Polish sovereignty and democracy were, paradoxically, largely negative.

Because of their previous policy, both the Western delegations to this conference, which was held not far from the ruins of Berlin, were condemned to accept both the outcome of the discussions held in Moscow and the fact that their main task in the future would be to counteract any attempt by the Soviet Union to expand its power unduly. Hence there were lengthy negotiations about German war reparations and about Poland's share in these, and about Poland's western frontier, which—in light of the uncertainty hanging over the future of Germany—was to be the only fixed western frontier of the Soviet empire. The Anglo-Saxons, particularly the British (and Churchill especially), were not enthusiastic about drawing the border along the Lausitzer Neisse or about transferring to Poland the left bank of the Oder near Szczecin, both of which were viewed by many Poles not only as compensation for the painful territorial amputation in the east but as an opportunity to strengthen the country. Thus the entire Polish delegation, which was now invited—in contrast to the situation at Tehran and Yalta—to present its point of view, maintained a show of unity even though its members included Deputy Prime Minister Mikołajczyk, who embodied the notion of a legal opposition to the PPR. He was able to take advantage of his relationship with Britain and the United States to obtain their agreement to arrangements of most benefit to Poland.

It was finally agreed that Poland would receive reparations from the overall amount accorded the Soviet Union and that the border would follow the line proposed by the Soviet Union (and Poland). Some intricate maneuvering on the question of Germany, which, after all, could not be simply wiped from the map of Europe, left Poland in an awkward situation in the long run. The Potsdam agreement was not viewed as equivalent to a peace treaty with Germany, which at that time had no status in international law, and the final confirmation of the border was postponed until such a treaty might be concluded. The decision to expel the entire German population from the area being transferred to "Polish administration" presented Poland with additional complications. If the Germans had remained, they would have constituted a national minority numbering several millions and thus a serious threat to the country, regardless of the future shape of Germany. But the drastic step whereby so many people were ejected from their homeland (and simultaneously deprived of their property) simply intensified the Germans' animosity toward the Poles, deepening the chasm that the war had opened up between the two nations and presenting the inevitable prospect of German revanchism.

The USSR thus became the de facto guarantor of Poland's territorial expansion to the west, a fact that increased the country's dependence on its neighbor and one whose significance could come to transcend all other political considerations. It was to be a major factor in Polish-Soviet relations for decades to come. The communists also made use of it, often in a brutal fashion, to legitimize their rule and as an effective weapon in their political battles with opponents at home. This proved effective, especially at the beginning, since the Western powers made no secret of their dissatisfaction with the Oder-Neisse line, which they used as a convenient means of influencing German public opinion. Stalin also exploited the border issue, although less provocatively and less consistently, in his efforts to help the German communists consolidate their position.

The sequence of decisions reached at summit meetings from Tehran to Potsdam constituted a kind of logical conclusion to the state of affairs brought about by the catastrophe of September 1939 and the subsequent partition of the Second Republic. Poland's position during the interwar years, when its foreign policy—regardless of how one views its merits—was that of a sovereign country, faded into history. Poland was now an actor on the international stage in formal terms only. In actuality, the country had become a fragment of a vast ideological empire, to which it was bound by a multiplicity of ties.

SUMMER 1945: HOPES OF NORMALIZATION

When the participants in the Moscow negotiations arrived back at the airfield near Warsaw, first to leave the plane were Bierut, Osóbka-Morawski, and Szwalbe, while Mikołajczyk found himself near the back of the group. However, when the car carrying the former prime minister entered the city, it was he who received a hero's welcome: "Women burst into tears," wrote one of those who welcomed them home, "and even men could be seen wiping a tear from their eye." People who had been tormented for so long, greeted him not only as the representative of a democratic and independent Poland but as a political leader supported by the democratic powers and as the harbinger of what they assumed to be impending changes in the way Poland was governed.

Among the general decisions taken by the Big Three, two were supposed to create a basis for change: the guarantee of "freedom of activity" to
all "antifascist" political parties and the requirement that free elections be
held "as soon as possible." On the other hand, the people who had the advantage of wielding power and enjoying Stalin's unqualified support had no
intention of departing from the course they had been following hitherto.
Both the Kremlin and the Polish Workers' Party regarded the "Moscow
agreement" as a tactical maneuver, a Leninist "one step backward" that was
to clear the way for "two steps forward." Their main directive as they followed this path was Gomułka's declaration that "now we have seized
power, we shall never give it up."

The country's political landscape changed fundamentally as a result of
the decisions reached in Moscow, the participation of Mikołajczyk and some
of his colleagues in the government, his role in the official delegations to
Potsdam and Moscow, and the dissolution of the underground Council of
National Unity and the Delegatura (and the impending dissolution of the
Armed Forces Delegatura). Hitherto there had been two main camps: on
the one hand, the PPR and its satellites (the PPS, SL, and SD, as well as such
organizations as the Peasant Self-Help Cooperative) and on the other, all
those groups that remained in the underground, both political and military.
There was now a third component, consisting of political groups and parties
that were anticommunist but functioned legally and openly. The position of
the Western powers and the emergence of a legal opposition (albeit one that
belonged formally to the governing coalition) had a major effect on both the
general situation and on the political structures already in existence,
whether associated with the PKWN or the underground.

Among the former, the main effect was a marked increase in the PPS's
aspirations to be treated as an equal partner by the communists. The majority of the few socialists who had returned from exile, such as Jan Stańczyk
and Ludwik Grosfeld, joined their PPS colleagues in Lublin, swelling the
ranks of those who had not previously cooperated with the PPR (Józef Cyrankiewicz, Dorota Kluszyńska, Adam Kurylowicz, and Kazimierz Rusinek).
These activists attempted, albeit inconsistently, to play the role of the political center between the communists and Mikołajczyk's supporters. In this
they were joined by the extremely ambitious Edward Osóbka-Morawski,
who remained prime minister, Stanisław Szwalbe, and Bolesław Drobner,
the *enfant terrible* of the party. Those socialists opposed to cooperation with
the communists wavered, but beginning in May they too tried to reach an

agreement with their Lublin colleagues. When these attempts ended in failure, thanks to the opposition of the PPR, Zygmunt Żuławski and others began to establish a second socialist party, called the Polish Social-Democratic Party.

As a result of the emergence of the SL-Roch from the underground, the enthusiastic welcome extended to Mikołajczyk everywhere he went, and the support he received from the "king of the peasants," Wincenty Witos, the Peasant Party that had officially reconstituted itself in the fall of the previous year quickly disintegrated. The party was abandoned not only by individual members but by entire district- and regional-level organizations. Party leaders such as Stanisław Bańczyk, Tadeusz Rek, and Bronisław Drzewiecki, who had not been directly associated with the communists, tried to force through a union with Witos and his supporters, or at the very least to make the party independent of the PPR; this further weakened the SL and reduced the communists' support in the countryside.

Although the government-in-exile had issued a statement declaring that the government framework established at the Moscow conference had no legal basis and could only "be recognized by the Polish nation under duress," a substantial proportion of the broad public and the political elite in the country accepted the diktat of the Big Three as a *fait accompli*. In July a group of moderate nationalists (including Stanisław Rymar and Jan Bielawski) set up the Committee for the Legalization of the National Party, which declared its desire that "all Polish forces take part in the rebuilding of . . . the country." Another organization that emerged, in the spring of 1945, was the Bureau of the Delegatura for New Territories. This was not so much a formal organization as a loose grouping of like-minded people, many of them associated with the nationalist movement. Their example was followed by nationalists in the Poznań region.

Bolesław Piasecki was released from prison following a meeting with Gomułka. Arrested by the NKVD in November 1944, he was an ambitious politician and radical nationalist who had become famous before the war for his efforts to reach an understanding with the Sanacja regime. The communists agreed (with General Serov's approval) to let Piasecki establish an organization that would appeal to some Catholics and nationalists and whose program would advocate coexistence between Catholics and communists. In November 1945 he began publishing a weekly, *Dziś i jutro* (Today and Tomorrow) and he succeeded, at least initially, in obtaining support from some sections of the church hierarchy and establishing contact with a number of Catholic intellectuals.

Karol Popiel's return to Poland shortly after that of Mikołajczyk led the Labor Party, a party that had played a major role in the underground state and in the émigré community, to begin open activity. The party had some support among trade union activists in Pomerania, Silesia, and around Kraków, and while underground it had gained a number of intellectuals as members, among them Jerzy Braun, Zofia Kossak-Szczucka, and Kazimierz Kumaniecki.

The Kraków weekly, *Tygodnik Powszechny,* expanded its circle of contributors and began publishing some lively political articles, especially those written by Father Jan Piwowarczyk. Father Zygmunt Kaczyński, a former minister in Mikołajczyk's government, also started to be active in public life. A good organizer and an experienced journalist, he began preparations for the publication of another weekly, *Tygodnik Warszawski* (Warsaw Weekly), a venture in which he had the support of the Warsaw Archdiocese. Cardinal August Hlond, who had spent the war years in France and in German captivity, returned to Poland on 20 July and began energetic efforts to organize the church in the new territories. Despite signs of government hostility toward the church (the decree making civil marriage compulsory), the communiqué issued on the occasion of the first postwar Conference of Bishops to be held in the presence of the primate (on 4 October) called on the faithful to participate in "rebuilding the Republic." Although the communiqué declared that the state should be based on a "healthy democratic spirit" and that believers should support those who aimed to implement "a social and political program in accordance with the teachings of Christ," it clearly urged people to engage in legal activity. In an address delivered on 28 October, Cardinal Hlond even declared that the "Catholic Polish nation loves its reborn state." This did not, however, signify capitulation but rather, in the words of the primate, "a peaceful crusade." Within a short period of time various Catholic associations and organizations (sodalities, rosary circles, youth and student groups) began to function again, seminaries were established, and a number of Catholic publications were revived.

Many organizations displayed strong opposition to the PPR: Mikołajczyk's supporters dominated the youth organization, ZMW Wici, and the Polish Teachers' Union; prewar journalists, many of them known for their liberal or even anticommunist views, played a major role in the Union of Journalists; a similar situation was to be found in the Polish Writers' Union. Thousands of officials, judges, lawyers, teachers (including university faculty), and engineers who had harbored serious doubts about the future now began to approach their professional duties in state institutions with greater optimism. Even some of the landowners and tenant farmers who had recently been dispossessed or evicted expressed their readiness to accept managerial positions in the newly created state farms. Many professionals took positions in various ministries—foreign affairs, industry and trade, agriculture and agrarian reform, and shipping—and one of the most outstanding economists of prewar Poland, Eugeniusz Kwiatkowski, returned to the country.

Professional military officers returning home from captivity, including those who had been captured following the collapse of the Warsaw uprising, were increasingly willing to sign up for military service and were frequently accepted. Senior commanders from the Polish Armed Forces also returned to the country, some of them to take up positions with the army. Regardless of its real purpose, the amnesty for members of underground groups, proclaimed on 2 September, also played a role, causing numerous individuals and groups as well as the entire organization of the Peasant Battalions to abandon clandestine activity.

Several private publishing companies reemerged, prewar textbooks were used in schools to teach humanities as well as science, and a number of prewar sports clubs and organizations reconstituted themselves. The changing atmosphere and the anticommunist attitude of the general public could be seen in the spontaneous celebrations on the first anniversary of the Warsaw uprising, in the enthusiasm of the crowds at Mikołajczyk's rallies, and in the huge number of people who took part in the pilgrimages to Częstochowa.

Thus the country began to rebuild the institutions of civil society that had been shattered by war, and they differed from the dummy institutions established by the Lublin government. The PPR was prevented from controlling or blocking these developments by its international commitments and by the fact that the process was both spontaneous and wide-ranging. Although the communists were not then in a position to come up with a precise plan, to forecast "phases" or "stages" of the country's transformation, they had no doubts about their overall aim: all areas of social life, including the economy, were to be subjected to communist party supervision or even direct administration. They could achieve this aim, generally speaking, by destroying all political institutions and organizations that were independent of the PPR and the central state authorities (or displayed strong tendencies toward such independence), by subjugating them, or by absorbing them. In their vision—and regardless of the extent to which, and for how long, "Polish specifics" were to be taken into account—there was no place for either autonomous organizations and institutions or even individual producers.

THE INSTRUMENTS OF POWER

Some communists no doubt believed that Polish socialism would be different from the Soviet version, which many of them knew from their own bitter experience. Nevertheless, when in 1944 the PPR became the dominant factor in the emerging institutions of power, it created an apparatus bearing all the characteristics of a totalitarian system, one in which terror, coercion, and control were combined with the ability to mobilize the population around centrally determined slogans.

The situation that arose after the creation of the Provisional Government of National Unity presented the PPR with a major challenge. While the presence of the Red Army guaranteed that the party would continue to wield power, it did not help it to gain the acceptance of the majority of the population. The communists faced major obstacles in the form of widespread mistrust and even hatred on the part of many people who saw them as the agents of a foreign power and the existence of various institutions that crystallized and gave voice to such sentiments. The party thus undertook an extremely intensive propaganda campaign aimed at convincing the public that only the PPR and the forces associated with it were capable of expressing the national will. At the same time, it fought hard against all those who were unwilling to submit to its dictates.

With the end of the war there were no longer any reasons—or rather, pretexts—to license and supervise the press or to maintain a centralized system of state propaganda. Nevertheless, the apparatus charged with these tasks was systematically expanded, and there emerged within the PPR central office a separate unit whose function was to plan and coordinate propaganda campaigns. This unit had at its disposal the Ministry of Information and Propaganda, which had direct control over a network of provincial and district agencies, print shops, publishers, newspapers, training centers for agitators, mobile cinemas, community centers, propaganda brigades, and so on. The communists ran the state radio network and the Polish Press Agency, the largest press agency in the country; the entire press, even the press published by the opposition, was condemned to use its the services. The PPR had a decisive influence in the *Czytelnik* (Reader) publishing cooperative, organized by Jerzy Borejsza with the aim of neutralizing the country's intellectuals and gaining their support. This institution was not only the country's largest book publisher, but also a major power in the press, and the owner of numerous printing works and distribution agencies (which were transferred to it by the government). Attached to this agency was a representative of the state censor's office, which not only engaged in preventive censorship of all publications, theatrical performances, and films, but also issued permits for periodical publications, allocated supplies of paper and newsprint, and supervised printing works. The PPR Central Committee also had de facto control over the vast propaganda apparatus belonging to the army, the Main Political-Education Agency, whose activity ranged far beyond the military and was particularly evident in the countryside and in the small towns where soldiers were stationed.

The press and publications of the parties associated with the PPR were also subjected to state censorship and generally participated, without much resistance, in the large-scale propaganda campaigns that were nominally a joint undertaking but in fact were organized at the dictate of the communists. Independent organizations found it difficult to penetrate the tightly woven network of licenses and allocations. The peasant movement, whose leader happened to be deputy prime minister, had to engage in lengthy negotiations before obtaining permission to publish a daily paper, *Gazeta Ludowa* (The Peasants' Paper), whose circulation was restricted to a level far below demand. Neither the church nor the Labor Party obtained permission to publish a daily paper. The communists also prevented the publication of any privately owned dailies and periodicals.

All this ensured the PPR almost total dominance in the field of information and propaganda. The party was able to use its control over the allocation of paper and newsprint and the mechanisms of censorship and publishing permits to hinder and prevent the articulation of alternative political or ideological opinions and, above all, the emergence of organized groups outside the sphere of influence of the communists and their zealous helpers. In view of the close relationship between the PPR and the government apparatus, this propaganda was actually official state propaganda, but although it contained elements designed to appeal to all—first and foremost the call to take part in rebuilding the shattered country and to settle the Regained Territories—its main purpose was political struggle, a struggle that was waged with considerable savagery.

Newspapers, leaflets, pamphlets, and radio programs were full of aggression directed with equal force at "the reactionary underground," "remnants of the aristocracy and bourgeoisie," "speculators and freeloaders," "Anglo-Saxon imperialism" and its "émigré lackeys," "obscurantist clergy," and members of the opposition peasant movement, who were consistently depicted as "representatives of the rich peasantry" and supporters of "foreign powers." This propaganda painted a black-and-white picture of the world, in which the PPR and its allies proved to be not only the sole guarantors of Poland's new territorial boundaries (which more or less coincided with the truth) but also the only force capable of raising the country from the ruins, of "repolonizing the ancient lands of our Piast heritage," and carrying out economic reforms.

The communists presented themselves as genuine and faithful heirs to the entire "progressive tradition" in Poland, from the eighteenth-century Commission on National Education (the struggle to eradicate illiteracy) to opposition to the authoritarian governments of the interwar period (which the communists called "fascist"). Figures such as Hugo Kołłątaj, Joachim Lelewel, Maciej Rataj, and Mieczysław Niedziałkowski were certainly no worse, and perhaps better, patrons than such early communists as Ludwik Waryński, Marcin Kasprzak, and Julian Marchlewski (not to mention Rosa Luxemburg). There were abundant references to anti-German elements in Polish history and frequent recourse to pan-Slavic rhetoric, which was intended to facilitate the newly launched notion of Polish-Soviet friendship and foster a positive attitude toward communist rule in Yugoslavia and elsewhere. The communists' overwhelming advantage in the sphere of information and propaganda was itself a factor that helped shape the new "truly democratic" reality, since it demonstrated the weakness of all those who were in various ways opposed to the PPR.

"In order for propaganda to be effective, it must be backed up by a sharp sword"—this motto of Joseph Goebbels, the master of totalitarian propaganda, was also the motto of the PPR. Throughout 1945, both before and after the creation of the Provisional Government of National Unity, work proceeded on the expansion of the repressive apparatus. In May 1945 the Ministry of Public Security (MBP) had approximately eleven thousand employees; by the fall the number was two-and-a-half times greater, and the network of agents and informers was growing at an even faster rate. A reorganization in September strengthened those units in the ministry charged with combating the underground, as well as those agencies that monitored and infiltrated legally functioning political parties, associations, and the church (the Fifth Department), and supervised various areas of the economy (the Fourth Department). These departments operated on the basis of agents recruited through the use of intimidation, physical terror, or so-called compromising materials. The police, or Citizens' Militia, employed 62,000 people (twice as many as the prewar State Police, which had to deal with a population of thirty-five million), and the Internal Security Corps employed some 3,200 officers and approximately 29,000 thousand NCOs and rank-and-file troops. The ministry had charge of more than one hundred prisons and camps, not counting the jails operated by the Office of Security (UB), the police, and the Internal Security Corps. Regular military units were used in many pacification operations, and throughout 1945 detachments of Soviet internal troops, together with various NKVD agencies and counterintelligence units were active in Poland. NKVD units carried out their last attack against partisans in the field in August 1946 (and they did not leave Poland until the spring of 1947). Because of the composition of its senior personnel and its subordination to PPR directives, the Ministry of Public Security essentially functioned as the party's own political police. The state of discipline in the security organs, especially the police, left much to be desired. Drunken brawls, insubordination, and skirmishes between groups of *ubeks,* as security service employees were called, and groups of police or soldiers were commonplace. There were numerous cases of theft carried out during searches, of rape, and even armed assault. Nevertheless, the security organs constituted a powerful and effective weapon in the struggle against the genuine opponents, open or clandestine, of the communists and Soviet domination, and in the effort to intimidate the broader society.

The army, whose top commanders were communists or people (like Żymierski) who were totally beholden to them, also played a major role. As mentioned above, the army was widely used to indoctrinate both the troops and the civilian population. It organized a large proportion of the resettlement campaigns in the western territories, and the traditional Polish sentiment of respect for the military was exploited to legitimize the authorities. The army itself was closely supervised by the PPR leadership, and its own counterintelligence service was oriented not so much toward uncovering spies as toward monitoring the political loyalty of the troops, especially the prewar officers who were signing up in increasing numbers.

The system of regional self-government based on national councils, an innovation in Poland, also proved to be a convenient tool in many of the PPR's political and propaganda campaigns. First established before July 1944, their members were selected through a process of nomination—a state of affairs that was to hold for many years to come. These bodies were, of course, dominated by the PPR and its most loyal allies; they generally passed resolutions and took decisions dictated "from above," providing a multiparty facade for single-party rule. A similar arrangement existed in the National Council of the Homeland, even after the Moscow negotiations. Members of the council were called deputies, although they were not elected but nominated or co-opted, and the communists and their allies occupied the overwhelming majority of seats. The council's presidium had a broad range of formal powers and was led by "President" Bolesław Bierut, who officially proclaimed that he was not a member of the party, although most of the PPR Politburo meetings took place in his government office in the Belweder Palace.

The PPR also ensured its influence over the ministries concerned with education and public administration, officially headed by Mikołajczyk and his party colleagues. They willingly employed "prewar" experts, who—with the exception of the armed forces and the security apparatus—constituted the majority of managerial employees and made a substantial contribution to education, the judiciary, the economy, banking, and so on. Everywhere, however, and at all levels, the PPR made sure that it had its own people to monitor their activity. The PPR leadership aimed to centralize personnel policy, but it was prevented from achieving the desired level of control by the need to maintain the appearance of power sharing and by weaknesses in its own resources.

This battery of instruments enabled the PPR to overcome its opponents and to emasculate those who had agreed to be its allies. Of course, the government administration at both the central and local level fulfilled normal organizational functions. The police combated common crime, which was extremely widespread, as is often the case after a war. The economy underwent a process of rapid reconstruction. Much effort and no small amount of material resources were devoted to settling and organizing the western territories and the Baltic ports. It was a difficult undertaking, but the authorities gradually gained control over the postwar economic chaos, which had been exacerbated by mass migration and the pillaging carried out by the Red Army, which had treated the former German lands as conquered territory. With the help of engineers and workers, factories were gradually reopened. Schools of all kinds, colleges, and universities reopened their doors to students. Despite chronic shortages of both human and material resources, the health service undertook a massive campaign of immunization and began to battle the two plagues of wartime—tuberculosis and venereal disease. The government made an attempt to balance the state budget and control the money supply. Czesław Bobrowski, a well-known economist and socialist, returned to Poland from London to draw up proposals for a system of national economic planning that differed substantially from the Soviet model, which was essentially unfamiliar to the Polish communists, even the PPR leadership. The traditional cooperative movement, both consumer and producer cooperatives, developed rapidly.

These were the areas of public life in which cooperation was most easily achieved. Few groups, even those most hostile to the communists, were inclined to call for sabotage, to advocate destroying rebuilt factories or blowing up mines and port facilities. Many members of the underground had regular jobs as engineers, teachers, and administrators. The Catholic Church stressed the need to stabilize social relations in the former German regions, in which it had the official support of the Vatican, and as result of this approach, a network of Polish parishes and dioceses was established there.

Regardless of differences in the human and material losses sustained during the war and regardless of geopolitical factors, many European countries were involved in rebuilding their economy and returning it to peacetime production. What happened in Poland was in many respects similar to what happened in the countries of Western Europe. They too were faced with acute food shortages, the total absence of everyday necessities, and raging inflation; they too were settling accounts with the war and occupation. What was characteristic for Poland and the other countries liberated by the Red Army was the creation at that time of the broad framework of the future communist totalitarian system: the emerging hegemony of a single party combined with total contempt for democratic procedures, the construction of a vast repressive apparatus, and the efforts to make the state omnipotent, with control over all areas of social life.

THE POLITICAL LANDSCAPE

The political landscape of Poland at the end of 1945 can be most accurately depicted if we distinguish three areas: the PPR and associated parties, the legally functioning opposition parties, and the anticommunist underground. Of course, the dividing lines were not always clear-cut, but the distance between the extremes was so vast that it completely precluded the possibility of not only agreement but even the faintest shadow of mutual toleration.

The key role was played by the communist party, which continued to camouflage its true identity. After a temporary slowdown in recruitment, it rapidly developed into a disciplined organization of over 200,000 members. Prewar communists constituted its elite, but the mass of the membership were new people. Some of them were careerists, but most of them came from those social groups and strata that suddenly found the way clear for their social advancement, partly because the intelligentsia had been decimated and partly because the PPR—quite rightly—did not trust those members of the intelligentsia who had survived.

It was young people from socially and economically underprivileged strata who flocked to the party, and in a country so poor there were many of them. One particular incentive to join was provided by the agrarian reform, which constituted a test of the scope and pace of changes to come. Those who were willing to volunteer were rewarded with access to tens of thousands of positions in the rapidly expanding power apparatus, in which the communist party was the decisive component. Many leftist and "progressive" intellectuals also joined the party, as did radically inclined members of the younger generation who dreamed of helping to "transform the world." The party played down revolutionary rhetoric when discussing political questions but was happy to emphasize it in relation to social issues.

Despite some differences of opinion, the PPR was internally cohesive, a factor that helped it to wage its political struggle and expand its control of public life. The party's activists were relatively young, energetic, and convinced of their ideological calling. The top leadership, too, did not display any serious differences of opinion, despite differences in wartime experience. The party itself was nimbly led by Władysław Gomułka, aided by Roman Zambrowski. Most of the top leaders—Bolesław Bierut, Jakub Berman, Hilary Minc, and Stanisław Radkiewicz—focused their activity on state institutions. With sole control over the main instruments of coercion, with various Soviet agencies and the Red Army behind—or rather, above—them, and with the "umbrella" of the Kremlin in international relations, Poland's communists were the winning team. The resources at their disposal allowed them to be ruthless in dealings with their vassal allies and even more ruthless with their opponents, and provided them with room to maneuver on the sociopolitical front, which they put to skillful use despite their lack of experience.

During a meeting of the Central Committee in May 1945 Gomułka declared that it was time for the PPR to pull its "spies" out of the allied parties. Such spies remained, nevertheless, a powerful instrument in monitoring and shaping party activity, and in some cases, communists were actually delegated to work in these parties. Not surprisingly, this was true of the Democratic Party, which really had no political identity of its own, and the Peasant Party, which had been established before the war by communists active in rural areas. It was also true of the Polish Socialist Party. The PPS leadership included such activists as Feliks Baranowski, Stefan Matuszewski, and Tadeusz Ćwik, who were able to draw the entire party toward the PPR and exert pressure on PPS members who might favor greater autonomy. Such pressure was effective in part because PPS members were as afraid of Stalin's power, and that of his Polish cohorts, as they were of any potential fundamental change in the international situation that might alter the balance of forces inside Poland. While they tried on several occasions to find common ground with Mikołajczyk and his supporters, it took only a reprimand from the PPR for them to abandon the effort. They also tried to bring more people into the party, not an easy task at the time since they were competing with the PPR, which was also seeking recruits among the working class, the socialists' traditional base. In some areas—Kraków, Łódź, and Wrocław, for example—this competition was out in the open. Nevertheless, on key issues the PPS, with varying degrees of enthusiasm, fell into line with PPR policy.

The combination of coercion and sociopolitical measures was at this time directed against any efforts to broaden the range of legal opposition. A number of nationalists submitted a petition requesting permission to engage in open political activity; not only was the petition rejected, but nearly all the signatories were arrested. The presidium of the National Council of the Homeland issued an ad hoc edict declaring that the number of political parties in the country was already sufficient, thus blocking the formation of the Polish Social-Democratic Party. Żuławski and his closest associates then joined the PPS—in somewhat humiliating circumstances because they were obliged to join as individuals rather than as a group. Their action did little, however, to strengthen the ranks of those socialists who were hoping to emancipate their party from dominance by the PPR. In this situation, the socialists who were most respected for their stand on Polish independence refused to join the party now led by Cyrankiewicz, Szwalbe, and Osóbka-Morawski. A few of them, such as Zygmunt Zaremba, left the country illegally. A similar argument was used to reject Stanisław Bańczyk's request to form a third peasant party, alongside the "Lublin" Peasant Party and the SL-Roch of Mikołajczyk. In this case, however, Bańczyk and his supporters joined the opposition. The PPR engaged in its most complex maneuvering when it decided to neutralize the Labor Party, which seemed to be in a position to gain the support of the Catholic Church and thus become a powerful force. Several days after Karol Popiel returned to Poland (6 July), a group of activists associated with the PPR and the Party for a National Upsurge, which had not been reactivated as a legally functioning party, sprang into action under the leadership of Zygmunt Felczak and Feliks Widy-Wirski. At the same time as the Labor Party emerged from the underground and was preparing its first national congress, the Upsurge group announced that it was resuming activity as . . . the Labor Party, from which it had split in 1943. The Labor Party leadership, which included prominent underground activists Jerzy Braun and Józef Kwasiborski, was refused permission from the state administration to reactivate the organization, and the congress intended to launch the party's legal functioning took place on 15 July in semi-clandestine circumstances. The PPR and the PPS informed Popiel that as a condition for formal recognition, he would have to join forces with the Upsurge group, which had already been formally recognized as a party. Despite support from Mikołajczyk, the KRN presidium, dominated by PPR members, refused to recognize the Labor Party. For several months the party was the target of harassment: newly established regional offices in Łódź and Katowice were subjected to petty annoyances, many party members were detained, and publishing permits were denied, while the Upsurge group obtained a permit for its own daily, *Ilustrowany Kurier Polski* (Illustrated Polish Courier).

The Labor Party leadership finally gave way, and on 14 November an agreement was reached whereby the Upsurge group would be assigned seven out of fifteen seats in the party's governing body. Similar proportions would obtain among the party's delegates to the KRN. The Labor Party thus gained legal recognition, but in these circumstances its central executive could at any moment be paralyzed. By agreeing to the entry of Upsurge, which supported the neopagan and decidedly anti-Catholic ideas of Jan Stachniuk, the party now experienced a marked cooling of relations with the Catholic hierarchy, especially with Cardinal Hlond. The situation within politically active Catholic circles now became somewhat complicated, which suited the PPR perfectly: despite the public pronouncements of Father Piwowarczyk, the Kraków Catholic community around *Tygodnik Powszechny* began to distance itself from purely political activity; in Warsaw Father Kaczyński was using his weekly paper to form his own group; Bolesław Piasecki was clearly aiming to become the leader of an independent Catholic grouping; and the Labor Party, the only institution capable of becoming a mass party, had been effectively shackled.

The PPR tried a similar maneuver in the case of the SL-Roch, aiming to leave Mikołajczyk in a position similar to that of Popiel. This effort ended in failure. The clandestine peasant movement had not only been a major political force of the underground state but, more important, it was extremely cohesive. The relatively few defections or attempts to cooperate with the PPR had done nothing to undermine the authority of its former leader, Wincenty Witos, who remained resolute, or that of the current leader, Mikołajczyk. The position that he had achieved in the government-in-exile was regarded not only as his personal success but as a success for the entire peasant movement. PSL members inside Poland constituted one of the most moderate resistance groups in terms of attitudes toward the Soviet Union, so Mikołajczyk's decision to take part in the Moscow talks aroused little opposition.

In the summer of 1945 the SL-Roch thus found itself in an exceedingly comfortable situation: it had expanded and decentralized its organizational network, it had no serious internal differences to deal with, its leadership enjoyed widespread respect, and there was no questioning of the support that Mikołajczyk had received directly from the Allies, especially the British, who had done the most to persuade him of the need to come to an arrangement with Moscow. Soon after Mikołajczyk—whose émigré political opponents now maliciously referred to him as the "Knight of Yalta"—had returned to Poland, the SL-Roch emerged from the underground, and although both Bierut and Osóbka-Morawski tried to persuade Mikołajczyk to come to an agreement with the "Lublin" Peasant Party, on terms agreeable to the weaker partner, this proposal was rejected decisively by the Central Executive Committee of Roch, which had been reactivated on 8 July. The pro-PPR peasant activists were intractable in their demand that they be given complete parity on all party decision-making bodies; in this they were motivated by their own self-interest and by the fact that they were under pressure from the communists. Given their opponents' refusal to compromise, the Central Executive Committee of Roch decided to rename their organization the Polish Peasant Party (PSL).

Members of the rival organization now deserted in droves to join the PSL, and within a few weeks it had become the largest political party in Poland. Neither the central nor regional authorities were able to counteract this process. The PPR made able use of the clause in the Moscow agreement specifying that "the Peasant Party" should be given approximately one-third of the seats in the national councils at all levels and the same proportion of managerial positions in the administration and in such economic institutions as banks and cooperatives. The party interpreted this to mean that both parties should share this quota between themselves, As a result, the failing SL not only had a substantial presence in various forums of public life but could now hold out the prospect of material gain or career advancement to all those who stayed with the party or were considering joining the organization. In view of the failure of its frontal attack on the independent peasant movement, the PPR launched a "war of attrition" against the PSL: in many regions of the country, the local administration, and especially the local organs of the repressive apparatus, harassed party activists; many were detained, many were beaten up, and some were even murdered by "unknown perpetrators." The party encountered obstacles in its publishing efforts, and its daily paper, *Gazeta Ludowa,* was the censor's favorite reading material. The Ministry of Public Security recruited a broad network of agents and informers within the PSL, while the PPR machine unleashed a stream of hostile propaganda that soon turned into real hate sessions, directed first and foremost against Mikołajczyk.

For tactical reasons and because it did not want to attract the attention of the censor's office, the PSL never published the twelve-point political platform that it adopted on 8 July. The platform demanded that Lvov and the Drohobych Coal Basin remain Polish territory, and that NKVD and Red Army units leave Poland. It called for the restoration of freedom of speech, and guarantees of the safety of "all citizens who fought the Germans" and their release from prison, "irrespective of the organization to which they belonged." It called also for the return of Polish troops from the West "in complete detachments," and for the elimination of "the excessive number of Soviet citizens" from the ranks of the armed forces. It demanded free elections and the organization of the country's internal affairs "in accordance with native models and aspirations and on the basis of free individuals who are responsible members of the community." This platform, moderate in tone but radical in substance, was clearly formulated in opposition to the PPR. Although the precise wording was not widely known, its contents were implicit in the speeches made by party leaders and in resolutions passed by conferences at the province and district level. Its political platform brought the PSL many new sympathizers and supporters from various anticommunist circles, and it became the main—if not the only—openly functioning opposition force.

The return of Mikołajczyk and the decision of the Western Allies to withdraw their recognition of the government-in-exile had a decisive influence in shaping the activity of those groups that remained in the underground. Although bloodied in its struggle with the invaders and devastated by the Red Army, the Polish resistance—especially its armed, and largest, component—still constituted a powerful force. Despite appeals from the underground leadership, since the spring underground fighters had been taking to the forests, where they were joined by thousands of young people fleeing from the NKVD and Ministry of Public Security. According to several estimates, which are still hard to verify, up to eighty thousand people (compared with the 300,000–350,000 sworn members of the AK in the summer of 1944) were involved in various underground organizations, although only a small proportion were involved in armed combat. The front that was passing across Poland left many weapons in its wake, and the widespread demoralization to be found in both the Polish forces and the Red Army made it easy for the resistance to replenish equipment. It would seem that the resistance was much better armed than it had been during the occupation.

The state of the underground does not seem to have changed much following the amnesty (passed on 22 July and announced on 2 August) and the establishment of the associated verification commissions. While some forty-two thousand people emerged from the underground, most of them had not been active and they handed over only a small number of weapons. The entire Peasant Battalions network renounced clandestine activity, but since at least July its members had been inactive, not engaging in even isolated, local actions. A substantial proportion of (post-) AK partisan units remained underground; some of them had been reorganized in 1945 or had even been formed from scratch and were thus trying to associate themselves with the AK tradition. Many units of the former AK were active under their own, local names, which frequently derived from the pseudonyms of their commanders, indicating the progressive disintegration of the military underground and the breakdown of the old territorial structure. Two of the largest units that had functioned independently since the dissolution of the AK were the Secret Polish Army of Lieutenant Stanisław Soczyński, and the Wielkopolska Autonomous Volunteer Group. Many groups took the name of the National Armed Resistance Movement, but not all of them had ties to the movement's central organization, established after the AK command had been dissolved. Nationalist groups neither emerged from the under- ground nor dissolved themselves: the National Party and its National Mili- tary Union, the Polish Organization and its National Armed Forces, and the National Military Organization remained as clandestine organizations. The National Party and the Polish Organization managed to some extent to re- create their territorial network (the former had six regional command cen- ters, and the latter, eleven). The nationalist partisan units had relatively few members, but they were among the most active. The liquidation of the Armed Forces Delegatura in 6 August did not mean that the Home Army was going to lay down its arms and abandon clandestine activity. AK com- manders had been considering various ways in which the organization could continue to be active, while making the best use of its human poten- tial and easing the return of its members, especially commanding officers and the younger generation of fighters, to civilian life. The amnesty and numerous arrests caused the final decision to be delayed, but on 2 Septem- ber Colonel Jan Rzepecki, the former delegate, together with the regional commanders of the Armed Forces Delegatura, established the Freedom and Independence Group (WiN), with the aim of transforming what had been a military structure into a secret political organization. Although Mikołajczyk refused all contact with the WiN leadership, the organization's program ini- tially had many points in common with that of the PSL.

WiN recognized the Polish émigré government in London, but its view of the current situation in Poland was closer to that of Mikołajczyk than Arciszewski. At least, this was the case at the beginning. The organizational structure of WiN was a direct continuation of the Armed Forces Delegatura, and despite the serious losses that the AK suffered in the spring and sum- mer of 1945, it was without doubt the largest and most respected organiza- tion in the underground. Out in the field, however, the leadership's overall political approach met with resistance, especially as the activities of the se- curity forces forced many groups to engage in self-defense. In addition, the activity of the nationalist underground—which constituted a kind of rival organization—encouraged WiN groups to undertake offensive actions. In fact, then, WiN did not constitute a purely political organization. Neither WiN nor the nationalist armed organizations had their own channel of communications with the Polish authorities in London. They maintained contact via the couriers who entered the country, occasionally bringing with them modest sums of money, and returned to London with reports of the situation at home. During the late summer and fall, traffic across the "green frontier" was especially heavy, and many people involved in underground activity, fearful of the growing number of arrests, left the country.

The purely political underground was weaker than its military counterpart. Apart from the National Party, none of the underground political organizations had much influence, and they actually seemed to function—when seen from outside (or above)—as a single entity. The situation was as it had been during the occupation: society as a whole was not that interested in which particular unit had rescued a group of prisoners or attacked a police station; the most important thing was that the underground was alive and active. A clearly visible ideological convergence was taking place, especially between the AK and the nationalists. The PPS -WRN also remained underground, as did the Piłsudski-ite groups, which had remained relatively weak during the war. Both the military and political underground concentrated their activity on propaganda. Dozens of newspapers were published by political parties as well as by WiN, the National Armed Forces, and even some autonomous partisan units.

The conditions in which the underground functioned were quite different from those of wartime. While a large number of people had a decidedly negative attitude toward the PPR, "people's democracy," and the Soviet Union, they were also exhausted by the war. Many counted on the outbreak of World War III, but this prospect by no means appealed to everyone, since it could only entail yet another cataclysm. Faith in the West, which intensified with Mikołajczyk's return, was accompanied by the feeling that Poland had been betrayed. This belief undermined public support for the underground, especially the military underground, because it came to be seen as causing unnecessary losses. Despite the fact that many people viewed the current situation as a "second occupation," the barriers between the power apparatus, the ruling group and its supporters, and the rest of the country were not as strong as under the Germans. At the same time, the partisans commanded much less public sympathy than previously. The underground expressed an attitude, but the public's hopes for change were focused on the PSL and the forthcoming elections.

While the communists used a variety of weapons to wage war on legally functioning political parties and groups, they went after the underground with ruthless determination. They resorted frequently to the principle of collective responsibility, organizing pacification campaigns across entire regions where the partisans were most active. These campaigns were carried out by troops belonging to the Internal Security Corps as well as regular military units, and in many cases captured partisans were simply executed on the spot. Detention centers were filled to overflowing, and the press carried a growing number of reports of trials that ended in the death sentence. According to fragmentary data (which exclude the results of NKVD activity), in 1945 nearly three thousand people were killed and tens of thousands were arrested. Communist agents infiltrated many underground organizations, where they operated as both spies and provocateurs; there are a dozen or so known cases in which the UB organized partisan units or underground groups.

The first severe blow came in the fall, when almost the entire central command of the National Armed Forces was captured, together with a large number of WiN leaders, including Colonel Rzepecki and district commanders Antoni Sanojec and Jan Szczurek-Cergowski. Since underground organizations were essentially a continuation of those that had existed under German occupation, the communists found it relatively easy to identify the groups involved, and it was certainly much easier to infiltrate professional intelligence agents into their ranks. As part of its investigative tactics the security service frequently offered various political concessions, often with success, as in the case of Rzepecki or that of Colonel Jan Mazurkiewicz (Radosław), who was arrested somewhat earlier and who, while in prison, called on underground fighters to take advantage of the amnesty and turn themselves in. The amnesty itself provided the Ministry of Public Security with valuable information—which was precisely one of the reasons for passing it in the first place.

The year 1945, then, set the stage—both legal and clandestine—for political developments over the next year or so.

TOWARD COLD WAR

Although the Great Powers managed for several years to prevent the escalation of the most important conflicts between them, their undeniable differences only deepened. While never coming to armed conflict, the "ideological wars" constituted, in a way, a continuation of the recently ended world war.

This was the case in Asia (China, Vietnam), and also in Greece, where civil war broke out in December 1944 between the government of the king and communist partisans led by General Markos, who were defeated only thanks to British intervention. Stalin provided no direct support to his Greek comrades. The ruler of the Kremlin may have been one of the most ruthless and bloody dictators in all of human history but in international relations he could be exceedingly pragmatic and circumspect. Even cautious. During the final stages of the war and during the first few years of peace he clearly had no wish to provoke the Western powers. In all probability the most important issues for him were Germany, and—as a bridge to Germany—Poland. The Soviet Union thus ceased to put pressure on Turkey, and after some wavering the Red Army withdrew from northern Iran. Stalin also adopted a conciliatory posture in relation to occupied Austria, deciding not to use the Soviet troops stationed in the eastern part of the country and to accept the results of the December 1945 elections in which the communist party suffered a crushing defeat. He also contented himself with Finland's strict neutrality, although there were clear signs of preparations under way for a communist coup d'état in the spring of 1948. As a result of some changes to its border with Finland, the Soviet Union gained a border with Norway, a development that gave rise to concern not only in Oslo but also in London.

In the Far East Stalin did not intervene directly, limiting himself to retaining the division of Korea and providing political rather than military support to the communists in China and Vietnam. Everywhere in that part of the world, however, even in Indonesia, then fighting the Dutch, and in Burma, World War II had given birth to communist parties, most of them having their own guerrilla units. National liberation movements were also growing in strength; directed against the colonial powers, they were, inevitably, natural allies as the Kremlin pursued its political aspirations. This gave rise to concern in the United States, which had always regarded the Pacific Rim as its own "security zone"; as a result, tensions between the two countries increased. In Western Europe, too, Stalin did not try to intervene directly—something that would have been beyond the powers of the Soviet Union at that time—but in both France and Italy the communist parties were extremely active, had considerable popular support (roughly one-third of the electorate), and played a major role in the governing coalition in each country. They constituted a major potential resource if the situation developed in Moscow's favor.

The situation in Eastern and Central Europe was quite different. The three Baltic states remained fully incorporated into the Soviet Union, and the Soviet authorities continued the deportations and "purges," whose victims included not only people who had collaborated with the Third Reich but also those who had been active in the cause of independence. The border with Romania remained much as it had been set out in the Ribbentrop-Molotov Pact, and thanks to the incorporation of part of Transcarpathia, the Red Army was now assured access to Hungary and Czechoslovakia. But neither these measures nor the presence of Soviet troops, which occupied Bulgaria, Romania, and Hungary and were stationed in Poland, were the decisive factor in determining the place of the Soviet Union in this part of the Continent.

In all these countries, Soviet pressure, regardless of differences in form and degree, led gradually but inexorably toward the seizure of power by the communists. This process went most quickly in Yugoslavia because of the real strength of the local communist movement. Tito was not content with the rapid successes he achieved at home—with the use of genuinely Bolshevik methods—but was also aggressive abroad, laying claim to Trieste.

In one way or another, the Soviet Union expanded and reinforced its presence over a huge part of Europe. If we add the substantial area of Soviet-occupied Germany, where both the local administration—dominated by communists—and the Soviet military authorities introduced changes that provided the basis for the country's future sovietization, the threat was palpable. In early 1946 the British and Americans began formulating a new political line. During a meeting at the White House, President Truman declared that he was "tired of baby-sitting the Soviets." On 5 March, speaking at a university in Fulton, Missouri, Churchill declared that a communist bloc was being formed and called for continuing military cooperation between the United States and Great Britain. This position was supported by the majority of the American public, and the enthusiasm for the Red Army that had been so widespread in the summer of 1945 melted away. In the West, people began to view the Soviet Union not as an ally but as an enemy.

The fact that in 1946 the communists visibly consolidated their position in seven countries of East-Central Europe—and dominated Yugoslavia, a country of major interest to Great Britain—and that they were enjoying major successes in the Far East, spurred the Western allies to take action. On 12 March 1947 President Truman told the U.S. Congress: "It must be the policy of the United States to support free people who are resisting attempted subjugation by armed minorities or by outside pressures." This remark was directed at Greece and Turkey, but it was interpreted as ushering in a new doctrine in American foreign policy, one that became known as the "Truman doctrine." Less than three months later, Secretary of State George C. Marshall (a career soldier who had held this position only since January) announced the creation of the European Recovery Program, the aim of which was to provide major economic assistance to countries that had been ravaged by war. The program would not offer the kind of short-term humanitarian aid provided by UNRRA and other agencies, but would provide funds for the countries' own rebuilding efforts. It was obvious that the Soviet Union would not agree to take part in the program, but Stalin forced Poland and Czechoslovakia to make the same decision.

When the Marshall Plan got under way in July 1947, Soviet domination and that of the homegrown communists was well entrenched everywhere in Europe to the east of the Iron Curtain, with the exception of Czechoslovakia. Opposition had been crushed, the communists' allies had been emasculated, the population was terrified or terrorized, and agrarian reform and the nationalization of industry—two of the main factors bringing the communists legitimacy and supporters—had essentially been carried out. This process proceeded in much the same fashion everywhere, although there were numerous variations, depending both on the international situation (whether a country had sided with the Allies or the Axis, whether a country was part of the anti-Nazi alliance from the very beginning of the war), and on local traditions. The speed with which the most vocal anticommunists were eliminated from the governing coalition varied—most rapidly in Yugoslavia and Albania, most slowly (February 1948) in Czechoslovakia—but everywhere the process moved in the same direction. Although specific regulations dealing with agrarian reform and the nationalization of industry varied from one country to another, by June 1948 such changes had been introduced everywhere. Everywhere, too, parliamentary elections had been held, and in those countries where the first attempt did not go too well (as in Hungary in November 1945), they were held again. Now it was not only the more or less known collaborators of the Germans (or Italians) and "class enemies" who ended up behind bars, but also members of the first coalition governments of 1945–46 and recently elected parliamentary deputies.

One event that helped further entrench Soviet domination was the signing on 10 February 1947 of a peace treaty with the former satellites of the Third Reich, which not only brought them official international recognition but also involved the Western powers in sanctioning the political status quo in these countries. All these processes also took place in the Soviet zone of occupied Germany, where nationalization and agrarian reform were accompanied, in April 1946, by the communist party's absorption of its social-democratic ally. This phase found ideological and political culmination in the conference of nine communist and workers' parties, held in September 1947 in Szklarska Poręba, in southwest Poland. The final, almost cosmetic, touch was the coup in Prague in February 1948, which gave complete power to the Czechoslovak Communist Party. The beginning of the Berlin blockade in mid-June 1948 signaled the beginning of a new phase: the arrival of the "Cold War," which signified not only open—although still not armed—conflict between the "socialist camp" and the Western democracies, but also the forced unification of the countries that found themselves within the Soviet sphere of influence and their forced adoption of the Soviet system.

THE FIGHT OVER ELECTIONS

The agreement reached by the Big Three at Yalta stipulated that parliamentary elections would be held in Poland, but such elections were also part of the standard political repertoire the communists had to go through in order to legitimize the changes under way throughout East-Central Europe and to acquire recognition abroad. Thus elections had to be held in all the countries within the Kremlin's orbit. The first to hold elections was Hungary (5 November 1945), where the Independent Party of Small Farmers, the equivalent of the PSL, won 57 percent of the vote. The results were quite different in the three Balkan states (Yugoslavia, Albania, and Bulgaria), where communist-controlled electoral blocs, usually called National Fronts, gained 88–93 percent of the vote, but the Hungarian case gave the PPR cause for concern while encouraging the PSL.

The creation of an electoral bloc, which the Polish communists proposed to call the Democratic Bloc (less militant sounding than the National Front, but equally false), became a short-term tactical goal, even though many speakers at the PPR congress (6–13 December) argued that it was time to settle accounts with not only the underground but also the legal opposition. The communists and their allies in the PPS, whose leadership feared an increase in tension between the PPR and the PSL, invited the latter to join them. However, the PSL congress (19–21 January 1946) did not make a final decision on the issue. With Stanisław Mikołajczyk now its undisputed leader following the death of Wincenty Witos, the party not only sensed its own strength as an organization with more than half a million members, but also was convinced of the rightness of its cause. The congress passed a resolution demanding, among other things, the liquidation of the Ministry of State Security and the Ministry of Information and Propaganda and the release of all political prisoners. The program adopted at the congress continued the line of previous programs from 1935 and 1943, drawing on agrarian traditions to provide a sober, democratic alternative to the communists' political platform.

Leaders of the PPR, PPS, and PSL met four times between 7 and 22 July 1946 for negotiations over the elections. During these discussions the PSL came under considerable pressure, often harshly worded, to agree to field a joint list of candidates. PSL representatives suggested that a coalition government be formed after the elections, potentially agreeing to the creation of a joint slate only in the western territories. When the PPR and PPS rejected this proposal outright, the PSL demanded that on any potential joint list 75 percent of places should be reserved for "representatives of rural areas," which would have guaranteed the party the decisive voice in drawing up the new constitution. The PPR and PPS agreed to accept a 20 percent parity for themselves and each of the two peasant parties, a proposal that would have ensured that the PSL did not get to play a major role in the Sejm and would also have discredited Mikołajczyk in the eyes of the most anticommunist groups. The PSL leaders did not, however, allow themselves to fall into this trap and, amidst an escalating propaganda campaign launched by the "democratic parties," they broke off negotiations.

Gomułka did not, however, wish to repeat the "Hungarian error" by calling elections while faced with an opponent as strong as the PSL and with continuing underground activity, which by its very existence encouraged people to express their opposition to the PPR. Nor did he have faith in the efficacy of the instruments that were supposed to ensure—through terror or falsification—a result favorable to the PPR. Taking advantage of a comment that Mikołajczyk made regarding the possibility of holding a referendum on the constitution along the lines of the referendum recently held in France, he postponed the elections. This provided yet one more opportunity to force concessions from the PSL. On 5 April the communists and three allied parties formally adopted the notion of carrying out a referendum—a "people's" referendum, of course.

The three questions contained in the referendum were to deal with the abolition of the Senate, the approval of agrarian reform and the nationalization of industry (while retaining small-scale private production), and support for the western border established at Potsdam. These questions put the PSL in a rather awkward position: at some point in the past the peasant movement had come out in favor of a single-chamber parliament; despite reservations regarding their implementation, the PSL supported the reforms themselves; and the party had long advocated moving Poland's border to the west. Nevertheless, the communists decided to treat the outcome of the referendum as a trial run for the forthcoming elections. They hoped to gain better information about the geographical distribution of PSL support, prepare an administrative framework to monitor the results, and mobilize and expand the repressive apparatus. The PSL decided to accept the challenge and expressed its readiness to carry out the referendum. Hoping to turn it into a genuine plebiscite, the party called on the population to vote no on the first question. The struggle had entered a new phase.

The public mood plainly did not favor the "bloc of four," which was identified with the ruling group. Throughout the spring acute shortages and rapid price increases led to a wave of short-lived but recurring strikes in many parts of the country. The main flash points were Upper Silesia, the Silesian Coal Basin, and around Łódź, at that time the most important working-class centers. Relief supplies from UNRRA were not enough to relieve the misery, and the distribution of these supplies was often the cause of the strikes. Official measures to combat speculation were more propagandistic than real in nature and thus did little to improve the situation.

Despite severe losses, partisan units remained active in the so-called old territories, especially around Białystok and Lublin, and in northern Mazowsze, where they controlled many districts, limiting the presence of the authorities in the countryside. The Ukrainian Insurrectionary Army continued fighting in the southeastern part of the country. Ejected from eastern Galicia by the NKVD, the Ukrainians were now not only fighting against forces belonging to the Ministry of State Security but were carrying out reprisals against the Polish population. The resettlement of the German population, which got under way in February, added to the economic dislocation in the western territories, which was further exacerbated by the fact that this was precisely the period that saw the largest influx of population from the east. Rural areas were hard hit by the system of compulsory deliveries of farm produce that replaced the system of services in kind (abolished in August 1945), especially as the relations between prices of agricultural produce and those of industrial goods were disadvantageous to the peasantry, and the little credit that was available was mainly channeled to the state sector. In the fall of 1945, roughly 78 percent of arable land lay fallow, and agricultural productivity was considerably lower than it had been under German occupation. After its congress, the PSL continued to grow and began to make inroads in urban areas, even organizing membership groups in factories. Patriotic sentiments—by definition, anticommunist—were spreading among young people and found expression in demonstrations on 3 May and, first and foremost, in the strikes and protest actions organized in every major academic center after security forces had disrupted a student march on 3 May in Kraków. The presence of UNRRA relief supplies, and even the growing number of American films playing in the cinemas, not only strengthened public conviction regarding the superiority of the United States but also gave people the sense that the West was actively engaged with the Polish question. A number of popular sayings were coined at this time, among them: "Truman, Truman, drop that bomb / We can't stand it here at home," and "Just one little bomb, and we'll be back in Lvov."

Hostility toward the authorities was intensified by the behavior of the Red Army, whose soldiers continued to plunder, unchecked, while their commanding officers lorded it over most of the western territories. While the security forces and police were putting most of their effort into fighting the underground, common banditry was flourishing in many areas of the country. Despite the resettlement of the Germans, ethnic conflicts persisted in the western territories. Autochthonous Poles were frequent targets of aggression, and in many towns and settlements Jews once more came under attack. Often these attacks were simply cases of banditry, but there were also frequent cases of aggression motivated by anti-Semitism. To the old stereotypes there was now added a new one concerning the Jewish-communist clique (żydokomuna) that allegedly ruled Poland, a new stereotype that was reinforced by the visible presence of people of Jewish origin in the power apparatus and the PPR. This allegation was repeated constantly by most of the underground newspapers. According to some estimates, several hundred Jews were murdered.

The situation was thus far from stable, but in this respect Poland was not much different from the other countries that had endured the war in this part of Europe. If we exclude Greece, the site of a protracted civil war, Poland—and the western Ukraine—was, however, the only country in which antigovernment guerrillas were still active.

Although the power of the Soviet Union provided the communists with both protection and support, the PPR did not underestimate the existing threats. Two draconian decrees were enacted on 15 November 1945, dealing with, first, "particularly dangerous crimes during the period of reconstruction of the state," and, second, the introduction of summary legal proceedings and the establishment of the Special Commission to Combat Embezzlement and Economic Sabotage. These decrees were zealously applied by the Regional Military Courts, which now had jurisdiction over civilians. Less than three weeks before the referendum the so-called Small Penal Code was published (which was to remain in force until 1969), together with a decree on censorship that was couched in such general terms that its application was virtually unrestricted. In February the Volunteer Reserve Citizens' Militia (ORMO) was formed. The ORMO provided the PPR with what were essentially fighting squads, whose members soon numbered more than one hundred thousand. To coordinate activity, the State Committee on Security was established. Under the control of the Ministry of Public Security and the Ministry of Defense, the committee mobilized a force of nearly 130,000, drawn from regular army soldiers, troops belonging to the security ministry, and members of ORMO, whose task was "to provide protection and undertake a propaganda-political campaign during the period of the referendum." This was a powerful machine that reached into the furthest corners of the country and, armed with both machine guns and leaflets, urged the population to vote "three times yes."

The PPR and its allies redoubled their efforts to force PSL members and sympathizers out of their positions in the administration and national councils. Several district-level PSL organizations were dissolved on the basis of trumped-up charges of collaborating with "reactionary underground organizations." Most of the PSL delegates to the congress of the Peasant Self-Help Cooperative were prevented—through arrest or intimidation—from taking part in the deliberations. The censor's office intervened with increasing frequency in the PSL press, and the largest press distributor, Czytelnik, refused to distribute *Gazeta Ludowa*. A group of peasant activists associated with the PPR and the Ministry of Public Security (including Tadeusz Rek and Bronisław Drzewiecki) also tried, with meager results, to undermine the PSL from within.

The PPR did not neglect "positive" measures: on 6 June the authorities announced that compulsory deliveries would be abolished, the distribution of UNRRA aid was speeded up, and efforts were made to increase supplies of food to the larger towns. A special task force, headed by Zenon Kliszko, worked out the details of the electoral law in the effort to eliminate PSL members from the district and ward supervisory commissions. The group enjoyed a fair measure of success: out of eleven thousand ward commissions, PSL members chaired only 461, and the PPR—four thousand. The task force also adopted a ruling extremely favorable to the PPR and its allies: a blank vote would be counted in the "three times yes" column.

Although the voting itself took place in relative peace, the prisons were filled with thousands of PSL members held in "preventive" detention, and nearly every polling station had an armed guard. The ballot boxes were frequently transported to the office of the district administrator or even the local premises of the Office of Security, where a "select group" counted the votes. The first partial results transmitted to the Warsaw office of the PPR were decidedly negative for the party and its allies, although turnout—something they had been concerned about—was relatively high. To this day it is not clear whether the party leadership had prepared a coherent plan for "improving" the results of the referendum.

In any event, not later than 3 or 4 July it was decided that the overall results had to be falsified. We can assume that the PPR leadership regarded this decision as a natural response to the situation, one that was not open to discussion, since the polling data gathered by party bodies and government agencies (including the military) were quite disastrous. In the country as a whole, only 27 percent had voted "three times yes," while at least 33 percent had voted "three times no." Taking into account the plebiscite nature of the vote, no fewer than three-quarters of the voters had come out against the PPR and its allies. In some areas fewer than 15 percent of voters had voted yes on all questions (this was the case in the Kraków and Rzeszów provinces). To all intents and purposes this amounted to total defeat. Days passed without the results being published, but when they were finally published, on 11 July, it was no doubt clear to everyone that the data had been falsified. According to the official communiqué, 67 percent of voters said yes to the first question, 78 percent voted yes to the second, and 92 percent voted yes to the third. Even before the communiqué was issued, the PSL lodged a protest. The party's complaint was rejected—two months later.

However, before Poland and the outside world discovered what the PPR regarded as appropriate referendum results, public opinion was shaken by one of the most horrifying events of a period already full of crime and violence. On 4 July in Kielce a crowd of several thousand carried out a pogrom against local Jews. The soldiers and police dispatched to protect those under attack simply stood by, and some of them even joined in. Forty people were killed. Anti-Semitism, widespread across the country, erupted here with destructive force, and for several weeks after the "Kielce events" the public mood in many towns was one of hysteria. While the PPR pointed at the underground and its "supporters," the PSL—whose statement condemning the pogrom was held back by the censors—made it known in unofficial statements that it considered the real instigators of the event to have been the security service, aiming to divert the attention of the outside world away from the falsification of the referendum results. To this day the circumstances of the pogrom have not been fully explained, but the notion that it was part of a political struggle does not appear to have any basis. Even if the authorities did instigate the attack on the Jews in Kielce, the massive participation by the local population, from all social strata, is evidence of the continuing strength of ancient social phobias and frustrations. In fact, the event seriously undermined the prestige of Poland (and Poles) in the eyes of the West. Jews were already leaving Poland before the pogrom, many of them going to Palestine, and one result of the event was a marked acceleration of the exodus. The pogrom also deepened divisions in public opinion, causing some members of the liberal intelligentsia to move closer to the parties of the "democratic bloc."

Although the actual voting favored the opposition, the fact that the PPR succeeded in falsifying the referendum results and forced people to accept them testified to the communists' cynicism as much as to their arrogance and self-confidence. It also, however, led to increased efforts on the part of some in the PPS leadership to regain their party's independence, since the voting had shown how little public support the PPR bloc could muster. During the summer the main antagonists conducted negotiations—unofficial in the case of the PPR, official in the case of the PPS—but discussions broke down over the PSL's steadfast refusal to abandon its demand for total independence. While these discussions were going on, the campaign against the opposition continued unabated. Ever more military units were drafted to fight the guerrillas, the security services expanded, the number of trials increased, and many areas of the country were under what amounted to martial law. The PPR also undertook a successful maneuver to transform the Labor Party into its obedient servant. In light of the fact that Popiel's supporters constituted the overwhelming majority of delegates to the party's congress, the authorities refused permission for the event to take place. When the party's Executive Board responded by suspending party activity, the Upsurge group immediately began referring to themselves as the party. The PSL thus lost its only partner and—if we exclude the underground, which was increasingly on the defensive—was left to face the increasingly powerful apparatus of control and repression alone. A sense of hopelessness took hold of the party, and gradually members began to leave, largely because of harassment on the part of local administration officials, who used blackmail and threats, which they sometimes carried out.

Slowly but surely the PPR prepared for the final attack on the opposition, while simultaneously fulfilling its obligation to hold elections. The State Committee on Security drew up the plan of operations, a great deal of work went into drafting an appropriate electoral law, propaganda attacks on the PSL intensified, and disputes between the PPR and the PPS were subjected to arbitration by Stalin, who determined the overall line of activity.

The pretext for launching a massive attack on the PSL, one that was to continue until the day of the election, was provided by U.S. Secretary of State James Byrnes. During a speech delivered in Stuttgart on 6 September 1946, he discussed the issue of Poland's western frontier in purely legal terms, reminding his audience that it would be subject to the "final treaty" (which was in accordance with the Potsdam agreement) without declaring that the exact course of this future frontier was a foregone conclusion. This speech formed part of the Americans' complicated maneuvering over Germany and was intended to counter Molotov's recent statements clearly courting the Germans. The Western allies treated Poland as a country belonging to the Soviet sphere of influence, and they were more interested in making sure that Stalin stayed on the far side of the Elbe than in advancing the cause of their erstwhile partner.

The anti-Americanism that was a constant feature of PPR and government propaganda intensified dramatically; Byrnes's words were seen as provided a convenient starting point for a campaign that would depict the Americans as enemy number one and Mikołajczyk and the PSL as the "lackeys of imperialism" and "allies of German revanchism." When several thousand people marched in an anti-American demonstration in Warsaw on 8 September, they were skillfully directed toward the offices of the PSL leadership, which they then proceeded to plunder, destroying much of the furniture and equipment in the process. The "people's anger" found an outlet in attacks on PSL members and on Mikołajczyk personally. In this way the PPR obtained propaganda support for activity carried out by officials of the Ministry of Public Security. During August Stanisław Mierzwa (one of the sixteen who had been sentenced in Moscow) was arrested in Kraków, together with several other leading PSL activists. After the editorial offices of *Gazeta Ludowa* in Warsaw had been searched numerous times, on 11 October the security service arrested Kazimierz Bagiński, who had also been among the sixteen, as well as several senior staff on the paper, including the editor, Zygmunt Augustyński. Numerous central party activists and an even greater number of local activists were summoned for "warning" conversations, the purpose of which was to persuade them to leave the PSL or to attack Mikołajczyk's line. The PPR also tried some political maneuvering in relation to Catholic groups, but this came to naught because of strong mutual antagonisms as well as the uncompromising attitude of Cardinal Hlond, who put a stop to all efforts to produce a "Catholic list" of candidates.

The electoral law, which was passed despite PSL objections, gave the authorities numerous possibilities to shape the electorate by removing people from the electoral rolls and determining the membership of the electoral commissions. Drawing on the experience gained during the referendum and information gathered by the Ministry of Public Security, the authorities divided the country into electoral districts, giving disproportionate weight to the western territories, since they exerted greater control over social behavior in that part of the country. In ten districts out of fifty-two, PSL candidates were struck off the ballot lists. Finally, the PPR ensured its electoral victory by preparing a "formula" that could be applied easily to the actual voting figures in order to obtain the desired official result (which had been approved by the PSS). Their assumptions regarding the real outcome were realistic, but pessimistic: they estimated that in the "politically reliable" wards, the democratic bloc could hope for no more than 28–35 percent of the vote. At the same time, they decided that the PSL should officially receive no more than 15 percent of the vote. This made it all the more necessary to conduct a massive propaganda campaign combined with intimidation of the population and terrorization of PSL members. Once again tens of thousands of people, organized in "protection-propaganda brigades," fanned out across the country; members of the PSL Central Council and the party's electoral candidates were thrown into prison; thousands of activists were arrested; couriers carrying documents needed to register lists of candidates were seized; in some parts of the country "unknown perpetrators" murdered local PSL activists; and more than thirty district-level PSL organizations were closed down. The PSL leadership ordered its grassroots organizations in the communes to hide their banners and cash boxes. Protests submitted by the party to the Soviet ambassador were ignored, and memoranda from Poland's Western allies were deemed to constitute "interference in the internal affairs of a sovereign country."

The day of the election, 19 January 1947, was nothing like the day of the referendum. Not only because the summer sun was missing: a large part of the country, especially the countryside, lived in an atmosphere of physical and psychological terror. Committees organized in advance of the voting staged group marches to the polling stations in the towns and organized convoys of trucks in the countryside. Those who voted in groups had priority, while those who went "individually" had to wait in long lines; ballots containing the numbers of the PSL candidates were torn up, while those for the democratic bloc were inserted in the ballot box; everywhere there were soldiers, police, security officials, and ORMO. Once the polling stations had closed, the "formula" was applied, and the PSL managed to obtain the actual results in fewer than 1,300 of more 5,500 wards. According to these data, the PSL received about 69 percent of the vote. But, in accordance with the popular saying of the time that "some people voted, but other people counted," the official result gave 80.1 percent to the democratic bloc, and the PSL was allowed 10.3 percent. The battle was over. The victors had only to clear the battlefield and take their prisoners. And look around for the next enemy.

1947: THE END OF A PHASE

The Sejm that was to pass a new constitution for Poland held its inaugural session on 4 February 1947. The Soviet Union and Poland's communists and their allies believed they had fulfilled the Yalta requirement that they hold "free elections." Despite obvious abuses committed during the counting of votes and the preelection campaign, and, of course, during the entire period since the PPR had seized power, the Western powers could do little apart from lodging verbal protests and "chilling" interstate relations. The PSL was, obviously, excluded from the governing coalition, and its twenty or so representatives constituted an opposition caucus that could play no role other than speaking the truth about the prevailing situation in the country. Both Stalin and Gomułka considered that they had no further obligations toward the participants in the Moscow talks, which boded ill for the future of the legal political opposition. After all, this was an institution that contradicted the very nature of the system, since the official ideology decreed that no legal institution could be opposed to a party that "expresses the interests of the entire nation" and any that did oppose it could not be legal.

The PPR took pains, however, to create the appearance of democracy and to acquire legitimacy by drawing on national and state traditions. For example, the first session of the Sejm elected its marshals and passed a constitutional law establishing the office of president of the Polish Republic. The following day Bolesław Bierut was elected to this position. He arrived to take his oath of office—full of lofty rhetoric and ending with the Christian entreaty "So help me God"—in the same kind of procession as that which used to accompany the president of the Second Republic. Nevertheless, the state and legal system that was adopted on 19 February 1947 (the so-called Small Constitution) departed from democratic principles regarding the separation of powers. For example, the new constitution established the Council of State, a body that combined both legislative and executive powers, and it accorded the government virtually unlimited powers to issue decrees with the force of law. On 22 February the Sejm issued a declaration on a broad range of "civil rights and freedoms," but in practical terms they were circumscribed, as is often the case, by political expediency. This legislative package was rounded out by an amnesty that resulted in the release of around 25,000 people from prison and detention and a reduction in sentence for many others.

The amnesty was intended both to lure people out of the underground and to facilitate the infiltration of groups hostile to the authorities. Some thirty thousand people emerged from underground organizations, but the majority reported the activity they had engaged in years earlier, during the occupation, and the number of weapons handed over was—as had been the case with the 1945 amnesty—disproportionately small in relation to the number of people who took advantage of the amnesty. Nevertheless, both the broader population and underground activists were tired, and the fact that the Western governments "took note of" the falsified election results without breaking off relations with the Warsaw government no doubt had a major influence on the decision to cease or suspend activity. Equally impor-

THE SPRING WILL BE OURS

tant was the intensification of the campaign against the "reactionary under-ground" during the period leading up to the elections and the continuation of the pacification campaign since then. The bloody fratricidal fighting, which in many parts of the country acquired the dimensions of civil war, passed its apogee and neared its inevitable end. In this final phase of the conflict the communists displayed undiminished—and possibly even greater—determination than their opponents. The authorities were pre-pared to use the most drastic measures, as they showed during Operation Vistula, when they made use of military convoys and concentration camps (including former German camps) to forcibly remove some 120,000 Ukrai-nians from southeast Poland. The main attacks were directed at under-ground leadership groups, and in 1947 nearly all of them were liquidated. All that remained on the battlefield was a small number of partisan units that became increasingly isolated and less able to cope effectively with tacti-cal demands. The leadership of the National Party and the PPS-WRN did not recover from a wave of arrests in late 1946 and early 1947, and the National Armed Forces simply disintegrated. The fourth successive imprisonment of the WiN Central Command effectively turned what had once been the largest underground organization into a front that the security service used until 1952 as a weapon in its counterintelligence operations. Nevertheless, battles, skirmishes, raids, pacification campaigns, and arrests continued throughout 1947. More than two thousand people were killed, and at least twenty-five thousand were imprisoned. The Office of Security, the police, the Internal Security Corps, and the PPR all suffered considerable losses at the local level.

The underground ceased to be a political force. Before long this was true of the legal opposition also. The independent Labor Party made several attempts to resume activity following the elections, but without success. Po-litical Catholicism was now represented in the Sejm by a tiny group of three deputies associated with Piasecki. Increasingly a disruptive force in relation to the church, in March he obtained permission to publish a daily paper, *Słowo Powszechny* (The Universal Word). Already at the end of January a factional grouping emerged within the PPS, this time not only much larger than the year before but also led by activists of some standing—Józef Niećko, Czesław Wycech, and Kazimierz Banach, all of whom had played a major role in the anti-German underground. Many local PSL organizations did not revive after the terror of the preelection campaign, many of its mem-bers stopped paying their membership dues, and activists were unceremoniously ejected from the few remaining positions that they occupied in the state administration. A growing number of members joined the procommunist SL or even the PPS, which caused alarm among the leaders of both these parties as well as the PPR.

In April PSL activist Kazimierz Bagiński went on trial, and only after he had been sentenced was he able to benefit from the amnesty. His colleague, Zygmunt Augustyński, was less fortunate: in July he was sentenced to fifteen years in prison and was not included in the amnesty. During trials of underground activists, prosecutors with increasing frequency referred to the PSL—and Mikołajczyk himself—as "collaborators of underground gangs." Some PSL leaders proposed that the party follow Popiel's example and suspend all activity, retaining only the Sejm caucus. It was not only in Poland that the legal opposition found itself under ever darkening skies. In Budapest the secretary general of the Peasant Party, Bela Kovács, was arrested in January; in May the Hungarian prime minister, Ferenc Nagy, did not return home from a private visit to Switzerland; on 5 June the leader of the Bulgarian Agrarian Party, Nikola Petkov, was arrested, on 15 August he was sentenced to death and the party was dissolved; on 14 July the leader of the Romanian Peasant Party, Iuliu Maniu, was arrested, and two weeks later the party ceased to exist.

Across the country, PSL offices, including the party's Warsaw headquarters, became deserted. *Gazeta Ludowa* was massacred by the censors, and in June the PPR leadership began preparing the "legal basis" for an indictment against Mikołajczyk. In this situation, on 21 October the former prime minister of the Second Republic fled Poland with the assistance of the American and British embassies. He was followed a few days later by Kazimierz Bagiński and Stefan Korboński. On 27 October the PSL, or rather its remnants, was taken over by secessionists, and Józef Niećko assumed the party leadership. This was the real end of legal opposition in Poland.

Neither the electoral victory of the democratic bloc nor the overall political situation in Europe favored those who advocated autonomy for the PPS. The dismissal of Edward Osóbka-Morawski as prime minister and his replacement by Józef Cyrankiewicz was clearly the result of pressure from the communists. In April 1947, at a meeting of the PPR Central Committee, the party leadership proclaimed the necessity for "a battle over trade." The cooperative movement, which hitherto had been a major source of support for the PPS, was to be the chief victim in this battle. PPR leaders made numerous public references to "social-democratic relics" in the PPS and the

need to "eradicate the influences of the WNR." The arrest in June of Kazimierz Pużak, the socialist of greatest standing at that time, suggested—
correctly—that the authorities would soon announce that they had
uncovered links between the independent socialists and a number of activists (selected by the PPR) in the legal opposition. Procommunist politicians
began to play an ever greater role in the PPS leadership. Often they were
simply careerists willing to adapt to a situation in which the PPR assumed
total control over public life and the economy and in which the two parties
would merge together in an "organic union"—to use the phrase that was
then popular all across East-Central Europe. Many activists, including many
intellectuals (such as Julian Hochfeld and Jan Strzelecki) considered it vital
to salvage something from the ideological tradition of the PPS, even at the
price of capitulation. The series of successive concessions to the communists that began in 1944 could not at this point have been halted even if
anyone had been willing to try. The PPS congress in December 1947 proudly
proclaimed that the party "was, is now, and will in the future be needed by
the Polish people." It was, however, no longer needed by Stalin or Gomułka.

Although the authorities were making progress in rebuilding the country's factories, towns, and villages and in organizing the western territories,
the economic situation remained difficult and far from stabilized. The authorities attempted to channel discontent over the miserable state of market
supplies with slogans concerning "the fight against speculation," which, of
course, did nothing to improve the situation. During the spring and summer
of 1947, industrial regions were hit by another wave of strikes, the largest
of them, in September, in Łódź. Among the strikers were thousands of PPS
and even PPR members. The situation only worsened when UNRRA aid,
which in 1946 amounted to 22 percent of national income (306 million dollars), was suspended. Since Poland refused to take part in discussions over
the Marshall Plan, the State Department discontinued all aid programs, and
all loans were cut off in mid-1946. The United States had no interest in aid-
ing hostile governments and thus strengthening the communist camp.

Nevertheless, the Polish government still had reserves that could easily
be mobilized, especially in the consumer industry. The Central Planning
Office, under the able leadership of Czesław Bobrowski and a group of prewar economists, had a major impact on the state's economic activity. Moreover, the PPR's chief economist, Hilary Minc, was not an advocate of
"jumping over" stages of development and proclaimed that the country still

needed "capitalist-market elements." Most factories were being managed by their former staff of engineers, while PPR (and PPS) organizations and officials were more concerned with political activity than with management issues. New methods were only beginning to germinate. Although Poland's first "Stakhanovite," made his appearance in July 1947, when miner Wincenty Pstrowski launched the slogan of "labor competition," generally speaking, rational principles of industrial production continued to prevail. Despite the cooling of political relations, trade with the West still accounted for 61 percent of all foreign trade in 1947, largely thanks to a boom in coal production after thousands of prisoners of war had been assigned to the mines. Tax discipline also improved, albeit as a result of drastic measures.

All in all, although life remained difficult, real wages increased markedly compared to the previous year and non-farm earnings were close to 1938 levels. For a large proportion of the rural population, the possession of their own farm was a source of satisfaction, some of it material satisfaction. As a result of the agrarian reform, more than one million families had received land, allowing them to establish a farm or expand their existing landholding. These people were not required to remember that land reform (although not necessarily this particular version) had been a central element in the program of the independent peasant movement. The road to social advancement was wide open, a road leading largely to positions in the rapidly expanding economic administration, and in the armed forces and the security apparatus. An increasing number of young people from rural areas entered institutions of higher education, and the measures taken to facilitate their access to higher schools and colleges after the student demonstrations of 3 May 1946 yielded their first fruit. The intelligentsia was under constant pressure, and the PPR managed to "capture" many intellectuals.

The direct influence of the ruling parties also expanded in scope as a result of the constant influx of new members. By the summer of 1947, the PPS had over 660,000 members, and by the end of the year the PPR had more that 820,000. A large proportion of those in possession of a party card undoubtedly had little interest in the finer points of ideology and felt little enthusiasm for party meetings. Many of them were practicing Catholics. But the very fact that they joined one of these parties helped to legitimize the authorities and made it possible for them to mobilize large groups, to organize rallies and demonstrations, and to expand their supervision of factories and social organizations. Given the destruction in 1947 of all institutions capable of crystallizing and articulating anticommunist sentiments, the population was deprived of any alternative programs and elites.

These functions were increasingly assumed by the Catholic Church. While refraining from involvement in directly political activity, the church presented, in a measured but emphatic manner, its position on all the major issues of public life. In protest against the falsification of the elections, the church rejected the authorities' request to hold a celebratory mass to give thanks for the "victory" of the democratic bloc. In a pastoral letter dated 8 September (in celebration of the birth of the Virgin Mary), the episcopate wrote of its desire for "an end to the unwarranted and unnecessary restriction of civil liberties." On 14 March 1947 church leaders delivered to Bierut a memorandum titled "Catholic Constitutional Demands." Alongside expressions of concern that Christian values should be respected when drawing up the new institutional framework for the state, the memorandum pointed to the need to respect civil liberties and private property, as well as the need to "ensure that the activity of state institutions will be based on law, that there will be no place for arbitrariness, the abuse of power, or the merging of police and political powers."

While still refraining from launching a direct assault on the church, the ruling group gradually expanded its interference in church life. In April 1947, for example, six monastic printing works were nationalized, and in May the Ministry of Public Security began to collect information about "the clergy's material basis." A pastoral letter read out in churches on 28 September 1947, in which the bishops protested against censorship, the abolition of religious instruction in schools, and "the pressure on Catholics to join political parties whose principles contradict our sacred faith," gave the PPR leadership the pretext it needed to declare war on the church. The next meeting of the Politburo "discussed a broad range of methods of struggle," and on 11 October, during a meeting of the Central Committee, many provincial party secretaries denounced the "clergy's offensive." The push to initiate a decisive "counteroffensive" was so strong that Gomułka felt obliged to restrain these moves, which he considered premature. At the same time, he declared that "for a long time to come the issue of the church will be the central political problem before us." On 29 October Prime Minister Cyrankiewicz told the Sejm that the church "is opposed to political stabilization." The era of relative tolerance and goodwill gestures—which had previously accompanied official attacks and harassment—was coming to an end.

Also coming to an end was the slogan of the "gentle revolution" in culture, whose chief spokesman (and enforcer) was Jerzy Borejsza. In the summer of 1947 Central Committee officials drew up a list of "themes to be addressed in creative activity" (including music) that were to be given priority by publishers and cultural institutions. At a meeting of the Central Committee in October, writer Jerzy Putrament declared that the party should "draw up a plan and undertake a systematic campaign to inoculate our work against the rotten influences of European capitalist backwardness." On 16 November, during the inauguration of radio broadcasting from Wrocław, Bolesław Bierut proclaimed that artistic works of all kinds should "reflect the great turning point that the nation is living through" and noted that, so far they had not "kept pace with the rapid and mighty current of present-day life." The era of "cultural revolution" had dawned, a revolution that was by no means confined to slogans and appeals, but involved the centralization of administration and the creation of agencies whose purpose was to steer the country's artists.

After 1947, when the legal opposition was eliminated, the possibilities of underground activity were drastically diminished, and the first "cleansing" of the PPS took place, the power of the PPR, which never been seriously under threat, became monopolistic in the literal sense of the word. The communists were in a position to cease their political struggle and turn their attention to putting their own house in order. They were also able to launch their battle against the church for "the hearts and minds" of the people.

THE STATE IN EXILE

When Poland's Western allies withdrew their recognition of the London government-in-exile, it was not only the large number of Poles in Western Europe at that time who faced an extremely difficult decision, but also, and above all, the political, military, and intellectual elites. During 1945–48 the vast majority of the 1.3 million Poles who had been forced laborers, prisoners of war, or concentration camp inmates in the western zone of occupied Germany or Western Europe returned home. They included around one hundred thousand out of 250,000 soldiers and officers of the Polish Armed Forces. A group of political activists who were associated with Mikołajczyk's government or supported his political line also decided to return; most of them were socialists, peasant movement activists, or Christian democrats. Returning military personnel included several dozen senior officers, among them several generals.

Most of those considered to be leaders or opinion formers elected, however, to remain in exile and continue activity within the existing institutions of the Second Republic—the state authorities, the army, and political parties and their newspapers and periodicals. By no means everyone was convinced that armed conflict between the British and Americans and Moscow was either imminent or inevitable, but most people assumed that the current state of affairs would prove temporary. The process of adaptation to the new environment and migration beyond Europe only began in earnest in 1947. At this point this new Polish diaspora dispersed, largely to the United States, Canada, Argentina, and Australia, where a series of ethnic Polish communities gradually emerged and only rarely took part in émigré political activity.

Although there was no shortage of political conflicts and polemics, until the summer of 1947 the focal point for the Polish émigré community was the president and the government, whose political composition had remained largely unchanged since Tomasz Arciszewski had become prime minister. At this time, however, apart from the issue of travel to Poland, the main problem for the émigré community as a whole was that of the army. The British, who were responsible for disbanding the army, clearly hoped that most of the soldiers would return to Poland, but tried to avoid bringing direct pressure to bear and did not agree to let Warsaw's nominee, General Karol Świerczewski, assume command of the forces. Nonetheless, the fact that the British were demobilizing their own enormous and costly war machine made it clear that there was no possibility in the long run of maintaining a Polish army, even one much reduced in size.

It was not until March 1946, however, that the first decisive steps were taken: the government-in-exile ordered the evacuation of the Second Corps from Italy to the British Isles, where the troops were to be demobilized gradually but without too much delay. On 3 September 1946, Arciszewski's government decided to disband the Polish Armed Forces and to recognize a unit newly created by the British, the Polish Training and Relocation Corps, headed by General Stanisław Kopański. It was the job of the corps to prepare soldiers for the return to civilian life, to teach them English, and to provide them with occupational training. The corps was finally disbanded in the spring of 1949, and most of its approximately 115,000 soldiers and officers remained in Britain. Other troops spent the transition period in the Polish Guard Units that were formed in the British and American zones of occupied Germany and initially involved nearly 100,000 soldiers.

The Poles considered that the continued existence of their exile state required that they retain at least the vestiges of a military organization. Military commanders and political leaders made numerous efforts to ensure that a military force of some kind remained in existence, even if in a much reduced form. In reality, though, there was no chance whatsoever of maintaining the Polish Army in exile. Even in the early 1950s, when the conflict between Moscow, London, and Washington was its height, the formation of a "Polish legion," for which General Anders argued (in France, Spain, and the United States), never got beyond the conceptual phase and was more of a political than a military project.

Nonetheless, the demobilized soldiers constituted—as did the former Home Army combatants in Poland—a formidable force that the politicians could not afford to ignore. It is not surprising that the Poles who stayed in the West after 1945 are frequently referred to as "the combat émigrés." A general armed forces organization, the Polish Combatants' Association, was soon (1946) formed, as were similar organizations for different branches of service—pilots and sharpshooters, for example. These émigrés, particularly those in Great Britain, were characterized by their high social status (among the members of the Training and Relocation Corps, about one in ten had completed secondary school at least, and one in a hundred was an engineer by training) and by their political commitment, which did not, however, translate into an influx of new people into political parties, old or new.

The second largest group was made up of the Displaced Persons (DPs) who inhabited dozens of camps on German territory. When these camps were finally closed down in the fall of 1951, they still contained about 120,000 Poles. Both in Great Britain and in the Western occupied zones of Germany, the new émigrés engaged in an exceptionally high level of social and political activity. They formed dozens of organizations; in Germany itself during 1945–49 they published some four hundred periodicals, and established Polish schools, nursing homes, quasi-academic colleges, and theaters. In the summer of 1945 an episcopal curia was established in Germany to serve both the DPs and Polish soldiers. All this meant that during the first few years after the end of the war there existed a kind of Polish state in exile. This state had several thousand "citizens" and was recognized by a substantial proportion of the population at home and by a large proportion of the old émigré community, especially in the United States, where the Polish-American Congress, founded in 1944, provided a focus for émigré activity and a network of communication between individual émigré organizations.

At this time the government and the army, as well as most of the political parties, maintained fairly systematic contacts with Poland. Many groups and organizations adopted a "dual-track policy" in one variant or another. In this regard the National Party was particularly active, taking advantage of the fact that one of its members, in his capacity as Minister of Internal Affairs, controlled the émigré government's channels of communication with the homeland. One of the tasks assigned to the couriers dispatched to Poland was to arrange for the most prominent members of the underground to escape abroad. Such arrangements were successful in the case of Jan Matłachowski (SN) and Zygmunt Zaremba (PPS). The underground sent its own, more or less official, representatives to London, among them Józef Maciołek, who set up the WiN Foreign Delegatura. From 1947 on, however, as the security service crushed the underground organizations, these contacts became increasingly rare, and the political life of the émigré community began to follow a different rhythm than that of the homeland.

For several reasons it can be said that the year 1947 brought to an end the first stage in the history of the postwar combatant and political émigrés. The last units of the Polish Armed Forces were disbanded, the main underground organizations in Poland were destroyed, several prominent politicians from the legal opposition (Mikołajczyk, Korboński, Bagiński, Popiel) made their way to the West, and émigrés, including Displaced Persons, resettled in ever more distant places. At the same time the agreement among the main political parties regarding the manner in which the president was to be appointed now broke down. President Raczkiewicz changed the procedures, in effect since 1944, for determining the selection of succeeding presidents and in so doing was considered to have broken the "Paris agreement" of 1939. Following his death on 6 June 1947 he was succeeded not by Tomasz Arciszewski, who had previously been designated to the position, but by the Piłsudski-ite Augustyn Zaleski, who had served as minister of foreign affairs during the years 1926–32 and 1939–41. He formed a new government, appointing General Tadeusz Bór-Komorowski as prime minister.

Most of the PPS now moved over to the opposition, as did the émigré group Independence and Democracy, the tiny Democratic Party, and part of the Labor Party. Together they formed, in June 1947, the Democratic Convergence (Koncentracja Demokratyczna). During 1948 Mikołajczyk and his party colleagues were quite active within the London émigré community. As a result, in November 1948 the PPS (except for a splinter group led by Adam Pragier), the PSL, and the SP signed the Agreement Among Democratic Parties. It should be noted that most of the signatories were people who had recently fled Poland (the three from the Peasant Party, together with Popiel, and Konrad Sieniewicz from the Labor Party) and that recent arrivals Zygmunt Zaremba and Franciszek Białas also played a major role in the Socialist Party. Despite the numerous differences among them, they represented a different way of looking at the Polish situation, one that emphasized the need to adapt émigré activity to the situation within Poland and the level of social resistance within the country, which was being expressed in forms other than that provided by traditional political parties.

The situation within the émigré political community—and the entire diaspora—was shaped by the fact that despite the deepening conflict with Stalin the Western powers (particularly the United States) had not yet worked out a coherent joint strategy. The doctrine of "containment" was in its infancy, and the Americans and British were most concerned to ensure political consolidation and economic stability in the part of Europe that was outside Moscow's direct sphere of influence. Their strategy toward Poland and the other countries of East-Central Europe was one of "passive presence," which implied that little attention would be paid to émigré circles. This was true even of the Polish émigré community, which was far ahead of others in terms of both its size and its level of organization.

CHAPTER 4

Constructing the Foundations

THE COMINFORM AND THE NEW COURSE

On 22 September 1947 a number of well-guarded villas in the foothills of the Sudety provided the setting for a meeting of communist party representatives from nine countries—the Soviet Union, Yugoslavia, Bulgaria, Hungary, Romania, Czechoslovakia, France, Italy, and Poland, the host of the event. The delegations were made up of high-level officials, but only in the case of Poland and Romania did the general secretary take part. Each party sent an official delegation of two people, usually activists responsible for international relations or ideological issues. The Polish delegates, Władysław Gomułka and Hilary Minc, were accompanied by four other members of the Politburo, one of whom, Roman Zambrowski, headed the secretariat that dealt with the organizational details of the meeting. The only members of the top leadership who remained in Warsaw were Marian Spychalski and Bolesław Bierut, still officially not a party member. A meeting at this level was a major event, and it is not surprising that virtually the entire PPR leadership made its way to Lower Silesia. Additional party representatives also accompanied the other delegations.

Preparations for the conference had been under way for at least six months, and more than a year earlier Stalin had referred to the need for closer cooperation and "exchange of experience" among the main European communist parties. The Soviet party made the formal, unpublicized, proposal to hold the meeting, seconded by the Yugoslavs. With the exception of Albania, which at this time was closely allied with Yugoslavia, all the ruling parties were represented, as were the two largest parties in Western Europe. A number of major parties were absent, including the German Socialist Unity Party from the Soviet-occupied zone of Germany and the German Communist Party from the western zones; also absent were the Finns and the Greeks, then involved in civil war. The French and Italian parties were essentially extras: both parties had resigned from a governing coalition in the spring of that year, each of them was becoming more and more extreme, and their chances of seizing power had diminished considerably.

Of the remainder—and leaving aside the Soviet and Yugoslav parties—only the Czechoslovak Communist Party still faced some problems at home and was not yet in complete control of the government. The conference agenda consisted of three items for discussion: the causes of differences in the "road to development" taken by individual countries, the prospects for the "people's democracies," and the reasons for the adverse situation of the French and Italian parties.

The principle report, "On the International Situation," was presented by Andrei Zhdanov. Its most important point was the assertion that the world was entering a period of confrontation between two camps, one of them "imperialist and antidemocratic," the other "anti-imperialist and democratic." One result of this emerging dichotomous world was the need for cooperation among communist parties and for these parties to acquire greater self-confidence. "The greatest danger at this time," declared Zhdanov, "is for the working class to underestimate its own strength and to overestimate the strength of the enemy." In virtually identical terms the discussants expressed their support for the argument advanced by one of Stalin's closest associates. The discussion did not specifically address the issue that Zhdanov had raised, concerning the need for "consultation and voluntary coordination of activity." The Yugoslavs and Bulgarians voiced especially harsh criticism of their West European comrades, and even Gomułka accused them of "opportunistic errors" consisting in the fact that each party had initially occupied a position in government similar to that of the Hungarian and Romanian communists but had failed to seize power. The critics overlooked just one minor detail—the Red Army had not marched into either France or Italy.

The main issue was, however, "coordination," or, to be exact, the creation of an organizational body that would undertake this activity. Despite the modest name—Information Bureau—to be given to this entity, there was reason to suspect that the Soviet Union, whose brainchild it was, intended the Bureau to function along the same lines as the Comintern. This possibility did not appeal to everyone, and it was Gomułka who most forcefully expressed reservations regarding the proposal. These focused on the broad scope of competence to be given to what came to be called the Cominform. Not everyone in the PPR leadership shared his opinion, however, and Gomułka, hitherto the party's undisputed leader, found himself at odds with his colleagues. Finally, with the approval of Stalin, who had maintained daily contact with Zhdanov, the meeting agreed to a somewhat restricted set of prerogatives for the Bureau. To emphasize that agreement had been reached, it was Gomułka who presented the concluding report: "Coordinating the Activity of Communist Parties." The meeting passed a resolution defining the tasks of the Bureau as "organizing the exchange of experience among parties and coordinating their activity—as the need arises—on the basis of mutual agreement." Initially the Bureau was to function without a permanent secretariat and would simply produce a joint publication, which was given a title couched in pure Orwellian Newspeak: *For a Lasting Peace, For People's Democracy.*

While Stalin now had at his disposal a convenient instrument of political pressure, the tone of Zhdanov's report and the statements of the other participants indicated an equally important development: the communist parties had to go on the offensive. The Sudety conference was a response to the end of the process whereby the communists had seized power all across East-Central Europe, making it possible to create a tightly knit and centrally steered bloc of satellite states. Although the Cominform was formally an interparty, not an intergovernmental, body, it was obvious, given the totalitarian nature of the system, that the aim was to create a unified state-military structure possessing both a united leadership and a common ideology. It was clear to the Western powers that while Moscow might not yet be ready for military or economic confrontation, it was now prepared to challenge them politically.

Going on the offensive had implications not only for the international situation but also for the internal situation of each country involved. For Poland, as for the other countries within the Soviet sphere of influence, it meant that the communist party had to "close ranks" and abandon the various elements of political camouflage it had hitherto been using. The first task was to liquidate the socialist or social-democratic parties, something that had so far been achieved (on 20 April 1946) only in the Soviet zone of occupied Germany. Of course, the slogan about the need for the "organic unity of the workers' movement" could be heard everywhere in 1945, but it was in the fall of 1947 that the issue acquired momentum. Formally speaking, Romania was the first (23 February 1948) to achieve this goal, but the other countries soon followed—even Czechoslovakia, where the communists were obliged to carry out what amounted to a coup d'état in order to gain complete power. "Organic unity" was achieved in more or less the same manner everywhere but with slight variations in terms of whether the process was initiated "from below" or "from above." In Czechoslovakia, for example, the maneuver was defined as unification "on the ideological and organizational basis" of the communist party, while in Hungary and Bulgaria the communists and socialists were merged at the local level before a national congress was held.

In Poland the process took a somewhat different course, and the country's "workers' movement" found itself bringing up the rear in the race for unity. At the PPS congress in December 1947, Gomułka declared that the two parties would "draw closer together not through the victory of one approach over another but through an intermingling." In February 1948, PPR leaders were still declaring—and this at an internal forum—that the party "will not insist on a faster pace." This did not, however, prevent them from simultaneously taking numerous steps to undermine the position of their socialist partner (for example, the Społem consumer cooperative, a PPS stronghold, faced a variety of bureaucratic obstacles, and Czesław Bobrowski was forced to resign as head of the Central Planning Office). Nevertheless, developments in other countries—where social democrats were joining the communist parties en bloc—and particularly the sudden changes in Czechoslovakia, caused the Politburo to declare, on 6 March 1948, that "events in the international area have created a new situation, a new stage in the workers' movement in Poland . . . in which the issue of its organic unity is undergoing rapid maturation." On 24 April leaders of both parties issued a joint circular dealing with preparations for unification. The pace of these developments was, however, slowed somewhat by a major crisis within the top leadership of the PPR.

Gomułka's reservations regarding the Cominform had already led to conflict between him and his closest associates and had also called into question his willingness to adapt to the new situation. At the beginning of April the CPSU Central Committee Department of International Relations compiled a memorandum titled "On Anti-Marxist Tendencies Within the Leadership of the PPR." Most of the accusations set out in the memorandum were backed up by quotations from Gomułka, although Spychalski and Minc were also cited.

The complaints became more serious with the escalation of the conflict between the Soviet Union and Yugoslavia, a conflict that played a major role in the Stalinization of East-Central Europe. Its basis lay in Moscow's mistrust of the Yugoslav communists, particularly their undisputed and sole leader, Josip Broz-Tito. An orthodox Leninist, he was the first to nationalize industry, establish a one-party system, launch a direct assault on religion, and begin collectivization. He also advocated a hard-line policy in relation to the West, supporting the Greek communists and advancing Yugoslavia's claims to Trieste. He and Georgi Dimitrov—the long-standing secretary of the Communist International and faithful executor of Stalin's wishes— considered creating a socialist federation of Balkan states. The Kremlin regarded this idea as highly undesirable and even dangerous, since it could undermine the Soviet authorities' power over the entire group of states.

Tito was a highly ambitious politician, and he doubtless assumed that as leader of such a federation he was destined to become "the Stalin of the Balkans." Yugoslavia differed from other states under communist rule in that it was less dependent on the Soviet Union for its very existence. While the Red Army had played a crucial role in liberating part of Serbia, Tito's partisan army was—at least, from mid-1943—the largest anti-Nazi force in the country. Thus Tito did not feel himself in any way obligated to Stalin and did not feel he owed him any thanks for "the victory of the Yugoslav revolution."

The conflict first erupted at the end of January 1948, when Yugoslavia produced a plan to send troops to southern Albania to resist any eventual intervention on the part of Greek government forces in their effort to eradicate base camps belonging to the communist guerrillas. Stalin strongly "reprimanded" Tito, arguing that the idea was irresponsible because it could give the British a pretext to meddle in the internal affairs of communist-ruled Albania. Although this was a relatively minor dispute and Yugoslav troops did not actually set foot on the territory of a neighboring state, Stalin clearly intended to heighten the conflict. Among other things, he recalled Soviet advisers from Yugoslavia and suspended existing economic agreements between the two countries. For a short time, sharply worded letters were dispatched directly to Belgrade, and the whole affair remained shrouded in secrecy. However, a letter dated 27 March, containing a long list of accusations and ominously comparing the Yugoslav leader to Trotsky, was distributed to all the parties belonging to the Cominform.

This constituted an unambiguous call to arms, a summons to take Stalin's side and jointly bring pressure to bear on the Yugoslavs. This simultaneously elevated the conflict to the international level. During the next few weeks, relations were further inflamed as Stalin searched for Yugoslav communists willing to oppose Tito. As a result, the whole conflict became public knowledge, and Tito took steps to maintain party discipline and loyalty to himself. A meeting of the Cominform was called in the second half of June. The first item on the agenda was "the Yugoslav question."

Gomulka—according to his biographer, Andrzej Werblan—"did not much admire Tito," but he nevertheless attempted to mediate the dispute, unmindful of the fact that the Kremlin did not care for uninvited go-be-tweens. The general secretary of the PPR had no idea that he had already been cast as a candidate "Polish Tito" (there were similar candidates in other countries). It is possible that his colleagues in the Politburo had no inkling either, but Gomułka's previous "slipups" could have been enough for them to begin distancing themselves. In all probability the division of labor between the nominally "nonparty" president and the leader of the PPR had begun to irk Bierut. Moreover, such a division was inconvenient at a time when power was becoming centralized; it did not mesh with the Soviet model and it disrupted the logic of the command structure. Gomułka, a tough and determined politician who also managed to be pragmatic and frequently condemned "sectarian tendencies," would have found his room for maneuver somewhat limited in a situation in which precisely such tend-encies were becoming a major element in the overall line.

The pretext for the attack was provided—as is often the case—by the candidate himself. On 3 June 1948, at a meeting of the Central Committee, Gomułka delivered an extensive report dealing with the historical, but im-portant, aspects of the "mutual intermingling" of the PPR and PPS. He re-called the "Luxemburgist errors "of the Social Democracy of Poland and the Kingdom of Lithuania and the Polish Communist Party, and after sharply criticizing the "reformism" of the prewar PPS he went on to state that, "the struggle for independence" was one of its "splendid traditions . . . that ought to form part of the basis of a united party." At a time when the unification of communist and socialist parties was everywhere accompanied by a chorus condemning the latter, Gomułka's statement sounded a discordant note, even if it was heard only by the initiated. Before the discussion was over, he was already in trouble. Five days later the Politburo, in the absence of the general secretary, issued a statement extremely critical of him. A week later Gomułka issued a reply, in which he retreated not one inch from the views he had expressed in his report, some of which he went on to express even more sharply.

The atmosphere became feverish. On 28 June the Cominform met in Bucharest (Berman and Zawadzki represented the PPR) to condemn Yugoslavia and take up the question of collectivization. A few days earlier the Soviet occupation authorities had begun a blockade of the Western sectors of Berlin. The Soviet Union's satellite states now had not only an external enemy in the shape of "imperialism," but also an internal enemy in the shape of "Titoism," and every country had to find its own Tito equivalent. It was the beginning of a period of internal communist party disputes, some of them more public than others; in all cases, however, the chief purpose was to identify victims for the sacrifice. In Bucharest, Lucretiu Patrascanu, one of the chief architects of the communist takeover, began to come under fire. The removal of László Rajk, one of the founders of Hungarian people's democracy, from his post as minister of internal affairs and his appointment to the essentially second-rank post of minister of foreign affairs marked the beginning of his road to the condemned cell. The clouds were gathering over the coleader of the Albanian communists, Koci Dzodze.

After 4 June Gomułka stopped attending meetings of the Politburo, which were now taking place with increasing frequency under the chairmanship of Bierut. At the beginning of July the formal head of the PPR left Warsaw to begin more than six weeks of compulsory vacation in Kowary, in the foothills of the Sudety. A meeting of the Central Committee on 6–7 July was attended by the "nonparty" president of the Polish Republic, who even gave a speech. His cospeaker was Marian Spychalski, Gomułka's close associate from their days in the underground and first deputy minister of defense, who categorically rejected Gomułka's line. Jakub Berman spoke about the PPR's ideological "contribution" and pointed to the need to "educate the party" in the spirit of intensifying class struggle. Aleksander Zawadzki discussed "the Yugoslav question." But perhaps the most important speech was delivered by Hilary Minc, who stated that "on the road of intense class struggle," "socialist elements" ought to subordinate and "expel" all elements of the capitalist economy. He also declared that the development of cooperative farming "will undermine the basis of rural capitalism and in the final analysis will destroy it."

Many people took part in the discussion, but only one of them (Władysław Bieńkowski) was bold enough to argue against Spychalski's position. The others generally "sharpened" the points that he and Bierut had made, and Bierut returned to the podium to emphasize the need to combat foreign intelligence and "the agents of imperialism." During July local party activists attended meetings where they discussed the recent deliberations and resolutions of the Central Committee. They were universally approved by acclamation, and the lower levels of the party were clearly "aroused" and ready to "intensify the class struggle." On 17 July, at a national meeting of the PPS, Cyrankiewicz simply stated that the socialist party "has arrived at the level of . . . Marxism-Leninism," thereby signaling the final and complete capitulation of his party.

In July and August the party leadership tried to persuade Gomułka to change his views, but he refused to yield. On 15 August, in a conversation with Stalin, Bierut outlined the situation in Poland, stating that "the rightist-nationalist deviation" had appeared "at the highest leadership level." He went on to suggest the personnel changes that could be made. Stalin's acceptance signaled his agreement to Gomułka now being condemned in public. Gomułka was still trying to defend himself, but additional arguments against him were produced by several members of the wartime underground PPR leadership, particularly Franciszek Jóźwiak and Kazimierz Mijal, who confirmed that their leader had indeed displayed a "defeatist" attitude during the first half of 1944.

It was not only among party leaders and local activists that tensions were increasing. Minc's July comments, repeated in numerous press reports and at party meetings, had given rise to great unease in the countryside. The peasants—as Minc himself reported to a meeting of the Politburo—began to bury stones along the boundary lines of their property to help them remember its exact location. There were also signs of a phenomenon well known to the Soviet architects of collectivization: peasants began to kill their livestock. Marked uneasiness was increasingly visible in the PPS, where the purge initiated from above was gathering strength and procommunist activists were becoming ever more bold. The process of ousting Mikolajczyk's supporters from the PSL had come to an end, and preparations to merge the party with the SL were under way. On 21 July 1948, in Wrocław, the country's youth organizations were merged; the newly formed Union of Polish Youth (ZMP) absorbed not only the communist Union of Fighting Youth and the socialist youth movement, but also the agrarian ZMW Wici and the youth organization belonging to the Democratic Party. The ZMP—whose first president was Janusz Zarzycki, a communist and previously head of the main Political Administration of the Polish Army—was an organization cut from the Soviet mold and was geared to a mass membership. The student organizations were also merged, to form the Union of Polish Academic Youth.

On 31 August yet another session of the Central Committee opened. The main report, "On the Rightist-Nationalist Deviation in the Party Leadership," was delivered by Bierut, who in this way officially took over the function of PPR leader. The report was actually one long political act of indictment against Gomułka, who offered a lengthy self-criticism while continuing to defend some of his views. This was considered inadequate, and during a marathon session lasting until 3 September the former party leader gradually retreated, admitting—under heavy pressure from committee members—that he had indeed made a series of mistakes. Finally he voted in favor of a resolution that itemized them all: he had undervalued the country's revolutionary traditions and the role in them of the struggle for independence; he had exaggerated the role of the PPS and had displayed erroneous tendencies in 1944; he had opposed the collectivization of agriculture advocated by the Cominform, and had defended the notion of the peaceful convergence of capitalism and socialism; he had shown mistrust of the Soviet Union, had downplayed the significance of the class struggle, and had demonstrated a conciliatory attitude toward Tito. Gomułka was finished politically; he and his closest associates were now relegated to the sidelines.

This phase of the struggle against "deviation," however, went no further than ideological incantation. Gomułka remained in the Politburo, and he remained deputy prime minister and minister for the reclaimed territories, although he was simply a figurehead. A few people were demoted in the party hierarchy. Several others, including Franciszek Jóźwiak and Edward Ochab, were promoted. All in all, these maneuvers were insignificant and, it would soon transpire, did not satisfy the party's "local *aktiv*," who demanded more severe penalties at meetings held several days after the Central Committee deliberations. On 6 September the PPS leadership expressed its full support for the new line and its satisfaction at Bierut's return "to an active and leading role in the workers' movement." On 11 September the Peasant Party expressed a similar opinion, on 14 September—the Democratic Party, and on 17 September—the PPR's trade union activists.

While all this was going on, the rest of the population remained passive onlookers. It was not until November that the public was mobilized in a campaign designed to demonstrate popular support for the unification of the PPR and PPS. Unification was preceded by a growing wave of "cleansing" in the party ranks. Some eighty-two thousand people (about 13 percent of the membership) were expelled from, or left, the PPS; in the case of the PPR, the number was twenty-nine thousand (3 percent). While the socialists expelled many party activists, including many at higher levels, the communists confined themselves to eliminating "alien-class elements," although some PPR meetings became a stage for a savage settling of accounts with "the carriers of deviation" and were conducted in an atmosphere of mutual distrust. There had been earlier polemics and sharply worded criticism—at which Gomułka, among others, excelled—but the mass campaign that began among the party elite in June and then spread to the lower levels after 3 September was (in the language of the then current Newspeak) "a new quality." Anyone could become the victim of hostile propaganda and of the security service—not just an actual or potential enemy of the authorities but literally anyone, regardless of the position that he or she held in the state or party hierarchy.

In this situation the unification congress of the PPR and PPS, which finally took place on 15–21 December in the building of the Warsaw Polytechnic, was essentially a ritual event. It was accompanied by countless pledges to increase production and accelerate "plan fulfillment" (usually to the detriment of quality of output), and by the launching of new investment projects; mass meetings were organized, and factories and streets were decorated with flags and banners; a "youth relay," in which 12,500 young people took part, raced into Warsaw; congress delegates received ceremonial send-offs from assembled crowds at their home-town train stations; the names of streets and squares were changed (the square in front of the polytechnic was renamed Worker Unity Square on the first anniversary of the congress).

The elevated tone of the proceedings themselves was not disrupted for long by Gomułka. At Stalin's unambiguous request, he was not only elected a delegate, but was allowed to address the congress and was even elected to the Central Committee, albeit with the fewest votes of all those elected. In a dramatic speech the former general secretary defended not so much his views as his good name, displaying, for all his communist orthodoxy, considerable courage and strength of character. On 9 December, during a lengthy discussion with Stalin, Molotov, and Beria, Gomułka had bluntly set out the reasons why he did not wish to take part in the work of the Politburo, despite pressure to do so on their part. At the congress, Bierut declared that Gomułka had demonstrated a remarkable disregard for party discipline, but the congress imposed no drastic penalties on the miscreant.

Bierut and Cyrankiewicz delivered the main congress reports, both of them similar in tone and content, while Minc presented an economic report in which he laid out the guidelines for the six-year plan (1950–55), a plan for "building the foundations of socialism." Implementation of this plan was to be directed by the Polish United Workers' Party.

COLD WAR: THE FIRST SKIRMISHES

The division of Europe that had become increasingly visible during 1947 became final in 1948, and in the fall of the following year it was strengthened even further by the creation of two German states—a situation that was to last more than forty years. Given the divergence in interests of the parties involved, there was no hope of reaching an agreement on the future of Germany, and the Western Allies came to the conclusion that unilateral action was the most appropriate course open to them. During lengthy negotiations lasting from 23 February to 2 June 1948 the three Western powers and the three Benelux countries worked out an agreement on implementing the Marshall Plan in the zones of Germany occupied by the Western powers and—more important—creating a single, federal, German state in that part of the country.

The first step was to demarcate the country's economic boundaries, and on 18 June a new currency was introduced. Stalin responded by blockading all roads into the Western-occupied sectors of Berlin, which gave the Americans an opportunity to demonstrate their technological strength: in record time they organized an airlift, which eventually flew in 800,000 tons of supplies a day. The success of this operation had a pronounced effect on attitudes in Western Europe, where communists had considerable influence, although the failure of the giant wave of strikes in late 1947 and early 1948 provided evidence that this influence was on the wane.

Both camps closed in on themselves, trade contacts diminished, and Anglo-Saxon and French culture were repudiated and replaced by "socialist realism" in the countries east of the Elbe. In January 1949, the Council of Europe was formed, and on 4 April, in Washington, twelve states signed the founding document of the North Atlantic Treaty Organization, creating a strong military alliance based on a common military strategy and integrated command structure. The fact that on 15 May 1949 the Soviet Army suspended its blockade of Berlin signified Moscow's acceptance of the status quo in Europe. It did not, though, signify a defeat for Stalin, particularly as less than three months later TASS announced that the Soviet Union had carried out a successful test explosion of an atomic bomb, an event that was confirmed shortly afterwards by U.S. Air Force reconnaissance flights. From that moment on, the "atomic umbrella" was extended over the entire globe.

Cold war became the only real form of conflict, at least in Europe. It raged with considerable force, and the Soviet Union appeared to have the advantage in that not only could it claim a monopoly on propaganda inside its own bloc but it was also able to take advantage of the democratic institutions in the West. Intellectuals in the Cause of Peace, a movement that began modestly, held its first demonstration in Wrocław in August 1948 and soon thereafter became a weapon in the Soviet Union's political arsenal. It was renamed The World Congress in Defense of Peace, and its slogans had little in common with those of traditional pacifism: "We are a growing and resolute force," proclaimed a resolution passed in April 1949, "capable of checking the ambitions of the warmongers and imposing peace." A popular saying of that time declared: "We shall defend peace until not a single stone is left standing." In March 1950 the Congress issued the so-called Stockholm Appeal, demanding a ban on all atomic weapons. According to the organizers, more than 270 million people (including eighteen million Poles) signed the appeal, and nearly 600 million signed the Berlin Appeal of February 1951.

In the countries belonging to the socialist camp, the campaign to collect signatures was conducted in an atmosphere of collective hysteria that was deliberately manufactured with the aim of drawing large numbers of people into activity directed from above. In Western Europe several factors undermined the effectiveness of Soviet policy, including the relatively rapid recovery from the postwar economic crisis. Despite continuing difficulties, industrial production was growing, unemployment was falling, and trade was on the increase. The Marshall Plan played a major role in this recovery: by June 1950, Europe had received an infusion of 9.4 million dollars. Germany had suffered the greatest destruction, but soon after the creation of the Federal Republic (21 September 1949) the country began to experience an "economic miracle" under the leadership of Ludwig Erhard and his ideas concerning the social market economy.

While the conflict in Europe remained within the limits of cold war, a new theater of confrontation opened in the Far East. During 1949 Chinese communist forces finally defeated the army of Chiang Kai-shek, and on 1 October in Beijing Mao Zedong ceremonially announced the birth of the Chinese People's Republic. Five months later in Moscow, China and the Soviet Union pledged their commitment to "friendship, alliance, and mutual assistance," in a treaty similar to those that the Soviet Union had signed with the European "people's democracies." There thus arose a powerful, Euro-Asiatic bloc with a shared ideology and common political and military aims—the first step toward the creation of Orwell's terrifying vision. Again, as in the years 1944–47, the scales seemed to be weighted in favor of Stalin; on the occasion of his seventieth birthday in December 1949 he was proclaimed the Father of Nations and the Standard-Bearer of Peace and became the object of an idolatrous cult reaching far beyond the borders of the Soviet Union.

This time, the test came not in the form of a defensive action along the lines of the Berlin blockade, but as an armed attack. On 25 June 1950, when signatures were still being collected for the Stockholm Appeal, the Democratic People's Republic of Korea, under the leadership of Kim Il Sung (a captain in the Red Army at the Battle of Stalingrad), dispatched seven army divisions across the thirty-eighth parallel, the line that the Yalta treaty had designated as the boundary between areas of Soviet and American military action against Japan. During a bloody struggle lasting nearly a year, the Republic of Korea was actively supported by the United States and its fourteen allies, which fought under the flag of the United Nations, while North Korea was directly supported by China and received indirect assistance (in the form of weapons, special training, and logistical support) from the Soviet Union and its satellites. The conflict, which resulted in at least 3.5 million casualties, nearly 150,000 of them Americans, ended in compromise. Nevertheless, the East-West confrontation that had initially centered on Europe intensified, helping Stalin to tighten his grip—in fact, his rule—over the entire "peace-loving bloc." The Americans searched frantically for ways to mount resistance, strengthening their military and economic presence in the Pacific region, a task that seemed all the more urgent as China had emerged from the Korean War without any sense of having suffered a defeat.

Despite the apparent peace in Europe, Western Europe felt itself severely threatened and took increasingly energetic measures to foster integration, which had begun in 1950 with the formation of the Franco-German coal and steel community, the brainchild of Robert Schuman. Two years later, this project was expanded to become the European Coal and Steel Community, made up of France, Italy, the Federal Republic of Germany, and the Benelux countries. Military integration proved more difficult to achieve and remained within the broad framework of NATO without expanding to the operational level. Although the countries of Western Europe—and only some of them, at that—actually drew closer together only in the economic sphere, the Kremlin viewed these measures with great suspicion, and its propaganda depicted them as tantamount to a *casus belli*. Also important was the fact that the these moves toward integration helped to strengthen the West European economies at a time when they were recovering from the postwar crisis and entering a phase of rapid development and modernization, a process that had a positive effect on the other countries of Western Europe, including Scandinavia.

Although economic rivalry was inevitable, none of the larger states acquired a dominant position, a factor that helped to give the region the stability it needed to deal with the perceived threat from the Soviet Union. The Soviet plan for economic integration was implemented by a body set up in 1949, the Council on Mutual Economic Assistance (CMEA, or Comecon). Apart from the shortcomings that derived from its high level of centralization and subordination to purely political directives, Comecon had an additional major defect as far as its non-Soviet members were concerned: it was dominated by one state and, despite its promising name, was essentially an instrument to control the weaker partners and make them dependent on the Soviet Union; it also hindered their contacts with outside countries.

With the rhetoric of its propaganda and the creation of separate economic institutions, the Cold War not only increased mutual mistrust but also laid a permanent foundation for the division of Europe, a division that was further strengthened by the fact that it corresponded roughly with the centuries-old division between the prosperous West and the impoverished East.

"LET US BUILD A NEW HOME"

The measures introduced in 1947 in the effort to restrict private trade and manufacturing (including handicraft production) and the considerable taxes imposed on midsized and larger farms had a perceptible impact in 1948; among other things, the number of private factories and shops declined. Nevertheless, living standards improved noticeably. Rationing was gradually abolished for many items (including, sugar, potatoes, bread, flour, coal, and knitwear), and increased investment expenditure resulted in more jobs. The PPR leadership considered the three-year (1947–49) plan of reconstruction to be proceeding successfully and assumed that the plan targets, which involved achieving 1938 levels in all major sectors by 1949, would be met. However, the changing international situation and the associated changes in the "ideological climate," so visible during the conference at Szklarska Poręba, caused the party leadership to outline a new vision of the process of accelerated industrialization. With the emasculation of the PPS, the moderate industrialization plan (the so-called Drewnowski plan) was cast aside, and preparations began for a far more ambitious plan covering a six-year period (beginning in 1950) that would "harmonize" the rhythm of Polish plans with that of the Soviet five-year plans (the six-year plan would end in 1955). In the fall of 1948 the banking system was reorganized to make it more similar to the Soviet system, and it was decided to incorporate into the state budget the surplus from insurance of all kinds.

The unification congress adopted the theses of the six-year plan, according to which industrial output was to increase by 85–95 percent in comparison with 1949, and agricultural output was to rise by 35–45 percent. The plan posited that national income would increase by 70–80 percent and living standards—by 55–60 percent. This was an ambitious program calling for a huge investment effort, but in favorable circumstances, with good harvests and assuming that enough investment capital could be found, it was actually quite realistic, especially given the relatively low starting point. The problem was, however, that after being occupied by its two neighbors—both of which essentially engaged in an enormous expropriation of assets—after nationalization and the seizure of the larger landholdings, after the blows aimed at private production, and after refusing all possibilities of foreign loans and foreign capital, the costs of this effort would have to be borne by the population. And, as future events were to show, by the very social groups that, according to official ideology, were supposed to benefit from the changes.

To achieve these goals the authorities introduced major changes into the whole system of economic administration and management. In February 1949 the Central Planning Office was replaced by the State Economic Planning Commission (PKPG), modeled on the Soviet Gosplan, which was to be the central overseer of what subsequently came to be known as the command-distribution system. At the same time, the Ministry of Industry and Trade, which had already grown enormously (25 departments, 20 administrative boards, 21 scientific-research institutes, 56 trade centers, and 17 supply and distribution centers) was divided into six "branch" ministries. These multiplied considerably over time and came to include ministries for meat and dairy products, urban and housing construction, industrial construction, building materials, wood and paper products, and so on. By 1952 there were already thirty-four ministries, of which two-thirds were branch ministries, while eight deputy prime ministers were members of the Government Presidium, a body that was established in May 1950. Below the ministries were several dozen "administrative boards," creating a second level of administration (or third if we include the Planning Commission).

An enormous bureaucratic machine rapidly emerged, which simultaneously served as a ladder for the social advancement of those members of the "lower" strata eager to occupy a place in the power structure, broadly defined. During the years 1945–49, then regarded as the years of "the Polish revolution," some seventeen thousand manual workers moved into managerial positions in the economy and in the party apparatus, but during the first half of the six-year plan alone (1950–52), as many as 115,000 people made a similar transition. They not only moved into newly created positions but also ousted "old specialists" from their posts. This whole structure became totally ossified, inflated beyond measure, and characterized not only by a strictly observed hierarchy but also by a total lack of competence.

Equally important, and perhaps more so, was the successive raising of plan targets. This was done first in May and again in December 1949, before the six-year plan had even started. The next, and largest, revision took place in July 1950 and was associated with the increase in international tensions following the North Korean invasion. The "Law on the Six-Year Plan of Economic Development and Construction of the Foundations of Socialism," passed at that time, proposed an increase of 158 percent in industrial output over the level achieved in 1949 and a 50 percent increase in agricultural production, including a 68 percent increase in livestock. The planners were more cautious when it came to the growth of real wages, leaving the earlier targets unchanged.

An important component in the revised plan was the Polish-Soviet agreement, signed on 29 June 1950, dealing with deliveries of investment goods and raw materials as well as armaments and military equipment. The agreement tied Poland's economy to that of the USSR; and while it provided access to an enormous raw-materials market, it also involved the import of energy- and material-intensive technologies that formed the basis for a wide range of investment projects, effectively condemning Poland to long-term dependence on an economy with an extremely low propensity to innovate.

Plan revisions were not confined to raising output targets, but also involved changes in the proportion of funds allocated to consumption and accumulation and in the amount allocated to different branches of the economy. The investment quota increased at the expense of consumption, and by 1953 accounted for 28.5 percent of national income (compared to 15.8 percent in 1949). At the same time, there was a marked increase in the resources allocated to the means of production (heavy industry and raw materials), which in 1952 amounted to 42.7 percent of all investment expenditure. Light industry and foodstuffs were "condemned" from the very beginning of the plan: in 1950, they accounted for nearly one half of gross output, but received less than 12 percent of investment expenditure. This state of affairs remained virtually unchanged during subsequent years.

Investment in agriculture was sharply restricted, falling to 7.8 percent of total investment in 1952. While the ratio of investment in agriculture and industry in 1948 had been 1:2.8 in favor of industry, four years later industry received 6.5 times the resources allocated to agriculture. A range of polices were devised to encourage collectivization, and the policy of establishing state farms remained in effect. In 1954, roughly 9,300 collective farms occupied about 8 percent of arable land, and state farms occupied nearly 10 percent. Despite the fact that the productivity of the "socialized sector" was considerably below that of individual peasant farms, the former absorbed an ever-larger proportion of agricultural investment credit and expenditure (about 72 percent in 1955), while private farmers were burdened with ever higher taxes. Although the Polish leadership did not introduce "anti-kulak" measures of the kind undertaken by Stalin in 1930–32, the lower levels of the police and security service harassed the peasantry in numerous ways. Particularly strong pressure was brought to bear in relation to the system of compulsory deliveries gradually introduced during 1951–52, first for grain, then for pigs, and finally for milk. In 1953 compulsory deliveries accounted for 85 percent of grain output, 51 percent of potatoes, and 50 percent of slaughter animals. Failure to meet one's quota of deliveries and "negligence" during sowing, harvesting, or ditch-digging campaigns were punishable not only by fines but also by a term in jail or labor camp.

The "construction of the foundations of socialism" was based on a strategy of extensive economic development, and the modernization of existing plants was a task for the distant future. The "investment front" was developed with great speed, while at the same time many decisions were essentially political in nature—for example, the well-known decision to build the massive iron and steel works on the outskirts of "reactionary" Kraków. The scale of the investment effort resulted in constant imbalances in the supply of energy and in industrial output, causing a succession of bottlenecks; success in dealing with one such inevitably gave rise to others in different branches or regions.

Migration from the countryside to the towns took place on a mass scale, involving more than 1.9 million people during the years 1951–55. For these people, flight from the overpopulated, impoverished, backward, and now persecuted countryside was the first step in social advancement, but the campaign nature of this mobilization and the fact that factory work was so poorly organized meant that productivity remained below the level of 1939. Some phases of large-scale investment, especially those carried out by the work brigades of the Polish Service, which provided employment and rudimentary wages to young people from rural areas and small towns, were more akin to public works projects than to the construction of modern industry. Various forms of forced labor were also used. Military draftees deemed to be "politically suspect" or of "undesirable class background" were dispatched to the Coal Mining Corps, established in the spring of 1949. By 1953, thirty-one thousand such people were "serving" in the corps. From their meager wages, one-fifth of those paid to civilian miners, they had to cover not only the cost of their food and board and work clothing, but also management salaries. It is not surprising, then, that daily per capita coal production fell from 1,328 kilograms in 1949 to 1,163 kilograms in 1955, just 38 percent of per capita output in 1938.

Perhaps this was an extreme example, but low productivity was the norm rather than the exception. The highly publicized periodic campaigns of labor competition did little to alleviate the problem, frequently disrupted the production process, and of course, generated resentment and hostility in the workplace. Even more propagandistic in nature—and negative in terms of effect on output—were the various kinds of "production pledges," involving the completion of an investment project or the start-up of a new assembly line to commemorate a state holiday or a political event without regard to technological requirements or real state of readiness. Industrial— and agricultural—production was also adversely affected by the "spy mania" aroused by official propaganda and by the search for "saboteurs" and "subversives" that accompanied every breakdown or even failure to fulfill the plan. People who had trained and worked as engineers and economists before the war were at particular risk of being targeted, as were former Home Army soldiers and "Anders's agents." Increasingly, production problems were investigated not by experts but by security service officials.

From the quantitative point of view, industry developed at a genuinely rapid pace, although the rate of growth declined—something that the CUP had predicted and the PKPG had rejected as a possibility. The highest rate of growth—27.7 percent—occurred in 1950; as the investment front broadened, the rate of growth in heavy industry declined. Moreover, plan indicators for growth in output were lower than the rate of growth before the six-year plan, when rebuilt factories were the main source of production. The lengthening of the investment cycle became a permanent element of the Polish economy, a feature that it shared with all other economies subject to central planning and administration. Nevertheless, the economic landscape underwent pronounced changes, and Poland gradually became an industrial-agrarian state. Numerous factories were built, and even if they did not meet the technological standards of the time, they produced goods that were needed in the modernization process. The flagships of socialist construction included the Lenin Iron and Steel Works in the new town of Nowa Huta, outside Kraków, which began production in 1953; electric power plants in Jaworzno and Miechowice; the aluminum plant in Skawina; the Fasty plant in Białystok; the factory producing penicillin in Tarchomina, near Warsaw; the Stilon plant in Gorzów; and the FSO and FSC automobile and truck plants in Warsaw and Lublin.

Similar processes took place in the other countries dependent on the Soviet Union, and the lower their level of development, of course, the more rapid the rate of growth of industrial output. Western Europe was also growing fast, and the German "economic miracle" brought particularly rapid results. Between 1948 and 1955, industrial production in France and Italy almost doubled, and Austria's growth rate was similar to that of Germany.

Even if we take account of the shortcomings in Poland's "great leap forward" in industrial production, it can still be counted a success in comparison with the situation in agriculture, which paid political and ideological tribute to policies favoring the socialized sector, with its low productivity and loss of manpower. In 1950 agricultural output still had some momentum and grew by 7.5 percent (compared with 27.7 percent in industry) but it then declined over the next three years until it was at the level it had been at the beginning of the six-year plan. This led to constant food shortages in the towns and to the pauperization of the villages, where peasant farms rapidly became decapitalized. The worker-peasants, who in later years increased the flow of money to the villages, were only just emerging as a social stratum and had little effect on the economic situation of the rural population. The small towns that had traditionally lived off trading and processing agricultural products also fell victim to the pauperization of the countryside and the emergence of the state agricultural purchasing apparatus. They were not usually chosen as the site of large-scale industrial investment, which tended to be concentrated in traditionally industrial areas or their immediate surroundings. Small towns and urban settlements in the Regained Territories were in a particularly difficult situation, since state farms occupied nearly one-third of all arable land in the region, and a large area was under the control of the Soviet Army and its network of firing ranges and military camps. This region, especially the whole northern belt, had been abandoned or neglected, and the new inhabitants continued to feel insecure. Their sense of insecurity was heightened by the endless "campaign for peace" and the constant references to the German threat, which seemed to suggest that war was imminent.

The enormous plan to transform the economy placed a huge burden on the entire population, a burden that was made even heavier by monetary measures that the authorities took with the aim of increasing the flow of resources to the state coffers. The first such measure was the monetary reform carried out on 30 October 1950, an operation in which the government's margin of profit, or seigneurage, amounted to roughly 9.5 percent of the annual budget revenue. While this maneuver undermined public confidence in the złoty, it did nothing to dampen inflation, and the amount of money in circulation grew far more rapidly than the supply of goods and services. The second attempt to mop up excess liquidity was carried out in a rather more subtle fashion—in the form of savings bonds issued by the National Fund for the Development of Poland, an agency established in June 1951. Nearly 8.5 million people purchased bonds, but despite strong pressure at the workplace and an intensive propaganda campaign, the funds generated barely amounted to 1.7 percent of the annual budget.

On a number of occasions the authorities carried out wide-ranging price increases without any compensating increase in wages or reduction in the price of selected items. The first price increase—on 31 December 1949—took place at the beginning of the six-year plan; and the second, much greater in its impact, was carried out on 3 January 1953, at the same time that rationing was abolished. The latter was especially painful as the country was entering its third year of widespread austerity. As a result of all this, in 1953 real wages in the socialized sector fell below the level of 1949, consumption of meat and sugar declined, and expenditure on food absorbed nearly 70 percent of family income in the towns.

The well-entrenched system of shortages created opportunities to re-distribute a small proportion of national income and to use the resources thus generated to fund a special system of remuneration and to foster a particular kind of corruption. Beneficiaries of this system included not only members of the political elite and (some) employees of the most vital ele-ments in the power structure, but also writers and artists, who were thus encouraged to legitimize the system, as well as "leading workers," who al-legedly were also exemplary citizens. Entire occupational groups or branches of the economy were promoted in the same manner. Great care was taken to conceal the fact that those who were showered with medals, who were provided with vouchers for a variety of consumer goods unavail-able in the stores, who were favored with a dignitary's handshake, those miners who fulfilled the plan ahead of time worked alongside the young men from the Mining Corps, rotting in the mines and starving in their dreary barracks.

One of the characteristic features of this epoch were the massive para-doxes of precisely this kind. "Thousands of hearts, millions of hands / but our hearts beat as one" was a refrain sung during countless parades and mass meetings. And hundreds of thousands of people of all ages and from all walks of life did indeed take to the streets on 1 May or 22 July. Banners and placards enlivened every demonstration, and broad smiles greeted whoever happened to have a place on the viewing stand. People who were awarded medals threw out their chest with pride. Young workers, who only a few years previously had left their impoverished villages, enthusiastically went through the motions of laying bricks, felling trees, and tightening screws. Led by a chorus of megaphones, the crowds shouted, "Long live . . ." or "Down with . . ." Perhaps this well-organized and carefully nurtured en-thusiasm became increasingly insistent as living conditions worsened, as fewer and fewer goods could be bought with the monthly wage, as power outages became more and more frequent. It seems as though by chanting people sought to stifle their doubts, to believe in the words of the slogans and the songs they heard everywhere. This enthusiasm was defended, not only by those who orchestrated or nurtured it, but also by many who had recently abandoned their family homes and who remembered the poverty and misery of a few years earlier, even the unemployment and bleak prospects of the prewar years.

Even though the economy was—as it soon came to be called—a make-believe economy, the whole country seemed to be one huge construction site in which there was a place for everyone who was willing and able. Towns were rebuilt, the countryside received electricity, and smoke rose from the chimneys of an ever increasing number of new factories. "Everything in Poland that is young and beautiful / marches under our banners," went another popular song of the time. Many, very many, people really wanted to be young and beautiful. If not immediately, then after a few years down the road, when they had finished building "the foundations of socialism."

THE APPARAT AND APPARATCHIKS

By 1944 institutions and organizations based on the Stalinist model were already emerging in Poland, the communist party had achieved dominance, and the country had become completely dependent on its powerful neighbor—all of this against the will of a decided majority of the population. Nevertheless, many features that did not fit the Soviet model of the totalitarian state remained in effect for a certain period of time. Since a similar situation existed in the USSR's other satellite states, this mixture could not really be called "the Polish road to socialism." Rather, it was a specific transitional stage, which reduced the external and internal costs of the great transformation that was the dream of the local communists and their counterparts in Moscow. Once the Cold War was severely restricting the influence of the Western powers, and the internal enemy—the opposition and the underground—had been totally destroyed, there was nothing to prevent the completion, in all spheres of public life, of the project that had been started.

The engine of change, and its chief executive, was the Polish United Workers' Party (PZPR). This party was essentially the former PPR in another guise, since it was the political platform and ideological credo of the latter that provided its basis. The PZPR—referred to then and for many years to come as "the Party" with a capital "p"—was, as the PPR had been before it, a party based on the principle of so-called democratic centralism, an organizational concept that essentially amounted to a variant of the military command system. After Gomułka had been removed from power, the PZPR had a single leader, Bolesław Bierut, who stood at the head of an extensive hierarchy. This stretched from the Politburo of the Central Committee and a few other central party agencies (such as the Central Committee Secretariat and the Organizational Bureau, known as the Orgburo) to the province (*województwo*) and district (*powiat*) committees and their de facto equivalents in some central administrative agencies and large industrial plants, to the commune (*gmina*) committees and the primary party organizations (POP). At each level there was a full-time staff, known as the "executive," and a committee, often referred to as "the plenum." In accordance with the classic separation of powers, the basic unit at each level was the party conference or congress. In addition to the executives, there were various control bodies—revision commissions and party control commissions. Although all positions were officially filled by election, the whole system was actually based on the principle of nomination and co-optation from above. This state of affairs resulted not so much from the fact that the party continued to function according to the principles required of an illegal (KPP) or clandestine (PPR) organization, as from Bolshevik tradition, and it confirmed the old thesis of Robert Michels concerning "the iron law of oligarchy."

A relatively large number of people occupied positions at the higher levels of the hierarchy, but the very "summit," the real central leadership, consisted of no more than a few dozen people, of whom a group numbering between ten and twenty were the real decision makers. They included members (and candidate members) of the Politburo, of whom there were never more than fifteen. It was they who simultaneously constituted other key agencies at the central level—the Secretariat (six persons) and Secretariat of the Orgburo; Politburo members included Central Committee secretaries (five or six people) and made up one half of the twenty-four members of the Central Committee Orgburo. They constituted the core of its two standing committees—on state security and defense—which did not have equivalent departments within the Central Committee apparatus. Thus although there were numerous central agencies, they were made up of the same small group of people, each of whom held numerous positions in the party leadership (Bierut, for example, held as many as five different posts at once). The principle was that each of them simultaneously occupied a position in the government, the Sejm, or the Council of State. During 1948–56 only eighteen people were either full or candidate members of the Politburo. This group was extremely stable: of the fifteen members elected in December 1948, only two (Marian Spychalski and Henryk Świątkowski) had left by the time Bierut died, and only three others had been co-opted (Konstanty Rokossowski, Zenon Nowak, and Władysław Dworakowski).

Bierut, born in 1892 and the oldest member of the group, was plainly and indisputably its leader, but among the remainder, some clearly were more equal than others, a fact that was not necessarily related to the importance of the additional positions they occupied in the state apparatus. Three of the four former PPS members—Henryk Świątkowski, Adam Rapacki, and Stefan Matuszewski—were clearly overshadowed by their colleague Józef Cyrankiewicz, chairman of the Council of Ministers (during 1952–54, deputy chairman). While Rokossowski had supreme command of the Ministry of Defense and Radkiewicz enjoyed a similar situation at the Ministry of Public Security, both of them were subject to oversight by separate Politburo commissions, each of which was chaired by Bierut.

It is generally agreed that both Jakub Berman and Hilary Minc played a decisive role alongside Bierut, and some analysts also include Roman Zambrowski in this inner circle. This is the configuration that most probably existed during the years immediately following the formation of the PZPR, but a number of factors suggest that it began to change in the spring of 1950, when Franciszek Mazur and Zenon Nowak, whose work focused on the party apparatus, began to move up the hierarchy. In the fall of 1952, after the election of a new Sejm, Mazur joined Bierut and Berman as one of the chief managers of the political arena, finally ousting Zambrowski from his position of influence. In 1954 Minc, for many years in charge of economic policy, was the one to be demoted.

In one way or another, all of them—apart from the four PPS members and Rokossowski—came from the prewar Communist Party, whose members played a major role in the PZPR; in 1954, for example, 27 percent of officials employed in the Central Committee apparatus were former members of the KPP or its youth organization. It should be noted that Mazur and Nowak, who advanced rapidly up the hierarchy, were the two most closely linked to the Soviet Union. The former had joined the CPSU in 1919, had been a member of the KPP Central Committee during 1930–38, and after returning to Poland in 1945 was for many years head of the Central Committee Organizational Department (in both the PPR and PZPR). Nowak had served in the Red Army and remained in the Soviet armed forces after the war, not returning to Poland until 1947. This central leadership was supported by the Central Committee—in its administrative rather than decision-making capacity. In December 1948 the committee had seventy-two full and fifty-eight candidate members, and there was little turnover in membership. During the five years preceding the Second Congress in the spring of 1954, eight people were removed from the committee, and a further nine were removed at the congress itself. The main targets of these purges were former PPS members and, in 1949, Gomułka supporters. Virtually all the Central Committee members were employed in the party apparatus, from the level of first secretary of the provincial committees on up, were heads of Central Committee departments, or held central positions in the state administration. Committee members thus constituted the real central *aktiv* of the PZPR. In the period immediately following the unification congress, they included many former PPS members who acquired posts in the leadership by virtue of their prominence in their former party and who were gradually relegated to secondary positions.

The relative stability of the committee membership did not mean that there was no movement within the executive apparatus. The heads of committee departments and their deputies changed quite frequently, and during 1949–51 positions within the regional apparatus were constantly being reshuffled. In 1949 changes were made in eleven out of the fifteen provincial committees, and there were cases (in Bydgoszcz, for example) where within a single year the position of first secretary was occupied by three people in succession. In Łódź province, the first secretary changed four times over the course of two years. Some apparatus employees wandered all over the organizational landscape, dispatched from one province to another, often three or four times. Mobility within the regional level was mostly horizontal: out of fifty-two people occupying the position of provincial first secretary during the period 1948–54, eighteen held the post in two provinces, and five—in three provinces. This movement calmed down in 1954, but was renewed the following year, when changes were made in the leadership of ten out of eighteen provincial committees.

There was even greater movement at the district level, and here too it largely involved the transfer of secretaries from one organization to another, even to regions some distance away, rather than promotion to first secretary. All this turnover in personnel was administered from party headquarters in Warsaw and in a manner more closely resembling that of a bureaucratic—or military—structure than that of a traditional political party. A large proportion of the people who made up what was called the leading local *aktiv*, had few, if any, ties to the region they administered and were kept in a state of complete dependence on those above them in the party apparatus.

Orwell's notion of the "inner party" can be used to define all those who were professional party officials or who—on behalf of the party—occupied responsible positions in the state administration or social organizations, or worked in the main organs of social control, which, in the case of Poland, included the Ministry of Public Security. During the period 1951–54 there were approximately one hundred thousand such people in the PZPR, just over 10 percent of total party membership. While this inner party grew relatively slowly (from around 88,000 to about 98,000), the party apparatus expanded rapidly, from some 5,500 employees in March 1950 to nearly thirteen thousand by the end of 1953.

It is not surprising, then, that these people were ill prepared to carry out functions that required, at the very least, some kind of professional or general training. As late as 1958, fewer than half of all full-time PZPR officials had been educated above the elementary level; although in some, but by no means all, cases, this education had been supplemented by party courses of one kind or another. A requirement for admission to the two-year course taught at the Higher Party School, established in 1951, was that students had completed seventh grade. Over a period of several years only about four hundred people graduated from the school, which was supposed to be the party's main source of trained cadres. Most party officials, including about three thousand at the central level, attended courses organized by the party itself, most of them lasting a year or less. Rapid training was also provided for people who were to go into teaching, and for the party and state officials who were to supervise education and culture. Much of this instruction took the form of three-year courses organized by the Training Institute for Education Cadres, established in 1950 and reorganized in 1953 as the Institute of Social Science, attached to the PZPR Central Committee. Below the central level was a regional network, consisting of sixteen provincial "schools" providing six-month courses, and six consolidated provincial schools that conducted courses lasting a year. Only later did it become customary for party officials to obtain educational credentials—some of them more or less fictitious—from regular educational institutions.

The "outer party"—to continue the use of Orwell's terminology—was, of course, a mass party. Nevertheless, despite a widespread belief to the contrary, the period under discussion was not one of rapid numerical growth in PZPR membership. Quite the opposite: the number of party members declined from around 1.443 million in December 1948 to around 1.298 million in December 1954. The party conducted a more or less permanent purge of the rank and file, and between April 1949 and September 1953, some 140,000 members were expelled and the names of a further 96,000 were simply removed from the membership lists. Record keeping was in a state of chaos: during this same period, nearly 250,000 members simply "disappeared" from the rolls. As a result, party "saturation"—the percentage of the population in the party—fell from 6 percent in December 1948 to 4.8 percent in 1954 (compared to 18.7 percent in Czechoslovakia—an all-time record that was difficult to match). Of the adult population, however, 9 percent—nearly one in ten—belonged to the PZPR in 1954.

This provided the party with enormous possibilities for mobilization, but the leadership plainly did not want to enlarge the party too much, no doubt for fear of diluting its level of militancy, and it continued to emphasize recruitment of people from those social classes and strata that the party claimed—by its very name—to represent. This pressure was as strong as it was ineffective: while manual workers made up nearly 60 percent of party members in 1949, by 1954 they accounted for only 43 percent (in absolute terms, a drop of about 200,000 people). Manual workers were replaced by white-collar workers—some of them freshly promoted representatives of the "proletariat"—whose number in the party increased by 180,000; by 1954 they made up 36 percent of the membership. The decline in party saturation at the factory level must have been noticeable; even so, in 1955 one worker in five belonged to the PZPR. The population as a whole was plainly in no hurry to join the ruling party; this was especially evident in rural areas, which were home to about half the country's inhabitants. Nevertheless, the party's network of primary organizations reached virtually everywhere. In December 1954 there were 56,4000 such organizations, although most of them were small, with fewer than fifteen members.

Although party members were, almost by definition, supposed to be active, and the nature of the party itself (and other communist parties) decreed that this activity should be systematic, there is plenty of evidence to suggest that a large proportion of PZPR members limited their participation in public life to taking part in various political campaigns. Of course, groups of people who were more active could be found everywhere, but party meetings and reports on levels of activity generally bemoaned the passivity of the membership, the low attendance at party meetings, the low turnout for ideological instruction, and the low level of interest in the party press; it became increasingly common for membership dues to be deducted directly from wages. Nevertheless, a political campaign of one kind or another was almost a daily feature, especially as economic activity of all kinds acquired campaign characteristics—from production pledges on the factory floor, to ceremonial deliveries of grain to state purchasing agencies, to the banners and placards hoisted by the groups involved in clearing rubble from the streets of Warsaw. In all these cases, party members were supposed to "lead the way," "set an example," and "be at the forefront." Usually, they were— under the watchful eye of the POP secretary or instructors from the district committee.

A major element in the party's omnipresence was its intervention in the functioning of every factory institution. The voice of the party secretary—or executive—was of vital significance, regardless of the fact that management functions were, in any case, increasingly in the hands of party members. The de facto institutionalization of the party's presence took place at every level, just as it had been institutionalized in the central state administration. Constant economic problems, which the party tried to resolve through mobilization and enthusiasm, reinforced these tendencies, frequently giving rise to tensions between the party organization and the factory management, a situation that also provided opportunities to defuse some social discontent. At the same time, this supervision, which became transformed into direct management, was an obstacle to rational decision making. Party organizations and agencies intervened in every area of the production process, often in a fashion that conflicted with technological requirements or real capabilities in the enterprise. In this they were simply following the example set by the central leadership, since even the highest party bodies concerned themselves with issues that were more technical than political in nature. An exquisite example is provided by the Central Committee plenum of 3–4 July 1954, at which the main topic of discussion was a report delivered by Zenon Nowak, "Current Tasks in the Field of Developing Agriculture, Particularly the Elimination of Uncultivated Land and the Management of Meadows and Pastures."

The "inner party," numbering tens of thousands of people, together with the even more numerous social *aktiv* (56,000 party organizations signified at least 120,000–150,000 secretaries and executive members), turned the PZPR into a formidable force that penetrated every corner of public and economic life.

"ALL POWER IN THE HANDS OF . . ."

The strength of the PZPR was based, first and foremost, on the fact that it appropriated the entire state apparatus and adapted it to the requirements of dictatorial power. This ensured that all existing organizations would be subordinated to the party and would become—to use Lenin's well-known formulation—its "transmission belts," although to tell the truth, the overwhelming majority of the party's members were themselves nothing more than a "transmission belt," since they had no role in shaping the policies they were supposed to implement.

The party rapidly and efficiently took control of all associations, large and small, frequently merging similar organizations to facilitate control. The organizations liquidated in this way included, for example, the Workers' Society of the Friends of Children and the Peasant Society of the Friends of Children, which were merged to form a single society; several veterans' associations were amalgamated into a single Union of Fighters for Freedom and Democracy (ZBoWiD); and the respected Polish Tatra Mountain Society was merged with the Polish Touring Society. Changes of this kind also involved replacing a large proportion of an organization's leaders with people who either belonged to the ruling party or were in some way beholden to it.

Under pressure that was frequently quite ruthless, associations changed not only their leadership but also their statutes and bylaws; they were forced to withdraw from international federations and to reshape themselves in accordance with the Soviet model. Traditional sports clubs disappeared, to be replaced by clubs corresponding to sectors of the economy—clubs for railroad workers, miners, construction workers, and so on—as in the Soviet Union. Given the low standard of living, state support played a crucial role in the activity of many associations and was yet another factor fostering their dependence and causing them to lose the characteristics of a social organization. The party was happy to make use of associations in mobilization campaigns of various kinds and in the processions and demonstrations that were a test of the organizational ability of local party leaders and provided alleged proof of the widespread popular support for the regime. Mountain climbers marched past the viewing stand girded with lines, pickaxes in hand; gymnasts carried parallel bars on which the best of them performed somersaults for the assembled dignitaries; weight lifters demonstrated their prowess. Social organizations, an essential element of civil society, were crippled.

The party also engineered a huge increase in the membership of some organizations, especially those with major social functions. One of these was the labor movement, traditionally of interest to socialists and communists. The PPR and PPS had already joined forces to ensure control over the trade unions in the fall of 1944, and a year later they made it impossible for Christian-democratic activists to be elected to trade union office. The party finalized the process of centralization with the formation in June 1949 of the Central Trade Union Council (CRZZ). The importance that the party attributed to the reshaping of the union movement can be seen in the fact that in the fall of 1948 responsibility for the final preparations was assigned to Edward Ochab, who had previously occupied a succession of high-ranking positions. The first chairman of the CRZZ was Aleksander Zawadzki, a Politburo member known for his hard-line stance while acting as head of the provincial administration in Katowice. The party leadership was also concerned that the unions should embrace all workers, and they did become the largest membership organization in the country: in 1949 they had roughly 3.5 million members, by 1954 membership had increased to 4.5 million, and a year later only some 750,000 employees in the socialized sector remained outside the unions. While union meetings were often the scene of worker complaints and conflict with management, the main task of the organization was to mobilize workers to increase output and to take part in propaganda campaigns.

Another large organization was the Union of Polish Youth (ZMP), which in less than two years acquired a monopoly (thanks in part to the disappearance of Catholic youth organizations) on "representing" the younger generation. In 1949 the ZMP had more than one million members; by 1955 membership had risen to two million, roughly 40 percent of young people. About half of all young workers and 60 percent of secondary-school youngsters belonged to the organization. Only in the countryside did the ZMP fail to take root, attracting only 15 percent of peasant youth. In both its organizational structure and its internal activities the union faithfully mimicked the Leninist Komsomol (and the PZPR). The life of the ZMP was governed by democratic centralism, the principle of nomination and co-optation, and the dominant role of the "executive." The organizational development of the union closely resembled that of the PZPR, especially the rapid expansion of its full-time apparatus.

The union provided a means both to exert pressure on teachers and to mobilize young people. Union members were especially visible during parades and other mass events, marching—or working—in the organization's uniform of green shirt and red tie. Young people frequently marched in their own separate columns, well equipped with banners and placards. For the leaders viewing the parade, it was these people, "young and beautiful," who afforded them the greatest satisfaction. But the ZMP was also a major transmission belt on the production front, organizing pledges and labor competition, both in the factories and the schools.

ZMP organizations also constituted a kind of pressure group at the lowest levels of the economic and educational administration that was particularly active—and often effective—in eliminating or intimidating people the party found inconvenient. A major element in the life of the organization was vigilance regarding the "enemy," who was said to be lurking inside as well as outside the union, although this did not prevent ZMP members from frequently taking part in acts of protest and resistance of various kinds. Everywhere—but most noticeably in schools—the ZMP constituted an important instrument of indoctrination and a watchdog of morality. Naturally, it was precisely among this age group that the authorities emphasized the need to conduct one's relations with members of the opposite sex in accordance with the norms of socialist puritanism. With the liquidation of the scouting movement and its replacement by an organization modeled on the Soviet pioneer movement, children too came within the orbit of ZMP indoctrination.

The creation of the PZPR and the progressive sovietization of all of public life called into question the future of the remaining political parties. At the end of 1948 there were four such parties, with a total membership of well over 500,000. All of them fell in line with the changes taking place in the communist movement and declared their readiness to make similar changes.

The Labor Party found itself in the most difficult situation, although it had ceased to espouse Christian-democratic traditions. Nor was it helped by its ceremonial declaration that it recognized "Polish people's democracy as a democracy of a new type." The PZPR had no desire to tolerate a party that aimed to engage in political activity among workers; and the interests of small-scale producers, the remnants of the private trade sector, and the intelligentsia were already being "served" by the Democratic Party. Thus in the summer of 1950, the Labor Party liquidated itself and took its few remaining members (22,000) into the SD. This party, too, encountered numerous difficulties despite the fact that it stood, in the words of its leader, Wacław Barcikowski, "firmly on the road to socialism." Its membership declined rapidly (from about 142,000 in 1948 to fewer than 50,000 a year later), and the party lost whatever remained of its identity.

The PSL never recovered from the disintegration that followed Mikołajczyk's flight abroad. It was plain to all party activists that they were expected to join the SL, but before they could do so they had to submit to a veritable political cleansing, renounce their agrarian traditions, repudiate everything to do with Mikołajczyk, and purge all "dubious" elements from their ranks. In 1949 the PSL, which now had fewer than 45,000 members, was merged with the SL—under the tight supervision of the Ministry of Public Security. The SL, too, was purged, and many members preferred to seek admission to the PZPR than to remain in a party that—it was widely believed at the time—was destined to be liquidated. When the United Peasant Party (ZSL) was formally established at its founding congress in November 1949, only just over two-thirds of former SL members joined the party, together with just over half of the PSL's members. Nevertheless, this gave the ZSL a membership of about 250,000. It seems that the PZPR leadership had no clear idea concerning the future of its erstwhile "allies." Some people argued the need to go further than simply limiting the—already illusory— independence of the ZSL and SD and advocated liquidating the two parties. Such opinions could also be found among peasant activists, including Józef Niećko, considered one of the fathers of the agrarian movement in Poland. Observing the process of collectivization and assuming that it would be successfully completed, he declared this would signify the "proletarianization" of the peasantry and hence there would be no need for a separate political party to represent its interests. The sense that liquidation was inevitable was so widespread that in 1950 about 25 percent of ZSL members left the party. Of course, this was also a response to the party's unequivocal support for collectivization.

In the final analysis, however, the PZPR concluded that the continued existence of the ZSL and SD was useful to it as long as their role was firmly circumscribed. This approach was set out by Zambrowski at a meeting between the PZPR Politburo and the SD National Committee in October 1950, when he stated that, "the idea of treating the ZSL as a partner in a coalition with the PZPR is now out of date." "It would not be correct," he continued, "to tell the broad masses of the ZSL and the PZPR that the ZSL is a transmission belt of the PZPR, but among the parties' leading *aktiv* there should be no doubt about the situation." Both parties survived, but at the price of their complete and utter subordination, a state of affairs that the majority—at least of the "leading *aktiv*"—accepted without demur. The PZPR not only determined which socio-occupational groups were be the focus of these parties' activity, but also imposed numerical limits on membership and reduced their opportunities to reach a broader audience by closing down their daily newspapers. Their role in the state administration was also reduced. In Bierut's government, which replaced that of Cyrankiewicz on 21 November 1952, the ZSL had three instead of seven ministries, while the SD had none at all; and the position of marshal of the Sejm was no longer assigned to a member of the ZSL. The PZPR had become sole master of the political stage.

The party was able, without hindrance, to arrange the institutional scenery in a manner to its liking. With this aim in view, it began work on a new constitution, an administrative reorganization, and changes to the law. As early as the fall of 1948 the party took steps toward abolishing the existing system of local authorities, which combined regional and local administrative institutions and self-government bodies—the national councils—although the representative functions of the latter were largely a fiction, since their members were nominated, not elected. In a system that adhered to the Soviet model, the existing system of local authorities undermined the unity of the power apparatus. The changes began with a massive purge, which eliminated from the councils activists of the former opposition parties as well as people who were, for whatever reason, viewed unfavorably by the real local leaders, the secretaries of the PZPR committees. According to some estimates, during the period 1948–50 a majority of council members were replaced every year as a result of personnel changes within the PZPR and the party's desire to adapt the composition of the councils to the social structure characteristic of their local area. It was at this time that "representatives" of young people, women, ironworkers, and collective farmers were appointed to the councils in proportions corresponding to their proportion in the population of a given province or district.

On 29 March 1950 the Sejm finally passed the "Law on Local Organs of Unified State Power," abolishing the erstwhile administrative positions as well as the self-government bodies. The national councils became the sole organ of state power at the local level, combining both functions. The council structure also incorporated most of those sectors of state administration that had so far remained independent of the local authorities, including economic administration and education. The councils did not however, take over agencies of the security service, police, or censor's office, which remained subordinated to their central headquarters. Elections did not take place until the fall of 1954, and until then the councils—whose scope of competence was actually quite broad—consisted of people nominated by the party, which thus had a more or less free hand to determine their composition.

Beginning in 1949, the authorities took a number of steps intended to "bring order" to the judiciary and to impose the Soviet model on judicial institutions. Some changes had already been made in the period since 1944, including amendments to the penal code and changes in the role of military courts, but although these possessed an internal logic they did not add up to a coherent system. The first steps toward creating such a system were taken on 27 April 1949 with the passage of four laws that changed the principles governing the functioning of the criminal justice system. Among other things, these changes replaced the three-tier system with a two-tier system, abolished the position of investigating magistrate, and expanded the role of "people's assessors" in court proceedings. The Supreme Court also acquired the power to establish norms independently of the appeals submitted to it; and the notion of "degree of social harmfulness" of an offense was added to the list of criteria to be taken into account in sentencing. Also in 1949 the government issued a decree on state and official secrets, which proved a convenient instrument in the permanent hunt for spies.

The next major step involved a legislative package of five laws (passed on 20 July 1950), which, among other things, separated the public prosecutors from the Ministry of Justice, reduced the number of courts of the first instance, and instructed the courts that their first obligation was to safeguard the political system, followed by the interests of the (socialized) economy, and only then the rights and interests of the country's citizens. This package included measures designed to speed up the influx of new personnel: qualifying examinations for would-be judges were abolished, the period of apprenticeship was substantially shortened, experience as a lawyer was no longer required, and positions in the judiciary were no longer to be filled on a competitive basis. That the party regarded a turnover in personnel as a matter of some urgency is suggested by the fact that in 1953 roughly 30 percent of judges had worked in the prewar judicial system. The government also continued, until 1952, the fifteen-month courses it had introduced in 1946 to train people with a secondary education for a place on the bench. The authorities further added to their legal weapons when the government issued, in March 1953, a number of decrees concerning tougher measures to protect socialized property.

The constant intervention in legal proceedings by security organs was not codified in law but was a major factor in practice. They took the place of the investigating magistrate, prepared "draft" indictments for prosecutors, monitored court proceedings, and so on. The judicial system became a major instrument of social control and—it is no exaggeration to use the term—"judicial terror." The system encompassed agencies and procedures that were clearly terrorist in nature. These included the Secret Section of the Warsaw Military Court, which during 1949–54 sentenced some five hundred people, and the so-called operational sanctions that allowed prosecutors to detain people for up to two months without the need to file official charges. Until the spring of 1955 military courts retained jurisdiction over civilians charged with "crimes against the state," although the number of such cases gradually declined. (During the period 1946–53 about 65,000 people were sentenced for such crimes, 22,500 of whom were sentenced during the period 1950–53.)

Although the Sejm elected in 1947 was referred to as a constituent assembly, there was no great rush to begin work on a new constitution. A specially formed group, attached to the PZPR Central Committee, began work in June 1949 but proceeded so slowly that it was necessary to extend the Sejm's term of office. One reason for the slow progress was the succession of changes to the state administrative system and the judiciary. The authors of the new constitution had great difficulty resolving the basic question: whether—and if so, to what extent—they should model the constitution on "the most democratic constitution in the world," in other words, the Soviet Constitution of 1936, and to what extent, if any, they should retain some traditional Polish institutions.

After nearly two years' work, conducted away from the public gaze, the draft was finished. After Stalin had personally approved the document (and made several changes), a Constitutional Committee of the Sejm was formally established (on 26 May 1951), and on 23 January 1952 the draft constitution was presented for public discussion. Meetings were organized in factories and offices; according to official data, eleven million people attended these meetings, and one participant in eight actually spoke. This was an enormous propaganda campaign, and the draft constitution met, declared Bierut, "with the complete approval and support of the millions of our nation."

On 22 July 1952, after a debate lasting three days, the Sejm passed the constitution, which recapitulated the ideological principles of "people's democracy." It confirmed the existing legal order and power structure, and it did so in extremely ideological language. This was a "class" document in its wording; it took "the working people of town and country" as its subject and declared it was the duty of the state to "restrict, uproot, and liquidate all social classes that live by exploiting workers and peasants." Affirming the right to personal property, it declared that private ownership of buildings, land, and means of production would be restricted to "peasants, and those engaged in handicraft production and cottage industry." Freedom of the press was supposedly guaranteed by the provision stating that printing works, paper, meeting rooms, buildings, the radio, and so on, were to be "put at the disposal of the working people and their organizations." (Andrzej Ajnienkel maliciously noted that the Soviet people had fared better under Stalin's constitution of 1936 because they had also been given the streets.) The constitution retained the Council of State, which acquired wide-ranging powers—including those that had belonged to the now abolished office of president—and jurisdiction over the regional national councils. The Central Control Chamber was abolished, and with it the Sejm's power to monitor regularly the activity of the state administration. This function was assigned to the newly created Ministry of State Control, which was itself part of the administration that it was supposed to monitor. The constitution contained a kind of wish list, granting citizens the right to work, education, rest, and so on, but much of this amounted to window dressing, not only because many of the provisions were vaguely worded but above all because citizens had no power to ensure that they were respected in practice.

In a certain sense, the first stage of building "people's democracy" in Poland ended with the election of a new Sejm, the first one to last a normal term. The electoral law stipulated that the number of candidates could not exceed the number of seats in any electoral district, and only committees of the National Front could present lists of candidates. The process of election was thus to be reduced to that of simply voting. And that is precisely what happened: according to the communiqué issued by the State Electoral Commission on 26 October 1952, 95 percent of the adult population turned out to vote, and candidates of the National Front received 99.8 percent of the votes cast. "The working people of town and country" had handed over power to their representatives.

CLASS STRUGGLE

The communists initially had to contend with a relatively strong movement of armed resistance and a political opposition that functioned legally until 1947, although it had lost much of its strength the previous year. It therefore seemed quite natural that the communists should launch a fierce struggle against the opponents of the new system. This struggle—in which Soviet troops and security services initially played a part—was waged with a ferocity that was especially shocking in light of the enormous disparities in strength between the two sides. The struggle claimed thousands of innocent victims; the principle of collective responsibility was applied on a massive scale; those who were arrested were tortured; and due legal process was violated—and not only during summary proceedings. The authorities frequently resorted to provocation and assassination; they falsified documents and confessions; they forced people to confess their guilt, and broke them psychologically; and they used blackmail to expand the network of informers and agents. This struggle, which many people saw as a war waged against the whole nation, was conducted by a formidable and constantly expanding range of forces that included regular military units and armed units of poorly trained civilians belonging to the Voluntary Militia. During the first half of 1947, the authorities had at their disposal up to 250,000 people, as well as the entire Polish Army in reserve, and an enormous contingent of Soviet Army troops in the background.

In 1947 armed resistance was essentially crushed, and only a few scattered units remained in action. Despite the amnesty, tens of thousands of people remained behind bars, and trials proceeded apace (around twenty-two thousand people were sentenced by military courts alone in 1947 and 1948). In the fall of 1947, the legal opposition was also broken, and all that remained were the Catholics associated with a few publications that were being squeezed to death by the censors. At the end of August 1948 they too were attacked, when *Tygodnik Warszawski*, the most overtly political of the Catholic publications, was closed down and most of its editors were arrested. As a result of the purge carried out in the PPS, those socialists who still believed in the possibility of taming the monster in their midst were deprived of a forum.

When the First Congress of the PZPR ended with the singing of the "Internationale," delegates might have thought that the words "this will be the final battle" referred to a historical event and that the phrase should be reworded in the past tense. The party now had more than one million members from all classes and social strata. It controlled all social organizations and had command of the entire state apparatus, the economic administration, and all quasi-self-government institutions. The "tyrants" denounced in the singing at the party congress were defeated—turned to dust and ashes, or flat on their backs in prison cells. The few who had refused to lay down their arms were reduced to a few tiny islands surrounded by a sea of fear, indifference, and servility—and belief in the slogans proclaimed by those in power.

Meanwhile, as early as the summer of 1947 Stanisław Radkiewicz, a member of the Politburo and minister of public security, stated at a briefing for senior ministry staff: "Today we have to dig very deep in our search for the enemy." Another high-ranking communist activist declared: "We don't need to see what's going on around us to know that the day when the enemy will begin to fight on the economic front is not far off." "This is the logic of history and experience," he concluded, "and this is how it will be now." No doubt he had in mind the Soviet experience of the 1930s, when the whole society was subjected to a campaign of terror that destroyed millions of people, created an all-pervading atmosphere of fear and suspicion, and led to an endless hunt for "spies." In the summer of 1948 the struggle against "the rightist-nationalist deviation" got under way with the introduction of the notion—forged by Stalin—of "intensifying class struggle." This signified not so much a change in methods, which were already sufficiently drastic, as a broadening of the struggle to search for the enemy in new areas. A year later Bolesław Bierut stated—in the traditionally ornamental language of Stalinist Newspeak—that it was necessary "to force out of hiding the concealed remains of the enemy and its cunningly disguised tentacles, which reach into every crevice of the social machine."

The hunt for the enemy took two different directions. One took as its starting point the idea that "sabotage and subversion constitute a system organized by the enemy within entire areas." This led to the surveillance, persecution, and terrorization of all social groups and strata. The other began with the assertion that "the enemy has penetrated the ranks of the party" and implied the possibility of a permanent purge within the communist party and the intimidation of those who were supposed to instill fear into the rest of society.

The first of these required a change of methods on the part of the security services. Up to now, said Radkiewicz, "we have focused on controlling all aspects of life of the country with the aid of our official employees." Changing conditions required, however, "a shift in emphasis from the official apparatus to a paid apparatus separate from the official one." He lamented the fact that the ministry's network of agents "does not have as many people as the official apparatus." Beginning in 1948, then, the security ministry began to expand this network so that it would be in a position, "with its assistance, to safeguard the security of economic, political, and social life and all other areas of life." By 1954, it had recruited between seventy and seventy-five thousand "pairs of eyes," and, as Radkiewicz had demanded, they "covered all organizational units in the country." The largest network belonged to the section of the ministry concerned with the economy, in which subsections dealt with industry, transport, and agriculture. These were eventually divided into narrower fields, covering such areas as heavy industry, light industry, railroads, private agriculture, and so on.

In the economy things were not going well. Roofs collapsed in the mineshafts, machinery broke down in the factories, and the peasants were late with their compulsory deliveries. . . . All such cases were treated as acts of sabotage and subversion, and a zealous search was mounted not only for the perpetrators but also, and above all, for the "instigators" and "organizers." The director of the Fourth Department of the Ministry of Public Security, which dealt with industry, considered that the Central Board of the Coal Industry effectively engaged in sabotage when it issued a circular, ordering all those signing up for labor competition to undergo a medical checkup and laying down an age limit for those wanting to take part. Minister Radkiewicz, for his part, when discussing the issue of fires in rural areas, remarked that it was wrong to blame children for setting the fires. "Everyone and everything is hiding behind the children," he declared. "Nobody sticks his nose any further than these children to check what lies behind them, who has put them up to it, who has created the conditions for them to set these fires." In the Katowice province, during the first quarter of 1953, security forces arrested roughly five hundred "subversives." "A large number of them, probably the majority," said the head of the provincial UB, "were young men about whom we could pick up absolutely no leads, either in the course of our investigations or during other operations; in other words, they were freelance subversives." It seems that the authorities detained, and interrogated, several hundred young men who worked on machines that broke down, in mines where accidents had occurred, in loading yards where the coal wagons came off the tracks, and so on. After a series of strikes around Będzin in April 1951, an official analysis of their cause pointed, first and foremost, to shortcomings in the work of the security services: "It is not enough to make a thorough study of the administration at a particular site . . . or to investigate breakdowns. . . . It is not enough to work with an antisubversion network." "What is needed is a thorough study of the workforce on the shop floor and at all levels of the administration, reconnaissance concerning the political coloration of the site, intelligence concerning the precise political influences to be found among the workforce, in the past and at present."

So they rummaged through the files, which had been systematically maintained in a uniform format. Everyone who belonged to—or was ascribed to—one of twenty-five categories ended up in the files. They included, for example, people who had been politically active before the war, who had been in the Home Army, who were active in the PPS, or who had returned to Poland after serving in the Polish Armed Forces. Over time, this list grew to include forty-three categories. By 1954 the "register of criminal and suspicious elements" contained nearly six million names—one in three of the adult citizens of Poland. In every suspicious situation they hunted for AK members, in factories and offices they searched for members of the WRN, in the countryside they also looked for kulaks, Mikołajczyk supporters, and members of the Peasant Battalions. The ministry's own files were no longer enough. In 1950, when they were preparing to issue identity cards, security officials discussed the need to design the document in such a way that not only "would it be possible at first glance to determine whether or not we are dealing with a person who earns an honest living" but also "on closer inspection to determine whether or not the person in question is dangerous in terms of political associations or class origin."

It is not surprising, then, that the number of political prisoners increased. According to official (but secret) data, on 1 January 1948 the country's prisons held 26,400 political prisoners, 44 percent of all those behind bars. A year later the number of "politicals" had risen to 32,200 (40 percent) and by mid-1950, to 35,200 (35.9 percent). At the beginning of June 1950 the two largest prisons for political prisoners, in Wronki and Rawicz, each held nearly four thousand prisoners. And this was a year before Operation K, "a single blow within an overall intensification of repression," in the course of which some 4,700 people were arrested simultaneously. They sat in prison alongside AK soldiers (who were persecuted with exceptional ferocity); leaders and activists of clandestine political parties and the legal opposition; underground "lads from the forests"; engineers whose machinery had broken down; students who had squirted ink at a picture of Bierut; prewar politicians; and "freelance subversives." Beginning in 1949 those who had been released from prison under the terms of the 1947 amnesty were once again arrested and returned to prison. The same fate even befell those (like General Emil Fieldorf and Jan Hoppe) who had been arrested in the spring of 1945 and deported to the Soviet Union and who thus had not had the opportunity to oppose the new regime.

The jails of the police and the security service were often extremely crowded, particularly when they detained large numbers of people as a preventive measure before party holidays, before price increases, or when the deadline for compulsory deliveries had passed. In the late fall of 1952 alone, several tens of thousands of peasants were detained. Five hundred of them were sentenced by administrative tribunals; 2,000 were sentenced by the courts; 1,000 sat behind bars awaiting trial; 5,000 signed a document pledging that they would complete their deliveries and were released only on condition that they do so; and 6,000 were released after being "cautioned." During 1949–53 tens of thousands of people wended their way through prisons and jails. To these we should add the many people sentenced by the special commissions to combat speculation, who often had nothing whatsoever to do with speculation, and those who were sentenced to jail by penal-administrative tribunals for failure to fulfill compulsory delivery quotas.

Hundreds of thousands of people were directly touched by the "avenging hand of the people's justice." Millions of family members, neighbors, and colleagues at work or in school felt its force. And this, it would seem, was the main point: a large part of the population was intimidated, many people were actually terrorized, there was widespread mistrust, and people feared even relatives and friends. This state of affairs was reinforced by conformism and by the habit of saying one thing in public and another in private. Society became atomized, and the absence of independent political parties and associations made it easy for the authorities to engage in a kind of "secondary organization," bringing people into mass organizations like the youth movement, trade unions, or the Women's League, whose functions were to mobilize and indoctrinate.

One can imagine that the terror and the omnipresence—real or imagined—of informers were also intended to help those who created and inflicted this terror to stifle their own fears regarding the hatred that millions of citizens felt for them. Around two hundred thousand people at least were "recruited," most of them blackmailed on the basis of "compromising material" or bought with the promise of better treatment in prison or early release. When the Ministry of Public Security was abolished in 1954, Radkiewicz himself admitted that the purpose of this recruitment was not only to obtain informers but also to break people, to degrade them and make them more afraid than ever. Given the mass scale of repression of various kinds and the scope of physical fear, it can be said that there really was a "class war" going on in Poland. On one side stood the party-state apparatus—what Djilas subsequently called the New Class—and on the other stood a large part of society, party members and nonparty members, the obedient and the insubordinate.

The broader population had only indirect experience of the second area in which the authorities conducted a campaign of terror. This was the war on the enemy that had had been "breeding" within the party. In fact, though, this campaign constituted a link in a single chain, just as the Moscow show trials of the 1930s had been a part, the tip of the iceberg, of the Great Purge. The "settling of accounts" with the rightist-nationalist deviation during the summer of 1948 was, it would soon turn out, only a political prelude, an overture, but one that lasted quite a long time. When the opening bars sounded—or perhaps we should say, when the conductor raised his baton—it was before a small audience, and softly.

On 13 November 1948 the security service arrested Włodzimierz Lechowicz, a personage of little renown in public life. An agent of military counterintelligence before the war, he had worked for the Delegatura during the occupation. After the war he joined the Democratic Party and became a senior official in the Ministry of Reclaimed Territories, headed by Gomułka. Before the war Lechowicz actually had ties to Soviet intelligence, and he took up his position in the wartime underground with the agreement of the intelligence unit of the People's Guard, which was headed by Marian Spychalski. Lechowicz was the first link in the chain that was to lead to the top. In February 1949 the PZPR leadership established the Politburo Commission for Security Affairs, whose members included Bierut and Berman, as well as the minister of public security and his deputy (and, ex officio, the secretary of the PZPR organization in the ministry). In this way the topmost party leadership took over direct supervision of the security service. It was obvious that in this case it was not a question of supervising the fight against the underground, the AK, or "freelance subversives," but of supervising the battle that was about to take place within the party. A few weeks later Spychalski was removed from his post as deputy minister of defense and immediately became the subject of an investigation, initially conducted by party bodies only. At the same time, the security service arrested Brigadier General Franciszek Herman, one of the top commanders of the AK, who had occupied a number of senior positions in the army (including that of chief of staff of ground forces). He was to be the second link in the chain.

During the period 11–13 November 1949 the first rumbling sounds could be heard. A meeting of the Central Committee (attended also by members of the central party *aktiv*), which opened with a report from Bierut titled "The Party's Tasks in the Struggle for Revolutionary Vigilance in the Current Situation," quickly turned into a hate session directed against the "deviationists" and "renegades." Gomułka and Spychalski, together with Zenon Kliszko, their close associate from the wartime underground, were expelled with great to-do from the Central Committee. It was high time for such decisive action, as Poland was clearly lagging behind: in June Koci Xoxe had been sentenced in Tirana, in September László Rajk had stood trial in Budapest, and the trial of Traicho Kostov was about to get under way in Sofia. The imported Central-European revolution was beginning to devour its children.

On 1 March 1950 a new unit, known as the Special Bureau (it later became the Tenth Department), was created in the Ministry of Public Security. During the next few weeks more senior officers were arrested, and on 17 May it was the turn of Spychalski. The authorities began arresting all of Gomułka's close associates until, on 2 August 1951, he himself was detained, together with his wife, and subsequently held in a specially prepared villa in Miedzeszyn, on the outskirts of Warsaw. Subsequent events took a well-known course, and one of the targets was General Wacław Komar, for many years head of intelligence, and his colleagues in the Intelligence Department of the General Staff. Preparations began for an enormous show trial, similar to those organized in neighboring countries. Despite the fairly unambiguous suggestions voiced in Moscow and the ambitions of Rokossowski, who wanted the military to carry out the investigation into Spychalski, the show trial never took place. Gomułka, who did not capitulate, was interrogated only a few times, and no physical coercion was used. And although the number of people caught up in the investigation continued to grow until as late as the summer of 1953, when Michał Żymierski was arrested (five months after the death of Stalin), the authorities never formulated a satisfactory indictment. Polish communists thus avoided the fate that befell their Czech, Hungarian, and Bulgarian comrades.

All the action came to focus, in fact, on those who were supposed to provide an indirect link to Gomułka and his party comrades. In August 1951, when the one-time general secretary of the PPR was being transported back from a vacation in the resort of Krynica, four generals, including General Stanisław Tatar, and five other high-ranking officers went on trial before the Supreme Military Court. All of them were accused of having established "a counterrevolutionary organization," and the person who allegedly facilitated their "infiltration" of the army was identified as Spychalski. A large number of the 1,200 or so officers who had served in the armed forces before the war were already in prison, and a series of secret trials resulted in the death sentence for nearly forty of them, of whom twenty were actually executed.

Of course, implicating the prewar military in "counterrevolutionary" activity was plainly linked to the preparations afoot to put Gomułka on trial, but this was not the only reason. On 6 November 1949, on the eve of the solemn commemoration of the anniversary of the Russian Revolution, the distinguished Soviet commander, Konstanty Rokossowski, then head of the Northern Armed Forces Group, which was stationed in Poland, was appointed minister of defense and Polish marshal. Rokossowski brought with him yet more Soviet colonels and generals to join the considerable number already in the Polish forces. In no time at all, Soviet citizens occupied virtually all high-ranking positions, except for that of head of the Main Political-Education Board. The largest European army of the communist bloc (after the Soviet Army), which in early 1953 had 410,000 troops (compared with 140,000 in December 1948, after demobilization), was completely under Soviet control. Red Army officers were in command at every level, from the minister to the chief of the general staff, to heads of the different services and military districts—a total of fifty-two generals and 670 officers, as well as 200 advisers, most of whom were attached to the arms industry. The Soviet aim was to have full control over Polish forces in the event that Moscow decided to initiate armed conflict in Europe, something that was seriously considered at the time. Another aim was to strengthen the fighting capability of the Polish forces and to bring about a complete unification in military doctrine, training, organization, and equipment.

This army, from its very beginning an instrument (and locus) of indoctrination, was also a major element in controlling and disciplining the whole of Polish society. This was one of the functions of the military counterintelligence unit known as the Main Information Office, which was subordinated not to the chief of staff but directly to the Ministry of Defense. The office, with subunits in the various branches of the armed forces and every military district, employed more than 1,000 people and had a network of informers that grew from just under 9,000 in 1948 to more than 23,000 five years later. In 1953 nearly 18,000 people, including 5,500 officers on active duty, were either listed in its files or under investigation. Known for its exceptional ruthlessness, the Information Office kept both the officer corps and the rank and file in a state of fear.

The office also played a major role in coordinating purges and selecting replacement personnel: during the period 1949–54, about ten thousand officers were dismissed and replaced by people who had been through a short training course. The same factors that brought about massive social mobility in civilian life were at work in the military, especially as appropriate class background was even more important there than in the state administration. Tightly controlled by its commanders and the Information Office, the army became a mainstay of the system and was active far beyond the confines of the barracks. It took part in a great many propaganda and other campaigns (collecting signatures for successive appeals in the defense of peace, for example), every year it released into the broader society tens of thousands of young men who had been through a two-year period of indoctrination, and it had in its charge a mass organization (the League for the Defense of the Homeland, renamed in 1950 the League of Friends of the Army). The army was an active participant in the "class struggle."

ÉMIGRÉS: IN THE SHADOW OF THE COLD WAR

As the Cold War intensified, the United States began searching for new instruments with which to influence developments. The State Department conceived a plan whereby émigrés from the countries of East-Central Europe could constitute such an instrument. This introduced new elements into the activity of the Polish émigré community while also giving rise to conflicts and rivalry between various groups over contacts with the State Department and the organizations established with its assistance. The Americans (and the British) insisted that the émigré communities put aside their differences and foster political cohesion. They remained, however, fragmented—the Poles, perhaps, more so than other nationalities—and the two powers then reserved the right to select the groups with which they would work.

The chief organizer of cooperation between émigré groups and the countries lying between the Gulf of Finland and Bulgaria's Rodopi mountains was the Committee for a Free Europe, founded in 1949, with headquarters in New York, and financed, first and foremost, by Western governments. Its main form of activity was propaganda, directed both at Western societies and—increasingly, as time went by—at communist governments. The most significant step in this propaganda campaign was the creation of Radio Free Europe, in which the Polish Service began regular broadcasts from Munich to Poland on 3 May 1952. Another major development was the establishment of the Assembly of Captive European Nations (ACEN), which began operations on 20 November 1954 from its headquarters not far from the United Nations building in New York.

The Central Intelligence Agency, established in 1947, also set up a covert communications channel. Many émigré groups (not just Polish) once again began hoping—especially after the outbreak of the Korean War—for an outbreak of worldwide conflict. The electoral campaign rhetoric of General Eisenhower, the Republican Party's candidate for president, was one of several factors reinforcing these hopes. In the United States these tendencies found support in statements concerning the need for a new doctrine in international relations, one that would "roll back" the Soviet Union's advance in East-Central Europe, and in the intensification of the anticommunist campaign inside the country.

These changes did not immediately have an effect on the Polish elites in London; while the Americans were emphasizing the need for unity, the London Poles were torn by yet another divisive conflict. This one had a far greater impact than the conflict that resulted in the PPS going over to the opposition in 1947 and its short-lived alliance with the PSL. Beginning in early 1949 a crisis gradually emerged within General Komorowski's government, which had already been abandoned by all the traditional political parties. This time it was the National Party that engineered the crisis and its leader, Tadeusz Bielecki, who initiated it. The political grouping associated with President Zaleski, known as the Castle, tried to save itself by reestablishing the National Council (in June 1949), but the opposition declined the invitation to join it. Komorowski also sought to retain influence among combat émigrés by establishing a body known as the National Treasury that would raise funds to support the struggle for independence at home. The opposition parties responded to these moves by establishing (in December 1949) their own collective body, the Political Council. However, most of the council's members harbored such serious reservations regarding Mikołajczyk that the PSL split; Bagiński and Korboński, who were not directly associated with the "Yalta betrayal," created a separate peasant party.

The core of the Political Council consisted of the Polish Socialist Party, the National Party, and the Independence and Democracy group, but General Komorowski also joined it. In the attempt to defend his position, Mikołajczyk organized the Polish National Democratic Committee (in May 1949), but succeeded in persuading only part of the Democratic Party and Popiel's Labor Party to join. The émigré political stage thus fragmented into three sections, which not only created an awkward situation for the Committee for a Free Europe but also alienated most of the émigré community, which had grown tired of the mutual recriminations and insults.

In the summer of 1950 the Homeland Commission of the Political Council established contact with American intelligence agencies and agreed to provide intelligence and subversion training (in Berg, outside Munich) in exchange for around one million dollars and some technical assistance. More than one-quarter of the couriers and intelligence agents sent into Poland were captured immediately, since all the channels of communication with the country—based on WiN networks—were controlled by the Ministry of Public Security. Until as late as 1954, when the "Berg affair" became a topic of public debate and outcry, these contacts had no perceptible effect on the course of events. During this period efforts to reach agreement within the émigré community were renewed. The decisive breakthrough seems to have come with the intervention of General Sosnkowski, who since 1944 had been living quietly in political retirement in Canada. In December 1952 he arrived in London and began seeking a way to establish a modus vivendi between the Castle group and the Political Council. An agreement was finally reached, and on 14 March 1954 the main political forces signed an Act of Unification. The consensus was, however, immediately broken by President Zaleski, who refused to honor his pledge to resign.

As a result, the overwhelming majority of émigré political groups refused to recognize his presidency. In June 1954 they established the Interim Council of National Unity, chaired by Tadeusz Bielecki, which then selected some of its members to form the National Unity Executive. The council proposed that three prominent representatives of the émigré community—General Anders, Arciszewski, and Raczyński—form the Council of Three, which meant that virtually all the political figures who enjoyed some measure of broad social support broke with the Castle group. Two years later, the Interim Council gave the Council of Three "presidential powers," reinforcing a division that would last until 1972. Mikołajczyk was excluded from all these political maneuvers, but he still had considerable influence with the administration in Washington. Those groups in the émigré community that stuck to traditional forms of activity through political parties and the already weakened state institutions started to become, as Raczyński wrote in 1959, "out of sync with the course of history." Groups proposing new forms of political activity came to the fore, such as Radio Free Europe, energetically and independently directed by Jan Nowak-Jeziorański, and the Literary Institute (Instytut Literacki) and its monthly journal, *Kultura,* established in 1946 by Jerzy Giedroyc. Both of these institutions focused on influencing the situation within Poland, and because of this had a much better sense than others of what was needed. For them, the need to save—and strengthen—cultural identity was more important than the issue of conflict over the presidency. Already in 1951 Giedroyc presented the London Poles with a major dilemma, when poet Czesław Miłosz, who had recently left Poland, published a book titled *The Captive Mind,* in which he offered a new interpretation of why some intellectuals had succumbed to communism. While London sharply attacked Miłosz, Giedroyc endorsed his views.

Émigré circles also faced problems because of infiltration on the part of the Polish security services, a process that intensified during the period when the first signs of an easing in international relations were making themselves felt. This infiltration affected all the émigré communities from East-Central Europe, and the process was accelerated under direct pressure from Moscow. One event whose significance was underestimated by the émigré community was the return to Poland in September 1955 of Hugo Hanke, a little-known Christian-democratic activist, who had just been appointed prime minister in the government-in-exile. A paid agent of the UB since 1953, Hanke landed at Okęcie just when the authorities were in the process of setting up the Polonia Association and the Homeland Radio Station was making its first broadcasts directed at Polish émigrés. Both these institutions served to sow dissension among the new generation of émigrés and attract supporters from among the ranks of the old émigré community.

The thaw had the effect of demobilizing many émigrés. After abandoning political activity and trying to return to Poland during 1947–49, Stanisław Mackiewicz, one of the most prominent of those who had earned a reputation for their unyielding opposition to communism, finally succeeded in returning. The events of 1956 also led to new divisions, when some politicians (among them, Jędrzej Giertych from the SN, Piotr Zaremba from the PPS, and Stanisław Wójcik who had parted company with Mikołajczyk's PSL) voiced their support—with greater or lesser degrees of enthusiasm—

for Gomułka, at that time frequently depicted (and not only among émigrés) as a "national communist." Radio Free Europe and *Kultura* also expressed support for liberalization in Poland, but the émigré politicians who did not believe in Gomułka's patriotism were probably in the majority. They included Mikołajczyk, who even thought for a time that he might be able to reach an agreement with Khrushchev and return to Poland.

A few politicians of the older generation, including Jerzy Zdziechowski and Juliusz Poniatowski, also decided to return home, but without any hope of playing any role in public life. A number of writers, including Teodor Parnicki, Maria Kuncewiczowa, and Melchior Wańkowicz, also decided to return. Others, such as Witold Gombrowicz, succumbed to the temptation of having their work published in Poland or agreed, like the well-known pianist Witold Małczużyński, to perform or otherwise promote their artistry in visits to their homeland. Even some military figures, such as General Antoni Chruściel, sought (in vain) permission to return.

During 1955–56 the Americans essentially abandoned their attempts to establish political bridgeheads within the émigré communities, limiting themselves to maintaining their influence through radio broadcasting and some support for publications. ACEN, along with one or two other initiatives, continued to function, but had virtually no impact on Kremlin policy. Émigré politicians had to rely on their own resources, ever smaller and increasingly fragmented. On the other hand, while politicians were caught up in endless quarreling, numerous writers, poets, essayists, and researchers were producing works that became part of the national culture and gradually began to circulate within the country. The work of such people as Kazimierz Wierzyński, Czesław Miłosz, Witold Gombrowicz, Marian Hemar, Władysław Pobóg-Malinowski, Marian Kukiel, and Oskar Halecki became the property of an independent intellectual movement, exerting a greater influence on developments in Poland than even the most worthy politician enjoying widespread respect in London, Chicago, or Melbourne.

THE LAST REDOUBTS

The underground was slowly dying away, the victim of ceaseless attacks. Even so, during the years 1949–55 the Internal Security Corps still managed to arrest about sixteen thousand people, one thousand of them captured during fighting. Trials were a daily accompaniment to the activities of the security organs. During 1950–53 more than 9,500 people were sentenced by military courts alone on charges of belonging to "an illegal association."

According to data compiled by the Ministry of Internal Affairs, security organs registered more than 500 groups and organizations engaged in, or intending to engage in, "antistate activity." Most of them were tiny groups, whose members were more likely to have been thinking about "doing something" than to have actually carried out an attack or act of resistance. Some of them were simply invented by security officials seeking to impress their bosses.

Nevertheless, it can be said that between ten and twenty thousand people at least (and perhaps several tens of thousands) wanted to express their opposition actively. And they did so on numerous occasions. Not a day went by without Warsaw headquarters receiving reports of such activity: leaflets and graffiti; flags torn down in schools, factories, and (more rarely) offices; propaganda displays smashed. The authorities treated every attack on police or security personnel and every robbery of a cooperative or some other institution of "social ownership" as an antistate, hence political, act (in 1951 even the theft of property belonging to foreign cyclists taking part in the Peace Rally was treated as such). On the other hand, there is no reason to doubt that some of these acts were indeed committed out of purely political motives.

Not all breakdowns were the result of technical errors, poor quality, or poor worker training. There were cases of deliberate sabotage, most of them committed by individuals rather than organized groups. Attempts to flee the country—usually unsuccessful—can also be considered active resistance. According to data compiled by the Border Defense Corps, 38 percent of those caught trying to leave the country in 1950, and 74 percent of those caught in 1954, stated that they wanted to leave for political reasons (a further 13 percent said their reasons had to do with "the system"). At least 1,000 people a year tried to escape from a country that was guarded by 300 kilometers of barbed wire fence, more than 10,000 flares, 100 kilometers of border alarms, and 1,200 observation towers.

The vast majority of those who took part in such activities were by no means "Anders' agents," "supporters of Mikołajczyk," or "fascist members of the NSZ," most of whom had long left the underground, were behind bars, and were identified in the files. It was young people, usually very young people, who wrote the leaflets and painted slogans on the walls. In late 1954 and early 1955 an investigation lasting a month-and-a-half finally ended with the arrest of a group that had distributed more than 2,500 leaflets. "We lost some of our comrades," complained one of the heads of the Warsaw UB, "and invested a lot of energy in the search, only to find that this was an organization made of boys aged 13, 14, 15. These kids went to see the film of Bogdan Czeszko's *Pokolenie* [*Generation,* directed by Andrzej Wajda] and they decided to take the characters in the film as their model. The first leaflets they printed said, 'Join the Union of Fighting Youth!'"

At the beginning of 1955 one of the high-level officials dealing with youth issues, Feliks Dwojak, estimated that during the previous few years the authorities had "liquidated" youth organizations with a total member-ship of some ten thousand people; he considered senior secondary-school pupils the most dangerous group (in terms of "the ease with which they engage in violent attacks" and "the large number of illegal leaflets" they published). Throughout the country numerous trials of youth groups took place, some of them were held in public, and in some such cases the author-ities did not manage to make adequate "preparations." A Colonel Józef Czaplicki reported reprovingly that at the public trial of a group going by the name of Katyn that took place in Sieradz in 1951, "the local population listened carefully. This was especially true of the high-school students. After the verdict had been pronounced they gathered outside the court building and the moment those who had been sentenced appeared in a convoy of open trucks, they began throwing them flowers and cigarettes and shouting out greetings." Even dragging young people into the PZPR's satellite organi-zations did not render them immune to the temptation to take part in resis-tance: 20 percent of the young people arrested in 1949 and 40 percent of those arrested a year later were members of the ZMP. The more the party and the ZMP became mass organizations, the less their members differed from the rest of the population in terms of their attitude to the regime.

This "youth resistance movement" no doubt involved a fair amount of ordinary rebelliousness and revolt against the adult world. At a time when the image of this world was defined by communist slogans and personified by the *ubek* or party member, protest was, naturally, directed against them. Most often it took the form of what used to be called "small-scale sabotage." In 1950, for example, in Grudziądz, an unidentified group "over a three-month period carried out a campaign of spraying paint or ink" at various objects of official propaganda, "bringing about a situation," said Czaplicki, "in which virtually all propaganda objects were removed from the town." Throwing an ink pot at a portrait of Bierut hanging above the blackboard can hardly be called childish when it is punishable by one or two years in prison and brings with it the possibility of being beaten up during the investigation.

For many people, the officers sentenced in the big show trials were celebrated heroes, and their unsung heroes were the unknown youths who wrecked bulletin boards and composed leaflets (often hand-written). Despite the authorities' assertions to the contrary, this resistance was spontaneous, scattered, not based on any clear-cut program or organization, and the members of various groups met each other for the first time in the prison cells. The same applies to the tiny groups that were all that remained of the underground that had its beginnings in the tragic fall of 1939. Armed attacks—usually against police and security personnel—continued until as late as 1954–55, and it was not until 1956 that the authorities announced the liquidation of the very last "gang." Those who were set on engaging in action more drastic than leafleting (amassing weapons, for example) also included many young people for whom the exploits of the AK or WiN were simply part of the Polish romantic tradition along the lines of the conspiracy to assassinate Tsar Nicholas I and a succession of failed uprisings. Older secondary-school pupils and university students also organized various kinds of "self-education circles," in which they studied the anticommunist interpretation of the nation's history, maintained AK traditions, and read forbidden literature. It was groups of this kind that frequently gave birth to proposals for more concrete action.

The crushing of the legal opposition and the underground brought to the forefront the institution that the majority of Poles had long considered the basis of national identity and their shield against foreign domination: the Catholic Church. Since the fall of 1946 at least, the PPR had been using both the Ministry of Public Security and the propaganda apparatus to prepare a sweeping attack, but it was only in the spring of 1948 that decisive action got under way. The party then initiated a major propaganda campaign in connection with a letter from Pope Pius XII to the German bishops that referred, among other things, to the fate of the twelve million Germans forced to leave the western territories. Although the party leadership was preoccupied with internal matters—the accelerated merger of the PPR and PPS, and the question of the rightist-nationalist deviation—it still found time to begin exerting ever-greater administrative pressure on the church, forcing it to close down schools and orphanages. The episcopate adopted a defensive posture, calling for calm and openly appealing for an end to underground activity. However, it also expressed (for example, in a pastoral letter, dated 24 April 1948) its hope for the future and its faith in the spirit of the nation, which "must remain strong, alive, capable of bringing about that which will determine its greatness tomorrow." The deputy security minister, Roman Romkowski, was certainly right when he warned his subordinates that the church would "not be as easy to deal with as the PSL."

Fate also intervened to complicate the war against the church, which the authorities simply viewed as yet another element in the secular class struggle. On the morning of 22 October 1948 the sixty-seven-year-old Polish primate, Cardinal August Hlond, died. He was replaced a few weeks later by Stefan Wyszyński, twenty years younger than Hlond, well known for his prewar pastoral work and numerous articles in Catholic publications, and recently ordained Bishop of Lublin. The authorities were to find Wyszyński a formidable opponent—a pastor and a politician who managed to combine the perseverance of a true son of the church and guardian of the spiritual world with the flexibility of a seasoned statesman.

In the second half of 1948, however, before the new primate could take office, the authorities succeeded in "dealing with" what they considered to be undesirable activity on the part of Catholic political groups. At the end of August and the beginning of September, *Tygodnik Warszawski* was closed down, and its founders imprisoned, both laymen (Jerzy Braun, Kazimierz Studentowicz, Jan Hoppe, Konstanty Turowski, and Antoni Antczak) and clergy (Father Zygmunt Kaczyński). In the absence of Karol Popiel, who had fled the country in October of the previous year, Christian-democratic circles were completely destroyed. The Kraków-based *Tygodnik Powszechny*, always less politicized and more willing to make concessions, came under intense pressure from the censors, shifted its focus to defending cultural values, and ceased voicing purely political sentiments. The monthly *Znak*, closely associated with *Tygodnik Powszechny*, strongly endorsed this line, especially in articles written by Stanisław Stomma.

Also in 1948, cooperation collapsed between Christian-democratic groups and those associated with the two weeklies on the one hand and Bolesław Piasecki and his associates on the other, although the two groups jointly signed a letter criticizing the pope's statement to the German bishops. The closing of *Tygodnik Warszawski* and the palace coup within the PPR—as well as the now obvious intensification of the campaign against the church—caused Piasecki and his supporters to crystallize their position. The turning point came on 5 December 1948, when *Dziś i jutro* carried an article by Konstanty Łubieński that set out their reasoning. Just like the satellite parties, the group that was to become known as PAX declared itself on the side of socialism, acknowledging that "in the current period" it was "the very best model for the material world" and, together with Catholicism, would constitute a force that would "create an era of a new 'golden age.'" Piasecki tried, with the encouragement of the authorities (including the MBP), to set himself up as a mediator between the ruling party and the church hierarchy. The activity of his group thus constituted both a doctrinal and institutional departure from Catholicism. The Polish church hierarchy and the new primate lost the possibility of seeking support among the lay political activists who had remained independent of the PZPR.

The year 1949 brought heightened attacks on the church, a development already presaged officially in speeches at the First Congress of the PZPR and unofficially at briefings in the Ministry of Public Security and sessions of various party bodies. On 14 March the newly appointed minister of public administration, Władysław Wolski, signed a government statement harshly attacking many members of the church hierarchy and stating that the clergy was "intensifying" its antistate activity. This document was followed by a carefully prepared propaganda campaign, in which MBP agents in Catholic circles were instructed to speak at "mass meetings and rallies and at meetings of mass organizations, and state that, as Catholics, they fully endorsed the line proposed by the government."

The atmosphere became more heated, but the increase in temperature also gave rise to "the Lublin miracle" (in which a young nun claimed on 3 July to have seen tears flowing from an image of the Virgin Mary), which drew thousands of the faithful (and the interested). In this situation, the papal encyclical of 13 July, threatening the excommunication of anyone belonging to the communist party—which in Italy was commonplace—was considered a suitable pretext to sharpen the attack. On 5 August the government issued a decree "On the Protection of Freedom of Conscience and Religion" that stipulated a prison term of up to five years for "anyone who infringes freedom of religion by denying religious rites or services on the grounds of political, social, or scientific activities or opinions." Nearly 5,500 priests were summoned for "explanatory and cautionary "talks. The Politburo adopted an expanded plan for seizing control of Catholic youth organizations and the Caritas charity, taking over hospitals from convents, and restricting religious celebrations outside immediate church environs. As part of a general campaign to restrict the number of publications, most of the Catholic press was closed down. In an attempt to protect believers from further harassment, the church suspended or "put to sleep" most of its youth and devotional organizations.

The authorities were helped in their activities by the fact that they had some success in recruiting collaborators among the clergy itself after the veteran's organization, ZBoWiD, founded in 1 September 1949, established a Circle of Priests. This development could have been viewed at the time as a first step toward creating something akin to a "national church" and provoking a schism. It appears, though, that the prevailing opinion among the agencies carrying out the campaign within the church was that the "patriotic priests"—as the members of the veterans' circle were called—were to be used to bring pressure to bear on the church rather than to establish a "counter-church." One high-level PZPR official dealing with these issues, Antoni Bida, even warned his subordinates that "those who would like to turn the class war into a war over dogma will lose." This "class war" was supposed to involve driving a wedge between church dignitaries and "rank-and-file" clergy, who were to be recruited by playing on personal ambitions, exploiting the long-standing conflicts between the vicars and older parish-priests, and by blackmail of the time-honored variety based on misconduct involving alcohol, money, or sex.

After lengthy negotiations, mediated by Piasecki and conducted in an atmosphere of constant pressure and unceasing propaganda, the "Agreement Between Representatives of the Government of the Polish Republic and the Polish Episcopate" was signed on 14 April 1950. With the support of virtually the entire episcopate, including the venerable Cardinal Sapieha, the primate agreed to far-reaching concessions: the church would recognize the need to include in its teaching respect for the law and state authorities; it would condemn the underground and the "anti-Polish and revanchist" statements of the German clergy; it would not oppose collectivization of agriculture; and it would support "the struggle for peace" and act in accordance with "Poland's raison d'état." In exchange, the government would allow religious instruction in schools; chaplains would be permitted in the armed forces and in prisons and hospitals; and the church would be allowed to operate seminaries and the Catholic University in Lublin, to publish its own periodicals, and to organize schools to be run by convents and monasteries. The problem, however, was that the state had the resources necessary to compel the clergy to behave in the desired fashion, while the church was obliged to rely on the good will of the other side. And this, of course, was nonexistent.

It is not surprising, then, that the pressure on the church was maintained. As early as May 1950, the authorities imposed severe restrictions on land ownership on the part of monasteries and bishoprics; and the bishop of Chełm, Kazimierz Kowalski, went to join more than one hundred priests already in prison. Religion was systematically eliminated from the schools, and any catechism instructors who resisted being ejected were treated as intruders; the MBP, which had jurisdiction over the whole prison service, regulated priests' access to prison inmates; and the church's publishing activities were severely curtailed by the restricted supply of paper and newsprint. In accordance with the principal of divide and rule, Piasecki was allowed to form a Commission of Catholic Intellectuals and Activists, attached to the National Front, a move that was intended to check the episcopate even further and—just in case—to keep the "patriotic priests" in line. Piasecki's group went ever further not only in terms of subservience to the authorities but also in doctrine. It was precisely at this time that the group adopted (in its internal guidelines) the assumption that Marxism would defeat capitalism and that, thanks to its own initiative, the "errors of Marxism" would then be rectified by Catholicism, leading to a syncretic system— Catholic in its philosophy and socialist in its institutions and politics.

In January 1951 the authorities forcibly removed the interim administrators of five dioceses in the northern and western provinces, pushing through the "selection" of vicars-general subservient to the government. On 20 January yet another member of the church hierarchy, the bishop of Kielce, Czesław Kaczmarek, was arrested. In March activists of the Labor Party were the subject of a show trial. The authorities circulated a falsified transcript of the proceedings with the inflammatory title, "Allies of the Gestapo." A dozen or so writers and editors of *Tygodnik Warszawski* were tried individually and sentenced to prison, some of them to life terms. Two of those sentenced, Antoni Antczak and Zygmunt Kaczyński, died behind bars.

Cardinal Wyszyński tried to salvage the situation, accepting the vicars-general and in several discussions with Bierut trying to find a modus vivendi, even if only a temporary one. He succeeded—during a visit to the Vatican—in obtaining the pope's agreement to the appointment of titular bishops to the five orphaned dioceses, but Bierut rejected this concession. The propaganda machine intensified its attack on the church, accusing the episcopate and the Vatican of obstructing the permanent incorporation of the western territories.

The maneuvering continued, however, one move being the formal establishment of the PAX Association on 9 April 1952, which gave Piasecki's group greater opportunities to participate in the impending elections. PAX received five places on the National Front electoral list and favorable treatment, including tax concessions, for its material assets. The formation of the new Sejm not only signified the success of PAX but also marked the point at which the authorities launched an all-out—and decisive—attack on the church hierarchy. In November the bishops in the Katowice province were forcibly removed from office, and five priests belonging to the Kraków Metropolitan Curia were arrested, as was Archbishop Antoni Baraniak. In January 1953 the authorities denied Cardinal Wyszyński a passport to visit Rome, and on the twenty-seventh of the month the trial of the Kraków priests came to an end, with stiff sentences being handed down in the midst of a deafening propaganda campaign. Work was finally completed on a decree "Concerning Appointments to Church Posts," published on 9 February. The accompanying executive order strengthened its provisions, giving the state administration authority over the church's entire "personnel policy." This was a clear attempt to subordinate the church, something that—in line with the Soviet example of the 1920s—had already been achieved in the rest of Moscow's dependent states. This operation required an expansion of the MBP agencies dealing with the church, and in January 1953 the relevant section within the ministry was replaced by a separate department (the Eleventh Department), with equivalent regional agencies down to the district level.

The episcopate and the primate decided to take up the challenge. On 8 May the Conference of Bishops agreed on the wording of a letter to be sent to Bierut, and—more important—on 4 June Cardinal Wyszyński read this letter to a crowd of 200,000 people taking part in the traditional Corpus Christi procession in Warsaw: "We cannot render unto Caesar that which belongs to God. *Non possumus!*" During the summer, after Bierut had visited Moscow to consult with the new, post-Stalin (and post-Beria) ruling group, the PZPR leadership decided on the next step aimed at securing the primate's subservience. On 14 September 1953 the public trial of Bishop Kaczmarek got under way; after proceedings lasting eight days the bishop was sentenced to twelve years in prison, and the authorities issued Cardinal Wyszyński a virtual ultimatum, demanding that he condemn the Kielce church hierarchy. In a letter to the Council of Ministers, dated 24 September, the cardinal rejected the charges against Bishop Kaczmarek. On the same day, the authorities decided it was time to "isolate" the head of the Polish church, and two days later he was arrested by a group of MBP officials.

The security apparatus was mobilized to deal with any potential "hostile demonstrations against the authorities' orders," but there were only scattered protests. One reason for this was, no doubt, the capitulation of those members of the episcopate who had not been arrested and who on 28 September adopted a declaration, written by Piasecki, affirming their loyalty to the regime and condemning Bishop Kaczmarek. The bishop of Łódź, Michał Klepacz, who was being groomed by Franciszek Mazurek, the Politburo member overseeing the campaign against the church, was now named chairman of the Conference of Bishops. Whether the episcopate's declaration signified its willingness to render unto the PZPR Central Committee "that which belongs to God" is open to debate, but the church had plainly ceased to be an autonomous entity in public life. Thus, six months after the death of Stalin, the ruling party achieved one of the main goals of Polish Stalinism.

CULTURAL REVOLUTION

"Tired and hungry, the mass of university professors can be rallied to our side if we show concern for their material well-being; individually, each professor can be bought if we show concern for the material needs of his workplace, because they all have a fixation where their work is concerned." These words were written, in an analysis intended for internal circulation only, by a high-level official in the Department of Science and Higher Education of the Ministry of Education. This document, written at the end of 1945, provides insights into how the state authorities, dominated by the PPR, intended to seduce the intellectual elites. Similar methods were used in the effort to persuade other groups to participate in the country's intellectual and artistic life. After all, actors, writers, painters, and musicians also had a fixation about their work. The limits of this participation were defined, on the one hand, by relatively stringent censorship and the system of licenses, and, on the other, by the forceful push to rebuild science and education, intellectual and cultural life, which presented artists and intellectuals with a number of moral and political dilemmas. These were somewhat mitigated by official policy, which sought to "rally people by showing concern" and by emphasizing the dual goals of reconstructing and disseminating culture, something that had long been the dream of many artists and teachers.

Although the restrictions were painfully evident, positive changes were being made in many areas. Theaters were opened in the western and northern territories; by 1947, 93 percent of the school-age population was attending school; in the same year the combined circulation of the daily press exceeded the prewar level; the number of book titles published in 1946 was greater than the record number published in 1938; and in 1945 alone six new institutions of higher education were established. Cinemas largely showed prewar films, theaters played a traditional repertoire, especially dramas of the romantic era, and books by Erskine Caldwell and John Steinbeck were published in translation. The younger generation of writers engaged in an "intellectual settling of accounts" that was generally honest and of high quality (Kazimierz Brandys's *Drewniany koń* [Wooden Horse], Stanisław Dygat's *Jezioro Bodeńskie* [The Bodensee], Artur Sandauer's *Śmierć Liberała* [Death of a Liberal], and Paweł Hertz's *Sedan*). Books dealing with the Era of the Gas Ovens were hampered by not being able to discuss the tragic events in the East, but still provided examples of powerful literature, among them Zofia Nałkowska's *Medalioni* and the electrifying work of Tadeusz Borowski.

The propaganda was savage, just as the fight against the legal and underground opposition had been, but in the cultural sphere, broadly defined, the basic aim of artists was to refrain from "antistate" statements and to remain neutral, which the ruling group interpreted as (and which did in fact function as) support for the new regime. The authorities gave preference to any initiatives that were based on more or less honest aspirations to bring about far-reaching changes and achieve what amounted to an "educational revolution." They encouraged people to think of the rewards that come from doing good for others, of the need for a "social patron" to protect art and culture from the commercialization that inevitably leads to vulgar trash, and the lofty goal of bringing literacy to the peasants.

As early as 1947 the attitude of the PPR gradually began to change, a process that was not perceptible to everyone. The Central Committee's Cultural-Educational Commission, established in February, together with the equivalent Central Committee department, rapidly began drawing up plans for the whole area they were to supervise. They compiled a list of "themes to be addressed in artistic endeavors" (including music). These included "contemporary Polish heroes and statesmen"—Bierut, Gomułka, Spychal-ski, and Cyrankiewicz among them; "the revolutionary results of agrarian reform"; and "the nationalization of industry—breaking the chains of economic dependence on private capital, foreign and domestic." The party considered that cultural life "lags far behind," and stated unequivocally that, "the aim is to transform human beings, to eliminate the distance that exists today between the new system . . . and the consciousness of its citizens, which generally remains deeply mired in the mental and emotional sphere of yesteryear." It also confirmed the existence of "an anachronistic ideal of falsely interpreted 'creative freedom.'" The directives produced within the PPR were "translated" administratively into the Ministry of Culture, established in July 1947, which was "to direct policy and coordinate the activity of all agencies, ministries, and institutions."

Education occupied a major place in a fairly broad range of activities. More than 500 PSL members were rapidly dismissed from the school superintendents' system, all textbooks and reading materials (about 2,500 titles) were reviewed, and nearly twenty thousand teachers were required to attend "ideology courses" during school vacations. In May 1947 a meeting of "candidates for the post of lecturer in politico-social doctrines" at institutions of higher education heard one of the speakers state that it was necessary "to destroy existing cadres and form new ones." The Central Committee of Democratic Faculty, established by the PPR and PPS in September, was to carry out this "destruction" under the slogan of eliminating the "kulaks of science" from universities and colleges. On 28 October 1947 a decree was published, "The Organization of Science and Higher Education," which eliminated the miserable remnants of university autonomy that had already been so restricted before the war. In the summer of 1947 the Department of Enterprises of the Ministry of Culture and Art was established. This body centralized control over the film industry, already totally nationalized, as well as the recording and printing industries.

At a meeting of the PPR Central Committee on 11 October, largely devoted to—in the words of Jerzy Putrament—"counteracting the penetration of capitalist mentality," party activists recommended not only limiting imports of "Anglo-Saxon" films, books, and newspapers but also restricting the activities of the British Council and English-language study groups in schools. It was also considered necessary to eliminate private publishing and strengthen censorship. In the same month, the Kraków censor's office banned a production of Juliusz Słowacki's *Kordian,* and it soon turned out that theaters would no longer be allowed to perform plays by Wyśpiański, Mickiewicz, and Norwid.

These aspirations were presented to the public—in rather general terms—in a speech that Bierut delivered on the occasion of the opening of Radio Wrocław on 16 November 1947. Stefan Żółkiewski, a promoter of the new esthetic norms, entitled his commentary on the speech, "Facing a New Stage in Cultural Policy." The December congress of the Polish Fine Arts Association took place—as the association's president, Stanisław Teisseyre put it—"under the aegis of the Wrocław speech," although participants clearly stressed that "art must not become a method of creative activity determined from above." Nevertheless, the majority of the congress participants were soon subordinating themselves to this method.

In the "plan of work for 1948," drawn up by PPR Central Committee officials, the scenario for change was plainly spelled out: "intensification and planned direction of the processes involved in the creation of a new cultural tradition," "the introduction of new, nonbourgeois content," and "the ideological transformation of institutions involved in the dissemination of culture." Poland followed the example of the Soviet Union, where the battle for socialist realism, following a short postwar breathing space was renewed in 1946, with a fierce propaganda attack on the renegades— Akhmatova, Zoshchenko, and Shostakovich. The first swallow heralding the approach of socialist realism in Poland appeared on 25 December 1946 in the form of a film by Eugeniusz Cękalski, *Jasne łany* (Sunny Cornfields), which told a tale of good poor peasants and evil kulaks. The nature of the campaign being waged in Leningrad and Moscow was made abundantly clear to delegates attending the Congress of Intellectuals in the Cause of Peace, which took place in Wrocław in August 1948, at the same time that the public phase of the conflict with Gomułka was beginning in Warsaw. Aleksandr Fadeyev, chairman of the Soviet delegation, gave a speech in which he stated: "If hyenas knew how to use a fountain-pen and jackals could type, they would write like T. S. Eliot."

The cultural revolution was a strange and frightening mixture of the much-needed educational revolution and the thesis that "the class struggle intensifies as the construction of socialism progresses." It entered a decisive stage at the beginning of 1949, in virtually all fields at the same time. A succession of congresses or working conferences, beginning with writers (Szczecin, 20–23 January) and ending with filmmakers (Wisła, 19–22 November), cleared the ground by eliminating from decision-making bodies all those who wanted to retain creative autonomy, and provided a forum for pronouncements concerning the "new stage." The next step toward centralization of control over cultural life was the establishment of the Central Bureau of Art Exhibitions (21 February), the Central Publishing Commission (29 July), and the Central Commission for Theatrical Repertoire (13 December). The press was "rationalized," with the number of dailies being reduced from 107 to 34, and the number of periodicals, from 745 to 592. The rate of increase in new book titles slowed, although there was a slight increase in the number of copies printed, and privately published books accounted for about 25 percent of the book market (compared with 8 percent a year later). The number of translations from Russian rose nearly threefold (from 63 to 174), while translations from English and other "imperialist languages" came to a halt. Arnold Szyfman's dismissal from his post as director of Warsaw's Polish Theater marked the beginning of a process whereby the great directors were relegated to the background, and Russian plays (increasingly, works of socialist realism, not the classics) came to feature prominently in the repertory. (One example was the First Festival of Russian and Soviet Art, staged by forty-seven theaters in October-December.)

Beginning on 11 January 1949, all the country's theaters were nationalized; a year later they had acquired the valued status of industrial enterprises, and their employees were subject to regulations concerning labor discipline. During 1949 the first Polish "tales from the factory floor" appeared: Jan Wilczyk's *Nr 16 produkuje* (Shop No. 16 is at Work), Jerzy Pytlakowski's *Fundamenty,* and Aleksander Jackiewicz's *Górnicy* (Miners). Large editions of poetry anthologies with titles such as *Armia radziecka* (The Soviet Army), *Młode ręce budują* (Young Hands Are Building), *General Karol Świerczewski,* and *O Gwardii i Armii Ludowej* (On the People's Guard and the People's Army) were published. A great deal of propaganda hoopla surrounded the opening in August of the First Exhibition of Portraits of Leading Workers.

Together with the sole remaining comic-strip publication, *Nowy Świat Przygód* (A New World of Adventure), the remnants of prewar "petit bourgeois" mass culture disappeared, to be replaced by an expanded network of factory-based clubs (of which there were more than ten thousand by 1953) with their artistic ensembles, mass editions of the "Soviet classics," and millions of propaganda pamphlets.

The PZPR Politburo decided to convene the First Congress of Polish Science, which—twice postponed—approved the establishment of the Polish Academy of Sciences (in 1951), and science and higher education were now included in the economic plans drawn up by the Planning Commission. An overall reorganization of higher education was begun; small departments were replaced by institutes, and medical and agricultural faculties were separated from universities. These changes were used as a pretext to remove a number of leading philosophers and humanities scholars (including Janina Kotarbińska, Maria Ossowska, Władysław Tatarkiewicz, and Roman Ingarden) from teaching and/or academic life as a whole. Lecture notes and textbooks were withdrawn from circulation, to be gradually replaced by books translated from Russian. Beginning with the 1949–50 school year, the main purpose of education was said to be "the formation of a scientific worldview based on the foundations of contemporary achievements of dialectical and historical materialism, and the formation of socialist morality."

These changes were summarized, and their "broadening and deepening" announced, in a speech that Jakob Berman delivered to the PZPR Central Committee in November 1949, the same meeting that finally disposed of Gomułka and "his clique." "Socialist realism," Berman proclaimed, "is a genuinely revolutionary leap, . . . a revelatory creative methodology." Stalin's seventieth birthday in 1949 provided an occasion to demonstrate the new artistic approach; the front pages of the newspapers and bookstore windows were filled with panegyrics exalting the Great Leader of Progressive Humanity.

Thus a pattern was established for the coming years. Socialist realism became compulsory in all fields of art, and cultural associations became instruments of control over their members, reinforcing the process of self-censorship. A few extreme radicals emerged in the process, people who in literary circles were referred to as "the pimply youths," although by no means all of them were young. In the humanities Marxists reigned supreme, most of them succumbing to the charms of the most vulgar version of this ideology. Biology was invaded by the views of Trofim Lysenko and his followers, which drove out "bourgeois" genetics. Some artists and scientists were silent, unable to express their own ideas and unwilling to express those that were expected of them. Others sought protection away from the ideological front lines: writing historical novels, researching the Middle Ages, or editing the work of others. Still others tried, *nolens volens,* to adapt to the situation, but without condemning other people or engaging in too rigorous a self-criticism. Against this background it was easy to identify those who considered themselves the standard-bearers of the new order.

It was their voices that were heard most frequently and most loudly, and together with the highly overgrown "cultural bureaucracy"—especially in science—they administered the entire " world of representation." Architecture students were instructed to follow "the methods of the former St. Petersburg Academy of Fine Arts during the years 1893–1905, the culmination of the old realist school." Painters were reminded that they were to accustom themselves to "independent creative work, corresponding to the requirements and tasks set by the society of People's Poland, fighting for peace and socialism." At a conference of university rectors, which more closely resembled a political briefing than a meeting of university lecturers, participants were told they had a duty "to use all methods available to prevent the penetration of universities and research institutes by foreign spies and agents of imperialism."

There were numerous propaganda attacks on individuals, and although the security forces were never directly involved, some of them sounded threatening, and even ominous. How did Adolf Rudnicki feel when he read that his novel *Pałeczka* (The Stick) "might call into serious question his further participation in the great process of creating literature"? Or Stanisław Pigoń, whose monograph dealing with the work of the writer, Tadeusz Orkan, revealed something more than "unconscious blindness to history"? Or Władysław Konopczyński, in whose work the reviewer detected "the stench of superstition, provincialism, and obscurantism"? Nothing could be done to harm Shakespeare, but actors and directors must have felt more than a little uneasy when they read that, at the National Congress of Polish Language and Literature, someone had stated that "our young people will no longer find greatness . . . in either Hamlet, standing beyond the pale of society or in Kordian, unable to live in the real world." Słowacki's Judym, "seeking through martyrdom to resolve class conflicts," was also unfit to be a hero.

Self-criticism was a frequent ritual, and we shall never know whether Borowski really considered he had made a mistake in "failing to depict the class divisions of the [concentration] camp," or whether Gałczyński was really ashamed of the fact that "he had not broken prison bread in fascist Poland alongside Broniewski and Wygodzki."

But cultural life proceeded at a brisk pace, and not only in the corridors, where some were chastised and others were praised. There were exhibitions and premieres; famous artists were awarded the highest state honors and prizes (in 1949 painter and sculptor Xawery Dunikowski received the Builder of People's Poland Medal, one of the first two to be awarded). Culture was a major factor of the epoch, and its dissemination was treated as a task of great political significance. Theater and cinema audiences grew in size, the annual Festival of Learning and Books was essentially a major effort to promote literacy, and dozens of books were published in mass, cheap editions. In 1949 the authorities began an energetic and wide-ranging battle against illiteracy (at that time 1.4 million people were registered as unable to read and write), public libraries and school libraries sprang up everywhere, and the popular women's weekly, *Przyjaciółka* (Girlfriend), had a circulation of two million—unimaginable before the war. In 1950 the Pioneer radio set went into production, at a rate of one hundred thousand radios a year, and radio stations rapidly increased the power of their transmitters (although some of this was neutralized by jamming stations). The trade unions, the women's organization, and the Peasant Self-Help Cooperative provided a base for an amateur dramatics movement that took various forms and whose task was to do battle with both "nationalism" and "rootless cosmopolitanism." "Artistic-agitation brigades" were dispatched to rural community centers across the country; in 1953, they gave a total of 152,000 performances that were seen by nineteen million people.

It is difficult to judge how much of this rapid growth in cultural interests reflected an authentic desire to read or go to the theater, resulting from the changes in social structure brought about by urbanization and industrialization, and how much was the result of official pressure to "organize an audience" and the availability of free subscriptions (and outright falsification of statistics). In either case, this "socialist mass culture" was a tool of indoctrination.

THAW AND FLOOD

On 5 March 1953, at 9:50 P.M. Moscow time, Kremlin doctors recorded the death of Joseph Vissarionovich Stalin, one of the founders of the greatest tyranny of modern times and for almost a quarter century its sole ruler. With its military power and its ideology this system exerted direct and indirect influence over a large part of Eurasia and reached into the remaining inhabited parts of the world. It was bound together by both ideology and an extensive apparatus of repression and control, and its keystone was the tyrant, the object of an unprecedented cult. The shock evoked by the news of the dictator's death was proportional to the scope of the power that he wielded: "The entire world realizes that with the death of Stalin a whole epoch has come to an end," declared Dwight D. Eisenhower on 16 April, four months after his election as U.S. president. In the Soviet Union and all the countries of the socialist camp, the day of Stalin's funeral was declared a day of national mourning, and tens (perhaps hundreds?) of thousands of people took part in solemnities. The people who were least surprised were the great autocrat's closest associates. They had witnessed his illness and had become increasingly alarmed by his growing mistrust of everyone around him, a state of mind bordering on persecution mania.

The system that Stalin had created now confronted a challenge on a scale similar to that of the German invasion of 1941. A fierce struggle soon broke out within the Kremlin leadership over how to respond to this challenge and over who would succeed the "cunning Georgian." Just under two weeks after the death of Stalin, the principle of "collective leadership" was adopted, whereby a triumvirate consisting of Grigory Malenkov, Lavrenty Beria, and Vyacheslav Molotov was to rule the empire in harmony. They quickly took steps to loosen the chains of terror. On 27 March a partial amnesty was proclaimed and some articles of the penal code were amended. A week later the new leaders rehabilitated the government doctors who had narrowly escaped falling victim to Stalin's last wave of purges, this one plainly directed against Jews.

Prime Minister Malenkov also signaled that the government was considering the possibility of a shift in economic policy that would increase the resources allocated to consumption. A few hesitant—not to say fearful— steps were taken to loosen the bonds of ideological orthodoxy, involving proposals to renew diplomatic relations with Yugoslavia. The leadership also took steps to "warm up" relations with the United States, and at the instigation of Moscow the North Korean government signed a cease-fire in Panmunjom on 27 July. The de facto end of the Korean War not only had enormous significance in the sphere of international relations, signaling the beginning of the—albeit still distant—end of the Cold War, but also made it possible for the East European regimes to make adjustments in response to the growing economic crisis that they faced.

All these countries, including Poland, were burdened by nearly three years of a massive buildup in armaments. During this period real wages fell, supplies of consumer goods fell further below demand, inflation appeared, and farm incomes declined drastically. As it turned out, Poland was the last country that managed to deal with the crisis relatively easily by "adjusting prices" (on 3 January 1953). Six months later a similar maneuver evoked widespread resistance on the part of people who were no doubt emboldened by the events that had occurred since Stalin's death. When Czech workers were confronted with the monetary reform combined with an increase in prices that accompanied the abolition of rationing, they reacted with widespread strikes and street demonstrations. While these were quickly suppressed and officially declared to be the work of "imperialist agents," they were a sign of things to come.

Far more violent was the response of German workers to new labor norms introduced on 16 June. For several days all major towns in the GDR were engulfed by a wave of strikes and demonstrations that were bloodily suppressed with the assistance of the Soviet occupation forces, including armored units. A highly disquieting situation also existed in Hungary, where the authorities decided—under strong pressure from Moscow—to undertake a "peaceful maneuver," appointing Imre Nagy prime minister on June 4. An opponent of previous economic policies, Nagy quickly followed Malenkov in announcing the introduction of a "new course." Apart from anything else, the fact that the Soviet leadership was obliged on more than one occasion to "admonish" its Budapest colleagues suggested a certain weakening of the Kremlin's authority, one cause of which was the internal power struggle taking place in Moscow. The most glaring sign of this struggle was the announcement—in classic Stalinist style—that the once all-powerful Beria had been dismissed from his post and arrested for "criminal antiparty and antistate activity." According to official sources, he was executed in December following a secret trial; other sources say he was shot immediately following his arrest at a meeting of the Politburo in the Kremlin. At the beginning of September, the next stage of the power struggle was resolved, this time—as is so often the case—in favor of the person occupying the position in the center (between the "conservative" Molotov and the "liberal" Malenkov): this was Nikita Sergeyevich Khrushchev, whom Poles from the borderlands remembered without fondness as the ruler of the Ukraine during 1938–47.

Beria's associates were finished off in truly Stalinist fashion, but Soviet society experienced a huge sense of relief that was also fostered by developments in the international arena. Malenkov put forward a proposal for "peaceful coexistence," something that Moscow found easier to countenance now that it had mastered the production of the second generation of nuclear weapons, the hydrogen bomb. During the period 25 January–18 February 1954, the foreign ministers of the Big Four met for lengthy discussions for the first time in several years. Almost three months of negotiations in Geneva yielded, on 21 June, if not agreement on the reunification of Korea, at least agreement on another flash point in Asia, the demarcation of a cease-fire line in Vietnam. On 15 May 1955 the occupying powers signed a peace treaty with Austria, whereby, in exchange for Austria's neutrality, the Soviet Army left the country.

A major event during this period, when the Cold War was showing the first signs of abating, was the meeting in Geneva of the leaders of the Big Four, almost exactly ten years after the Potsdam Conference, which had brought together Stalin, Truman, and Churchill/Attlee. Two months later, on 13 September 1955, Moscow established diplomatic relations with the Federal Republic of Germany. What diplomats and journalists started calling "the spirit of Geneva" began to waft around the world.

For Poland and the other countries of the socialist camp, the easing of tensions between the superpowers was not the only important development at this time; equally significant was the barely perceptible but nevertheless real loosening of Moscow's control. In October 1954, the Sino-Soviet Agreement was signed in Beijing; this guaranteed the equality of each party and bound each of them to respect the internal sovereignty of the other. The approach to China would not necessarily be applied to Moscow's European satellites, but it could herald a broadening in their freedom of maneuver, on the condition, of course, that they did not disturb ideological fundamentals. Similarly significant was Khrushchev's unexpected visit to Yugoslavia (27 May–2 June 1955), where he queried Stalin's charges concerning the alleged Titoist conspiracy that provided the basis for purges across Eastern Europe in the late 1940s and early 1950s. The signing of the Warsaw Pact on 14 May 1955 provided further evidence that the Soviet Union was becoming more concerned about the form of its relations with its satellites than had previously been the case. While the pact constituted a response to the inclusion of West Germany into NATO in October the previous year and stipulated the subordination of "amalgamated armed forces" to Soviet command, it gave this dependence a legal and contractual basis.

The perceptible, if inconsistent, changes that took place in the three countries closest to Poland during the months immediately following Stalin's death seemed to pass Warsaw by. In the summer of 1953 Marshal Rokossowski, undoubtedly at the instigation of Moscow, proposed at a Politburo meeting that "Soviet officers be gradually detached" from the Polish armed forces and that they be replaced by a system of advisers, similar to that existing in other countries of the Soviet bloc. At a briefing for the *aktiv* in the security ministry and prosecutor's staff, Radkiewicz referred, among other things, to a "breakdown in law and order, consisting in a whole range of incorrect and unjust methods in our work, not only at the stage of investigation." At the same time, a commission was established to investigate prison conditions. All this took place, however, in deepest secrecy and resulted in no actual changes: Soviet officers remained in their positions and prison cells remained full. In fact, it was precisely at this time that the authorities launched their all-out attack on the church, and they continued their campaign "to root out those enemies concealed deep below the surface" by arresting Marshal Żymierski.

It was not until the fall that the first signs of the "new course" appeared. At a meeting of the PZPR Central Committee on 29–30 October 1953, Bierut delivered a report with the highly complicated title, "The Party's Tasks in the Battle for Faster Growth in the Living Standards of the Working Masses During the Current Stage of Socialist Construction." Shortly afterward, on 14 November, the prices of some foodstuffs were reduced, very slightly, for the first time in living memory. Stronger whiffs of change, of what came to be known as the thaw—after Ilya Ehrenburg's novel of that name—could be detected the following spring. The Second Congress of the PZPR (10–17 March) adopted Malenkov's prescription and decided on a clear reorientation of economic policy, reducing growth targets for the remainder of the six-year plan. On the political front, the Poles established their own "collective leadership"; Cyrankiewicz replaced Bierut as prime minister so that the latter might "devote himself to party work" in his position as first secretary of the Central Committee.

Interference in culture and the arts also eased, the shift in policy being announced by the slogan of "the struggle against whitewash" and "the need to do away with schematic approaches." The chief official charged with introducing socialist realism, Włodzimierz Sokorski, personally lauded "the real turn-around in our cultural policy," by which he meant the abandonment of "the administration of art." In the background, and still in secrecy, the first real changes began to take effect in the security apparatus. At a meeting in the Ministry of Public Security in March speakers referred to "impermissible cases of the infringement of people's law and order." Decisions followed soon thereafter. The long-term head of the Investigation Department, Jozef Różański, was dismissed, the Tenth Department was dissolved (on 11 June), and the first ever reduction in security ministry personnel was ordered. There were also unpublicized reductions in military personnel, and factories hitherto producing for the defense industry began producing goods for the consumer market.

It is difficult to determine what the scope and pace of further change might have been had external events not intervened, although the main direction had already been laid out: an "economic maneuver" had been initiated with the aim of raising living standards and reducing the proportion of resources allocated to investment, mass repression (apart from the persecution of private farmers) had been abandoned, and a substantial number of people had been released from prison. A powerful stimulus that accelerated these changes now came from outside, but not from Moscow, which probably regarded with favor the relatively stable situation on the Vistula.

On 28 September 1954, the Polish Service of Radio Free Europe began broadcasting a series of programs narrated by Józef Światło, former deputy director of the Tenth Department of the Ministry of Public Security, who had "disappeared" in West Berlin in December of the previous year while traveling on official business. Światło's broadcasts, titled *Behind the Scenes of the Security Service and the Party,* amounted to a genuine propaganda coup. They not only laid out the facts of unprecedented terror, but also provided a wide range of sensational details and gossip about the lives—and sexual liaisons—of the party elite. Its members were described as a bloodthirsty, demoralized, and fractious clique. According to data collected by the Ministry of Public Security as part of its efforts to monitor the public mood, tens of thousands of people listened to Światło's broadcasts, Essentially, the whole country knew about them.

The reaction was swift. Within a week or two a commission had been established to examine the activity of the security ministry, and Radkiewicz was trying to salvage his career by drawing up a plan to reorganize the ministry into two separate institutions, a Ministry of Internal Affairs and a Committee on Public Security. The party leadership, however, had decided that far-reaching changes in personnel were needed. The authorities began releasing from prison the communists arrested by the Tenth Department, and one of the places thus vacated was taken (at the beginning of November) by Różański. The time had come for a more serious form of self-criticism.

After a series of briefings for the staff of the security ministry itself and for the first secretaries of the party's provincial committees, more than two hundred officials belonging to the so-called central *aktiv* were obliged to engage in public self-criticism. During the two-day session (29–30 November 1954), some people called for the entire leadership of the ministry to be called to account, and some even voiced criticism of the Politburo. There were references to Gomułka and calls for his release. The formal division of the Ministry of Public Security took place on 7 December; Radkiewicz was exiled to the post of minister of state farms, and people from the party apparatus were brought in to head the new institutions (Władysław Wicha became head of the Ministry of Internal Affairs, and Władysław Dworakowski chaired the Committee on Security). On 13 December, Gomułka was discretely released from house arrest, with the proviso that this move was to remain secret for the time being. He had spent three-and-a-half years in confinement, without confessing to anything. He could now wait for his moment to come.

All this was spelled out in January 1955, during discussions at a meeting of the PZPR Central Committee and in a committee resolution stressing the need "to observe the Leninist principles of party life" and "to eradicate bureaucratic distortions." Although Bierut retained his authority within the party, which undoubtedly helped consolidate the leadership, the process of "controlled relaxation" gave rise to many problems and carried with it the possibility that disagreements over its scope and pace would emerge. The first signs of such disagreements could already be detected in the spring of 1955, although they perhaps had less to with any specific issues than with the widespread hopes of further change engendered by the appearance of new people in the party leadership—Władysław Matwin and Jerzy Morawski (known as the "young secretaries"). Given that the reorientation of economic policy had so far yielded little in the way of visible results—although prices had been reduced for a third time in April—the "new course" was most visible in the sphere of culture and in the gradually expanding freedom of speech. This found expression in widespread criticism, in the public repudiation of socialist realism by many artists, a process that its most zealous supporters (among them, Leon Kruczkowski) were powerless to prevent. A number of people began to organize various initiatives "from below": Stefan Kisielewski began preparations to publish a periodical (a project that was nipped in the bud), and a group of Warsaw intellectuals founded, with the party's blessing, the Club of the Crooked Circle (Klub Krzywego Koła). The younger generation—already "corrupted" by Western films, underground jazz, and Radio Luxembourg—was much influenced by the International Youth and Student Festival, which provided an opportunity to rub shoulders with thirty thousand foreigners, some of them extremely exotic. Evidence of artistic ferment and the abandonment of socialist realism was on display at an exhibition featuring the work of young painters and sculptors that opened in Warsaw on 31 July. It was a paradox of history that, ten days earlier, Soviet construction workers had presented "a gift to the Polish nation" in the form of the Palace of Culture and Science, the quintessence of socialist-realist architecture.

Of special significance in the world of symbols was the publication of Adam Ważyk's "Poemat dla dorosłych" (A Poem for Adults) in one of the August issues of *Nowa Kultura.* In a journal intended to provide a platform for, and advance the cause of, socialist realism, one of the leading theoreticians of the esthetic norms descended from the era of the Moscow show trials rejected not only these norms but the whole practice of socialist industrialization. The poem depicted the other side of the coin: the lives and state of mind of the young people erecting the Great Edifice of Socialism. As was so often the case, the party authorities added oil to the fire, fiercely attacking both the author and the publisher; even members of the Politburo (Berman and Ochab) spoke out alongside the party writers and literary critics who were drafted into action. While the party leadership called for a struggle against "all forms of disorientation and ideological confusion," it was becoming increasingly difficult to wage such as struggle, especially as the PZPR itself was becoming a breeding ground for what Berman called "revisionist" and "democratic-liberal" tendencies. A widening gulf was plainly visible between the upper echelons of the party, which under Bierut's watchful eye remained relatively united, and intellectuals, the intelligentsia, and the younger generation. It only needed a jolt that would divide the upper echelons for the "revisionists" to become equal players in the political maneuvering.

Such a jolt was delivered in the late winter of 1956, and its effect in Poland was considerably stronger than in any other country of the Soviet bloc, including the USSR. Khrushchev's speech, delivered on 25 February at a closed session on the last day of the Twentieth Congress of the CPSU, was an event of worldwide significance. The title of the speech, "On the Cult of the Personality and its Consequences," was not itself shocking, since this cult had been the subject of discussion and commentary for over a year.

Khrushchev did not, however, confine himself to generalities, but cited hundreds of specific and horrifying examples of "errors and distortions," attributing responsibility for these to Stalin personally. Although he did not attempt to analyze the system as such, the fact that he produced in public such a powerful litany of accusations and criticisms put an end to the authority of the late "fourth founding father" of Marxism. With Khrushchev's speech the CPSU simultaneously distanced itself from Stalinist terror and claimed the position of the one legitimate critic of the past, thus reserving the right to "reform" itself.

Before the text of the speech had been made public, PZPR activists used the speeches delivered during the open sessions of the congress as the basis for a two-day meeting (3–4 March) at which they developed some of the themes raised in Moscow, particularly those relating to the rightist-nationalist deviation, the 1938 dissolution of the Polish Communist Party, and the "abuse of power" on the part of the security apparatus. On 10 March an editorial in the party daily, *Trybuna Ludu*, broadened Khrushchev's critique, but the most notable feature of the article was that it constituted a statement that went beyond the party to address directly the whole population.

It was to be expected that the divisions within the party would become deeper and that conflicts would erupt at the top, but a succession of events accelerated the process and gave it added strength. On 12 March, just before midnight, Bolesław Bierut died in Moscow. Taken ill toward the end of the congress, he never recovered sufficiently to return home. (The first signs of a serious deterioration in Bierut's health had been noted in January.) The loss of the first secretary deprived the PZPR leadership of the person who had kept control over public life and created the problem of choosing his successor. From this moment on the issue of how much and how fast to reform became the subject of intense infighting in the party, with the result that change became more radical in scope and proceeded at an accelerating pace.

Conflict erupted into the open at the first Central Committee meeting (20 March) following Bierut's death, although the committee did follow the Politburo's recommendation (made with the approval of Khrushchev, who was in Warsaw at the time) that Edward Ochab be elected first secretary. At the most general level, the controversy centered on how to continue to legitimize the system and retain power. The differing viewpoints were rarely formulated in a straightforward and politically coherent fashion, and were often articulated as personal squabbles. Some people thought the best solution would be to sacrifice a large number of those officials most responsible—in their eyes—for the "errors and distortions" of 1948–55, to rehabilitate Gomułka and his period as first secretary of the PPR, and to increase wages in order to reduce popular discontent. This was an essentially conservative position, and the scapegoats selected by its proponents suggested that they harbored strong anti-intelligentsia and anti-Semitic tendencies. These people later became known as the Natolin group, after the small town of that name near Warsaw, the site of numerous villas for government dignitaries. At the time, their opponents referred to them as *konserwa* (the Polish word for canned food), "dogmatists," or "sectarians" (in the Leninist sense of the word). Their leaders included Franciszek Jóźwiak, Aleksander Zawadzki, Kazimierz Witaszewski, Zenon Nowak, and General Kazimierz Witaszewski, who became famous at that time for his remark that the best way to deal with discontented intellectuals was "with an iron gas pipe."

The rival faction, subsequently known as the Puławska group, after a government apartment complex on Warsaw's Puławska Street, defined itself as the champion of "renewal" and "democratization." Its members argued that changes needed to be made in various parts of the system: reforms were needed in economic administration, censorship should be liberalized, the scope of individual freedoms should be broadened, and the PZPR should be democratized. The main representatives of this line included Roman Zambrowski, Janusz Zarzycki, Jerzy Morawski, Władysław Matwin, and Stefan Staszewski.

The Natolin group was entrenched in the party and state apparatus (including the military), while the Puławska faction drew support from the more radical sections of the younger generation and party intellectuals. Decision-making positions in the party were, however, largely in the hands of "centrists," people who feared that any ostentatious liberalizing measures could raise the temperature of public debate and conflict but who also harbored numerous reservations about the Natolin line. The centrists included Ochab, Cyrankiewicz, and Jerzy Albrecht. Bierut's closest associates, Berman and Minc, became complete outsiders. The former lost his position in the Politburo on 3 May 1956, while the latter had already been ousted as head of the planning commission in 1954 and was by now just a figurehead.

The "war at the top" was largely conducted behind the scenes rather than in full view of the public. At the same time, a growing number of social groups were publicly advancing a range of economic and social demands and calling for compensation for past acts of repression. The party leadership found it increasingly difficult to control the public mood, partly as a result of the factional infighting. The slow and cautious changes in economic administration and the allocation of resources had yielded barely perceptible results. Virtually every step in the direction of liberalization evoked an even greater jump in public expectations. These were usually articulated and introduced into the public domain by the journals that dealt with social and cultural topics, the most consistent in this regard being the weekly *Po prostu* (Speaking Frankly), which became for many people both the symbol and the standard-bearer of increasingly radical proposals for change. These publications attacked the privileges of the state and party apparatus, described the living and working conditions of teachers, researchers, and workers, called for the rehabilitation of the Home Army, attacked the canon of "dogmatic Marxism," discussed workers' self-management, and demanded far-reaching changes in the organization of the party's youth movement. Even though nearly all of this could be fitted within a Marxist framework and was accompanied by frequent quotations from the nineteenth-century classics (and from Lenin), such pronouncements and debates indicated that the party had lost its internal cohesion. They destabilized the entire system constructed on the basis of unity of opinion within the hegemonic ruling party. Another cause for alarm within the party leadership were the unmistakable signs of restlessness—as yet unorganized—among the satellite political parties and among the groups and institutions, including the Catholic Church, that were outside the framework of official political life.

At the end of April the Sejm proclaimed an amnesty. Within the space of a few weeks this was followed by the rehabilitation of those who had been sentenced in the trial of General Tatar and the arrest of yet more officials from the former Ministry of Public Security. There were also personnel changes in the government and at the highest levels of the judiciary and the public prosecutors' office. So many changes at such a speed were perceived as a sign that the authorities' grip on power was weakening. The result was considerable disorientation within the state apparatus, including the security service, and increasing boldness on the part of the general population, which voiced its demands with growing insistence. The text of Khrushchev's secret speech was widely distributed and all across the country it was the focus of lengthy discussions. At party meetings, generally open to the public, participants asked thousands of questions that until recently they had been afraid to ask themselves. Resolutions were passed demanding the truth about crimes and punishment for the perpetrators, the swift introduction of changes, and the country's emancipation from dependence on Moscow.

A key moment for this stage of the crisis—and for the entire course of events in 1956—was the short-lived revolt of the workers and citizens of Poznań. It erupted early in the morning of 28 June in the form of a strike over economic grievances in the Stalin Locomotive Works (ZISPO, formerly the Cegielski Factory). The ZISPO workers who took to the streets and started marching toward the center of town were joined by passersby and workers from other factories. The demonstration gathered outside the headquarters of the local authorities—the national council, and the provincial party committee. In the absence of any contact with representatives of the local authorities, who had no idea how to deal with the situation, the demonstration transformed itself over a few hours into a series of assaults on public buildings, including the prison.

The slogans rapidly changed from economic to political: "Down with the communists," "Free elections," "Down with the Russkis!" The crowds sang the national anthem and the patriotic hymn "Rota." They tore down the red flag. They threw portraits of dignitaries from the windows of official buildings. Across the front of the building that housed the party committee they draped a banner demanding "bread" and "freedom." Before midday they attacked the local UB headquarters, and the demonstration then rapidly turned into an armed revolt, which the participants themselves viewed as a national insurgency. Some demonstrators were fortified by rumors to the effect that similar events were being played out in other towns and cities and that only in Poznań was the UB continuing to defend itself.

In the afternoon the authorities mobilized units from four army divisions, involving more than four hundred tanks and armored vehicles and around ten thousand troops. Additional units began moving toward Poznań. The rioting was suppressed within twenty-four hours. About seventy civilians died in the fighting, together with eight soldiers, policemen, and security officials; several hundred people were injured. Of the 250 or so people who were arrested, 196 were workers. Although the disturbances were quickly, and unanimously, deemed to be the result of "a conspiracy of imperialist agents," and Prime Minister Cyrankiewicz threatened, in a radio address, to "cut off the hand" that would raise itself to strike people's power, the question of how to assess the Poznań events became an additional element in the divisions within the ruling group. These divisions were force-fully expressed at the next Central Committee meeting (18–28 July), but only the faintest signals of what was going on reached the public, such as the fact that Gomułka, Kliszko, and Spychalski had been readmitted to the party.

The shock of Poznań's "black Tuesday" put an end to public demonstrations, but public opinion remained at fever pitch. In hundreds of factories and institutions employees passed yet more resolutions; antistate slogans appeared on the walls, and thousands of leaflets were suddenly in circulation. In many industrial regions, workers were in the mood to strike and keen to demonstrate their solidarity with workers in Poznań. There was a widespread belief that the changes introduced since the Twentieth Congress had been too slow and too cautious. Workers also demanded that the authorities honor their promises of wage increases. One of the most spectacular examples of social mobilization was the enormous flood of pilgrims to the ceremonies at Jasna Góra on 26 August. Within the main "transmission belts"—the trade unions and the ZMP—criticism was voiced with increasing frequency and ever more forcefully, even at the central level. The authorities were also uneasy about the imminent start of the academic year, since students and the younger generation of the intelligentsia were among the most active and radical groups in the developing popular movement. In several cities, including Warsaw and Kraków, they had established contact with groups of factory workers.

After an internal debate lasting several weeks, the top party leadership finally decided to try to find a way out of this dangerously protracted crisis by making some drastic personnel changes at the very top. On 13 October the public was informed that Władysław Gomułka had, on the previous day, taken part in a meeting of the Politburo—a clear signal that Gomułka had returned to the political arena. The same Politburo meeting had also decided—and this was not announced—to appoint Bierut's former prisoner first secretary of the Central Committee. The "centrists," who had the decisive voice in determining policy of the party's topmost body, had come to an agreement with the Puławska faction. Attempts to destroy this alliance by the rival Natolin group served to radicalize even further those who had been demanding far-reaching changes and who had been mobilizing public opinion since the beginning of October.

On 16 September Bolesław Piasecki had published an article in *Słowo*

Powszechne in which he referred to the possibility of "the ruthless mainte-nance of *raison d'état* in circumstances similar to the declaration of a state of emergency." This clumsy formulation was interpreted as a signal that the Natolin faction was threatening to engineer a coup, and caused further pub-lic anxiety. Students in many towns—but mainly Warsaw—became highly agitated, a mood that was easily passed on to others. The process reached its apogee early in the morning of 19 October, shortly before the start of the Eighth Plenum of the Central Committee—the meeting that was to appoint Gomułka to the highest office in the state—when a plane from Moscow landed near Warsaw bearing Khrushchev, a large number of CPSU Polit-buro members, and an impressive group of senior Soviet Army command-ers. Many parts of the country reported that Soviet troops were moving toward the capital, and several units of the Polish Army under the command of Marshal Rokossowski were put on a state of alert. Troops belonging to the Internal Security Corps, commanded by the erstwhile prisoner, General Wacław Komar, were moved discretely to guard strategic nonmilitary loca-tions in Warsaw.

After day-long negotiations—and a private discussion—Gomułka man-aged to convince Khrushchev that personnel changes in the leadership were not only not a threat to the system but were the best means of relieving tension. That night the CPSU delegation and most of the Soviet generals flew back to Moscow, and Soviet troop movements came to a halt. When the Central Committee meeting resumed on 20 October Gomułka delivered a wide-ranging speech, amounting to a powerful indictment of the era of "er-rors and distortions." "It is necessary," he said, "to replace all the bad parts of our model of socialism with better ones, to improve the model." He em-phasized that Polish-Soviet relations "ought to be based on mutual trust and equality" and that each country ought "to possess complete autonomy and independence." He also stated unequivocally that, "our party stands at the head of the democratization process." "We shall not allow anyone to turn the process of democratization against socialism," he declared. The follow-ing day the Central Committee elected a new Politburo, which no longer included Nowak, Mazur, Jóźwiak, or Dworakowski. Marshal Rokossowski, nominated "from the floor," failed to secure enough votes.

Gomułka's return to the leadership was greeted with enormous enthu-siasm, which he doubtless did not expect. Across the country the event was celebrated in hundreds of public meetings and rallies, many of them turning into street parades. Resolutions were passed, endorsing "the course of democratization and renewal" and supporting the new leadership and Gomułka in particular, At this point similar activity was to be seen in military institutions, agencies of the security apparatus, and in the central state administration, all of which had so far maintained an awkward silence.

The new first secretary proved adept at taking advantage of the public mood. At a mass rally of 500,000 in the center of Warsaw on 24 October, for example, he emphasized "the right of every nation to its own sovereign government in an independent country." Economic demands now took second place in popular expectations, which were dominated by nationalist emotions, demands for independence from the "Russkis," and calls for the repudiation of Stalinist practices and institutions. For several weeks in different places across the country people continued to gather in mass meetings that turned into demonstrations, unorganized marches, and even outbreaks of violence. Such was the case, for example, on 23 October in Legnica (headquarters of the Soviet Army's Northern Group), on 24 October in Katowice, 11 November in Płock, and 10 December in Szczecin. Peasants disbanded the collective farms; factory workers ran the most hated directors and supervisors off the premises; those who had collaborated with the security service were forced out of their jobs; and the equipment used to jam foreign radio broadcasts was destroyed. The authorities, especially at the local level, received a flood of complaints, and officials frequently found themselves confronting groups of angry citizens who invaded their offices. There were numerous calls for the dismissal of officials at all levels and their replacement by "new people" untainted by the Stalinist years. Local leaders emerged; often they turned out to be simply people whose oratorical skills enabled them to establish a rapport with a group of workers or mass meeting.

Nevertheless, on 24 October, in front of a huge crowd of local citizens gathered on Warsaw's Parade Square and with the rest of the country listening to the live broadcast, Gomułka told his audience: "An end to meetings and demonstrations. It is time to get on with daily work." He took a number of steps designed to ensure that he had control over the situation and commanded the loyalty of the state and party apparatus. At meetings with the party *aktiv* he tried to reassure those who feared the system was disintegrating. At the same time, he made a number of decisions in response to popular demands. On 26 October Cardinal Wyszyński was released from detention, members of the Catholic intelligentsia were then given permission to set up their own organizations, and it was agreed that *Tygodnik Powszechny* would resume publication. In December the Joint Government-Episcopate Conference began work, restoring religious education to schools, and those bishops who had been removed from their post were able to return to their dioceses. Marshal Rokossowski departed for Moscow, and with him went nearly all of the Soviet officers in the Polish Army. Major changes were made in the composition of the Council of Ministers (to the detriment of the Natolin faction). Personnel changes were also made in the CRZZ and the writers' and journalists' unions. Most of the party's provincial secretaries were replaced. The Committee on Public Security, the State Economic Planning Commission, and the Ministry of State Farms were abolished. The Polish Scouting Association resumed activity; an agreement was signed regulating the presence of Soviet troops; and university professors who had lost their teaching jobs were allowed to return to work.

These measures were designed to "improve the system," strengthen Gomułka's position, and satisfy popular demands. The popular mood was somewhat restrained by the moderate stance of Cardinal Wyszyński and by the news from Hungary, where the leadership's violent reaction to a peaceful demonstration on 23 October had caused an explosion of discontent. When Soviet forces joined in the action, the revolt turned into a national uprising that was suppressed with extreme brutality. Events in Hungary had the effect of bolstering the position of Gomułka, who was seen to be implementing change in a situation of relative stability, and in any event in a peaceful fashion. They also brought home the determination with which Moscow was prepared to retain control over East-Central Europe and the costs that would have to be paid for any attempt—without much chance of success—to free Poland from its dependence.

The abandonment of Stalinism in its pure form was, on the whole, a process that took place gradually over a lengthy period. Because of the way it came about, the "October turning point" was perceived as being far more significant than just a change of course and leadership. The mass mobilization of many social strata, the tensions of the Eighth Plenum, and the repercussions of Soviet military intervention in Hungary meant that a large part of society felt that a far-reaching and irreversible transformation of the entire system had taken place. This system was identified with terror, arrogant control over the whole of public and social life, interference in private life, contempt for and destruction of national traditions, deprivation and poverty, humiliating subjection to the Russians, and the surrender of state sovereignty. All this was publicly condemned by Gomułka, who came to be seen as the embodiment—and guarantor—of a change of fortune, at both the individual and national level. He also guaranteed continuity, since he managed to stem the tide that had been rising since the spring of 1956 and prevent it from bursting through the dike as it had done in Hungary.

CHAPTER 5

Real Socialism: The Iron Fist

STABILIZATION AND CONSOLIDATION

October was both a personal and political victory for Władysław Gomułka: personal because he became the country's unquestioned leader, and political because he did not have to abandon any of his political principles; these remained intact, as did the political tools he needed to put them into practice. These tools had been forged during the years when Gomułka belonged to the narrow ruling elite (1944–48), but they were subsequently honed during a period when he was far removed from public life (1948–56) and even a prisoner (1951–53). Several of them had been created, in a sense, for use against him (the Special Bureau and the Tenth Department of the Ministry of Public Security, for example). Although some of these tools had been dismantled—or rather blunted—in the years leading up to Gomułka's triumphal return to power, the main elements of the system survived the upheavals that followed both the death of Stalin and Khrushchev's speech to the CPSU Twentieth Congress. These were the hegemony of the communist party, which had seized control of the entire state apparatus and constructed a system of dependent organizations; the principle of democratic centralism that turned this party into a hierarchically managed machine; and the legitimization of both these elements by a utopian vision that called on people to construct "the realm of freedom," of social justice, and prosperity, supplemented by the assertion that, given the balance of world power, only the communist party could guarantee the nation's existence.

Although Gomułka was accused in 1948 of renouncing ideological orthodoxy, the "deviation" that he represented did not actually transcend the communist doctrinal framework and was really a matter of tactics. It was only natural, then, that he rejected neither the elements that legitimized the system nor the basic components that ensured its effectiveness in practice (the hegemony of the centralized party). Nevertheless, this came as a complete surprise to a large part of the population, even the radical groups that had invested so much energy and emotion in supporting the former general secretary of the Polish Workers' Party. Even though Gomułka had no plans to dismantle the system, it took him some time to achieve stability and gain control of the levers of power, and this period came to be known as "the abandonment of October."

Gomułka maneuvered skillfully, avoiding any major upsets, although the process was by no means easy. The "renewal" that he wanted to bring about had to take place more or less simultaneously in two major areas: within the communist party, and within the surrounding society. Perhaps it was something of a paradox that he achieved a relatively rapid, albeit short-lived, success in the case of the latter, while the situation regarding the former was just the reverse. In 1970 society rejected both his person and his policies, but the elimination of unorthodox tendencies within the party—which he did not achieve until 1968—proved effective until at least the end of the 1970s, when Gomułka was living out his days in the depths of the countryside.

It was Gomułka's aspirations for independence from Moscow that met with the greatest public enthusiasm, although in reality his aim was not so much total independence as a new definition of international relations, especially in the economic sphere, together with respect for "Polish specifics." Popular support for the new rulers was guaranteed by the individual measures they took and—most of all, perhaps—by the overall atmosphere that emerged following the decisive abandonment of the Stalinist model. After the years of universal terror and all-embracing controls, people attached enormous value to their sense of personal security, and the fact that Gomułka continued with the kind of measures he had introduced earlier guaranteed that the change was irreversible.

Yet more state and party functionaries responsible for "errors and distortions" were dismissed from their posts. (Among others, Berman and Radkiewicz were expelled from the party in May 1957, and Romkowski, Różański, and Fejgin received stiff prison sentences in November.) Regional units of the Security Service (SB), which replaced the notorious Office of Security, were subordinated—formally, at least—to local police chiefs. Nearly all those who had been sentenced for political activity were released from prison, and many people were officially rehabilitated. The army's Main Information Office was also reorganized, and a more traditional Military Internal Service was established. Soviet advisers disappeared from both these agencies. The new ruling group did not go as far as to allow independence of the judiciary, but political influence was exercised with far more discretion, especially after the trials relating to the Poznań events, and was essentially confined to cases concerning corruption and embezzlement, which met with widespread social acceptance. Lawyers were given a somewhat greater scope for activity. Another process, also begun before October, that had similar results was the abandonment of the aggressive "anti-imperialist" propaganda that for years had exacerbated social unease and had been associated (correctly) with unceasing activity on the part of the security organs. The cessation of direct attacks on the church and the muting of official atheistic propaganda also had a major impact on public opinion.

The new leaders also continued the "economic maneuver" cautiously initiated in 1954. They substantially reduced the investment effort, and the proportion of resources allocated to capital accumulation did not exceed the plan indicators of 1949. Investment in the consumer industry increased. Centralized administration was reduced in many branches of industry, opening up room for "economic experiments" that soon brought an increase in output. The armed forces were further reduced in size, by about forty-five thousand troops, and factories producing arms or other goods for the military used their spare capacity to produce consumer goods. A "green light for handicraft production" resulted in numerous new ventures in both trade and production, and the revival of the cooperative movement had a similar effect. As a result, during 1956–58 national income grew at a faster rate than investment for the first time in many years, and real wages increased at an average annual rate of nearly 8 percent (almost 10 percent during 1956–57). The loans obtained on favorable terms from both the Soviet Union and—after almost ten years—the United States also helped to improve the economic situation, as did the numerous investment projects begun under the six-year plan that finally came on line.

Similar results could be seen in agriculture, where a major role was played by the fact that the authorities made no move to prevent the peasants from dismantling the collective farms, of which only around 1,500 (15 percent) survived. The peasants no longer had to face pressure to collectivize, and they no longer feared being branded as kulaks, but perhaps the most important factors were the influx of credit, a reduction in taxation, increased production of agricultural tools and machinery, and all the factors that automatically flowed from increasing real wages in industry. During 1956–58 the growth in agricultural output was greater than that during the entire six-year plan.

Market equilibrium proved impossible to achieve, partly because of strong inflationary pressures, but the economy was, nonetheless, another sphere in which Gomułka and the policy of "renewal" found widespread popular support. There were numerous conflicts over economic grievances, including several strikes (in January 1957 in Wrocław, in March in Bydgoszcz, and in August in Łódź), but these did not spill out onto the streets, and Gomułka met personally with a strike delegation from Bydgoszcz. The proposals for reforms and the much discussed issue of worker participation in management, already introduced in some factories, meant that people viewed the improved economic situation as a permanent development, with a legal and institutional basis.

Stabilization was also aided by the fact that divisions within the top party leadership, visible in 1956, did not exist on the same scale within the apparatus of power, especially its key components. Following Khrushchev's decision of 19 October, Marshal Rokossowski made no attempt to hang on to his position, and immediately following the Eighth Plenum, the officer corps unequivocally came out in support of Gomułka. The security apparatus also remained loyal, and although somewhat weakened as a result of reorganization, it was never in danger of collapse.

The PZPR went through a period of internal conflicts, but it had sufficient "reserve cadres" to refill the positions vacated by departing Soviet specialists and by those people who were (or were considered to be) most compromised. The majority of party officials supported the new line, some more enthusiastically than others, and sweeping changes were made at the top levels of the apparatus. The party thus demonstrated, as it had in 1948, a high level of organizational discipline. While changes in personnel were not as wide-ranging as many in the population would have liked, the fact that many senior officials quietly made way for people who had previously been imprisoned or relegated to secondary positions helped to bolster public support. People were prepared to forget Gomułka's radical statements and actions of 1944–47, and they were similarly inclined to ignore the intransigence that his former colleagues had displayed in fighting against the one-time opposition. Spychalski, Kliszko, Loga-Sowiński, Bieńkowski, Moczar, Korczyński, and Komar gained public acceptance more easily because most of the top positions were occupied by people like Ochab, Cyrankiewicz, Zawadzki, and Zambrowski, who had held such posts for the whole period of communist rule.

The extent of Gomułka's popular support was expressed in the elections to the Sejm that took place on 20 January 1957, close to the anniversary of the 1947 elections, which had been carried out under enormous pressure, in an atmosphere of terror, and with falsified results. Now elections were being held under a somewhat modified electoral law that allowed the number of candidates to exceed the number of seats to be filled. The Front of National Unity (hastily established on the basis of the former National Front) decided, however, that voters' choices would be limited to a single "joint" list of candidates representing all political parties and other organizations eligible to field candidates. The short election campaign was marked by the echoes—the hopes and emotions—of the October ferment, but the party retained control over both the selection of candidates and the course of the campaign. Although this time there was no direct pressure to vote, turnout was relatively high—94.1 percent according to official data. A major element in the campaign and the elections themselves was Gomuł-ka's frequently repeated appeals for people to vote without deleting any names from the ballot, which meant that every vote would be counted as going to those candidates at the top of the list. Since the lists were arranged not in alphabetical order but in order of political priority, it was not really the voters who decided who entered the Sejm but the state and party agencies that drew up the lists for each electoral district. This enabled the party leadership to eliminate candidates who could not be refused permission to run for office but whom it did not wish to endow with the rights and privileges of Sejm membership. This is precisely what happened to the most popular worker activist during the October events, Lechosław Goździk from the FSO car factory in Warsaw. It was notable that across the country PZPR candidates received fewer votes than nonparty candidates, but they still received an average of 88 percent of votes cast.

Mass voting without deletions signified unequivocal support for Go-mułka and the policy of "renewal." Given his unequivocal position concerning the country's continuing adherence to the "road of socialist transformation" begun in 1944, it also signified that the majority of the population assented or at least acquiesced to the continued existence of the system. At least in the form that seemed to have emerged from the October upheaval.

After the bloody campaign against the underground and the opposition, after the traumatic experiences of Stalinism, and in light of the fact that the institutions of coercion and control remained intact, it is not surprising that not a single group hostile to the system reemerged. With Cardinal Wyszyń-ski's support, Catholic groups close to the church adopted the position of a "moderate opposition," without any clear-cut goals of a purely political kind. The activity of former PSL members, independent socialists, and Christian democrats was confined to semi-social events (which the security service kept under close surveillance), and while the members of WiN and the NSZ were no longer behind bars, their ranks had been more than decimated. Home Army soldiers could now visit the graves of their comrades in arms without fear, and could even read the first relatively objective accounts of the anti-German underground, but they had no possibility of joining together in their own veterans' organization.

The years of Stalinist repression and the earlier campaign against the opposition had destroyed traditional political tendencies and elites, which survived only among émigrés. This obviously made the job of Gomułka and his group much easier; they had little difficulty in retaining control of the satellite parties, the ZSL and SD, by offering such relatively minor concessions as allowing them to resume publication of a daily paper and establishing the largely sham Central Consultative Commission of Political Parties. They also managed to ensure that the leadership of the PAX Association remained unchanged, which gave them a useful means by which to exert pressure on the church and other Catholic groups.

There was, then, not a single meaningful political institution, whether new or reactivated, that escaped the control of the communist party, and society was left without any clear alternative program or ideology of a purely political kind. This lack of alternatives served to enhance the significance of various groups and tendencies inside the party itself, or in its immediate surroundings, whose members disagreed with the leadership over some points of doctrine or, more commonly, the party's current political line. In 1956 differences of opinion over the scope and pace of change gave rise to a number of such groups. Most visible were the "revisionists," whose emergence was a characteristic feature of the whole period of the thaw, not only in the countries governed by communist parties but throughout the entire world communist movement. As we noted above, they were Gomułka's most passionate and energetic supporters in October, and their radical proposals paved the way for change. The new leader was not, however, an advocate of far-reaching reforms, nor did he wish to become a captive of the reformists. For this reason, he viewed the consolidation of power within the party as a major and urgent task.

With the support of both the broader society and the revisionists, Gomułka dealt relatively quickly with those who had occupied a conservative position in October, resisting the changes he championed. Given the nature of the proposed reforms, the new leadership viewed the conservatives— referred to at the time as "dogmatic sectarians"—as a relatively minor threat. They based themselves on the same principles as the leadership, and Gomułka could assume that they would submit to party discipline once they were deprived of external stimuli (from Moscow). And indeed they did, although at a Central Committee meeting in May 1957 Gomułka still felt obliged to engage in public debate with Kazimierz Mijał, while another leader of the hard-liners, Wiktor Kłosiewicz, received a party reprimand.

Since the dogmatists lacked a social base, it was not they who became a problem, but the revisionists, who advocated measures likely to garner considerable support and rejected a number of principles dear to Gomułka. He and some of his closest associates, as well as high officials in the party and state apparatus, believed that if the process of change went any further, it would inevitably transcend the boundaries of ideology and permissible political practice. They thus took steps to restrict the activities of those who advocated moving on to what Gomułka critically termed "the second stage." A number of personnel changes were made in the party apparatus and in the mass media. The party leadership skillfully blocked the spontaneous effort to liquidate the ZMP, and on 25 April 1957 the party's youth movement was reborn as the Union of Socialist Youth (ZMS). Liberal writers were prevented from establishing a new publication, whose very name, *Europa,* must have aroused misgivings in the leadership. The party leadership also formed its own "ideological front" for intelligentsia and intellectual circles in the form of a weekly, *Polityka,* whose first issue appeared on 27 February 1957 and which was intended as a counterweight to *Po prostu.*

At the end of the summer Gomułka decided to strike: on 21 September, at a party meeting in the FSO plant, he declared, "We shall not allow . . . counterrevolutionary activity! Either *Po prostu* will accept the party line . . . or *Po prostu* will simply not be published." "There is no other way, comrades," he added. The first issue of *Po prostu* following the summer vacation did not appear, and university and high school students expressed their protest in street disturbances that lasted several days (3–6 October). These were suppressed with the help of units belonging to the recently established ZOMO, the motorized police; more than five hundred people were arrested, and several dozen were brought before the courts. At a Central Committee meeting held in the same month it was decided to carry out a verification of the membership, the purpose of which was clearly defined by Gomułka

when he referred to "the need to deal a blow . . . to revisionism and liquida-
tionism." By May 1958 nearly 16 percent of party members had been expelled, the largest purge in the party's history. Although Gomułka had been
in control of the situation all along, from the beginning of 1958 he was the
indisputable master of the entire power apparatus—the party, the state (including the army and the security organs), and the machinery of propaganda.

The revisionists did not manage to form a tightly knit group with its
own clearly defined boundaries and program; indeed, they did not really
try to do so. The leadership therefore managed without much difficulty to
disperse and divert them to a level of opposition more intellectual than political. Another factor that made it relatively easy to marginalize the revisionists was their own ideological and political ambivalence. Since they
continued to base their ideas on Marxism (and even "real Leninism"), they
failed to develop a convincing program of overall political change and they
saw both the dogmatists and the reinvigorated Catholic Church as a threat.
Those who decided to rupture the organizational umbilical cord that tied
them to the party were few in number (they included the writers who had
hoped to publish *Europa*). While they thought that remaining in the PZPR
would give them the opportunity to engage in public activity, it essentially
crippled them. Many revisionists were also burdened by the fact that they
had played an active role in Stalinist indoctrination.

The Third PZPR Congress, held on 10–19 March 1959, marked the end
of Gomułka's consolidation of personal power and the stabilization of relations both in the country as a whole and in the ruling party. Within a relatively short time, following the emotional and hope-filled events of October
1956, the system had acquired new strength and had made the transition to
maturity, a stage in which it could dispense with bloody excesses like those
of 1944–47 and with the brutal, open, and mass coercion that had characterized the period of "full Stalinism." Both on a global scale and in Poland, the
system had shown its political effectiveness and staying power, emerging
relatively unscathed from a far-reaching crisis. Stripped of its most violent
"errors and distortions," it became something that was taken for granted:
just as the Vistula flowed from south to north, and spring followed winter,
so Poland was a socialist country.

THE ECONOMY—ENCHAINED BY IDEOLOGY

Although Gomułka's speech to the Eighth Central Committee Plenum was
highly critical of the economic policy of the six-year plan and he subse-

quently continued with the changes initiated by his immediate predecessors, he did not—and could not—find a solution to the challenge of
modernization confronting Poland other than the one that had been dictated
to all communists over the decades by ideological fundamentals. Of these,
the most important was the belief in the superiority of "social ownership"
over private property, a superiority that was supposedly expressed not only
in greater justice in the distribution of goods and services but also in greater
efficiency in their production. The utopian origins of the imperative of
social ownership had long ago been translated into the dry prose of the om-
nipotence of the state. From 1956 on Polish economists made numerous
unsuccessful attempts to escape from the economic maze erected in the
effort to square the circle, a task imposed on the party at the beginning of
the first Stalinist five-year plan. It seemed to many people, including Gomułka, that proposals to decentralize management, change the principles
of price formation, and introduce some market mechanisms, as well as
(cautious) musings on the consequences of abandoning the Marxist schema
of the "productive" and "nonproductive" spheres of the economy, led
straight to the "free play of forces" in both the social and political sphere.
Reformers were not helped by the renewal of polemics between Moscow
and Belgrade, which caused the self-management model to lose its ideological seal of approval. The horizon of systemic change in the economy was
remarkably restricted. Even when such distinguished economists as Oskar
Lange, Michał Kalecki, Czesław Bobrowski, and Edward Lipiński claimed
they could see beyond it, what they saw was the mirage of "market socialism," an internally contradictory notion, rather than a vision of the kind of
changes that would make it possible to satisfy social aspirations.

When the post-October ferment died down, most of the population more
or less passively accepted the system; in contrast to the days when one had
to fear it, one might actually—in the words of a popular saying—come to
like it. The PZPR once again became the obedient machine of the ruling
group, and it was possible to resume the process of rapid industrialization
that had been interrupted in 1953. From the point of view of everyday living,
there were two major departures from the Stalinist model: the use of semi-
forced labor (which had never, in fact, played as important a role in Poland
as it had in the Soviet Union) was abandoned, as was—even more important—the forced collectivization of agriculture. With regard to the former,
Polish policy was similar to that of other communist countries, although
there were instances, both then and later, in which mass terror and prison-

camp labor were revived (largely in the Asiatic branch of communism). With regard to the latter, on the other hand, Poland constituted a notable exception, even in comparison with its European neighbors, which completed the collectivization of agriculture by the end of the 1950s. True to his old beliefs, Gomułka counted on introducing socialism to the countryside though the back door, by giving preferential treatment to the state and cooperative sector and by socializing wholesale trade in agricultural products and farm machinery, as well as services for private agriculture—which essentially meant keeping them under state management. This was an enormous concession that was sometimes treated as an ideological blemish, but it had little impact on the efficiency of the system as a whole and did nothing to change its two immanent characteristics: low propensity to innovate and constant shortages.

In 1959 the pace of industrialization began to accelerate once more. Regardless of variations in national income, the share allocated to investment continued to grow: after 1965 accumulation never fell below 25 percent, and in 1968 it reached the previous record level of 28.5 percent, set in 1953. Of the total amount going to investment, the proportion allocated to Group A, producer goods, reached two-thirds in 1970. The preference for new investment over modernization of existing capacity meant that increases in output were achieved by increasing employment rather than labor productivity. Members of Poland's postwar baby boom were provided with costly jobs in the heavy and extractive industries, rather than less costly jobs in manufacturing or the much neglected services sector. Most new machinery and equipment was still obtained from within Comecon, and it was difficult to export to the West goods that were, by definition, out of date.

The familiar bottlenecks and supply shortages reemerged as a constant problem that could not be solved by the centralization of management: in the fall of 1959 the competence of the Planning Commission was broadened, and a number of senior officials from the former PKPG returned to high office, among them Tadeusz Gede, Eugeniusz Szyr, and Julian Tokarski. During the 1961–65 five-year plan, the only output targets to be achieved were those for industry; plan targets were not met in the case of agricultural output or national income. Not to mention real wages.

Although the peasants no longer had to fear collectivization, it was they who bore the brunt of these costs. Compulsory delivery quotas were constantly being increased, and in 1968 reached the level of 1952. Taxes and other charges that drained financial resources from the peasantry increased with no regard to growth in output. On the other hand, cooperative and state farms, which in 1968 farmed less than 15 percent of the land under cultivation, received nearly 75 percent of all the resources allocated to agriculture. The production of farm machinery and equipment was adapted to the needs of the socialized sector and the agricultural circles, first established in 1959 as part of Gomułka's effort to construct a back door for socialism in the countryside. Nearly four-fifths of agricultural output was in the hands of the state, which inevitably led to enormous waste. Restrictions on the sale and purchase of land led to increased fragmentation of landholdings: in 1950, farms of two hectares or less accounted for 26 percent of the total and those with more than twenty hectares accounted for 1.3 percent; by 1968, nearly 38 percent of farms had two hectares or less, and only 1 percent had more than twenty hectares. This prevented any increase in the total area of farmland: in 1956, some 15.4 million hectares were under cultivation, while in 1968 the figure was 15.3 million.

Despite restrictions on the growth of real wages, the amount of money in circulation continued to increase, unmatched by any equivalent increase in goods available in the stores. Shortages of consumer goods and periodic breakdowns in market supplies of meat were commonplace. The sole remedy that the authorities could offer was further increases in tightly controlled prices, especially the frequent (and painful) increases in the price of meat (in 1959 and 1967) and bread (in 1957, 1958, and 1963). They also resorted to other administrative maneuvers with the aim of reducing consumption—for example, the famous "meatless Mondays" in canteens and restaurants, introduced in July 1957. The lack of growth of real wages was offset by a considerable increase in employment and in so-called collective consumption. In accordance with the egalitarian principles of official ideology, the latter played a particularly significant role and was much favored by Gomułka. The authorities thus maintained a kind of "socialist welfare state," subsidizing not only education and health care, but also transport, rents, energy, vacations, and so on. The hitch was, however, that the resources available were far from sufficient to meet demand. Moreover, this system stifled initiative, did nothing to encourage increases in individual productivity, and generated a system of privileges—for entire branches of the economy or particular groups—that is characteristic of every economy marked by constant shortages. These privileges were extended to a large proportion of the constantly expanding bureaucracy—the state and economic administration and the party apparatus—and to those sectors of the economy connected with raw materials and heavy industry. This tended to reinforce the anticonsumption allocation of investment resources and further increased the amount of money in circulation that was not matched by market goods and services.

Gomułka and a number of his closest associates, as well as the older generation of communist activists, not only launched the notion that it was necessary to make sacrifices in order to safeguard the future (a characteristic slogan of all communist parties since Lenin's time), but advocated a particular anticonsumption model that is effectively summed up by the term "homespun socialism." Although the system was more broadly, and more genuinely, accepted than before the October upheaval, people no longer felt the kind of enthusiasm or excitement about their own social advancement that had previously been so widespread, especially among the young people who had been able to abandon the backward countryside.

The endless references to the positive changes that had taken place relative to the prewar period sounded anachronistic. Gomułka himself was an expert at this, delivering interminable speeches in a monotonous voice, and with a characteristic accent. These lent themselves to parody: "Before the war, the Polish economy was on the edge of a precipice. Since liberation, we have made great strides." The atmosphere of enthusiasm and hope gave way to disappointment, alienation, and quiet but widespread criticism and complaints about low wages and shortages. The point of reference was no longer the past, but the standard (and style) of living in Western Europe and the United States, which were then going through a period of economic boom and modernization that the Polish leadership could not conceal from its citizens, given the considerable influx of Western fashions. In any case, Khrushchev's often repeated pledge to "catch up with and overtake" the West encouraged such comparisons.

The other people's democracies of East-Central Europe faced similar problems as they tried to reconcile "catching up with" the developed economies of the West with the requirements of ideology and the dictates of imperialist doctrine. But even cooperation among them did not solve the problem, since all their economies were essentially autarchic in nature, and each of them had precisely the same range of goods available for export. The lack of a convertible currency hindered foreign trade within Comecon, which by force of circumstance was conducted on the basis of barter, and any trade surplus that might accumulate could not be used to purchase goods in the "hard currency" zone. It was almost impossible to break into Western markets with goods produced in the East, if only because of their poor quality. The Comecon countries thus remained traditional suppliers of raw materials and agricultural products, usually products that had undergone only minimal processing. The success of the Soviet space program (beginning with the first Sputnik flight in the fall of 1957) and the healthy state of the defense industry, including nuclear weapons, created the illusion of strength. Although economic relations with the "imperialists" developed considerably after Stalin's death, Comecon was essentially a collection of countries with only weak links to world markets. This was also true of Poland, and the small number of investment projects based on licenses and loans from the West, such as the production of Fiat cars at Warsaw's FSO plant or the construction of a fertilizer plant in Włocławek, was not enough to break down the barriers.

Thus despite a substantial investment effort, a considerable increase in employment, and statistically quite good results in industrial output—which grew at an annual rate of 7–10 percent during the years 1960–70—Poland's citizens felt they were living in a world of permanent shortages. After several years of intensive investment the ruling group acknowledged the need for a correction, since tensions in the economy had reached a dangerous level and popular discontent was palpable. It is probable that one of the reasons why it was so easy to mobilize people, especially factory workers, during the "March events" of 1968 was their desire to use the situation to express their dissatisfaction with the policies of the ruling elites. The public perceived the ensuing purge of the upper echelons of the apparatus—this time along ethnic lines—as an occasion to get rid of those responsible for economic stagnation and low living standards.

The purpose of the "economic maneuver" proposed by Gomułka and his associates was not, however, to bring about an improvement in living standards—not even temporarily, as had been the case in 1954 and subsequent years—but to instill discipline in the production process, raise labor productivity, and increase industry's export potential. All this was to be achieved while keeping a lid on increases in real wages and without any hope of soon restoring equilibrium to the market in foodstuffs. During 1969–70, national income grew at a declining rate, but the proportion of investment resources allocated to Group A continued to increase. The end of yet another five-year plan was a difficult period, and the ruling group decided that the new plan (1971–75) should begin with a clean slate. This involved an increase in prices that came on top of the authorities' efforts, begun in 1969, to raise labor productivity norms and to rein in the growth in take-home pay that had come about as a result of overtime working (in some occupational groups, including shipyard workers, wages declined by about 15 percent in 1970). On 30 October 1970, the Politburo approved a program of price increases for a substantial number of food items. On the evening of Saturday, 12 December, the Council of Ministers issued the appropriate communiqué: the new prices were to take effect on 14 December. The meat dishes to be served during the approaching holidays were suddenly 20 percent more expensive, the price of fish to be eaten on Christmas Eve rose by 12 percent, and the price of a morning cup of (ersatz) coffee increased by 92 percent. The Sunday newspapers printed lengthy justifications, a letter from the Politburo was read out at party meetings, and those who had assembled in celebration of Foundry Workers' Day assured the hero of 1956 that, "the tried and tested ranks of foundry workers will not disappoint Your trust and will give their utmost to fulfill the program presented by the party and the government." These were, of course, ritual words, and it is hard to imagine that these workers were happy about the new prices. Nonetheless, the years in which Gomułka ruled supreme in Poland had brought many people real change for the better: consumption grew slowly and in fits and starts, but it grew; factories hired new workers; the educational infrastructure expanded; and more housing was constructed. People lived modestly but securely. However, this ceased to be enough, especially as there was nothing to suggest that things would change for the better anytime soon.

FACTIONS AND DISSENT

The year 1956 brought a marked acceleration in the flight from the closed world of socialist realism and "progressive culture." Writers such as Zbigniew Herbert and Miron Białoszewski, whose work had been held back by the censors, now found themselves in print. Books that had languished in the drawer, such as *Rojsty* (Swamp) by Tadeusz Konwicki or *Buty* (Shoes) by Jan J. Szczepański, finally saw the light of day. American classics of the "lost generation"—Erskine Caldwell, John Steinbeck, and Ernest Hemingway—returned to the bookstores. Avant-garde artists, such as Maria Jaremianka, Tadeusz Kantor, and Władysław Strzemiński, condemned to obscurity by socialist realism, now held exhibitions of their work. More than one-third of the films shown in cinemas were produced in the West. Even émigré writers returned to the cultural marketplace: Witold Gombrowicz's *Ferdydurka* was republished, and the December 1956 issue of the Kraków-based *Życie Litera-ckie* (Literary Life) was bold enough to print an extract of a story by Czesław Miłosz. One sign of the times was a documentary film series depicting life on the social margins, and another was Marek Hłasko's novella, *Pierwszy krok w chmurach* (The First Step Through the Clouds). The events of October reinforced these developments, and Polish artists, as well as their readers and viewers, bid a final farewell to socialist realism. Dramas of the romantic era were rehabilitated (although not without exceptions); Sartre and Witkacy took up residence in the theaters; Kafka and Faulkner were printed, as were the émigré works of Gombrowicz (*Trans-Atlantyk*); exhibitions of Polish painting were dominated by abstract and nonfigurative art; and composers began composing atonal works. A whole literary genre sprang up to settle accounts with the immediate past. Sometimes the issues were addressed in the form of the historical novel—*Ciemności kryją ziemię* (Darkness Covers the Earth) by Jerzy Andrzejewski—and sometimes more directly—*Matka królów* (Mother of Kings), by Kazimierz Brandys. Also popular were a number of works in the realm of the absurd that reexamined national myths and contemporary attitudes (such as Andrzej Munk's film, *Eroica,* and Sławomir Mrożek's *Policjanci*). Surrounded by neighbors who continued to follow the precepts of socialist realism, Poland became an island of the avant-garde, a place that people used to call "the liveliest barracks in the camp."

These developments were not only a sign that popular expectations were becoming more modern and that Poland's artists were in the avant-garde, but also indicated a state of intellectual ferment, an indispensable characteristic of modernity. The central leadership of the PZPR (and Gomułka personally), as well as members of the party and state apparatus, observed all this without any satisfaction and with some alarm. It was evident that culture was no longer being directed from above, and artistic circles, with their many ties to political and philosophical revisionists, nurtured—so the leadership thought—too many aspirations that transcended the world of art. In the fall of 1957, Gomułka gave a speech in which he reminded his audience that "the conscience of the working class is the party," not the writers. In February 1958, Włodzimierz Sokorski, the leading activist on the "cultural front" during 1948–56, categorically declared that the state "cannot, and has no wish to, relinquish influence over what is presented in theaters, what kind of paintings are bought and from whom, or what is transmitted by radio and television" and that "it has the right to defend its citizens from trash and art that is destructive and openly hostile." At a series of briefings organized by various departments of the Central Committee, party activists examined publishing policy, the state of the social sciences, and the situation in the universities and in literary circles. Changes in personnel were called for (including the dismissal of culture minister Karol Kuryluk), and participants agreed that "publishing houses, especially their managerial positions, should be staffed only by people who implement the party line with conviction."

In mid-1958 a specially established commission reduced the number of periodical publications by 255. Censorship was tightened, and increasingly it was the censor's office that decided how many copies of each book should be printed or how many performances of every play should be staged. The trial in July 1958 of Hanna Rewska, who had provided material to the Paris-based *Kultura*, was the first in a series of trials of people who maintained contact with the émigré community. This trend received considerable publicity with the campaign against Marek Hłasko after Jerzy Giedroyc had published two of his books banned by the Polish censors, *Cmentarze* (The Graveyard) and *Następnego do raju* (The Next One for Heaven). The disobedient author refused to return home from abroad, thereby beginning a long procession of those who "chose freedom" over the new, post-October reality. At the Third PZPR Congress Gomułka not only sharply criticized intellectual circles, but reestablished the Central Committee departments dealing with culture and with science and education, which had been abolished in the fall of 1956. In December 1959, after intensive preparations, the much-respected writer Antoni Słonimski was replaced as president of the Polish Writers' Union by Jarosław Iwaszkiewicz, who was not burdened by what the authorities regarded as inappropriate political opinions and contacts.

These were not drastic steps and did not bring with them the danger of a forced return to socialist realism, but they were extremely painful to intellectuals, especially writers, because they involved restrictions not only on creative freedom but also on publishing opportunities: during 1957–62 the total annual number of copies of all books printed fell from eighty-five million to seventy-eight million, and the number of poetry and prose titles fell from 1,120 to 720. The authorities continued to issue ominous statements addressed to artists. In June 1963 *Nowa Kultura* and *Przegląd Kultur-alny* were closed down on the grounds that they were "unreformable," and the lead article in the first issue of the journal that replaced them, *Kultura*, declared that what the country needed was a "struggle against reactionary ideology, which is still being regenerated on Polish soil." A few weeks later (4–6 July), at a meeting of the Central Committee devoted to ideological problems, Gomułka declared: "The party does not wish to intervene in creative issues," but added that "the party will do its utmost to support works of socialist realism." Although the distance between words and deeds was considerable, these discouraging statements sounded like a warning.

Discontent was growing, and it is hardly surprising that it spread beyond private conversations and discussions at informal gatherings. On 14 March 1964, thirty-four writers and scholars sent the prime minister a letter, just two sentences in length, protesting against "restrictions on the allocation of paper and newsprint" and "the tightening of press censorship." The fact that the text of the letter made its way to foreign journalists and was read on Radio Free Europe evoked a rapid and sharp reaction on the part of the authorities, which launched a veritable campaign against the signatories. They mobilized "the mass of the members" of the writers' union, collecting six hundred signatures under a rebuttal letter; they forced ten professors to withdraw their signatures, and imposed a publishing ban on some of the signatories. Delegates to the Fourth PZPR Congress, which took place two months after this declaration of discontent, adopted a resolution declaring that "there should be no place for works of art whose ideology is directed against socialism."

The subsequent propaganda campaign and, in particular, the trial of Melchior Wańkowicz during the fall of that year (other prominent signatories—Jan N. Miller, January Grędziński, and Stanisław Mackiewicz—were charged later) signified a public breach between the Gomułka leadership and a large proportion, although not the majority, of Poland's artists. The mutual antipathy, or even outright hostility, between members of the intellectual elite and the authorities became a permanent feature of Poland's political landscape, and writers came to constitute a breeding ground for opposition.

Alongside the conflicts between writers and the party-state apparatus, growing ferment was visible within some of the groups that had been most radical in 1956. Many of the October radicals submerged themselves in the new reality and kept away from politics (as did Jerzy Grotowski, who had such great success in the theater); others adapted to party discipline and dutifully did what was required of them. The majority engaged in daily skirmishes with the censors and their new bosses in editorial offices, publishing houses, research institutes, and university departments, expressing opinions similar to those harbored by the discontented writers. Quite a large group—including many former "officers in the ideological front"—became leading philosophers, sociologists, and economists. Those who persevered with Marxism and continued their revisionist analyses faced growing difficulties in finding a forum in which to express their opinions; nonetheless, Leszek Kołakowski, Bolesław Brus, and Bronisław Baczko played a major role in intellectual life and enjoyed considerable prestige among the younger generation. All in all, the anti-intellectualism of Gomułka and his closest associates served to increase the number of his opponents.

For several years the Club of the Crooked Circle in Warsaw served as a focus of activity for some revisionists and for scholars, writers, and journalists of various generations who were concerned with maintaining their intellectual independence. The authorities viewed this institution with growing displeasure, and not without reason: speakers at the club included Paweł Jasienica, Stefan Kisielewski, Kazimierz Moczarski, Władysław Bartoszewski, Julian Hochfeld, and even Central Committee member Adam Schaff. His talk, delivered on 1 February 1962, turned out to be the last. A few days later the club was closed down. There were signals more ominous than this ban on peaceful meetings. On 19 December 1961 the security service arrested Henryk Holland, a sociologist popular in revisionist circles and once one of the most militant party journalists. Two days later, during a search of his apartment, he died after falling from a window. It was widely believed that Holland had been murdered by the SB, although it is difficult to say whether or not this was the case. Many party activists, scholars, and journalists who had been shunted to the sidelines of political and cultural life attended his funeral. Gomułka regarded this as an act of insubordination, and the Politburo set up a commission that, together with the appropriate party control commissions, exacted punishment for this disobedience. Three months earlier Anna Rudzińska, active in the Club of the Crooked Circle, had been arrested. In February 1962, when Rudzińska was being sentenced, Jerzy Kornacki, a writer associated with the far left before the war, was arrested, and the *Przedwiośnie* literary group, which he had helped to found, was closed down. These individual steps combined to form a fairly consistent policy that relegated revisionist and liberal groups to the margins of official public life. This policy was aimed not only at the world of culture and academia. As early as 1959 Żółkiewski and Bieńkowski were dismissed from their government posts, in 1960 Morawski was dismissed from his position as Central Committee secretary, and he was followed in 1963 by Zambrowski and Matwin. The army also dispensed with the services of "the people of October," including Generals Janusz Zarzycki, Adam Uziembła, Jan Frey-Bielecki, and Zygmunt Duszyński. These people were hardly revisionists or party dissidents, although some of them, like Bieńkowski—who would soon begin publishing abroad (with Giedroyc's publishing house)—had long parted company with Marxist orthodoxy. Nevertheless, they still considered their membership in the PZPR as indicating that they accepted its basic ideology, even if they disagreed with its current political line. None of them left the party. For these people, participation in public life meant remaining within the framework of the broad elite; to place oneself outside the elite was to leap into the political void.

In one way or another, after the purges of the late 1950s, a substantial proportion of those who were most attached to the slogans of democratization found themselves outside the power structure. On the other hand, some pre-October activists returned to power. Alongside Szyr and Tokarski, the most spectacular return was that of Kazimierz Witaszewski, the notorious "general of the gas pipe," who in 1959 was appointed to the general staff and in March 1960 became head of the Central Committee Administrative Department, with oversight of the armed forces and the Ministry of Internal Affairs. Despite the October upheaval, a considerable number of people referred to as "the indestructibles" remained in high office, especially in the state apparatus. During the period under consideration, they included Józef Cyrankiewicz, a member of the government since November 1946; Stefan Jędrychowski, a member of the government (with some short gaps) since the days of the PKWN; Adam Rapacki, the holder of several ministerial portfolios since 1947; Piotr Jaroszewicz, a permanent member of the government since leaving the army in 1950; and Eugeniusz Stawiński, the "iron" minister of light industry since April 1949. The presence of these holdovers strengthened the public's perception of the ossification of Gomułka's ruling group and seems to have resulted from his deep conservatism.

Because of this conservatism, the rapid abandonment of the slogans of the fall of 1956, and a clear stagnation in personnel turnover, the leadership lost the support it had once enjoyed and began to encounter first objections and then resistance to its policies. This hostility emanated from a number of groups, with varying, and often contradictory, motives, but it was aimed directly against Gomułka and his closest associates.

A group that can be called the "true communists" was the least important and essentially nonthreatening, although its members were a nuisance
to Gomułka personally. These were people nostalgic for revolutionary slogans and practice who agreed with the Chinese communists that the thaw
and the policies introduced under Khrushchev constituted a betrayal of
communist ideals. Led by Kazimierz Mijał, who had been Bierut's secretary
for many years, the group began to engage in more decisive action in the
spring of 1964, when it distributed a few leaflets. One of these called on
people to "get rid of Mr. Gomułka's clique." The security service searched
several apartments and made a number of arrests, and although Mijał's
group had many sympathizers among those who had belonged to the KPP,
the group did not manage to create an organization or continue its activity.
After setting up the illegal Communist Party of Poland (consisting of a few
former dignitaries), Mijał fled in 1966 to Albania, where he was given control of Polish-language radio broadcasting. The activity of Mijał's group was
clearly linked to the split in the world communist movement, which constituted a potential threat to Gomułka. However, apart from Albania, which
came out on the side of Mao Zedong—and Romania, which tried to play a
mediating role—the pro-Chinese elements were not a significant presence
in any of the countries of East-Central Europe.

Another group, made up of Trotskyite critics of Stalinism, also exerted
little influence—and not only because its members were arrested quite
quickly (in April 1965). Led by Ludwik Hass, a historian who had spent the
years 1939–56 in labor camps and in exile in the Soviet Union, the group
established contact with the Fourth International, active in Europe and
Latin America. Three members of the group were sentenced to prison for
having printed and distributed a translation of the resolution passed by the
1957 congress of the Fourth International in the form of a pamphlet titled
The Decline and Fall of Communism. The fact that the group based itself on
the theories espoused by the chief organizer of the Bolshevik revolution and
the war of 1920 made it unlikely—especially in Poland—that it would garner
broad social support or even acquire much influence among the older generation of communists.

Another grouping that also had its roots in Marxism had a quite different fate. Its leaders, Jacek Kuroń and Karol Modzelewski, belonged to the
generation formed by the events of 1956, and rather than looking for a solution in one version of Bolshevism or another they went beyond it. They both
took as their starting point the most radical slogans of October but in con-

trast to many writers, for example, they tried not only to analyze the existing state of affairs but also to formulate a vision for the future. The people associated with them came from the universities and youth organizations. The group had ties to revisionist tendencies well as liberal intellectuals, and could be regarded as their most radical and most directly political wing.

Kuroń and Modzelewski wrote a document with the pointed title, *An Anti-Communist Manifesto*. When this was confiscated, they produced a new document, which on 18 March 1965, they presented to the PZPR and ZMP organizations at Warsaw University. This document, later known as *The Open Letter*, contained a wide-ranging critique of the system based on principles derived from nineteenth-century syndicalist critiques of Marxism, on Milovan Djilas's concept of the New Class (Kuroń and Modzelewski referred to the "central political bureaucracy"), and on some of the demands then being advanced by Western social-democratic parties. In a key statement the authors declared that "given the impossibility of overcoming the economic and social crisis within the framework of the bureaucratic system, revolution is inevitable" and that "the possibility of armed intervention on the part of the Soviet bureaucracy . . . cannot be measured in terms of the number of tanks and airplanes in its possession but by the intensity of class conflicts in the USSR." The day after delivering *The Open Letter* both Kuroń and Modzelewski were arrested. Four months later, after what was a relatively short investigation at that time, they were sentenced to prison.

This group did not, however, break up, but remained active in a number of places, largely universities, conducting lively internal debates. To a large extent, this activity was the work of the youngest people associated with the group, among whom Adam Michnik distinguished himself. Perhaps the limited opportunities for discussion, which made it difficult to crystallize a set of beliefs, were the reason why it was an émigré journalist, Juliusz Mieroszewski, who provided an overall survey of the group's political program. The group referred to its strategy as "evolutionism" and took as its starting point the assumption that, "because we cannot overthrow communism in Russia, we must start to influence the evolution of both communism and Russia." Essentially, this was just what the revisionists and party liberals had been saying when they functioned as a kind of pressure group in relation to the party leadership.

Both the security service and PZPR bodies, including the top party leadership, paid considerable attention to the activity (and creativity) of the groups and broader circles that developed out of Marxism and the liberal

intellectuals who were close to them. Party officials engaged in public polemics against them and employed a variety of administrative measures,
such as banning them from publishing or appearing on radio and television,
and denying them passports; concentrated propaganda attacks were organized. When the need arose, the courts would hand down prison sentences.
The leadership attempted to impose discipline on the party by establishing,
in the fall of 1963, the Central Committee Ideological Commission and by
restricting the already minuscule choice that members had when selecting
delegates to party conferences or members of party committees. Gomułka
and his associates still saw the greatest political danger as coming from
what they viewed as the "right." In the long run, they were largely correct.
In the short run, however, they were wrong. In the shadows of the public
scolding meted out to Kołakowski and Brus; the sentencing of Wańkowicz,
Rewska, and Rudzińska; and the liquidation of the Crooked Circle, another
threat to the ruling group emerged, a threat that was far more dangerous to
the individuals in power, but not to the system itself.

The basis of this threat was twofold: first, the lack of opportunities for
promotion of the younger generation of apparatchiks, whose careers were
blocked by the many prewar communists who remained in the state and
party apparatus; second, the search for new ways to legitimize the system
that would also constitute an effective response to revisionism, a response
that would resonate with the broader society. Also important were the personal ambitions of some of Gomułka's comrades from the wartime underground, who felt they had not achieved the prominence they deserved after
October.

All in all, this was a situation in which motives, attitudes, and personal
histories combined to give rise to a political tendency, although one that
never produced a political program. Its importance lay in the fact that it
was situated in the very heart of the party apparatus and in such crucial
institutions as the Ministry of Internal Affairs and the army. It was also an
unflagging opponent of revisionist and liberal tendencies and thus, in this
regard, a loyal ally of Gomułka, one that even outstripped, if not the first
secretary himself—which would have been difficult—some of his closest associates.

This group probably expressed the views of the majority of the rapidly
growing party apparatus, which by 1965 had the same number of employees
(12,500) as ten years previously. It undoubtedly also expressed the views of
a substantial proportion of the constantly expanding PZPR membership. In

1964 the party had more than 1.5 million members, and it not only continued to grow but grew at an increasingly rapid rate: by 1970, more than 2.3
million people belonged to the party, which meant that membership had
doubled during the previous ten years. The PZPR's youth movements also
grew rapidly: in 1970 nearly 1.3 million young people belonged to the ZMS,
and nearly 1.1 million to the ZMW. Even though propaganda, indoctrination, and education persistently inculcated communist views—albeit with
varying intensity—it is obvious that the mass of people who joined the party
and its youth organizations were far removed from the style of thinking of
the old elite, most of whom had been members of the prewar KPP. It is also
doubtful whether they actually internalized the ideology to the extent the
leadership would have liked and whether the old communist canon still
served to bind the membership together. While this was a period of accelerating decolonization in Africa, this was a process that took place under the
overall slogan of national liberation rather than that of socialist revolution.
The tensions manifest in several countries of Western Europe, although
largely initiated by communist parties, no longer aroused in the communist
bloc—and certainly not in Poland—any hopes for a worldwide social upheaval. Alongside external factors, such as the western border and the interests of the Soviet Union, the main source of legitimacy was supposed to be
the system's efficiency and its guarantee of constant economic growth and
the modernization of everyday life. This loosened the old ideological bonds
and deepened the differences between generations within the party.

The tendency under discussion here is usually referred to as "the Partisans," since the core of the group, led by Mieczysław Moczar, was made up
of former members of the communist resistance, who also sought support
in the ranks of the noncommunist (once anticommunist) resistance. The
group emerged in the public arena at the beginning of the 1960s, although
it did so discretely, presenting its views behind the mask of literary or historical questions. The broader public first became aware of the group
through the publication in 1961 of Moczar's memoirs, under the title *Barwy
walki* (Battle Colors), and a collection of wartime accounts by members of
the People's Guard, *Ludzie, fakty, reflekcje* (People, Facts, Reflections). It
was characteristic that Moczar, then deputy minister of internal affairs, was
warmly received on the pages of PAX publications, which had devoted considerable space to systematic and credible accounts of both the Home Army
and Poland's wartime military effort alongside its Western allies. This was
not the result of either an accident or a hasty decision. Bolesław Piasecki,

who had managed to survive the crisis caused by his behavior in the fall of 1956, remained an implacable enemy of those whom he called the "advocates of a new October." On the other hand, he wrote favorably about a tendency that he defined as "patriotic-socialist," in whose ranks he undoubtedly included both Gomułka and himself.

The Partisans publicly defined themselves in essentially similar terms, which became particularly evident with the publication of *Siedem polskich grzechów głównych* (The Seven Polish Deadly Sins), by Zbigniew Załuski, himself a partisan in the literal sense of the world. The main thrust of Załuski's book, the subject of heated debate for more than a year, was the attempt to draw a connection between the tradition of the workers' movement and the Polish tradition of national uprisings. In the former, Załuski included not only the "conspirators from Proletariat," or "the fighting men and women of 1905," but also the "terrorists of the KPP," and those who, on workers' marches, had confronted "police rifles with their bare fists." Among the latter he included the partisans and soldiers of World War II (he himself had fought in the Kościuszko Division) who "flew the red-and-white alongside the red." The official end to the debate came in the form of an editorial in *Trybuna Ludu* (26 April 1963) stating that the author had lost sight of "the historical sense" of the armed struggles of the past and had detached them from "their role in the conflict between the forces of reaction and progress." Despite this condemnation, the PZPR now had at its disposal—and permanently—new tools of legitimization prefiguring the later slogan concerning "the moral and political unity of the nation."

Some party writers and journalists now contrasted the notion of a community based on bonds of fate and struggle with the "scoffers" and "mockers" who were questioning the romantic-insurrectionary stereotype and thereby undermining the fundamentals of national identity. Many noncommunists treated this as a genuine bid for support, and, according to Andrzej Micewski, even the episcopate "took a bona fide interest in the patriotic argument." At that time it was quite widely believed—as it had been in 1956 or, in the case of Yugoslavia, in the years 1944–50—that if communism were imbued with national elements it would be transformed into a more democratic system, one free of the doctrinal straitjacket that constrained everyone.

The public viewed the lessening of dependence on Moscow and the new emphasis on national identity as a step in the right direction. These tendencies were most in evidence, not in Poland but in Romania, especially after the spring of 1965, when Nicolae Ceaușescu took over the leadership of the country's communist party. It seems that it was far easier for a large proportion of noncommunists in Poland, including the church, to accept "national communism" than the "democratic socialism" advanced by the liberals and revisionists. We can assume that the majority of PZPR members felt the same way.

The Partisans matched their activity in the field of propaganda and in the public forum with activity behind the scenes, wooing supporters and creating an institutional base. Their main base of support was ZBoWiD, an organization in which it was easy to build a community of interests with noncommunist veterans and to establish a network at the local level, outside the control of the central party apparatus. Moczar consolidated his position as leader in the summer of 1964, when a Russian translation of *Barwi walki* was published in Moscow. This made it more difficult for his opponents to attack him for the nationalism that they discerned in some of his statements, especially in the undertone of his "patriotic" slogans. It was hard to believe it was pure coincidence that the Russian edition of Moczar's memoirs appeared just before the Fourth Congress of the PZPR (15–20 June), at which delegates elected to the Central Committee a number of young apparatchiks—including Stefan Olszowski, Stanisław Kociołek, and Jerzy Łukaszewicz—who were the natural allies of the Partisans in their attacks on revisionists and liberals and who were ever more insistently pushing their way to the top of the party.

It was at this congress that General Wojciech Jaruzelski, the head of the Main Political Administration of the Armed Forces—and thus Colonel Załuski's boss—was first elected to the Central Committee. In the army, too, after "the October generals" had been removed, a new leadership was in the making. Moczar rose rapidly: in September he became chairman of ZBoWiD's Main Council, in December he was finally appointed minister of defense. Although he was only a regular member of the Central Committee, many people saw him as a possible successor to the "Old Man," as Gomułka was called with increasing frequency (Moczar was actually only eight years younger, but this amounted to a whole generation's difference in the party).

Of course it was coincidence that all these events—the Letter of the 34, the public statements of Mijał and his supporters, the creation of the first political program on the part of the most radical October groups, the arrival of the younger generation of apparatchiks in direct proximity to the center of power, and the promotion of the leader of the Partisans—took place in the same year. But this coincidence brought about a situation in which Go-mułka's position, and especially that of his closest associates and members of the party elite, was subject to questioning from within. And these were by no means the only political problems facing the first secretary.

THE WAR OVER THE MILLENNIUM

Cardinal Wyszyński's return from internment was the reason why, "virtu-ally every day," according to Andrzej Micewski, "we were approached by politicians who wanted to resume activity and sought moral support from the church." The cardinal generally confined himself to listening, advising them to be cautious and circumspect, but refrained from "giving guidance of a political kind."[1] The leader of the church and the unquestioned author-ity for the Catholic community followed this pattern for many years, avoid-ing public statements or intervention in social and political issues outside the realm of church teaching or freedom of worship. He supported very few initiatives to create, or revive, purely political organizations or even politically tinged publishing efforts. He stood for the "minimalism" advo-cated in 1946 by Stanisław Stomma and opposed the "maximalism" then represented by *Tygodnik Warszawski*. Despite clear overtures from the post-October party leadership, he plainly realized the opportunistic nature of the concessions offered and had no desire to go to war with the authori-ties over political issues.

The group associated with the former *Tygodnik Powszechny* subordi-nated itself to this doctrine more or less completely, an essential condition for gaining the authorities' agreement to the revival of the publication. This took place at the end of 1956, and Jerzy Turowicz became editor once again. The authorities also gave permission for a small group of Catholics to be elected to the Sejm—where all nine of them formed the Znak Caucus—and for the creation of discussion groups, known as the Clubs of Catholic Intelli-gentsia (KIK). Just five of these were established. Despite some major dif-ferences of opinion within this circle of activists, the group as a whole was generally referred to as "neopositivists," whose guiding principles were mainly drawn up by Stanisław Stomma, Stefan Kisielewski, and Antoni Go-lubiew. They took as their starting point the view that it was impossible to free Poland from its dependence on the Soviet Union ("Despite our Latin culture, we belong to the East," Kisielewski used to declare) and that, in the

1. Andrzej Micewski, *Kardynał Wyszyński. Prymas i mąż stanu* (Paris, 1982), 149.

existing situation, the most important task was to speak out on "specific, empirically observable problems." They advocated a constructive approach, which by no means signified an endorsement of the system, and they contrasted this with "romanticism" and with the efforts of Piasecki and others to "Christianize socialism." Some KIK activists were, however, drawn to the latter approach, especially the founders of the monthly journal, *Więź* (The Link), and its editor in chief, Tadeusz Mazowiecki. Another group could be distinguished from PAX and the various people who had seceded from Piasecki's organization (Jan Frankowski, for example). This consisted of "left-wing Catholics" who remained independent of the PZPR, adhered to the French school of Catholic personalism, and advocated a more authentic interpretation of the notion of social justice.

Despite a strong common foundation in the form of shared faith and acceptance of the authority of the institutional church, the Catholics who were active in public life did not create a unified group. This was because of personal ambitions (particularly apparent in the case of Piasecki), differences of opinion regarding the organization of social life, differences in attitude toward "real socialism," and manipulation on the part of the authorities, who used the security apparatus to good effect. The differences that had emerged in 1945–46 subsequently broadened into a chasm that proved impossible to bridge. Nor did the church make any effort to do so, although it undoubtedly would have benefited from the existence of a cohesive cohort of politically active believers.

During the years that Gomułka was in power new differences were added to the old, partly in response to the divisions that emerged after 1956 in what had previously been a unified ruling group. PAX and some of its former members, such as Janusz Zabłocki, now belonging to the *Więź* group, reacted favorably to the emergence of the Partisans, whom they considered to be "national communists." Other Catholic activists were more sympathetic to the position of liberal writers, revisionists, and other advocates of an antitotalitarian socialism. However, their contacts with representatives of these tendencies were somewhat sporadic and hampered by mutual mistrust: one side was alienated by the anticlericalism and virtual atheism that characterized even the ex-Marxists, while the other identified the church and Catholics with obscurantism, intolerance, and chauvinism (or simply with "the forces of reaction").

The rapprochement between PAX and the Partisans proved to be beneficial to Piasecki. His organization, which had turned itself into an association in 1957, grew from 150 members in 1956 to more than 7,000, organized in seventy-eight regional chapters, by 1967. Three PAX representatives were elected to the Sejm in 1961; in the following election their number rose to five, equal to the number of deputies from the Znak group, and Piasecki was now among them. The PAX press had considerably greater opportunities for activity (access to paper and the state distribution network) than did *Tygodnik Powszechny:* the PAX daily, *Słowo Powszechny,* had a circulation of 100,000 copies, and its three weeklies had a joint circulation in excess of 120,000.

With great self-confidence Piasecki developed the notion of "multiplicity of worldviews." In *Wytyczne ideowopolityczne* (Ideological-Political Guidelines), published in 1965, he wrote: "In Poland it is impossible to build socialism without an allied socialist party with a nonmaterialist worldview." He proposed abolishing the existing "allied parties" and creating in their place a party of "nonmaterialist socialism." More important than ideological declarations, however, was Piasecki's willingness to subordinate his organization to directives issued by the central leadership, or at least one of the factions within it. In the mid-1960s this behavior earned PAX the sharp condemnation of the church hierarchy.

Even though the institutional church, according to Micewski, at one point "took a bona fide interest in the patriotic argument" of Moczar's group, it distanced itself completely from the divisions within the PZPR. This was all the more understandable insofar as none of the groups inside the party showed the slightest inclination to continue the soft line in relation to the church that Gomułka had adopted after the October meeting of the Central Committee. This line was actually very short-lived: in June 1957 Gomułka publicly stated: "If we were obliged to reach a certain modus vivendi with the church . . . , it was because of our situation. . . . We are taking account of the facts and this is bringing us some positive results."

Soon the party was no longer obliged to take account of the facts; the wave of social unrest that brought Gomułka to power died down and the situation within the PZPR was brought under control. Policy toward the church became characterized—like policy in other areas of public life—by what was then popularly called "the return of the new." The first visible sign of a shift came on 21 July 1958, when security officials searched the premises of the Primate's Institute, situated in the monastery at Jasna Góra (which only added to the drama of the situation). Shortly afterward, a member of the party's top leadership declared that "the clergy must realize that

Poland does not have two states, that there is only one state and one governing power, people's power."

The concern of the "one governing power" was exacerbated by the fact that Cardinal Wyszyński was clearly determined to undertake a long-term, mass mobilization of the faithful. In 1956 the church inaugurated a ten-year-long celebration of a thousand years of Christianity in Poland, called the Great Novena of the Millennium. The celebration was to take the form of hundreds of individual religious ceremonies, varying in scope but most of them at the local level. It was also to include numerous mass pilgrimages. The authorities decided to counter with their own celebration, proclaiming 1966 the year of the Thousandth Anniversary of the Polish State and launching the slogan of "A Thousand Schools for the Thousandth Anniversary" (the schools were actually much needed). In the summer of 1958 believers and practicing Catholics in the PZPR were prohibited from holding party office. At the same time, the Office of Religious Affairs and the Ministry of Internal Affairs began to work together in coordinated fashion. At the province, town, and district level, special "staffs" were established, whose members included the appropriate party secretaries, chairmen of the national councils, police commanders, and heads of the security service sections dealing with the church.

During the 1958–59 school year the authorities inaugurated a campaign to remove crosses from schools; shortly afterward crosses were being removed from factories, and a ban was imposed on new church construction. For several years these measures resulted in widespread clashes between groups of believers and the police. The best known of these took place in Nowa Huta on 27–28 April 1960, when the authorities tried to remove a cross erected on a site where a church was supposed to be constructed. But similar incidents took place elsewhere, including Zielona Góra, Głuchołazy, Gliwice, and Toruń. Evidence of the authorities' determination in this endeavor was provided by the liquidation of the country's only school for church organists, founded in 1916 in Przemyśl, a move that provoked local disturbances lasting three days. All this was accompanied by various routine difficulties and obstacles relating to such issues as taxation and military service on the part of the clergy. A major long-term blow was delivered in the summer of 1961, when the authorities abolished religious instruction in the 21,500 schools in which it had been introduced (out of a total of 28,000 schools). There were also attempts to take control of the catechism instruction centers that had sprung up everywhere like mushrooms after the rain:

in 1962 they numbered around fifteen thousand, and four years later the number had grown to nearly twenty thousand. According to data gathered by the church, nearly four million children attended classes and nearly ten thousand people gave instruction.

In the fall of 1961 the SB expanded its Division on Church Affairs into a department (the Fourth Department), whose central office employed more than 120 people. Two years later, the minister of internal affairs, Władysław Wicha, recommended that the ministry broaden the scope of its interests. Addressing a national briefing for ministry employees, he stated: "The operational work of the SB consists of more than just gathering information. It also involves activity among the clergy, instigated by us and carried out by agents engaging in operational maneuvers with the aim of disrupting and paralyzing the church hierarchy." In addition to PAX and Frankowski's Christian Social Association, which had some influence among lower-level clergy, and in addition to direct pressure exerted by the state administration and security service at various levels, the authorities also reactivated the old "patriotic priests" movement, this time in the form of "priest circles" attached to the religious charity, Caritas.

The episcopate reacted by sending letters of protest to the authorities, informing the clergy of its position, and expressing its objections in pastoral letters addressed to the faithful. After 1961 Cardinal Wyszyński demonstratively refused to vote during elections. In 1963 he met for the last—and only third—time with Gomułka, and when he met that same year with two well-known party dissidents, Leszek Kołakowski and Jan Strzelecki, he sent the authorities a signal that they must have interpreted as a warning. The first, still feeble, threads of dialogue and understanding between the church and left-wing antitotalitarian activists (at that time, thinkers rather than activists) were gradually being established. Nevertheless, the episcopate's public pronouncements continued to be dominated by its concern to defend the church, the faith, and the faithful; its references to social issues were scarce, although in their pastoral letter to the clergy of 28 August 1963, the bishops did declare: "At every moment and in every situation we must be at the service of the people, ready to defend its rights, its freedoms, and its dignity."

The great battle with the church began shortly before the millennium celebrations reached their culmination. On 18 November 1965 the Polish bishops taking part in the deliberations of the Second Vatican Council wrote a letter addressed to their German counterparts. After a brief exposition dealing with the thousand-year history of Polish culture and statehood, the bishops described the martyrdom of the war and occupation, explained why the Poles had to take over the western territories, and called for a dialogue: "We hold out our hands to You . . . and we extend our forgiveness and ask for the same." Both the spiritual and political sense of these famous words was fairly obvious—more than twenty years after the end of the war it was time to establish good-neighborly relations. This also constituted an attempt to create, if not a breach, at least a wide fissure in the Iron Curtain that still divided Europe, despite the changes that had taken place since the death of Stalin, and whose existence had acquired a new—and material—expression in the form of the Berlin Wall, erected in the summer of 1961.

Disregarding (or perhaps not) the noble intentions of this document, the authorities treated it as a *casus belli*. Gomułka felt personally offended: the church had not only trespassed onto territory reserved exclusively for the party, but it was territory that the first secretary considered his personal domain, where only he could plow the land and plant the seeds—and he wanted to be the only one to reap the harvest. To "punish" the primate, the authorities withheld his passport, and the press unleashed a massive propaganda campaign, in which PAX and Frankowski's group also took part.

As the authorities made the practical arrangements for the approaching millennium celebrations, they gave the entire proceedings a clearly confrontational character. In February they established a special "party-state commission," chaired by none other than Kazimierz Witaszewski, whose members included, of course, representatives of the Ministry of Internal Affairs and the Office on Religious Affairs, as well as representatives of several ministries, including transport, culture and art, education, and the State Committee for Radio and Television. This team of officials even included the chairman of the Main Committee for Physical Culture and Tourism. The authorities' aim was not only to hinder the organization of the church's celebrations, but to come up with their own "counteroffer"—sports contests, variety shows, and television performances. They made intensive preparations for "the parade of the millennium," which took place, of course, on 22 July.

The confrontation lasted for several months and began in mid-April 1966, in Gniezno and Poznań, where religious ceremonies led by Cardinal Wyszyński were simultaneously matched by "patriotic" displays attended by the Minister of Defense, General Spychalski, and Gomułka himself. On 7 May, in Kraków, the counterweight to Cardinal Wyszyński was the prime minister, Cyrankiewicz. The festivities culminated in Warsaw, where crowds dispersing after the final mass clashed with ZOMO units blocking access to the streets around the PZPR Central Committee building. More than a hundred people were detained, and eight people were brought before the courts. Clashes also occurred in Kraków, Gdańsk, and Lublin, the site of the most serious incident, in which 290 people were detained. In all these disturbances, organized groups of "worker activists" took part alongside regular security forces; some of them were actually SB officials, whose behavior toward the public was aggressive and on occasion simply provocative.

The millennium clashes caused the authorities to suspend for a time the application of more subtle methods in their fight with the church, the main element of which involved attempts to draw a contrast between the "progressive" pope (Paul VI) and the "backward" primate. Among other things, they attempted to establish direct contact with the Vatican, bypassing the church hierarchy, and they discretely supported similar efforts on the part of the Znak group in 1963–64. The hardening of official policy toward the church following the letter to the German bishops, and the pope's unambiguous expressions of solidarity with the Polish episcopate resulted in the authorities' refusal to agree to let Pope Paul VI visit Poland, which they hoped to use as a means to blackmail the Polish hierarchy.

Considering the massive and spontaneous participation in the religious festivities, the emotion and determination displayed by many of the people who took part in ceremonies that were disrupted and hindered by the authorities, as well as the international repercussions of all this, the primate seems to be the one who emerged victorious from this confrontation. In any event, the church had now become the focus for not only the rank-and-file faithful but also for those members of the Catholic intelligentsia who had reservations regarding the caution with which Cardinal Wyszyński was reacting to the changes introduced by the Vatican Council. The unmistakable muting of antichurch propaganda, including the personal attacks on Wyszyński, provided indirect evidence that the authorities thought they had lost more than they had gained during "the war over the millennium." The campaign of ostentatious petty annoyances came to an end, and the authorities even agreed to some major concessions, such as granting permission in the fall of 1967 for the construction of a church in Nowa Huta. This lull may well have resulted from the fact that, during 1967, other tensions were increasing, both inside the party and in its relations with dissident youth and intellectual circles.

The military intervention in Hungary in November 1956 established fairly clear limits to the "Leninist principles of equality among nations" that provided the guidelines—as Moscow stated in a declaration of 30 October 1956—for its relations "with other socialist countries." While it restrained the aspirations of Gomułka and his group to achieve greater independence in relation to the Soviet Union, the new first secretary by no means advocated cutting all ties with Moscow or even drastically weakening them. In this he was guided both by ideology and by his assessment of Poland's geopolitical situation. In fact, Gomułka's inclinations were just the opposite: doctrinal principles, and fear of "the reemerging forces of reaction" at home and of the growing power of Germany were combined into a coherent set of attitudes and actions, the cornerstone of which consisted of keeping Poland in the communist bloc and strengthening the bloc itself.

As a result, the PZPR (and Gomułka) did not, in fact, lose control of the situation in Poland, and the country did not become "the weak link" in the communist bloc, as Khrushchev feared it would in October 1956. With the passage of time, Poland actually became a strong point in the Kremlin's policy, both on a global scale and within the world communist movement. Not only did the country not display any separatist tendencies, but once the domestic situation had more or less stabilized in 1958, it began to play an active role in all the major developments in the international workers' movement, an area in which Gomułka personally was much involved. He found this easier once Moscow overcame its initial hesitations, eased the pressure it had exerted during his first years in power, and finally gave its blessing to the entire inventory of Polish specifics—private agriculture, the position of the church, and a considerably greater degree of creative, cultural, and even intellectual freedom.

Poland's membership in the Soviet bloc tended to cushion the effect of events in the outside world that shaped the global balance of power. The population did not experience directly their impact on developments inside the country, except, perhaps, in the case of the economy. The authorities no longer exerted as much pressure as previously to mobilize society around slogans concerning "the struggle for peace." Propaganda campaigns became less importunate and burdensome; the campaign relating to the Vietnam War, for example, was nothing like the campaigns that had once been organized over the war in Korea.

Although Poland's dependence on Moscow in the field of foreign policy was only slightly less than before, after 1956 both sides strenuously observed the formalities, out of concern for world opinion, which had more weight in political calculations than during the period 1949–53. Poland acquired some room for maneuver, but the current state of research makes it difficult to assess whether and to what extent particular actions were really based on Polish initiatives and whether the procedure of "reaching agreement" with Moscow was conducted in a fashion typical of the normal obligations between allies. It is possible that Polish initiatives were simply "trial balloons" in the politics of the whole bloc. In fact, of course, they were few in number. The most famous was the so-called Rapacki Plan, a proposal to create a nuclear-free zone in Central Europe, consisting of Poland, Czechoslovakia, and East and West Germany, that was put forward by Poland's minister of foreign affairs in a speech to the United Nations in September 1957. While the proposal dealt with crucial issues, it was clear that only the major powers were in a position to make any binding decisions.

This proposal, similar to plans suggested by a number of other countries, including Bulgaria and Finland (the so-called Kekkonen Plan), was further elaborated in following years, one of these elaborations becoming known as the "Gomułka Plan." The first secretary plainly wanted to show himself capable of diplomatic successes. This became evident in 1960, when he led the Polish delegation to the annual session of the UN General Assembly and spoke three times during the plenary discussions. Khrushchev was also attending the UN session, and the fact that Gomułka met with him three times suggests that he probably consulted him about some of his remarks. Despite what seemed to be an initial antipathy but may actually have been only mutual distrust, Gomułka met frequently with both Khrushchev and his successor. During more than fourteen years in power the leader of the PZPR held over forty bilateral meetings, both official working visits and confidential meetings that were kept secret. The first secret discussions between Gomułka and Khrushchev took place as early as 1 November 1956 and dealt largely with the national uprising in Hungary. The meetings that they held almost every January at the government resort in Łańsk became a ritual.

An issue of special interest to Poland was that of persuading the Western powers and West Germany to recognize officially the Oder-Neisse border. Under Gomułka this issue lost none of its significance either at home or abroad, in Poland's relations with the West. The threat of "German revanchism" remained one of the main weapons in mobilizing public opinion and a growing number of émigré groups to rally around the government—or more precisely, the communist authorities—as the sole guarantor of Poland's borders. On several occasions Gomułka was personally involved in trying to resolve what was one of the most crucial issues facing the country, but he had very little chance of exerting any real influence over the course of events, and the persistence with which he returned again and again to the subject suggested that he did so for domestic political reasons. The most significant success was a certain warming of relations with France, but this probably took place at the initiative of Paris, based on de Gaulle's personal desire to counteract the American domination of Europe and the bipolar division of world power. The French president's visit to Poland, in September 1967, was considered a genuine achievement of Polish diplomacy. We can assume, however, that the warm welcome de Gaulle received from the Poles was more a function of the fact that he was a distinguished guest from Western Europe—a rarity in Poland—than the result of his support for the country's demands regarding the western border.

Gomułka—and the politicians below him in the hierarchy—based Poland's diplomacy on maintaining a firm position in relation to the border and backing this up with strong words addressed to West Germany. A permanent fixture of the diplomatic repertoire was to point to the numerous statements made by politicians, organizations, and even state institutions in the FRG questioning the existing border. The Germans responded in kind, and until the second half of the sixties public opinion in West Germany remained firmly against recognition of the status quo. The relatively frequent contacts between Poland and the GDR also served to increase the pressure on Bonn, although it was obvious that East Berlin was totally dependent on Moscow. It was not until the spring of 1969 that Polish diplomacy showed signs of a new approach. At this time new tendencies were clearly visible in the FRG, especially on the part of the Social Democratic Party but also in some Catholic and Protestant circles, and Bonn had finally achieved a breakthrough in East-Central Europe by concluding agreements with Romania and Hungary. On 17 May 1969 Gomułka publicly stated that Poland was prepared to sign a treaty with West Germany as long as it contained a clause recognizing the Oder-Neisse border. In February 1970 working discussions finally got under way, the Polish group working under the direct supervision of the first secretary.

The difficult negotiations proceeded quite rapidly, but it turned out that they constituted just one fragment of a broader diplomatic initiative: less than three weeks after the fifth round of talks, on 12 August, a German-Soviet treaty was signed in Moscow. In one article of the treaty both signatories guaranteed the inviolability of . . . Poland's border (only the western border, of course). In this situation the completion of the Polish-German negotiations became a formality, although this by no means diminished the legal and political significance of the treaty that was finally signed on 7 December in the presence of its architect, Gomułka. The fact that the treaty was concluded in the shadow of the Moscow-Bonn agreement did not dampen the triumphalist tone of Polish commentators. The treaty gave Poland, in my opinion, one important asset that went unmentioned in official statements: it undermined (to some extent, at least) the legitimacy of communist party rule, since it was now more difficult to resort to the argument regarding the necessity for close ties with one of the powers guaranteeing the western border. This did not prevent the authorities from continuing to use this argument later, when prompted to do so by the situation within Poland and by the persistent opposition to the treaty voiced by many groups in West Germany.

While Polish diplomacy was fairly active, there were few international contacts at the highest level. Apart from de Gaulle's visit and that of Willy Brandt in connection with the treaty of 7 December 1970, official meetings were conducted with "second-tier" officials: the queen of Belgium in 1960, Finnish president Urho Kekkonen in 1964, the shah of Iran and King Hassan of Morocco in 1966, Indian prime minister Indira Gandhi and her Swedish counterpart, Tage Erlander, in 1967. Polish government delegations at the prime ministerial level also traveled abroad rarely, and the only important such visits were to France and Austria, both in 1965. This seems to have been the result of a kind of deliberate self-isolation, since Poland had opportunities, especially during the years immediately following 1956, for a considerably greater involvement in the international diplomatic arena. Gomułka limited his—and Poland's—international interests to the issue of the Oder-Neisse border, relations with Moscow, the circle of states belonging to Comecon and the Warsaw Pact, and the affairs of the international communist movement. It is possible, but difficult to establish with any certainty, that the Kremlin hindered Poland's independent initiatives, only supporting those that fitted in with its own global strategy.

The PZPR—and hence the Polish state—played an active part in everything taking place in the world communist movement, which in the 1960s experienced enormous numerical growth and far-reaching internal fragmentation. The expansion of communism—both as an ideology and in its state-imperialist form—was most pronounced in the late 1950ss and early 1960s. It was particularly visible after the successful coup in Cuba (1 January 1959) that began as a revolt against dictatorship and ended as a revolution based on Marxism. Its leader, Fidel Castro, not only introduced a Soviet-style political system, but also established military ties to the Soviet Union, a development that was facilitated by U.S. opposition to the coup. Cuban communist guerrillas, led by Ernesto "Che" Guevara, also attempted to transplant rebellion to the South American continent.

Less visible was the expansion of communist influence in countries liberating themselves from colonial rule. The process of decolonization erupted in the early 1960s, with the rapid creation of independent states in Africa, usually as a result of the withdrawal of the colonial power. Nearly everywhere that decolonization was taking place or other forms of dependence on West European countries were being overthrown, Marxist ideological influence was to be found ("Arab socialism," "African socialism"), as was Soviet political influence and, more rarely, that of the Chinese People's Republic. Numerous incentives existed for this state of affairs. After freeing themselves of the guardianship of Western states and in a situation of bipolar global division, it was natural for postcolonial countries to seek support from the opponent of the Western democracies, whose reputations were tarnished by more than a hundred years of colonialism. Moscow and the states of the communist bloc actively encouraged these tendencies, even going so far as to agree, if the need arose, to abandon the principle of ideological solidarity (for example, in most of the Arab states the communist party was illegal and persecuted).

A great deal of energy was expended on propounding far and wide the thesis regarding the effectiveness of the Soviet model of accelerated modernization and industrialization, whose crowning achievement was the position of the USSR as a global military and industrial power. This model was frequently said to be universally applicable to all countries at a low level of economic development. In countries without parliamentary traditions and a democratic political culture it was easy to adopt features of the Soviet system—rule by a single party and dictator ("the cult of the personality")—which were also fostered by the emergence, during the struggle for independence, of a strong leader. Gamel Abdel-Nasser, Ahmed Mohammed Ben Bella, Kwame Nkrumah, Jomo Kenyatta, and Sekou Touré all became charismatic leaders with pronounced authoritarian tendencies who frequently found inspiration (and justification) in Lenin, Stalin, Khrushchev, Mao Zedong, or Tito.

The Movement of Nonaligned States, initiated when the Cold War first abated somewhat, always distanced itself more from the United States than from the Soviet Union, and during the 1960s clearly drifted even closer to Moscow. An impetus was provided by developments in Indochina, where in 1964 the Americans gradually became drawn into the war between communist North Vietnam and the pro-Western government in the southern half of the divided country. At this time, however, the communist bloc exerted its influence in the "classic" mode of a great power—by providing weapons, technology and equipment, as well as advisers and specialists, by educating students (at Moscow's Lumumba University), and by training fighter pilots, all of which was financed by credit offered on favorable terms or even given as an outright gift.

A major element in the political maneuvering that acquired truly global dimensions after Castro's partisans had marched into Havana was the developing situation in the Middle East and the continuous tensions in that part of the world. Some historians and commentators are of the opinion that while Stalin was still alive the Soviet Union began maneuvering toward the side of the Arabs in the conflict between Israel and its Arab neighbors (and virtually the entire Muslim world). This is one explanation for the wave of official anti-Semitism that was evident in some of the political trials in the Soviet bloc (the Slánsky trial in Prague, for example). The short-lived conflict over the Suez Canal (29 October–6 November 1956) gave the Arab countries an additional incentive to seek support in Moscow, where it was readily provided. Nasser, since 1954 the de facto dictator of Egypt, was one of the most important figures of the Third World and after a series of bloody coups in Iraq (1958, 1963) he became a key figure in the Middle East, a region that was of crucial significance to the great powers' global strategy because of its oil reserves. Moscow became seriously involved in the region, conducting an increasingly decisive anti-Israel policy. This became especially apparent in 1967, when the Soviet Union broke off diplomatic relations with Israel after the outbreak of the Seven Day War (5–10 June), which had been started by the Arabs. The Soviet example was followed by all the countries of Comecon and the Warsaw Pact, with the exception of Romania.

The emergence of the Third World also provided the Soviet Union with an incentive to maintain the influence of Marxism in some Western countries, especially those which had until recently possessed colonies. The local communist parties regained much of the influence they had lost when the Soviet Army crushed the Hungarian uprising. A wave of solidarity with postcolonial countries—laced with strong feelings of guilt—caused a large proportion of the younger generation to feel, if not exactly admiration for the USSR as a world power, then a desire to engage in revolutionary struggle against a system that was seen as "rotten," "ossified," and simultaneously "oppressive."

All this created the impression—to a large extent justified—of communism's increasing expansionism, and encouraged the West to continue its own integration. Given the very nature of democracy, this process inevitably involved conflict and friction, which Moscow did its best to exacerbate. More or less traditional treaties of alliance were organized under the aegis of the United States (the South-East Asia Treaty Organization, for example), but more important were those concluded—amidst the greatest contradictions—in Europe. During the period under discussion the treaty establishing the European Economic Community, signed in Rome on 25 March 1957 by France, the FRG, Italy, and the three Benelux countries, was of major significance. Together with the Council of Europe, which was founded in 1949 and had a broader membership (fifteen countries in 1957), the EEC became the central integrating institution of democratic Europe.

The trend toward European integration caused alarm in Moscow, but its influence on the global situation was indirect and, in the 1960s at least, it did not hinder the expansion of communism elsewhere in the world. One way in which the Soviet Union responded to the process was by erecting the Berlin Wall (12 August 1961), an enormous construction project intended to seal the cracks in the Iron Curtain that had opened up since 1956. These were partly the work of Poland, which was far more liberal than other communist bloc countries in allowing its citizens to travel abroad and foreigners to visit the country. In essence, however, the Berlin Wall was a defensive measure; it strengthened the status quo in Europe and could be seen as an attempt by Moscow to safeguard its rear while it expanded its influence elsewhere.

At the level of both propaganda and the real balance of power, Moscow built a strong foundation for its policies in the form of arms programs whose enormous cost was borne by the Comecon countries and, above all, by the peoples of the USSR itself. The arms race proceeded apace, and Moscow took the lead in the second half of the 1950s when it sent its first satellite into orbit round the earth (4 October 1957) six months ahead of the Americans. This position was confirmed when Yuri Gagarin made the first manned space flight (12 April 1961). The United States took up the challenge, and Neil Armstrong became the first man to land on the moon (on 21 July 1969) as part of the Apollo 11 mission.

The rivalry in space was undoubtedly spectacular, but it was not then as important as the nuclear arms race and the related issue of weapons delivery systems. The crisis point came when the Soviet Union installed missiles in Cuba, giving rise to a massive escalation of tensions in the fall of 1962. On 28 October, after a week in which it seemed that the world was only a hair's breadth away from World War III, Khrushchev gave way, and the missiles were dismantled. The Cuban missile crisis came to be seen as the culmination of the Cold War; it was followed by the agreement to install a telephone hot line between the Kremlin and the White House (20 June 1963) and by the treaty concerning a partial ban on nuclear testing, signed, after five years of negotiations, on 5 August 1963. Two major powers that did not sign the treaty were France, then entering a period of pronounced anti-Americanism in its policies, and China.

Beijing's refusal to follow Moscow's lead seriously weakened the position of the Soviet Union, and the Sino-Soviet conflict became one of the major factors hindering the further expansion of Moscow's influence. The origins of this conflict, which escalated during the 1960s to a point that no one anticipated, could be traced back to the first phase of de-Stalinization, when the Chinese communists made their first attempts to play an independent role in the international arena. Its basis was similar to that of the Stalin-Tito conflict of 1948, but because of China's potential it was of far greater significance for the balance of world power and for the communist movement. The conflict emerged gradually, beginning in the fall of 1957, when the CPSU took steps to centralize the communist movement and the Soviet Union came out strongly in favor of peaceful coexistence and the policy of détente. Mao Zedong proclaimed himself the "real" successor to Lenin and Stalin, and the Chinese Communist Party began to compete with the Soviet party for supremacy in the communist movement.

The Chinese advocated "a revolutionary war" against the West and argued that shifts in the Soviet Union's economic policy were evidence of the victory of revisionism and constituted a corruption of Marxist principles. The first controversy arose in the fall of 1957, during a meeting attended by representatives of sixty-four communist parties from around the world. Gomułka adopted a cautious position at the meeting, declining to support the proposal to include in the wording of the closing declaration a reference to action taken "under the leadership of the Soviet Union," and twice meeting with the Chinese party leader. Shortly afterward, however, when new controversies between Beijing and Moscow erupted during 1958–59 (among other things, over Soviet criticism of the Great Leap Forward and over the Soviet Union's neutrality in the border dispute between China and India), the PZPR leader became more vocal in his support for Khrushchev. In January 1961 he declared, "History has assigned the CPSU a place generally recognized by all the parties of the avant-garde." During a speech at the Kremlin in 1964 he stated that "the supreme interests of our movement must take precedence over the factional passions kindled by our Chinese comrades."

The Sino-Soviet conflict escalated. Advancing the thesis that socialist revolution was becoming a struggle "of the world's poor" against "the rich," Beijing tried to gain influence in the newly created postcolonial states and openly supported all kinds of guerrilla movements. The dispute caused a split in many communist parties, including some in Western Europe. China's position was strengthened in the fall of 1964, when it exploded its first atom bomb (only three years later it had the hydrogen bomb) and when, almost simultaneously, Khrushchev was overthrown in a quiet coup and replaced by Leonid Brezhnev. In 1966 Mao Zedong unleashed his Cultural Revolution, and in May the first detachments of the young Red Guards took to the streets.

The Guards were directed against the governing elite, and their slogans also sharply attacked the Soviet Union, declared to be the chief enemy of world revolution. On several occasions crowds of demonstrators stormed the Soviet embassy (and other embassies). These developments acquired added significance in light of the fact that Beijing was persistently pressing territorial claims, demanding the annulment of the nineteenth-century Chinese-Russian border treaty. In March 1969 tensions escalated following a number of serious border incidents along the Ussuri River. Mao, who shortly beforehand had called off the Cultural Revolution, agreed to diplomatic negotiations, and the tension subsided. One reason for this change of course was undoubtedly the fact that the United States had decided to begin discrete peace negotiations after several years (1965–68) of heavy military involvement in Vietnam (in 1969, half a million U.S. soldiers were in the country).

Polish communists proved resistant to the Chinese virus, but the conflict between Beijing and Moscow had repercussions within Comecon and the Warsaw Pact. From the strategic point of view, Albania, the smallest country of the bloc, was of little significance to Moscow, but from the point of view of prestige, the position it took was galling. Enver Hoxha came out strongly on the side of the Chinese, and in 1961 Moscow broke off diplomatic relations, and Albania was suspended from Comecon and the Warsaw Pact.

More important was the position of Romania, which in 1957 had already declared China and the Soviet Union to be equals and had then gone on to display signs of distancing itself from Moscow. These differences in policy were exacerbated by changes within Comecon that generally favored the more industrialized members. In April 1964 the Central Committee of the Romanian Communist Party passed a resolution stating, "There can be no father-party or son-party, no superior party or subordinate party." A year after the death of Gheorghe Gheorgiu-Dej, Nicolae Ceaușescu became the new general secretary and proceeded to distance his party from some of Moscow's decisions. Not only did he not condemn China, but he did not break off diplomatic relations with Israel in 1967, and he did not take part in the invasion of Czechoslovakia a year later. Some chauvinist elements made their way into official propaganda, which began to stress national traditions and to argue that the Romanian state could trace its origins back to ancient Dacia. Romania became open to cooperation with the West, and in 1967 the country established diplomatic relations with the FRG, the only communist country apart from the Soviet Union to do so. Ceaușescu did not, however, follow the example of the Albanians, and although he caused trouble for Moscow, the Kremlin also considered him a useful mediator in the international arena. While neither the Albanian secession nor the Romanian "deviation" undermined the Soviet position in East-Central Europe, they undoubtedly contributed to a loss of authority on Moscow's part, a development that perhaps facilitated—and even encouraged—a number of experiments.

One of these, although one that had few external repercussions, was the reform of the Hungarian economy, modeled on the Polish reform proposals of 1956–57. Unlike Gomułka, however, János Kádár decided he would actually introduce these reforms, which he did on 1 January 1968. Changes in Czechoslovakia, on the other hand, took an unexpected and dramatic turn. They began with a program of economic reforms that were vitally needed after a period of falling growth rates during the early 1960s. The situation was complicated by the fact that the process of de-Stalinization in Czechoslovakia had been proceeding slowly and with considerable delay. In the summer of 1967 communist party revisionists joined forces with liberal writers and intellectuals to voice their discontent. The Czechoslovak Communist Party reacted swiftly, but it failed to silence the dissidents and could not prevent the emergence of divisions within the party elite. A meeting of the Central Committee (30–31 October) revealed a split between the proponents and opponents of reform. A visit from Brezhnev on 5 January 1968 did nothing to resolve the situation, and an apparatchik of the younger generation, Aleksander Dubček, took over as first secretary.

The conflict in the party deepened, with the reformers gaining the advantage and forcing the resignation of Antonín Novotný from his post as president of the republic, the last official position that he held. On 6 April 1968 the Central Committee adopted an "Action Program," containing proposals for far-reaching political changes, including the abolition of censorship. The general direction of the reforms was summed up in the statement that the aim was to create "a new model of socialist society, deeply democratic and adapted to Czechoslovak conditions." The main point, however, was not the words themselves; after all, the Soviet authorities had proclaimed their commitment to "real democracy" during the Moscow purges. In this case, words were backed up by legal changes, and the public began to demand that civil rights and freedoms be respected and began to organize around such issues (forming the Club of Involved Nonparty People, and a club made up of former political prisoners). The reformists forged ahead: Novotný was replaced by General Ludvík Svoboda, Oldřich Černik became prime minister, the reformist economist Ota Šik took charge of the economy, and Josef Smrkovský became speaker in the parliament. The reform movement gained further impetus with the publication of Ludvík Vaculík's declaration, known as "Two Thousand Words," which was rapidly signed by several thousand people. Ancient conflicts between Czechs and Slovaks also reemerged. The party leadership tried to prevent events from getting out of control and did not go beyond their April program, even though the conservatives were on the decline. Dubček also received expressions of support from Romania and Yugoslavia, and commentators even began discussing the possible revival of the prewar Little Entente.

All this aroused growing alarm on the part of both Brezhnev and Gomułka, who was vitally interested in the changes taking place in Prague. In February 1968 he had a private and confidential meeting with Dubček, warning him that he was in danger of losing control of the situation. In early spring, communist party leaders from the Warsaw Pact countries began holding regular meetings—on 23 March in Dresden, on 8 May in Moscow, on 14–25 July in Warsaw, and on 3 August in Bratislava—but representatives of the Czechoslovak party attended only the first and last of these. Party leaders discussed ways of averting further democratic developments on the Vltava and pressured their Czechoslovak counterparts to rescind the most far-reaching reforms already enacted.

Gomułka firmly believed that what was taking place in Czechoslovakia was "a new type of counterrevolution," one that did not involve bloodshed but one that was, nonetheless, taking place before their eyes. He hotly defended this view against reservations voiced by János Kádár. Party propaganda in Poland became more aggressive, as it did elsewhere in the bloc, the mass media emphasizing "the danger developing on our southern flank," and publishing reports fabricated by TASS concerning the discovery of arms caches collected by "West German revanchists." At the same time, military preparations were under way, including exercises on Czechoslovak territory involving staff officers and signals troops.

At a meeting on 18 August, the leaders of five communist parties were informed of the decision to intervene militarily. The invasion began on the night of 20–21 August. Some 200,000–250,000 soldiers and about 4,200 tanks from the Soviet Union, Poland, Bulgaria, and Hungary took part in the first wave (East German forces were standing ready on the border). At the order of defense minister Martin Dzur, the Czechoslovak army put up no resistance and remained confined to barracks. The leadership—Dubček, Smrkovský, and Černik—was detained and taken to Moscow, where they were joined by Svoboda. The leaders of the countries taking part in the military intervention were summoned to Moscow, where they were kept informed of the state of "negotiations." After discussions full of threats and blackmail, the Czechs and Slovaks were forced to make far-reaching concessions. Although no immediate changes were to be made in the leadership—these took place gradually during the winter and spring of 1969—further political reforms were blocked and many were rescinded. Moscow could tolerate the insubordination of Bucharest in the field of foreign policy, but it could not permit the model of socialism proposed by Prague to take root. One major outcome of Operation Danube was that the numerically powerful Central Group of the Soviet Army was now stationed in Czechoslovakia, which closed an operational loophole.

For many people on the left, including communists, the military intervention and the crushing of the Prague Spring were proof that all hopes for a gradual transformation of the system were vain—unless, of course, it was initiated by the Kremlin. For these people the events of August 1968 were more significant than the crushing of the Hungarian uprising, which they tended to associate with "reactionary" forces. The tanks on Wenceslas Square destroyed the vision of "socialism with a human face."

In November 1969, speaking as a guest at the Fifth Congress of the PZPR, Leonid Brezhnev officially declared that the sovereignty of socialist states was "limited" by the interests of the entire community. Among those applauding was Gomułka, whom the CPSU leader had four years earlier described as "a faithful son of his people, an outstanding activist of the international workers' movement, and a great friend of the Soviet Union."

MARCH

On 9 June 1967, the fourth day of the Arab-Israeli war, party and government officials from the Warsaw Pact countries, at a special meeting in Moscow, decided to break off diplomatic relations with Israel. On 19 June, addressing the Sixth Trade Union Congress, Gomułka declared that "every Polish citizen should have only one Homeland—People's Poland," and he condemned "the Zionist circles" in Poland that "have come out on the side of the aggressors, the destroyers of peace, imperialism." On 28 June a meeting of the Administrative Council of the Ministry of Internal Affairs heard a report to the effect that 382 persons of Jewish origin had been "exposed" as taking the side of Israel. According to information gathered by the Third Department, they included 76 journalists and writers, 57 state administrative officials, and 51 employees of the economic administration. The department was instructed to "investigate the Zionists," beginning with the office of state reserves, atomic scientists, and the Polish Press Agency. The meeting considered it vital that directors of enterprises or administrative agencies in which "an exposed Zionist" was employed be informed of the fact and encouraged to dismiss the person concerned.

So began the initial phase of a conflict, whose main participants were, on one side, the joint forces of the Partisans and "young apparatchiks" and, on the other, young dissidents, revisionists, and liberal intellectuals. Members of the power elite who had once been members of the KPP also came under attack, the strongest blows being aimed at people who were—or were thought to be—of Jewish origin.

After the unrest of 1964—the Letter of the 34, the trial of Wańkowicz, the publication of Kuroń and Modzelewski's *Open Letter,* and their subsequent arrest and sentencing—and after liberal party members and intellectuals had been consistently deprived of all opportunities to voice their opinions in public, it seemed as though dissident circles had been completely silenced. This was not, however, the case: on the tenth anniversary of October, Leszek Kołakowski and Krzysztof Pomian addressed a meeting organized by dissident students in Warsaw and voiced sharp criticism of current party policy. The two speakers and several people who supported their views were promptly expelled from the PZPR, a move that caused several dozen others to resign from the party in protest. The dissidents were not, however, ready to organize, and their opposition remained within its existing limits. This remained the case even when Kuroń and Modzelewski emerged from prison, although the political debate among the small groups of young people associated with them acquired increased vigor and—partly as a result of the "war over the millennium"—began to demonstrate new elements: a rethinking of the attitude toward the church and a new emphasis on the traditions of the nationalist and independence movements.

The Partisans' undoubted success in capturing the post of interior minister for Moczar was followed by a further strengthening of their position, a process in which Gomułka seems to have been instrumental. In 1965 Grzegorz Korczyński became deputy minister of defense and chief inspector of homeland territorial defense, and Tadesz Piętrzak was appointed police commander in chief. The Partisans began collaborating more closely with PAX, and ZBoWiD expanded its range of activities, establishing its own Writers' Club in 1966. When Gomułka began hunting for "the Zionist fifth column," the Partisans saw a new opportunity. In the summer of 1967 "reviews of cadres" got under way. Given that the Ministry of Internal Affairs had already been thoroughly "reviewed," the first institution to be purged was the army, where about two hundred senior officers were dismissed or transferred to civilian employment—without the slightest sign of opposition from the defense minister, Spychalski. In the central state apparatus the atmosphere was that of a veritable witch hunt, which rapidly spread to the lower levels of the official ladder.

Official propaganda began beating the patriotic drum ever more loudly. A stage show featuring partisan songs and titled *Dziś do ciebie przyjść nie mogę* (Today I Cannot Come to You) created a furor and was described by one critic as showing "our colors"—a reference to Moczar's book, published a few years earlier. Harsh criticism was directed at the émigré community and its institutions, especially *Kultura* and Radio Free Europe, both of which were exceptionally sensitive to the rhythm of events in Poland. The persecution of defiant individuals continued unabated, with the trials of Nina Karsów and Janusz Szpotański, and the security service intensified its activity. The Ministry of Internal Affairs exerted constant pressure on the church, renewing its efforts to foment strife within the hierarchy. In September the authorities refused to give Cardinal Wyszyński a passport so that he could attend the opening of the Synod in Rome, although (as the press emphasized) the other bishops going to the meeting did receive passports. Among them was Cardinal Karol Wojtyła, whom the authorities had clearly identified as the leading competitor to Wyszyński.

Events in the outside world exacerbated the domestic situation. Dissent was growing in neighboring Czechoslovakia, dissidents were emerging in the Soviet Union itself, and university campuses in the United States were being rocked by student strikes and demonstrations. The Vietnam War and the protests against it increased in intensity. Incomprehensible reports about marauding Red Guards began to filter out of China.

The Partisans and their increasingly numerous and vociferous supporters in the Polish media became ever more aggressive and brutal. They were thirsting for a fight. The explosion came, as is often the case, from an unexpected quarter, but one that was by no means unusual in an authoritarian state. On 10 January 1968 the Ministry of Culture and Art informed the management of Warsaw's National Theater that its production of *Dziady* (Forefathers' Eve) by Adam Mickiewicz would be closed down on 30 March. The production had aroused concern among senior officials in the culture ministry, who detected an emphasis on the play's anti-Russian elements. News of the decision swept through intellectual circles and the young dissidents—named "Commandos" by their opponents—decided to launch a public protest. After the final performance some three hundred people marched to the nearby statue of Mickiewicz, where they laid flowers. At this point, the police joined in the action, arresting several dozen people. Since 1 February the Commandos had been collecting, in a semi-open fashion, signatures to a petition protesting against the decision to close *Dziady;* in the course of two weeks they collected more than three thousand in Warsaw alone, and more than a thousand in Wrocław. The writers, too, had begun to mobilize. At an extraordinary session of the Warsaw branch of the writers' union, on 29 February, the majority of those present voted for a resolution protesting against the closing of *Dziady*—which they interpreted as a sign of the authorities' "increasing intervention" in the arts—and against "the arbitrary and secretive" activities of the censors and the institutions in charge of culture. This resolution went much further in its criticism than the Letter of the 34, and during the discussion Stefan Kisielewski coined a phrase that became one of the most popular terms for the system—"the dictatorship of the ignorant."

At the beginning of March the Commandos decided to organize a mass meeting at Warsaw University. The purpose of the meeting was to protest against the closing of *Dziady* and against the university's expulsion (at the behest of the security service) of Adam Michnik and Henryk Szlajfer as punishment for their having provided information about the protests to foreign journalists. The meeting was set for 8 March.

At this point the initiative appeared to lie with the young dissidents and their allies in the artistic community. However, their most dangerous opponents were quietly preparing to move. On 2 March the Warsaw party *aktiv*—led by the newly appointed first secretary of the Warsaw committee, Józef Kępa—passed a resolution stating that it was following "with concern and outrage the actions of a reactionary group . . . , which under the guise of defending Polish culture is attacking the Party and People's Power with ever greater ferocity and enmity." The mass meeting at Warsaw University came as no surprise to either the party *aktiv* or the security apparatus. Quite the opposite: Moczar and the Partisans were better prepared than the event's organizers, whose plans did not go beyond ensuring that the meeting pass two short resolutions. When the rally got under way at midday, buses full of ORMO units were already nearby, together with ZOMO detachments, and several Commandos had been under arrest for several hours already. ORMO units and "worker activists" entered the university campus, followed by police units armed with batons and helmets. They rapidly dispersed the students, many of whom managed to escape to the surrounding streets.

The next day students at Warsaw Polytechnic held a rally, and a rapidly growing crowd then marched toward the offices of *Życie Warszawy,* the city's local daily, chanting, "The press lies." The police reaction was no less brutal than at the university. On 9 March not only were all the forces of the Ministry of Internal Affairs (including the Internal Security Corps) in a state of readiness, together with thousands of ORMO and party activists, but so also were the central military authorities, which ordered a full mobilization of the kind normally seen only in the case of serious rioting or a general strike. Gomułka and a few other dignitaries had spent 6–7 March at a Warsaw Pact meeting in Sofia, so it is possible that the scale of the disturbances caught him by surprise, but he took no steps to reduce the level of tension and remained silent for several days. Subsequent events went in two different directions.

Beginning on Monday, 11 March, demonstrations and strikes were held in a number of universities: 11 March—Kraków; 12 March—Poznań, Łódź, Wrocław, and Gdańsk; 14 March—Toruń; 15 March—Upper Silesia and Lublin. High-school students in many small towns also organized protest demonstrations, although in less spectacular fashion and less frequently. Students at some institutions organized sit-ins—in Wrocław and on 21–23 March in Warsaw (at both the university and the polytechnic). Skirmishes with the police also took place, some of them lasting several hours and most of them occurring in downtown areas. Altogether about 2,500 demonstrators were detained, and several hundred people were arrested. Some 1,500 students were expelled, and many university departments were obliged to organize a new round of admissions; hundreds of students were called up for "military training." Mass demonstrations came to an end on 28 March when a meeting of Warsaw students approved a resolution entitled, "Declaration of the Student Movement." Despite efforts to do so, they failed to establish contacts with factory workers, and although there were numerous expressions of sympathy and even support from the public, the student movement remained largely isolated.

It did, however, obtain support from another direction. On 11 March, the five deputies of the Znak parliamentary caucus sent a formal note to the prime minister, demanding that "the government take political steps aimed at reducing the level of tension." Another document was of even greater significance. On 21 March, while student strikes were still taking place, the bishops attending the 107th Conference of Bishops sent the prime minister a memorandum in which they pointed out that "society has long been concerned about the methods used by the security authorities," and that, "the right to accurate information guaranteed to our citizens by the Constitution of the Polish People's Republic and the UN Declaration requires freedom of the press, restrictions on the scope of censorship, and objective information." The stand taken by the church was especially significant in that this was the first time in many years that it had gone beyond defending the rights of believers or of the church itself to speak out in defense of a specific social group and the aims it had expressed. The bishops' statement could also be read as expressing support for the demands raised by a group whose members included people known for not only their atheism but also their hostility toward the church.

The student movement developed spontaneously, expanding far beyond the expectations of those who had set it in motion and who had done so without reference to any specific political program. The appeal to basic values—national traditions and freedom of speech—and to social solidarity struck a chord with a large number of young people, regardless of their beliefs. In the course of a few weeks the range of slogans and demands broadened and became more varied. Demands were voiced for "democratic freedoms," "freedom of the press and of assembly," freedom to establish "opposition parliamentary caucuses," "guaranteed freedom of association," and "independence of the courts and openness of all judicial proceedings." There were frequent references to the example of the Prague Spring. The declaration of 28 March provided the most elaborate exposition of the students' demands, attempting to situate them within the framework of a specific interpretation of socialism; the document's frequent references to the constitution—which were to be found also in the statement issued by the episcopate—do not seem to have been simply a tactical maneuver. Although the movement had no single organizing center, every group produced a similar list of demands. They all fell within the boundaries of an idealistic version of socialism and had little in common with "real socialism" functioning in a situation of "limited sovereignty." In a certain sense, the crushing of the Polish student movement prefigured what was to come several months later in Czechoslovakia. For many people, both these events put an end to their belief in the possibility of bringing about peaceful change in the system to give it "a human face." For many young people "the March events" became a formative political experience that shaped a whole generation, one that was to play a major role in organizing various forms of social protest in the future.

This experience was all the more intense because the authorities did not confine themselves to unleashing the brutality of the law enforcement agencies or to propaganda directed against those who actually participated in the events. For the people who acted on behalf of the state and party leadership—and there can be no doubt that these were the Partisans—the students who were beaten, arrested, expelled or slandered were simply "victims of opportunity." Their real target was not situated located on university campuses. On 12 March the Polish Press Agency issued a number of news bulletins reporting that the prime minister had dismissed several senior state officials. For the next several weeks, this issue was a prominent daily feature in the press. On the same day, Warsaw's *Kurier Polski* published an article by Ryszard Gontarz titled "Inspiratorzy" (Instigators), which became the key text in a campaign that combined vulgar anti-Semitism with—as is often the case—attacks on the intelligentsia.

To get some idea of how even leading party activists saw the world—and how they presented their view to the public—we can turn to a speech given by Edward Gierek in Katowice on 14 March. Referring to agitators trying to make their way to Silesia, he stated: "They are the same frustrated enemies of People's Poland . . . , assorted offspring of the ancien régime, revisionists, Zionists, and lackeys of imperialism." Although Gomułka referred on occasion to "the sometimes erroneous interpretation of the struggle against Zionism," the term was actually interpreted in a uniform fashion and in accordance with the aims of the leaders of the campaign.

While Gomułka emphasized the anti-intelligentsia aspect of the campaign, most public statements stressed the anti-Semitic element, but regardless of where the emphasis lay, the public reception was the same. A wave of mass meetings in factories and "hate sessions" in administrative offices swept across the country; "Zionism" was condemned, but there were also frequent demands that "its carriers" be rooted out. This strand of the March events had clear-cut goals: to eliminate a part of the old elite and the revisionists, as well as liberals of all stripes. In some cases victims were easy to track down because they belonged to both these categories; both contained a considerable number of people of Jewish origin, most of them completely assimilated (some of them from families that had been completely assimilated for several generations). Official anti-Semitism was nothing new in the history of the communist movement, the most flagrant example occurring in 1948–53 in the USSR itself. After the 1967 June War it emerged again, albeit in a less blatant form and without such tragic consequences as twenty years earlier. The Soviet anti-Semitic campaign was also on a smaller scale than Poland's, although it undoubtedly served to encourage the latter. Anti-Semitism also appeared at this time in Hungary and Czechoslovakia, where it was used as a weapon in the efforts to hold back democratization.

It proved easy to gloss over the central paradox of a campaign that linked—as did Gomułka and Gierek—"Zionists" with "reactionaries" of undisputed "Aryan" ancestry. A third term—"imperialism"—helped overcome the inconsistency, since members of both groups were, of course, identified as its "lackeys." And so the names of such postwar communists as Zambrowski, Staszewski, and Berman were uttered in the same breath as those of liberal intellectuals like Jasienica, Kisielewski, and Szpotański. Misleading juxtapositions of this kind were by no means confined to the brazen propaganda campaign. Gomułka genuinely believed that herein lay the cause of the March outburst in the universities, a belief that he expressed at Politburo meetings, where he added Cardinal Wyszyński's name to the list. On 8 April Gomułka told the Politburo: "Today Brystygierowa is going to Laski to see Wyszyński. Kołakowski was also one of Wyszyński's clients."

While there were many cynics and ordinary opportunists ready to carry out the authorities' every command, this approach to the analysis of social reality—known at the time as "detectivist materialism"—was an expression of the deep frustration to be found among many groups. They included, without a doubt, those members of the state and party apparatus who considered their career prospects to be blocked. They also included many people in artistic and academic circles who felt similarly about their own careers. Frustration was also to be found frequently at lower levels of the social hierarchy, among poorly paid office and factory workers, among overworked owners of small farms who needed additional income from factory jobs to survive, and among young people living in workers' hostels who could see no possibility of getting their own apartments. It was largely to these people that the March propaganda was addressed, pointing out who was to blame for the poor state of the economy and the difficulties of everyday life, and condemning those who were "living in luxury" at the expense of the hardworking nation. It was not difficult, therefore, to ensure a large turnout at factory meetings, although to be on the safe side they were organized during working hours. At this level the propaganda was especially crude, involving egalitarian slogans—which some members of the party leadership considered too far-reaching—and even, on occasion, the demand for "a return to democracy."

The deeply rooted distrust of communists and memories of recent excesses on the part of the security forces also made it easy for people to identify those who bore responsibility for the Stalinist years as "enemies of the nation." "Zionists," "revisionists," and unregenerate "reactionaries," all mixed up together, became the classic scapegoat, to be blamed for the existing—and highly unsatisfactory—state of affairs. It is not surprising that, despite some reservations, Gomułka and his associates let the propaganda campaign run on for three months, and it was only on 24 June that the government press office issued an instruction forbidding "the display and accumulation of publications dealing with Zionism." The attack increasingly focused on "revisionists," a development that was reinforced by the increasingly hard line taken by both Moscow and Warsaw toward the situation in Czechoslovakia.

According to incomplete data, in the space of about two weeks at least 700 people were dismissed from central government institutions, and 800 journalists and editors were sacked from RSW Prasa, the state publishing agency. The most spectacular incident was the dismissal from Warsaw University of six professors and docents (including Leszek Kołakowski, Bronisław Baczko, and Włodzimierz Brus), an event that was given considerable publicity. The hate mongering and slander, as well as fairly frequent incidents of aggression, resulted in a wave of emigration. Roughly 15,000 people left Poland as a result of the anti-Semitic campaign (most of them during 1968–69). They included nearly 500 academic researchers and lecturers, nearly 1,000 students, and 200 people employed in the press and in publishing, as well as filmmakers, actors, and writers. More than 200 former employees of the Ministry of Internal Affairs (and its predecessor institution) and army officers, most of them specialists in political indoctrination, also left the country.

Once they were freed from prison and detention, a large number of the Commandos also emigrated. Emigration brought with it innumerable personal dramas and, of course, a campaign of defamation. Most of those who left had nothing to do with revisionism (not to mention Zionism) and were loyal members of the PZPR, many of them with a history of activism going back to the prewar KPP. For these people the experience of the anti-Semitic attack directed by their party comrades was extremely painful, and they left Poland with a sense of injustice that frequently turned to hatred—and not only toward those who had initiated or sanctioned the whole campaign.

For those who initiated and carried out the campaign, however, the exodus was not as important as the opportunities for career advancement and the pacification of dissidents and liberals. Just as the Commandos had not expected to rally tens of thousands of students, so the Partisans certainly had not expected their actions to bring about the emigration of several thousand people and cause Poland's reputation abroad to sink abruptly. Initially, it seemed as though the Partisans and their allies would achieve all their aims, including the ouster of Gomułka, whose position—it was widely assumed—Moczar was hoping to take over. The first secretary remained silent, but on 14 March, at a rally in Katowice, Edward Gierek, the leader of the largest provincial PZPR organization and a member of the Politburo, publicly expressed his support for the party leader. On 19 March Gomułka finally spoke. At a meeting of the Warsaw party *aktiv* in Congress Hall (the third such meeting in less than three weeks), Gomułka faced a hostile audience far more radical than he, but managed to retrieve the situation by endorsing a large proportion of the slogans and demands launched by the Partisans.

Gomułka hung on to his position but he was plainly weakened, especially as several allies at higher levels were forced out of office. Edward Ochab, a member of the Politburo since 1948, resigned, as did foreign minister Adam Rapacki; several other ministers were ousted. Spychalski, Jędrychowski, Szyr, and Cyrankiewicz found themselves under renewed attack. However, while many new people assumed posts at lower levels, at the very top Gomułka remained in control of the situation. The most significant changes took place in two ministries. When Spychalski replaced Edward Ochab as chairman of the Council of State, General Wojciech Jaruzelski, the forty-five-year-old chief of staff, succeeded him as minister of defense. Gomułka retained his mastery of personal intrigue, and in July he engineered a change at the top of the Ministry of Internal Affairs. Citing the example of the Soviet Union—"There is a danger [of disloyalty], which is why we must control this department," he told a meeting of the Politburo—he ensured that Moczar was promoted to candidate membership in the Politburo and the post of Central Committee secretary. In his place as head of the ministry Gomułka appointed his confidant, Kazimierz Świtała, who had been working in the ministry for only a year.

The pressure from below was checked at the threshold of the top leadership, and it was only at the next PZPR congress in the fall that the attackers finally began to consume the fruits of their labor. It was not Moczar's people who were the main beneficiaries but the younger apparatchiks. Relatively speaking, the fewest changes occurred at the lower and middle levels of the party apparatus, while more changes took place in the state and economic administration and—most important—on the so-called ideological front: in the press, radio, television, universities, and research institutes. Pseudo-patriotic phrases and poorly camouflaged nationalistic slogans once again made their appearance, despite official guidelines urging restraint. Propaganda became more strident in late 1968 and early 1969, with the trials of those who had taken part in the student protests (including the trials of Kuroń and Modzelewski, and of Adam Michnik and three others).

For several months propaganda also focused on events in Czechoslovakia, exacerbating public tensions over Poland's participation in military exercises, including those of 22–30 June in Czechoslovakia, and, eventually, in the invasion itself. At 11:40 P.M. on 20 August General Florian Siwicki, commander of the Silesia Military District, received the order to begin Operation Danube. Within a few hours, the Second Army—about 26,000 troops, 600 tanks, 3,000 motor vehicles, and 450 pieces of artillery (about 10 percent of the total invasion force)—had crossed the border. In accordance with the invasion plans, some 20,000 square kilometers (roughly 15 percent) of Czechoslovak territory was "in the care" of Poland.

The invasion itself, and especially the participation in it of Polish troops, roused to action the student forces that had been crushed in March. Many intellectuals, including Jerzy Andrzejewski and Sławomir Mrożek, issued public protests. On 8 September, during harvest festival celebrations in Warsaw's largest sports stadium, attended by members of the top leadership, including Gomułka, Ryszard Siwiec, a former AK officer, burned himself to death in a desperate act of protest. (Four months later Jan Palach would do the same in Prague.) His death passed unnoticed by the broader public; the same was true of the leaflets and graffiti that appeared in the towns and the slogans scrawled on the highways. The country succumbed to a tidal wave of propaganda that aroused ancient anti-Czech prejudices and lauded Poland's supposed military superiority. It seems probable that the invasion of Czechoslovakia helped Gomułka regain control of the situation at home, but it also destroyed all belief in the socialist myth, especially among politically aware members of the younger generation. As a result, some of those who had hitherto nurtured such a belief began looking for something new. In general, however, the Poles passively watched this demonstration of the "limited sovereignty" to which they had become accustomed. They concentrated instead on the difficulties of everyday life and on surreptitiously complaining about them.

CULTURE: BETWEEN HERBERT AND MACHEJEK

Under Gomułka Poland's cultural infrastructure developed perceptibly, if slowly. This process was perceptible enough to be perceived positively and slow enough for the country to continue lagging behind Western Europe, which experienced a real boom in many fields. The level of education rose, with an increasing proportion of young people continuing their studies after completing elementary school. The authorities placed particular emphasis on the development of occupational training, and by the 1967–68 school year, roughly three-quarters of all young people studying at postelementary level were enrolled in vocational courses. This approach was based on the view that school was a place where young people acquired the skills needed for a specific, life-long occupation, an approach that was in sharp contrast to the growing tendency of wealthier countries to treat school as a place in which young people were socialized and acquired a range of more general skills.

Similar developments took place at institutions of higher education, where some 210,000 students were enrolled at the end of the Gomułka era, with a further 100,000 engaged in correspondence courses. The authorities assumed that the number of students in any given discipline should correspond to long-term plan forecasts concerning the demand for specialists in particular sectors of the economy or even branches of industry. These tendencies were especially visible in technical institutions, but limits on student numbers were enforced throughout the system. The education authorities supported local ambitions and during the fourteen years of Gomułka's rule, seven new institutions of higher education were established in towns that lacked an academic tradition (including Koszalin, Radom, and Rzeszów). This lowered the already low level of Polish higher education, but also provided opportunities to young people from smaller urban centers. The construction of two new universities—in Silesia (1968) and in Gdańsk (1970)—was motivated more by political considerations than substantive concerns. The former, in particular, was intended to function as a counterweight to the traditional institutions that had so disappointed the authorities in 1968. In the mid-1960s the authorities revived the notion of "political" education, which had been abandoned after 1956, introducing the relevant courses into the curriculum of both higher institutions (1964–65) and secondary schools (1967–68).

The number of institutions concerned with the dissemination of culture continued to grow, as did the number of instruments at their disposal, giving rise to public discussion regarding the emergence of "socialist mass culture." The growth in the number of televisions was especially noticeable: by 1970 they were to be found in roughly 4.2 million households, a tenfold increase over 1960 (the number of radios remained unchanged, at around 5.5 million). Although television broadcasting was subject to rigorous scrutiny by the censors, and despite the fact that it had enormous potential in terms of its range and technical possibilities, the authorities continued to focus on the press as their number one medium of communication with the public. After demand for PZPR daily papers collapsed in 1956, the leadership used political means to rebuild the market, and by 1966 party dailies accounted for roughly 57 percent of the circulation of the entire daily press. The trend toward decentralization was successfully countered: the number of dailies stabilized at 53–55, one-third of which were published in Warsaw. The authorities also managed to prevent any increase in the number of weekly publications. In 1970, 203 weeklies were published, while 420 had been published in 1937, when literacy levels were much lower. Readership of the daily and weekly press grew rather slowly (from 62 copies per inhabitant in 1960 to 73 in 1965), probably the result of both a relatively high level of market saturation and the absence of new and attractive offerings.

In the effort to increase literacy, the authorities resorted to some unusual—and largely unsuccessful—methods, such as expanding the network of rural "café clubs" organized by Ruch, the state agency with a monopoly on press distribution. The clubs were supposed to become local cultural centers, which were in fact sorely needed. It was characteristic of a centralized and bureaucratized system that instead of helping people establish something new of their own, the authorities created a network of institutions that implemented a program imposed from the center. By 1969, nine thousand café clubs were in existence, causing Gomułka to grumble on occasion about the new fashion for drinking coffee in the countryside instead of kvass or juice.

While the new—or newer—media of radio and television enjoyed modest numerical growth, traditional cultural institutions were going through a period of stagnation. The number of books published each year could not break through the magic ceiling of one hundred million copies, roughly 2.5–

3.0 per person. The only kinds of books to show numerical growth were textbooks (although they remained in short supply) and pamphlets, usually of a propaganda kind. It was not until the second half of the 1960s that the decline in the number of titles and copies of works of fiction (domestic and translated) came to a halt. Policy regarding translations continued to reflect the changes made after 1956. Characteristically, however, translations of children's literature were virtually monopolized by translations of Soviet works (in 1965, these accounted for one million out of 1.2 million books printed), although in the field of adult fiction, translations of Soviet writers (including the Russian classics) and American authors were published in a more or less equal number of volumes (in 1965, roughly 750,000). Slowly but surely the library network expanded, especially in villages and small towns, compensating to some extent for the stagnation in the number of books published. The central cultural budget continued to reflect political priorities: in 1965, for example, 40 percent of Ministry of Culture subsidies intended for social organizations were allocated to the Polish-Soviet Friendship Society.

The number of cinemas gradually increased, but audiences declined, a fairly typical tendency at this stage in the development of mass culture. Television was becoming an ever more powerful competitor. After a marked increase in the number and variety of foreign films on offer during the years 1956–58, the number of films imported stagnated and even declined. One thing that did not change was the position of Soviet films and those produced in other "fraternal" countries. In 1964 Soviet films made up more than one-quarter of all films shown in Poland, roughly the same number as American, British, French, and Italian films combined. The number of theaters, opera companies, and symphony orchestras remained unchanged. This was true of audiences also (except for the Philharmonic Orchestra, which benefited from attendance at its concert series, Warsaw Autumn, begun in 1957). This probably reflected the spread of television, still in its early stages of development and now seeking its own place in the world of culture by broadcasting theatrical performances. The theater repertoire was far more varied than that of the cinema, with a predominance of Polish plays, more than half of them contemporary works. Plays from the Soviet Union and other socialist countries virtually disappeared from the stage.

In comparison with the previous period, popular culture underwent an enormous change, although a certain ambivalence was plainly visible in the activities of state institutions. The administrative authorities supported some cultural forms that had been highly favored during the years 1949–55 (folklore song and dance ensembles, for example), but they made no effort to prevent the appearance of a Western-style youth culture that was ideologically suspect, to say the least. The music heard on the radio came to be dominated by melodies and songs written and performed by Polish bands that assiduously mimicked their Western counterparts. The times when jazz was a semiclandestine art form were long gone, but the fact that during the 1960s the "socialist youth organizations" ceased urging their members to "compete with each other in work and study" and became places of entertainment (usually "bourgeois" entertainment) aroused concern—especially among the party leadership. For the youth organizations, however, entertainment became a vital condition of retaining any kind of influence among the country's youth. Excursions, including trips abroad, festivals, pop groups, amateur theatricals, and cabarets—often with quite generous financial support—attracted young people. The words of some of the songs and sketches were sometimes subversive, and far more people wanted to go on a trip to "the West" than to the Black Sea.

"Socialist mass culture" was a mish-mash of what the public really wanted and timid attempts to stem the influx of American or West European models. "Papa, buy me jeans," sang the popular Karin Stanek, expressing the aspirations of her generation to a leadership that realized that a Russian peasant shirt was no longer regarded as attractive attire. The pragmatic desire to win over the younger generation often conflicted with ideological principles that could not be instilled by reminding people that the Beatles came from poor proletarian families oppressed by capitalists.

The public holidays belonging to the old revolutionary tradition, inherited from previous years and still celebrated en masse, especially the May Day holiday, remained an integral part of public life. The authorities tried to give the mass rallies and parades that were a compulsory component of the occasion the appearance of spontaneity, and militancy was replaced by joyfulness. There were fewer symbols of struggle—and even of labor; there were more flowers and balloons, and sometimes there were no red neckties to be seen. At festivals and picnics organized during the afternoon, the brass bands of railroad workers or firefighters played alongside young musicians doing their best to imitate the major pop stars of the West. All attempts to repel the influx of models from the far side of the Elbe were doomed to failure. As it was, two nineteenth-century stalwarts, Jósef Kraszewski and Henryk Sienkiewicz, still topped the list of the most widely read writers.

The party leadership made clear its preference for "socialist content" in even high-level artistic endeavors, and from 1957 on there was growing discord between a large part of the intellectual and artistic elite and the authorities. Nevertheless, until at least the mid-1960s Poland produced a culture that was both fertile and original. Many works of enormous value were created, and these often also played a political role, since the censorship restrictions against which writers and directors rebelled were nothing like the PZPR monopoly in the field of ideology.

Cinematography enjoyed a moment of glory, in terms of both films produced and success in reaching a broader public. The films of Andrzej Wajda (*Kanał*, 1957; *Ashes and Diamonds*, 1958; *Lotna*, 1959; and *Popioły* [Ashes], 1965) and Andrzej Munk (*Eroica*, 1958; *Zezowate szczęście* [Bad Luck], 1960; and the unfinished *Pasażerka* [The Passenger], 1963) set the tone, but they were soon followed by a series of works produced by a younger generation that made its debut after 1956—Roman Polański, *Knife in the Water*, 1962, and Jerzy Skolimowski, *Walkower* (Walkover) and *Rysopis* (Identification Marks: None), 1965. The first epics were produced—Aleksander Ford's *Krzyżacy* (The Teutonic Knights, 1960) and Jerzy Kawalerowicz's *Faraon* (Pharaoh, 1965). The films of Tadeusz Konwicki, which began with *Ostatni dzień lata* (The Last Day of Summer, 1957), followed their own specific course, closer to Polański than to Wajda, The films of Wojciech Hass were also praised by public and critics alike, from the bleak and existentialist *Pętla* (The Noose) to the sentimental *Pożegnania* (The Parting), both made in 1958.

Although the censors made it difficult or impossible to bring many major projects to fruition, the generation of the 1960s managed to cut through the restrictions to produce such significant works as Krzysztof Zanussi's *Struktura kryształu* (The Structure of Crystals, 1970) and Marek Piwowarski's comedy *Rejs* (The Cruise, 1970), a tale of drunken passengers on a cruise ship that has run aground, which the audience had no difficulty interpreting as a metaphor for the world around them. Polish cinema also produced its own stars, the most famous being Zbigniew Cybulski, whose persona combined characteristics of James Dean with those of a Polish Hamlet unable to let go of his wartime experience with the Home Army. With his accidental death in January 1967 (he fell while trying to board a

moving train), Cybulski came to be something of a symbol: the Polish intellectual, tortured by his inability to act had died to be replaced by the man of
action.

Such men were presented, as though in opposition to the "anti-hero-
ism" of Munk and Wajda, in films inspired by the Partisans. In 1966 some of
the most prestigious awards were given to Jerzy Passendorfer's film, *Barwy
walki,* and to the extremely popular television series, *Stawka większa niż
życie* (Stakes Greater than Life), in which a Polish intelligence agent—
clearly working for the Red Army's intelligence agency, the GRU—waged,
as is usually the case in such a series, a successful war against the entire
might of the Third Reich. A year later the award went to the equally popular
series, *Cztery pancerni i pies* (Four Tank Officers and a Dog), an adventure
story devoted to Polish-Soviet friendship. Lieutenant Hans Kloss and his
men (together with the "Soviet" dog, Sharik), steadfastly pushing on to Berlin in tank number 201, became the leading figures of the long-awaited "socialist mass culture": resourceful young people who were not afraid to fight,
were untroubled by doubts, and fought hard for "our freedom and yours."
And under the "correct" colors, moreover.

The post-October years brought interesting and even major developments in literature, which emerged relatively unscathed from the short, but
intense, period of socialist-realist leveling. Zbigniew Herbert's delayed
debut, *Struna światła* (A Ray of Light, 1956) proved to be the first of a whole
series of thoughtful poetic statements, and his collection of essays, *The Bar-
barian in the Garden* (1962)—one of the most influential contributions of
Polish twentieth-century culture on the subject of the great traditions of European civilization. Miron Białoszewski, in some ways the opposite of Herbert, combined linguistic intuition with a civic courage that he
demonstrated in his *Memoir of the Warsaw Uprising* (1970), written in defi-
ance of the established stereotypes that were then being energetically promoted by influential forces.

A group of writers of the 1956 generation associated with the biweekly
Współczesność (Modernity) played a major role in literary discussions. During the period 1958–61 in particular, a number of "angry young men" (Stanisław Grochowiak, Bohdan Drozdowski, Ernest Bryll, Marek Nowakowski,
and Ireneusz Iredyński) wrote regularly for the paper. These were also good
years for Tadeusz Konwicki, who wrote *Dziura w niebie* (A Hole in the Sky,
1959), *A Dreambook for Our Time* (1963), and *Wniebowstąpienie* (The As-
cension, 1967). Władysław Terlecki demonstrated his talent, penetrating the

innermost world of conspirators and traitors in *Spisek* (The Plot, 1966) and *Dwie głowy ptaka* (The Two Heads of the Bird, 1970). Stanisław Lem set out on his quest to conquer the world of science fiction (*Star Diaries*, 1957, and *Solaris*, 1961) and also ventured into the territory of futurology (*Summa technologiae*, 1964, and *Filozofia przypadku* [The Philosophy of Chance], 1968). Jarosław Iwaszkiewicz, the party's loyal servant, wrote some of his best poetry at this time (*Tatarek*, 1960), and also published his magnum opus, *Sława i chwała* (Fame and Glory, 1956–62). Jerzy Andrzejewski produced his subtle allegory, *The Gates of Paradise* (1960), and Julian Stryjkowski ventured into the nostalgia-laden territory of the Galician shtetl (*Austeria*, 1966). The publication of Stanisław Barańczak's *Jednym tchem* (In a Single Breath, 1970) marked the debut of the generation of 1968, a group that was to lay the foundations of the independent publishing movement during the coming decade. Tadeusz Parnicki, who returned permanently to Poland from exile only in 1967, caused a stir with his finely wrought novels, *Nowa baśń* (New Fairy Tale, 1962–70) and *Zabij Kleopatra* (Kill Cleopatra, 1968). The incomparable epigrams of Stanisław Lec (*Unkempt Thoughts*, 1957) were republished many times and found a wider readership in numerous translations. Tadeusz Różewicz reached the peak of his talent (*Conversation with the Prince*, 1960, and *Nothing Dressed in Prospero's Cloak*, 1962), but he preferred to write for the stage. Thanks to his *Card Index* (1960), *Nasza mała stabilizacja* (Our Small Stabilization, 1964), and *Akt przerywany* (The Interrupted Act, 1970) and thanks also to Sławomir Mrożek's great series—*Policja* (1958), *Indyk* (The Turkey, 1960), *Śmierć porucznika* (Death of a Lieutenant, 1963), and, above all, *Tango* (1964), Polish theaters had something worth performing, and Polish audiences—something worth watching. Roman Bratny caused a furor with his two-volume epic devoted to the Home Army, *Kolumbowie. Rocznik 20* (The Columbus Generation, 1957). And this still left the novels of Jacek Bocheński (*Boski Juliusz* [Heavenly Julius, 1961] and *Nazo poeta* [Nazo the Poet, 1969]), and the essays of Kazimierz Brandys (*Letters to Mrs. Z.*) and Stanisław Dygat—all of them full of political allusions.

Not far removed from the world of literature was Paweł Jasienica's magnificent series of "history for the people," *Polska Piastów* (Poland of the Piasts, 1960), *Polska Jagielonów* (Jagiellonian Poland, 1963), and *Rzeczpospolita Obojga Narodów* (The Republic of Two Nations, 1967). Marian Brandys began his adventures in history with the documentary epic, *Kozietulski i innych* (Kozietelski and Others, 1967). Stanisław Cat-Mackiewicz continued to produce new work (*Był bal* [There Was a Ball, 1961] and *Europa in flagranti*, 1965), as did the greatest Polish storyteller of the twentieth century, Melchior Wańkowicz. If we add to this the lively disputes, with strong political overtones, among literary critics (Andrzej Kijowski, Ludwik Flaszen, Jan Błoński, and Artur Sandauer), the renaissance of the great Witkacy (*Dramaty*, 1962), the writings of Juliusz Kaden-Badowski, Antoni Słonimski, and Julian Przyboś, and the enormous success of Jan Kott's essays on Shakespeare (published in English as *Shakespeare Our Contemporary*) we have a picture of a vibrant and varied literary scene.

Controversies within the world of culture seem to have been more often rooted in political attitudes than in differences of opinion on esthetic issues, although Poland also had writers whose style combined hack writing and political servility. One such writer was Władysław Machejek, whose prose (*Partyzant sługa boży* [The Venerable Partisan, 1970] or *Wypiękniałaś w lesie* [You Grew More Lovely in the Forest, 1964]) was often primitive or even coarse. This whole range of writers, from Kott, the subtle Shakespearean scholar, to Machejek, the primitive defender of "people's democracy," was watched over by Zenon Kliszko, the supreme cultural overseer and number two in the party. Declaring himself a student and admirer of Cyprian Norwid, one of the Great Four of Polish romantic literature, a writer whose work—philosophical poetry in the best sense of the term—is difficult to fathom and dense with meanings, Kliszko suggested that he provided a shining example in counterpoint to the work of liberal dissidents. At least this meant that Norwid's work was reprinted.

While the theatergoing public had plenty of reasons to complain about the censors, they also had much to be happy about. Poland's leading directors frequently staged productions of major contemporary dramas—Bertolt Brecht's *The Career of Artur Ui* (1962), with a magnificent performance by Tadeusz Łomnicki, a series of plays by Friedrich Dürrenmatt, the well-known *Witches of Salem* by Arthur Miller, and William Gibson's *Two on a Seesaw*, directed by Wajda and starring Cybulski and Elżbieta Kępińska. The amateur actors of the Stodoła student club also treated the public to that classic work of political provocation, *King Ubu*, by Alfred Jarry, in which the action takes place "in Poland, in other words nowhere" (1959). Jacek Woszczerowicz gave a great performance in the title role in Shakespeare's *Richard III*. Kazimierz Dejmek had great success with his rendering of *Żywot Jozepha* (The Life of Joseph, 1958) and *Historya o Chwalebnym Zmartwychstaniu Pański* (The Story of the Glorious Resurrection, 1961). After he had finished working with Brecht, Konrad Swinarski returned to Poland full of wonderful ideas, staging a memorable production of Zygmunt Krasiński's *Un-Divine Comedy* (1965). The works of Różewicz and Mrożek, mentioned above, made their way from one theater to another, with Erwin Axer staging a major production of *Tango* in 1965. In 1962 Jerzy Grotowski staged his first major production, *Akropolis,* thereby initiating some of the most original developments in Polish—and subsequently world—theater. During the critical years 1968–69 two plays by Ernest Bryll, *Rzecz listopadowa* (November Incident) and *Kurdesz,* caused a stir, attributable in part to the political context of the time.

The above constitutes just a fragment of the repertoire that during those years made its way, often with difficulty, through the restrictions erected by censorship and by the tastes of the "decision makers." The enormous public interest in the work of Witold Gombrowicz was suppressed, productions of Kafka ran into difficulties, Witkacy disappeared from the stage, and numerous plays from the great romantic repertoire were taken out of production, among them Juliusz Słowacki's *Ksiądz Marek* (Father Marek). In December 1957 *The Un-Divine Comedy,* one of the greatest works of Polish culture, was banned; Wyśpiański's plays did not have an easy time either.

Symphonic music remained virtually untouched by the years of socialist realism. In 1959 Krzysztof Penderecki launched his career as a world-class composer (*Psalms of David, Threnody—In Memory of the Victims of Hiroshima,* and *Stabat Mater*). Polish soloists, conductors, and orchestras were welcomed abroad, and Polish composers wrote works commissioned by foreigners. The Chopin competition became known around the world, and contemporary music was well represented at the annual festival, Warsaw Autumn. Achievements in the fine arts did not acquire such an international reputation, but the field was characterized by considerable variety and creative freedom. The administration did not flaunt its preference for the "realism" that became increasingly visible from the mid-1960s.

The year 1970 was not a clear-cut turning point in the world of the arts, but the Gomułka era did have its own specific characteristics, one of them being considerable ambivalence. On the one hand, for political reasons manuscripts were rejected and books already printed were even destroyed, films were left on the shelf and screenplays were put on ice, plays were taken out of production at the order of state officials, and some writers were banned from publishing or had their work withdrawn from the bookstores. On the other hand, the era produced a considerable amount of wonderful poetry, interesting novels, great plays and theatrical productions, and a long list of outstanding films. On the one hand, many established writers and intellectuals left the country (Marek Hłasko, Aleksander Wat, Leopold Tyrmand, Sławomir Mrożek). On the other hand, many returned to "the bosom of the homeland" (Michał Choromański, Zofia Kossak-Szczucka, Melchior Wańkowicz, Teodor Parnicki, and Maria Kuncewiczowa). On the one hand, there were persistent efforts to maintain links with the great native and European traditions. On the other hand, these coexisted with the primitive—which is not to say unpopular or ineffective—art of propaganda, often heavily laced with vulgar chauvinism (as in the "eReF" Theater of Ryszard Filipski). But then where is it written that artists are supposed to have an easy life, with generous and undemanding patrons?

THE BLOODY FINALE

While Gomułka succeeded to a large extent in resisting the pressure from those who were pushing for far-reaching personnel changes, the Fifth PZPR Congress in November 1968 sanctioned the influx of a new generation into the leadership. The main beneficiaries were not, however, the Partisans—who were feared not only by Gomułka but also by the increasingly powerful Edward Gierek—but the people belonging to what was known as the ZMP generation: Stanisław Kociołek, Józef Tejchma, Jan Szydlak, and Stefan Olszowski. Dynamic and ambitious, they enjoyed a fair amount of support at the middle and lower levels of the party apparatus. Like Gierek, they claimed to be pragmatic modernizers and could also count on the support of people involved in economic management, whose interests were espoused by the weekly, *Polityka*, then launching the notion of "managerial socialism."

After the tumult of 1968, public life in Poland returned to its former pattern, and elections to the Sejm (1 June 1969) brought no surprises in terms of either turnout (97.6 percent) or the percentage of voters (92.2) who faithfully voted for the candidates of the Front of National Unity. Nevertheless, it is worth noting that these "indicators" were considerably lower in Poland than elsewhere in the Soviet bloc. Pressure on the church was eased, the "anti-Zionist" propaganda was toned down, and no further efforts were made to arouse the public during the trials of those who had participated in the March events. The Partisans had some impact on the world of journalistic commentary—and scholarship—in terms of a partial rehabilitation of the Second Republic, although efforts were made to keep historiography within the confines of a "class analysis" of the most recent history. The majority of people promoted to fill the vacancies resulting from the March purges had no difficulty in adapting to the exhortation that they "keep quiet and work hard," although some could not refrain from injecting a note of triumphalism into their behavior. For the leading members of this new, younger group, this was a transitional period after their great leap forward during 1967–68.

After the emotional spring and summer of 1968, the public mood seemed to calm down, but new ideas continued to percolate among active members of the younger generation. In the spring of 1969 the authorities arrested a group of people involved in providing material to the Paris-based *Kultura* and distributing in Poland books published by its sister publishing house. This was the first attempt to set up a regular network, and also the first attempt in many years to forge such close links between émigré institutions and groups in Poland. A number of people were already writing for *Kultura.* The most active of these was probably Stefan Kisielewski, who not only published (under the name Tomasz Staliński) his novel *Widziane z góry* (The View from the Top), but also passed along manuscripts written by Gomułka's once close associate, Władysław Bieńkowski (*Motory i hamulce socjalizmu* [The Motive Forces and Brakes of Socialism], published in 1969). Nevertheless, few copies of *Kultura* or books published by Giedroyc found their way to Poland.

A group with the enigmatic name Ruch—meaning "movement" or "activity"—emerged in 1966–67 from a different background. In contrast to the few other clandestine groups then in existence, most of which were not serious, Ruch not only survived for several years but also drew up its own program and saw itself as continuing the struggle of the clandestine groups that fought for independence during 1945–47 (one of its founders was Marian Gołębiowski, sentenced during the trial of WiN leaders in January 1947). The organization was headed by Stefan Niesiołowski, Andrzej Czuma, and Emil Morgiewicz. Ruch published an irregular bulletin and had several dozen members. Following in the tradition of the clandestine independence movement of the early twentieth century, it advocated theft, or "expropriation," as one form of political activity. Times and circumstances had changed, however, and no one was planning armed raids or attacks on trains—just how to get hold of typewriters and duplicating machines. In the spring of 1970, during massive celebrations of the 100th anniversary of the birth of Lenin, Ruch decided to blow up the statue of the leader of the Bolshevik Revolution in Poronin. On 20 June 1970, the day the conspirators were to leave Warsaw to carry out the plan, eight of them were arrested by security forces, and within a few weeks virtually the entire group had been taken into custody. They went on trial a year later, some of them receiving sentences as high as seven years in prison.

During the first ten months of 1970, the Ministry of Internal Affairs seized 5,000 leaflets, and recorded 770 graffiti, and 766 anonymous letters of an antistate nature; several hundred authors were "identified," and more than twenty people were tried and sentenced. Several other illegal organizations were uncovered, in addition to Ruch. Ruch was not, then, the only such organization, but it distinguished itself not so much in terms of its attempts to undertake "direct action" as by its level of political consciousness—a characteristic not often found among the clandestine groups that existed after 1947—and by its ability to express this in the form of a political declaration. Adopted in January 1969, this declaration has become known by its opening words—"The years are passing." In many respects it drew directly on the political thinking of the opposition—both open and clandestine—of the 1945–47 period, emphasizing the struggle for independence and against totalitarianism and links with the other nations of East-Central Europe ("who share with us at this moment a common fate"). The group accepted the major features of the socioeconomic system while stressing the need for equality and social justice.

All this, however, took place "beneath the surface," and the broader public learned about opposition activity only from reports of political trials or from listening to Radio Free Europe. This activity had meaning for its participants, and it also confirmed—albeit largely symbolically—the fact that the system did not have universal support. The security service provided an effective barrier between opposition groups and the rest of society, and it was not from this direction that the real threat to Gomułka's position emerged. It was here, however, that the threat to the entire system would take root and flourish.

Gomułka's fate was sealed in less than a week. On 30 October 1970, after lengthy preparations, the Politburo decided to raise the price of most food items. On 16 November this same body decided on the political preparations that had to be made before the price increases went into effect on 13 December. At the same time, other preparations, decidedly nonpolitical, were also being made. On 8 December the Minister of Defense issued the order "Concerning the Principles of Cooperation Between the Ministry of

Defense and the Ministry of Internal Affairs in the Sphere of Combating Hostile Activity, Ensuring the Peace, Protecting Public Security, and Defensive Preparations." On 9 December the internal affairs ministry began preparations by creating a special staff (under General Tadeusz Piętrzak), which the next day adopted a plan of action code-named "Autumn"; on 11 December all ministry units were placed on full alert. That same day the Politburo approved the text of a letter to be sent to all party organizations. Early on the morning of 12 December motorized and mobile police units, as well as units of the volunteer reserve police, were assembled in readiness, together with police and security service trainees, and police special operations groups.

In contrast to the price increases of the 1960s, this round of increases was more akin to the last enormous "price adjustment" of the Stalinist years (3 January 1953), as it covered the majority of food items. Prices went up by between 13 and 30 percent (the price of meat, by 17 percent), and compensatory wage increases were introduced only for families with a large number of children and did not exceed 5–10 percent of monthly income. The following day, a Sunday when the stores were open to allow people to shop for the holidays, customers had their first opportunity to compare the money in their wallets with the new prices. Everywhere people were distressed, but only in one place did they react. On the morning of 14 December, workers in departments S-3 and S-4 in the Lenin Shipyard in Gdańsk went on strike. Workers from other departments joined them, and they soon filled the square in front of the management offices. At around 11:00 A.M. a crowd numbering two thousand or so left the shipyard and started marching toward the headquarters of the PZPR provincial committee. At this time, members of the party's Central Committee were attending a plenary session in Warsaw, where they were acquainting themselves with a report titled "The Economic Situation in the Country and the Key Tasks of Economic Policy During 1971." At 1:00 P.M. they learned of the strikes and demonstrations in Gdańsk. Deputy Prime Minister Stanisław Kociołek flew to the city, accompanied by General Henryk Słabczyk, deputy minister of internal affairs. The first street skirmishes occurred at around 4:00 P.M. Demonstrations that had been noisy but not aggressive now turned violent as neither the party authorities nor the local administration made any attempt to talk with the hastily formed group that represented the strikers. That afternoon, several thousand people demonstrated in the center of Gdańsk, and the units dispatched to restore order became ever more brutal. It was late at night before the crowds were dispersed; hundreds of people were beaten and detained, the first shots were fired, and automobiles and newsstands were set on fire. By this time, a whole group of senior political, police, and military officials had arrived in Gdańsk: Zenon Kliszko; Ignacy Loga-Sowiński, chairman of the CRZZ, the trade union umbrella organization; General Grzegorz Korczyński, deputy minister of defense and Gomułka's confidant; and "unofficially" Franciszek Szlachcic, deputy minister of internal affairs. Additional police units were rushed to the Tri-City area of Gdańsk, Gdynia, and Sopot, local military units were placed on a higher state of combat readiness, and internal security forces were sent into action.

Beginning early in the morning of 15 December other enterprises joined the strike—the port of Gdańsk, the Refitting Shipyard, and the Railroad Rolling-Stock Repair Yard; the Paris Commune Shipyard in Gdynia also went on strike, as did the Zamech plant in Elbląg. The strikers held mass meetings and hastily established strike committees. At 8 A.M. the provincial party headquarters in Gdańsk went up in flames, and troops were called in to clear the surrounding area. Shots were fired, and the strikers had their first fatality. Meanwhile, at Central Committee headquarters, Gomułka was chairing an emergency meeting of senior officials, including the chairman of the Council of Stare (Marian Spychalski), the prime minister (Józef Cyrankiewicz), the minister of internal affairs (Świtała), the minister of defense (Jaruzelski), the chief of police (Piętrzak), the head of the Central Committee Administrative Department (Stanisław Kania), and three Central Committee secretaries (among them, Moczar). After a brief discussion Gomułka decided to authorize the use of firearms. This decision, transmitted by telephone, was confirmed by an order (no. 108/70) of the Ministry of Internal Affairs, and formally took effect at midday.

Additional armored and motorized military units, from Elbląg, Koszalin, and Słupsk, joined the action. In addition to the Coastal Military District, whose units had already left the barracks, two other districts were briefed in preparation for action. At approximately 2:00 P.M. it was decided to create a local staff in Gdańsk, under Korczyński, and to assign to it the chief of the general staff, General Bolesław Chocha. By this time, one-quarter of Politburo members were on the spot, together with three deputy ministers and the chief of the general staff. The army made preparations to enter the larger towns—Gomułka was not underestimating the situation. Quite the opposite: he considered that the strikes and violent protests amounted to a counterrevolution. And he knew, if only from the works of Lenin, how to deal with counterrevolution. In Gomułka's view of the political world, every act of protest in the communist system was a counterrevolutionary act, and if he had once considered the Poznań workers' strike in 1956 to be "a justified protest of the working class," it was doubtless because he was not then the country's leader.

The clashes lasted until late in the afternoon; shots were fired, and buildings went up in flames. At 6:00 P.M. columns of armored vehicles began moving into place along the main streets. The workers proclaimed a sit-in strike, and the police and army blockaded the shipyard and the docks. During the night of 15–16 December the members of the Gdynia strike committee were arrested; serious clashes had so far been averted there, partly thanks to the activities of the committee. Demonstrations took place in Gdańsk for the whole of 16 December, but troops surrounding the shipyard opened fire at gate number 2, preventing the workers from taking to the streets. Clashes also occurred in Elbląg, and strikes broke out in Słupsk. The wave of protest was engulfing the entire Coast.

Early on 17 December a massacre took place in Gdynia: when workers on the early shift arrived at the blockade surrounding the shipyard, the troops fired several rounds. On that day the shipyards in Szczecin went on strike and demonstrations began on the streets of the city that were to last two days, just like the earlier events in Gdańsk. Units from the Warsaw and Silesia military districts began regrouping in the vicinity of Wrocław, Kraków, and Warsaw. Disturbances continued in Elbląg, Gdynia, and Słupsk. In the afternoon Brezhnev called Gomułka to tell him that the Kremlin leadership was "deeply concerned" and even "unable to sleep all night." The head of the PZPR assured Brezhnev that order would be restored and that, if the need arose, "We will of course ask for help." That evening Prime Minister Cyrankiewicz appeared on television to make the first official statement on the strikes. Its tone and conclusions were reminiscent of his radio address following the revolt in Poznań, when he had threatened to "cut off the hands" of striking workers.

According to information received by Central Committee staff in Warsaw, work stoppages and improvised rallies had been recorded in roughly one hundred factories in seven provinces. In several towns—Białystok, Wałbrzych, Nowa Huta—workers had attempted to organize street demonstrations. By 18 December, at least 41 people had been killed (including 17 in Gdynia and 15 in Szczecin) and more than 1,000 had been injured (400 of whom had been admitted to hospital); roughly 3,200 people (of whom two-thirds were factory workers and 13 percent, students) had been detained, most of them brutally beaten after being taken into custody. The authorities had already regained control of the streets—with the aid of 5,000 police and, in the Coastal region alone, roughly 27,000 soldiers (and 550 tanks, 750 armored trucks, and some 100 planes and helicopters)—but the entire country remained in a state of unrest. News of the dramatic events on the Coast began spreading, numerous flyers began circulating, and graffiti made their appearance. Workers continued their occupation of the Szczecin shipyard.

By 17 December at the latest, the crisis had entered its second, "governmental" stage. The impetus may have been provided by the return to Warsaw of Deputy Prime Minister Piotr Jaroszewicz, who had spent the previous two days at a Comecon meeting in Moscow. Before leaving, Jaroszewicz met privately with Soviet Prime Minister Aleksei Kosygin to discuss the situation in Poland. Several high-ranking officials had urgent discussions about how to resolve the crisis or, more precisely, the need to get rid of Gomułka. They assumed that such a move would be effective in reducing social discontent; it would allow blame for "errors and distortions" to be assigned to a few members of the leadership, while simultaneously opening up the possibilities for advancement that Gomułka had partly blocked off in the spring and summer of 1968.

It appears that Gomułka, increasingly isolated (or isolating himself) in his office, was completely unaware of the meetings that were taking place in a variety of configurations and locations. His mood worsened, and he became increasingly stubborn, refusing to give way in the face of what he described several months later as "unbridled anarchy, unrestrained lawlessness, and contempt for law and order." On 18 December he decided to award the police and the army a wage increase. That same day, Tejchma met with Kania, Kania with Jaruzelski, and Jaruzelski with Moczar. In the afternoon Szlachcic, who had already talked by phone with Gierek in Katowice, flew to Gdańsk. That evening he met with Kania and Babiuch in Jaruzelski's office. That night, accompanied by Kania, he went to Silesia, where Gierek was waiting for him. The cards had been dealt. Or perhaps we should say that the players were now free to show their hand, since that evening Cyrankiewicz received a letter from the Kremlin. In it Brezhnev declared that the crisis could not be resolved "without appropriate political and economic measures" and that it was "important" that these be taken "as quickly as possible." This amounted to a de facto repudiation of Gomułka's line and an endorsement of personnel changes.

On 19 December Józef Tejchma presented Gomułka with the proposal that he resign. Gomułka still tried to defend himself—suggesting an increase in family allowances and a three-month postponement of price increases for most kinds of meat—but his colleagues were adamant. After discussions lasting several hours the Politburo decided, in Gomułka's absence, to convene the Central Committee and to nominate Edward Gierek for the post of first secretary. This proposal was difficult to reject. The committee was unmoved by Kliszko's warnings that "the underground will mobilize" and that "AK members are well prepared," or by Bolesław Jaszczuk's fears that Gomułka's removal would constitute "a signal that the enemy should prepare for action."

After fourteen years and two months of increasingly personal rule, Gomułka went into political retirement. What really mattered, though, was that the upheaval caused by the workers' revolt left the structure and principles of the political system intact. What actually happened was a palace coup, but this is not to say that the system itself was not weakened.

CHAPTER 6

Real Socialism: La Belle Epoque

The ouster of Gomułka and several of his closest associates at the Seventh Central Committee Plenum on 20 December 1970 came as a surprise both to the public at home and to observers abroad. But the appearance on television of a new first secretary who promised to uncover the truth about events on the Coast and to "examine in the next few days what measures might be taken to improve the material situation of the lowest-paid families" did not immediately allay the unrest.

On 22 December the strike in Szczecin was still going on, and it was ended with some difficulty. Along the Coast almost every factory held meetings, at which workers raised hundreds of demands and complaints, ranging from various local issues of a technical, organizational, and social kind, to demands that the price increases be rescinded and that those responsible for the use of armed force and for the state of national economic and social policy be punished. Virtually everywhere workers demanded trade unions independent of the party and the administration. They also demanded that the mass media provide an accurate account of the course of events and an accurate list of worker demands: "We ourselves can explain our actions to the whole of society," said one Gdańsk worker at a meeting in department S-3, where the strike wave began, "but you must give us the opportunity to speak to the public." In this context, workers demanded the restriction, or even abolition, of censorship.

The wave of criticism continued unabated throughout January. Some people voiced cries of desperation: "I don't care if I'm going to die of starvation," said one elderly pensioner who happened to have been associated with the communist movement before the war, "but I'll tell everything. You can lock me up tomorrow, but you won't be able to lock up all of us." People frequently blamed the whole party for the use of armed force and for the crisis: "Was it really only five people in the Politburo who were guilty?" was one question asked. In many cases, workers demanded the right to strike, and even voiced demands for democratic elections ("in accordance with the constitution"). While such demands and opinions were often voiced in an ineffective manner, with major issues being mixed up with small-scale problems affecting a single workplace, they still constituted a register of grievances and a list of demands and accusations directed against real socialism. Gierek realized this, and in a conversation with Brezhnev on 5 January 1971 he pointed out: "At this moment the country is calm, but . . . beneath this calm is a powder keg."

He was right. In mid-January strikes broke out once again. On 18 and 20 January public transport in the Tri-City region came to a halt for several hours. Work stoppages of varying length took place in dozens of factories and enterprises. On 22 January workers at the Szczecin Shipyard went on strike in protest at a false report in the local press that they had pledged to increase output (in mid-January many such pledges, "to show support for the new leadership," were made in Silesia). The next day, twenty-three plants were already on strike. Just when it seemed as though the strike wave might be dying out, a strike was declared at the Marchlewski Textile Plant in Łódź on 11 February, and six other plants quickly followed suit. Three days later, thirty-two factories were on strike in the city.

The new rulers made various attempts to stamp out the unrest. On 30 December 1970 they announced increases in the lowest wages, pensions, and disability payments, as well as family benefits. Factory directors paid out bonuses and promised an increase in overtime. It is estimated that wages increased overall by some 5 percent. On 8 January 1971 a government communiqué announced that the price of basic foodstuffs would be frozen for two years. Moscow provided additional credit in dollars, and maneuvering continued at the highest levels. On 31 December Gierek held a widely publicized meeting with workers at the Warsaw Iron and Steel Works. The most effective and energetically publicized events were the surprise meetings that Gierek and Jaroszewicz (now prime minister) held with striking shipyard workers in Szczecin (24 January) and Gdańsk (25 January). Gierek made a particularly positive impression, listening to a string of complaints and demands, patiently explaining, and promising improvements. The crowning success came at the meeting in Gdańsk, when he ended his remarks by asking the crowd, "So what do you say? Will you help?" He received the hoped-for reply, "We will help!" albeit delivered with little enthusiasm. This fragment of dialogue, seized on and repeated endlessly by official propaganda, became the first slogan of the new decade.

On 26 January, after enthusiastic announcements in the press, the Citizens' Committee to Rebuild the Royal Castle in Warsaw held its inaugural meeting. The next session of the Central Committee (6–7 February) condemned the previous leadership and made further changes in senior personnel; among others, Ignacy Loga-Sowiński and Stanisław Kociołek left the Politburo, and the latter also lost his position as Central Committee secretary. Gomułka's membership in the committee was suspended, while Zenon Kliszko and Bolesław Jaszczuk were expelled from the body. A considerable number of ministers were replaced, and changes were made in the membership of the Council of State, now chaired by Cyrankiewicz, "iron Józef," who had tenaciously occupied high-ranking government positions since February 1947.

To a large extent the statements and decisions emanating from the church were conciliatory. In a report compiled on 23 December 1970 the Fourth Department of the Ministry of Internal Affairs noted that both Cardinal Wyszyński and the bishops were favorably disposed toward the change of leadership, and that observations conducted over the holiday period in 1,800 churches "with the aim of establishing the content of public statements made by bishops and clergy" yielded positive results for the authorities. The primate canceled plans for the clergy to read out, on 27 December, a pastoral letter approved in September and titled "The Voice of Polish Bishops in Defense of the Threatened Life of the Nation" (only the Bishop of Przemyśl, Ignacy Tokarczuk, ignored the order). In his New Year's sermon Cardinal Wyszyński declared: "I am convinced that understanding will reemerge in our sociopolitical life, as will the hope that after these painful, bloody experiences . . . we shall deepen our understanding of the meaning of God's laws, the spirit of the Gospels, and the spirit of love and justice."

Nevertheless, tensions remained and the strike wave continued until 15 February, when the authorities finally announced that the December price increases would be rescinded, while the increases in wages and benefits would be retained and food prices would be frozen for two years. But the dramatic (and obviously rhetorical) question asked by one of the participants in the Gdańsk meeting with Gierek—"Why must the workers pay for every change with their blood?"—remained unanswered.

THE STRATEGY OF ACCELERATED DEVELOPMENT

Gierek and his associates had few options in economic policy from which to choose, and they opted for the one that flowed logically from tendencies that had been developing inside the party since the mid-1960s—

modernization of the economy, increased consumption, a quasi-managerial style of enterprise administration (by "socialist captains of industry"), an opening up to Western markets and technology, and the modernization of agriculture. These tendencies were associated, first and foremost, with Gierek himself, who had made a reputation as the "manager" of Silesia and as someone who knew the West, where he had spent his younger years (as a miner in France and Belgium). Similar opinions were to be found among the younger generation of party officials who were looking for an alternative to the "homespun socialism" of Gomułka. The weekly paper, *Polityka,* had fostered this approach, as had a number of party intellectuals searching for a "modern socialism" (a phrase coined by Stefan Bratkowski in his essay, *Polski problem nr. 1*).

During 1971, when social tensions had finally eased, the leadership drew up its guidelines for a new economic strategy. The first draft was approved on 1 June at a joint session of the Politburo and top government officials. The proposals were ambitious but seemed to be realistic: over the course of the 1971–75 five-year plan they envisaged that national income would increase by roughly 40 percent, industrial output by 50 percent, agricultural output by 20 percent, and real wages by 18 percent. To help achieve these results, economic and financial reforms were to be introduced in industry, with the creation of Large Economic Organizations, a kind of state corporation possessing broad powers and a considerable degree of autonomy. The proposals included plans to borrow money in the West, something that could be done relatively easily given the overall situation in world capital markets. The aim was to obtain loans to finance both investment and consumption. The proposals also envisaged a number of incentives for farmers. The leadership moved quickly to begin implementing the whole package, taking advantage of investment projects begun under Gomułka.

Before the end of 1971 production began at the country's first large factory manufacturing prefabricated housing components, a licensing agreement was signed with Fiat to produce small automobiles, state health care benefits were extended to cover private farmers, and a package of measures concerning agriculture was adopted. On 1 January 1972 the government abolished the system of compulsory deliveries, a relic of the past dating back to the period of "war communism." A number of major investment projects, somewhat akin to public works projects, were started; they included the complete modernization of the Warsaw-Katowice highway, the construction of many bypass roads and overpasses in urban areas, a modern railroad station in Warsaw, and the huge new Port Północny near Gdańsk. The large state farms raising livestock were expanded and oriented toward the production of meat, which was then viewed as the product with the greatest strategic significance in terms of social peace. The network of hard-currency stores (Pewex and Baltona) was developed, and the goods that they stocked began to offer a glimpse of consumer culture. Developments such as the licensing agreement with Coca-Cola and the appearance of Marlboro cigarettes in news kiosks acquired almost symbolic significance.

The rate of growth really was impressive: during 1972–74 national income increased at an annual rate of roughly 10 percent, and industrial output—by 11 percent. During the period 1972–73 agricultural output grew by nearly 16 percent. Real wages grew at a faster rate than at any time since the war—an annual average of 7 percent. According to some estimates, the entire consumption fund (wages, benefits, pensions, and so on) increased by roughly 51 percent over the course of the five-year plan period. Many social groups were overcome by a genuine consumer frenzy. This was fostered by the easing of restrictions on foreign travel, beginning with the opening of the border with East Germany, which took effect on 1 February 1970. Propaganda touted the construction of a "new Poland"; to many people it appeared to be within reach.

The economy prospered, and many social groups experienced a genuine improvement in their standard of living. The country's leaders drew on the shallow, but nonetheless real, reserves generated in previous years, and they signed a succession of financial and manufacturing agreements with Western firms. Party and state dignitaries were in almost constant contact with the outside world; they came to focus largely on the West, and American financiers and businessmen were frequent guests in the drawing rooms of those in power. The five years of "dynamic development" were a genuine, albeit short-lived and superficial, success. However, no serious effort was made at structural reform of economic management; this could not be done without major political changes, and no one in the party leadership had any interest in these. According to official sources, during the period 1971–75 national income grew by nearly 60 percent, industrial production—by 64 percent, agricultural output—by more than 19 percent, and real wages—by nearly 41 percent. Even more important was the fact that the mood of the public to a large extent mirrored the optimism of the Central Statistical Office. Such popular slogans as "A Pole Can Do It" seemed to be confirmed by the new highways, buildings, and factories springing up everywhere. The country seemed to be repeating the "Gomułka miracle" of 1956–58, but at a higher level. Once again a wave of young people from the countryside moved into the towns and new industrial centers, and the number of "worker-peasants" grew, bringing a visible improvement to the lives of innumerable smallholders.

The man or woman on the street had no way of knowing, and the leadership ignored the fact, that this success was to a large extent—and literally—"success obtained on credit." In 1975 at least 25 percent of all export earnings had to be allocated to debt servicing, and Poland's international debt exceeded eight billion dollars, forcing the country into a debt crisis. The cause of the problem was not so much the country's borrowing as the fact that, without far-reaching structural changes, Polish products stood very little chance on world markets. The mass of the population, which still lived in an economy of shortage and constant imbalances, was less susceptible to the euphoria that engulfed the political elite and deadened all warning signals. Discipline was thrown aside with the adoption of "open planning," and a veritable frenzy of investment was begun in conditions that remained those of a wasteful command economy. A classic example was the decision to build the Katowice Iron and Steel Works (the first large furnace began production in 1977). The massive investment projects of the six-year plan were nothing compared with the projects initiated under Gierek, which reflected both the old Leninist and Stalinist precepts concerning the primacy of heavy industry and the power wielded by the "Silesian lobby."

"Dynamic development" became "accelerated growth," following exactly the same formula that had been followed in 1949 and 1960. In 1973 accumulation absorbed 33 percent of national income and a year later—more than 35 percent. This investment effort exceeded even that of the Korean War years, and the pattern of resource allocation was similar (in 1975, 75 percent of investment resources were allocated to Group A). Small-scale and medium industrial enterprises were liquidated and absorbed into gigantic "socialist corporations." All of this took place in conditions of total disregard for the environment—and for those who were actually engaged in production (in 1978 a four-shift system was introduced in mining). The great leap forward became a race to the bottom: in 1975, the leadership decided to go ahead with the construction of mines in the Lublin coal basin, opencast mines in Bełchatów, and part of the natural gas pipeline leading from the Orenburg fields. More foreign loans were obtained to finance copper mining and processing in Lower Silesia. Every year the plan targets for coal mining were increased. In 1976 work began on a broad-gauge railroad track to the Katowice Iron and Steel Works, while at the same time, work was continuing on the new high-speed railroad track between Katowice and Gdańsk.

In what was by now a typical pattern, one sector that fell victim to this process was agriculture. Fewer and fewer resources were allocated to the inefficient but superficially modern state farms. The focus on heavy industry led to a decline in industrial production for the countryside—in building materials and artificial fertilizers, for example—which inevitably resulted in a lower growth rate in grain production and thus in the need for imports, obtained, of course, with further foreign loans.

The situation spiraled out of control, and nothing slowed it down: not the energy crisis following the Arab-Israeli War of 1973, which brought a recession to the whole of Western Europe; not the growing proportion of export earnings absorbed by debt repayments (36 percent in 1976, 56 percent in 1977); not the growing inflationary pressure for which the only remedy was a worsening of market imbalances. Partly out of good faith, partly out of fear of social unrest, and partly because they sought confirmation of success, the authorities left the price of basic foodstuffs unchanged, even after 1972. Food subsidies therefore increased considerably, and because of the constant growth of the money supply—largely because of the wages paid to those employed in the investment sector—goods simply disappeared from the stores. The authorities resorted to the tactic of "disguised" price increases, achieved by modifying the assortment of goods available, and introducing what was called "commercial pricing" for some items. They finally realized that they needed to take steps to reduce investment and stabilize the market in foodstuffs.

They began with the latter. On 24 June 1976 the government presented the Sejm with a proposal to raise food prices by 30–100 percent (the price of meat and meat products was to increase by as much as 70 percent) and to provide partial compensation in the form of wage increases. The authorities' desire for a parliamentary seal of approval for this decision was clear evidence of their uncertainty regarding its reception and their desire to share the responsibility. Trying to avoid the mistake that Gomułka had made in December 1971, they announced that the proposal—although approved unanimously by the recently elected Sejm—would be subjected to "public consultation." This consultation was to take place in the course of a single day, plainly indicating that it was to be nothing more than a propaganda ploy. Nevertheless, people took the matter seriously: on 25 June, in Radom, Ursus, and Płock, strikes and street demonstrations took place, and in many other towns work was "disrupted"—the enigmatic term used to cover unrest, work stoppages, and improvised factory rallies. In the three towns mentioned above protesters scuffled with police. In the evening the government issued a communiqué rescinding the proposed price increases on the grounds that they had met with criticism in the course of the "consultation" and postponing a final decision until an unspecified future date.

This was a painful blow to the prestige of the ruling group—the prime minister in particular—and the Sejm. It was also a powerful blow to Gierek's entire economic policy to date. It took little time to restore calm to the streets, but the economy had no opportunity to "catch its breath," if that was in fact possible. The country's indebtedness was now growing at breakneck speed ($8.4 billion in 1975, $14.9 billion in 1977, and $23.8 billion in 1979); loans were becoming more difficult to obtain and only on terms and conditions less favorable than previously; and debts could be repaid only with the aid of further loans. The continuing recession in the West made it even more difficult to sell Polish goods that were already selling badly, and trade with Comecon partners, accounting for roughly 50 percent of Poland's international trade, generated no hard currency. On the contrary—it stimulated its outflow, since a considerable proportion of the components that went into products sold to Comecon members were purchased with hard currency.

This was most evident in the shipbuilding industry. The Soviet Union was virtually its only client, but the ships were fitted, in accordance with world standards, with equipment purchased—usually on credit—in the West. The Orenburg gas pipeline proved to be another such trap, and an unavoidable one. In the fall of 1976 the leadership announced that it would undertake an "economic maneuver" with the aim of reducing considerably the investment front, curtailing the excess money supply, and changing the focus of investment. Given that the country had become—as the slogans had been proclaiming triumphantly for several years—a "giant construction site," this maneuver was extremely hard to carry out, especially after the June compromise over food prices. Euphoria was replaced by chaos. Construction projects were "frozen" even if the equipment and machinery needed for their completion had already been purchased. Sometimes these decisions were taken in a fairly random manner, but often they reflected the preferences of departmental or regional interest groups. Bureaucratic administration from above was unable to ensure a sensible and fluid allocation of resources; bottlenecks multiplied, and inflationary pressure continued unabated. An increase in the price of meat was out of the question, and other measures to restrict demand, such as the introduction of sugar rationing in August 1976, proved inadequate.

In 1979, 75 percent of export earnings went to service the debt. As a result, imports of components needed for industrial production and the purchase of grain and fodder came to a halt. State banks began obtaining foreign loans for extremely short time periods and, of course, at appropriately high rates of interest. The slowdown in the rate of growth in industrial output was visible from one quarter to the next, despite the fact that the domestic market still had excess demand and new factories continued to come on line. Meanwhile, in 1975–76 agricultural output had already declined by more than 3 percent (partly as a result of climatic factors) while the money supply continued to increase, as did the disproportion between the prices of foodstuffs and those of industrial goods. The lines in front of the stores grew longer. Purchasing officers from even the most powerful enterprises roamed the country with a mad glint in their eye (and bribes in their pocket), searching for needed parts and components. Production lines ground to a halt with increasing frequency because of power outages or lack of raw materials. In 1979, for the first time in Poland's postwar history, national income was lower than it had been in the previous year—2.3 percent lower, according to official data. Despite official forecasts, output of industrial consumer goods fell more sharply than output in the metal industry, for example. Energy shortages became a constant feature. Farmers not only lost the possibility of investing or replenishing their stocks, but the law that provided them with a state pension in exchange for transferring their land to the state land fund had the effect of reducing the area under cultivation, since the state authorities did not sell or transfer the land thus acquired to private farmers. During the Gierek decade, urban and industrial areas attracted a large proportion of young people away from the countryside, and in many regions what had once been family farms were now run by a single generation. Other regions (in the west of the country, for example) were simply depopulated, and the land left fallow.

The cycle ran its course; the economic boom and relatively harmonious development of 1971–73 had given way to a period of wasteful and unplanned industrialization, followed by incompetent and inconsistent attempts to reign in expenditure that only led to economic breakdown and a rapid increase in social discontent. Poland was poised to repeat the events of June 1956 or December 1970. It needed only the final drop to make the bucket overflow. When "commercial prices" for meat were introduced in workplace canteens on 1 July 1980, the first strikes erupted. At that time probably no one imagined that this would constitute not so much a "drop" as a "spark," a spark that would—to use Lenin's famous phrase—"ignite a fire."

THE LEADING FORCE

Just as Gomułka had done after October, Gierek dealt quickly and effectively with members of the party elite who might prove to be too ambitious or disloyal. The most impressive such maneuver was the elimination of Moczar, who was dispatched, as early as the summer of 1971, to the Central Control Chamber, a typical parking spot for those on their way down from the upper echelons of the power apparatus. Many diplomatic missions were headed by newcomers—Stanisław Kociołek in Brussels, Zenon Nowak in Moscow, Artur Starewicz in London, Grzegorz Korczyński in Algiers, Ignacy Loga-Sowiński in Ankara. In the spring of 1972 Józef Cyrankiewicz disappeared, to resurface a year later as chairman of the National Committee for the Defense of Peace, an insignificant sinecure. Stefan Olszowski, one of the most dynamic of the young apparatchiks, was shunted away from the mainstream to the foreign ministry for several years (1971–76). In March 1972 Józef Tejchma, one of the prime movers behind the ouster of Gomułka, was assigned a government post and required to leave the Central Committee Secretariat, a key position in the power apparatus.

The next major reshuffle came in 1974, when Franciszek Szlachcic, for several years considered number two in the party leadership, was relegated to the sidelines. Kazimierz Barcikowski was assigned to the unenviable post of minister of agriculture, and Stefan Jędrychowski, one of the most experienced members of the government leadership, suddenly found himself heading the embassy in Budapest. Considerable changes were made at the lower levels, and in less than eighteen months after the election of the new first secretary, the majority of his counterparts at the provincial level had been replaced. At the same time there was a shakeup in the Central Committee: only 49 of the 115 members elected at the Sixth PZPR Congress in December 1971 had previously been committee members. Nevertheless, there was no question of a genuine rejuvenation of the party *aktiv:* in 1975 nearly 60 percent of provincial first secretaries were aged over forty-five and had been employed in the party apparatus for more than fifteen years (30 percent had been in the apparatus since before 1956). Not only at the highest levels but also in the regions there were many people with more than twenty years' experience in party bodies and so-called responsible positions: from the prime minister, Piotr Jaroszewicz, to the new head of the CRZZ, Władysław Kruczek, to the chairman of the Council of State, Henryk Jabłoński.

After a strong start in December 1970, when the rapidly aging young apparatchiks made the most gains, relatively few new people made their way to the highest levels of power in the following years. The most spectacular careers were those of Jerzy Łukaszewicz and Jan Szydlak, but it was still Edward Babiuch, Stanisław Kania, and Jan Szydlak who were the most active. Stanisław Kowalczyk, appointed head of the Ministry of Internal Affairs in 1973, remained in a strong position, as did General Wojciech Jaruzelski. There was constant surreptitious jockeying for position, but it had little bearing on the general situation in the country and essentially lacked an ideological or even political basis. There seems to have been no group equivalent to the Partisans of the Gomułka era.

The revolving door revolved unceasingly, and the fact that so many appointments were made in the absence of apparent qualifications served to intensify the public's negative perception of the political elite. The most important changes were carried out at the beginning of 1980, when the economic collapse was obvious to everyone. Jaroszewicz lost his position as prime minister and was left with only his seat in the Sejm; Olszowski went off to be an ambassador, as did Tejchma shortly afterward. Stanisław Kruczek, the senior member of the PZPR leadership in terms of length of party membership, was demoted to chairman of the Central Party Control Commission. Gierek's own position does not seem to have been threatened at any time, and relations within the party elite more closely resembled those between a ruling monarch and his courtiers than at any time previously. Gierek was adept at playing the role of pragmatic leader open to the outside world; he loved to travel and receive guests; he met with "working people" and appeared on television.

This impression was strengthened by Gierek's numerous visits—accompanied by his wife and a large entourage—to foreign heads of state, and their return visits to Poland, during which he behaved like a proud manager demonstrating his achievements. Openness to the outside world was an element in his economic strategy, but it also fulfilled political functions, one of which was to maintain Gierek's personal prestige. Alongside the leaders of the "fraternal countries," with whom he met frequently, favored interlocutors included Austrian chancellor, Bruno Kreisky (five meetings during the period 1973–79), and the leaders of West Germany (four meetings in the years 1975–79). France occupied a special position, and contacts between the two countries took place every year after 1975 at the very highest level. Gierek's frequent meetings with Tito (five during the period 1972–78) were something of an occasion, although Poland and Yugoslavia had few political or economic ties. Gierek also established a strong position in relation to the United States: all three U.S. presidents made official visits to Poland—Richard Nixon in 1972, Gerald Ford in 1975, and Jimmy Carter in 1977. When Gierek visited the United States in 1974, he did not miss the opportunity to address the UN General Assembly.

Increased contacts with the West overshadowed Gierek's far more frequent meetings with the leaders of the GDR, Hungary, and Czechoslovakia, and his constant contacts with Brezhnev. The master of the Kremlin was the most frequent visitor; he was usually treated with considerable pomp, and the route followed during his travels around the country was carefully prepared according to the principles of "Potemkin villages." The rapidly aging Soviet leader was feted and no longer treated as an "elder brother" but more as a "father" and guardian. His speeches and books were published in large editions and given wide publicity. One example of this extreme fawning came on the thirtieth anniversary of the founding of People's Poland, when Brezhnev was awarded the highest of all military honors, the Grand Cross of the Order of Military Valor. Gierek clearly wanted to play the role of go-between in East-West relations, and it appears that he had Moscow's consent to do so. Confirmation of this can be found in the meeting that took place in Warsaw (on 18–19 May 1980) between Brezhnev and French president Valéry Giscard d'Estaing, another favored interlocutor of Poland's first secretary. The range and number of Gierek's official contacts also made him seem more like a head of state than a party leader. In this regard he was more akin to Bierut than to his immediate predecessor. This was a major element in the increasingly fashionable notion concerning the "moral-political unity" of the nation and the progressive reduction in the role of ideology in public life.

Gierek intervened in the work of the government far less often than his predecessor had and gave the prime minister a relatively free rein, but personnel policy—including policy within the state administration—was entirely in the hands of Central Committee officials. The party leadership had declared its intention to solicit input from experts as part of its effort to modernize management methods. In fact, the full-time party apparatus continued as the sole source of not only policy decisions but also broad proposals and background studies. One example is provided by the fate of a report on the state of the education system and proposals for reform, compiled by a distinguished panel of experts under the chairmanship of the well-known sociologist, Jan Szczepański. The report included a number of detailed studies that ended up on the shelves, and the reforms that were actually introduced followed a completely different approach. Similarly, the Panel of Economic Advisors, a permanent body established after the crisis of June 1976 (under the chairmanship of Professor Paweł Bożyk), had absolutely no influence over the decisions made at the center. Various "councils" and "commissions" made up of nonparty experts multiplied, but their role was largely decorative. Gierek's meetings with researchers, writers, and journalists served a similar function. There was far more apparent "consultation" than real exchange of views. Nevertheless, in comparison with Gomułka, this onetime miner in northern France seemed to be a dynamic, attractive, and self-assured politician. In other words—a man of the world.

This persona harmonized well with the vision of "consumer socialism," in which it was taken for granted that various levels of the party elite would provide examples of the new style. Corruption and exploitation of one's official position to ensure access to goods of various kinds became commonplace, and the slogan "enrich yourselves" was implemented with enthusiasm. The expanding party and state apparatuses were linked to each other by innumerable ties that were used for purely private gain. The allocation of apartments, automobiles, building materials, plots of land, and official positions developed into a real trade. Major industries and local authorities were able to ensure themselves a friendly press, a share in state subsidies, and positive responses to proposals for investment.

People occupying positions at ever-lower levels of the official hierarchy began to derive privileges resulting from their office. One element in this process was the formalized and strictly enforced system of the nomenklatura, which at the end of the 1970s comprised more than half-a-million positions that could be filled only with party approval. Each party body wanted to have its own nomenklatura, and in the regions political considerations played a far smaller role than personal relations and private interests. A large part of the elite—including (and perhaps especially) at the local level—essentially became a "new *szlachta*," not simply administrators but also owners. Those who wielded power were increasingly referred to, by a growing number of people, as "owners of the Polish People's Republic"—even if only the owners of one rural commune. This was symbolized by the party pin that activists took to wearing on their lapel, which depicted the letters "PZPR" superimposed on an outline of Poland.

One of the most striking—and of course discrete—examples of the tendency to treat the state as the property of the PZPR were the decrees issued by the Council of State (on 5 October 1972) concerning "Pensions for Persons Occupying Leading Party and State Positions and Members of their Families" and "Salaries of Persons Occupying Leading State Positions." The first of these extended pension rights not only to spouses and children, but also to siblings, parents, and grandchildren. The second allowed officials to continue drawing their salaries for up two years after leaving their posts. And these posts continued to multiply: in 1972 there were twenty-four ministries, and in 1980 there were thirty-four; the number of deputy prime ministers was never less than five (there was a moment when ten such officials were in office at the same time); and there were more than 150 deputy ministers and secretaries of state and their deputies. At the lower level of this treasure-trove of positions were the provinces, whose number increased to forty-nine as a result of an administrative reform introduced in 1975.

From the 1960s on fewer and fewer people joined the PZPR for political or ideological reasons, and under Gierek party membership became something akin to a diploma, a qualification required to occupy a managerial position in any branch of the state administration. People rushed to join the ruling party: at the end of the Gomułka era the PZPR had 2.3 million members, by 1980—roughly 3.1 million. During the 1970s there was a constant influx of new people, and young people (aged 18–29) made up one-quarter of the party's membership. The number of manual workers also increased gradually, although they did not make up more than 46 percent of the membership. It was striking that, during a decade in which everything developed so rapidly, the "allied parties" simply stagnated, the United Peasant Party with around 420,000 members and the Democratic Party with around 100,000. Of course, some limits were imposed by the PZPR, but probably the enormous "sucking power" of the hegemonic party and the tightly sealed nomenklatura system were the key factors. In contrast to the upheavals of

1956, when the coalition allies—especially the ZSL—tried to loosen somewhat the bonds of dependence, the 1970 changing of the guard evoked no major reaction. The "transmission belts" so laboriously assembled in the years 1945–48 functioned without problems, and only at the lower levels of the CRZZ did the events along the Baltic Coast lead to minor disturbances.

Although economic development would seem to lead to decentralization and an increase in the number of players in both economic and social life, the 1970s actually brought clear signs of a centralization of power. Some of these, such as the amalgamation of the youth movement, were obviously political in nature. In 1973 the various youth organizations were brought under the umbrella of the Federation of Socialist Unions of Polish Youth, which in 1976 was replaced by a single organization, the Union of Socialist Polish Youth, with roughly five million members. Other centralizing measures served to ensure greater control over agriculture and were intended to achieve both political and economic goals. In 1976 three enormous (pseudo) cooperatives were merged to form a single gigantic organization, the Central Association of Agricultural Cooperatives: Peasant Self-Help. In 1973 the state publishing agency, RSW Prasa, was merged with the Książka i Wiedza publishing enterprise and the Ruch distribution network into an enormous corporation (RSW Prasa-Książka-Ruch) that controlled 85 percent of all press circulation (92 percent, in the case of daily papers), one-quarter of all printing capacity, and 34,000 distribution points. With 90,000 employees, it was the largest enterprise in Poland. It gradually acquired additional agencies (two more publishing enterprises in 1974 and the fine arts export enterprise, Ars Polona, in 1977) to become a veritable money-making machine for the PZPR, which owned 90 percent of the "shares" of what was nominally a cooperative.

The most spectacular measure, however, was the reorganization of the local state administration, which was carried out in two stages. In 1973 the position of provincial administrator (*wojewoda*) was introduced, together with equivalent positions at lower levels, making the regions more closely dependent (in formal, legal terms at least) on the center. In 1975 the country's regional administration was restructured; the districts (*powiaty*) were abolished, and the number of provinces was increased from seventeen to forty-nine. This was followed by a similar reorganization of the judiciary and all administrative institutions that did not come under the local government agencies. Many observers concluded that the main purpose of the reform was to reduce the power of the provincial party apparatus and state administration. Whatever the intention, it did severely weaken the local chieftains and thereby increased their dependence on the center. In addition to the chaos that usually accompanies such measures, the reform also resulted in a massive increase in the budget (because of the need to construct "appropriate" office buildings for the new provincial agencies) as well as an increase in the number of nomenklatura positions. The unexpected administrative promotion of several towns was accompanied by the downfall of smaller local centers, many of them with a history stretching far back into the past.

Although the Constitution of 1952, drawn up with invaluable assistance from Stalin, had fulfilled its main functions fairly well, the leadership considered that it failed to meet the requirements of the era of "developed socialism," whose onset was loudly proclaimed in the mass media (and with the help of some obliging university professors). The constitutional changes introduced during the years 1972–75 were essentially a consequence of the reforms in local administration, but the legislative machinery had more ambitious goals in mind: to enshrine in law the de facto monopoly of the PZPR and its general ideology, which remained more or less stable despite occasional about-faces and upheavals. The proposed changes were set out in September 1975 in a resolution of the PZPR Central Committee, bombastically titled "On the Dynamic Development of Socialist Construction, on the Higher Quality of Labor and Living Conditions of the Nation." Three months later the party congress approved the proposals, and the Sejm elected a Constitutional Commission, which immediately, and without any fanfare, set to work.

When the proposals were unveiled to the public, the party leadership seems to have been surprised by the outcry they evoked among many intellectuals and the church. Protest letters came pouring in, and the collection of signatures to such letters became a major element in crystallizing opposition sentiments. Relations with the church became extremely tense. In an official, but unpublicized, memorandum the episcopate protested against the proposal to recognize the "leading role" of the PZPR on the grounds that it would lead, "de facto, to a situation in which the state would become an object of the ideological system" and "the remnants of democracy would be eliminated." The episcopate also objected to the proposal to make a connection between the fulfillment of civil obligations and the enjoyment of civil rights, and criticized the proposal to add to the constitution an article guaranteeing "indissoluble fraternal ties" with the USSR and the socialist states.

This would lead, wrote the bishops, "to restrictions on Poland's sover-eignty."

Intellectuals voiced protests that were similar in tone. The first—and best known—was the "Letter of the 59," dated 5 December and organized by Professor Edward Lipiński, one of Poland's most distinguished econo-mists. The letter demanded guarantees of freedom of conscience and reli-gious worship, freedom in the workplace, meaning "the possibility of free choice of one's own occupational representatives," freedom of speech, and scientific freedom. The letter also demanded that the authorities observe "the right of all citizens to nominate and select their representatives in free and fair elections."

Strong social pressure caused the leadership to withdraw some of the proposed wording that evoked the most opposition. Instead of the party's "leading role in the state," the organization was referred to as "society's leading political force in the construction of socialism"; "alliance" with the Soviet Union was replaced by "friendship and cooperation"; and the uncon-ditional linkage of rights and responsibilities was abandoned. On 10 Febru-ary 1976 the Sejm approved the constitutional amendments. There was no difficulty in ensuring a majority: nobody voted against, and only one Catho-lic deputy, Stanisław Stomma, abstained—an act for which he was punished by being kept off the electoral list at the next election.

Several days later, the PZPR, the ZSL, and the SD decided that the pro-gram resolution passed by the Seventh PZPR Congress (in December of the previous year) would automatically become the "election platform" of the Front of National Unity. "The Party's Program is the Nation's Program," pro-claimed the slogan, the latest in an era renowned for its slogans, an era when more attention was given to propaganda than to the economy. In a sense this was a sign of the leadership's lack of faith in the power of the economic data, whose social impact the leadership hoped to increase by propaganda. The appropriate measures were set in motion in 1971, and the Sixth Party Congress devoted a separate section of its final resolution to "mass information and propaganda media." In April 1972 the party paper, *Trybuna Ludu* (Tribune of the People), acquired a special status, becoming a "leading" newspaper. The Central Committee's propaganda apparatus was reorganized, gradually expanded, and eventually divided into powerful agencies. In 1973, as mentioned above, the RSW Prasa-Książka-Ruch super-enterprise was formed. In addition, the government and the Politburo adopted a joint resolution that subordinated the whole of radio and television programming (including entertainment) to the task of "strengthening society's trust in the party and people's power." At the same time, audiovisual media were given priority over the press in the propaganda effort, and the evening edition of the television news became the "number one medium," under the personal supervision of the appropriate Central Committee secretary (from 1971 on, this was Jerzy Łukaszewicz). Maciej Szczepański emerged as the strong man in the media. In the fall of 1973 he was appointed chairman of the Committee for Radio and Television, replacing Włodzimierz Sokorski, one of the old KPP generation, who had managed to navigate his way around all the reefs to be encountered in postwar Poland. Szczepański, like many others promoted during the 1970s, belonged to the "Silesian group," which was still being touted as the model of modernity.

The leadership expanded the system used to "inspire" and steer the media from its Warsaw headquarters, and the censorship network was increased in size and given additional tasks (including internal supervision to ensure that censors complied with directives). The closed nature of this system is suggested by the composition of the editorial boards created for every party newspaper: they were headed by Central Committee representatives, and their members included not only journalists but employees of the relevant section of the censorship office, the Central Office for Supervision of Press and Performances. On important occasions Central Committee officials "hand steered" both the appearance and the content of the entire press. This was the case, for example, in 1979, during the visit to Poland of John Paul II, when newspaper editors were provided with instructions concerning the length of particular texts and their exact placement in the paper.

The leadership did not skimp on investment and was keen to modernize the mass media with new printing presses, new recording equipment for television, open-air festivals organized by party dailies, tens of thousands of propaganda billboards with resounding slogans (centrally dictated), weekend editions of the daily papers, a proliferation of concerts and other events, and hours of television coverage of colorful ceremonies in one part of the country or another. And always and everywhere the same tone of self-satisfaction that verged on persistent bragging.

This system was popularly and pejoratively termed "the propaganda of success," largely because the propaganda attack was launched against society when nothing much remained of the economic success of 1971–74. The public mood was made worse by the fact that the material aspirations that the new leadership had done so much to arouse now collided with the solid wall of the crisis—worsening shortages of consumer goods, restrictions on the growth of real wages, a decline in farm incomes, and obvious cases of waste. At the same time, the ostentatious consumption of all those individuals associated with the state and party apparatus only increased. A sense of deprivation seems to have spread rapidly across society, accompanied by the perception of a widening gap between a stratum of people who were politically and economically privileged and the rest of the population. Although the standard of living was undoubtedly higher than during the Gomułka era, and the enclaves of modernity far more numerous, the crisis that overtook the country after 1976 to a large extent obliterated any sense of positive change in the broader society.

The incredible clumsiness of the "price adjustment" of June 1976 severely undermined the leadership's authority. The loss of authority could not be reversed by the wave of rallies that party and state bodies staged across the country over the next few weeks to demonstrate support for the leadership and to condemn the "troublemakers of Radom." In fact, these events served to strengthen people's sense of the significance of the spontaneous protests and demonstrations. While the change in leadership after the revolt of December 1970 had been seen as a change that would make a real difference, the departure of Jaroszewicz in 1980 was simply perceived as yet another personnel maneuver and thus had no measurable effect on the mood of the public. The promotion of the relatively unknown Edward Babiuch to the post of prime minister only strengthened the public's impression that the PZPR believed that it held exclusive rights to govern the country.

BETWEEN HELSINKI AND KABUL

Poland's impressive international contacts during the 1970s were to some extent the result of Gierek's own efforts and his policy of opening up to the outside world, but to a greater extent they were part of the Soviet Union's general strategy and the long-term successes of the policy of détente. Poland played a prominent role in this strategy; alongside Romania, whose leader, Nicolae Ceauşescu, continued to play a "semi-neutral" role in international relations, Poland was the most active of all the member states of Comecon and the Warsaw Pact—except, of course, for the USSR, which set the tone and issued directives to the whole bloc. Even what seemed to be such a Polish specialty as good relations with Paris was actually preceded by the Soviet-French agreements signed in 1971.

Major changes took place on the world economic map, consisting, at the most general level, of the exceptionally strong entry into world markets by the two powers defeated in World War II, the Federal Republic of Germany and Japan; but in the political and military sphere the bipolar division remained largely intact. American "ping-pong diplomacy," whose chief practitioner was Henry Kissinger, bore fruit in the form of President Nixon's visit to Beijing in 1972, but the vision of a new "big three" came to nothing. For the Americans, rapprochement with China was first and foremost a form of blackmail directed at the Kremlin, although it was not as effective as it might have been, since Sino-Soviet relations had left behind the stormy years of the late 1960s to enter a phase of undisguised, but nonaggressive, mutual antipathy, and Mao Zedong's infamous *Little Red Book* was now just one of many propaganda pamphlets. China did not possess the economic— and hence military—power that would allow it to catch up with the two superpowers, and potential clients and allies were more interested in tanks and helicopters than in advice, even the even the best advice, on how to make a revolution.

The situation in the Arab states and the Muslim countries of west Asia was probably more important in terms of the overall balance of power. Two events in the early 1970s indicated that this region had emancipated itself from the direct influence of the superpowers. The first was the unexpected decision by Egyptian president, Anwar Sadat, to expel all Soviet advisers in the summer of 1972, and the second was the oil crisis of 1973, when the price of oil more than doubled within a few months, partly as a result of the Arab-Israeli war (the Yom Kippur War of 6–22 October 1973). At the same time, Islamic fundamentalism—a constant presence in the region— underwent a major revival, and only the deep divisions between various branches of Islam and personal rivalries between the region's leaders prevented a genuine "third force" from emerging.

The 1970s turned out to be a decade of genuine gerontocracy, since world events largely proceeded according to the dictates of Moscow, where a number of ailing men in their seventies wielded power—Leonid Brezhnev (born 1906), Aleksei Kosygin (1904), Mikhail Suslov (1902), Andrei Gromyko (1909), and two marshals, Andrei Grechko and Dmitri Ustinov, who were not much younger. The Kremlin's approach to public life remained utterly Byzantine, continuing in every way—apart from the bloody terror—

the practices of Stalin's time. Brezhnev was awarded two Lenin Prizes (for peace in 1972, and for literature in 1979); he promoted himself to marshal (1976), and took over the position of chairman of the Presidium of the Supreme Soviet (1977). Gromyko, known as "Mr. Nyet," had reigned supreme in the international arena (obviously, without stepping ahead of his boss) since at least the beginning of the 1950s, and the prime minister, Kosygin, had been sitting in a government chair without a break since 1939. Suslov, at this time the chief ideologue, had a similar amount of experience, as a Central Committee secretary since 1947 and a member of the Politburo since 1952. Although the policies of these old men contained—in increasing size and number—the seeds of future defeat, the 1970s saw the Soviet Union's greatest successes since 1944–45, when Stalin succeeded in conquering all of East-Central Europe. The greatest failure—on "the Arab front"—was offset by the fact that the Americans could not really consider themselves the victors in that part of the world, despite Kissinger's success in prizing Egypt away from the anti-Israel Arab bloc. Evidence of this was provided by both the civil war in the Lebanon and, especially, the victorious "Islamic Revolution" (1979) in Iran.

The first half of the decade was marked by the United States's political— and to a large extent also military—defeat in Vietnam. In light of the withdrawal of American troops, the cease-fire agreement signed in Paris on 27 January 1973 became just a piece of paper, and two years later the communists from the north seized Saigon and renamed it Ho Chi Minh City. Pro-American governments also collapsed in Laos. The radical Khmer Rouge seized power in Cambodia and proceeded to go much further than even Stalin had dared in pursuit of its own totalitarian utopia—and genocide. The role of the United States in the Vietnam War gave rise to a severe political crisis at home, and, together with the Watergate affair, plainly weakened Washington's position in the international arena. A number of agreements concerning strategic arms reductions (SALT I in 1972, SALT II in 1979), the production of antiballistic missiles (1974), and nuclear weapons testing (1974), sealed at a series of summit meetings between Brezhnev and successive U.S. presidents, essentially served the interests of the Soviet Union more than those of the United States. The former had the advantage— especially in Europe—in terms of conventional weapons, and it had been successful in finding friendly governments among the countries of the Third World.

In terms of medium-range strategy, one of Moscow's successes was the

371

signing of the final act of the Conference on Security and Cooperation in Europe (CSCE), which took place after several years of negotiations—in which Poland played an active role—in Helsinki in the summer of 1975. For the Soviet Union, the most important part of the document was the first part, signed by thirty-five states, including the United States and Canada, which guaranteed the inviolability of European borders and thus formally confirmed all of Stalin's territorial gains. From Poland's point of view, a major positive feature was the recognition of the Oder-Neisse border, but the CSCE also sanctioned the incorporation into the USSR of Bessarabia (Moldova), Trans-Carpathian Ukraine, the former Baltic States, southern Karelia, and the Petsamo district, which cut Finland off from the North Sea. The CSCE also sanctioned the existence of two German states. The fact that the Helsinki Agreement was signed almost exactly thirty years after the end of the Big Three meeting in Potsdam gave it a symbolic dimension and thereby enhanced its significance.

In Moscow, as in Warsaw or Budapest—and undoubtedly in Paris and London also—less attention was paid to what was termed the third basket of the final act, which guaranteed civil rights and personal freedoms to the citizens of the signatory states. The West—in this case, essentially the United States—was only now beginning to think in terms of using this part of the agreement to influence developments on the other side of the Iron Curtain. Leaders in the East held the view that the principle of "nonintervention in the internal affairs" of signatory states would allow them to continue dealing with political opposition and dissident groups as before. Their unwillingness to use more radical methods, and, even more important, their growing dependence on credit from the West led to their becoming embroiled in a series of skirmishes with the growing dissident movements, but nobody then imagined that these movements would grow into a permanent network of opposition groups. The formation in 1971 of the Moscow Committee for Human Rights, whose chief founder was one of the fathers of the Soviet hydrogen bomb, Andrei Sakharov; the multiplication of dissident groups; the birth of *samizdat*, involving the creation of networks to distribute manuscripts that had been typed and retyped—all this activity, conducted with the main aim of defending freedom of religion and national rights, was cause for alarm. The award of the Nobel Prize for Literature to Aleksandr Solzhenitsyn (1970) provided further cause for alarm, as did the award of the Nobel Peace Prize to Sakharov (1975), which was seen by the Soviet leadership as even more provocative; the publication of Solzhenitsyn's *Gulag Archipelago* in several languages (1973) exploded much of what was left of Moscow's already eroded prestige. Alongside the final triumph of Hanoi and the immediate domino effect that this had on the rest of the South-East Asian peninsular, Brezhnev had one more major success to his name. In 1974 Emperor Haile Selassie of Ethiopia was overthrown, and a group of radical army officers seized power and soon asked Moscow for help. Moscow also established a presence in South Yemen and Somalia. Shortly after proclaiming Angola's independence, that country's leftist radicals received assistance in their struggle against their pro-Western opponents in the form of a Cuban army corps of several thousand troops, who arrived in Angola courtesy of the Soviet navy and air force. Cuba, whose trump card was the racial mix of its people, also sent troops to Ethiopia. In 1976 another newly liberated Portuguese colony, Mozambique, found itself in the hands of pro-Soviet leaders. Also in that year the deaths, within several months of each other, of Mao Zedong and Jou Enlai reduced the likelihood of danger from the direction of China, which was now absorbed in domestic issues. In 1978 Afghan communists, although quarreling with each other, overthrew the government of Mohammed Daud. The old Russian plan to reach the "warm seas" seemed to be close to realization, especially as Pakistan had difficulty maintaining control of its provinces that lay to the south of Afghanistan. Procommunist guerrilla groups—openly supported by Fidel Castro—intensified their fighting in Central America and in the summer of 1979 one such group seized power in Nicaragua. The possibility that the case of Nicaragua might prove contagious seemed all the greater given that four ministerial portfolios in the new government were held by Catholic priests, followers of "liberation theology," which took as one of its symbols "Christ with a gun in his hand," the personification of class struggle and concern for the oppressed. In Iran—a neighbor of the USSR and an ally of the United States—growing unrest led in early 1978 to demonstrations and disturbances, which lasted throughout the year until the shah, Mohammad Reza Pahlavi, finally left the country in January 1979, to be replaced by the fanatical leader of the Islamic opposition, Ayatollah Khomeini. The Soviet leadership realized that it faced a potential long-term threat when the capital of militant Islam moved from the distant Libya of Colonel Muammar Qaddafi to a country only a stone's throw from the Central Asian republics inhabited by millions of Soviet Muslims; in the short run it drew comfort from the fact that Washington had become "the Great Satan" for the increasingly powerful fundamentalists.

In Europe, the activities of numerous terrorist groups with close ties to the Palestine Liberation Organization and Libya had a destabilizing effect, and thus served Moscow's interests. Some of these groups were degenerate offshoots of the 1968 student protests (the Red Brigades in Italy, the Baader-Meinhof gang in Germany), while others were nationalist in orientation (the Provisional Irish Republican Army, and fascist gangs in Italy). Several rival Palestinian groups engaged in widespread terrorist activity in Europe, as well as elsewhere. Urban guerrillas (Tupomaros), who normally sowed panic among and evoked bloody reprisals from autocratic governments in Latin America, were also active in Europe.

According to incomplete data, 279 terrorist attacks took place in 1979, and more than 1,700 in 1980. The best-known attacks included the bomb planted by the IRA in a Birmingham pub, killing twenty-one people (1974); the murder of Aldo Moro, one of Italy's most popular politicians (1976); the bomb explosion in the Bologna railroad station that killed eighty-five people (1980); the hijacking of airplanes to Entebbe, Uganda (1976), and Mogadishu, Somalia (1977); the murder of eleven Israeli athletes during the Olympic Games in Munich (1972); and the massacre at the Israeli airport in Lod (1972), carried out by Japanese terrorists with ties to the PLO. The Soviet Union and other countries of the Warsaw Pact provided discrete and usually indirect support for such activity (in the form of training and shelter, for example).

The collapse of authoritarian regimes in Greece and the Iberian Peninsula during 1974–75 gave the socialist bloc some hope of communist success in Western Europe. After some initial gains on the part of the local communist parties, however, center-right or centrist forces gained the upper hand, and the prophecies of Warsaw's jesters, who collected reservations for a "Friendship Train" to Lisbon, went unfulfilled. In 1973 Great Britain finally overcame a long-standing impasse, based largely on the opposition of General de Gaulle, and joined the European Economic Community, together with Denmark, the first Scandinavian country to do so. This provided a considerable impetus to the further integration of Western Europe, but of course it had no immediate economic consequences. NATO, on the other hand, faced a crisis on its "southern flank," when Greece resigned from its military structures in the wake of the conflict with Turkey over Cyprus. The oil crisis of 1973 had a negative impact on the countries of Western Europe, triggering a recession that lasted several years, but the oil price increases imposed by the cartel of oil exporting states weighed most heavily on the impoverished countries of the Third World, which were unable to afford further oil imports. In the industrialized countries, after a brief period of panic the situation stabilized, partly thanks to the ability of the world financial and capital markets to absorb tens of billions of "petro-dollars." Only a tiny percentage went to finance terrorism, and doubtless not much more to aid Palestinian refugees, in whose name most terrorist attacks took place.

The entrance of the postcolonial countries onto the stage of world diplo-macy in the 1960s allowed the Soviet Union to eradicate the advantage hith-erto enjoyed by the United States and its allies in the United Nations. In the following decade, their roles became reversed, and Washington found itself complaining that the UN had become "an anti-American voting machine." Moscow had to take account, however, of a powerful bloc of Arab (and Is-lamic) states that frequently allied itself successfully with some African countries, and it was no easy task to steer a course among 150 or so delega-tions. Nevertheless, the adoption of resolutions expelling South Africa from the United Nations (1974) and condemning Israel (1975) could each be counted a success by Moscow.

The position of the Soviet Union—and that of the whole socialist camp—was somewhat strengthened during the 1970s, but the enormous defense effort and the costs of expansion to virtually every continent were accompa-nied by growing economic problems. The arms race, which continued de-spite several international treaties and agreements, was particularly burdensome for the inefficient economy. It was becoming increasingly costly both in absolute terms and in the sense that the Soviet economy was faced with a widening gap between the defense sector and the rest of indus-try, which was finding it increasingly difficult to produce out-of-date goods for the consumer market. Agricultural productivity remained low, and it was becoming increasingly necessary to import grain, which the country could only do with the aid of loans from its greatest enemy. With the United States's deployment in the second half of the 1970s of a new generation of tactical and operational weapons (including the cruise missile) based to a large extent on sophisticated electronics, which the Soviet Union could match only thanks to espionage, the situation became increasingly compli-cated.

Any possible expressions of concern about the future were drowned out, not only by the mighty propaganda machine but also by the success enjoyed hitherto. The crowning achievement of the 1970s was, therefore, the attack on Kabul carried out by the 4th and 105th Paratroop Divisions on 24 December 1979. In all likelihood, nobody in the Kremlin foresaw that the Soviet Union was embarking on its own Vietnam—a guerrilla war whose material and political costs would grow year by year. This time the fighting would take place not in the Mekong Delta and subtropical jungle, but in the mountains of the Hindu Kush.

THE NEW OPPOSITION

When the revolt on the Baltic Coast was bloodily suppressed and a new group took over the leadership of Poland, dissident groups were probably at their weakest in a long time. The Commandos, ex-revisionists, and liberal intellectuals were still recovering from the shock of the March events, some of them had emigrated, and some were in prison. Ruch had been paralyzed by the arrest of seventy-five people associated with the group. Catholic activists from Znak and Więź, the most active groups at this time, were faced with deepening divisions within their ranks. The new situation exacerbated these tendencies, and Janusz Zabłocki approached the authorities with a proposal to start his own Catholic weekly. Many people who were decidedly anticommunist deluded themselves that the change in leadership, and the circumstances in which it had taken place, would help to bring about liberalization. For example, a group of activists from the Labor Party of 1945–46 (including Władysław Siła-Nowicki, Józef Kwasiborski, and Stefan Kaczorowski) produced a memorandum proposing the revival of the party, which had suspended political activity as far back as the summer of 1946.

Hopes for change were fairly widespread, although neither Gierek nor anyone else in the top leadership of the PZPR had actually promised anything concrete. The Ruch affair became a litmus test of the leadership's attitude toward opposition groups. The group's leaders went on trial in October and received some of the longest sentences to be handed down since 1955 (Andrzej Czuma and Stefan Niesiołowski were both sentenced to seven years). The Ruch trial provided intellectual groups with an incentive to undertake joint activities, which took the now traditional form of letters signed by well-known public figures. A year later, when a petition was organized urging the Council of State to commute the death penalty imposed on Jerzy Kowalczyk (together with his brother he had blown up the Opole assembly hall, where the police and security service were to celebrate the anniversary of their founding), several thousand signatures were collected, suggesting that the possibilities for mobilizing public opinion were similar to those that had existed in February-March 1968.

For the next several years opposition activity did not transcend the forms that it had taken to date—private social gatherings, discussions, and polemics. None of these tiny conspiratorial groups—whose members were almost always young people or even adolescents—turned into an organization on the scale of Ruch. The general public knew little or nothing about them, and only the security service and the top party leadership realized the extent of various forms of dissent and opposition. In comparison with the Gomułka era, however, some major changes were taking place. Opposition groups established ongoing contacts with émigré organizations, especially with Jerzy Giedroyc's monthly, *Kultura,* and the quarterly journal, *Aneks,* founded in early 1973 by a group of Commandos who had emigrated from Poland. These publications provided a forum for discussion about the possibilities for different kinds of opposition activity. Another qualitative change, which was partly the result of an easing of restrictions on travel abroad, was the increased influx of émigré publications into Poland.

The beginnings of this public debate can be traced back to Leszek Kołakowski's article, "Tezy o nadziej i beznadziejności" (Theses on Hope and Hopelessness, June 1971). Major contributions included Jan Drewnowski, "Jedyna droga" (The Only Way, March 1972); Leszek Kołakowski, "Sprawa polska" (The Polish Question, April 1973); Jacek Kuroń, "Opozycja polityczna w kraju" (Political Opposition at Home, November 1974); Zdzisław Najder, "O potrzebie programu" (The Need for a Program, May 1975); and Antoni Macierewicz, "Refleksje o opozycji" (Reflections on Opposition, summer 1976). We should also include in this debate Jakub Karpiński's book, *Ewolucja czy rewolucja* (Evolution or Revolution) published in 1975 by Giedroyc, who had already published in 1971 *Drogi wyjścia* (The Way Out), by Władysław Bieńkowski. Juliusz Mieroszewski, a regular contributor to *Kultura* also joined the debate, as did historian Adam Bromke, who argued the need to support the "unorthodox communism" of the post-Gomułka era. Although this discussion proceeded fairly slowly, it served to crystallize opinions among contributors and readers, and it allowed participants to decide what forms of activity were possible. Despite some substantial differences of opinion, there was growing agreement that efforts to bring about change ought to focus on exerting constant and widespread social pressure on the authorities.

Another development was the increasingly close cooperation between left-liberal intellectuals and the groups associated with *Więź* and *Tygodnik Powszechny*. One outward sign of this was Antoni Słonimski's regular column in the latter publication. A major source of intellectual inspiration was Bohdan Cywiński's *Rodowody niepokornych* (Genealogy of the Defiant Ones), which rehabilitated in the eyes of the Catholic intelligentsia the left-wing social activists of the turn of the century, a tradition that was much valued by the majority of ex-revisionists. A similar role was played by *Próby świadectwa* (Attempts to Bear Witness) by Jan Strzelecki, a onetime advocate of "socialist humanism" and still a member of the PZPR. Both groups moved closer to each other without arousing any serious reservations on the part of the church. One reason for this was that Cardinal Karol Wojtyła, metropolitan bishop of Kraków, maintained close ties to the people at *Tygodnik Powszechny*. Contacts between the two groups also had a purely personal element: several of the Commandos excluded from the state universities were studying at the Catholic University in Lublin, and the Club of Catholic Intelligentsia in Warsaw provided a forum for many meetings and discussions. Other groups were also formed, including one led by Leszek Moczulski, whose book, *Wojna polska* (The Polish War), published in 1972, was subsequently withdrawn from bookstores and libraries. Several PAX organizations also experienced a certain amount of political ferment, although on a much smaller scale than during 1955–56. Home Army and other war veterans made bolder efforts to commemorate their dead comrades in arms and Polish military tradition, but they stayed away from political territory. Some student groups drew up a document setting out the reasons for their opposition to the unification of the youth organizations and, especially, the attempt to turn the Polish Student Association into a political organization. Church bodies that ministered to students played a major role, together with the Oasis Catholic youth movement, in getting young people interested in social activity and helping them develop a sense of independence. Despite the extremely tight controls on information, several dissident groups did establish links with each other, usually on the basis of friendship ties. Such contacts were facilitated by the fact that the whole dissident grouping was small and almost totally concentrated in a few of the larger towns—in Warsaw, Kraków, and Łódź—and in the Catholic University in Lublin. Although the number of people belonging to such groups did grow, they did not manage to take the step taken by Soviet dissidents, people who were in far greater danger and had far more at risk.

For the time being, however, there was nothing to light the fuse. The campaign of protest against the amendments to the constitution played a major role, but once they had been passed the situation returned to its former state, except for the awareness that the scale of the campaign had been greater than anticipated. This trend continued with the publication of an open letter by Edward Lipiński, warning the leadership of the dangerous consequences of current economic policy, and with the protests against the persecution of some students for "statements hostile to the state." There was some discussion about creating a human rights committee, as Soviet dissidents had done. At this point, the London-based weekly, *Tydodnik Polski*, caused a stir by publishing (in May 1976) the program of the Polish Independence Compact (PPN), a highly secret group founded by Zdzisław Najder. The PPN document, which was copied and distributed in typescript form, presented the opposition with far-reaching tasks, including the struggle for independence, and it emphasized the need to reach an understanding with the nations living to the east of Poland. The group was, however, extremely small, and saw its role as that of shaping public opinion rather than organizing society.

The scale of events changed after the unsuccessful price increases of June 1976, or more precisely, after the repression directed against the workers of Radom and Ursus. Although the strikes of 25 June were not as drastic in form as those of 1970 and the police did not resort to firearms, the subsequent crackdown was on a similar scale to the repression that followed the earlier strikes. In many towns—including Gdańsk, Grudziądz, Łódź, Warsaw, Starachowice, Nowy Targ, and Płock—several thousand factory workers were sacked or suffered a marked reduction in wages. Some 2,500 were detained, more than 350 were sentenced, in summary proceedings, to jail and steep fines, while legal proceedings were opened in about 500 additional cases. The police and security service were particularly brutal in Radom, where they created an atmosphere of fear, engaging in extralegal activities with total impunity and with the connivance of the local courts.

By mid-July a number of "open letters" and appeals were in circulation. On 17 July, in the corridors of the Warsaw courts where workers from Ursus were on trial, a group of people involved in opposition activity made contact with the families of those who had been sentenced. They began collecting money to assist the families of workers who were under arrest, and lawyers began providing free legal advice. The sentences were extremely severe— four to ten years. After some hesitation, a group of fourteen people issued, on 23 September 1976, a document titled "An Appeal to Society and the Authorities of the Polish People's Republic." Most of the signatories were members of the older generation, people with considerable moral authority but not well known among the broad population. They included Antoni Pajdak (sentenced to prison shortly after the trial of the sixteen in 1945), Ludwik Cohn (sentenced during the PPS-WRN trial in 1948), Józef Rybicki (commander of the AK Warsaw District Kedyw, a member of the WiN command, imprisoned during the Stalinist era), and Father Jan Zieja (head chaplain to the wartime clandestine scouting movement). Edward Lipiński was better known, as was Aniela Steinsbergowa, a lawyer who had played a prominent role in a series of trials in 1956–57 to rehabilitate the victims of the Stalinist years. The best-known member of the group was, without a doubt, Jerzy Andrzejewski, considered one of the best Polish writers of the postwar period. The fourteen signatories also included some much younger people, who took the lead in formulating the appeal and in organizing aid for the Ursus workers: Jan Józef Lipski, Piotr Naimski, Antoni Macierewicz, and Jacek Kuroń. It was they who took the initiative in forming the Workers' Defense Committee (KOR), and the name was then adopted by all signatories to the appeal. On 28 September the group issued the first *KOR Communiqué*, thereby inaugurating what would become an uninterrupted stream of uncensored, unofficial publishing in Poland.

Although KOR set itself the limited goals of defending workers persecuted after 25 June 1976 and publicizing cases in which the authorities had violated the law, the very nature of the political system meant that it became a political organization, and it was treated as such by the authorities. On 22 October 1976 Stanisław Kania, the Central Committee secretary responsible for the internal affairs ministry and the judiciary, held a meeting at which security officials demanded decisive action against the members of KOR. The party leadership, however, considered extreme measures to be inadvisable, a position that it continued to uphold, with only rare exceptions. An internal party document issued two years later under the title "Counteracting Antisocialist Elements" stated that the basic task was to ensure "the political isolation of antisocialist groups" and that "important tasks in the struggle with the political enemy fall to the Ministry of Internal Affairs and the public prosecutor's office." The authors went on to note: "To date we have not resorted to . . . methods based on imprisonment and trials. This is evidence of our strength, not a sign of weakness. It is possible that we shall also have to resort to these most severe measures in the future. Now, however, we are correctly pursuing the line of harassing our opponent and we must continue to implement it consistently."

The PZPR leadership did, in fact, find itself in an awkward situation. For a number of reasons related to international prestige and the economic situation, it was concerned to maintain Poland's image as a country that was not only undergoing "dynamic development" but was also governed democratically. Brezhnev, too, displayed a certain amount of elasticity in dealing with dissidents: at the beginning of 1974 Solzhenitsyn was expelled from the Soviet Union, and in December 1976 Vladimir Bukovsky was exchanged for Chilean communist Luis Corvalan. The leadership's feeling of self-confidence and its view that the opposition was weak—an essentially correct assessment—also played a role. The existence of the opposition was a kind of luxury that it could allow itself. The leadership continued, then, "harassing" its opponents and it did so consistently. The few attempts to tighten the screws—as in May 1977, after the death in unexplained circumstances of KOR activist Stanisław Pyjas in Kraków—simply strengthened rather than weakened the determination of the opposition and produced an immediate reaction on the part of world public opinion.

Harassment consisted largely of short-term detention, apartment searches, confiscation of property, dismissal from work, denial of a passport, and fines. Beatings (by "unknown perpetrators") were, however, common, and there were numerous incidents of damage to automobiles, and situations in which gangs forced their way into apartments where meetings or lectures were in progress. Security forces also engaged in various kinds of "operational maneuvers" designed to sow dissension between different opposition groups and cause rifts within individual groups. The authorities also conducted a propaganda campaign that varied in intensity and was aimed at discrediting particular individuals or groups through defamation or ridicule. They also frequently accused the opposition of acting "in the service of non-Polish interests," but stopped short of accusations of espionage.

All this had little effect, however, and the opposition gradually increased in size and expanded into new areas of activity. The institutional church did not disown the opposition, and some priests were directly involved in dissident activity (including—in addition to Jan Zieja—Ludwik Wiśniewski, Czesław Sadłowski, Stanisław Małkowski, and Bronisław Dembowski), something that would have been impossible without at least the tacit consent of the bishops. From the fall of 1976 on the opposition was a permanent feature of the political landscape, although it had little direct impact on the life of the average citizen. There were relatively few occasions when it was possible to mobilize a large number of people: in May 1977, following the death of Pyjas, several thousand students demonstrated in Kraków; in 1978 and 1979 crowds numbering a few thousand gathered outside the Gdańsk Shipyard to commemorate the December anniversary; and several hundred people regularly gathered in Warsaw to commemorate 11 November and 3 May. Nevertheless, some activities designed to pressure the authorities had the desired effect. This was true of KOR and its main goal: by 1977 all those sentenced to prison for their role in the disturbances in Radom had been released from prison.

The creation of KOR, which—in contrast to the PPN—published the names of its members, opened up a new phase of opposition activity. It was also new inasmuch as other groups soon followed KOR's example, adopting a tactic of openness. This tactic was more typical of groups involved in civil disobedience than in clandestine political work, but much activity—particularly printing and anything to do with finances—was, of course, conducted in secret.

On 25 March 1977 several people, including Andrzej Czuma and Leszek Moczulski, signed an appeal "To Polish Society" and established the Movement in Defense of Human and Civil Rights (ROPCiO). This new group saw itself as a competitor to KOR, but the real reason for the formation of ROPCiO was not so much personal differences (although there were plenty of those) as differences in ideology and in the perception of immediate options and longer-term goals. In a sense, KOR developed naturally out of the concerns of left-liberal groups and Catholics drawn to personalism; ROPCiO, on the other hand, drew on the tradition of the Piłsudski-ite independence movement, combined with elements of Christian democracy and nationalism. A deep split developed within the group in 1978, between those (like Czuma) who stressed the nationalist elements and those (like Moczulski) who emphasized the Piłsudski tradition. In Gdańsk a group of young people, under the leadership of Aleksander Hall, broke from ROPCiO to form the Young Poland Movement (RMP), and Moczulski then left to create the Confederation for an Independent Poland (KPN), formally established on 1 September 1979. This was the first organization to refer to itself as a political party.

During 1977–79 these broad groups gave rise to numerous narrower initiatives directed at specific social groups: the Student Solidarity Committee (SKS), formed in Kraków following the murder of Stanisław Pyjas; the Association of Academic Courses (TKN), established in January 1978 and whose name and activities drew on the traditions of the left-wing "defiant ones" of the turn of the century; the Interim Peasant Self-Defense Committee for the Lublin Area (associated with ROPCiO), also established in 1978; and the similar Committee for the Grójec Area (associated with KOR). From the political—and strategic—point of view, the most important initiatives were those that aimed to reach the workers. In September 1977 KOR made a start by publishing the bi-weekly *Robotnik* (The Worker), whose title evoked both the socialist tradition and the figure of Piłsudski. In March 1978 Kazimierz Świtoń from Katowice attempted, with only partial success, to set up the Free Trade Unions (associated with ROPCiO), and several weeks later a similar organization (but associated with KOR) was established in Gdańsk. The Gdańsk Free Trade Unions, supported by KOR and a group from the Young Poland Movement, not only organized successful demonstrations on the anniversary of the 1970 strikes, but also published *Robotnik Wybrzeża* (The Coastal Worker). The Gdańsk initiative was the more successful of the two, partly because people retained fresh memories of the blood shed eight years earlier, and partly because a strong group of intelligentsia joined forces with them. The leaders of the Gdańsk Free Trade Unions included KOR member Bogdan Borusewicz, Joanna and Andrzej Gwiazda, and Anna Walentynowicz. A thirty-five-year-old electrician, Lech Wałęsa, soon began to make a name for himself as someone who was willing to be active and could be counted on not to give up easily.

Although the Gdańsk trade union only functioned in the Tri-City area, the authorities soon realized that this form of opposition activity could spread like wildfire. Gierek's ruling group considered "the protection of industrial plants ... from infiltration by the enemy to be a task of major importance." At the beginning of 1979, the SB set up a new unit, Department Three A, whose function was "to protect the national economy"—but not from spies. One of the most important forms of opposition activity was the underground publishing movement, which not only fulfilled organizational and information functions, but also provided a forum for the crystallization of programs and for political debate. Equally important were publications that undermined the legitimacy of the system by stripping away the official lies surrounding the country's traditions and filling in gaps in historical consciousness, and by relentlessly criticizing the state of the economy and the principles on which it was managed. KOR's series of communiqués and its *Biuletyn Informacyjny,* as well as the anonymously published journal *U progu* (On the Threshold), were followed by a wave of journals that were published more or less regularly: the literary journal *Zapis* (Record, first published in January 1977); two periodicals published by ROPCiO, *Opinia* and *Droga* (The Road); *Gazeta Polska,* published by the KPN; *Puls,* a periodical featuring the work of a younger generation of writers; two journals focusing on theoretical, historical, and political issues—*Głos* (The Voice) and *Krytyka*—published by two different tendencies within KOR, personified, respectively, by Macierewicz and Michnik; the journal *Spotkania* (Encounters), published in Lublin; and *Res Publica,* published by a group of young Warsaw intellectuals. All told, several dozen different periodicals were published.

Underground publishers became a major element in opposition activity—especially in the "battle over consciousness." The first organization to print books and pamphlets (as well as periodicals) regularly, and the organization that proved to be the most effective, was the Independent Publishing House (NOWa), which published nearly a hundred titles over the course of several years. Other publishing groups, which did not survive as long or published fewer titles, included the Third of May Constitution Publishers, the Kraków Student Printing Press, the Głos Library, and the Spotkania Library. Reprints of émigré books, especially books dealing with history, were a major feature of underground publishing, but many original works also appeared, including Tadeusz Konwicki's *Polish Complex* (1977) and *A Minor Apocalypse,* Julian Stryjkowski's *Wielki strach* (The Big Fear, 1980), and Jerzy Andrzejewski's *Miazga* (Pulp, 1979). Works by foreign authors also appeared for the first time in Polish translation, including *The Tin Drum,* by Günter Grass (1979), and Bohumil Hrabal's *Too Loud a Solitude* (1978). Polish readers were also introduced to émigré editions of the poetry of Czesław Miłosz, the five volumes of Witold Gombrowicz's *Diaries, Inni świat* (Another World), by Gustaw Herling-Grudziński, and George Orwell's famous antitotalitarian works, *1984* and *Animal Farm.* Underground publishing also produced, of course, political books and pamphlets. The best-known of these were Adam Michnik's *The Church and the Left* (1977), which was to some an extent a response to Bohdan Cywiński's *Rodowody niepokornych,* and Leszek Moczulski's *Rewolucja bez rewolucji* (Revolution Without a Revolution, 1979).

From the moment the first issue of *Zapis* appeared, a small—but growing—number of writers deserted official, state publishers in favor of independent journals and publishing groups. This was a natural development, given that many writers and poets of different generations had long been involved in various forms of dissident activity. Data compiled by the security service give some idea of the scale of underground publishing: during 1976–79 security officials confiscated an estimated 440,000 copies of flyers, periodicals, books, and pamphlets; 121 duplicating machines; 106 typewriters; 1,770 reams of paper; and 113 kilograms of ink.

It is difficult to judge the precise scope of opposition activity. The number of those who were actively involved or closely associated varied from several hundred—in 1976—to several thousand. Some publications were distributed in editions of two thousand or so, and some demonstrations drew four to five thousand participants. The Polish Section of Radio Free Europe, whose audience always grew at times of increased social tension or during major events, played a crucial role in informing the public about the existence of opposition groups and their activities. Official propaganda directed against opposition groups also gave them involuntary publicity. The formation of the opposition provided the impetus for several journalists belonging to the PZPR to try to revive reformist tendencies in the party. The well-known journalist, Stefan Bratkowski, established a group with the name Experience and the Future (DiP), whose members also included people associated with the opposition.

At the level of society as a whole, however, the influence of the opposition was confined to a few enclaves: it was relatively strong among students and intellectuals (and, more broadly, among the intelligentsia), in several industrial areas (especially Gdańsk and Gdynia), and in a number of widely scattered rural communities. The Gierek ruling group was essentially correct in its view that the opposition was not in a position to provoke protest on a mass scale. Some groups, particularly KOR, actually feared such events on the grounds that mass demonstrations would provide the authorities with a pretext to stifle the still fragile structures of the underground. Nevertheless, considerable organizational potential in terms of contacts, printing facilities, and practical experience of illegal activity was created after 1976, and the barriers erected by fear were much lower than they had been in the past. The opposition also offered a foretaste of a pluralistic political arena. At the same time, the public was becoming increasingly ill disposed toward the authorities, and would become more hostile as the economic situation worsened. An opposition that was differentiated and quarrelsome, but organized and growing, combined with increasing discontent on the part of a large proportion of the population and a considerable decline in the authority of the ruling group—this posed a real threat.

The "softening" of the émigré community that had begun in 1956 continued during later years, albeit at a varying pace and with varying results. Although the decided majority of combat émigrés maintained their distance from the activities of the Polonia Association, boycotting the events and performances that it organized, the institution—closely supervised by the foreign and internal affairs ministries—acquired many contacts among the older generation of prewar émigrés, people who had left Poland for economic reasons. These contacts multiplied during the 1970s, when numerous events in Poland—folklore festivals, sports contests, and children's camps—attracted participants not only from Western Europe but also from Canada and the United States.

Many people with roots in the prewar wave of emigration broke with the boycott and visited Poland. Even ZBoWiD, an organization totally subordinated to the PZPR, tried to establish relations with émigré combat veterans. The émigré community continued to be divided in terms of attitudes toward events in Poland, but these differences were less pronounced than during 1956–57. They did, however, provide the basis for a split in the PPS (into groups led by Adam Ciołkosz and Zygmunt Zaremba), and the security apparatus continued to meddle where it could (provoking yet another, third, split in the PSL).

Such conflicts were accompanied by constant efforts to overcome the divisions, which were a source of embarrassment, perpetuating the negative image of the émigré community, and providing an easy target for the intense propaganda directed against the London Poles by the Polish authorities. Biological processes helped to diminish the controversies. During the 1960s many of the protagonists of various political conflicts died, among them Jan Kwapiński (1964), Stanisław Mikołajczyk and Tadeusz Bór-Komorowski (1966), Marian Seyda and Zygmunt Zaremba (1967), and Kazimierz Sosnkowski (1969). In 1970, in light of the advanced age of President August Zaleski, contacts between the Castle and the opposition National Unity Executive increased until—thanks to mediation on the part of the president of the Polish-American Congress, Alojzy Mazewski—a compromise was achieved. Following Zaleski's death (7 April 1972), his deputy,

Stanisław Ostrowski, undertook to uphold the agreement, and all opposition institutions were dissolved (the Council of National Unity, the Council of Three, the Executive). In 1979, after completing a seven-year term, Ostrowski stepped down to be replaced by Edward Raczyński. "The Ark of independence," as the London government was called during the immediate postwar years, regained its symbolic significance, but this could no longer change the political position of the London Poles. The remnants of the government-in-exile had no influence whatsoever in the international arena, and their authority among the émigrés—both the combat veterans and the older generation—was insufficient to imbue the leadership and institutions of the Second Republic with any real significance.

The combat émigrés, who were the dominant group in Britain, remained influential in France, and were plainly joining forces with the older Polish-American community in the United States, did not lose momentum in the nonpolitical arena. A number of research institutes (including the New-York based Piłsudski Institute, the Institute of Arts and Sciences in America, and the Sikorski Institute in London) continued to function and even expanded their activity. Periodicals and newspapers were still published; in 1971 the Polish Socio-Cultural Center was established in London. The Congress of Poles in the Free World, held in Washington in November 1975, mounted an effective counteroffensive against the increasingly insistent attacks on the part of intellectuals and intelligentsia associated with the Polonia Association in Warsaw. Measures making it easier for people to leave the country provided new recruits to the émigré community, although it was somewhat slow to embrace those who had now decided to leave. This was largely because most of the new migrants had left for economic reasons, and they looked to the émigré community for material assistance rather than spiritual sustenance. Nevertheless, they became readers of émigré periodicals and books, and thus partly compensated for the dying off of the older generation and the loss of Polish identity among their offspring.

In the 1960s institutions of a nontraditional kind came to predominate in émigré political and cultural activity. Radio Free Europe, despite the renewed jamming of its broadcasts, had a considerable audience in Poland, and the Paris-based *Kultura* expanded its reach, despite the unceasing efforts of the Polish authorities. Both these organizations were profoundly affected by the events of March 1968, or rather by their repercussions: a group of people who had essentially been made to feel most unwelcome in Poland began to collaborate with Nowak and Giedroyc. The appearance of these people in the West also made it easier to establish contacts with dissident groups at home. Giedroyc and his publishing house, Institut Literacki, played an especially crucial role, even seeking to organize some early opposition activities (the so-called affair of the "mountain climbers," a group of people who collected materials for *Kultura* and smuggled the journal into Poland). The post-March émigrés also had their own political ambitions, expressed in the various articles by Leszek Kołakowski that appeared in *Kultura* and in the journal *Aneks,* published by Aleksander Smolar. Thanks to their good contacts with the generation of 1968, both *Kultura* and Radio Free Europe began to expand their role beyond that of simply providing information.

This became evident in 1976, when an organized and open opposition emerged in Poland. The opposition was also helped by the combat émigrés, who in March 1978 set up the Fund for the Defense of Free Speech and Human Rights in Poland. Now it was not only *Kultura* and RFE but also the institutions symbolizing the independent Republic that had meaningful contacts with the homeland. This was the surest way to enhance their authority. The émigré community's state of mind improved considerably with the election of a Polish pope, an event that enhanced Poland's prestige in the eyes of the outside world, as well as the prestige of those who had migrated from Cardinal Wojtyła's motherland. The strikes during the summer of 1980, and particularly the emergence of Solidarity, had a similar effect. All of this together aroused a widespread sympathetic interest in Poland that was felt also by émigrés and led them to rethink their attitude: virtually all émigré groups now wanted to have an impact on developments in the country. This state of affairs intensified—and not just at the emotional level—after the imposition of martial law, which resulted in, among other things, increased migration from Poland. The Iron Curtain installed by the Red Army in 1945 not only divided Europe into East and West. It also divided the Poles. Drawn tightly shut during 1949–56, it subsequently developed an increasing number of holes, until, under pressure from both sides, it turned into a veritable sieve.

"HABEMAS PAPAM!"

The church welcomed the changes of 1970 with cautious optimism. Meeting on 29 December, the Chief Council of the Episcopate discussed a ten-point list of demands, but decided to postpone any initiative until after the next meeting of the Central Committee, on the grounds that the Seventh Plenum

(20 December) had dealt only with changes in the leadership without defining future economic policy. And thus it was that Cardinal Wyszyński met, on 3 March 1971, with Prime Minister Piotr Jaroszewicz and presented him with a number of proposals. The most important of these concerned the church's demand for formal legal status and for guarantees of its right to operate freely, including the right to develop lay organizations without outside interference, as well as demands for restrictions on the activities of the Office of Religious Affairs, for church access to the media, and for an end to the ban on construction of new churches. In a communiqué issued several months later, the church declared that it had no wish "to create a political opposition or to mobilize social forces to struggle against the constitutionally established system" and that it would not "question or undermine the alliances entered into by the government."

This amounted to a proposal for a kind of Truce of God, but while the PZPR leadership had no wish to worsen relations with the church, it had no intention of offering any concessions relating to its legal status, access to radio and television, or religious education in schools. Building permits for new churches were more readily granted, most of the public harassment—in any case, less frequent since 1967—came to an end, and the position of the church in the provinces formerly belonging to Germany underwent a marked improvement. A law passed in June 1971 regularized property rights in the region, and a year later, after both sides had ratified the Gomułka-Brandt treaty, Pope Paul VI published a papal bull titled "Episcoparum Poloniae coetus," establishing seven dioceses in western and northern Poland. In the spring of 1971 representatives of the Polish leadership and the Vatican began talks that culminated in a visit to Rome by the minister of foreign affairs, Stefan Olszowski, (in November 1973) and the establishment of "permanent working contacts" between the two sides. In this diplomatic maneuvering, the Polish authorities continued efforts, first begun in 1946–47, to establish relations with the Vatican without the mediation of the Polish hierarchy; yet again they were doomed to failure.

Official policy toward Catholic organizations also showed that the line adopted during the days of the PPR had not been affected by any "renewal." In June 1976 Bolesław Piasecki was elected a member of the Council of State, signifying that the new ruling group considered PAX a privileged partner. The authorities continued to interfere in the activities of other associations, especially the most troublesome group, Znak, and the associated Clubs of Catholic Intelligentsia, which now had 1,700 members. The administration supported Zabłocki's group in its demands for a share of Znak's resources, and in the 1976 elections the Znak members who were approved for the electoral list were people who favored cooperating with the authorities in a similar manner to PAX. The Christian Social Union, which fulfilled the role of a PAX "double," continued to receive official support. The church stood no chance of regaining control over its former charitable organization, Caritas, which had proved to be a convenient tool with which to organize members of the clergy willing to follow the directives of the Office for Religious Affairs. No measures were taken to relax security service monitoring of the clergy's activities. Quite the opposite: the Fourth Department was expanded and in 1973 employed a staff of around nine hundred in its central and regional offices; it also added to its network of agents. Petty harassment also continued, and the construction of new churches still encountered numerous obstacles. Although there were no serious public disputes, church-state relations could be considered, at best, correct. In fact, apart from clear concessions concerning the position of the church in the western provinces, none of the episcopate's other demands was implemented, and the authorities' centralizing measures were creating—in the view of the primate—new threats. The episcopate did not hesitate to express its concern. In September 1973 it issued a document dealing with the educational reform then under discussion, pointing out that, "any genuinely humanistic educational system must be based on the truth about human dignity." The bishops also cited the encyclical of Pope John XXIII, *Pacem in terris,* concerning the close relationship between international peace and respect for human rights.

Cardinal Wyszyński sounded a particularly strong note in a sermon on the subject of secular power, delivered in Warsaw's cathedral on 27 January 1974. He pointed out that the divine origin of power did not mean that power was limitless, but just the reverse: it was subordinate to both "the creator of power" and "the natural order." He also emphasized—having in mind the recent unification of youth organizations—the inalienable right to "freedom of coalition, in other words, freedom of association in the pursuit of one's goals," and he referred specifically to the right to "freedom of the press, public opinion, publishing, discussion, and scientific inquiry and research." The overall thrust of these remarks was echoed in the position of the episcopate and the primate on the changes to the constitution, and it was the voice of the church that seems to have had the greatest influence on the amendments to the original proposals.

In 1976, a difficult year for the party, the church avoided arousing the faithful in any way, but came to the defense of those who had been beaten, thrown out of work, and sentenced. In a letter written in July, the episcopate called for an amnesty for those in prison, and a communiqué issued by the Conference of Bishops (8–9 September) calling on people to "work efficiently," also pointed out that a precondition for this was "trust in the authorities." This was followed by a document published in November that raised the issue of the relationship between resolving the country's economic problems and "broadening and guaranteeing civil freedoms." It was clear, however, that the primate had no intention of exploiting the failings of the state and party leadership and its painful loss of authority. The church hierarchy remained silent on the subject of the organized opposition; and not until June 1978—in an exchange of letters with the Office for Religious Affairs—did Cardinal Wyszyński come out in defense of the TKN and the "flying university," whose lectures were being attacked by gangs of youths.

Nevertheless, as we have already noted, neither the episcopate nor the primate took any steps—in public, at least—to restrain those priests who supported the opposition or were themselves involved in its activity. During the whole postwar period, churches never really ceased to be places where the broader public could express its dislike for, or hostility toward, communism, or at least listen to sermons critical of the system, and they now provided an asylum for many opposition groups. Churches provided the site for the three collective hunger strikes organized by KOR, and many demonstrations to commemorate a particular anniversary began with a mass. An important role was also played by the annual Weeks of Christian Culture, inaugurated in the mid-1970s, which dealt with issues of national culture by no means confined to religious artists or religious themes. Churches became a major forum for opposition artists or those who had fallen out of official favor. The faithful were no longer surprised to hear the verses of Słonimski or Miłosz recited in church. Cardinal Wyszyński sanctioned such events himself when he introduced (May 1977) an evening devoted to the poetry of Mieczysław Jastrun and Wiktor Woroszylski, one of the organizers of the underground publication *Zapis* and a zealous proponent of the "new literature" during the 1950s. "The word must not be allowed to die," declared the cardinal.

Relations with the church assumed increasing importance for the Gierek leadership as economic problems worsened. Nevertheless, extremely strong barriers of both an ideological and political kind caused official policy toward the episcopate to be characterized by about-faces and duplicity. The communists, too, had their *non possumus:* fulfilling the demands of the church and the recommendations set out in bishops' homilies or official documents would have required a fundamental change in the entire system. Thus, while trying to maintain appearances, taking care to treat the primate with reverence, and occasionally even praising the pope, the party leadership did not actually budge an inch: it took no steps toward granting the church legal status; the return of religious instruction in schools was out of the question; atheistic propaganda continued; publishing was strictly controlled and circulation restricted; and building permits were issued grudgingly and sparingly.

The Office for Religious Affairs and its regional outposts, together with the Ministry of Internal Affairs, infiltrated the clergy and congregation, and the functions of the Fourth Department included analysis of sermons delivered by the bishops and monthly reports of any statements "containing negative sociopolitical overtones." The authorities' anxiety was heightened by the sympathy for opposition activity displayed by many priests, but their main aim was not to annoy the church. "Although there are numerous grounds for a critical assessment of the activities of individual bishops and the contents of the episcopate's official pronouncements," wrote the author of a confidential document, "it is necessary to implement with complete consistency the line of cementing the political unity of the nation. This requires both determination and patience." This "cementing" was even given formal endorsement at a high level. For example, in January 1978 the Front of National Unity added to its declaration the statement that "socialist Poland . . . respects and values the church's concern for the affairs of the nation."

This statement, like the majority of such statements, was nothing more than a rhetorical flourish that had no practical effect, and it was formulated in the wake of what the authorities considered the crowning achievement of party policy to date: on 1 December 1977 Pope Paul VI granted Gierek an audience, and Cardinal Wyszyński, then visiting (not by coincidence) the Vatican, attended the official reception at the Polish embassy. Although the Polish church viewed the meeting between the first secretary and the pope as a positive development, it yielded no new initiatives or concessions on the part of the authorities. Since neither side wished to take more radical action—the primate, to call for disobedience, Gierek, to order arrests—the result was a stalemate that continued despite the existence in the power apparatus, especially the internal ministry, of people who favored abandoning this soft line. Both sides actually found it rather convenient.

The church was increasingly seen as the only strong and consistent opponent—ideological and political—of the monocratic party, and this opinion was by no means confined to believers. Even the Western left seems to have gradually come to appreciate the position of the Polish clergy. On the other hand, the PZPR—and Gierek personally—continued to accumulate points for its obvious (and genuine) liberalism compared with the situation in other socialist countries. The authorities therefore turned a blind eye, or perhaps condoned, such initiatives as the visit to West Germany by a large delegation of Polish bishops (20–25 September 1978), something that would have been unthinkable during Gomułka's time. Germany had, after all, become the country's largest supplier of credit.

This was the state of affairs when an event occurred whose consequences are difficult to overestimate: on 16 October 1978, on the eighth round of voting, the conclave of cardinals elected a new pope—the metropolitan bishop of Kraków, Cardinal Karol Wojtyła, who took the name John Paul II (to honor his predecessor, who had held office for only one month). The election of a Pole as head of the Catholic Church came as an enormous surprise, particularly as every pope for the preceding 455 years had been Italian. For the Poles it was a joyful shock. The prestige of the Polish church rose enormously, and Cardinal Wyszyński became "Primate of the Millennium." For many people, including opposition activists and dissident artists, the elevation of a lecturer from the Catholic University also elevated the prestige of Polish intellectuals, and the fact that Cardinal Wojtyła had collaborated closely with *Tygodnik Powszechny* was cause for hope that the church would continue its discrete support of the opposition. The Polish leadership, for its part, reacted positively, reminding the world that the new pope came from "socialist Poland." A message of congratulation was dispatched on the very day of the election, and the authorities agreed to the live transmission of the entire inaugural ceremony, which was attended by the chairman of the Council of State.

There was no doubt that the election of a Pole as head of the Catholic Church was hard for the PZPR to swallow and augured further, even greater difficulties. The authorities nonetheless stuck hard and fast to the line they had followed hitherto, and the only real relaxation of policy occurred in relation to church construction. The natural—and expected—proposal that the pope visit his homeland became the subject of considerable maneuvering, with the authorities trying to obtain, in exchange for their agreeing to the pilgrimage, an end to the church's support for the increasingly active opposition. Confidential and difficult talks took place about the route to be taken by the pope, the tone and nature of his public pronouncements, the number of meetings with state and party leaders, and the date for the start of the visit (the authorities rejected the proposal that this be linked to celebrations in honor of St. Stanisław, the eleventh-century bishop of Kraków killed by King Bolesław). There were several highly inflammatory issues, such as the decision to continue construction of a tunnel at the point where the main route of the pilgrimage entered the monastery of Jasna Góra. Security service monitoring of the clergy intensified, a fact that did not go unnoticed by those who were under surveillance. All in all, however, the authorities realized that refusing permission for the visit would be more harmful than allowing it to take place.

The authorities probably did not fully anticipate that the pilgrimage, which lasted from 2 to 10 June 1979, would turn out to be one long string of triumphs—for the church, the pope, the primate, and the millions of people who attended the masses celebrated by the pope and lined the roadside to see him pass by. Observers were amazed at the size of the crowds and the orderliness of the proceedings, which were guarded by police and volunteer "papal guards," side by side. John Paul II did not venture into political territory in his homilies, but nearly every one of his sermons contained elements that the security service could easily have considered "negative." This was the case, for example, in Warsaw, where the pope declared that "Christ cannot be excluded from human history," and in his farewell address in Kraków, when he urged the faithful "never to lose hope, become discouraged, or give up." His sermon in Gniezno struck a particular chord in urging community with the other nations of East-Central Europe, while simultaneously emphasizing that because of its Christian faith, Poland was part of the greater European community.

Party and state officials were cordial, they accorded the pope all the honors due to him, and were plainly interested in making the most of their presence alongside—as they said—"our great fellow countryman." At the same time, however, the entire propaganda machine was precisely calibrated to downplay the significance of the visit and, above all, to conceal the size of the enthusiastic crowds. The reporting was tightly controlled, the images transmitted on television cutting out the crowds and focusing on priests, nuns, and old women. The manipulation was obvious to anyone who took part in even one encounter with the pope, and cautious estimates put the total number of participants at around eight to ten million.

Externally, nothing changed after the pope's departure, and each of the two protagonists continued to behave as before. Similarly, opposition groups, which had not tried to take advantage of the pope's visit to promote their views, continued their previous forms of activity. Nevertheless, the influence of John Paul II and the words that he spoke, together with the size and discipline of the crowds that attended papal masses and lined the streets, undoubtedly changed the country's psychological climate. "In bowing before the Holy Father, Poland got up off its knees," commented one observer. It is easier to fight standing up.

"BEHIND THE FACADE"

The Venice Biennale held at the end of 1977 was devoted to independent and dissident movements in communist Europe; the Polish exhibit—smuggled abroad by members of KOR—was presented under the title "Behind the Facade." It included uncensored books and periodicals, photo essays on the annual pilgrimages to Jasna Góra and Piekary Śląskie, photographs of the funeral service following the death of Stanisław Pyjas, and a number of graphics. In a report presented at a symposium accompanying the exhibit Stanisław Barańcak, one of the founders of KOR, wrote: "Behind the dead mass of the facade . . . and in total opposition to it there is feverish activity." While there was a good dose of exaggeration in this juxtaposition of the "dead facade" and the liveliness of everything unofficial, this decade was characterized not only by the emergence and conscious creation of independent culture, but also by the fact that an increasing number of artists were fleeing from the closed world of the censors.

The exaggeration of Barańczak's formulation was a function of polemical rhetoric as well as his use of the imprecise term "facade." If we define the facade to include everything that was written in censored publications, performed in state theaters, shown in state cinemas (and made with state funding), then it is clear that the facade was by no means dead. Before 1976 Barańczak himself, like everyone else, published a great deal in censored publications. After all, ever since 1955 the PZPR's cultural policy had been characterized by considerable ambivalence and numerous fluctuations. Censorship existed and made its presence felt: artists who in some way crossed the line politically encountered difficulties or lost completely their access to their readers or audience, but if they simply remained neutral and imposed a certain amount of self-censorship, they would not encounter any obstacles and might even be awarded state prizes.

If we use the word "facade" to include everyone who received a state prize, it is undeniable that some awards were handed out to obedient or obliging mediocrities, but awards were also given to such people as Jerzy Grotowski (1972), Maria Ossowska (1972), Stanisław Lem (1973, 1976), Marian Brandys (1974), Konrad Swiniarski (1974), Bogdan Wojdowski (1975), Andrzej Wajda (1975), Kazimierza Iłłakowiczówna (1976), Ryszard Kapuściński (1976), Gustaw Holoubek (1978), Tadeusz Łomnicki (1978), Leopold Buczkowski (1979), Teodor Parnicki (1979), and Zygmunt Hubner (1979). People who unequivocally spoke out on the side of the opposition or openly opposed the authorities were, indeed, usually bypassed. Among the people who remained "unnoticed" in this way were Jerzy Andrzejewski, Jacek Bocheński, Kazimierz Brandys, Andrzej Kijowski, Tadeusz Konwicki, and Jan Józef Szczepański, but the honorees mentioned above really did belong to the "major league" of Polish culture.

The leadership's feeble and selective liberalism in cultural policy was dictated by political tactics. Such was the situation in the case of the "amnesty" accorded the work of Sławomir Mrożek, who returned to the Polish stage in 1973, and to the plays of Witold Gombrowicz, who reappeared with the Polish preview of *Ślub* (The Wedding), produced by Jerzy Jarocki in 1974. In 1977 a work by composer Andrzej Panufnik, who had emigrated in 1954, was performed for the first time in Poland, and in the National Philharmonic Concert Hall, to boot. Kazimierz Wierzyński was "rehabilitated," posthumously and selectively, when a volume of his poetry was published in 1972. The political decision makers also took into account the international renown of particular artists. For example, they discussed the behavior of Krzysztof Penderecki following a performance of one of his works—most of which dealt with biblical themes—when he publicly knelt and kissed the ring of Cardinal Wyszyński, who had been among the audience. The then head of the "cultural sector" in the PZPR Central Committee, Wincenty Kraśko, decided that Penderecki's international position (the UN secretary general had commissioned work from him) demanded that the incident be passed over in silence.

The facade was not actually dead, then, not even after 1976, when a growing number of new young artists decided to flee from the area controlled by the authorities, and when those who did not wish, or were unable, to do so—such as people involved in the theater or cinema—fought with the censors, publishers, editors, and officials "in charge of" culture. The pile of queried or rejected manuscripts grew, the number of films that ended up in the archives instead of in the cinemas increased, and KOR's *Black Book of Censorship* depicted the scope of the devastation, but the Gierek decade was by no means a "black hole" in Polish culture.

The 1968 generation expressed itself in the much harassed but still performing student theaters, such as the STU Theater in Kraków and Poznań's Theater of the Eighth Day. In the first half of the decade its representatives made a name for themselves in the realm of poetry, and they happily analyzed the work to date and future prospects of young writers (in numerous commentaries by Stanisław Barańczak and Stanisław Stabro, and *Świat nie przedstawiony* [The World Not Represented] by Julian Kornhauser and Adam Zagajewski). In 1974 Zbigniew Herbert published the first volume of *Mr. Cogito,* which began its triumphant conquest of the imagination of successive generations of young people. Several outstanding novels or other works of prose appeared, both before and after 1976, which—as Barańczak justifiably argued—turned out to be one of the major turning points in the history of twentieth-century Polish culture. Kazimierz Brandys's *Wariacje pocztowe* (Postal Variations) or Andrzej Kijowski's *Listopadowy wieczór* (November Evening), both published in 1972, certainly would not have appeared later, when these writers were signing protest petitions, but in 1980 one of the most outstanding novels of the postwar era *was* published—*Obłęd* (Madness), by Jerzy Krzysztoń. The second half of the decade saw the publication of Tomasz Łubieński's slim volume of essays, *Bić się czy nie bić* (To Fight or Not to Fight, 1978), a major contribution to the debate on Polish national consciousness; after a long delay, Kazimierz Moczarski's *Conversations with an Executioner* (1977); Ryszard Kapuściński's marvelous reportage, *The Emperor* (1978), immediately hailed as a classic; and Hanna Krall's extraordinary conversation with Warsaw ghetto survivor Marek Edelman, *Shielding the Flame* (1977).

In the theater, Andrzej Wajda directed two great productions, *The Devils,* based on the story by Fyodor Dostoyevsky (1971), and Stanisław Wyśpiański's *November Night* (1974). Before his tragic death (19 August 1975) Konrad Swiniarski presented a couple of fine productions—Shakespeare's *All's Well That Ends Well* (1971) and Stanisław Wyśpiański's *Wyzwolenie* (Liberation). Jerzy Jarocki staged one high-quality production after another (Witkacy-Witkiewicz's *The Shoemakers* in 1971 and *Mother* in 1972; Gombrowicz's *Ślub;* Shakespeare's *King Lear* in 1977 and *A Midsummer Night's Dream* in 1979); and Kazimierz Dejmek, still searching for new forms of expression, was also a notable presence (Gombrowicz's *Operetka* in 1975; *Dialogues de passion* in the same year). In 1975 Tadeusz Kantor and his troupe (Cricot II) began touring the world with his play *Umarła klasa* (The Dead Class). Jerzy Grotowski became the guru of the theatrical avant-garde around the world, inspiring numerous "theater workshops" that attempted to create new values in small-scale or street theater, while Tadeusz Różewicz went against the current of the romantic-combat stereotypes with his play, *Do piachu* (To Dust), produced by Tadeusz Łomnicki (1979).

The 1970s saw the emergence of a new Polish school of cinematography that parted company with the epic tendencies of Wajda to follow in the footsteps of Krzysztof Zanussi (*Illumination* in 1971, *Protective Coloring* in 1977) and that became known as "the cinema of moral disquiet." This new school included work by Krzysztof Kieślowski—*The Scar* (1975) and *Amator* (1978), Feliks Falk—*Wodzirej* (Top Dog, 1978), Agnieszka Holland—*Aktorzy prowincjonalni* (Provincial Actors, 1979), and Janusz Kijowski—*Kung Fu* (1980). One of the veterans of Polish cinema, Jerzy Kawalerowicz, directed a major film, *Śmierć prezydenta* (Death of a President). Almost every year Andrzej Wajda brought out a new film, including such outstanding productions as *The Promised Land* (1975) and *Man of Marble* (1977), his settling of accounts with Stalinism, with screenplay by Aleksander Ścibor-Rylski, an extraordinary film despite the "improvements" made by the censors. The decade also produced a number of major epics—the sentimental *Nocy i dni* (Nights and Days) of Jerzy Antczak (1975) and Jerzy Hoffman's *Potop* (Flood, 1974). A new generation of actors emerged onto both screen and stage, among them Krystyna Janda, Jerzy Stuhr, Wojciech Pszoniak, Jerzy Radziwiłłowicz, and Jerzy Trela.

Polish symphonic music maintained its high level and was well received around the world. Marek Rostworowski's carefully researched and imaginative exhibition, *A Self Portrait of the Poles* (which opened in September 1979), was a major event, a splendid lesson in Polish history that forced one to think about the present day.

It seems indisputable that Barańczak read these books, applauded these performances and concerts, and watched these films. It is equally obvious that during the 1970s, especially after 1976, the divide between some intellectual and artistic circles and the state-party leadership entered a qualitatively new phase. This became evident in the case of the journalists and writers of all kinds for whom underground publishing provided a forum. At the same time, an ever-wider circle of people became involved in dissent, either directly, by participating in opposition ventures, or indirectly, by depicting reality in a way that did not favor the authorities (or the system). Uncensored publications provided a space for writers and intellectuals of all generations, from Jerzy Andrzejewski and Kazimierz Brandys via Julian Stryjkowski, Tadeusz Konwicki and Zbigniew Herbert, Marek Nowakowski, and Kazimierz Orłoś to Jacek Bierezin and Leszek Szaruga. The exodus from the censored world was most widespread among the poets of the 1968 generation. Although there was no hard and fast boundary between those who decided to publish exclusively in the realm of "feverish activity" and those who struggled with censorship within the walls of the "facade," people associated with uncensored publishing naturally tended to construct their own value system, in which aesthetic norms frequently took second place to ideological and political criteria. When critics from the facade ignored or brutally attacked writers involved in underground publishing, those who wrote for *Zapis* or *Puls* responded—with a few exceptions—in kind.

While the divisions deepened within artistic circles in Poland, the 1970s—particularly the years following the emergence of underground publishing—brought a merging and interpenetration of domestic and émigré culture. I have already mentioned that Miłosz's work reached Poland, as did those works by Gombrowicz considered "unsuitable" for official publication, together with Wierzyński's poetry and Herling-Grudziński's essays. But there was movement in the other direction too. Stefan Kisielewski steadfastly published his political novels with Jerzy Giedroyc's publishing house, under the pseudonym Tomasz Staliński (Tomasz was Bierut's wartime underground code name). In 1973 Kazimierz Orłoś published his book *Cudowna melina* (Amazing Den of Thieves), also with Giedroyc, but under his own name, thereby provoking an enormous row at the congress of the Polish Writers' Union in February 1975. After 1976 it became easier—and more natural—to publish abroad. The authors whose work appeared in émigré publications included Stanisław Barańczak, Bogdan Madej, Wiktor Woroszylski, Tadeusz Konwicki, Jerzy Ficowski, Roman Zimand, and Marcin Król. By placing their work with émigré publishers and in émigré journals, Polish writers not only freed themselves from the noose of censorship but also broke the monopoly of their state patron. A similar role was increasingly played by the independent—although censored—Catholic publica-

399

tions: *Więź, Znak* (and their book series), *Tygodnik Powszechny,* and the more elite journal, *W drodze* (Along the Way), published by the Dominicans.

Whether part of the facade or part of the movement behind the scenes, Poles continued to read Sienkiewicz and Kraszewski more than anyone else. And they also enjoyed the homegrown and imported products of mass culture that were created by the climate of "dynamic development" and genuine modernity: "the red flag flying above the discotheque," as someone called it. While the police did round up hippies, the country's completely socialist youth organizations spent more time organizing discos that invariably played imperialist hits than running ideological education programs. One of the creators of the "propaganda of success," radio and television chairman Maciej Szczepański, did not hesitate to launch domestically produced variety shows and to import American television series. Every summer season brought more song festivals, energetically and successfully promoted by television and watched in most of the nearly eight million households with a television set. Sporting victories excited the public, and the exploits of Kazimierz Górski and his soccer team (Olympic gold medal in 1972, third place in the 1974 World Cup) were presented by the propaganda machine as firm proof of the vitality of the system.

The number of books published remained well below the level of demand but slowly rose (from 112 million copies in 1970 to 147 million in 1980). Educational levels rose—formally, at least; in the academic year 1978–79, roughly 470,000 people (including external students) were enrolled in ninety institutions of higher and further education. The total circulation of all dailies and periodicals reached forty-one million. The figures were eloquent, and the authorities cited them constantly, using them to conceal, above all, the fact that the whole of culture—from school programs to the repertoire of major theaters—was subordinated to the political goals of the hegemonic party.

A HOT SUMMER

Although the events that shook Poland in August 1980 were predictable, their scale took everyone by surprise—both those who had been looking for a signal that the system was in decline and those who now found themselves forced out of office and facing personal disaster. The leadership's usual weapons—increased security service activity, stepped-up propaganda, and changes in top personnel (carried out during the previous winter)—were to no avail. Growing discontent suddenly erupted into the open when the leadership announced what it regarded as a "moderate" increase in the price of a relatively small number of meat items. Despite their tough demeanor and their manifest self-confidence, Gierek and his associates had little authority left. It had been eroded by their clumsy retreat from the price increases of 1976, and by their striking inability to deal with the economic crisis and their visible fear of factory workers during the first wave of strikes in July.

Since the fall of 1978, and especially since June of the following year, most Poles had come to believe that the pope and the primate were their real, powerful, spiritual leaders. It seems that this feeling, together with the obvious floundering of the state and party authorities, gave people an unexpected sense of self-confidence. Opposition organizations had little to do with initiating the strike wave; it was triggered by the authorities' ill-considered but inevitable decisions. The presence of dissidents did, however, provide a stimulus to strike action. In the course of just under four years, opposition groups had taken root and gained strength, in terms of both political experience and their thinking about long-term change.

Although there were many groups in existence, open opposition activity was dominated by KOR, which in the fall of 1977 had changed its name to the Social Self-Defense Committee KOR (KSS KOR). Internal debates and polemics with other groups did not really produce a clear program of the political changes that KOR wanted to bring about, but many elements were obvious. The main guiding principle was to work for a Poland that would be democratic and sovereign, but everyday activity was based on the notion that "the movement is everything," and focused on creating "an alternative society." In fact, the very name of the group referred—in the words "self-defense" and "social"—to the underlying premise of its activity: step by step, self-organizing groups would liberate their members, who would then proceed to liberate the whole of social life from the tutelage of the omnipotent state and the communist party. Only rarely did KOR and the relatively numerous embryonic "self-defense" structures associated with it engage in public demonstrations. The group advocated grassroots activity of a kind that would affect people's consciousness rather than their emotions. This involved publishing newssheets, pamphlets, books, and leaflets, organizing discussion meetings, and providing information about abuses on the part of the authorities (which was the province of the Intervention Bureau, ably run by Zofia and Zbigniew Romaszewski). KOR took the view that change would follow an evolutionary course, a view that it stressed frequently in the hope of avoiding the harshest forms of repression and reassuring the authors of the doctrine of "limited sovereignty" that change in Poland would not destabilize the international situation. But this approach also derived from the group's negative view of the revolutionary tradition and its belief that an all-out and immediate push for democracy could easily turn into an antidemocratic, if not dictatorial, regime. It seems to me that KOR's approach was also shaped by the ideological and intellectual legacy of such people in the old left as Edward Abramowski, who believed that changes in the world were the result of changes in human beings and argued against the view that a new system would create a new person.

The KOR view of Polish political realities and how to shape them led the group to adopt a positive attitude toward even the weakest reform tendencies in the PZPR and to welcome "repentant sinners" who had taken their time in deciding to associate with the opposition. This issue was the subject of a major public dispute between Piotr Wierzbicki, who sharply attacked those intellectuals unable to make up their minds to abandon "the state payroll," and Adam Michnik, who was opposed to oppositionist fundamentalism. This attitude, which formed part of what Jan Józef Lipski referred to as "the ethos of KOR," meant that the group easily established contacts with intellectual and artistic circles. KOR also developed increasingly strong ties with opposition tendencies within the Catholic intelligentsia—*Więź, Znak,* the Clubs of Catholic Intelligentsia in Warsaw and Kraków, and *Tygodnik Powszechny*—whose already growing influence became even greater following the pope's visit to Poland.

At the same time, KOR was the group with the most influence among those factory workers actively engaged in opposition, and its *Charter of Workers' Rights,* published in December 1979, was widely distributed. Among other things, the document stressed the value of strikes, "even small ones," and argued that it was vitally important for strikers to create a representative body to monitor the implementation of strike demands in the event that a strike was successful. The charter was signed by representatives of all the existing Free Trade Unions. Several dozen of the signatories were workers, the largest number coming from the Gdańsk Shipyard and the Lenin Iron and Steel Works in Nowa Huta, and many of the others were engineers and technicians from the lower levels of management. The charter was published in *Robotnik,* whose circulation reached several tens of thousands of copies. While the document did not call for direct confrontation, it was unequivocal in its call to action ("even covert action, initially") and its support for the formation of the Free Trade Unions. The KOR members who worked among, and eventually with, factory workers included a number of people with a long history of opposition activity (among them Jan Lityński, one of the best known of the Commandos, and Henryk Wujec).

Contact with oppositionists in other socialist countries was a crucial part of KOR activity. After an exchange of declarations and documents, representatives of KOR and Charter 77, the chief opposition group in Czechoslovakia, met in August 1978, the tenth anniversary of the Warsaw Pact invasion. In January 1979 Zbigniew Romaszewski visited the best known of all Soviet dissidents, Andrei Sakharov. This meeting was the result of a consistent policy on the part of KOR and contributed to the group's popularity in the international arena.

Other significant opposition groups engaged in many of the same tactics and forms of activity as KOR, but they placed their emphasis elsewhere and drew their strength from other sources. This was particularly true of the Confederation for an Independent Poland, which emphasized the need for political change within the country and in its relations with Moscow. The KPN started from the assumption that reform, no matter how far-reaching, was not the goal; the basic and most urgent task was not to change the system but to "exchange" it for something entirely different. The group believed that independence and democracy were inseparable and that one could not be achieved without the other. The KPN advocated that society establish its own organizations, seeing this as a step toward the creation of alternative political institutions that would select their own representatives at the national level. The process of change would thus involve an intermediate stage characterized by a kind of dual power. The KPN did not rule out the possibility that the final overthrow of the regime could be triggered by a general strike, organized and coordinated by these national representatives. The group assumed that the Soviet Union would not intervene directly, partly because Moscow would be offered the possibility of establishing genuinely good-neighborly and peaceful relations with Poland. KPN literature therefore devoted considerable space to geopolitical issues and to discussion of an alternative political system. The group emphasized the need to establish a disciplined and centralized organization, and the names it devised for its components harked back to the underground AK and WiN ("sectors," "operational command," and so on). The KPN also advocated street demonstrations, especially to commemorate the anniversary of Poland's regaining independence (11 November). The group had a small but generally disciplined and committed network in nearly all the larger towns, including Warsaw, Gdańsk, Lublin, Kraków, and several towns in Silesia.

The third opposition group, ROPCiO, had a similar organizational structure to that of KOR but was closer to Moczulski in ideology than to Kuroń. Decidedly less influential than KOR and less radical in its program for independence than the Confederation, ROPCiO never really regained its breath after the splits of 1978, but the energetic group led by Antoni Macierewicz, which published the journal *Głos,* was close to it in terms of ideas, and this became particularly apparent toward the end of 1979. Macierewicz's group did not actually part company with KOR, which it had helped to found, but it came to place increasing emphasis on demands for national independence. While ROPCiO emphasized its ties to Catholicism and its support for the so-called social teachings of the church, this did not mean that the group enjoyed a privileged relationship with the hierarchy, as the church it did not single out any opposition group, either positively or negatively. ROPCiO drew support from people formerly associated with Ruch and also had numerous contacts with war veterans; these contacts were largely kept up by Wojciech Ziembiński. The members of Ruch, which was still led by Andrzej Czuma, were active in organizing patriotic demonstrations, and their writings contained frequent references to past struggles for independence.

The Young Poland Movement was an especially important member of the opposition in the Tri-City area. The group saw itself as continuing the traditions of the national democrats from the period before their turn to radical-totalitarian politics at the end of the 1920s. The RMP journal, *Bratniak,* was much involved in the ongoing ideological disputes, and members of the group were active in the Gdańsk Free Trade Unions and in organizing patriotic demonstrations. Several Student Solidarity Committees became a permanent fixture in the opposition, although they lacked a coordinating structure. They frequently supplied people to carry out activities organized by other groups, mainly by KOR, and they were a visible presence on campuses in Kraków, Wrocław, and Warsaw.

All in all, then, the opposition, although sharply divided—and still dividing—was a presence in many towns and social groups, and in several large industrial plants. It had a fairly reliable information network within the country, and good channels of communication with the outside world. Despite the systematic confiscation of equipment by the security service, the opposition possessed its own printing capacity and had gained considerable experience in both printing and distribution. Its members were also highly committed, although they had only a somewhat hazy notion of the various ways in which the situation might development and had few specific answers to the question: "What next?"

The strikes that began leaping like wildfire from one factory to another and from town to town in early July did not initially constitute a serious threat to the Gierek regime. The flames were speedily extinguished, largely by acceding to the workers' wage demands, which were generally quite modest. "We have averted a great danger," declared Stanisław Kania on 11 July; he was seriously mistaken. The previous day a strike had broken out in Lublin. Over the course of the next week, the strike spread to a number of plants, including the facilities at the local railroad junction, a vital link in transport to and from the Soviet Union. At this point the Politburo intervened, appointing a government commission, headed by Deputy Prime Minister Mieczysław Jagielski, to review the strikers' demands. This yielded positive results from the authorities' point of view. The strike wave died down, but almost everywhere around the country workers had only to threaten a strike or forcefully raise demands, and enterprise directors and senior administrative officials began offering at least partial concessions.

The opposition reacted to these events immediately. In two communiqués, issued on 2 and 11 July, KOR called on workers to organize and to avoid any kind of action that could provide an opportunity for provocation. The group also reiterated its list of immediate demands: changes in agricultural policy, legal recognition of the right to strike, the creation of independent trade unions or committees to represent workers, and the abolition of censorship. In some places people who worked with KOR went to aid the strikers (this was the case during the final phase of the Lublin strike); other groups (the KPN, for example) did likewise. Probably more important was the fact that the opposition provided the public—largely via Radio Free Europe—with information about the nature and scope of the strikes. This was especially significant given that the strike wave died down but did not completely die out. In first one place and then another, tension turned into protest. The most spectacular strikes were those of Warsaw's sanitation and urban transport departments (11 August).

The turning point came in mid-August, when a strike broke out in the Gdańsk Shipyard. From the very beginning, the strike that erupted on 14 August was somewhat different from the others: it was organized by members of the Free Trade Unions, and their first demand was the reinstatement of two workers who had recently been sacked, Anna Walentynowicz and

Lech Wałęsa. They also demanded the building of a memorial to the victims of December 1970. And, of course, an increase in wages. On 15 August workers in other enterprises also began coming out on strike. On 16 August the shipyard management agreed to the strikers' demands, and Wałęsa, as chairman of the strike committee, announced that the strike was over. This decision was queried by some of the strikers, who pointed out that workers elsewhere had come out in solidarity with the shipyard strike. Wałęsa rescinded the decision to end the protest.

During the night of 16–17 August representatives of twenty-one striking factories met in the shipyard to set up the Inter-Enterprise Strike Committee (MKS). Strikes spread like lightning: on 18 August the MKS represented 156 factories. The Gdańsk provincial administrator was handed a list of twenty-one demands. The first of these called for "the acceptance of free trade unions, independent of the party and employers, in accordance with Convention 87 of the International Labor Organization concerning trade union freedoms, ratified by the Polish People's Republic." That same day workers went on strike in the Szczecin Shipyard and a large number of factories in the city. They immediately established their own MKS, which drew up a list of thirty-seven demands; the first of these, strikingly similar to the number one demand of the Gdańsk workers, called for "the establishment of free trade unions, independent of the party and government, and the creation of conditions for independent activity."

The strike that erupted in Gdańsk on 14 August aroused considerable concern among the leadership: "The whole business is being orchestrated by two members of KOR and . . . Wałęsa, an associate of Kuroń's group," someone asserted during discussion at a meeting of the Politburo, which decided to ask Gierek to return from vacation—which he usually spent on the Crimea—and to have the prime minister, Edward Babiuch, deliver a televised address. Babiuch's statement, delivered on 15 August, had no immediate effect whatsoever, apart from irritating viewers and signaling that the authorities were on the defensive. Subsequent Politburo sessions discussed the possibility of taking a hard line with the strikers, and set up a Crisis Group, consisting of security and military officials. However, the leader of the group, Stanisław Kania, acknowledged that the authorities "wouldn't stand a real chance if it came to a confrontation."

Cardinal Wyszyński had no more effect than Babiuch when, during a visit to Wambierzice in Lower Silesia, he appealed for peace and order. On the same day, 17 August, Gierek appeared on television to deliver a contentious and unconvincing address to "the working class." The old communist Władysław Kruczek was undoubtedly right when he told his colleagues: "We must show that we're not afraid"; except that it was not at all clear how—apart from resorting to the police (and perhaps the army)—they were to demonstrate self-confidence. Meanwhile, the strikes began to spread. On 19 August workers in Elbląg formed a strike committee, and by 20 August the Gdańsk MKS had come to represent more than three hundred factories. The same day, sixty-four intellectuals signed a letter in which they expressed support for the strikers and called on the authorities to engage in talks. In light of the fact that the signatories included several PZPR members and people considered to be "progovernment," the party leadership saw the letter as signaling a "deep crisis of confidence." The leadership was even more alarmed by the fact that, despite a massive propaganda campaign in the media, public opinion across the country sympathized with the strikers, and workers elsewhere had begun to come out in solidarity (among them, workers at the tractor plant in Ursus, near Warsaw).

The first arrests of opposition activists, carried out on 20 August, also had little effect. Several of the most active members of KOR were detained, along with the leader of the KPN. Both the main strike committees were well organized and virtually in control of the Tri-City area and Szczecin. Despite the news blackout and the suspension of telephone service, information about the committees and their activities spread rapidly across the country. Dozens of journalists arrived in Gdańsk, where the strike committee happily welcomed foreign correspondents. In almost all the larger towns opposition activists distributed leaflets and the August issue of *Robotnik*, of which several tens of thousands of copies had been printed. The authorities hesitated to use force, although both the internal and defense ministries had begun preparations. Two Politburo members and deputy prime ministers, Kazimierz Barcikowski and Mieczysław Jagielski, were dispatched to Gdańsk with authorization to begin talks with the strikers. After unsuccessfully attempting to resolve the situation without involving the MKS, they finally began negotiations with the committee (on 20 and 23 August). On 23 August a delegation of the Szczecin MKS arrived in Gdańsk, and it was decided that the basic demand of both committees would be for official agreement to the formation of free trade unions.

Moscow was discrete in expressing its concern over the situation in Poland, by no means urging a "forceful" solution. The PZPR leadership decided on a tried and tested maneuver: "We need to carry out a regrouping of the top leadership," declared Prime Minister Babiuch on 22 August, adding that, "in order to save the party and the country, all criticism should be directed at the government." On 24 August a plenary meeting of the Central Committee adopted a proposal for major personnel changes: six people left the Politburo, and the prime minister and two of his deputies were dismissed from their posts. Also dismissed was the chairman of the Committee for Radio and Television, who had become a symbol of corruption. The party leadership decided, nevertheless, to aim for a "political settlement," meaning that wage concessions would be offered in exchange for the strikers dropping all political demands. To help achieve this end, it stepped up the propaganda campaign and mobilized the party membership. Neither tactic achieved the desired result, although the party-state negotiators attached some significance to the fact that both the strike committees had been joined by members of the opposition, who set up two advisory panels. The authorities hoped to find a common language with these people and assumed that they would be willing to compromise, as the "Appeal of the 64" had suggested.

The strike negotiators were, however, determined, and in this they were supported by the mass of the strikers. The general atmosphere of nervous excitement was fed by the religious services organized on the grounds of the striking factories and the pervading mood of religious exaltation, and by the rapid development of what might be called "strikers' folklore"—songs, live performances, graffiti, and banners. It was not only the crowds gathered outside the gates of the shipyard but also the influx of foreign radio and television reporters that strengthened the public's conviction regarding the significance of the events and the role of those who had locked themselves in behind the walls of the plant. Staging a sit-in strike and not taking to the streets—in line with Kuroń's slogan: "Don't burn down party committees, set up your own"—turned out to be extremely effective.

A number of well-known politicians (Stefan Olszowski, Andrzej Żabiński) had returned to the leadership, but neither this "renewal" nor the appointment of an old party hack, Józef Pińkowski, as prime minister had any effect on the strikers, who simply ignored this "regrouping." Yet another televised appeal by Gierek was similarly fruitless. The strikers even ignored a sermon delivered by Cardinal Wyszyński on 26 August in Jasna Góra, extracts from which (those most favorable to the authorities) were broadcast on television the same day. The primate's call for people to "conserve, save, and respect" the material progress that had been made to date plainly constituted an appeal for no more strikes, although he did not, of course, spare his criticism of the authorities, whom he held responsible for the situation in which the country found itself. That same day top party leaders came the closest they had ever come to a change of tactics. They fully realized the far-reaching implications of agreeing to the strikers' first demand: "If we agree, the strikes will come to an end, but at the price of bringing to life a permanent structure that will be stronger, more dangerous, with millions of members," said Kania. "This would be a political act," declared Gierek, "with unforeseeable consequences for the country and the entire socialist camp."

It was on 26 August that an MKS was formed in Wrocław, a strike committee was established in the Lenin Iron and Steel Works, and strikes broke out at the Cegielski Plant in Poznań and the Thorez Mine in Wałbrzych. The wave was sweeping, unhindered, across the country. The authorities had their backs to the wall. And they were surrounded on all sides. The Soviet ambassador, Averky Aristov, transmitted a sharply worded message from Brezhnev, who expressed surprise that the border with the West remained open. President Giscard d'Estaing, a great admirer of Gierek, appealed for "a resolution of these problems in line with the wishes of the people." Both the Gdańsk and the Szczecin MKSs refused to budge. For its part, the Politburo nervously reviewed various options: "intensify the blockade of the coastal region," "introduce a state of alert in the main industrial centers," "carry out more arrests," or "consider declaring a state of emergency." Someone also suggested advancing the slogan, "Communists, step forward!" To each of these options there was a reply: "At the moment, we don't have a party"; "Communists, step forward, but we don't know that they will step forward. We could end up all on our own"; "How can we impose martial law if the whole country is on strike?"; "Who will get the machinery working once we've seized the ports?"

On 27 August factories in Warsaw and Łódź came to a standstill; on 28 August workers went on strike at the copper plant outside Legnice; and on 29 August miners from the Manifest Lipcowy Mine refused to go below ground, coal miners in Jastrzębie formed their own MKS, and a strike began in the Katowice Iron and Steel Works. . . . The revolt had spread to "the most faithful of the faithful," and Gierek had lost his chief base of support. There was no alternative: the party leadership decided to "consult the allies," namely, Moscow, and, without waiting for a reply, to call a meeting of the Central Committee at which they would agree to the formation of free trade unions.

Early on 30 August, before the "owners of the Polish People's Republic" had convened to accept a decision made, as usual, by the Politburo, Barcikowski signed an agreement in Szczecin, while the more cautious Jagielski had drafted another with the Gdańsk MKS. Both committees were now receiving pilgrimages of delegates from other town and factory strike committees, or from work crews that had not yet decided what to do. For the past few days, power really had been divided between Central Committee headquarters in Warsaw, where the PZPR leadership was in constant session, and the health and safety hall in the shipyard, where the MKS was meeting without interruption. On 31 August, after receiving a solemn promise that all opposition members would be freed from detention, Lech Wałęsa and Mieczysław Jagielski signed the agreement. Euphoria seized everyone in the room, everyone in the shipyard, and the thousands of people gathered outside the gates. The whole country listened spellbound to the radio broadcast of this extraordinary moment.

The next few days were given over to cosmetics. On 3 September a third agreement was signed in Jastrzębie. Two days later, at the next meeting of the Central Committee, Gierek resigned. Although these few weeks in August brought little more than a further "regrouping of the leadership," they shook the country. The seismic movement, with its epicenter in Gdańsk, was to be felt by the whole of Europe. Few people realized at the time that it signaled the approach of the beginning of the end of real socialism in its classic, Soviet-European form.

CHAPTER 7

The Long March—Prologue

On 1 September 1980 the Inter-Factory Strike Committees in Gdańsk, Szczecin, and Wrocław renamed themselves Inter-Factory Founding Committees (MKZs), and when the strikes ended in Silesia, the strike committees in that region followed suit. Despite the fact that agreements had been signed, the strike wave moved into most of the regions that had hitherto been unaffected. Everywhere workers demanded wage increases and changes in social policy, but the main cause of the unrest was the attempt of the authorities, at both the national and the local levels, to restrict the scope of the "independent, self-governing trade unions" by arguing that they could function only in those areas where an agreement had been signed with an MKS. In many smaller industrial centers the local administration and PZPR committees placed numerous obstacles in the way of those seeking to form union organizations, which only fanned the flames of hostility and suspicion. The information blockade continued across virtually the whole country, and the media provided no information about the formation of the new trade unions.

Everywhere opposition groups joined in the push to set up the new organizations, offering to help workers in regions where the two groups had not previously been in contact. In some towns the Clubs of Catholic Intelligentsia or parish organizations sympathetic to them played a major role. In some cases, local branches of PAX lent their premises to the organizing effort. In the main areas of opposition activity, union organizing benefited from the presence of the underground, which made available its printing equipment and the services of people who knew how to operate it and had some editorial experience. A large number of journalists, economists, and sociologists also offered their knowledge and organizational skills to the MKZs. Members and associates of KOR, ROPCiO, the Society for Academic Courses, the Young Poland Movement, and the Clubs of Catholic Intelligentsia collectively reinforced the emerging union structures at the factory, regional, and national levels. Some of them were co-opted to provisional decision-making bodies, while others formed advisory groups or provided technical assistance.

The KPN, which was less active in the emerging trade unions, was the object of particular concern on the part of the state authorities. Fearing, no doubt, that the Confederation would rally the movement around its slogan of national independence, they arrested its leader, Leszek Moczulski (on 23 September). Some of the new union organizations also adopted the notion, then being heavily promoted in official propaganda, that the movement should be "apolitical," an argument directed against both the KPN and KOR. The Gdańsk MKZ was naturally viewed by many as the center of the movement, but this position was questioned in some regions, especially Silesia. Nevertheless, people from across the country made the pilgrimage to Gdańsk. Some of them went out of curiosity; and others, would-be union organizers, went in search of advice, resources, and assistance, and to be "anointed," not only to satisfy their own ambitions but also to strengthen their authority in the continuing skirmishes with the state administration. Despite numerous obstacles people flocked en masse to the new organizations, whose membership soon exceeded all expectations. Within two weeks founding committees had been established in all larger factories, including those producing armaments, and in many central administrative institutions and the courts. On 17 September a meeting in Gdańsk brought together delegates from thirty MKZs across the country, representing more than three million people who, it was estimated, had already joined the union or declared their desire to do so. Up to this moment it had been more appropriate to refer to "unions," since it was not clear whether a unified organization would emerge or whether the movement would consist of disconnected regional and factory structures—as the PZPR hoped would be the case.

However, after lengthy and heated discussions and despite strong opposition from the Gdańsk delegates, it was decided to create a unified trade union based on a single statute that would be binding on all members. Those who argued most forcefully for this position were Warsaw lawyer Jan Olszewski and historian Karol Modzelewski from Wrocław, who suggested the name for the organization—the Independent Self-Governing Trade Union (NSZZ) Solidarity. The creation of a single union was also favored by delegates from the smaller MKZs, fearful of confronting their local authorities. But the decision was also dictated by the very logic of a situation in which political and economic power were so highly centralized.

Solidarity did not, however, intend to duplicate the PZPR model, and decentralizing tendencies were always present in the union. Nor did it replicate the traditional, vertical, model of trade unions based on individual branches of industry, with regional and national structures. The basic organizational units of Solidarity were factory commissions organized into regions (branch organizations were established later and never played a significant role in the union). The Gdańsk meeting also decided to set up a National Coordinating Commission (KKP), whose very name indicated an instinctive aversion to centralization. All the MKZs were represented on the KKP, each of them with a single vote regardless of the size of its membership. The regional structure, which emphasized the importance of local interests, gave the union additional opportunities to mobilize its members and encouraged activity in the smaller factories and urban areas; it also enhanced the status of local leaders.

The first, improvised, session of the KKP elected its chairman; to no one's surprise, the post went to Lech Wałęsa. An electrician by training, a participant in the Gdańsk strike of December 1970, an activist in the Free Trade Unions, an able negotiator during discussions with government officials, and a speaker who easily commanded the attention of a room full of strike delegates and the crowds occupying the shipyard (as well as advisers and dozens of journalists), Wałęsa had come to personify August 1980. For a large number of people he also personified the workers, the social group that yet again had galvanized the country and forced concessions from its communist rulers. For many people, especially the intelligentsia, Wałęsa was also the ideal "man of the people," worthy of being anointed "leader of the nation." In many regions, young and dynamic workers and engineers from large factories emerged to become leaders at the local level and then part of the union elite. Within the movement, one could discern the revolt of a younger generation, whose aspirations had been stifled by the nomenklatura system and bureaucratic rigidities.

The main division, though, and one that was clearly visible when Solidarity was being formed, was that between the broadly defined "ruling class" and its subordinates. This division was formalized in one of the articles of the union's statute, which prohibited anyone in a managerial position from occupying union office. The division also became translated, at the most general level, into the confrontation between Solidarity as the organizer of the grass roots and the PZPR as the epitome of power at all levels of society.

This did not mean that rank-and-file party members did not flock to the union. It was not so much that they wanted to control the new movement from within (although such motives played a part) as that they wanted to voice their shared opposition to the way the country had been governed and the resulting economic situation. The majority of the population probably perceived Solidarity as a protest movement and a means of bringing pressure to bear on the authorities, rather than as an organization that would create an alternative system. This was the view of the party leadership, which revived the old slogan "Socialism—yes, distortions—no," but it was also shared by a large number of Solidarity leaders. This opinion was typified by union activists from Silesia, who stated in an interview with the party weekly, *Polityka,* that "people don't want to change the socialist system, they just want to improve it," and that society wanted a socialism that was "authentic and just." The first of these statements was made by Kazimierz Świtoń, associated with ROPCiO and the founder of one of the first independent unions, the second—by Andrzej Rozpłochowski, soon to become one of Solidarity's most radical activists.

Moscow was becoming increasingly concerned about the turn of events in Poland. At a meeting on 3 September, the CPSU Politburo declared unambiguously that the compromise that had been achieved was "clearly of a provisional nature" and urged its Polish counterpart to "prepare a counterattack." While the Politburo recommended "political flexibility" and the use of progovernment mass social organizations, it went as far as to suggest "the use, if the need arises, of forceful administrative measures." The Kremlin leadership was already suggesting that "experienced political employees of the Polish Army be assigned to leading positions in Party bodies."

The key to Moscow's position lay in the reference to the "provisional nature" of the agreements between the Polish leadership and the striking workers. The birth of Solidarity was seen as a dangerous systemic anomaly. However, the way in which it had emerged and the scale of the movement were such that direct action had not been possible. Not even using "forceful measures." Not to mention the army.

The new union was not established, however, without serious difficulties. On 24 September a KKP delegation submitted the union's statute and a request for union registration to the Warsaw Provincial Court, which had been hastily selected by the Council of State to register the new trade unions. The leadership's obvious opposition to the form of organization that Solidarity had chosen and the obstacles that the union faced in many parts of the country when trying to function suggested that registration would be a difficult process. Social tensions were further heightened by the delay in implementing wage demands. The emerging organization felt the need to test its organizational strength and demonstrate its potential, so the KKP decided to call a nationwide warning strike. This took place on 3 October in the form of a one-hour work stoppage or—depending on the decision of local union leaders—a symbolic demonstration of the union's position (using flags, placards, sirens, armbands, and so on). Most observers considered that the strike demonstrated widespread support for Solidarity and a high level of discipline within the union.

It did not, however, dissipate social tensions. These grew in tandem with the delay in registering the union, and protest actions over wages were renewed (these included a hunger strike carried out by railroad workers in Wrocław on 21–27 October). The court's decision to amend the statute unilaterally by, among other things, deleting the section concerning the right to strike and adding a statement regarding the "leading role" of the PZPR provoked widespread public outrage and demands for a general strike. The Politburo weighed the possibility of imposing martial law, but some members, including the minister of defense, General Wojciech Jaruzelski, expressed doubts "whether we can effectively impose martial law on millions of strikers." The leadership found itself on the defensive, even its most hardline members—subsequently referred to as *beton*, the concrete faction—opting for gradual measures. The authorities were counting on Solidarity losing its initial impetus and on being able to weaken it by exploiting the (visible) divisions within the union. They also entertained hopes of being able to restore the party's ability to mobilize its members and the broader population as a means of limiting the growth of Solidarity. Some party leaders seem to have thought they might be able to incorporate Solidarity into the system. This is one possible interpretation of Kania's remark concerning "a compromise of a structural kind," which he made, not in statement designed for propaganda purposes, but at a meeting of the Politburo.

For the time being the only solution was to withdraw the court's proposed amendments to the Solidarity statute. After tense negotiations and a number of discrete meetings between KKP and government representatives, Solidarity was formally legalized on 10 November. The strike was called off, and a gala celebration was held in Warsaw's Grand Theater. For the first time since the liquidation of Mikołajczyk's PSL, communist leaders were forced to acknowledge that an organized opposition had the legal right to function in Poland. There were grounds for satisfaction.

The forced recognition did not, however, signify a permanent easing of tension. During the following weeks tension again increased. This was caused by events within the country and by a number of moves on the part of Warsaw Pact members. These developments occurred more or less simultaneously, although it is hard to say whether this was a matter of coincidence or design. It was obvious that Moscow's anxiety over the course of events had not evaporated with the end of the strike wave and the signing of the agreements, to which the CPSU leadership had signaled its agreement. The Kremlin had greeted the elimination of Gierek, his replacement by Stanisław Kania, and the other changes in top party personnel as a traditional and welcome development. The Soviet Union promised additional deliveries, and the TASS communiqué issued after Kania's visit to Moscow (on 30 October) referred to "a complete unanimity" of views, signifying Soviet agreement to the political line represented by Poland's new first secretary.

Soviet consent to this approach did not, however, mean consent to Solidarity's uncontrolled development. What the Soviet leadership found particularly alarming was that the union led by Wałęsa, with the considerable and visible involvement of an opposition that had been termed—not without reason—"antisocialist," had set an example that was proving contagious. On 16 September the Coordinating Committee of Creative and Scientific Associations was formed, largely at the initiative of TKN and DiP members. On 18–19 October the National Founding Committee of the Independent Students' Union (NZS) announced its formation and soon thereafter applied for official registration. At its congress, held during 29–31 October, the Union of Journalists elected a new governing body in which the majority of members were drawn from the opposition, or circles close to it, and were in any event extremely critical of the way in which the mass media were being steered from behind the desks of the Central Committee. The new president was Stefan Bratkowski, a party member but one who had rebelled against real socialism to become the main founder of DiP.

A development that was far more threatening to the leadership—and the system as a whole—than the creation of organizations among the intelligentsia was the formation, on 21 September, of the Founding Committee of the Independent, Self-Governing Farmers' Union, which also applied for registration. Although the organizers of the independent movement in rural areas had far less influence than their urban counterparts, no one could be sure that the fragmentation and weakness of the villages would not evaporate if the union were officially registered. The prospect of a second Solidarity must have aroused something more than alarm among the party leadership. The court rejected the applications of both the students and peasants, which only resulted in Solidarity lengthening the list of its demands. As if this were not enough, the plague invaded the citadel: on 27 October a group calling itself the Consultative-Coordinating Commission of Party Organizations met in Toruń. This created a dangerous precedent infringing the principle of democratic centralism, which dictated that party organizations maintain no contacts with each other, only with the body immediately above them in the hierarchy. The "horizontal structure" that emerged in this fashion threatened, should it spread, to deprive the leadership of its ability to steer the party ship through the stormy seas building around it.

In this situation the first public response of Poland's neighbors was not long in coming. On 30 October the GDR suspended the agreement on freedom of movement across its border with Poland, a move that was followed by Czechoslovakia on 18 November. On 9 November TASS announced that Polish and Soviet troops were engaged in military exercises on Polish territory. On 21 November the central party newspapers in Berlin and Prague attacked Wałęsa directly, and *Rude Pravo* issued a clear warning against Kania's far-reaching liberalism, drawing a comparison between the situation in Poland and the Prague Spring. Although it could not be excluded that Gustav Husak and Erich Honecker were running ahead of the pack commanded by Brezhnev, it was fairly clear that at the very least they would not have taken the initiative without Moscow's assent. While the economic situation in the neighboring countries to the west and south was far better than in Poland and the opposition far weaker (in Czechoslovakia) or barely in its infancy (in the GDR), both countries had reason to fear contagion by the Polish disease.

These multiplying signs of growing disquiet on the part of Poland's allies were accompanied by a severe crisis that erupted (not necessarily by accident) on 21 November. After searching the offices of Solidarity's Mazowsze Region security forces arrested Jan Narożniak, who had been helping out at the office, and one of his friends, who worked in the public prosecutor's office, on charges of having given the union a copy of a secret circular issued by the general prosecutor, Professor Lucjan Czubiński. The document contained suggestions as to how to combat the opposition and included a number of tricks that were in clear violation of the code of penal procedure. On 24 November workers at the Ursus tractor factory began a strike in protest against the arrests, demanding that a Sejm commission be established to investigate the activity of the police, security service, and the prosecutor's office. Two days later the KKP expressed its full support for the Mazowsze MKZ, protests began in several towns, and the Politburo requested a report on the incident from the deputy minister of internal affairs, General Adam Krzysztoporski, who declared outright that "the apparatus [of the MSW] is convinced that this is the beginning of the end." Indeed, the demand to call "the apparatus" to account, a process that could have stretched all the way back to 1944, was read as an attack on "the hard core of the system" and an attempt to disarm people's power. While the two sides avoided a confrontation of the kind that was feared by both Kania (and his supporters in the party leadership) and Solidarity leaders and influential intellectuals, the level of tension within the country rose markedly. On 29 November the GDR issued an order restricting the length of time that Western observers could spend in the zone along the border with Poland. On 3 December the prime ministers of Czechoslovakia and the GDR held a surprise meeting.

President Jimmy Carter publicly confirmed the presence of "an unprecedented concentration of Soviet forces along the Polish border," and on 4 December the Central Committee issued a dramatic appeal that opened with an invocation previously unheard in the Polish People's Republic: "Fellow countrymen! The fate of our nation and our country hangs in the balance!" The next day the head of the Central Committee press department declared at a press conference: "If power slips from the hands of democracy, . . . Poland's communists will have the right and duty to call for assistance." On the evening of the same day the very top PZPR leadership, together with the ministers of defense and internal affairs, flew to Moscow for an extraordinary meeting of the Warsaw Pact Political Advisory Committee.

This meeting, which took place on 5 December, did not reach a decision regarding military intervention in Poland. The Polish leaders were asked to take more decisive measures against the growing social movement, but in a personal conversation Brezhnev assured Kania: "I won't invade without your say-so." Perhaps the allies really intended to render armed assistance to the Polish leadership, which plainly did not feel strong enough to engage in a once-and-for-all showdown. Perhaps the obvious military preparations and the publicly expressed threats were both meant as a form of blackmail directed against Kania and his closest associates.

A SECOND COMPROMISE

Somehow or other, crisis was averted, and the ceremonial commemoration of the tenth anniversary of the workers' revolt on the Baltic Coast took place without disruption, on 16–17 December 1980. It looked as though Solidarity had become—in Kania's words—an integral element of the sociopolitical landscape and a part of the structure of the system. That this was a delusion was made clear in the following months, when a number of major conflicts erupted. At the regional level, general strikes broke out in the Beskid region (27 January–6 February 1981) and in the Sudeten region (30 January–10 February). Farmers in Rzeszów staged a sit-in strike (2 January–18 February), and students went on strike in Łódź (21 January–17 February). At the national level the authorities were involved in a conflict over the union's demand that Saturdays be free of work, and over union members' refusal to report for work on Saturday, 10 January.

At the beginning of 1981 Soviet propaganda sharpened its tone: on 29 January TASS issued a communiqué, "On Developments in Poland," asserting that Solidarity was engaged in "counterrevolutionary" activity. Divisions deepened within the PZPR, whose activists—it was stated at a Politburo meeting—"demand that we take principled steps [while] the party masses demand that we negotiate and reach agreement." The party leadership decided to convene an extraordinary congress, which was seen by the hard-liners as a concession to "revisionist" forces and others ready to "capitulate." They had a point: in a similar situation Gomułka had not only rejected all suggestions for an extraordinary congress but had even managed to postpone the scheduled congress by a year (the Third PZPR Congress took place in 1959 instead of 1958).

It was becoming increasingly obvious that Solidarity would not allow itself to become absorbed into the system. The union was growing in strength; by the end of 1980, it had roughly nine million members—some 54 percent of all those employed in the socialized sector and about 28 percent of the entire adult population. Solidarity provided an umbrella for efforts to organize other social groups: in addition to those already mentioned, people engaged in small-scale handicrafts had formed their own union; Solidarity was forming a section for retirees; efforts were under way to organize a trade union for civilian employees in the Ministry of Internal Affairs; and in December 1980 committees in defense of prisoners of conscience began springing up all over the country. At the end of January 1981 activists involved in the union press held their first conference, which established the Solidarity Press Agency, thereby giving additional impetus to the already rapid development of newspapers and other publications appearing beyond the reach of the censors. Factory commissions in the larger enterprises had access to a telephone and telex network, which ensured reasonable distribution of internal information. During the "December crisis" a few activists whose role appeared somewhat ambiguous were removed from the union's regional organizations (one such person was Jarosław Sienkiewicz in Silesia).

After a lengthy debate in mid-February Solidarity issued a preliminary draft program, which served to consolidate the movement and gave it a new political significance. The document was characterized by a certain ideological eclecticism, with references to "the best traditions of the nation, Christian ethical principles, the political challenge of democracy, and socialist social thought," but it also stated forcefully that there could be no economic reform without changes in the political system. The draft called for changes to the electoral law and for new elections to the national councils to be held in 1981. It declared unequivocally that "the only possibility open to us is to move forward, toward a complete renewal of the country." The union retained its cohesion despite continuing internal conflicts, some of them based on personal ambitions and some of them provoked or nurtured by the authorities (attempting to divide "healthy worker tendencies" from "antisocialist elements"). It was seen by its party opponents as a tightly knit organization, highly disciplined and subordinated to its central leadership. While this was an exaggerated view, a number of factors did foster unity within Solidarity. One of these was the unassailable authority of Wałęsa.

Wałęsa's position was further enhanced when he, together with a Solidarity delegation, was granted an audience by Pope John Paul II (15 January) and then met twice with Cardinal Wyszyński (19 January and 6 February). Although the church did not encourage radical actions or demands, it was nonetheless unambiguous in its support for the union and spoke out firmly in favor of recognizing the independent peasant union (in Cardinal Wyszyński's sermon of 2 February, for example). Playing the role of intermediary, as it did during the Beskid strike, the episcopate strengthened its own position vis-à-vis the party-state leadership, while simultaneously acquiring prestige in the eyes of all those who supported Solidarity but wanted the union to avoid any action that might lead to physical confrontation.

While independent groups grew in strength, the government suffered a parallel lost of authority, as it was blamed for delays in implementing the agreements, for provoking local conflicts, and above all perhaps, for the drastically worsening economic situation. Industrial output was declining rapidly, partly as a result of the strikes during the second half of 1980, and a poor harvest had reduced agricultural production by nearly 10 percent. Given that the total wage fund had increased by roughly 13 percent, the inevitable result was empty shelves in stores that had long been poorly supplied. There were shortages of industrial goods, which increasingly were to be had only on payment of a bribe, as well as foodstuffs. Standing in line became a daily (and sometimes all-night) event, and by the afternoon it was usually hard to find milk, cheese, and bread, let alone meat. There were increasing public demands for the introduction of rationing.

The party leadership decided that the state administration needed to be strengthened, especially as some people at the top of the party were beginning to entertain apocalyptic visions of the way the situation was developing. At a meeting of the Politburo on 7 February, Kania said: "Perhaps a catastrophe really is approaching, forcing us into a situation where our neighbor will come to our aid. [It is a question of] creating a situation here that will be the beginning of a major upheaval in the world." Although the state of social consciousness by no means suggested that political programs calling for a complete change in the system would gain widespread public support, Kania's fears were not totally groundless: just under ten years later it would turn out that Solidarity was one of the levers that had uprooted the system. In that sense, "a major upheaval in the world" really had begun, although its mechanism was not the one that the leadership feared—Poland's neighbor left the party to face Solidarity alone.

The decisions taken by the ruling group were atypical for the system of real socialism: on 11 February the Sejm dismissed the colorless Józef Pińkowski from his position as prime minister, appointing in his place General Wojciech Jaruzelski, who retained his defense ministry portfolio. A week later General Michał Janiszewski was appointed head of the Council of Ministers' Administrative Office, an important position that involved supervision of the regional administration. Gradually the state administration underwent what amounted to a process of militarization: by the summer of

1981 General Jaruzelski's cabinet contained three other generals who held ministerial positions, while two more held the position of deputy minister in "civilian" departments. General Jaruzelski proved to be the strong man of the regime. This was the result of his personal characteristics, which at that time were known only to a small group within the leadership, and the force that he represented as the long-standing head of the army, a highly disciplined institution that also enjoyed considerable social prestige.

Both Solidarity and the broader public reacted positively to General Jaruzelski's appointment as government leader. Party officials, nearly all of them in favor of taking a hard line in dealing with the enemy, were also reassured—and spurred on to increased activity. The prime minister called for "ninety days of calm," and in mid-February the main areas of strike activity did indeed quiet down. The PZPR delegation to the Twenty-Sixth CPSU Congress (23 February–3 March) had to listen to many strong words regarding the situation in Poland (the communiqué issued after bilateral discussions referred to "the existence of anarchy and chaos"), but the Soviet leaders again assured their Polish colleagues, as they had done four months earlier, that they would not invade Poland without their agreement.

It seemed as if there really would be a period of relative calm. On 10 March Wałęsa and Jaruzelski held a meeting. Negotiations concerning the introduction of meat rationing were completed (the decision was announced on 27 February and was to take effect on 1 April), new laws on censorship and trade unions were being debated, and a commission was in the process of compiling a report on the state of the economy and proposals for economic reform. On the other hand, the issue of the independent peasant organization continued to be a major source of ongoing conflict, and its founders decided, undoubtedly with the assent of Cardinal Wyszyński, to present the authorities with a fait accompli: on 13 February the three main groups of peasant activists, meeting in Bydgoszcz, reached an agreement, and on 8–9 March a conference in Poznań formally established the Independent, Self-Governing Solidarity Trade Union of Individual Farmers (known as Rural Solidarity) and elected a young activist, Jan Kułaj, as its chairman.

Although the situation in the country was far from calm, and everyday life was becoming ever more difficult, the sudden escalation in tension took most people by surprise. On 16 March a group of farmers demanding the registration of Rural Solidarity occupied the premises of the ZSL's Provincial Committee in Bydgoszcz and began a sit-in strike. On the same day Warsaw Pact exercises, scheduled to last ten days and code-named Soyuz

81, began in Poland. On 19 March, at a meeting of the provincial national council in Bydgoszcz, members of the council presidium provoked a conflict with a delegation of local Solidarity activists who had been invited to take part in the meeting. As a result of intervention by the police (including special units), three members of the delegation were badly beaten, among them Jan Rulewski, Solidarity regional chairman and a member of the KKP presidium. In a communiqué published on 20 March the KKP declared the police action to be "a clear provocation directed against the government of Prime Minister Jaruzelski," but it also considered the attack to be aimed at the union and ordered a strike alert.

A war of nerves broke out between Solidarity and the authorities, who stubbornly clung to the line that "law-enforcement agencies . . . acted in accordance with the law." While representatives of the KKP and the government were engaging in more or less confidential talks, and efforts to mediate were being undertaken by Cardinal Wyszyński (his appeal of 22 March, his meeting with the prime minister on 26 March and with Wałęsa on 28 March) and by groups of intellectuals, Solidarity was mobilizing. For two days (23–24 March) the KKP engaged in heated discussion, with many speakers calling for an open-ended general strike and others (most notably KKP advisers Jan Olszewski and Władysław Siła-Nowicki) warning that the union could be putting itself in "mortal danger." The KKP finally decided to call a four-hour general strike on 27 March; in the event that the union's demands were not met, an open-ended general strike would begin on 31 March. On the day the KKP meeting came to an end, an official communiqué announced that the Soyuz 81 exercises would be prolonged indefinitely.

The strike of 27 March was widely perceived as an impressive success, not only in terms of its scope and the accompanying intensive propaganda campaign, but also because of the high level of discipline among the strikers. The Soviet press escalated its attacks on Solidarity, an example that was immediately followed by the media in the rest of the Warsaw Pact. The Soviet Army's western military districts and the units stationed in Poland and the GDR had already been in a state of higher combat readiness for several months. In the United States, the Departments of State and Defense now warned Moscow, as they had done in December, against military intervention. On the day of the strike General Jaruzelski signed a number of documents setting out the procedures to be followed in the event of a final test of strength, including a text titled "The Guiding Principle in the Imposition of Martial Law."

Solidarity had put the PZPR leadership in an awkward position by linking short-term demands (punishment of those guilty of events in Bydgoszcz) with strategic issues: guaranteed security for all union members, union access to the mass media, and the registration of the farmers' union. At a meeting of the Politburo (24 March), Kania noted that "agreement to register the union today means agreement to elections to the Sejm tomorrow, in other words, a peaceful finale to the seizure of power." The leadership was also alarmed by the fact that massive numbers of party members had taken part in the warning strike and dozens of party organizations had expressed support for Solidarity's demands. The atmosphere in the country was like that on the eve of a decisive battle. The entire apparatus of the Ministry of Internal Affairs was placed on full alert, and the evening television news program frequently showed pictures of the continuing military exercises. Workers prepared to occupy their factories for an unspecified period of time, collecting blankets, food, and medical supplies (even supplies needed to treat any wounded). Telex machines were churning out information and recommendations, every piece of printing equipment at the disposal of Solidarity's regional and factory organizations was pressed into service, and slogans and images of the three activists beaten in Bydgoszcz were pasted the length of city streets across the country. A Central Committee meeting on 29 March concluded with the publication of a toughly worded communiqué. In discussions with union representatives, government officials implied that military action would be inevitable if the general strike went ahead.

On the afternoon of 30 March, the day before the strike was to begin, negotiators for the two sides began their final round of talks. On the evening television news KKP deputy chairman Andrzej Gwiazda, one of the most radical Solidarity leaders, read a communiqué announcing that an agreement had been reached and calling off the strike. The government admitted that the conduct of those in charge of the Bydgoszcz national council meeting had violated "binding legal regulations," expressed regret at the beating of the three activists, announced that those guilty would be prosecuted, and committed itself to speeding up work on the trade union bill and to "avoiding conflicts" over the issue of the farmers' union, which meant, in practice, agreement to the official registration of Rural Solidarity.

For the second time in seven months a major conflict between a large part of society and the party-state leadership ended in a compromise. The first was known as the "August agreement"; and the compromise of 1981 was known, rather pejoratively, as the "Warsaw concession." Although both events were accompanied by a natural sense of relief, there was a wide-spread perception that there were crucial differences between them. After August the strikers and their supporters had an overwhelming sense of victory, while the country's leaders felt they had done their duty by avoiding a total national tragedy. After 30 March many Solidarity members felt the union had not taken advantage of the situation and had agreed to a "rotten compromise" that would only prolong the stalemate in which the country was mired and would put the union on the defensive. Within the state and party leadership a fierce internal struggle flared up, the attack being led by those in the party who advocated a confrontation to destroy the "creeping counterrevolution" once and for all.

MUSTERING THE TROOPS

Crisis erupted first in Solidarity. After a stormy two-day debate (31 March–1 April), the National Commission declared the 30 March statement to be "a preliminary agreement, providing the basis for negotiations with the government," but a crisis of confidence in the union chairman and his advisers was plainly visible. Solidarity's press spokesman, Karol Modzelewski, resigned in protest; Andrzej Gwiazda resigned as deputy chairman; and Andrzej Celiński, Wałęsa's closest political associate, was ousted from his position as KKP secretary. Wałęsa and the other participants in the negotiations were accused of having violated democratic principles and of failing to respect decisions of the KKP, which had passed a resolution on 24 March stating that the strike could be called off only by a decision of the full commission. Attitude toward the "concession" became a major factor in the round of general membership meetings that began on 26 April to elect the union's first regular decision-making bodies as well as delegates to the national congress. At many meetings the dominant mood was radical, and there were bitter conflicts between individuals and groups supporting one line or another. The election procedures dragged on, partly because of the large number of candidates and the policy of subjecting them to a public "interrogation," which raised the temperature of the meetings considerably. While the former leaders generally managed to defend themselves, the merciless electoral struggle intensified existing divisions.

The flames were fanned by the authorities' visible unwillingness to implement the agreement signed on 30 March, apart from the registration of Rural Solidarity (12 May). The "Bydgoszcz affair" was the subject of increasingly blatant evasions, and no agreement was reached on the question of access to the media. Accusations of failure were leveled at advisers, negotiators, and Wałęsa. Despite these intense disputes, however, no clear-cut factions emerged to destabilize the union or cause it to split.

One consolidating factor was, without doubt, the presence of an exceptionally strong opponent, an opponent shared by every tendency in the union; another was the union's decentralized structure. From the very beginning, Solidarity activists had displayed a propensity for radical debates followed by moderate decisions. The Bydgoszcz conflict, however, became one of several factors that served as a catalyst for opinions and proposals that went further and further in the direction of demanding fundamental changes in the whole political system. A group that was not part of Solidarity's statutory decision-making structure was becoming increasingly active. The Network of Organizations in Leading Factories (the Network), which was formally established on 17 March and brought together more than a dozen of Solidarity's largest factory-level organizations from across the country, began to argue forcefully that workers' self-management committees should take over factory management. The group even tried to organize a Polish Labor Party (PPP), whose first documents were distributed in May. The PPP assumed that, after changes to the electoral law, it would win a democratic election (fulfilling Kania's bleak projections of early March). The committees in defense of political prisoners began to expand their activities and held their first national conference on 9 May. On 25 May marches (of varying size) in defense of political prisoners were organized all over the country, and the movement received additional impetus from the trial of Moczulski and three other KPN leaders, which opened on 15 June. The demonstrations of 25 May were the first street demonstrations (apart from the so-called white marches following the attack on the pope) organized by Solidarity and its supporters.

There was now a proliferation of political parties and groups—from the Polish Communist Party–Proletariat, to the fascist Polish Union of National Community, led by Bolesław Tejkowski—but most were of little significance, with a purely local following and quaint political programs. On the other hand, independent publishing of both periodicals and books (largely pamphlets) was developing rapidly. These provided a forum for debate on the state of the country and (more rarely) visions of the future, and for attacks on the political system and its leaders at their weakest point—their efforts to claim legitimacy on the basis of the past. The party leadership watched with growing alarm the battle to fill in the "blank pages" in Poland's recent history and to revive the traditions associated with the great public figures and political tendencies of the Second Republic, a battle that now raged far and wide.

Each Solidarity regional body had established Workers' Universities, and these spent far more time on lectures, discussions, and publications devoted to historical subjects than on training people to run a trade union. The topics most frequently requested by those who organized and attended the lectures included the story of those who died in the East during 1939–45, the Katyn massacre, the history of the Home Army (especially in the eastern borderlands), the kidnapping of the underground leaders (and their trial in Moscow), the campaign of terror waged by the security apparatus against the legal opposition during 1945–47, the partisans and the underground struggle for independence, and the mysterious history of the PPR during the occupation (the death of Marceli Nowotko). The fifth anniversary of the strikes in Radom and Ursus and the twenty-fifth anniversary of the blood-shed in Poznań were commemorated not only by demonstrations and the erection of monuments but also by publications that tried to answer questions about the functioning of the political system and personal responsibility.

The commemoration of the Radom-Ursus anniversary involved direct references to the emergence of KOR, and together with the anniversary of the March 1968 events, reminded people of the ideological roots of what had become one of the most influential and active tendencies in public life. Solidarity displayed a characteristic ambivalence toward the May Day holiday. The union leadership gave the regions and factory committees a free rein, and in some towns the PZPR authorities tried to persuade Solidarity activists to organize a joint parade. Virtually everywhere Solidarity refused to take part, and in some places the union revived an old working-class tradition by organizing picnics. Solidarity preferred to celebrate the 3 May anniversary of Poland's constitution of 1792, a holiday that the authorities had "awarded" to the Democratic Party.

The breakdown of taboos and prohibitions in the field of culture also played a major role in shaping attitudes. Cinemas began showing the films that the censors had consigned to the shelves. It was a major event when the Golden Palm, the most prestigious prize at the Cannes Film Festival, was awarded to Andrzej Wajda's *Man of Iron,* which dealt with the formation of the Free Trade Unions and the August strikes. On 27 July, two months after the prize was awarded, the film had its triumphal premiere at home and finally made its way to cinema screens across the country. Censored periodicals began referring to émigré literature, giving it particular prominence during a visit to Poland (5–19 June) by Czesław Miłosz, whose work had been banned in Poland until 1980, when he was awarded the Nobel Prize for Literature. During his visit, Miłosz met with workers at the Gdańsk Shipyard. Other creative associations followed journalists and writers in holding elections to their decision-making bodies, and on 31 July, after months of discussion and negotiation, the Sejm passed a law on censorship. Its provisions included one that allowed censorship decisions to be appealed in the courts, but few people actually bothered to do so.

The education authorities were forced to make changes to history and literature programs. Solidarity factory commissions created union libraries, consisting mainly of uncensored books and periodicals. Stalls selling the same kind of literature were to be found in Solidarity's regional offices, in the larger factories, and in colleges and universities. *Tygodnik Solidarności* (Solidarity Weekly), which was edited by Tadeusz Mazowiecki and began publication on 3 April with a circulation of half a million, devoted considerable space to the recent past. Some censored periodicals (especially weeklies and monthlies), as well as the entire PAX press, adopted the new tone, a process that was facilitated by the disruption of the censorship process and the party leadership's efforts not to be left behind. The only limits that remained in place were those concerning discussion of the Soviet Union's relations with Poland and the Poles. The effect of all this was to arouse broad groups of the population and increase their mistrust—and even hatred—of the country's communist rulers. References to past struggles for independence (Józef Piłsudski, the 1920 battle for Warsaw) and the even more obvious efforts to fill in the blank pages in the history of the years 1939–45 had strong anti-Soviet connotations. Discussion also touched on the Brezhnev doctrine of "limited sovereignty," an issue that was particularly topical in light of the events of late November and early December 1980 and during the period of the Bydgoszcz crisis.

Another problem was the drastic worsening of market supplies, and it became increasingly difficult to obtain the goods that were now added to the ration books: on 22 April butter, flour, rice, and grits were added to the list; on 1 June—powdered milk, semolina, and detergent for baby clothes. In many regions alcohol and cigarettes were in short supply. Standing in line gave rise to its own subculture, one that combined collective condemnation of the party-state leadership with aggression toward everyone else in the line. The reason for the drop in output was not so much strikes as slackness in the whole management system and difficulties in obtaining inputs, which also affected enterprises dependent on imported components or raw materials. The traditional incentives used by the system (labor competition, for example) had long lost their motivational force, and efforts to replace them with such measures as preferential treatment in the purchase of foodstuffs or industrial goods generally met with an unenthusiastic or hostile response. This was the situation, for example, after the introduction on 11 April of "motivational" food supplies for miners willing to work on Saturdays.

Speculation became increasingly widespread and now included a wide range of food items. After the announcement (23 July) of a reduction in the meat ration and an increase in food prices, many Solidarity regions not only issued verbal protests but also promised street demonstrations. The high point of these protests was the "hunger march" by women and children in Łódź on 30 July. The National Commission issued a statement (on 26 July), in which it declared: "Our union faces no issue more important than guaranteeing the elementary living conditions of the nation."

Emotions were inflamed by recurring cases of legal violations—and physical abuse—on the part of the police; government propaganda painted a stark picture of collapsing public order and safety. This was a double-edged sword, as it led people to repeat demands for "the restoration of order" and it reduced the authority of the country's leaders. The prestige of official institutions, except for the army, continued to fall. According to an official survey carried out in June 1981 by the Center for Public Opinion Research, 24 percent of respondents expressed confidence in the government, barely 6 percent—in the PZPR Central Committee, and 62 percent—in Solidarity. Public opinion was variously affected by two major events—the attack on Pope John Paul II (on 13 May), who narrowly escaped death, and the death of Cardinal Wyszyński (on 28 May). On the one hand, they led many people to focus on concern for the pope and mourning for the Primate of the Millennium; on the other hand, they intensified fears that the church might not be strong enough, should the need arise, to mediate between the leadership and society or to take its side should the communists initiate a confrontation.

Many people were on edge, either because of political events or because of difficult living conditions. Solidarity leaders found it hard to control the behavior and attitudes of union members and sympathizers. Despite re-

429

peated radical statements—usually on the part of mid-level union activists—the dominant opinion was that the movement needed to stick to the principle of "self-limiting revolution," especially in regard to any demands and actions that might provide Moscow with a pretext for intervening. Nevertheless, pressure was increasing in many circles for a change in the system of economic management and distribution. The idea of workers' self-management was gaining in popularity, as was the principle of enterprise independence, together with demands for social control over economic decision making (including control over the food sector), although only the last was fully understood and widely supported, as evidenced, for example, by the hunger marches.

Many union leaders and activists, especially at the regional and factory levels, were convinced that society was "in revolt" against the system, a belief that reinforced their sense of strength. They constantly referred to society and the authorities in terms of opposition between "them and us," and this went beyond the level of propaganda to become viewed as an established fact to be taken as the basis for predictions and plans. In reality, as public opinion surveys indicated, the opposition movement was a powerful force but one that involved the majority of society, not the whole of it. It was, moreover, highly differentiated, and different groups often had quite contradictory motives for their opposition. Nevertheless, the legitimacy of the party-state leadership continued to unravel.

For its part, the leadership was for several months in a state of crisis. The signing of the "Warsaw concession" and the conclusion of the Soyuz 81 exercises did not mean that external pressure on the Kania-Jaruzelski team had now lessened. Soviet propaganda (and that of Czechoslovakia and the GDR) added a new element to the now customary attacks on Solidarity and other manifestations of counterrevolution. At the end of March *Rude Pravo* declared that dangerous "revisionist tendencies" existed within the PZPR and that these had found "a common language with extremists in Solidarity." On 2 April TASS criticized the Warsaw party organization for not having responded effectively to the counterrevolutionaries at Warsaw University. The Bydgoszcz events had, in fact, helped to broaden and strengthen reformist tendencies inside the ruling party; from the ideological point of view this development could be considered just as dangerous as the openly anticommunist opinions voiced by Solidarity. On 15 April the party's "horizontal structures" held a national conference, attended by roughly 750 delegates from fourteen provinces. They demanded not only changes in the leadership but also the abolition of censorship and guarantees that democratic principles would be respected in the selection of delegates to the forthcoming extraordinary party congress and during the course of the congress itself. The division that was plainly visible within the broader society—and presented such a danger to the leadership—had replicated itself within the "leading force."

The depth of this division became particularly evident when the most hard-line communists began to organize. On 8 May a hitherto little-known group, which called itself the Grunwald Patriotic Organization (after the site of a Polish victory over the Teutonic Order in 1410), made its public debut with a rally outside the headquarters of the former Ministry of Public Security, at which it revealed itself to be a "national communist" grouping, whose slogans combined elements of chauvinism (largely anti-Semitism) and populism with references to Marxism-Leninism. With the encouragement of the group, some members of the top party leadership—including Stefan Olszowski, Tadeusz Grabski, and Stanisław Kociołek—established a weekly, titled *Rzeczywistość* (Reality), the first issue of which appeared in kiosks on 21 May, a new addition to a whole string of hard-line publications advancing a view of the world essentially close to that of the Grunwald group. On 28 May the rickety Bolesław Bierut club, active in party circles in Silesia, renamed itself the Katowice Party Forum and issued a declaration that was greeted with great enthusiasm by TASS. In Moscow's opinion, the Forum was the first group in Poland to provide "a genuinely Marxist-Leninist analysis of the situation." Several other groups of party members followed in the footsteps of the Silesian communists. Since the summer of 1980 the central party and military press had not deviated an inch from a hard-line position, but they now began publishing a growing number of statements directed not just against Solidarity and associated intellectual circles but also against revisionists and reformers in the party itself. Publications such as *Polityka*, whose long-time former editor, now deputy prime minister, Mieczysław F. Rakowski, was considered the leader of the liberal wing of the party elite, were suddenly called to account by the party apparatus. The same was true of the Warsaw-based weekly, *Kultura*.

The emergence of organized and active groups of "true Marxist-Leninists" coincided (not accidentally) with a sudden intensification of Moscow's attacks on the governing tandem in Poland. An internal document issued by the CPSU Politburo on 16 April stated that "the PZPR has to a large extent lost control of the processes taking place in society" and that some party organizations were controlled by "opportunist elements." On 5 June the CPSU Central Committee sent a letter to its Polish counterpart; this in itself was something of an event since such communications were usually handled at Politburo level (or by first secretaries). The letter declared that the PZPR had "given way, step by step, to the pressure of domestic counterrevolution," which had "brought the country to a critical point." The fact that the Soviet leadership addressed its assessment to the entire Central Committee was seen as signaling its consent to—or encouragement of—an attack on Kania. This seemed all the more likely in that the contents of the letter were rapidly leaked (not without assistance from the Soviet ambassador) to the public. The atmosphere in the party and in intellectual circles became extremely tense, the "horizontal structures" tried to mobilize their supporters, and a group of twenty-four intellectuals issued a declaration rejecting the assertion that "influential groups" in Poland were "aiming to break off binding alliances."

After heated debates within the top leadership and in the absence of an agreed position, the Central Committee met in plenary session on 9–10 June. The meeting was the scene of ferocious attacks on Kania. Grabski simply asked: "Are the current members of the Politburo, under the leadership of . . . Comrade Kania, capable of leading the country out of the crisis?" He answered the question himself: "I don't see any such possibility," and then went on to demand that the committee approve a vote of no confidence in the first secretary. During a break in the deliberations, the Politburo held an emergency meeting at which a number of people, including Wojciech Jaruzelski, Mieczysław Moczar, and Mieczysław Jagielski, expressed their readiness to resign. In the end, however, it was agreed that, given the current situation and in light of the approaching congress, it was vital that the leadership remain united. The existence of a strong opponent had a similar effect as it had on Solidarity; both sides were condemned to keep to a minimum any personnel changes that might lead to destabilization.

Kania's power derived not only from his position as first secretary, but also from the fact that he enjoyed the full support of General Jaruzelski—and hence the army. Moreover, Jaruzelski had already positioned some of his people in the security apparatus and internal affairs ministry: more than a month earlier General Czesław Kiszczak, head of military counterintelligence, had been appointed chairman of the government Coordinating Commission for Law Enforcement, Legality, and Public Order. In the final analysis Kania was able to defend his position as well as his policy of defeat-ing the party's opponent "through political confrontation, confrontation car-ried out under our own strength." At a meeting of the Central Committee Secretariat the day after the Central Committee plenum, Kania even stated that "this psychosis [namely, the CPSU letter and the debate at the plenum] may bring positive results," since the two things "have created a climate that is advantageous in a situation of danger." Doubtless he had in mind both the consolidation of the party and the "intimidation" of public opin-ion—and the Solidarity leadership—that could result from the prospect of hard-liners seizing control of the party. The success of Kania and Jaruzelski in fending off attack by no means signified success for the "horizontal struc-tures" or any other reformist group. Rather the opposite: out of fear of his own orthodox wing and Moscow, Kania had to prevent the advocates of far-reaching change from taking part in the congress. This was not a difficult task, since the middle and lower rungs of the party apparatus held the reins firmly in their hands. While considerable changes in personnel at all levels had taken place since August 1980, those who had been newly promoted, even those who had come from outside the full-time apparatus, differed lit-tle in mentality and opinions from their predecessors. The situation was similar in the case of congress delegates, and in the party as a whole the role of "the barons," the first secretaries of large provincial organizations, had grown. The Ninth Extraordinary Congress took place on 14–20 July. Nearly two thousand delegates, representing about 2.8 million members, took part. Since the summer of 1980 the party had lost roughly 300,000 members, and members were still leaving (and being expelled from) the organization. The proportion of manual workers and young people in the membership was declining, while the proportion of retirees was increasing. The number of full-time party officials was also growing, and now exceeded 19,000—roughly one apparatchik for every 150 members.

In contrast to all such previous events, the congress took place in a fe-verish atmosphere of sharp polemics and personal attacks, and the Polit-buro had difficulty in controlling the proceedings. The delegates were new people but by no means advocates of change; they generally viewed with disfavor all well-known members of the party elite, regardless of their posi-tion on the main issue dividing the organization. Many activists from both the hard-line and liberal wing failed to win election to the Central Commit-tee. Kania won reelection quite easily but had considerable difficulty in selecting people for the Politburo and Central Committee Secretariat from among the relatively unknown and undistinguished members of the party's highest collective body.

The congress resolutions reflected the dominance of the "centrists," under the banner of the first secretary. Declarations about renewal and change concluded with the adoption of half-hearted measures, and the language of the official documents remained within a well-established format: the resolution setting out the party's program bore the title "A Program to Develop Socialist Democracy and Strengthen the Leading Role of the PZPR in Building Socialism and Stabilizing the Socioeconomic Situation of the Country." Official pronouncements emphasized that the congress had approved "the line of seeking agreement," but this was interpreted in terms of the same old story—Solidarity was supposed to get rid of its extremists and become part of the system on conditions laid down by the communists. Nor was anything new said on economic issues. All this meant, however, that the PZPR had survived an internal crisis and had once more become a controllable mechanism, although it was clear that the days when the first secretary had total control of the organization had not yet returned.

In any event, on 20 July Kania and his closest associate, General Jaruzelski, left the Congress Hall in Warsaw's Palace of Culture and Science in a stronger position than when they had entered it six days earlier. They soon gained total control of the crucial Ministry of Internal Affairs, on 31 July appointing General Kiszczak its head, and they rapidly expanded their intelligence staff and network of informers. Although preparations for the imposition of martial law had been under way since at least the early fall of 1980—as Kania frequently informed high-ranking PZPR members—it was obvious that such a step would require support in the form of a disciplined and obedient party. By the time the congress was over, this condition had essentially been fulfilled.

The public followed the congress debates on radio and television with interest but without much emotion. Most people concentrated on coping with everyday problems and did not expect the congress to achieve a major breakthrough. Others focused on Solidarity's election campaign and the endless battle of wills with the government and local authorities. Negotiations were going nowhere because Solidarity had no intention of submitting to control by the communists, and the latter were tenacious in blocking any step that might weaken the system or lead to what they called its "dismantling." The result was an enormous number of conflicts.

434

The best known of these included the blockade of Warsaw's main intersection by a column of buses and trucks, the breaking off of talks during the night of 5–6 August, and the "days without newspapers" (19–20 August), when the daily papers were neither printed nor distributed. The date of the First National Congress of Solidarity Delegates was approaching. While union members had high expectations of this event, the party leadership and apparatus took an a priori negative, or at best skeptical, view. At least two decisions announced before the congress indicated that the authorities were preparing a major political confrontation: on 21 August Jerzy Urban, a nonparty, talented journalist who took pride in his cynicism, was appointed government press spokesman; on 2 September the provincial prosecutor in Bydgoszcz announced that it had proved impossible to identify those responsible for the beatings of 19 March and that the investigation would therefore be discontinued.

The Solidarity congress began in the solemn atmosphere of a mass celebrated by Cardinal Wyszyński's successor, Cardinal Józef Glemp. The congress program called for deliberations to take place in two rounds—during 5–10 September and 26 September–7 October—in the massive sports arena in Oliwa, near Gdańsk. Nearly 9.5 million Solidarity members were represented by nearly nine hundred delegates from thirty-eight regions. The atmosphere was tense, partly because of internal conflicts and partly because of considerable distrust of the union elite, which various groups had accused of manipulation. Tedious procedural and formal disputes dragged on for hours, but outside the hall the atmosphere was that of a festive picnic and popular holiday. The proceedings were not even dampened by the fact that the day before the congress opened, military exercises, code-named Zapad 81, began across the whole of the southern Baltic, in Belorussia, Lithuania, and the Kaliningrad district. According to NATO these were the largest exercises the Soviet Army had conducted since 1945. From the beach in Oliwa one could see warships on the horizon. Despite this hostile patrol, the congress proceeded as planned. A whole range of resolutions dealing with issues of varying degrees of importance were adopted, and thirteen working groups were established, together with a Program Commission charged with compiling a list of the proposals produced by the groups. The most important decisions dealt with workers' self-management, but the greatest furor—and applause in the hall—was caused by the "Message to the Working People of Eastern Europe," adopted on 8 September. The declaration expressed support for those "who have decided to enter the difficult path of struggle for a free trade union movement" and the hope that "before long your representatives and ours will be able to meet to exchange union experience." Many members of the union leadership were surprised and taken aback by the "Message," but the audience in the main body of the hall overwhelmingly approved it. What seemed to many people at the time to be political adventurism, an "infantile" step, or an outright provocation acquired a symbolic dimension ten years later. Although trade unions akin to Solidarity did not emerge anywhere else in Eastern Europe, the Polish experience became a fundamental element in breaking the grip of real communism across the entire region.

On 10 September TASS described the first round of the congress as "an antisocialist and anti-Soviet orgy" and stated—in a thinly veiled threat—that it had given rise to "a growing wave of indignation." Indeed, government propaganda launched a particularly strong attack against the "Message," the congress, and Solidarity as a whole. On 16 September the Politburo issued a statement to the effect that it considered the agreement of August 1980 to have been violated and "replaced with a program of political opposition that conflicts with the vital interests of the nation and the state." Two days later the Central Committee issued a declaration stating that it expected the leadership to take "decisive and radical steps." Apart from these statements, however, there were no outward signs of change. The government took yet more decisions that Solidarity regarded as provocations (for example, the unpublished resolution no. 199 that provided for high payments to miners who worked on free Saturdays), but they were actually taken in the attempt to salvage the economy without introducing any major changes in the system of management. The authorities provoked a stir when they forcibly removed from a Warsaw sports arena the organizers of the Police Trade Union, who were planning a protest strike. Independent intellectuals tried—as usual—to calm things down; the Joint Government-Episcopate Commission met; and the Sejm's decision to approve a bill on workers' self-management and industrial enterprises also helped calm the atmosphere.

The second round of the congress proceeded more efficiently, although much time was taken up by the drawn-out elections to the National Commission and by debate over the union program. On 28 September Professor Edward Lipiński, the elder statesman of KOR, read a statement concerning the cessation of activity on the part of the organization (which had not actually functioned for the past year). During discussion of a motion urging the congress to express its thanks to KOR and other groups of the democratic opposition, a sharp political dispute erupted, which revealed the depth of the divisions not only within Solidarity, where anti-KOR and anti-intelligentsia sentiments were being voiced with growing frequency, but also within the opposition as a whole. The previous day people associated with ROPCiO, RMP, and a loose grouping led by Antoni Macierewicz had established the Club in the Service of Independence, a quasi-political party with a right-wing-independence orientation. But for most delegates, not to mention most union members, these were minor issues that in no way affected the significance of the congress.

The congress adopted a wide-ranging program titled "The Self-Governing Republic," a title that accurately reflected its general thrust. In contrast to the draft program drawn up in February, the program adopted at the congress made not a single reference to socialist tradition, even though the very notion of self-management was strongly rooted in some trends in non-Marxist socialism of the turn of the century. Emotions ran high during the election for the post of Solidarity chairman. With 55 percent of the vote, Lech Wałęsa, the hero of August, easily beat Marian Jurczyk, Jan Rulewski, and Andrzej Gwiazda. Wałęsa's widely anticipated victory confirmed the relatively moderate stance of the majority of delegates, since the other candidates represented political views and programs that were somewhat more radical.

The adoption of the new statute and program, and the election of the union leadership—all of this carried out with scrupulous attention to democratic procedures—gave the organization, almost ten million strong, a legitimacy that could not be undermined by accusations that it was a tool in the hands of a tiny group of anticommunists. The majority of delegates had clearly proclaimed that they were all equally anticommunist.

PREPARING FOR BATTLE

The economic situation became dramatic—even by Comecon standards. Output fell, supply lines fractured, and factories found themselves bartering goods on a daily basis. According to the Central Statistical Office, the cost of living rose 15 percent in the first six months of 1981 alone, and many food items were only available on the private market, where prices were considerably higher than the prices charged in state stores. "How do you say butcher's shop in Japanese?" went a popular joke. "Nagiehaki" was the correct reply, which means "bare hooks" in Polish. Inflationary pressure increased, the excess money supply reaching 300 billion złoties in the spring; deposits in the PKO savings bank also grew, to reach 600 billion złoties by the end of September. This was "hot money," to be thrown into the market the moment any kind of consumer goods appeared in the stores.

People began using U.S. dollars when conducting (and calculating) some private transactions, such as buying an apartment or a car. The country's foreign indebtedness rose, and exports fell. Creditors took an increasingly negative view of government requests for debt rescheduling. Both the government and Solidarity came up with apocalyptic visions of the coming winter—electricity shortages, no central heating, shortages of coke and coal, disruptions in the supply of gas, bread rationing. Some Solidarity factory commissions, with assistance from the farmers' union, distributed potatoes and onions to their members. A growing number of people were going abroad, and camps for Polish refugees in Austria and West Germany were bursting at the seams. The union's regional offices set up special groups that were to spring into action during the expected winter emergencies. In the summer the government had already established the Operational Crisis Group, an emergency group to deal with agriculture, and a body called the Special Commission to Combat Speculation (all of them headed by deputy prime ministers).

Work on economic reform was going nowhere, all progress blocked by ideological fundamentals and external constraints. There was some discussion about "introducing market mechanisms into the socialist economy" and decentralizing administration to give autonomy to industrial enterprises, ideas that had first appeared in 1956–57. Agreeing under pressure to broaden the powers of workers' self-management, the government drastically reduced the number of enterprises that would be affected by the new regulations, thereby salvaging the nomenklatura system. But Solidarity, too, lacked any clear-cut program of the changes it wanted to bring about in the economy, something that became evident during discussion at the union congress. The idea of self-management had the most support; this did not involve breaking with the principles of the socialized economy but rested on the example of Yugoslavia, which seemed to be doing quite well in comparison with the other countries of Eastern Europe. An alternative proposal, drawn up by Stefan Kurowski, also remained within the overall existing economic framework. It called for a rapid restructuring of industry, sharp price increases, and the introduction of a convertible currency, all of which was to be centrally administered.

The basic difference between the government's proposals and those of the union was more political than economic in nature. Solidarity demanded "social control" over the reform process and the whole economy. The union proposed that this be achieved by creating a new body with overall authority over the economy, to be named the Social Council for the National Economy; the introduction of democratic principles and free parliamentary elections would inevitably follow. The PZPR found it impossible, of course, to accept such a program: free elections would mean the end of its rule. The party thus renewed its efforts—at this point without much conviction—to incorporate Solidarity into the network of institutions that it controlled, proposing the formation of a Council of National Understanding, which would actually have been a new version of the Front for National Unity. This proposal was out of the question for Solidarity and the organizations associated with it, since it would have involved their consent to the party continuing its "leading role" and thus to everything remaining as before. A growing number of people realized that the two forces confronting each other—the PZPR and the entire state apparatus and Solidarity and its associated organizations—were preparing for the decisive encounter.

Many people were plainly alarmed at this prospect. Many people also began to step back from the idea that Solidarity offered the only chance for an improvement in the situation, as all the union's actions hitherto had proved ineffective. Public opinion surveys carried out in late fall showed a slight drop in public confidence in the government and the Sejm, but a perceptible increase in confidence in the Central Committee (from 6 to 12 percent) and a sharp drop in support for Solidarity—from 62 percent in June to 41 percent. The union leadership appeared to have much less control than previously over the movement as a whole, and its more active members, especially the regional leaders, were becoming more radical. One idea that was becoming more popular was that of an active strike, meaning that the union would take direct control of the management of industrial enterprises. Solidarity also intensified its propaganda campaign demanding access to the official mass media, which was seen as the most fundamental of all the union's demands. The party, of course, viewed the campaign as an attempt to extort from it one of the main attributes of power.

In some factories Solidarity began campaigning to get the party organization removed from the premises. Nationwide opinion surveys indicated that roughly 60 percent of the population (and nearly 50 percent of PZPR members) favored a reduction in the role of the party. The exodus from the organization continued, with a further 200,000–300,000 members having left since the ninth congress. The general sense of unease was heightened by the activity of the independent peasant and student organizations, which found themselves in a worse situation than Solidarity, as the authorities did not consider them partners with whom they needed to negotiate (or pretend to do so). Dozens of "mini-parties" were engaged in feverish activity, although they found little support among either the broader society or Solidarity activists. The attempt to channel growing unrest into a one-hour warning strike on 28 October showed that Solidarity still had an impressive capacity to mobilize its supporters, but the atmosphere of the strike was quite different from what it had been in March.

Although the party leadership was under no illusion that the Solidarity congress might result in the union laying down its arms, once the union delegates had left Oliwa it began preparing for the final showdown. The turning point came with the appointment of a new first secretary. At a three-day meeting of the Central Committee (16–18 October) Stanisław Kania tendered his resignation, which was accepted by a vote of 104 to 79. As the speakers at the meeting made clear, the motives were fairly obvious: "the party needs a demonstration of strength," "the party wants a change of course," "it rejects the search for an agreement," "everyone in the Politburo in favor of extraordinary measures should stay, the others should go," "we are in a revolutionary situation and need to act with revolutionary measures." One such measure suggested was "the assumption of power by the military."

The strategy of procrastination and harassing the enemy had been exhausted. To a certain extent it had fulfilled its role. Kania's successor was General Wojciech Jaruzelski, who received the votes of 180 Central Committee members, with 4 opposed. A meeting of more senior party leaders decided that he should remain as prime minister (and, formally, as defense minister) to ensure speedy and coherent decision making. Ten days later the deputy defense minister, General Florian Siwicki, who was effectively acting minister, was co-opted as a candidate member of the Politburo, while General Tadeusz Dziekan was appointed head of the Central Committee Personnel Department. On 24 October the government issued a communiqué concerning the deployment, initially in rural areas, of Regional Military Operational Groups. A month later their operations were extended to urban areas, in other words, to factories and local administrative institutions. On the last day of the Central Committee plenum in October the Council of

Ministers passed a resolution extending by two months the period of military service for soldiers who were about to return to civilian life. This particular class had been drafted in 1979 and was thus considered by the leadership to be largely immune to "counterrevolutionary" influences. Preparations for the attack on Solidarity were entering their final phase.

In the negotiations between the government and the union, which had been going on virtually nonstop, it was only with the greatest difficulty that the two sides reached agreement on anything, and only in the case of second- or third-rank issues. The meeting between Jaruzelski and Cardinal Glemp (21 October) and between the "Big Three" of Glemp, Jaruzelski, and Wałęsa (4 November) yielded nothing apart from some curt communiqués. Local strikes were erupting all over the country; some of them dragged on, others ended without satisfying either side. The authorities were clearly interested in creating a picture of growing anarchy. On 30 October the presidium of Solidarity's National Commission warned that "protest actions have become spontaneous and unorganized." When one strike died down, another flared up. Shortly after the beginning of the academic year, strikes erupted in the universities, partly over the protracted discussions about a new law on higher education. On 5–6 November a prison riot in Kamieńsko was bloodily suppressed. Rumors were circulating among party officials and activists—as well as employees and officers of the internal affairs ministry—to the effect that Solidarity was drawing up "proscriptive lists" and creating armed bands of thugs. On 30 October the government sent to the Sejm a draft bill dealing with "Extraordinary Measures to Defend the Interests of Citizens and the State." A meeting of the Central Committee on 27–28 November approved a resolution referring to "a direct threat to the existence of the state." On 2 December special units of the Ministry of Internal Affairs conducted a spectacular action, involving a rooftop landing from a helicopter, when they broke up a strike organized by students at the Firefighter Officer Training Academy, who were demanding that the institution be removed from the ministry's jurisdiction. This sent a clear signal that the authorities had moved on from "well-considered administrative methods" to the use of force and also provided an occasion to check the level of preparedness of the troops to be used. The commander of the Warsaw Pact troops, Marshal Kulikov, was visiting one member state after the other, and spent 24–25 November in Poland. On 1–2 December a conference of foreign ministers took place in Budapest, on 1–4 December defense ministers met in Moscow, and on 1–3 December heads of the regions' press agencies convened in Prague. The allied support troops were getting ready for what was about to take place in Poland.

A meeting of the Politburo on 1 December agreed that the situation was "dramatic" and decided to introduce "immediately" a state of alert, involving "forces on duty twenty-four hours a day, communications, and increased patrols," as well as "protection of state and party buildings." Mirosław Milewski, until recently minister of internal affairs and now Central Committee secretary responsible for overseeing the ministry, asked dramatically: "Are we not now actors on a mournful stage?" The PZPR leadership was well aware that to all intents and purposes the party had ceased to exist as a force capable of mobilizing its members or, at the very least, was no longer capable of independent action. Several days later there was even some discussion of whether the organization should be dissolved and "a communist party" created in its place.

At the same Politburo meeting Marian Orzechowski stated: "We have reached the limit." The same could have been said about Solidarity—all its basic demands had been rejected. At an emergency meeting of the KKP presidium on 3 December in Radom there was nothing else to do but to reiterate, yet again, the union's list of demands: cease all attacks on the union, pass the law on trade unions, hold democratic elections to the national councils, establish the Social Council for the National Economy, and give Solidarity access to the mass media. In response to the government's proposal that the Sejm grant it extraordinary powers, Solidarity declared it would order a twenty-four-hour strike in the event such powers were granted and a general strike of unlimited duration should the government actually make use of such authority. Harsh words were uttered, and the official statement adopted by the meeting used the same formulation as the PZPR had used six weeks earlier: "Further talks on the subject of national agreement have become pointless."

The propaganda campaign assumed unprecedented dimensions. Among other things, a security service informer (one of the union's regional chairmen) had secretly recorded the meeting in Radom; extracts were broadcast on the radio. The church called on the Sejm not to pass legislation giving the government extraordinary powers. A conference of Solidarity delegates from the Mazowsze Region decided, after furious debate, to hold a protest rally in Warsaw's Victory Square on 17 December, the anniversary of the 1970 massacre in Gdynia. The decision was taken on 6 December and was subsequently presented by official propaganda as the proverbial straw that broke the camel's back. In fact, the imposition of martial law had been approved by the Politburo the day before, at the same time that Cardinal Glemp was holding his second to last meeting with Wałęsa. The party leaders who gathered in the conference room of the Central Committee building in the center of Warsaw were essentially of one mind. Zbigniew Messner warned that failure to act would mean that "in a few weeks there will be no one left to impose martial law." "Major historical crises," declared Józef Czyrek, "have never been resolved by expanding democracy but by giving extraordinary powers to rulers, by introducing dictatorship." Jaruzelski mournfully and emotionally stated that he was "counting on the workers' class instinct, " and that "it is a terrible, horrible discredit to the party that after thirty-six years in power, we have to defend it with militia [*sic!*] force. But we now have no alternative." The few who were more moderate (Hieronym Kubiak, for example) thought that martial law should be imposed when Solidarity called a general strike. The overwhelming majority, however, favored a preemptive move. The choice of timing was ceded, without discussion, to the general–first secretary–prime minister. Nobody mentioned the allies, who were more than ready to offer assistance if the first blow was unsuccessful. Six months earlier, in this same forum, Mieczysław Moczar had stated: "Poland must disarm its own minefields," adding that "future generations would curse us if our friends had to come to the rescue in their tanks." On 5 December 1981 probably all those involved in the decision shared this belief and were prepared to accept the risk.

The wintry days and evenings were full of tension. On 9 December a small Solidarity delegation, whose members included Wałęsa, met with the primate, who expressed concern over the way the situation was developing and warned that the authorities might act. But what could the union leadership do? Announce its capitulation? Solidarity leaders were aware of the sharp increase in tension, but they assumed that the confrontation would be initiated with the full majesty of the law, in other words, after the Sejm had passed the required legislation. The vision depicted in *Tygodnik Solidarność* on 11 December by Krzysztof Czabański—"tanks at all intersections, police and military patrols swarming the streets"—seemed impossible unless preceded by the appropriate legislative procedures. This was how most people interpreted the rumors about what was called "the state of emergency," the activities of operational groups, and the attack on the firefighters' academy. The visible signs of mobilization on the part of the police were simply viewed as a continuation of the war of nerves that had been going on for more than a year.

On 11 December the Congress of Polish Culture opened in Warsaw. The organizers had invited several government officials to attend the opening ceremony; among those who took part were Politburo member Hieronym Kubiak, Deputy Prime Minister Mieczysław Rakowski, and Minister of Culture Józef Tejchma. The Congress, an event that had been in preparation for several months, was supposed to last three days. The day of the opening, Solidarity's National Commission began a two-day session that was to discuss the proposals put forward at the Radom emergency meeting, which had no formal decision-making power, and make a final decision as to further action by the union. The discussion in Gdańsk was long and heated, chiefly because everyone present realized that they were confronting a total stalemate: "People are determined not to reconcile themselves to the system," said Olszewski, "and the government is not prepared to change it." That had been the situation since at least August 1980. "Up till now," said Wałęsa, "we have only been dealing with small issues, and now we're dealing with issues of unbelievable importance." Most of the speakers took a radical, even reckless, view of how to proceed, even after six advisers representing a broad range of political opinion (Geremek, Macierewicz, Mazowiecki, Olszewski, Siła-Nowicki, Strzelecki) urged the union to stay within the framework of the proposals accepted at Radom. In the end the proposals were adopted and a further decision was made to hold a referendum—nationally or within Solidarity—on "fundamental issues," meaning, among other things, "the ways in which national and regional organs of the state administration wield power." This was followed by a more relaxed discussion of the possible composition of the Social Council for the National Economy, which some of those present viewed as a substitute government.

The twelve-hour meeting, held in the now historic health and safety hall of the Gdańsk Shipyard, took place in a tense atmosphere. Late in the evening on 12 December, when discussion was winding down, some disturbing signals were noted: at 10:30 the telex machine stopped working; half an hour later the telephones went silent. Meanwhile, typists in the Ministry of Defense had been taking dictation from Wiesław Górnicki, recently appointed adviser to the prime minister and for many years one of the best-known journalists in Poland. Górnicki was dictating the text of a speech that his boss would deliver on radio and television first thing in the morning. At exactly midnight Polish television interrupted the broadcast of a film and without comment ceased all further transmission. At half past midnight the National Commission wound up its meeting. Half an hour later members of the Council of State met in extraordinary session in the Belweder Palace to approve the immediate imposition of martial law.

CHAPTER 8

The Long March—War and Peace

"THE TANKS ARE COMING"

At 1:00 A.M. on Sunday, 13 December, members of the Council of State met in the Belweder Palace to pass the decrees concerning martial law. Once a quorum (11 out of 16) had assembled, the hour-and-a-half-long meeting began; at this point, martial law had already been in force de facto across the country for some time. At 3:40 P.M. the previous day a coded message had been sent to all provincial police headquarters ordering the start of the operation, and those military units selected to take part were put on alert. At 11:30 P.M. units belonging to the Ministry of Internal Affairs—special groups, ZOMO detachments, antiterrorist units, groups of security service officials, and forces belonging to the Vistula Defense Units of the Ministry of Internal Affairs—went into action, supported by the army. They shut down all domestic and international telecommunications and took control of all radio and television facilities. Groups of police and security officials were dispatched to thousands of apartments with orders to take into custody the individuals who were to be interned. ZOMO units occupied the offices of Solidarity's regional bodies with orders to destroy communications and printing equipment (or prevent their being used) and to detain any persons found on the premises. Armored and mechanized units set off for transport hubs, highways and major intersections, government buildings, and strategic facilities of various kinds. And embassies. General Jaruzelski and his closest entourage were in the building of the Council of Ministers, where Wiesław Górnicki was putting the finishing touches to the text of the statement to be delivered by the prime minister–first secretary–minister of defense–and chairman of the still secret Military Council of National Salvation (WRON). The Solidarity activists who had been taking part in the National Commission meeting began leaving the shipyard. This was the signal that the forces of law and order, which had been brought to Gdańsk in large numbers, could move into action without having to fear resistance from the assembled leaders of an organization with ten million members. The PZPR provincial first secretary, Tadeusz Fiszbach, had been ordered by party headquarters to talk to Lech Wałęsa and persuade him to go to Warsaw "for discussions with state representatives." Shortly after 1:00 A.M. ZOMO units surrounded a number of hotels in Gdańsk and began detaining the Solidarity leaders and advisers who were spending the night there. At 3:00 A.M. Wałęsa declared he was prepared to go to Warsaw under duress. While he was being taken under security service escort to the Gdańsk airport, General Jaruzelski was making his way to the studio located in the barracks of the air force communications group, where he recorded his speech for radio and television.

The soldiers who under cover of tanks and armored vehicles had taken up position in deserted city streets across the country on this cold December night began to light their coke fires. At 5:30 A.M. government representatives woke Cardinal Glemp to inform him that martial law had been imposed. Police trucks took the first internees to jail after they had been interrogated at local police stations, while other people who had been detained were released after signing an undertaking to refrain from further political activity. In the West the major press agencies, ministers of defense and foreign affairs, and intelligence agencies had known for several hours that a massive action against Solidarity was under way. At 4:20 A.M. the U.S. State Department issued a laconic communiqué stating: "No movement on the part of Soviet troops has been noted."

At 6:00 A.M. Polish radio played the national anthem and then began broadcasting General Jaruzelski's speech: "Our homeland was on the edge of a precipice . . . , we found ourselves facing a difficult test. We must show ourselves equal to this test, we must demonstrate that 'We are worthy of Poland.'" The general went on to inform the public of the imposition of martial law and the formation, "this very day," of the WRON. Only once did he use the word "socialism" ("the measures taken today will serve to preserve the basic prerequisites of socialist renewal") Not once did he mention the party. The speech was rebroadcast every hour, and was supplemented at 10:00 A.M. by a proclamation issued by the WRON. At noon Polish television channel 1 began broadcasting a filmed version of the speech.

The proclamations issued by the Council of State were read out on television: the decree on martial law, resolutions concerning its introduction, and decrees on the prosecution of crimes and misdemeanors and on changes to procedures in military courts and the military prosecutor's office. They were read in a monotonous voice by a succession of popular television announcers dressed in military uniform. Their attire was sanctioned

447

by a communiqué issued at 4:30 P.M. by the Committee for the Defense of the Homeland concerning the militarization of some parts of the state administration, as well as transport, telecommunications, energy, mining, ports, and 129 "crucial factories." More than eight thousand military commissars, most of them officers on active duty, were dispatched to the institutions that were to be put under military command (four hundred of them went to central institutions and ministries). Martial law allowed the authorities to retain in the army the "senior class," whose term of service had already been extended by two months (until 15 December). The minister of internal affairs, for his part, issued instructions ordering all weapons and ammunition to be turned in and forbidding people to move from their current locations. The Ministry of Defense called up tens of thousands of reservists. Roughly 70,000 soldiers and about 30,000 functionaries belonging to the internal affairs ministry took part in the action, while 1,750 tanks were dispatched to patrol the streets, together with 1,400 armored vehicles, 500 infantry combat vehicles, and 9,000 automobiles; about one quarter of all these forces were concentrated in Warsaw and the surrounding suburbs.

Since the country had no regulations concerning a national state of emergency, once the leadership decided to use force, martial law was the only option available. Its provisions were draconian and designed to deal with a range of circumstances unlikely to arise as a result of domestic conflict (for example, citizens were required to provide shelter to civilians from neighborhoods that had been destroyed—presumably by bombs). Telephone communications were cut, gas stations were closed, and a curfew was introduced (from 10 P.M. to 6 A.M.); people wishing to travel beyond their place of residence were required to obtain permits from the authorities, railroad stations were patrolled, and road blocks were set up on major highways leading out of the cities. The authorities introduced censorship of the mail, closed the borders and all civilian airports (including domestic airports), suspended the publication of all papers expect for the party paper, *Trybuna Ludu,* and the defense ministry daily, *Żołnierz Wolności* (Soldier of Freedom). The martial law decree suspended all activity on the part of social and professional organizations and prohibited all meetings, public gatherings, and demonstrations.

Early in the morning the security service went back to Solidarity offices across the country, confiscating documents, money, books, and banners, tearing down posters, dispersing crowds that had begun to gather, and detaining Solidarity staff and activists who had not been interned during the night. Disoriented people were wandering the streets, and those who wanted to (or had to) return home were gathering at train and bus stations. Columns of army trucks and police vans were driving around, and troops armed with rifles were patrolling the streets. Columns of tanks and motorized infantry units could be seen on highways across the country, moving toward the larger towns and industrial centers. Forty-nine "isolation centers" were rapidly filling with internees, whose number rose to more than five thousand during the course of a week. A large proportion of Solidarity's national and regional leaders were in detention, together with leaders of Rural Solidarity and organizations associated with the union, as well as advisers, members of union commissions in the larger factories, activists from the democratic opposition, and intellectuals associated with Solidarity (the authorities had suspended the Congress of Polish Culture, which had been taking place in Warsaw). For propaganda reasons the authorities also interned several members of the former ruling group, including Gierek, Jaroszewicz, and Babiuch. The red flag that normally fluttered above the PZPR Central Committee building was replaced with the Polish national flag.

Western governments were unequivocal in their reaction, but they by no means suggested they were willing to intervene. "The Polish people," declared U.S. Secretary of State Alexander Haig, "must find their own way to overcome their current problems and achieve a compromise between the different forces existing in the country." French Prime Minister Pierre Mauroy stated that the French government "desires a renewal of dialogue between Poles and a return to civil and trade union freedoms." For the outside world, the most important aspect of the whole operation was that it had been undertaken without any involvement on the part of Warsaw Pact forces. Late in the evening, shortly after returning from a weekend away from Washington, President Ronald Reagan told journalists: "The United States has made it clear to the USSR that it will not take lightly interference of any kind in the internal affairs of Poland."

This was what both the Kremlin and the organizers of martial law had assumed all along and what both the former first secretary, Kania, and General Jaruzelski had pointed out many times. External assistance of any overt kind was considered a final recourse, to be used only if the army, law enforcement agencies, and party activists proved incapable of seizing control of the situation, or in the highly unlikely event that one of these institutions itself went out of control. The game—if that is an appropriate word to describe what happened in Poland after 13 December—carried a certain amount of risk. The greatest risk was probably borne by General Jaruzelski and his closest associates: if the initial crackdown failed, there were plenty of others in the top party leadership ready to take his place, even at the price of calling in the Soviet Army. Moscow, which since the summer of 1980 had been urging the Poles to "deal with the situation," was by no means eager to intervene, aware of both the political and material costs, which it could ill afford, given its protracted intervention in Afghanistan.

In many towns and factories on this Sunday, various efforts were being made to reconstruct the Solidarity organizations that had been smashed. Many regional leaders escaped arrest in Gdańsk, arrived in their home-towns the following morning, and immediately established regional or in-terfactory strike committees. There was no real need to formulate new demands: both the union statute and resolutions adopted by the National Commission declared that in the event of "an attack on the union," a gen-eral strike would automatically be called. Solidarity members in the port of Gdańsk set up the National Strike Committee, headed by Mirosław Krupiń-ski; in Wrocław Władysław Frasyniuk formed a regional committee; in the Lenin Iron and Steel Works the Working Commission of Miners was headed by Mieczysław Gil; and an interfactory strike committee was established in Szczecin.

In most cases the initiative now lay with factory-level activists who had escaped the pogrom. In some of the factories that were working on Sunday, strikes began that afternoon. The crackdown had, however, disrupted virtu-ally all channels of communication, not only between regions, but also within individual towns, and coordinated action was essentially impossible. Because of the rapidity of the attack and the size of the forces deployed, people were left paralyzed—which was precisely what the authorities had hoped for. Solidarity was not prepared—nor had it tried to prepare—for physical confrontation on such a scale, even though many of its activists had frequently resorted to strong words and put forward maximalist demands. Union leaders had not designated covert deputies to take their place if the need arose, and the organization had no reserve communications network or concealed printing equipment in working order. Not to mention any means of defending itself. The strikes of December 1970 and August 1980 had derived their strength from the fact that both the scale and the form of the action had taken the authorities by surprise. This time it was the agents of martial law who had surprise on their side.

Two sermons delivered on that Sunday by Cardinal Glemp (in Częstochowa in the morning and in Warsaw in the evening) reflected not only the position of the church but also, in all probability, the state of mind of a large proportion of the population. "We must calmly reflect on the situation, the aim of which should be peace and the saving of lives, so that we avoid bloodshed," he told students taking part in a pilgrimage. His evening message, delivered to a crowd gathered in a church belonging to the Jesuits—and broadcast over the radio (without the knowledge of the church hierarchy) at 10 P.M.—was even clearer: "I am going to call for reason even if it means laying oneself open to insult, and I shall ask, even if I have to go barefoot and beg on my knees: Do not begin a fight of Pole against Pole. Do not lose you heads, brother workers . . . every head and every pair of hands will be invaluable in rebuilding the Poland that will exist, and will have to exist, after martial law has ended." He also pointed out that, according to the authorities, "martial law has been dictated by a higher necessity, it is the choice of a lesser rather than a greater evil." "The average person," he added, "will subordinate himself to the new situation," and he assured his congregation that the church would defend the persecuted. The cardinal was plainly calling on people to forego physical resistance.

Nevertheless, on 14 December, beginning with the early-morning shift, a wave of strikes engulfed the whole country. Strikers issued appeals and produced flyers. Sit-in strikes were proclaimed in several hundred of the largest enterprises: in all the shipyards, ports, mines, iron and steel works, and in most factories in the metal and light industries. Calls for strike action in urban transport systems were generally unsuccessful, and no real attempts were made to organize strikes on the railroads or intercity bus services. Despite the fact that lectures had been suspended, students and faculty members gathered in most colleges and universities and in some cases prepared to occupy the premises. In nearly all institutions—apart from central government agencies—and even in the courts, work came to a halt, although efforts to organize sit-in strikes (such as those organized in a number of research institutes and in the National Library) were rare.

The authorities used the same tactics virtually everywhere, but because of the scale of the protest and the number of flash points, they were not able to act everywhere simultaneously. The operations, usually preceded by a more or less *pro forma* warning, were carried out by large numbers of armed ZOMO and other police units. Larger buildings were surrounded by armored vehicles or tanks. In most cases specially trained groups also took part, including groups from antiterrorist and guerrilla units, which attacked with considerable brutality. Many such operations were conducted at night, largely during the night of 14–15 December, and involved the use of petards, tear gas, and search lights. Special units moved from one location to the next, and transport aircraft and helicopters were used to transport them from one town to another.

The places where large-scale pacification operations were carried out included the Szczecin Shipyard, the Lenin Iron and Steel Works, the Manifest Lipcowy coal mine, and a group of factories in the Grabiszynek area of Wrocław. The strike in the port of Gdańsk was finally crushed on 20 December; the strike in the Katowice Iron and Steel Works ended on 23 December; the underground sit-in strike at the Ziemowit coal mine ended on 24 December; and four days later the strikers in the Piast mine ended their resistance. In many places strikes were accompanied by street demonstrations that turned into disturbances; the most violent of these took place in Gdańsk (17–18 December).

Workers in Silesia mounted strong resistance, and the strikes organized in the depths of the mines were the most difficult to break. It was there, too, in the Wujek mine, that the authorities resorted to the massive use of firearms. Early on the morning of 16 December the mine was surrounded by armored troops. Tanks broke through into the area adjoining the mineshafts, followed by ZOMO units and a platoon of Special Forces. The soldiers from this platoon opened fire on the miners: six people were killed immediately, and three who were severely injured subsequently died in the hospital. Firearms were used in many attacks and to disperse crowds from the streets (in Gdańsk, Huta Katowice, and Wrocław, among other places); at least five people were killed on the spot or subsequently died, but the crushing of the strike in the Wujek coal mine was the most dramatic and bloody of all the confrontations. The resistance mounted by the workers in this coal mine came to symbolize the attitude of all Solidarity members and supporters toward the imposition of martial law. The events were also recorded in the popular poetry that flourished at the time, and a refrain from one of the songs went: "They are coming, the tanks are coming to Wujek." Given that Solidarity organizations had been thrown into chaos and the authorities were determined to prevail, the strikes were bound to be short-lived. Resistance was, in fact, confined to isolated incidents, even in those areas—such as Silesia or Gdańsk—where such incidents were most widespread. Almost nowhere did resistance take the form of a general strike; in most factories only some of the workers occupied the premises; street demonstrations erupted spontaneously and were not coordinated with the sit-in strikes; in most factories—and in all the smaller ones—there were only chaotic mass meetings. To a large extent, this situation resulted from the force and scope of the crackdown, the arrest of those who organized or participated in the strikes (according to official data, around four thousand people were charged, and the first trials took place on 24 December), and the large-scale dismissal of workers who had gone on strike (at least two thousand workers lost their jobs at the Piast mine, for example). The authorities also undertook a wide-ranging operation to "discipline" the state and economic administration, as well as the PZPR. During the first week some five hundred people were dismissed from positions in the party, and several dozen party organizations were dissolved; several dozen provincial administrators and their deputies were removed from their posts, as were several hundred factory directors and heads of institutions. Military commissars took over the management of several hundred enterprises and administrative agencies. In all provinces special plenipotentiaries of the Central Committee were appointed, and Provincial Defense Committees supervised the regional administration. The authorities were helped by the overall social mood, which since the fall of 1981 had become less supportive of Solidarity's most far-reaching demands. A considerable proportion of the population was tired of the unending difficulties of everyday life, of the chaos and constant tension aroused by the propaganda of both sides. Within Solidarity itself—or rather within the remnants of the organization and among the leaders who had evaded internment—several days of resistance gave way to a tendency to discourage mass confrontations, which had so clearly shown themselves to be ineffective. On 21 December one of the leading activists of the Mazowsze region, Zbigniew Janas, issued an appeal "To All Activists of the Solidarity Trade Union," in which he declared himself opposed to active resistance and argued that the basic tasks facing the union were to organize assistance to those who were being persecuted and their families, to rebuild contacts, to engage in information (publishing) activity, and to establish clandestine committees that would make the necessary preparations to call a general strike in the event that "a spontaneous rebellion" erupted. This was the beginning of a great debate on "what is to be done."

When the members of the Politburo met on 22 December, resistance had largely been crushed. Although they were hardly euphoric, it was clear that the imposition of martial law had achieved its immediate goals: "We have won the first battle," declared General Jaruzelski. He warned, however, that "we have not yet won either the campaign (which will require several months) or the war (it will take ten years to repair the ravages of social consciousness and revive the economy from its state of ruin)." As so often happens, time would show that victory in the first battle, and even the first campaign, is no guarantee of victory in the war.

THE UNDERGROUND SOCIETY

Active resistance did not come to an end when the sit-in strikes were crushed or died down. Resistance was renewed at the end of January 1982, and mass protests were to be repeated for nearly ten months. While the first strikes (Wrocław) and street demonstrations (Gdańsk) were organized in protest against the introduction (on 1 February) of drastic price increases, nearly all the subsequent protest actions were organized around symbolic dates and anniversaries. Beginning in February, Solidarity members organized short strikes and public demonstrations of varying size on the thirteenth of every month to mark the imposition of martial law. These resulted in clashes with police, arrests, and dismissals from work. Although such protests took place in various towns and cities, they occurred most frequently in Gdańsk, Wrocław, Nowa Huta, and Warsaw, confirming their reputation as Solidarity strongholds. Large demonstrations were organized on 1 May, when groups of Solidarity demonstrators either joined, or tried to join, official parades, or, as was more often the case, organized counterdemonstrations. Encouraged by the evident success in terms of the number of participants, Solidarity members, together with a large number of high-school students, came out en masse on 3 May, the traditional national holiday. Several tens of thousands of people gathered in the narrow streets and on the squares of Warsaw's Old Town, and crowds numbering several thousand gathered in more than a dozen cities.

The most widespread demonstrations were those organized on the second anniversary of the Gdańsk agreements and the founding of Solidarity. According to official communiqués issued on 31 August 1982, demonstrations took place in thirty-four provinces, and over five thousand people were detained, of whom more than three thousand were brought before the courts or misdemeanor tribunals. In Lubin, a town in the Legnica copper mining region, ZOMO units opened fire: two workers were killed immediately and a third died in the hospital. There were also fatalities in Wrocław and Gdańsk. The last demonstrations and strikes in this phase of what General Jaruzelski called "the campaign" took place in October—after the Sejm had passed a law dealing with trade unions and the formal dissolution of Solidarity—and November, on the anniversary of the union's formal registration and Independence Day. From then on, street demonstrations took place with diminishing frequency and were generally organized on the occasion of national holidays (3 May and 11 November) and the main Solidarity anniversaries (31 August and, on the Coast, 17 December).

During the first weeks of martial law, protest actions were more or less spontaneous in nature; the word was spread by flyers, graffiti, the first underground newssheets, and the well-functioning network of rumor and gossip. Traditional forms of protest were supplemented by such innovations as turning out all the lights at home and placing lighted candles in the windows (on the thirteenth of every month), or evening strolls through the streets during the time of the main evening television newscast (initiated in Świdnik). In towns across the country, walls were covered with thousands of slogans, the best known of which included the following: "WRON beyond the Don," "The Winter Is Yours But the Spring Will be Ours," "CDN" [the Polish acronym for "to be continued"], "the crow will not defeat the eagle" [a play on the acronym WRON and the Polish word for crow, *wrona*]. Others drew on wartime symbols, such as the stylized anchor that was the sign of Fighting Poland and which now served as a symbol of Fighting Solidarity. Special teams dispatched to paint over these graffiti at night sometimes wrote their own (for example, "KOR = Jews," or "S = $").

Traditional melodies were given new words, and copies of these songs—either handwritten or produced on primitive duplicating machines—were passed from hand to hand. Tape recordings of songs broadcast by Radio Free Europe soon appeared. The folklore of protest was fed by contributions from internment centers and prisons. People bought resistors, which they pinned to their clothes. The universally known V for victory sign was much in evidence and led, for example, to the widespread use of drawings featuring a hare, whose long ears create the sign. Also popular were a small medal depicting a spread eagle superimposed on a cross, and various miniature buttons with such inscriptions as CDN, or Solidarity. During the Easter period, postcards featuring Solidarity propaganda appeared, which, together with Solidarity "postage stamps," were a means of raising money for clandestine groups. A whole "underground market" eventually developed, not all of it working on behalf of the real underground.

Appeals for a boycott of the government mass media were repeated over a lengthy period but with little success. A considerable number of artists and intellectuals honored the boycott, refusing to appear on television and even—for a certain period—on the stage. In November 1982 Ewa Dałkowska organized the first performance of her "Theater at Home," staging a play banned by the censors. Simultaneously, an unprecedented number of actors, painters, writers, and scholars took part in the annual Weeks of Christian Culture organized by many dioceses. The boycott of government cultural institutions and the media was accompanied by the "verification," or purge, of journalists, a process that resulted in at least eight hundred people losing their jobs; some of them then went to work for the underground press—which had certainly not been the authorities' intention. In intellectual and intelligentsia circles and in factories it became common to boycott managers at various levels, together with PZPR members, and people who expressed support for martial law.

Political divisions, already so evident during 1980–81, became ever deeper and wider, a process that was initially fueled by the numerous cases in which party members exacted revenge for the fears and frustrations of what they called "the period of legal Solidarity." The hostile atmosphere was exacerbated by the government's aggressive and unrestrained propaganda campaign, whose tone was set by Jerzy Urban in his weekly press conferences. The aim was to discredit individual Solidarity activists, as well as the entire movement, with the abundant use of falsifications and distortions. The authorities set out to demonize the union by presenting evidence, much of it fabricated, concerning its plans to "unleash civil war" and its ties to the "special services of Western countries," both before and after 13 December. They spread slanderous rumors about leading Solidarity members, many of them couched in chauvinist language. Solidarity's own propaganda responded in black-and-white terms, fueled by the official terminology of martial law, as well as the rhetoric of the government mass media. In this way, terms such "a war against the nation" and "the new occupation" came into widespread use, while Radio Solidarity chose as its broadcast signal a well-known tune dating back to the time of the German occupation. Regardless of the clashes on the streets, the country was in the grip of what amounted to a "cold civil war," one that divided not only colleagues and friends but often families.

Although resistance was largely spontaneous, especially at the beginning, organizational support was provided by clandestine factory commissions and the growing number of regional organizations. Within six months regional bodies had been established in all major centers; they were headed either by people known for their activity during Solidarity's period of legal existence (among them, Władysław Frasyniuk and Józef Pinior in Wrocław, Zbigniew Bujak, Zbigniew Janas, Zbigniew Romaszewski, and Wiktor Kulerski in Warsaw, and Bogdan Borusewicz and Bogdan Lis in Gdańsk) or by less well known members of the union's regional bodies. On 13 January a body calling itself the All-Poland Committee of Resistance issued its first communiqué, but it was the Interim Coordinating Commission (TKK), established on 22 April, that came to be widely regarded as the central leadership of the underground union, its proclamations being signed on behalf of four regions by Zbigniew Bujak, Władysław Frasyniuk, Władysław Hardek (Małopolska), and Bogdan Lis.

Differences of opinion over tactics led to the formation of groups that either did not fully acknowledge the leadership of the TKK (such as the Inter-Factory Workers' Committee in Warsaw) or declared their complete independence (such as Kornel Morawiecki's Fighting Solidarity, based in Wrocław). In July the TKK set up its Foreign Coordinating Bureau, headed by Jerzy Milewski in Brussels. At the same time, the clandestine Council of National Education was established in Warsaw, the first of what would become a whole group of independent organizations concerned with education (the Committee on Independent Education), artistic life (the Committee on Independent Culture), and university-level reaching and research (the Social Committee on Science). On 15 August the All-Poland Farmers' Resistance Committee, an offshoot of Rural Solidarity, published its first statement.

The Independent Student Union reemerged in a clandestine form, and a number of high-school students made use of their former contacts to set up the High-School Student Movement for Renewal. Ephemeral committees of social resistance, based on friendship networks, sprang up in many places. The Confederation for an Independent Poland was less significant for a period of time, largely because so many of its members had been arrested. The same was true of the Gdańsk-based Young Poland Movement. Neither KOR, which had disbanded in September 1981, nor ROPCiO, which had effectively merged into Solidarity, reconstituted itself. The numerous political parties that emerged in 1980–81—all of them, without exception, "drawing-room" organizations—also disappeared.

A clandestine press grew up alongside these secret organizations. The first newssheets already began to appear during the December strike wave (the Warsaw-based *Wiadomości* [News]), and within a few weeks several publications were being produced in all the larger centers. The best known included *Z dnia na dzień* (From Day to Day), published in Wrocław; *Obserwator Wielkopolski* (Poznań); *Solidarność* (Gdańsk); *Biuletyn Małopolski* (Kraków); *Głos Wolnego Hutnika* (The Voice of the Free Iron and Steel Worker), published in Nowa Huta; *Informator* (Lublin); and *Wola* (Will) and *Tygodnik Wojenny* (Wartime Weekly), published in Warsaw. *Tygodnik Mazowsze* (Mazowsze Weekly), founded on 11 February by a group formerly involved in producing the information bulletin of the Solidarity Agency, rapidly came to play a crucial role thanks to its ties to members of the TKK. During the course of 1982 at least eight hundred illegal periodicals appeared, most of them associated with Solidarity groups and organizations.

The first pamphlets and books were published not later than February 1982, most of them issued by two publishing organizations, NOWa and Krąg, well known for their activity in pre-December days; by the end of the year at least three hundred titles had been published. The scale of underground publishing was confirmed by the security service, which claimed, in November, to have "liquidated" 360 print shops and to have seized nearly 1,200 duplicating machines and 730,000 flyers. On 12 April Radio Solidarity, established by Zbigniew Romaszewski, transmitted its first broadcast (in Warsaw). Transmitters began functioning in several other cities during the summer, and even though they had only limited ability to disseminate information, the very fact of their existence was a stimulus to further activity.

While underground publications and flyers circulated quite widely, the main source of information for most people was foreign radio. The lively Polish-language broadcasts of Radio France International were extremely popular, as were the BBC and the Voice of America, but it was the Polish Service of Radio Free Europe, headed by Zdzisław Najder, a founder of the Polish Independence Compact in 1976, that had the largest following. The sources of information used by foreign radio stations included not only press agencies and reports from Poland filed by correspondents for the major Western newspapers, but also underground publications and information and commentary smuggled out of Poland, either with the help of embassy staff or via the groups involved in the frequent shipment of aid (food, medicine, clothing) into the country. In time, these sources came to provide foreign radio stations with most of their information concerning developments in Poland.

After the surprise attack that allowed the authorities to win the first battle, Solidarity activists spent some time debating tactics. One issue was what kind of organizational structure to create. The majority opposed any attempt to centralize activities and create a hierarchical structure. This reflected what had been the main tendency within the union since its very beginning and was also seen as offering some protection from infiltration by the security service. Some people held the opposite view, among them Jacek Kuroń, who argued, in an article smuggled out of prison, titled "Theses on a Solution to a Situation without Solution," in favor of "organizing around a central body" and "displaying a high level of discipline in carrying out its decisions." Some people even proposed creating an underground state similar to that of World War II. In the end, despite the reservations expressed by many well-known activists over several months, both the TKK and regional bodies were established. They did not form a close-knit structure, but loyalty toward the clandestine leadership proved to be long lasting, even on the part of those who had criticisms and complaints about its actions.

In the many articles published between February and May 1982 a division was evident between those who advocated preparing for an active operation—a general strike—that would take place in the near future and those who favored a "positional struggle." The case for the first was most eloquently argued by Kuroń, in the article mentioned above, and his chief opponent was Zbigniew Bujak. Romaszewski and one of the most popular underground journalists, Maciej Poleski (the pseudonym of Czesław Bielecki), were among the radicals who argued in favor of a general strike and "active resistance involving the use of force" against "the terrorist state." The emotional tension of this debate was heightened by recurring public protests on the streets, by the numerous trials of people who had taken part in the December strikes (Ewa Kubasiewicz received the highest sentence— ten years), and by the fatal shooting of a policeman by a group of teenage boys who were trying to steal his handgun. Many people feared that the situation would develop into terrorism, which they both condemned and saw as likely to lead to increased repression. In May Adam Michnik advocated (from prison) the notion of "the long march," declaring himself in favor of activity that was "tedious" and "often ineffective" but necessary for "the reconstruction of civil society."

Despite the differences of opinion, the majority favored trying to achieve some kind of agreement with the authorities. Even the then radical Kuroń saw a general strike as "the means to accelerate the concluding of an agreement." In its first declaration, the TKK stated that "the resolution of the problems facing Poland is impossible without negotiations between the authorities and society"; the only precondition that it laid down for such negotiations was the release of all those who had been interned, arrested, and sentenced.

This position found considerable support in statements made by members of the clergy and by John Paul II, who addressed the issue many times during the early months of martial law; it was also endorsed in a document titled "Theses of the Primate's Social Council Concerning Social Agreement," published on 5 April. Cardinal Glemp plainly favored a compromise, even at the cost of changes in Solidarity's organizational structure and the ouster of those activists considered to be radicals, a position that earned him frequent criticism in the underground press. Although few at the lower levels of the clergy shared this position (and even some bishops had reservations), it accorded with the general line laid down by Cardinal Wyszyński, who had always tried to protect the church from direct attack on the part of the state. In consequence, Cardinal Glemp frequently offered the church's assistance in establishing a dialogue; the authorities, however, ignored all such offers. One reason for the conciliatory tendencies of the episcopate was the papal visit to Poland planned for 1982. Negotiations on the matter took place over two months or so, and it was only on 21 July that the Vatican officially announced that the visit would be postponed. The authorities used the visit as a tool to pressure the church into adopting a conciliatory position. This was blatantly evident when the primate and General Jaruzelski met on 8 November 1982, two days before the planned strikes on the anniversary of Solidarity's registration; shortly afterward an official communiqué announced that the pope had been invited to visit Poland in June 1983.

Although the primate and the episcopate adopted a cautious approach, the church as an institution provided a haven for the Solidarity underground and a place where a good part of "the battle for social consciousness" was waged. Many priests spoke the truth about martial law and even provided assistance to the underground. The masses for the homeland that were celebrated in many churches (the best known being those in the Church of St. Stanisław Kostka, where Father Jerzy Popiełuszko officiated) played a major role in maintaining the will to resist among the broad ranks of believers. The Primate's Aid Committee and equivalent committees in the dioceses, established during the early days of martial law, were an important element of the church's overall activity. They collected money and distributed packages sent from abroad, providing assistance to tens of thousands of people—

internees, prisoners, and their families. Priests quickly gained access to the prisons.

In the fall of 1982 the wave of street demonstrations died down and successive calls for strikes proved unsuccessful, confirming General Jaruzelski's prediction that the authorities would win this campaign. Life itself resolved the dilemma of whether to mount "active resistance" or take "the long road": the latter was the only option. The martial law authorities also realized that Solidarity no longer posed a direct threat. As proof of this they released Lech Wałęsa from his place of internment, where he had been detained alone. On 14 November, when he was back at home, an official commentary issued by the Polish Press Agency stated: "The former leader of the former Solidarity trade union is currently a private citizen." On 19 December the Council of State issued a decree suspending martial law, and on the day before Christmas Eve, the minister of internal affairs, General Kiszczak, ordered the release of all internees and the closure of the centers in which they had been held. This did not, however, mean leniency for those whom the authorities regarded as the most dangerous. Four KOR members in internment had already been arrested in September; in December they were joined by seven well-known union activists, and this "representative eleven," as they were then referred to, became a collective hostage. Nor was there an end to the prosecution of people involved in clandestine activity. Martial law was actually replaced by a state of "special legal regulation," which retained in force the most important provisions needed to continue the repression.

In a program statement, "Solidarity Today," issued on 22 January 1983, the TKK maintained its previous position: "The goal of our struggle is still to implement the program . . . of democratic reforms needed to raise the country from its state of collapse." This demanded, the document continued, "the creation of a situation in which the authorities are forced to seek a compromise with society." When the TKK held its first, clandestine, meeting with Wałęsa in April it was clear that there were no major differences between them on the question of tactics. This state of affairs was reinforced by a statement calling for union pluralism, signed on 6 May 1983 by Wałęsa and other Solidarity activists and by representatives of several unions that had by no means formed part of the opposition before 13 December (the so-called autonomous unions that had emerged from the old, official union movement, and the Polish Teachers' Union).

After early 1983 no further attempts were made to organize strikes at the national or even regional level; demonstrations did continue, although they rarely achieved the dimensions of those that took place during the first year of martial law. The opposition focused its energy on publishing, education, culture, and propaganda. Solidarity remained the core of "the underground society," but many initiatives, even those claiming to emanate from Solidarity, were actually independent.

A permanent feature in the life of the opposition, and one that was of crucial significance, was the highly active underground press. During the period 1982–85 at least 1,700 different titles were published. In 1983 a larger number of sociopolitical and cultural journals began to appear, some of them substantial—*Obecność* (Presence) in Wrocław, *Obraz* (Image) in Szczecin, *Arka* (The Ark) in Krakow, and *Vacat* (Vacancy) in Warsaw. They published analyses of the domestic and international situations, articles and documents dealing with the most recent history, and fiction and poetry. *Tygodnik Mazowsze* achieved a circulation in excess of 10,000, and the leading regional publications printed several thousand copies. The Ministry of Internal Affairs calculated that underground printers had a "combined printing capacity" of about one million sheets of A4 format.

During the same period at least 1,800 books and pamphlets were published, with a circulation that reached as high as 5,000–6,000. Nearly half of these dealt with political issues: polemical pamphlets, analyses of the current situation, and anti-WRON propaganda. A fair amount of fiction and poetry was also published, much of it political in nature: satires and parodies as well as sentimental works of a martyrological kind. At least two hundred books on historical topics appeared, nearly all of them dealing with the history of Soviet totalitarianism, the fate of the Poles deported to Siberia, and the establishment of the communist system in Poland. The underground also produced a large number of reprints from émigré publications. In some cases selected articles from émigré journals were published in collected form (as in the case of *Kultura*), in others, entire issues of a given journal were reprinted (*Aneks, Zeszyty Literackie*).

The largest printing and publishing center was Warsaw, where nearly one-quarter of all newspapers and periodicals and nearly two-thirds of all books and pamphlets were produced. NOWa retained its position as the largest publishing operation, but other "old" publishing groups, Krąg and Głos, also produced a large number of books and journals. They were joined by many new publishers, including (in 1982) CDN, Słowo, and Przedświt, and (in 1983) Pokolenie, Rytm, and Unia. The underground press and publications attracted many people making their debut as writers—and also as editors and publishers—but the very nature of the situation demanded anonymity or the use of pseudonyms.

Various forms of culture sprang up to provide an alternative to what was offered by official institutions. In this area the church played an indispensable role. Virtually every religious ceremony associated with major traditional anniversaries was accompanied by artistic events—poetry readings, art exhibitions, and live performances. The Weeks of Christian Culture, which were probably held in all the dioceses and even in some larger parishes, were more patriotic and nationalist than purely religious in content. Parish premises, and sometimes even churches, were the site of popular lectures and discussions—usually on Polish history—as well as scholarly symposia. While the Catholic Church had always attracted its share of artists and intellectuals, their participation in the events organized by the clergy was unprecedented in its scale. Moreover, there were only a few cases where a priest refused to invite a given individual on the grounds that he or she was an atheist. Some political commentators did argue that people who previously had nothing—or little—in common with Catholicism were now treating the church instrumentally, but most of the clergy refused to be drawn into argument on the subject.

Various forms of "secular" opposition culture also developed, and even blossomed. By definition these tended to be intimate in scale: plays and cabarets performed in apartments, private showings of films recorded on video (including material recorded by the underground or by émigré groups), displays of graphics and paintings. Funding for activity of this kind, as well as for some scholarly research and educational campaigns, was provided from abroad, by private foundations, trade unions, and individual donations. The divisions that had emerged within creative and scholarly circles after 13 December deepened, and a number of researchers and critics withdrew from the official media (less frequently, from official institutions) and published exclusively in underground periodicals or in Catholic journals, whose number had increased markedly since 1982.

The consolidation of the situation brought about by martial law and the evident stabilization—and even conservatism—of Solidarity's organizational structure and political proposals led to the emergence of a growing number of independent initiatives outside the framework of the underground movement associated with the person of Wałęsa. At the end of 1982 some erstwhile political groups began to resume activity; and more important, a number of completely new groups began to emerge. The conviction that martial law was actually the swan song of real socialism took root among some groups, which naturally began to produce and popularize political programs whose starting point was not reform of the system but its total collapse. Some of these groups, such as the Wola Political Group and the Liberation Political Movement, remained within Solidarity but argued the need to politicize the movement and to advance more radical proposals than those then being put forward by the TKK or by Wałęsa and his advisers.

A sign of the times was the fact that support for the idea of national independence was spreading rapidly, and the notion of state sovereignty moved to the forefront of demands raised in political programs and journalistic essays. The idea of "Finlandization," once regarded as sheer adventurism, now came to be viewed as nothing short of opportunism (if not national betrayal). Groups that thought along these lines generally had their own publications, and although producing these was sometimes their only activity, they contributed to a gradual broadening of the range of political views and to the diversification of the underground political scene. Another characteristic feature, especially among the newly emerging groups, was the rejection of both central planning and Solidarity's proposals for self-management, and an emphasis on the free market and economic liberalism.

The overwhelming majority of these groups had no influence on the broader society and did not even try to achieve any. In this context, two groups distinguished themselves in terms of the radicalism of both their programs and their activities. One of these was the Confederation for an Independent Poland, which began to assume a higher public profile in 1984. The second was Fighting Solidarity, which, as early as 1983, enjoyed considerable support among young people. The Movement for an Alternative Society emerged in Gdańsk as an offshoot of the youth groups that took part in various Solidarity demonstrations and quickly grew to occupy a special place extending beyond the city. The generation that had lived through the years 1980–81 at the side of its politically active parents or older siblings wanted, after 1982, to take an active part in events. Generational rebellion was expressed, first and foremost, in attitudes toward the authorities, but also in opposition to the caution of the older Solidarity generation and the passivity of the majority of the population, who had quickly reconciled themselves to the situation. This rebellion was marked by pronounced countercultural features, expressed most vividly in music (both in the lyrics and in the behavior of the audience during concerts).

Although the possibilities for mobilizing the opposition were much reduced compared with 1982, participation in clandestine activity continued all over the country. The underground press and publishing certainly involved more than ten thousand people—perhaps several tens of thousands—as printers, editors, writers, and distributors. Union dues were collected in thousands of factories and institutions, and a large proportion of illegal factory commissions paid benefits and provided assistance to those who had been arrested or dismissed from work. Thousands of people were actively involved in cultural activity. The same was true of political parties. Several hundred people lived in hiding, which required an entire conspiratorial network of couriers (usually female), local contacts, and safe apartments. The activity of recent émigrés, who had numerous links to their homeland and were referred to as the Solidarity emigration, formed an integral part of the movement. They included people who had been abroad for some years (including those who left after March 1968) and those who simply happened to have been abroad when martial law was imposed, as well as union activists and strike participants who had left the country, often straight from internment or prison. According to official data, in the years 1982–83 roughly four thousand people emigrated in this way.

While the idea of creating an underground state was never carried out—in part because of firm opposition on the part of Solidarity—the underground reached far and wide, and was highly organized. Although many of the people who were still active in 1982 subsequently withdrew from activity, and the influence of the underground diminished, a considerable number of Poles—although far from the majority—continued to give it their steadfast support.

CHANGE WITHOUT CHANGE

The success of the first battle, conducted solely with the forces of the Ministry of Internal Affairs and the army, raised the question of the role of the PZPR and its place in the administration of martial law. Leadership of the country was in the hands of the so-called Directorate, whose members, under the command of General Jaruzelski, included internal affairs minister General Kiszczak; deputy defense minister General Siwicki; a deputy prime minister, Mieczysław Rakowski; and three (out of nine) Central Committee secretaries—Barcikowski, Milewski, and Olszowski. The WRON was a purely decorative institution, the government was a purely executive agency, while the Politburo had actually become, it would seem, an advisory body. The first plenary session of the Central Committee under martial law did not take place until the end of February. Even the Sejm convened earlier (25–26 January), since it was required to ratify the decrees and resolutions passed on 12 December (actually, on the thirteenth). The session went smoothly, with five abstentions and one vote (that of Romuald Bukowski) in opposition.

The Directorate, the Central Committee Secretariat, and the Politburo all discussed what should be done with the PZPR. Some people advocated the "Hungarian variant," which would have involved disbanding the party and forming a new one under another name. Others favored a far-reaching "verification" of the membership, involving an exchange of party cards and even, as Kociołek suggested, the requirement that members "sign a political declaration." In the end the leadership decided against radical measures but agreed on the need to "activate" the organization and, in the words of General Jaruzelski, "to rid the party effectively of alien elements." To a certain extent, this was a nonissue, since the exodus from the PZPR that began after August 1980 had continued without interruption. In mid-1980, the party had roughly 2.9 million members, and a year later, roughly 2.3 million (from 1984 on membership stabilized at around 2.1 million). The PZPR thus remained a mass organization, which plainly had a negative effect on its level of militancy.

Some party members reacted in a radical fashion to the introduction of martial law. Some local committees set up activist groups with such names as Workers' Militia, the Party's Guard, or Self-Defense Groups. In some places some members of these groups were armed, and occasionally they even set up their own barracks. In an effort to control such groups the Central Committee Secretariat ordered in February that they be incorporated into "politico-defense units," which would "carry out specialized tasks under the strict supervision of party bodies." A similar development, although one that was more civilian in nature, involved the creation of Citizens' Committees of National Salvation all across the country. Retired party officials appear to have taken the lead in all this, together with former employees of the internal affairs ministry (and its predecessor), retired military personnel, and people of various generations who favored "a return to revolutionary origins." The "real communists" from the Katowice Forum and *Rzeczywistość,* who had been muffled after the ninth congress, now seized the opportunity to raise their voices. The veterans' organization, ZBoWiD, was also part of this broad movement, and the proposal adopted (11 February 1982) by the organization's governing body, urging the construction of a monument to those who had died in the defense of people's power, meshed well with the radical ideas then being floated. When combined with a propaganda campaign that made plentiful use of populist, "anti-imperialist," and, especially, anti-intelligentsia slogans, the end result in many circles was an atmosphere reminiscent of both civil war and "cultural revolution."

Although radicals such as Kociołek, Olszowski, and Siwak were firmly entrenched in the top leadership, and the majority of full-time party officials (who then numbered twenty thousand) undoubtedly favored a hard line, Jaruzelski quietly went on implementing his own line. Viewed in the context of the PZPR, his approach was essentially centrist. At a Politburo meeting he declared: "We must come out . . . with a program that unequivocally emphasizes the Marxist-Leninist character of the party," but one that is simultaneously "reformist in nature." He used martial law not only to defend and consolidate a system that had been shaken by eighteen months of "anarchy" but also to strengthen his personal power and to implement his own program, which certainly did not enjoy universal support within the party.

There was no doubt, however, that the draconian regulations introduced on 13 December and the subsequent personnel changes in the party and state administration were directed against Solidarity, the opposition, and those sections of the broader society that were in revolt against the system. They were not intended to crush the party or to question the dogma concerning its leading role. The centrist nature of General Jaruzelski's policy was evident in the stabilization that took place at the top levels of the power elite: three people active in the "horizontal structures" movement were removed from the Central Committee; Olszowski and Kubiak lost their positions as Central Committee secretaries (although they remained in the Politburo); only Jan Łabęcki, PZPR secretary in the Gdańsk Shipyard, was removed from the Politburo, and he was replaced by another worker-activist.

While the presence of "communists in uniform" in state and party positions became a permanent feature of the martial law landscape, it became clear, as this landscape changed, that real power still lay with the party authorities. The military commissars disappeared, the defense ministry inspectors returned to their barracks, and provincial administrators with the rank of general were replaced by civilians. The changes in the party apparatus carried out after 13 December resulted in a return to an earlier state of affairs. Paul Lewis has calculated that in terms of age and length of service in the apparatus, the provincial first secretaries of 1985 were closer to those of 1975 than those who had held office in 1981.[1] Although the restrictions imposed on 13 December 1981 on the lower levels of the party were lifted, there were no changes in the internal mechanisms of the organization: democratic centralism remained the guiding principle, together with the principle of co-optation rather than election. The leadership used the old tactic of "cutting off both wings": when someone was dismissed or a particular group among (the remnants of) the reformists was closed down, a more or less similar fate was simultaneously meted out to the hard-liners. It would be hard to imagine that a party run in this way could actually promote democratic reforms. Changes were constantly being made in the composition of the government, but the structure of the central state administration remained unaltered and based on principles dating back to the time of Bierut and Minc. In November 1985—just before the end of the Sejm's term of office, which had been extended by a year—the Council of Ministers had thirty-nine members (compared with forty-one in 1980), including eight deputy prime ministers. Even if we assume that three of them held their position because of the "coalition" involving the ZSL, SD, and PAX, this was still a large number. Especially as all the key administrative and economic decisions—not to mention political, military, and internal security decisions—were taken by the party leadership. Reforms of the central administration were confined to small changes in the scope of competence of individual ministries. The situation was no different at the local level; the regional self-government institutions remained totally under the control of the center, as could be seen from the fact that elections to the national councils were conducted (17 June 1984) in exactly the same way as previously. It is, then, true to say that in terms of the functioning of state and local institutions, "there was no return to the situation as it was before December": there was actually a complete return to the situation as it was "before August." There were more people in uniform holding high office, but there was nothing to be expected from them other than increased discipline and further bureaucratization, particularly as most of them were staff, not line officers. The nomenklatura system remained untouched: the central nomenklatura (controlled by various Central Committee agencies) consisted of nearly 5,000 positions, while the local system included nearly 300,000.

1. Paul G. Lewis, *Political Authority and Party Secretaries in Poland, 1975–1986* (Cambridge, 1989).

The troops did withdraw to their barracks in 1982, and only units from the internal affairs ministry were used to break up demonstrations, which were still frequent in 1983; the machinery of "law enforcement" strengthened its visible and covert presence. The security service now employed more people—at least 40,000, of whom 22,000 were officers—than during the Stalinist period. The police had a force of roughly 90,000, not counting part-time units, which were used only to deal with street disturbances. In 1984 these consisted of nearly 13,000 persons with special training, organized in eighteen battalions (and this still left the Vistula Defense Units, which had a similar number of personnel). A substantial number of full-time security officials worked outside the department, trying—often with success—to infiltrate Solidarity and opposition groups; internment and imprisonment provided new opportunities to recruit secret collaborators. The scale of operational activities can be seen in the expansion of specialist sections and the creation (in the fall of 1984) of the Sixth Department to deal with "the protection" of food production, forestry, and the timber industry. The security service thus returned to its old structure, in which separate sections monitored all the major areas of the economy. A separate Bureau of Analyses was established and charged with disinformation and disrupting the underground from within. The records section was bursting at the seams with new case files. In the Fourth Department, which dealt only with the church, a new and aptly named D section was created: its task—disinformation and disintegration.

Although there was no return to the strategy of bloody terror on a mass scale like that of the years before 1956, both the expansion of the security apparatus and the brutality that it unleashed during the early days of martial law became a permanent element in the power structure. In addition, force was used on a massive scale to disperse demonstrations, and frequently involved the use of firearms. Underground activists were constantly being attacked—and even murdered—by "unknown perpetrators." Undercover security officials in the Toruń area were the most active in this regard. The police and security forces eagerly and frequently beat people taken into custody, and the work of the new D section involved the use of physical aggression and provocation. Leaving aside the question of who issued the order and in what form it was issued, the murder of Father Jerzy Popiełuszko by three officials from the Fourth Department on 19 October 1984 was not really outside the operational norm.

While wielding the stick, General Jaruzelski did not forget the carrot.

Since the state of the economy did not improve during the first year of martial law—thus preventing him from producing a carrot in the form of improved living standards—he feverishly sought social support and tried to reanimate the "transmission belts" (with the exception of the trade unions). A fair number of intellectuals (generally members of the older generation) appeared in the mass media to support the government, usually citing the notion of raison d'état and sometimes drawing on old Piłsudski-ite slogans. The leadership reasserted control over PAX by engineering the removal of its chairman, Ryszard Reiff (the only member of the Council of State to vote against imposing martial law), and managed to put a stop to the feeble efforts of the ZSL and ZD to become autonomous. On 3 May 1982 the Sejm adopted a declaration "Concerning National Understanding," and on 20 July the PZPR and its satellite parties (including the Catholic parties) announced the establishment of the Patriotic Movement for National Rebirth (PRON). Its president was Jan Dobraczyński, a well-known Catholic writer associated with PAX.

The PRON was intended to provide a platform on which various groups that supported the status quo could rally to the side of the party and to take over the role of the Front of National Unity, a more traditional instrument designed to create the appearance of a ruling coalition. To help the PRON gain credibility, Jaruzelski ceded to it a number of tasks: it submitted to the military authorities proposals to mitigate the rigors of martial law, issued the order to release internees and prisoners, and proclaimed an amnesty (in July 1984). Some of its actions were undertaken in an effort to court public opinion while at the same time depriving Solidarity of its traditions: official ceremonies were organized on 25 June in Radom and on 28 June in Poznań to commemorate the events of 1976 and 1956 (a similar ceremony was held in Gdańsk in December).

Although Jaruzelski and his associates declared many times that "there will be no return to the situation as it was before 13 December" or to that of pre-August 1980, the techniques of government were completely identical to the old methods. "We wanted renewal," Rakowski recalled years later, "but . . . at a given moment the old ways always came knocking on the door." It seems that no one in the PZPR leadership actually tried to turn the key in the lock to prevent the reentry of the "old ways." In December 1981 General Jaruzelski spoke in a somewhat pompous tone to his colleagues in the Politburo about the need for "a second revolution" that would be made by "people who are law-abiding, modest, and courageous, fighters for social justice." Leaving aside the lawlessness and brutality of martial law itself, there are grounds for arguing that this "revolution" was actually carried out by preserving—and even strengthening—all the former power structures.

General Jaruzelski's team espoused the formula: "He who is not against us ought to be with us"; but out in the regions and at the lower levels of the party and state apparatus there remained a strong tendency toward political vendettas of various kinds and the purge of people regarded as undesirable. The use of this formula had no effect on practice: "to be with us" simply meant to subordinate oneself. This applied not only to individuals but also to organizations. Although the authorities feared to raise the question of the legal abolition of Solidarity, they had no qualms about "punishing" several associations. On 20 March 1982 the Union of Polish Journalists was dissolved, as was (in 1983) the Polish Fine Arts Union, the Polish Writers' Union, and the governing board of the Polish PEN-Club. To avoid creating a vacuum, the authorities set up new organizations in place of the old ones—which generally carried on functioning illegally.

In accordance with tradition, PZPR activists remained in the background and recruited, without any difficulty, nonparty journalists, writers, and actors to assume the leadership of these new organizations. In some associations—which were known as "legal" organizations to distinguish them from those that were "underground"—there were clear signs of the desire to exact revenge on those who had taken the side of the opposition. The groups involved became divided, each side ostracized the other, each had its own hierarchy of prestige and authority, but even the most radical organizers of the "neo-unions" did not suggest a return to the esthetic norms of socialist realism. It was not possible to "dissolve" the universities (although it was suggested that a new institution be established in Warsaw to take over some of the departments belonging to Warsaw University). Instead the authorities dismissed all rectors, deans, and institute directors who had ties to the opposition; in some institutions where the faculty mounted only weak resistance and there was little solidarity, many people lost their jobs (this was the case at the University of Silesia, for example).

The authorities went to considerable lengths—although it is hard to say whether they actually believed they might be successful—to persuade some Solidarity members to cooperate in establishing control over the union under the general slogan, well known in earlier times, of "separating the healthy worker tendency from the filthy scum." Although they managed to find several regional activists who made the required statement (sometimes under pressure and even under blackmail), none of the widely known leaders gave in; nor—more important—did Wałęsa. The clandestine union organizations decisively rejected the government's proposals concerning "the future of the trade union movement," published on 20 February 1982.

The authorities considered the formal liquidation of Solidarity such a delicate matter that they postponed it until the fall. On 8 October 1982 the Sejm passed a law on trade unions, which rendered null and void all previous registration proceedings. The wariness and apprehension of the authorities could be seen in the fact that the law stipulated that new trade unions could be formed at factory level only and not until 1 January 1983. Formally, then, for more than a year after the imposition of martial law—which suspended the activities of all trade unions—no union organizations were allowed to function in Poland.

The formation of the new, "tame" unions was begun with care. Not until June 1983 was the first supra-factory organization registered (the Federation of Iron and Steel Trade Unions); two months later the first "all-Poland trade union meeting" took place, the second being held nearly a year later (in May 1984). At the end of November 1984, that is to say, more than two years after the passage of the trade union law, the All-Poland Trade Union Agreement (OPZZ) was formed. Its president was Alfred Miodowicz, hitherto head of the iron and steel workers' union and a member of the PZPR. Although the "neo-unions" encountered considerable resistance and mistrust among the workforce, they did attract some Solidarity members, although joining them was considered apostasy. The organizations that joined the OPZZ had several million members, a considerable force that, during the early years, was almost totally subservient to the guidelines and directives emanating from the PZPR. But building the new unions was a laborious process, especially in the large factories, where special efforts were made; there were cases where even party members refused to join, despite official orders to do so. In many factory organizations, a large percentage of the members were actually retirees looking for material assistance. On average, about 30 percent of the workforce joined the new unions; the percentage was higher in smaller factories and in administrative offices, and lower in large factories and among such groups as university faculty and those working at research institutes.

The OPZZ's mobilizing capacity was considerable but far below that enjoyed by its predecessor, the CRZZ, until 1980. It is true that from 1983 on a considerable number of people took part in May Day parades, but the organization made no attempt to revive such practices as labor competition. The majority of the unions belonging to the OPZZ tended to emphasize the demands of their members, respecting the traditional task of syndicalist organizations—to defend the immediate interests of their membership. The leadership of the OPZZ was, however, far more attuned to the political preferences of the PZPR. It seems that the emphasis on member demands, while burdensome for the economic apparatus, had been factored into the costs of reviving the union movement. After all, this strategy deprived Solidarity of its monopoly in representing the material interests of wage earners.

The old "transmission belts," such as youth associations and the women's organization, continued to function, publishing papers, calling meetings, and passing resolutions, but they did not manage to acquire any momentum. For example, less than 5 percent of students belonged to the two official political youth organizations active on college campuses (the ZSMP and the ZMW), despite intense agitation and despite the fact that members had certain privileges; fewer than 20 percent belonged to the ZSP, which had once been very popular. This did not mean that most students belonged to underground organizations, since this was impossible, if only for technical reasons.

But these were not the only reasons. Among students, as among other professional groups, a kind of "no man's land" was expanding and becoming a space occupied by a "silent majority." In a survey carried out in the fall of 1983, 16.4 percent of respondents described their attitude to the imposition of martial law as "highly positive," and a further 26.3 percent considered it "generally positive." While we can assume that some of these responses resulted either from fear or from the desire to give what respondents considered to be the answer preferred by the pollsters, it is certain that a significant percentage of the population supported the actions of the authorities or was positively inclined toward them. Although the state of public opinion did not give the party leadership cause for excessive triumphalism, given what happened between August and December and in 1982, it did provide cause for satisfaction. The crushing of Solidarity in the manner prescribed by General Jaruzelski and his associates required that the majority of the population be neutralized, a crucial step on the way to regaining total control.

The Catholic Church was a major element in this maneuvering on the part of the PZPR. At a meeting of the Politburo on 22 December 1981 Jaruzelski presented what he considered to be three possible models of relations

473

with the church—conflict, fraternization, or "constructive coexistence." The leadership chose the last. In fact, the central slogan of its political tactics— "struggle and understanding"—was of greatest relevance to the church, since only the first part of the slogan applied to the Solidarity underground and the rest of the opposition. As far as the church was concerned, official pronouncements emphasized only the second half, although—as I noted above—the authorities did not miss any opportunity to increase security service monitoring of the clergy and the church hierarchy, and propaganda remained dominated by anticlerical statements. Various kinds of harassment continued, sometimes taking a violent form, such as the gang attack on the premises of the Primate's Social Council (3 May 1983). At the end of 1983 the authorities launched a campaign to remove crucifixes from school classrooms, which resulted in numerous protest demonstrations organized by parents and students, the best known being those in Miętno, near Garwolin, and in Włoszczowa (March and December 1984).

The ambivalence and instrumentalism of the party's attitude toward the church were reflected in the official welcoming ceremony for Pope John Paul II at the Belweder Palace, when he began his second pilgrimage to Poland on 16 June 1983. It was plain to everyone watching General Jaruzelski deliver his address that he was extremely agitated. And he had good reason to be: in a private meeting before the official ceremony the pope had told him that saw Poland as "one great concentration camp." In a certain sense, the very fact that they agreed to the pope's visit constituted "a heroic act" on the part of the authorities, who had no reason to expect the Polish pope to urge his compatriots to subordinate themselves totally to the communist state. Nevertheless, unless they were going to move to the "second stage" of the revolution—the use of mass terror—the only possibility of calming the public mood and stabilizing the political situation lay in reaching an understanding with the church and recognizing—in the words of Rakowski—its role as "a great mediator."

Cardinal Glemp, the episcopate, and it would seem, the majority of the clergy not only agreed to play such a role but saw it as fulfilling the church's mission and as an opportunity to broaden its influence. The situation was similar to that of the fall of 1956 and the winter of 1970, but the scale of the problems was different and the amount of time needed to achieve normalization much greater. From the party's point of view the danger lay in the possibility that the church might become a permanent presence on the political stage, where it had been an active player since August 1980 at least.

The authorities therefore tried to maintain the full range of pressures on the church and politically active Catholic groups. Thus they allowed the Catholic periodicals that had been suspended on 13 December 1981 to resume publication and even honored earlier agreements regarding the establishment of new publications (some of which were actually reappearing after having been closed down many years previously), and they made it relatively easy to establish new Clubs of Catholic Intelligentsia. At the same time, however, the authorities maintained their support for PAX and the other Catholic political groups loyal to the regime. They issued numerous permits for church construction but kept up the barrage of hostile propaganda. They were also on the constant lookout for people among the clergy and bishops who would be willing to engage in a public display of loyalty. Party officials and activists at the regional and local level were largely opposed to the policy of "constructive coexistence" and the thesis that the church would continue to function "as long as the faithful want it to." General Jaruzelski simply ordered that they "consistently observe the principle of 'stick and carrot' so that the church and the clergy understand what is beneficial and what isn't." "We must improve this policy," he said, "with concrete actions to punish, to reward, to impose taxes. . . . We must skillfully point out the weak side of the church."

It was obvious to everyone, especially the party elite, that the course and success of "normalization" would depend on the state of the economy. Economic reform, in preparation since the fall of 1980 and the subject of numerous disputes with Solidarity's experts, was finally initiated, as planned, on 1 January 1982. It involved a considerable broadening of enterprise autonomy, the abolition of the intermediate management units (enterprise associations), a greater role for market mechanisms, the abolition of restrictions on the private sector in small-scale industry, and an end to the underprivileged status of private agriculture vis-à-vis cooperatives and state farms in terms of access to credit and means of production. However, regardless of the criticism voiced by those who advocated more radical measures, the reform conflicted with martial law, which tended to strengthen rather than weaken the elements of rationing in personal consumption and the "command-distribution" elements in relations between enterprises.

The Anti-Crisis Group, established in the summer of 1981, not only continued to function but also broadened the scope of its activity. Many management units now showed signs of the command methods preferred by the military commissars. In fact, the only components of the reform that were actually introduced were those relating to prices, including a drastic increase in prices: the price of food items rose by an average of 241 percent, and fuel and energy, by 171 percent. As a result, real incomes in 1982 (according to official data) were 32 percent lower than in the previous year. The problem, however, lay not simply in the public reaction to the first effects of the reform. Like all previous reform efforts this one, too, became mired in the nomenklatura system, in the incompetence of the economic apparatus and its defensive posture in the face of any innovations that might reduce its power. Above all, it was strangled by the indestructible noose of ideology, the dependence of economic policy on current political tactics and on decisions made in Moscow.

While the decline in national income was halted in 1983 (in 1985 it was almost at the level of 1978), and there was a sharp increase in industrial production (during 1982–86 gross output increased by 20 percent) and agricultural output (by 12 percent during the same period), market equilibrium was not achieved. Shortage of food items and industrial goods remained severe, forcing the authorities to continue rationing many items, including, of course, meat. Inflationary pressure increased, aggravated by wage concessions and the payments made to some groups in compensation for the price increases, which the authorities regarded as necessary to safeguard the process of normalization: during 1981–85 the average annual rate of inflation in government prices was 15 percent. Despite far-reaching restrictions amounting to a virtual ban on all investment, the state budget showed a constant deficit, which was covered by the printing of "empty money."

All the old management mechanisms that had been mothballed were now reactivated. So-called government programs, intended to restrict the flow of government subsidies and direct them to where they were most needed (the food processing industry, children's items, and so on) proliferated under the pressure exerted by interest groups in various sectors of the economy and elsewhere in the political system. The policy of "steering by hand" the flow of producer goods made it impossible to rationalize the economy at the level of the enterprise. The powerful network of branch ministries remained in place, and the enterprise associations reemerged in new forms. The Consultative Economic Council established (on 1 April 1982) at the Council of Ministers under the chairmanship of Czesław Bobrowski, the architect of the "economic miracle" of 1945–49, became—and was, no doubt, intended to be—a typical sham institution. Although the government gradually came to an agreement with foreign creditors, the country's indebtedness increased (reaching 33.5 billion dollars in 1986), and a serious deficit emerged in trade with other Comecon countries, especially the USSR (6.5 billion transferable rubles in 1986).

Economic reform, which had been so intensively popularized both before and after the imposition of martial law, was now not so much at an impasse as simply floundering in an unfavorable—even hostile—environment. Nor was any encouragement for the reform process to be found among the general public, who nurtured a widespread conviction that it would fail and that the authorities lacked the determination to see it through. Many opposition groups, especially those not linked to Solidarity, began to voice with increasing frequency the opinion that it was necessary to introduce a liberal market economy. The public became accustomed to such a view, especially as it seemed to be linked naturally to such notions as democracy and sovereignty.

General Jaruzelski and his team were plainly satisfied with the results of their labors, although the repercussions of the murder of Father Popiełuszko caused disarray in some parts of the power structure and undermined the authority that Poland had so painstakingly built up in the international arena—despite the fact that the authorities acted speedily and forcefully to bring to trial the four people accused of direct responsibility (they were sentenced, on 7 February 1985, to between fourteen and twenty-five years' imprisonment). The atmosphere created by this savage crime also presented a new challenge to the authorities, as some Solidarity activists began to act in a semi-open fashion, establishing committees to defend human rights. From the fall of 1983, when Wałęsa was awarded the Nobel Peace Prize, it became increasingly difficult to attack "the former chairman of the former union" and to prevent him from engaging in political activity. Nonetheless, the authorities considered they had laid the foundations for "normalization," as proof of which, elections to the Sejm were scheduled for 18 October 1985 and were to be conducted in accordance with the old principle of a single list of candidates (this time officially drawn up by the PRON). According to official sources, 78.8 percent of the electorate took part in the voting, confirming that the authorities had regained control over social behavior. Although Solidarity conducted a partial check of the turnout and declared that turnout in urban areas did not exceed two-thirds, such a result could still be considered positive for the PZPR.

KREMLIN BELLS

During Solidarity's first congress, when Soviet warships were standing ready off the Baltic coast, one of the union's most popular activists declared that the time would soon come when "the Kremlin bells will play Dąbrowski's Mazurka." Although this prognosis was widely viewed as just another "Polish fantasy" that also expressed a sense of superiority, the very existence of an independent organization with several million members had a decidedly destabilizing effect on relations between the superpowers, as did—and perhaps even more so—the effort to crush it by imposing martial law. These developments deepened the age-old conflict that had recently intensified when the Soviet Union rendered "fraternal assistance" to the Afghan communists, thereby bringing it closer to warm seas and the oil fields of the Middle East.

The Polish authorities may have tried to crush Solidarity on their own, but democratic governments and the world at large were well aware that Moscow had pressed strongly for decisive action. Responsibility for the imposition of martial law was assigned to leaders of both the PZPR and the CPSU and to the system of real socialism as a whole. The decision taken on 12 December 1981 was seen abroad as yet one more proof of the unreformability of communism, a system that could not tolerate the loss of control over society (and the state), and led to renewed criticism regarding its aggression and the dangers associated with this. Some of General Jaruzelski's statements, such as his comments concerning "the choice of the lesser of two evils," although addressed to a domestic audience, were interpreted as an attempt to shift the blame to Moscow. Although the Soviet Union's expansionism, so much in evidence during the 1960s and 1970s, had clearly waned, it was always possible that it was simply gathering strength before the next great leap. Both the presence of a powerful Soviet Army force (more than 50,000 troops) in Afghanistan and Poland's use of the army and police to crack down on a mass movement that laid claim to the principle of nonviolence raised a question mark over the future of détente. They certainly sounded the death knell for the theory of convergence, which had been a major component in shaping the policy of détente.

It is not surprising, then, that Western governments—and the United States in particular—reacted strongly and on a variety of levels. One of these involved the de facto freezing of official state contacts and the imposition of carefully chosen sanctions on Poland. Government loan guarantees were suspended and restrictions imposed on fishing quotas and on the landing rights of the Polish airline, LOT (23 December 1981). A stronger warning came in October 1982, after passage of the new law on trade unions and the formal banning of Solidarity: President Reagan ordered that Poland be deprived of its most favored nation trade status. Although other Western countries did not rush to imitate Washington, they eventually took similar decisions. This forced Jaruzelski's team to seek alternative partners (Austria, Denmark), and its nervous reactions—particularly those of government spokesman Jerzy Urban, who one minute threatened that French would no longer be taught in schools and another minute threatened to "break off scientific cooperation with the United States"—tended to deepen Poland's isolation rather than force Western leaders to moderate their approach.

It was, however, highly unlikely that the NATO countries would behave in complete uniformity and that sanctions against Poland would become a permanent fixture. Beginning in early 1984 they were gradually lifted. Their purpose had been to exert pressure on the country's rulers, not to declare economic war. The country of underground Solidarity was still—despite martial law and the achievement of some degree of "normalization"—a weak link in the socialist camp, sensitive to external stimuli. After all, the main enemy was Moscow, not Warsaw.

A major factor that strengthened the position of the West in relation to the Soviet Union during the first half of the 1980s was the economic boom that began in the United States in early 1983. The skillful policies of the Reagan administration not only paved the way for the boom but also managed to sustain it for several years, which strengthened the West's military potential and ensured that it had strong leadership. During 1982–87, that is to day, in the period before a new recession made itself felt, the gross domestic product of the United States grew by 27 percent and industrial output—by 33 percent. Almost all the free-market economies enjoyed relatively rapid growth. In addition to the majority of the EEC countries, the main beneficiaries were Japan and the four "Asian Tigers" (South Korea, Taiwan, Hong Kong, and Singapore), and the European countries that remained outside the EEC. Reagan also acted forcefully when he believed America's strategic interests to be threatened (the intervention in Grenada in October 1983), or acted as a "security guard," attacking states connected with international terrorism (the bombing raid on Tripoli in April 1986).

Although the United States continued to take part in disarmament negotiations, which dragged on into infinity, it increasingly did so from a position of strength. Despite sharp protests from the Kremlin, numerous objections from pacifists, and hesitation on the part of some governments, a new generation of Pershing and cruise missiles was installed in Europe, and in March 1983 the U.S. government announced plans to proceed with a costly program involving construction of an anti–ballistic missile shield, which became known as "star wars." This system of laser-guided weapons would not only be extremely expensive but would also demand the most sophisticated technology. The rapidly developing information technology would be the key component, and the disproportion between the capabilities of the Soviet Union and the West in this field was becoming increasingly evident. Even the best spy network assigned to stealing (and more often simply buying illegally) advanced equipment could not bridge the widening technological gap. The Soviet economy continued to suffer from its age-old ailments: lack of innovation, limited use of advanced technology, market imbalances, and inadequate food production. The country's indebtedness was increasing, and it was obliged to sell ever more gold in Western markets. While all the major economic indicators showed continuing growth, they did not accurately reflect the real state of affairs. The Afghan war was becoming increasingly burdensome for the Soviet economy, as was the need to provide continuing support to the equally inefficient economies of satellite states in Africa and Central America. An additional but essentially predictable problem was the biological—so to speak—instability at the very pinnacle of the power structure.

In November 1982, seventy-six-year-old Leonid Brezhnev died. His successor, Yuri Andropov, ruled for eighteen months before he was buried beneath the Kremlin wall at the age of seventy. He was followed by Konstantin Chernenko, who held office for an even shorter time; in March 1985, at the age of seventy-four, he shared the fate of his predecessors. Brezhnev was preceded by Mikhail Suslov, a Central Committee member since 1941 and chief party ideologist. And we must not forget the "indestructible" Gromyko (head of the foreign affairs ministry since 1957) and a number of other leaders who also came to the end of their days. Changes in the highest position in the party-state were accompanied by a more or less visible struggle over the succession, which disrupted the decision-making process and helped conserve the existing power structure. Although Reagan belonged to the same generation as the Soviet gerontocrats, he was, by contrast, the very personification of vitality and activity (the older Chinese leaders also managed quite well). The "dirty war" in Afghanistan and the brutality demonstrated in Poland provided an occasion to intensify anticommunist propaganda, to the point at which Reagan made his famous remark, calling the Soviet Union "the evil empire." The economic, military, and also psychological advantages of the great democracies became ever more obvious, while the USSR continued to stagnate.

It is difficult to say which factors—and in what proportion—caused Mikhail Gorbachev, the fifty-four-year-old successor to Chernenko, to decide that he would try to reform the power structure and the mechanisms of economic management. This brought with it a reduction in tensions between the two superpowers. Each one of a succession of meetings with Reagan (November 1985—Geneva, October 1986—Reykjavik, November 1987—Washington, May 1988—Moscow) brought a marked improvement in the climate between the two countries and increasingly significant concessions. The most important international decisions—the agreement to eliminate short- and medium-range missiles and to withdraw from Afghanistan—were reached in the fall of 1987. And—just as important—they were actually implemented: evacuation began on 15 May 1988, and nine months later General Boris Gromov was the last soldier of the Soviet Army to leave that inhospitable territory. Shortly afterward Reagan could take satisfaction in declaring that, during his presidency, "not one inch of the globe has fallen to communism." This assertion was backed up by the cease-fire, in mid-1988, between the communist government of Nicaragua and the anti-government guerrillas (supported by the United States).

Equally important from the point of view of the stability of the system were the changes taking place within the Soviet Union, beginning almost exactly a year after Gorbachev took office, at the Twenty-Seventh Congress of the CPSU (27 February–7 March 1986). The slogans under which these changes were introduced were not new; *perestroika* (transformation) and *uskorenie* (acceleration) had been watchwords as far back as the end of the 1920s, when the process of Stalinization was beginning in earnest. This time, however, perestroika meant almost the complete opposite—liberalization, not the unleashing of terror. Although Gorbachev's reform efforts encountered considerable resistance within the state and party apparatus, he gathered together a group of supporters and slowly but surely introduced one change after another. The reform process acquired impetus from an event that dealt a severe blow to the authority of the leadership—the catastrophe at the nuclear power station in Chernobyl, on the border between Ukraine and Belorussia. Despite efforts to hush up the disaster—which cast doubt on the real meaning of yet another slogan of the time, *glasnost* (openness)—it had a major impact on public opinion, both in the Soviet Union and abroad.

Turnover of state and party personnel accelerated, and the search for social support acquired added urgency. A moment of major symbolic significance was the phone call that Gorbachev made to the undisputed leader of the opposition, Andrei Sakharov, who had spent the years since January 1980 in internal exile in Gorky. On 16 December 1986 Gorbachev issued the order to release Sakharov from his banishment, thereby making it clear that he no longer considered it possible to make far-reaching changes without broader public support. This did not mean that dissidents were actually being invited to share responsibility for the country, nor did it signify consent to unrestricted activity on their part. Nevertheless, this telephone conversation was far more than just a grand gesture of magnanimity.

Changes in language and personnel gradually began to make their way down from the top leadership. On 23 August 1987, the anniversary of the signing of the Ribbentrop-Molotov Pact, hundreds of thousands of inhabitants of Lithuania, Latvia, and Estonia demonstrated in support of their demand for independence. Gorbachev's "thaw" had also unfrozen latent social conflicts that had been suppressed or stifled at birth. As some Western sovietologists had predicted (Hélène Carrere d'Encausse, for example), the first ruptures occurred along the seams that had for so many years held the multiethnic empire together. The massacre of Armenians in Azerbaijan in February 1988 ushered in a succession of intractable ethnic conflicts that raged from the Pamirs to the Dnieper.

The process of reform controlled from above began to give way to a process of overall destabilization. Despite a number of gestures designed to instill discipline (such as the expulsion of Boris Yeltsin, whose ideas were considered too radical), the CPSU leadership was no longer able to steer the process of change. As a consequence, it also lost the ability to retain control over its "internal empire" in East-Central Europe. The communist leaders of the rest of the Soviet bloc suddenly found themselves abandoned to their fate. The Soviet tanks they had used over the years to blackmail their citizens had begun to run out of gasoline. The bells in the Kremlin still played the "Internationale," but fewer and fewer people were willing to arise when summoned by the song.

FLEEING TOWARD THE ENEMY

The tactical goals of martial law were realized only in part: Solidarity was severely injured but not defeated; the economy recovered from its steep decline but no reforms were carried out. The fact that General Jaruzelski had won the first battle and then the campaign did not mean that he had won the war, for which he had allowed himself ten years. After several years of economic revival, accompanied by all the traditional systemic failings and shortages, the situation once again began to deteriorate. Output declined, bottlenecks multiplied, and inflationary pressure increased. The authorities sought relief in a succession of "price-wage maneuvers," which had only a limited effect, partly because they were afraid of provoking social unrest. Nevertheless, the leadership put a good face on a bad situation, as could be seen not only—and not so much—in the claims of propaganda as in the elections to the Sejm. A sense of stabilization was also evident in the fact that the PZPR held another congress (29 June–3 July 1986).

The leadership viewed the congress as an event that would help reactivate the party, which remained in a state of lethargy despite martial law and despite the insistent efforts of the hard-liners. Membership remained unchanged numerically, but in terms of the party's interests, its social composition deteriorated. In 1984 manual workers made up 38.5 percent of the membership, and people aged 18–29 constituted barely 7.6 percent (compared with 23.5 percent in 1978). The PZPR was aging at an alarming rate, with a growing proportion of its membership consisting of retirees and administrative employees. Despite the existence of the far-reaching nomenklatura system, the party was clearly losing its attraction. Mistrust and antipathy outweighed the benefits of membership. The party apparatus, on the other hand, was expanding. In 1985 the PZPR was one of Poland's largest employers, with a workforce of some 20,500, of whom 1,300 worked in the Central Committee apparatus. General Jaruzelski, doggedly implementing his centrist policies, made a few, but largely insignificant, personnel changes.

The newcomers to the top party leadership had no authority in the eyes of the public, and most of them were mistrusted by regional officials and activists. Since the first secretary totally dominated the congress, those he selected were people who would not threaten to have their own opinions on important issues but who could pass for "intelligent executors." Further evidence that everything was to continue as before was provided by the fact that Miodowicz was elevated to the Politburo. This promotion may have satisfied his personal ambition, but it certainly undermined the credibility of the trade union organization that he headed. Despite his control over the party, Jaruzelski did not abandon his practice of having his own—almost private—group of advisers, which included Wiesław Górnicki, Jerzy Urban,

Stanisław Ciosek, and General Władysław Pożoga (deputy minister of internal affairs). Other close associates included Rakowski, General Józef Baryła, and Generals Siwicki and Kiszczak. There was semi-official talk of the need for presidential government, and the term "enlightened absolutism" made its appearance; this was supposed to indicate that ideology was of diminishing significance in the power structure.

Nevertheless, the ideological rhetoric continued unabated in the press, on television and radio, and in the speeches of Jaruzelski himself. This did not make it easy to "repair the ravages of social consciousness." In fact, ever broader swathes of social consciousness were "ravaged," largely thanks to underground publications, popular lectures organized under the auspices of the church, and the Polish-language programs broadcast by foreign radio stations (in the mid-1980s, 25 percent of the population listened to Radio Free Europe). The authorities created extensive "educational programs" in history and economics, and there was an increase in the number of agencies concerned with the struggle "on the ideological front." In April 1984 the Academy of Social Sciences was formed, a powerful party institute with all the powers of a state university. Central Committee officials inundated Academy employees with requests for opinion surveys and analyses of all kinds, but none of their recommendations, not even the most competent, was suitable for implementation. Unless, perhaps, someone was planning to initiate a decisive policy change.

There was a growing realization that such a change was needed. The fundamental issue gradually tipping the balance in the direction of far-reaching reform was the impasse in the economy, which threatened at any moment to erupt in social unrest whose impact would be all the greater in that it would be channeled by underground Solidarity organizations. In a situation in which the authorities had barely managed to neutralize a large proportion of the population, this meant that clandestine activists would be operating from a position of strength. The situation that had arisen after the murder of Father Popiełuszko also led the church to stiffen its position. Increasing signs of pluralism within the broad opposition movement posed no immediate danger but could do so in the long term. Various youth groups were particularly active, especially the Freedom and Peace Movement (WiP), formed in April 1985, and the anarchist Movement for a Social Alternative. Small political groups were proliferating, and the radical Fighting Solidarity was gaining support. By force of circumstance Wałęsa and the TKK began to look like a moderate opposition.

The party's coalition allies, fearing that they would go down with the PZPR, again began to manifest their desire for autonomy. Some petty disputes erupted, including a row with the ZSL over the erection of a monument to Witos. The OPZZ was gaining strength. It now had some six million members, and Miodowicz was in no position to control the whole movement, which was becoming increasingly focused on articulating members' demands. These tendencies derived their impetus not only from the economic situation but also from the existence of underground Solidarity organizations, especially in the large factories. There was no sign that the sense of frustration, especially evident among the younger generations, was diminishing; in fact, it seemed to be increasing. This was indicated by sociological surveys and by the endless wave of people "voting with their feet": during 1980–86 more than 700,000 people remained abroad, more than two-thirds of them aged under thirty-five. Thousands of highly qualified specialists—engineers, doctors, and scientists—left the country. Although the immediate reasons for the wave of emigration were economic, both the authorities and those who emigrated viewed the decision to leave as a political one, indicating lack of confidence in the country's future.

With their backs once more against the wall, it seems that General Jaruzelski and his colleagues came to realize that they faced a stark choice: they could engage in another display of force along the lines of 13 December or they could try to involve some of the opposition in the decision-making process. The international situation, particularly the emergence of Gorbachev and his policy of perestroika, made the first option less feasible; and in any case, the first secretary and his group were by no means convinced that it would be successful. The "second stage" of economic reform, launched in a fanfare of propaganda, made no impression on either the public or the economic administration; and the accompanying campaigns, such as the "review of administrative positions," had done nothing to rationalize management and production and were no substitute for real change. Even such measures as the appointment of economist Zbigniew Messner to the post of prime minister, a move intended to emphasize the government's professional competence, had aroused little public interest and certainly no hope that the situation might suddenly improve. What was needed was a political gesture (and action) on a grander scale.

Such a gesture was made on 11 September 1986, when General Kiszczak announced the release of all political prisoners, some 225 people according to official data (among those not released was a group convicted of murdering a policeman in February 1982). The second half of the gesture involved the formation of the Consultative Council, a body that was to advise the chairman of the Council of State, a post held by General Jaruzelski since November 1985. The release of political prisoners was intended to be—and it was—a gesture of good will addressed to many constituencies. They included Western governments, whose assistance the leadership needed in view of the country's intractable economic problems. They also included the Catholic Church, which—as General Jaruzelski stated at a meeting of the Central Committee Secretariat in October 1986—had "adopted the position of critic" and should be "drawn into a position of joint responsibility for the country." The measure was all the more important in light of the fact that the pope would make yet another pilgrimage to Poland the following year. They were also intended to make life difficult for underground Solidarity by depriving it of one of its most important, and widely supported, demands.

The formation of the Consultative Council—which would have been impossible without the release of political prisoners—was a step in the same direction. The authorities also had other hopes of the new body, in light of the total fiasco of the PRON, which had done more to repel than attract those groups whose support the party was seeking. The Consultative Council was intended as a weapon to divide the opposition and to enlist from it a small group of people with enough prestige to function as a counterweight to Wałęsa, the intellectuals who operated as his advisers, and the TKK.

These intentions were only partly fulfilled. Although the TKK issued a statement welcoming the release of political prisoners as "fulfilling one of Solidarity's main demands," it went on to remind the authorities of the union's remaining demands, more important and more difficult to implement: "the restoration of pluralism in the trade union movement," "transformation of the economy," and the creation of conditions for "independent social activity." More important than Solidarity's verbal response was the action that it took. On 29 September 1986 Wałęsa, presenting the authorities with a fait accompli, announced that he had established the Interim Council, a body that would function openly and whose members were seven of the underground's most prominent activists. In a statement accompanying the announcement, Wałęsa noted that "dialogue must be institutionalized, but not in sham institutions." "This means," he continued, "the acceptance of the principle that all social bodies be independent and representative."

Solidarity's regional underground organizations followed suit, creating their own openly functioning committees. Similar developments took place in some factories, and at the beginning of November the first factory-level "founding committees" began applying to the courts for formal registration. For his part, Wałęsa made a good-will gesture of his own on 10 October when he signed, together with eight other opposition activists, an appeal to President Reagan requesting the lifting of economic sanctions against Poland.

The position of the Solidarity leadership thwarted the plans associated with the Consultative Council and was supported by, among others, the Warsaw Club of Catholic Intelligentsia, which voted not to delegate a representative to the council. As a result, the council, which convened in early December, had only one or two members who could be considered associated with the opposition (Władysław Siła-Nowicki) or the episcopate (Andrzej Święcicki and Krzysztof Skubiszewski), and none of them had a social mandate. Although council members could speak freely during its debates, and transcripts of the proceedings were widely distributed, its activities aroused little public interest and it certainly did not become a forum in which the opposition aired its views.

Other measures taken by Jaruzelski and his colleagues in 1987 were similarly ineffective and essentially timid. Neither the legalization of the uncensored periodical, *Res Publica,* nor the discussions that Central Committee Secretary Józef Czyrek held with a group of activists from the Catholic intelligentsia clubs yielded any results in terms of changing opposition attitudes. On the other hand, liberalizing gestures simply paved the way for further demonstrations of independence: from the happenings staged by the Orange Alternative in Wrocław (the first of these took place on Children's Day, 1 June 1987), to events such as the international conference organized by WiP, and the creation of private businesses by "positivistically" inclined opposition activists (among them, Mirosław Dzielski in Kraków).

Although the opposition and Solidarity did not enjoy any spectacular successes, they gradually acquired a self-confidence that could not be undermined by new forms of harassment (confiscation and fines). The changing atmosphere could be felt during the visit (8–14 June 1987) of John Paul II, during which he celebrated mass in two cities that had been out of bounds in 1983—Gdańsk and Szczecin. Crowds numbering in the millions were not as emotionally wound up as during previous pilgrimages, but everywhere people carried placards with the Solidarity symbol. A group of opposition intellectuals assembled by Wałęsa greeted the pope's arrival with a declaration in which they noted that "the Poles—like every other nation in the world—have the right to independence" and democracy, and "the right to freely shape their economic order." The authorities discretely displayed their dissatisfaction with the course of the pilgrimage. They were concerned by the meeting between John Paul II and Wałęsa, which acquired quasi-official status by virtue of being held in the official residence of the bishop of Gdańsk. They were also concerned by the substance of the pope's public pronouncements, listening in vain for him to urge obedience to the state and support for General Jaruzelski's initiatives.

Party leaders could not, however, neutralize this atmosphere—just as they could no longer isolate Wałęsa from the government's official foreign visitors. They were too dependent on good relations with the West, or more accurately, with the country's creditors. Thus in January 1987, the (former) head of a (former) trade union met with Deputy U.S. Secretary of State John Whitehead, and in September he met with Vice President—and as yet unofficial Republican candidate for the White House—George Bush.

These meetings, together with the increasingly numerous discussions that foreign visitors and Western diplomatic personnel had with Wałęsa's advisers and Solidarity activists, enhanced the public perception of the union as an opposition force—at the very least, in opposition to the ruling group and, essentially, in opposition to the whole system. Given that Gorbachev's reformist faction was gaining strength, the Kremlin might have viewed liberalization in Poland as welcome support. The opposition, however, offered no visible gestures of the kind the authorities were hoping for. Instead, it reiterated at every opportunity its demands for the relegalization of Solidarity and the creation of a legal framework allowing the formation of independent social and political organizations. While General Jaruzelski's ruling group might have been acquiring a "human face," this did not mean that it was thereby acquiring either legitimacy or support. Given the changes taking place in Moscow, the notion of "the lesser of two evils" had lost its resonance, and the number of people who held a positive view of martial law began to decline from the high point in 1986 (when 32.5 percent of those surveyed were "highly positive" and 33.3 percent were "generally positive" in their opinion).

The party leadership, unable to gain institutional support from Wałęsa and Solidarity—which it probably still considered superfluous and definitely considered dangerous—decided it would try to engineer a show of public support through a plebiscite. The idea seemed promising in that it involved no obligation toward any particular political force or social group. On 29 November 1987 the public was given the opportunity to vote in a referendum, which had been preceded by a spectacular reorganization of the central state apparatus, abolishing virtually all the branch ministries. Out of a total of twenty-six ministries, nineteen survived, and the number of deputy prime ministers was reduced to the rational number of three. The questions posed in the referendum were somewhat general (to do with "restoring the economy to a healthy state" and "the far-reaching democratization of political life") and reminiscent of the reformist incantations, repeated ad nauseam over the years and which had never led to anything concrete. On the other hand, the leadership set (itself) a very high threshhold: a positive result required a "yes" vote on the part of 50 percent of all those eligible to vote, not simply 50 percent of those who actually voted. This made things much easier for the opposition, which called on voters to boycott the referendum or vote "two times no." This time, the opposition did not challenge the official results to the extent that it had following elections to the Sejm and the national councils. Turnout was officially reported to be 63 percent. The first question was answered positively by 66 percent of voters, and the second received a positive response from 69 percent. This meant that in neither case did the authorities achieve their 50 percent goal. They missed it narrowly, by about 5 percent, but they missed.

The opposition in the meantime was rallying around Wałęsa, whose position was unassailable, despite the fact that alongside Kornel Morawiecki there had emerged a second group of opposition malcontents in the form of a body calling itself the Working Group of the National Commission. In October 1987 Solidarity established the National Executive Commission, headed by Wałęsa. Opposition intellectuals associated with the union were also busy, holding numerous meetings. In December Solidarity circles began floating the idea of an "anti-crisis pact" between the opposition and what they took to be reform-minded centrists in the PZPR. In February 1988 the PRON weekly, *Konfrontacje,* published an interview with Bronisław Geremek, in which he argued in favor of the idea. Before this (in December) the party weekly, *Polityka,* and the opposition *Tygodnik Powszechny* had each published an open letter from Jerzy Holzer, a well-known historian active in the opposition, urging Wałęsa and Jaruzelski to meet without any "preliminary preconditions."

Although the authorities had reason to be suspicious of these initiatives, to reject them would have signaled to the outside world that they were confident of their own strength. As early as September 1987 Jaruzelski's advisers were warning him that "the situation is more dangerous than at any time since 13 December 1981," suggesting that he "preempt the situation" and even that "the first secretary should stand at the head of the discontent." They imagined, however, that this kind of leadership would involve no more than "severe criticism of the poor, sloppy, inconsistent implementation of the policy laid out by the party." The most radical proposal involved "inviting Wałęsa to the Consultative Council" and the suggestion that the referendum contain a question regarding the desirability of introducing the position of president. Assuming that everyone would understand that this post was being created for Jaruzelski, he would gain "national legitimacy."

Thus on 8 February 1988, in accordance with the program on "the second stage of reform"—and in keeping with reform custom—the government raised prices. Although these increases were partly offset by wage increases for some groups, even OPZZ members found them hard to take. The atmosphere became increasingly tense, and a detonator was provided when the city transport department in Bydgoszcz called a strike (24 April) in support of purely economic demands. The iron and steel works in Nowa Huta and Stalowa Wola soon followed suit. On 2 May some workers at the Gdańsk Shipyard began a sit-in strike, and political demands, concerning Solidarity, were added to the strikers' economic demands. A new element, particularly evident in Gdańsk, was the participation of workers too young to have been part of legal Solidarity. After some hesitation, and despite mediation efforts undertaken by people designated by the church, the authorities decided to use force. Several strikes were crushed by ZOMO units, while others collapsed when faced with the threat of force. On 10 May the Gdańsk strike ended without any formal talks having taken place. Strike participants, led by Wałęsa and Mazowiecki, marched to the Church of Saint Brygida, the "home" of the Gdańsk opposition.

While many people found these events dispiriting, the state and party authorities could draw comfort from them. It looked as though they were no longer in imminent danger, the strike wave would not be repeated any time soon, and the prestige of Wałęsa and Solidarity had suffered a serious blow. General Jaruzelski undoubtedly felt his own position strengthened by the relatively friendly reception that Mikhail Gorbachev encountered during his visit to Poland, although he disappointed those who had been hoping that the Soviet communists would beat their breasts and express repentance for the crimes committed against Polish officers in 1940. True, all was not quiet in the country: radical groups took no heed of efforts to restrict their activities, and the opposition essentially functioned in a semi-open manner, concealing only its technical base, as it had done "before August." But it might have seemed to the authorities that this situation provided grounds for a certain stabilization, one that would satisfy both sides, at least in part.

"THE SPRING WILL BE OURS"

The forecast that "the spring will be ours," expressed in the slogans of the underground during the early days of martial law, began to come true in the middle of summer, although—as is often the case with spring—there were several sudden cold spells. On 15 August 1988, miners at the Manifest Lipcowy coal mine went on strike. Within a few days work had come to a halt at several other mines and at the port of Szczecin and Port Północny in Gdańsk. After a week, the strike wave reached the cradle of Solidarity, the Gdańsk Shipyard. To some extent this took both the authorities and the opposition by surprise.

This time, nearly all the strikes and the interfactory strike committees were headed by new people, most of them young. On 20 August, two days before the Gdańsk Shipyard came to a halt, when both the authorities and Solidarity were clearly losing control of the rising strike wave, the two sides began exploratory talks, in which Andrzej Stełmachowski acted on behalf of both the church and Wałęsa. The purpose of the talks was to come up with a formula that would allow the two sides to begin "a dialogue." Jaruzelski had all the more need of this as the OPZZ, defending the principle of "one factory = one trade union," was not only sharply criticizing the government's economic policy but had called on the marshal of the Sejm (as usual, a "peasant" from the ZSL) to convene an extraordinary session to discuss the issue. The "neo-unions," whose members now made up nearly half the workforce, could not afford to remain silent without losing influence. This was yet another source of pressure on the Jaruzelski team, as well as a convenient instrument with which to persuade the party apparatus and *aktiv* of the need to make concessions to the opposition.

On 26 August the Conference of Bishops, meeting against the backdrop of the annual pilgrimage to Jasna Góra, stated that it was necessary to "search for ways leading to union pluralism and to the creation of associations." The next day General Kiszczak announced the authorities' willingness to engage in discussions with "representatives of a variety of social and occupational groups." While the word "Solidarity" could not (yet) pass his lips, it was clear to everyone, including those attending a meeting of the Central Committee, who was supposed to be the main partner in such discussions. Perhaps it was no coincidence that it was on 31 August, the anniversary of the Gdańsk Agreement to which everyone was now referring, that the head of the Ministry of Internal Affairs met with the leader of Solidarity. The authorities stated that a precondition for beginning negotiations about organizing a "round table" was an end to all strikes, which Wałęsa was able to achieve, with some difficulty, within a few days. The authorities did not, however, forget that they had at their disposal means other than dialogue. On 20 August the Committee for the Defense of the Homeland had already decided to begin preparations for a state of emergency. It issued the appropriate instructions to both the army and the state administration and established a deadline for the completion of preparations: 31 October.

Discussions between representatives of the authorities and Solidarity took place on 15 and 16 September and were attended by observers—essentially mediators—from the church. Talks soon came to a halt, however. They collapsed over Solidarity's unyielding position regarding its legalization and its refusal to accept the authorities' right to veto its selection of delegates to take part in the round table. Kiszczak would not agree to let people who "do not respect the constitutional order" participate in the talks, by which he was referring specifically to Kuroń and Michnik. For their part, the OPZZ and virtually the whole party apparatus protested against the principle of union pluralism, but the authorities seemed to be satisfied with the fact that the strike wave was dying down and to be convinced that they would achieve an outcome totally to their liking. Miodowicz finally got one thing he wanted: on 19 September the Sejm dismissed the Messner government, a move that also gave Jaruzelski additional room for maneuver. Messner was replaced by Mieczysław F. Rakowski, since 1981 one of Jaruzelski's closest associates and someone who still enjoyed a somewhat tattered reputation as a reformer. He tried an old trick, looking for people in the opposition willing to accept a ministerial appointment, but everyone he asked turned him down.

This was no doubt a tactical maneuver on the part of this impulsive, eloquent, and (as his memoirs suggest) supremely self-confident politician. In any event, Rakowski decided (with the obvious assent of the Politburo) to dispense with negotiations and go it alone. One of his trump cards was to make further changes in the state administration, including another reduction in the number of ministries and the transformation of the Planning Commission into the Central Planning Office, a move that brought back memories of the 1945–48 period and the principle of the "multisector economy" that prevailed at that time. He also made some unexpected appointments, particularly that of Mieczysław Wilczek as minister for industry. While Wilczek was a PZPR member, he was also the owner of a highly successful business, and he was meant both to implement and symbolize the new economic policy. The new government dispensed with all political maneuvering and simply drew up a whole range of economic decisions, the main thrust of which involved a considerable liberalization of policy toward private business, the abolition of restrictions on foreign currency transactions, and the easing of price controls. This was meant to be yet another attempt—and the boldest to date—to introduce market principles into the economy.

Evidence that Rakowski saw no reason to "stroke" the opposition was provided by the fact that he kept as government spokesman Jerzy Urban, a figure who was by now widely despised (but watched with masochistic pleasure). A stronger signal was Rakowski's statement that people preferred "a table that is well laid to one that is round," but the real sign—of both proposed economic changes and his contempt for Solidarity—was the decision, announced on 31 October, to close down the Gdańsk Shipyard.

These gestures, redolent of a hard-line approach, were accompanied by feverish debate within the party. An attempt was made to replace the notion of "union pluralism" with that of "social pluralism." At the very highest levels of the PZPR there was even discussion about whether it would be more opportune to allow the formation of opposition political parties than to allow the relegalization of Solidarity, which most party officials and members of the Miodowcz unions vehemently opposed. The leadership commissioned dozens of opinion surveys and analyses and invited various groups—including anti-Solidarity nationalist groups—to take part in "a national debate on the future of the Homeland." Increasing emphasis was given to the idea of distinguishing between "extremists" and the "constructive opposition." At the same time, General Jaruzelski and his colleagues spared no effort to convince the party apparatus of the need for change, waging a kind of war on two fronts as they did so: to Solidarity they argued that major concessions were impossible, since they were opposed by the "base" of the party, and to the latter they presented the danger of further social explosions that could destroy the entire system. In the end, however, despite another meeting between Wałęsa and Kiszczak (18–19 November), the impasse remained.

Paradoxically, the first major step toward breaking out of this impasse was taken by one of the most decided opponents of an agreement with Solidarity: Miodowicz publicly proposed that he and his greatest enemy, Wałęsa, meet in a debate that would be transmitted live on television. The Politburo gave its consent, although it had the foresight to tell the OPZZ leader that he could not appear in the name of the entire party leadership. The debate took place on the evening of 30 November 1988 and was an undisputed triumph for the Solidarity leader, who appeared calm, moderate, and self-assured. "I don't know what happened to Miodowicz," Jaruzelski moaned to a group of close associates. "Something dreadful. And he so badly wanted this debate, like a moth round a flame." He admitted, however, "I thought he would destroy Wałęsa."

The ease with which Wałęsa upset Jaruzelski's prediction largely resulted from the fact that he spoke simply about simple truths and gave his opinions without regard to tactical considerations. The very appearance on television of someone so recently branded with infamy was a strong stimulus for millions of viewers. The course of the debate made many people realize, even the opponents of Wałęsa and Solidarity, that they were dealing with a serious partner and with a genuinely different view of official doctrine. Wałęsa's success at home was augmented by his visit to France (9–12 December), where he met with Andrei Sakharov, an event that the Polish media could not ignore.

Although party leaders were more disconcerted than satisfied by this television duel, its effect was to encourage them to carry on rather than abandon their reform efforts. Perhaps it was not simply that they were convinced of the necessity for and correctness of their measures; perhaps a certain defense mechanism came into play once they had decided on a course of action, and the opposition of "the base" simply strengthened their determination. During the next meeting of the Central Committee, which was divided into two sessions (20–21 December 1988 and 16–18 January 1989)—a sharp conflict erupted between Jaruzelski and his associates and the majority of the central party *aktiv*. Jaruzelski had so committed himself to the political line he was advocating that to abandon it would have been to court total defeat and the likelihood that most of his close associates, if not he himself, would be forced out of office. After dramatic debates, in which many people voiced complete opposition to Jaruzelski's policies—frequently referred to as "capitulation"—the position of the "centrists" was, nevertheless, adopted. At a crucial moment, the three generals (Jaruzelski, Kiszczak, and Siwicki), together with the prime minister, threatened to resign. While a vote of confidence in the entire Politburo did pass, the fact that as many as 32 out of 178 Central Committee members voted against (and 14 abstained) suggested that Jaruzelski was far from exerting complete control over the situation. Such a state of affairs did not often occur in communist parties. In the end, the Central Committee adopted a document titled "The Position of the PZPR Central Committee on the Question of Political and Trade Union Pluralism," opening the way for discussions with Solidarity.

In contrast to the struggle taking place within the party, the opposition was preparing itself for a new—but as yet unknown—role in an atmosphere of peace and quiet, or at least in what passed for such. On 18 December 1988, 119 people selected by Wałęsa took part in the first meeting of the Citizens' Committee, a body that was to help prepare for negotiations with the authorities. This group included opposition intellectuals of various ideological tendencies, people who had been acting as advisers to "an ordinary citizen"—as the government's press spokesman liked to refer to Wałęsa—and union activists, both those who had played a role in the underground and some who had organized the strikes of 1988. The Citizens' Committee, whose secretary was former KOR member Henryk Wujec and whose de facto leaders were Bronisław Geremek and Tadeusz Mazowiecki, was divided into working groups, whose task was to determine who would represent the committee at the Round Table negotiations. Not all opposition tendencies were represented on the committee. Virtually all political parties and groups were excluded, including those, such as Fighting Solidarity, that had their roots in August 1980. The opposition was becoming increasingly polarized between "the moderates" and "the radicals," the latter objecting to the whole notion of negotiating anything with "the commies." This group included long-standing oppositionists, such as Leszek Moczulski and his party, younger people who had entered political life during martial law (the most active of them belonged to the Federation of Fighting Youth and the RSA as well as the NZS), and some Solidarity leaders who had fallen out with Wałęsa (among them Marian Jurczyk, Jan Rulewski, and Andrzej Gwiazda). Although the radical groups were active and visible, they were fragmented and in no position to threaten the position of Wałęsa and his Citizens' Committee. They played a role similar to that played on the other side of the barricades by the OPZZ. Compared with them, Wałęsa and his supporters appeared as a moderate group, ready to cooperate, just as Jaruzelski and Kiszczak appeared moderate in comparison with Miodowicz or Kociołek.

The committee's preparations for negotiations took as their starting point the notion that the basic goal was to achieve a situation in which the ban on Solidarity (together with Rural Solidarity and the NZS) was lifted, and independent political parties and groups could function legally. Most of the demands raised were those of the years 1980–81, such as the liberalization of censorship, access to the state-run media, the opportunity for the opposition to publish its own newspapers, abolition of the nomenklatura, vigorous implementation of economic reform (including reform based on workers' self-management), freedom of association, the abolition of all organizational monopolies (including that of the state-run scout movement), independence of the judiciary, and an end to administrative and party control of regional self-government bodies. These were accompanied by an imposing package of economic demands, including the demand that wages keep pace with the cost of living.

Most of the committee's members, including Wałęsa himself, were not thinking about seizing power or even about sharing in it. Many people considered that too risky in light of the deepening economic crisis, the power of the army and the security apparatus, and the uncertainties regarding Moscow's position in the event of sudden and overall change. This moderation was partly tactical, but the ambivalence of the "constructive opposition" was evident not only in public statements but also in the private preparatory discussions conducted in the government villa in Magdalenka, outside Warsaw. The presence of a representative of the episcopate, which was decidedly opposed to radical proposals, was an additional moderating factor.

Nevertheless, a crucial question was clearly posed during these discussions, although perhaps just for bargaining purposes. "For us, the people of Solidarity," Geremek remarked on 27 January, "the basic issue is free elections. We understand the need for limits . . . that would allow an evolutionary arrangement and simultaneously move toward the freedom that society is justifiably demanding." "You are not in a position to block freedom," added Wałęsa. "It's not possible to develop without freedom." The opposition sought to undermine the party's control over the legislative process by gaining parliamentary representation while not sharing in executive power. Nevertheless, the issue of how to achieve this representation, and what date to set for elections, became a major element in the maneuvering. Józef Cz-yrek, reporting to the Central Committee, quoted the position of the church as being: "Call elections whenever you like, as long as they are free." In this approach, an "evolutionary arrangement" was one in which the elections would be "nonconfrontational."

The PZPR leadership started from quite a different position. Jaruzelski told the Central Committee Secretariat that the decision to hold the Round Table negotiations had been taken "because of the growing danger of a strike, because of the possibility that Wałęsa would seize the initiative, be-cause we had to play for time." Władysław Baka, the Central Committee secretary responsible for the economy, noted that "we have been forced to hold discussions by our forecast of how the economic situation would de-velop, and the worst possible variant of this forecast has been confirmed." Jaruzelski justified the party's willingness to strike a compromise in similar terms during a conversation with East Germany's Erich Honecker, who was highly alarmed at developments in Poland. The party's top leaders saw the success of their plans as hinging on what they called "joint elections," in-volving a joint electoral program and joint lists of candidates (including the national list), on which there would be room for "nonparty" candidates. They were ready to assign such candidates 30–35 percent of seats in the new parliament. The party's proposal did not contain that much of a risk, since it would, in effect, have drawn the opposition into a coalition govern-ment, in which the key ministries would remain in the hands of the commu-nists while responsibility for the inevitable economic collapse—the advent of which could only be hastened by acceding to worker demands—would be shared by everyone. "The party wishes to share power, but wisely": such was the general tenor of comments made at the highest levels.

Although Jaruzelski noted "disturbing signals concerning the behavior of the party's allies, which are in deep trouble," he contented himself with General Kiszczak's proposal that "we make them realize in no uncertain terms that we are providing them with protection." The leadership had greater problems with the OPZZ, which feared that the relegalization of Solidarity would cause a mass exodus from its member-organizations and relegate them to the sidelines. To the consternation of Jaruzelski and his colleagues, especially the prime minister, and despite sharp public criticism on their part, OPZZ activists went all out, attempting to arouse a wave of strikes and outdo Solidarity in the radicalism of their demands (the abolition of censorship, free elections). In essence, the PZPR leadership was in a worse position than the Citizens' Committee, in the same way that someone on the retreat is usually in a worse position than someone on the offensive. "We are putting the noose around our own necks," said Kiszczak in a moment of despairing frankness. "We are going to the slaughter like sheep."

When the plenary sessions of the Round Table began in the great hall of the Namiestnikowski Palace on 6 February 1989, the country was in a state of nervous anticipation. In the background of the political struggle now being played out increasingly in the open, in full view of the public, the wave of strikes was rising as a result of worker discontent over the accelerating pace of inflation, and radical groups were becoming increasingly energetic and bold. The strike that erupted in the Bełchatów brown-coal mine threatened to spread to the rest of the mining industry, and the organizers included a union belonging to the OPZZ. On 17 February a number of opposition groups—the Independent Student Association, the Confederation for an Independent Poland, and the Federation of Fighting Youth—began a series of demonstrations in Kraków that lasted a week and led to clashes with police. Fighting Solidarity also organized demonstrations, as did a radical wing of the Polish Socialist Party. In late March and early April, police clashed with environmental activists demonstrating in Poznań, and every Sunday in Gdańsk the Movement for a Social Alternative organized a "smoke-in."

The Round Table had split into working commissions, and every evening the television news broadcast pictures of their sessions, interspersed with scenes of ZOMO units charging at young—often juvenile—demonstrators. The ceaseless problems of everyday life, the empty stores and long lines, did nothing to lighten the public's mood, which was further worsened by the visible signs of speculation and the beginnings of the free market, stimulated by the government's decision to free, within the country, the exchange rate of the złoty against the dollar and other hard currencies.

General Jaruzelski and his associates were counting on the church to exercise a moderating influence, but while the episcopate certainly refrained from calling for action of any kind and continued to support all moderate groups, it had no influence over the public's feelings. "With regret we must admit that the church's activities are limited," Archbishop Stroba told Rakowski during one of several private discussions. The church was concentrating, we can assume, on piloting the Round Table discussions, which time and again erupted in clashes that could have brought the negotiations to an end.

The Round Table turned into a powerful machine, with several hundred participants divided into three groups (the economy and social policy, union pluralism, and political reforms), nine subgroups (whose topics included legal reform, the mass media, mining, agriculture), and three working groups (one of which dealt with wage indexation). Fifty-seven people took part in the plenary sessions, which were opened by General Kiszczak, in his role as host of the proceedings. On one side of Wałęsa sat his chief adviser, Tadeusz Mazowiecki, and on the other, the "underground legend," Zbigniew Bujak. While the opposition-Solidarity side was united, the government-coalition side was troubled by internal conflicts, most of them concerning OPZZ representation at the talks.

The discussions dragged on, the public grew impatient, and to avoid having the talks end in failure there had to be—in addition to totally informal and even private conversations—a series of "working meetings," nearly all of which took place at the increasingly notorious Magdalenka. The eight-week marathon, which was in itself a great spectacle, dealt with hundreds of problems of varying degrees of importance. Its greatest achievement was a wide-ranging political agreement, referred to, half ironically, half critically, as the "contract of the century." It involved a package of measures concerning a fundamental reorganization of the highest state organs—the creation of a second chamber of parliament (Senate) and the office of president—and a new electoral law. The government abandoned its central demand that elections take place on the basis of a single list and a joint program. After lengthy bargaining it was decided that all seats in the Senate and 35 percent of seats in the Sejm would be filled on the basis of a free vote, while the remaining 65 percent of Sejm deputies would be elected from a single list divided among candidates from the PZPR and its allies in the PRON (thirty-five of whom would be on the list of national candidates).

In this way the communists ensured themselves—or so they thought—a "controlling share" of parliamentary seats, enough for the day-to-day business of running the country and enough to block any one-sided constitutional changes, which required a two-thirds majority. Given that the Senate was limited to a hundred seats, they also created the very real possibility of electing their candidate as president, since this election was to be conducted by both chambers, meeting together as the National Assembly. According to the letter of the provision, the elections really would be "nonconfrontational." The party thought this also meant the election campaign would be a gentle business.

A crucial element in the "contract" were the prerogatives of the president, since it was obvious—and even agreed—that General Jaruzelski would be the most serious candidate. The agreement did not go as far as introducing presidential rule, but the office of president was accorded a broad array of powers—first and foremost, command of the armed forces and responsibility for the country's internal and external security. The president (Jaruzelski) was to be a guarantor that further changes in the political system would be of an evolutionary nature. In exchange for its agreement to these arrangements, the opposition secured a strengthening of the position of the Senate, whose legislative veto could only be overturned by a vote of at least two-thirds of deputies in the Sejm.

On 5 April the negotiations came to a ceremonial end, with the signing of the main documents: "Position on the Issue of Political Reforms," "Position on the Issue of Social and Political Policy and Systemic Reforms," and "Position on the Issue of Union Pluralism." General Kiszczak solemnly promised to respect the principle of *pacta sunt servanda,* and Wałęsa recalled the slogan that demonstrators used to chant—"*Nie ma wolności bez Solidarności*" (There is no freedom without Solidarity). The rules had been established, and formalized by appropriate measures on the part of the Sejm, but it was impossible to predict precisely the outcome of the elections. The answer would be known on 4 June.

The Round Table, widely reported on radio and television and in the press, became an event that reached far beyond the borders of Poland. The negotiations were followed closely in both the West and the East. Gorbachev, increasingly preoccupied with domestic matters (elections of deputies, constant ethnic unrest) did not speak publicly on the issues. The Western democracies emitted numerous signals in support of Wałęsa and his entourage, but they did not get involved and were even happy to maintain official contacts—including economic contacts—with the Rakowski government. It was communist leaders elsewhere in East-Central Europe who followed events most carefully. Some, such as Honecker and Zhivkov, watched with increasing alarm, others, such as the Hungarians, with a certain amount of hope, because they themselves were already involved in the process of reform, having proclaimed, in January, freedom of association and assembly. At the end of March the Budapest Round Table began deliberations, except that for the time being it was made up entirely of opposition activists preparing for their own battle with the communist party.

Yet again in the course of ten years Poland was the focus of world interest, although, for understandable reasons, observers were paying close attention to Moscow. Credit for the peaceful and rational manner in which the Polish crisis was resolved was attributed jointly to Wałęsa, Jaruzelski, and the master of the Kremlin, giving new impetus to "Gorbymania" in the West. More important, though, was the pronouncement of President Bush, only recently sworn in, when he emphasized, in a speech delivered on 17 April, the important of "the Polish experiment" and expressed the hope that "other countries will follow in its footsteps." He added, in encouragement, that "Western aid will come with liberalization."

In the meantime, both sides in Poland were preparing for the election campaign, which had been the subject of some discussion during the Round Table negotiations. On 7 April the Solidarity National Executive Commission passed a resolution declaring: "It is a matter of utmost importance to make maximum use of the opportunities that have arisen, despite the fact that these will not yet be fully democratic elections." The next day, at the suggestion of both Wałęsa and the Executive Commission, the Citizens' Committee took on the role of promoting the electoral campaign of the opposition-Solidarity forces, and on 23 April the committee held its first meeting with representatives of regional citizens' committees, during which they confirmed the list of candidates and the election program.

All this took place in record time, partly out of fear that the party machine, constantly at the ready, would drown out the poorly organized opposition. During this process conflicts erupted when some members of the committee (including Mazowiecki) protested against the undemocratic selection of candidates and the imposition on the regions of candidates from the center. The campaign conducted by groups opposed to the "capitulation at the Round Table" also intensified and was joined—not necessarily for reasons of personal ambition—by activists who had fallen out with Wałęsa (and even more so, with his advisers). Some of them, like Władysław Siła-Nowicki, decided to run for election outside the list of the Citizens' Committee. The Confederation for an Independent Poland also decided to field candidates.

None of this detracted from the momentum of the campaign waged by the decisive majority of the opposition under the auspices of the Citizens' Committee. On 1 May a whole series of Solidarity parades took place—the largest of them, in Warsaw, had nearly 100,000 participants—demonstrating the union's organizational agility and rapidly growing capacity to mobilize (despite a number of smoke-ins organized in competition). On 8 May the first issue of the daily *Gazeta Wyborcza* (Election Paper) appeared, its publication having been agreed at the Round Table. The paper was run by people who had previously produced the now discontinued *Tygodnik Mazowsze*, including its editor, Helena Łuczywo, who now became the managing editor, alongside Adam Michnik, whom Wałęsa had personally designated editor in chief. On 9 May Polish television transmitted the first program produced by the Solidarity Studio, whose call signal was the wartime melody used by underground Radio Solidarity.

Tens of thousands of people spontaneously became involved in the election campaign, from high-school students handing out flyers and pasting up posters to elderly ladies tenaciously holding the fort in committee premises that were usually ad hoc and ill-equipped, to the stars of stage and screen and sport (such as Himalayan mountain climber Wanda Rutkiewicz, and Krystyna Chojnowska-Listkiewicz, the first woman to sail solo around the world). A poster printed by Italian supporters created quite a stir: it depicted Gary Cooper in a scene from *High Noon*—wearing a Solidarity button.

It was the radicals who gave the campaign its fierceness, and the most notorious and "spectacular" event were the disturbances (17–18 May) in Kraków initiated by the anarchist Freedom and Peace Student Action group. Despite the intentions of the organizers, these disturbances played into the hands of the PZPR, which resolutely presented itself as a stabilizing and responsible force. The tone of the Solidarity campaign posed a greater threat to the communists, in that it devoted less space to economic issues and demands, focusing instead on describing and unmasking the despotic nature of party rule and the regime's dependence on the Soviet Union.

The PZPR, which was simply unable to keep pace with events, had already lost the struggle for social consciousness, particularly historical consciousness. By the time the party obtained Gorbachev's consent to the formation of a commission of historians who were supposed to cast light on the "blank spots" in the history of Polish-Soviet relations, hundreds of uncensored books, pamphlets, and articles had already appeared on the subject, and, in addition, the party had not yet managed to get Moscow to acknowledge the truth about the Katyn massacre. Evidence of this futile attempt to catch up was provided by the fact that in April the Politburo was still debating a document titled "Proposals Relating to the Issue of Eliminating the Remnants of Stalinism in Poland" and was considering how to carry out this maneuver without endangering the good name of tens of thousands of "builders and defenders of People's Poland." The opposition was helped in its propaganda efforts by almost every church in the country, although most of the clergy did not become personally involved.

Although the PZPR leadership had been the first to envisage elections and had even determined the precise date on which they were to be held, it was clearly surprised by the speed with which its opponents became organized. On 18 April the Politburo was still discussing a document stating that "the strategic goal of the party is to involve . . . the constructive opposition in a jointly conducted election campaign." If the joint list of candidates had been a failure, they could at least engage in a joint campaign. The trouble was, the party lacked a partner for such a campaign, and even its allies, especially at the regional level, were increasingly inclined to attack communism. The Central Committee's election staff worked feverishly, with intellectual support provided by the Academy of Social Sciences. On 9 May the Politburo adopted a set of guidelines recommending, among other things, that the party "point out the duplicity and hypocrisy of opposition candidates, remind the public that they used to be party members, and emphasize their lack of religious belief, their involvement in anticlerical activities, and their participation in Stalinist practices"; it was also suggested that during election meetings opposition candidates be asked about their "attitude toward proposed legislation on the rights of the unborn child." Some candidates on the PZPR list mounted an energetic and costly American-style campaign. To strengthen the campaign, and maintain full control over the number one medium, the party leadership called on the talent (and cynicism) of Jerzy Urban, appointing him head of the Committee for Radio and Television. All in all, the propaganda campaign was far from nonconfrontational.

The PZPR, of course, freely took advantage of its monopoly of power. Unpopular economic decisions were postponed; efforts were made to improve the supply of goods to the stores; the state administration, especially at the regional level, was brought into the campaign; and local self-government bodies were closely controlled. The party also tried to use official international contacts to its benefit, including the visit to Poland of Italian president, Francesco Cossigi; a treaty with the GDR settling a dispute over the boundaries of territorial waters off the Baltic coast was hastily finalized.

The results of final opinion polls, which were kept secret and circulated only among a small group in the leadership, showed the opposition with a growing lead over the party and its "coalition" partners (40 percent versus 15 percent), but the party leadership took comfort in the considerable number of undecided voters, who typically vote for the party they think will guarantee stability. But even within the PZPR, many members had decided to vote for Solidarity. The same was true to an even greater extent of the ZSL and SD. "Despite the fact that the future was starting to look bleak," Rakowski later wrote, "I did not lose heart." It seems that most of his colleagues were in a similar frame of mind, and the most optimistic of all were those involved in organizing the party's campaign.

The opposing camp was also in a good mood, even without confidential polling data, which would no doubt have increased the level of optimism. The atmosphere of endless chaos, like that of a light-hearted picnic, largely resulted from the fact that Solidarity had no professionals and certainly no political bureaucrats on its election committees and among its organizers. Its great trump card, which the movement exploited ceaselessly, was its sense of unity. This was not disrupted by a number of local incidents, such as the situation that arose in Radom when the local bishop came out in support of a candidate running against KOR-founder Jan Józef Lipski. All the candidates of the Citizens' Committee had campaign posters on which they appeared side by side with Wałęsa, even those who had met him for the first time when they had their picture taken together. "Wałęsa's Team" was their common slogan. Although they were confident of a positive result, the more cautious among them talked of obtaining 50–60 percent of the seats to be assigned by a free vote in the Sejm and a similar percentage in the Senate. They also paid attention, understandably, to the selection of people to sit on the electoral commissions, and everywhere, even in electoral districts abroad, Solidarity made sure to have its electoral agents on hand.

The voting took place without incident, apart from a few scattered cases of people distributing flyers calling for a boycott of the proceedings. Public opinion was more concerned about the news of the massacre of the peaceful student demonstration in Beijing, although this did not, of course, affect the elections in Poland. Late in the evening, when PZPR election officials looked at the early results, they realized that "a major defeat was taking shape." By the afternoon of 5 June it was clear to everyone that the "coalition" had suffered a disaster. Its defeat was far greater than even the greatest optimists in the Solidarity camp had predicted: out of 161 Sejm seats contested in a free vote, "Wałęsa's team" had won 160, and out of the 100 seats in the Senate, it had won 92. Out of 35 candidates on the national list, which consisted exclusively of top officials from the PZPR and its two allied parties, only two received enough votes to qualify for a seat, and the remainder were eliminated, since the electoral law made no provision for a second round of voting on the national list. That evening the Central Committee press spokesman acknowledged defeat, an admission that could perhaps have been interpreted as signifying that the party would now abandon its efforts to counteract the will of society.

After fierce discussion, one of the Round Table working groups agreed to transfer the thirty-three vacant seats from the national list to the local lists of the PZPR and its coalition partners. The second round of voting (18 June) did not result—nor could it—in any change. Solidarity won the remainder of the "democratic seats" in the Sejm and seven of the eight remaining seats in the Senate. As a result, it held 260 out of a total of 560 seats in the National Assembly; given the hesitation on the part of deputies from the ZSL and the SD, General Jaruzelski's election as president was by no means a foregone conclusion.

The electoral plebiscite yielded an unambiguous result: the Poles had rejected communism. This outcome was not affected by the more detailed analyses suggesting that in some respects a more cautious interpretation would be appropriate. Fewer than 62 percent of eligible voters went to the polls, indicating a degree of social apathy that was especially disturbing given the nature of the elections, and the possible influence of the radicals who had called for a boycott. Such a high rate of absenteeism also meant that real support for Solidarity was less than that suggested by the choices of those who actually voted. Candidates fielded by the Citizens' Committee garnered 72 percent of actual votes cast, equivalent to 40 percent of the total eligible vote. As Stanisław Gebethner has pointed out, roughly 25 percent of voters opted for candidates of both the Citizens' Committee and the PZPR (on different lists), making it difficult to consider them as being single-minded in their determination to end communism. In elections to the Senate, Solidarity candidates obtained 99 percent of the seats, but slightly fewer than 68 percent of the votes.[2]

These calculations did not, however, affect the overall assessment of the situation, especially that expressed by public opinion, free of statistical nuances. In the eyes of the public, the PZPR had suffered complete defeat, one that totally negated all claims regarding its mandate to rule—both its former mandate obtained by coercion and the party's more recent mandate

2. Stanisław Gebethner, "Wybory do Sejmu i Senatu 1989r. Wstępne refleksje," *Prawo i Życie*, 1989, no. 8.

allegedly obtained by its reform efforts. The opposition was the first to draw conclusions from the lesson that history had taught the communists. A few days after the first round of voting, Lech Wałęsa sent a signal, via Michnik, to General Jaruzelski and his colleagues: it is possible that, in the event of the (expected) election of the first secretary as president, Solidarity would be interested in taking over the post of prime minister. The party leadership considered this a violation of the Round Table agreement, but confirmation that such a turn of events was perfectly realistic came from the most authoritative source. When Gorbachev's adviser, Vladimir Zagladin, was asked what he thought about the article that Michnik had published on 3 July in *Gazeta Wyborcza* under the provocative title, "Your President, Our Prime Minister," he calmly replied: "This decision is an internal matter for our Polish friends." Only with the greatest difficulty could one interpret this response as an encouragement to negate the election results by the use of tanks. And if so—only Polish tanks.

The facts spoke for themselves, with implacable eloquence: the elections were not the high point in the process of reforming the political system of the Polish People's Republic, but marked the beginning of a period in which the system would be completely transformed—and not only in Poland. On 13 June the Hungarians began discussions of similar issues at their own Three-Cornered Table. On 26 June the Czechoslovak opposition called for talks in a petition circulated under the title "A Few Sentences."

Poland After Communism

THE BEGINNING

The elections of 4 June 1989 gave rise to a situation that none of the Round Table participants had envisaged, one that could not be adequately addressed by either General Jaruzelski's proposals for reform or Solidarity's plan to restrict the monopoly of the communist party. Nevertheless, it was some time before either side fully realized the political implications of this state of affairs. The reason for the delay was that neither of them had anticipated such election results and each feared that, given the high level of popular discontent and the collapse of the economy, any destabilization would open the way to an uncontrollable social explosion. Such a development was all the more likely given that some opposition groups openly opposed the Round Table agreement and argued that conditions were ripe to overthrow communism "from below," with the aid of mass strikes and demonstrations. At the same time, it was not clear what kind of reaction was to be expected from party officials and security service functionaries, the majority of whom took a highly negative view of the concessions made to Solidarity. While those who opposed the agreement with the opposition lacked a leader, and Jaruzelski's authority remained unassailable, it was not inconceivable that they would attempt to provoke an open conflict. The Poles were urged to be cautious by both Moscow and Washington, which regarded stability in Poland as a major factor in the European order and as an element that would make it easier for Gorbachev to continue his reforms. During his visit to Poland (9–11 July), President Bush voiced unequivocal support for Jaruzelski's candidacy as president, and the U.S. ambassador to Warsaw actually urged opposition members of parliament to ignore the fact that he had been the chief author and administrator of martial law and help ensure his election. Their assistance was vital in view of the "rebellion" mounted by some of the deputies belonging to the satellite parties, and it was only because a few deputies belonging to the Citizens' Committee abstained from voting that General Jaruzelski was elected president on 19 July, by a margin of just one vote more than the minimum required for election. He thereby suffered a major humiliation, and the opposition showed that even though it was not in the majority it could still influence key decisions of state.

When Jaruzelski became president, he resigned as first secretary of the PZPR, thereby initiating a number of personnel changes at the highest levels. At first it seemed as though these changes would be of a secondary nature, since the communists—still the governing power—had not responded to Michnik's challenge to appoint "our" prime minister, in other words, someone associated with Solidarity. For example, a few days after his election as president, Jaruzelski met privately with Wałęsa and offered Solidarity only a few minor government posts. The position of first secretary was taken over by Mieczysław F. Rakowski, who in the fall of 1988 had pronounced himself in favor of far-reaching economic reforms combined with only minimal changes to political institutions. The party's candidate for the post of prime minister was General Kiszczak, the chief organizer of the Round Table negotiations but also minister of internal affairs since the fall of 1981 and thus personally responsible for the repression of Solidarity and the activity of the security apparatus. This was one reason why the opposition decisively rejected his candidacy and the proposal that he head a coalition government containing a small number of Solidarity representatives. Wałęsa sounded out opinion in a series of meetings that were largely unpublicized (although General Jaruzelski was kept apprised of the results), and on 7 August he publicly proposed that Solidarity form a government together with the former satellite parties. This coalition had an arithmetical majority in parliament, but Jaruzelski was prepared to accept the proposal only if communists were also included in the government. This would result in a grand coalition of the kind proposed by Kiszczak, except that the center of gravity would be quite different—the core of the government would be formed not by the PZPR but by Solidarity.

The political maneuvering and the constantly deteriorating economic situation produced a high level of public tension. On 1 August, the last day on which the Rakowski government was in office, a decision to introduce "market prices" took effect, opening the door to a rapid increase in inflation and giving rise to numerous outbursts of protest and the threat of a general strike. It became obvious that any future government would bear an enormous responsibility and that without the participation of Solidarity there would be little chance of defusing tensions and stabilizing the situation. It appears that this was the factor that had the most influence over Jaruzelski.

In his new role as first secretary, Rakowski tried to stave off the defeat that loss of leadership of the government would signify for the PZPR—a party that had been created, and had for several decades served, as "the ruling party." He drew up an appeal that called on party members "to undertake a mass struggle," since the formation of a government headed by a noncommunist would "endanger the integrity and sovereignty of Poland." This appeal was not, however, published, since General Jaruzelski had already decided to entrust the formation of a government to the opposition. He was supported in this position by Gorbachev, who in a telephone conversation urged Rakowski to reconcile himself to the situation. As a result, on 24 August the overwhelming majority of members of parliament (378 voting in favor, 4 against, and 41 abstaining) elected as prime minister sixty-two-year-old Tadeusz Mazowiecki, a Catholic activist, prominent in the opposition since 1977. Mazowiecki was editor in chief of *Tygodnik Solidarności*, had been interned during martial law, and was now one of Wałęsa's advisers. This decision was confirmed just under three weeks later, when the Sejm approved by an even greater majority (402 in favor, 13 abstaining, and none opposed) Mazowiecki's proposals regarding the composition of the government. Half of the twenty-four cabinet members were people associated with Solidarity, and the remainder consisted of one minister belonging to no party, four each belonging to the PZPR and ZSL, and three from the SD. Four deputy prime ministers were appointed—one each from Solidarity, the PZPR, and the two satellite parties. While Solidarity had the largest number of ministers, two key posts were in the hands of the communists—Kiszczak remained as minister of internal affairs (and was also appointed deputy prime minister), and General Siwicki remained minister of defense. Both of them were formally members of the PZPR Politburo and, more important, were close associates of General Jaruzelski. The president thus retained control of the power apparatus and continued to have the support of a considerable proportion of those in the state and economic administration who belonged to the party's nomenklatura, as well as the support of the party as a whole. There thus existed the possibility that two rival power centers might emerge, that conflict might erupt between them, and even that an attempt might be made to restore the dominant role of the communist party.

The likelihood of such developments was quickly ruled out by the domino effect exerted across the region by *perestroika* in the Soviet Union and, especially, by the changes taking place in Poland. Signs of social assertiveness, already visible in the countries of East-Central Europe in 1988, gradually increased during 1989. Antigovernment demonstrations erupted in Czechoslovakia in January and in the GDR and Bulgaria in May. In September, when the Mazowiecki government was beginning to govern in Warsaw, an avalanche of changes took place. In Hungary the communists and the opposition reached agreement on transforming the country into "a democratic state based on the rule of law and a multiparty system," and opened the border with Austria, thereby giving rise to a mass exodus of Germans from the GDR. In the GDR itself, mass demonstrations began on 7 October, eventually forcing Erich Honecker to resign from all his posts; on 9 November the authorities decided to open the border with West Germany, a decision that allowed thousands of Berlin inhabitants to tear down the Berlin Wall with their bare hands; this was followed by further changes in the leadership, which then began talks with the opposition. At the beginning of November a number of opposition parties and groups emerged in Bulgaria (among them the trade union, Podkrepa, modeled on Solidarity); on 10 November a crisis erupted within the communist party, and Todor Zhivkov, who had held the post of general secretary since 1954, was removed from the leadership. On 17 November mass demonstrations began in Prague; two days later the opposition movement, the Civic Forum, emerged, with Vaclav Havel as its leader, and began talks with a new communist party leadership, which resulted in the formation of a coalition on 9 December. In mid-September opposition groups even emerged in Romania, for decades ruled with an iron fist by Ceauşescu; rioting broke out on 16 December, a week later the Front of National Salvation was formed; the group called for the overthrow of the Ceauşescu dictatorship and then, after several days of street clashes (and the execution of the dictator and his wife), took power.

Although these were just the first steps, and there were considerable variations in the extent to which different countries distanced themselves from communism, it was obvious that the system as such was in the process of collapsing and that the political-military bloc led by the Soviet Union was disintegrating. Although it initially seemed that Poland might become an isolated enclave within this bloc, it actually became one of many participants in a process that embraced a substantial part of Europe and, before long, the Soviet Union itself, which collapsed in the second half of 1991. This process was remarkable not only for its scope and its unprecedented, truly revolutionary, speed, but also for the fact that it took place without bloodshed: the skirmishes in Romania (and Moscow's later attempts at armed intervention in Lithuania) were essentially the sole episodes involving the use of force in the attempt to prevent the collapse of the system. Other countries followed the example of Poland, where despite the recent experience of martial law, the opponents—or as they were often referred to, the enemies—reached agreement. Thanks to this, despite the fears of most analysts and politicians, there was no broad-scale use of force. It was only in some parts of the Soviet Union (in the Caucasus and some regions of Central Asia) and in disintegrating Yugoslavia that bloody conflicts erupted between the newly emerging nation states. However, if we take into account the fact that all the collapsing states were authoritarian regimes whose existence had for years been based on the use of force, the human costs were—with the exception of the events in Chechnya and former Yugoslavia—relatively small or nonexistent. In fact, these conflicts erupted after the collapse of communism and were not a factor in bringing about the collapse itself.

In these changing circumstances Jaruzelski and his supporters and the PZPR as a whole were in no position to rein in the transformation process, or even to influence its scope and course. This was most evident in relation to the economy: on 28 December the Sejm (in which the communist party had a majority) adopted a package of ten laws drawn up by Leszek Balcerowicz, Solidarity's deputy prime minister and minister of finance. These were designed to improve the health of the state's finances and bring about macroeconomic stability, and they supplemented laws passed before the elections to create a solid basis for the introduction of market mechanisms. While a number of key legislative issues, such as reprivatization, were not included in the package, Poland's economic landscape underwent a profound change on a scale that no one could have imagined six months earlier. The entire operation, referred to as "shock therapy," was based on monetarist principles, whose chief proponent in Poland was Harvard economist Jeffrey Sachs, and it was carried out in consultation with the International Monetary Fund, which ensured that Western governments would create a stabilization fund of one billion dollars and made it possible for the country to obtain foreign loans. Action to rescue the economy was urgently needed if only because inflation was running at an annual rate of several hundred percent and threatened to bring about total economic collapse. Nevertheless, the social costs of shock therapy were enormous, since the introduction of market mechanisms brought with it a decline in production and thus a rapid growth in unemployment and a drastic decline in personal incomes: during the first year of shock therapy gross national output fell by 8 percent, and real wages by nearly 25 percent, while unemployment—a phenomenon that Poland had not experienced for decades—reached a rate of more than 6 percent. This caused serious social unrest among industrial workers and in rural areas, and resulted in a large number of strikes and protest demonstrations. It was obvious that such rapid and far-reaching transformation of the economic system could only be carried out by a government that enjoyed strong social support, which at that time could be provided only by Solidarity, and only if a large part of society believed that, along with these painful reforms, Poland was becoming a sovereign state and was setting out along the road to democracy.

Changes in the political sphere took place in a more evolutionary manner. The day after passage of the "Balcerowicz Program" the Sejm amended the constitution, restoring the traditional name of the country (the Republic of Poland), removing the article referring to "the leading role" of the communist party, and inserting a declaration to the effect that Poland was "a democratic state based on the rule of law [that] realizes the principles of social justice." Nevertheless, the balance of forces in the government remained unchanged, even after the formal dissolution of the PZPR at the party congress on 27 January 1990 and the formation in its place of the Social Democratic Party of the Republic of Poland (SdRP). The Polish communists employed the same strategy that their Hungarian counterparts had used a few months previously: they changed the party's name and turned the leadership over to younger, but experienced apparatchiks—in this case, Aleksander Kwaśniewski and Leszek Miller. A similar maneuver was carried out in November 1989 by one of the communists' former satellites, the United Peasant Party, which changed its name to the Polish Peasant Party while also bringing new people into the leadership. The Democratic Party retained its old name and within a short time faded from the political scene. Some Solidarity activists and radical anticommunist groups, as well as Lech Wałęsa, believed that since the PZPR, the chief partner at the Round Table negotiations, had ceased to exist, the agreement finalized in April 1989 had lost its rationale and the moment had come for fundamental changes at the highest levels of the state, including a change of president.

Meanwhile, the Mazowiecki government, supported by many influential politicians and journalists, including such leading opposition activists as Adam Michnik, Jacek Kuroń, and Bronisław Geremek, continued with its strategy of gradual change, which it justified in terms of the need to avoid creating a basis for new conflicts at a time of social uncertainty and while international maneuvering was taking place over the unification of Germany, which generations of Poles had feared as they had Russia. For this reason, the system of real socialism was dismantled slowly, but nevertheless consistently: 8 November 1989 saw the abolition of the Patriotic Movement for National Rebirth, a sham institution created after the imposition of martial law; two weeks later the Volunteer Reserve Militia (ORMO), widely viewed as the armed detachment of the PZPR, was dissolved; and on 12 April 1990 censorship was abolished. The Sejm authorized the state authorities to seize the property of the dissolved PZPR and to liquidate its powerful press and publishing conglomerate. Most important of all was the passage on 6 April of a legislative package that abolished the Security Service of the Ministry of Internal Affairs, whose chief task (alongside counterintelligence and intelligence directed largely toward stealing civilian and military technology in the West) had been "combating enemies of the state" and monitoring its citizens. The Sejm ordered a review of the SB's 22,500 functionaries and established in its place the State Protection Agency, which was given the task of counterintelligence. Gradual changes continued at the middle levels of the state administration—provincial administrators, heads of ministerial departments, directors of the some of the largest industrial enterprises. Finally, personnel changes in the most sensitive positions were cautiously initiated: in March one of Solidarity's senators, Krzysztof Kozłowski, was appointed deputy minister of internal affairs, in April two new deputy defense ministers were appointed from the ranks of Solidarity, and on 6 July Jaruzelski's two close allies in the government, Generals Kiszczak and Siwicki, were dismissed, the former being replaced by Kozłowski. In this way General Jaruzelski was deprived of any possibility of exerting a direct influence over the government; and although he managed to expand the newly created Presidential Office, he was clearly becoming nothing more than a figurehead, and his office—a parking place for the politicians associated with him.

A similar caution characterized the Mazowiecki government's foreign policy, whose architect was Krzysztof Skubiszewski, a professor specializing in international law and not a member of the PZPR or its former satellites. The appointment had to be approved by Jaruzelski, who initially wanted to appoint a PZPR member as minister of foreign affairs. However, he agreed to Skubiszewski, whom he knew from his time on the Consultative Council during 1986–89. During the first few weeks that the government was in office, both West German Chancellor Helmut Kohl and the Soviet foreign minister, Eduard Shevardnadze visited Poland, as did—surprisingly—the KGB chief, Vladimir Kryuchkov. Poland had no desire to provoke Moscow, which although weakened remained a nuclear power, with troops stationed not only in the GDR but also in Poland. The desire to establish good relations with the Soviet Union was also evident in the fact that the government entrusted the position of ambassador to Moscow to one of Jaruzelski's factotums, Stanisław Ciosek, a long-standing high-level party activist with no diplomatic experience. Gestures of goodwill toward Moscow were partly connected to the fact that the ten-point "Kohl Plan" concerning the principles governing the reunification of Germany made no mention of recognizing Poland's western border, which caused Mazowiecki to go as far as to declare that until the German problem had been resolved, Soviet troops should remain in Poland. He and Skubiszewski invested considerable energy in efforts to have Poland participate in the talks taking place between the two Germanys and the four great powers, known as the "Two-Plus-Four Talks." This was essentially unnecessary insofar as neither of the German powers questioned the Oder-Neisse border, although nationalist groups of "expellees" renewed their criticism of the federal government's policy. A major element in Polish diplomacy was the initiation of what became known as a dual-track policy in relation to Eastern Europe. During a visit to the USSR in October 1989 Skubiszewski not only met with Soviet leaders but also visited the neighboring republics of Ukraine and Belorussia, anticipating the disintegration of the Soviet Union. The government began cooperating with neighboring countries undergoing changes similar to those in Poland, and on 9 April 1990 the leaders of Poland, Czechoslovakia, and Hungary held the first meeting of what became known as the Visegrad Group. In light of differing interests—and to some extent also ambitions—this initiative never acquired great significance. Mazowiecki quickly submitted the relevant memoranda regarding Poland's joining the Council of Europe (January 1990), and the European Economic Community (April 1990), but this was just the first step in a process that was clearly going to take many years. While Mazowiecki's first trip abroad was to the Vatican, this was not really a matter of foreign policy. The prime minister had a personal desire to bend his knee before the pope, whom he had known for many years, and a political desire to gain the support of the person who was viewed by virtually all Poles as their highest moral authority, a factor that was obviously related to the government's domestic policy.

Because of the consequences of shock therapy and the cautiousness in liquidating communist state institutions and initiating personnel changes, Mazowiecki's government gradually lost support not only among the broader society but also within its primary political base. Lech Wałęsa was disappointed that Mazowiecki ignored his suggestions when forming his government and failed to contact him to discuss the country's most serious problems. The Nobel laureate argued that it was time to deal more firmly with the communists. He also nurtured ambitions regarding the presidency, which was not surprising in light of his position at home and abroad. The members of Wałęsa's political entourage were even more radical and grew impatient with Mazowiecki's slow and cautious approach and with the fact that he kept them at arm's length, offering none of them a position in the government. They also believed that the former opposition needed to establish political parties to replace the amorphous Citizens' Committee, which was, moreover, largely dominated by Mazowiecki's supporters. Until the fall of 1989 the Confederation for an Independent Poland was the only active anticommunist political party, but it had no representatives in parliament. The end of October saw the formation of the right-wing Christian National Union (ZChN), a party that drew support from among the Catholic clergy, Solidarity deputies, and Catholic activists. Its leader was Wiesław Chrzanowski, who had been active in anticommunist movements as far back as 1945–47 and had spent many years as a political prisoner. In the spring of 1990 the two most energetic politicians in Wałęsa's entourage, the twins Jarosław and Lech Kaczyński, set about organizing a center-right political tendency, under the slogans of "acceleration" and "decommunization," meaning the rapid expulsion of communists from all top positions and the election of Wałęsa as president; on 12 May they announced the formation of a political party named the Central Alliance. A few weeks later, in a fairly brutal but effective manner Wałęsa ousted from the leadership of the Citizens' Committee all those who favored continuing the process of evolutionary change and maintaining organizational unity. He also tried to reduce the influence of *Gazeta Wyborcza*, which supported Mazowiecki and opposed radical decommunization, and was the most widely read daily paper in Poland. Wałęsa withdrew permission for the paper to appear under the Solidarity logo and tried, unsuccessfully, to have Michnik dismissed from his post as editor; not only did the paper not lose readers but it gained a reputation for being independent of Solidarity. *Gazeta Wyborcza* became the voice of a center-left party, the Civic Movement—Democratic Action, formally established on 16 July 1990. Its leaders included several members of KOR as well as some of the younger Solidarity leaders, such as Zbigniew Bujak and Władysław Frasyniuk. The conservative-liberal Forum of the Democratic Right, created somewhat earlier, was yet another actor on the increasingly crowded political stage.

These developments signaled the disintegration of what had become known as the "post-August camp." This fragmentation was hardly surprising, since only the existence of an enemy as powerful as the communist system had enabled such ideologically disparate groups to work together. What was surprising, however, was the viciousness of the disputes among them, the impassioned rhetoric and negative stereotypes, which not only coarsened public life but deepened the chasm between adversaries. Inevitably, this reduced the level of cooperation among different groups in parliament and the government and tarnished the image of the former opposition in the eyes of the broader population. The church, and Cardinal Glemp personally, attempted to mitigate some of the conflicts, but without success. Wałęsa referred to these polemics as "the war at the top," a war that was intended, in his opinion, to ward off the possibility of "war at the bottom," by which he meant an explosion of social discontent directed against the entire process of transformation. In the long run, this "war" created a negative image of political life in general and undermined the authority of parliament and the government, regardless of whether or not individual criticisms and accusations had any basis in fact. So many people felt so frustrated because of their loss of a sense of social security that even if they ignored the violent diatribes and accusations—in which Wałęsa's supporters excelled—they were susceptible to populist slogans and the search for scapegoats, which was not, of course, conducive to building a state based on the rule of law. Nevertheless, the disputes did not degenerate into violence or physical aggression, and Mazowiecki's supporters exaggerated when they presented Wałęsa as a threat to democracy.

The scorned postcommunists found themselves constantly on the defensive, but the fact that they came under such relentless attack meant that they created a tightly knit group based on absolute loyalty. They did not, however, provide General Jaruzelski with an adequate basis of political support, and he did not feel strong enough to take up the challenge. In mid-September 1990, one month after Wałęsa had demanded that he step down, Jaruzelski announced that he would agree to a shortening of his term as president. Parliament amended the constitution accordingly and passed a law providing for the election of president by popular vote. This did not, however, mean that a presidential system was now being introduced, since the government was still headed by the prime minister, who, together with his or her fellow ministers, was responsible to parliament. The first round of presidential elections took place on 25 November, and to everyone's surprise, not only did Wałęsa receive only 39.9 percent of the vote, not enough to declare victory, but his chief rival, Prime Minister Tadeusz Mazowiecki, received fewer votes (18.1 percent) than the hitherto unknown Stanisław Tymiński (23.1 percent). Tymiński, a businessman who for the past twenty years had been living in Canada and Peru, ran an election campaign based on primitive demagoguery and vicious attacks on the entire post-Solidarity establishment. Another striking aspect of the elections was the relatively low turnout of approximately 60 percent. Both the success of Tymiński and the fact that two-fifths of the electorate could not be bothered to vote attested to the scope of social frustration and the widespread sense of alienation in relation to the changes begun in 1989. Another fact worth noting is that while Włodzimierz Cimoszewicz, the SdRP candidate, came in fourth, the 9.2 percent of the vote that he received meant that 1.5 million people voted for him—almost as many as the number of PZPR members when the party was dissolved. The Tymiński phenomenon galvanized the fractious "people of Solidarity" to cooperate with each other. Both Mazowiecki and *Gazeta Wyborcza* called on voters to cast their ballot in the second round for Wałęsa, who after a fierce but short campaign won 74.2 percent of the vote. The turnout, however, was still lower (53.3 percent) than in the first round; even a hotly contested election could not persuade more than twelve million people to exercise their right to determine who would occupy the most important position in the state.

President Wałęsa took the oath of office on 22 December. On the same day, Ryszard Kaczorowski, who had been serving in the émigré community as president and guardian of the traditions of the Second Republic, handed over to Wałęsa the prewar presidential insignia that had been stored in London. General Jaruzelski was not invited to either the swearing-in or the ceremonial transfer of the insignia, a gesture that was as hostile as it was insulting but one that fully accorded with the strategy of decommunization and a radical break with the ancien régime. Although the composition of the parliament elected on the basis of the Round Table agreement remained unchanged, the departure of General Jaruzelski effectively brought the transition period to an end: there was no further need for a guarantor of

POLAND AND ITS NEIGHBORS AFTER 1993

① RUSSIA, KALININGRAD REGION

peaceful political change. A new constitution had yet to be written, the political scene remained—as the Tymiński episode indicated—volatile, and there was still much to do to reform the state and the economy, but during 1990 there emerged in Poland the foundations of a democratic system and the free market.

THE INTERNATIONAL SITUATION

One major change in comparison with the years 1945–89 was the unification of Germany, which grew to become the greatest economic power in Europe and a crucial partner in Poland's efforts to join NATO and the European Community; another was the collapse of the federated states—the USSR and Czechoslovakia—that bordered Poland to the south and east. The most significant change, of course, was the breakup of the Soviet Union (December 1991), as a result of which Poland now had not one but four neighbors to the east—Ukraine, Belarus, Lithuania, and the Russian Federation. Continuing the dual-track policy initiated in 1989, Poland was the first to recognize the newly independent states and quickly established diplomatic relations with them.

From the strategic point of view, the country's main partner was Ukraine. Polish politicians generally agreed that Kiev's independence from Moscow guaranteed that Russia could not reassert any imperial ambitions and that maintaining friendly relations with Ukraine would help strengthen its sovereignty, a policy that was strongly advocated by Zbigniew Brzezinski, who had considerable influence in Poland. Despite the numerous grudges on both sides, most of them historical in nature, successive governments and presidents viewed rapprochement with Ukraine as one of the central elements of foreign policy. Poland tried to take the initiative in drawing Ukraine into Europe, although the possibilities for action were limited, largely because of the weakness of its economy. Efforts were made to compensate for this with a number of political initiatives, and the two countries held high-level meetings several times a year. Relations with Lithuania were somewhat cooler, as the anti-Polish sentiments dating back to the interwar years remained strong. Vilnius was not enthusiastic about Poland's ambition to become a "bridge" to Europe and was more interested in cooperating with Latvia and Estonia and obtaining assistance from Scandinavia. Although no serious conflicts existed between Poland and Belarus, the fact that Minsk made strenuous efforts to strengthen its ties with Russia, together with the autocratic nature of the government led by Aleksandr Lukashenko, meant that the country was not regarded as a trustworthy partner. Poland's relations with Czechoslovakia and, after its breakup (1993), with the Czech and Slovak Republics, were correct but far from cordial. In the case of Polish-Czech relations, which had never been warm, what amounted to a "race" to join Europe played a role: Poland argued that joint action on the part of the candidate states, especially those that made up the Visegrad Group, would facilitate the process of integration. The Czechs, on the other hand, believed that, as the most economically stable country, they would have a greater chance of success by going it alone.

The most complicated international relations, and the worst, were with the Soviet Union and then Russia. While the Soviet Politburo recognized at the end of September 1989 that it had to accept the new Polish reality and cooperate with the existing government, it also decided to provide assistance to its "Polish friends," in other words, the communists. Although Moscow was then embroiled in enormous internal conflicts that reached their apogee with the unsuccessful attempt to overthrow Gorbachev (August 1991), the Kremlin tried to maintain its influence in Poland, partly by postponing the withdrawal of its troops, which was not completed until September 1993, and by proposing that sites formerly occupied by the Soviet Army be used for a variety of Polish-Soviet joint ventures, a proposal that the Poles rejected. Nevertheless, the dissolution of Comecon in June 1991 and the liquidation of the Warsaw Pact shortly afterward took place without any major problems. After the collapse of the Soviet Union it seemed as though Poland and Russia would establish correct and stable relations, as was suggested by the positive results of Wałęsa's official visit to Moscow (May 1992) and Yeltsin's visit to Warsaw (August 1993). However, it turned out that the two countries had divergent interests: Poland was most interested in developing economic relations, since the collapse of Comecon was one of the chief causes of the country's economic difficulties, and in obtaining a final accounting of Stalinist crimes against Poles; Russia, on the other hand, was interested in keeping Poland from joining the European Economic Community and, first and foremost, in preventing it from joining NATO. Most Poles feared a resurgence of Russia's expansionist power and took a skeptical view of the country's conversion to democracy. In Russia Poland was frequently referred to as an age-old enemy and the advance guard of American imperialism. Poland's joining NATO and the negotiations regarding membership in the European Union hardly made Poland a strategic partner for Moscow in Central Europe, and the lack of surplus capital in Poland meant that Russia had little interest in developing economic ties. Thus despite some changes in Russia's global policies—such as participation in the anti-terrorist coalition formed after 11 September 2001—there was no change in Moscow's policy toward Poland. The same was true of Poland's policy toward Russia.

Public opinion was most interested in, and Polish diplomats and political leaders concentrated most of their efforts on, relations with the West, and with Germany and the United States in particular. Alongside current issues, the most important of which, of course, concerned the economy (loans, investment, the free flow of goods and services), the main focus was Poland's integration into the European institutional framework. In the case of policy toward Germany, the fundamental issue was Poland's joining the European Community; in the case of the United States, joining NATO. Poland initiated both these processes shortly after the Mazowiecki government was formed, but they were not accompanied by any concrete actions, since neither institution showed any signs of willingness to accept new members. Given Poland's size, there was a certain asymmetry regarding its chances of gaining membership in NATO and the European Community:

the presence of a country with thirty-eight million inhabitants and a sizable (although poorly equipped) army, situated at a major strategic point in Europe, had some value to the alliance, while European politicians shuddered at the thought of the Community subsidies that such a large country (especially its agricultural sector) would absorb. A similar asymmetry was to be found in Polish public opinion. While the majority of the public was in favor of joining NATO and the EU, there was a far greater consensus concerning the former, and virtually no political force opposed membership. The situation was quite different in the case of the EU: although those who favored membership were in the majority, opposition was voiced by many groups on the far right—usually those that viewed the world in xenophobic or Catholic fundamentalist terms—and by populists of various stripes, who were always plentiful. While no significant political party made opposition to NATO membership a central plank of its political platform, opposition to membership in the European Union became the standard rallying cry of several parties that were well represented in parliament (such as Catholic Electoral Action in 1993–97 and the League of Polish Families and the Self-Defense movement, after the elections of 2001).

The slow pace of negotiations regarding joining Western alliances was more the result of fears and uncertainties on the part of the West than of any doubts in Poland. In the case of NATO, for several years both the United States and its allies were anxious to avoid doing anything to annoy Russia. They thus came up with various ideas, such as the North Atlantic Council for Cooperation, the Partnership for Peace program, and the Organization for Security and Cooperation in Europe. It was not until April 1996 that Warsaw, Prague, and Budapest could submit a formal application to join NATO, and the documents of accession were initialed in December 1997. On 12 March 1999, a date that coincided with celebrations commemorating NATO's fiftieth anniversary, the three countries finally became full-fledged members. Without doubt the decision to expand NATO was influenced by developments in Russia: Yeltsin's antidemocratic tendencies, the war in Chechnya, and the numerous anti-Western statements on the part of Russian politicians. Although NATO's role in world politics was considerably smaller than it had been during the Cold War, for Poland—and the Poles— membership in the alliance was of enormous significance, protecting them from being trapped in the "gray zone" between Russia and Germany. Once it was clear that the communist system would be dismantled not only in Poland but throughout the Soviet bloc, Poland's importance diminished considerably, a fact that most Poles well realized, but they counted on Washington's support on the question of NATO membership and its assistance—indirect or via investment—in the process of restructuring the Polish economy. In neither case was Poland disappointed.

Entry into the European Community proved to be much more difficult, both because of resistance on the part of its members and because of the fact that the community itself was undergoing its own transformation (the Maastrict Treaty of December 1991). On 16 December Poland and the other Visegrad countries signed a treaty of association, but they could not formally apply for membership until the treaty had been ratified by all member states. Poland finally submitted its application to Brussels in April 1994. Long and tedious procedures began within the European Union itself, which had not decided how many states would be admitted. It was only at the Nice Conference, on 8 December 2000, that the member states officially agreed to admit new members and established the year 2004 as the time for doing so. Meanwhile, complex and controversial negotiations between Poland (and the other would-be members) and EU representatives got under way in November 1998. These focused on bringing Polish laws into line with those of the Union, and the main problem was to establish a transition period in a number of areas, during which EU regulations would not be fully applicable. The most contentious issues included the right of foreigners to buy land (which was opposed by a substantial proportion of Poles), free movement of labor (opposed by Western states, chiefly Germany and Austria), and agricultural subsidies. The would-be members were disturbed by the fact that EU expansion was opposed by a large proportion of the population in the three largest member countries: opinion polls conducted in mid-2002 found the majority of French to be opposed; in Great Britain, the public was more or less evenly divided; and in Germany those in favor slightly outnumbered those opposed. Although the Polish foreign service and government officials (including the president) lobbied hard in all member countries for Poland's entry into the European Union, Germany played a particular role in the process—because of both the strength of its economy and Berlin's political calculations. Poland was Germany's largest eastern neighbor, economic ties soon developed between the two countries, and the Polish market had the greatest absorptive capacity of all the would-be EU members by virtue of its size—its population was larger than that of the other countries combined. From the mid-1990s an increasing number of people in Germany voiced the opinion that the Germans had already "made good" the wrongs inflicted by the Third Reich, and even that it was time for the world to recognize the wrongs done to Germans during 1945–46, when some three million were forcibly resettled from territory transferred to Poland. However, Germany's policy toward Poland and the Poles was still marked by the sense of past wrongdoing and the desire for reconciliation. It was obvious, of course, that any reconciliation depended on the good will of the victims themselves; and since it was the Poles who had been the victims, good relations with Poland were a major element in legitimizing German democracy in the eyes of the rest of the world. The result of all this was that, regardless of the changes in the governing coalitions in each country, Polish-German relations were good, often very good, and the two sides had frequent contacts at the highest levels and at the level of local communities and associations. Of course, conflicts existed in relation to the transition period for Poland's entry into the European Union, and over the question of those who had been "expelled" and the issue of restitution of property or payment of compensation for loss of property. All in all, despite the existence of some conflicts with its neighbors, Poland acquired a sense of stability and security in international relations.

ECONOMY AND SOCIETY

During the final decades of the twentieth century a number of countries in southern Europe, Latin America, and Asia made what was usually a peaceful transition from authoritarian or dictatorial regimes to democracy. When the communist states set out along this road in 1989, the creation of democracy was not the only task they faced. In Spain, Chile, South Africa, or Taiwan there was no need for changes in the political system to be accompanied by changes in property relations and the creation of a free market. In Poland, on the other hand, although agriculture had never been completely collectivized and private ownership had been retained in handicrafts and small industry, the state played a key role in the economy, and even at the end of the 1980s, when the private sector had some possibilities to develop, it never accounted for more than 25–30 percent of gross domestic product (GDP). While some democratic countries, such as France, have a substantial state sector, there is widespread agreement that democracy is associated more with the free market than with state ownership and central planning. It was thus inevitable that Poland and the other countries of the former Soviet bloc should dismantle not only the communist political system but also the communist economic system. I have already mentioned the first measures taken within the framework of shock therapy and their immediate impact. The process of transforming the economy proved, however, to be more complex and considerably more painful for the majority of the population than anyone expected. It was not simply a question of introducing market mechanisms but also of simultaneously restructuring out-of-date industry and backward agriculture, something that had taken some countries in the West many decades to accomplish and had been the cause of enormous social conflicts, one such example being Margaret Thatcher's epic battle with Britain's miners.

Without going into details, I will note the main measures that the government and parliament took to create an economy based on the free market and private ownership. They included a law on the privatization of state enterprises (1990); the opening of the Warsaw stock exchange (1991); the introduction in 1992 of personal income tax and, in 1993, of value-added tax for producers and retailers; the liquidation and sale of state farms (1992), which caused the proportion of arable land farmed by these generally inefficient enterprises to fall from 19 percent to roughly 5 percent; currency reform; and the introduction of a floating exchange rate (1995). As a result of these measures, the private sector accounted for one-half of GDP in 1993 and for more than three-quarters in 2000.

The greatest problem was posed by unprofitable state enterprises, especially in heavy industry—mines, iron and steel works, shipyards, tractor factories—and agriculture. Poland's opening up to the world market, which was a major precondition of economic transformation, caused an influx of not only capital and new technology but also cheaper (and often subsidized) goods from the countries of the European Union, and from the former Soviet Union and Asia. The influx of goods, including food items, from the EU was particularly large, and Poland's efforts to join the Union made it difficult to impose drastic import restrictions or high tariffs. The economic crisis of the Soviet Union and subsequently of Russia and all the countries that emerged after the disintegration of the USSR led to the collapse of the markets that had once been so important for Polish industry and agriculture. In addition, these economies were also opening up to the outside world and were now able to offer their consumers goods from highly industrialized countries—the United States, the European Union, and East Asia—with which Polish products could not compete in terms of either quality or price. Even more important for international trade was the fact that the wealthy countries could provide incomparably greater export credits to their exporters than Poland could. All this meant that not until 1992 was it possible to halt the decline in output; GDP then began to rise slowly, reaching a respectable but still unsatisfactory annual growth rate of 5–7 percent during the period 1994–2000. When it seemed that annual growth was assured in 2001, recession set in, largely as a result of a slow-down in Western Europe, and the rate of increase in GDP fell by 1–2 percent. Real wages did not begin to grow until 1994 and generally grew more slowly than GDP, and the budget was burdened with enormous social expenditures inherited from the communist version of the welfare state. To these were added new welfare payments to the unemployed, whose number increased to 16 percent of the labor force in 1993–94; after falling for a couple of years, the unemployment rate again rose, to reach 18 percent in 2002. The state's financial situation was also affected by the foreign debts inherited from the previous regime, and considerable effort was invested in protracted negotiations to reduce them. Debt repayments to Western governments were partially rescheduled in 1991, but it was not until the fall of 1994 that loans from private banks were similarly renegotiated. Even so, repayments consumed 8–10 percent of export earnings—and a substantial proportion of these earnings went to private enterprises, not directly to the state coffers. Inflation caused enormous problems, and efforts to combat it required high interest rates, high taxes, and reductions in state expenditure on such items as salaries for teachers, the police, and the armed forces, which reduced personal incomes and hence purchasing power. The struggle against inflation was one of the priority tasks of successive governments, and in the end it was successful: the annual rate of inflation fell from 586 percent in 1990 to 3 percent in 2002.

The influx of investment capital did not get under way on a broader scale until 1996–97. Although the amounts involved were fairly small (from around five billion dollars in 1996 to around eleven billion in 2000), given the shortage of domestic capital and the lack of investment in the economy, they provided a major impetus to development. Part of this capital went to new investment, and part went to the state treasury in the form of payment for the purchase of state enterprises. New technology flowed into the country alongside this capital, together with export possibilities for Polish products, which could now take advantage of the trademarks and distribution networks of large Western corporations. The largest amount of investment went to the machine, chemical, and food industries, but only a few large state enterprises found foreign purchasers or investors. Few foreigners were willing to put their resources into mining or iron and steel production, while the state wanted to retain control of some sectors, such as telecommunications. The influx of capital provided a considerable stimulus to privatization. But the process had begun even before shock therapy was introduced, since some of the steps taken by the government in 1987–89 had made it possible to establish new private companies—albeit small ones—and allowed various kinds of ad hoc partnerships to make use of machinery and equipment in state enterprises. It was therefore possible to begin a business without a large amount of capital. After 1989 deals of this kind proliferated and became known as "the nomenklatura privatization," since, not surprisingly, those who were most able to take advantage of the new situation were people who had occupied management positions that had formed part of the communist nomenklatura system. This form of privatization aroused considerable resentment and even anger among those groups that lost out as a result of the changes taking place, such as workers in factories that reduced output or collapsed entirely or former employees of the now-liquidated state farms. If we add to this the fact that not all the new owners managed their property effectively, that not all foreign investors proved to be efficient, and that some of them encountered problems and often began restoring their firms to financial health by liquidating their foreign (in this case, Polish) operations, it is easier to understand why most Poles were unhappy with privatization, particularly that part of it undertaken with foreign capital. There was also extremely strong resistance to the notion of reprivatization. Despite pressures brought to bear by those lobbying on behalf of the former owners of apartment buildings, factories, and country houses, no satisfactory solution could be found. It was not simply that the communist era had instilled in people the conviction that collective property was superior to private property or that the notion of "social equality" had become firmly entrenched in society; there was also a widespread fear that full restitution would open the door to the return of property or payment of compensation to Germans forcibly resettled from Poland or to the heirs of Holocaust victims now living abroad.

The privatization of state property contributed to corruption, since the question of who would get to buy a particular factory and how much he or she would pay for it was decided by government officials, who were easily bribed. The more important privatization decisions were political in nature, so it was not surprising that some politicians also became involved in corrupt practices. It was simply impossible to devise and enforce new regulations in a hurry, which created opportunities for corruption and other forms of malfeasance. As a result, there was a veritable explosion of economic crime. While this had been an everyday feature of the communist system, after 1989 there was a complete change in the scale of such crime: it was no longer a question of products or spare parts being stolen by workers, but of tax fraud involving huge sums, sham companies, counterfeit products, evasion of import duties, smuggling—by the truckload—of goods (largely cigarettes and alcohol) into the country, and the production and smuggling of narcotics. International crime, hitherto unknown in Poland, made its appearance, partly because, day after day, tens of thousands of small-time smuggler-traders made their way to Poland from beyond the eastern borders and fell prey to criminal gangs of their fellow countrymen. The public's sense of personal security diminished considerably; perhaps not so much because of gang activity, although armed gangs sometimes settled accounts with each other on the streets of the larger cities, as because of the amount of common crime—break-ins, assaults, car thefts. The number of reported crimes increased from roughly 880,000 in 1990 to roughly 1.7 million in 2000. During this same period, the number of murders rose from 730 a year to 1,270. Thus a large proportion of Poles simultaneously lost their sense of social security (growing unemployment) and personal security (thefts and assaults). In addition, public opinion was constantly being aroused on the issue of crime: the media were now free to print whatever they liked and faced fierce competition, so every scandal, both large and small, every assault or incident of gang warfare, together with the names and pseudonyms of the most notorious bandits, featured prominently on the front pages of the newspapers or in prime-time newscasts.

Farm incomes rose even more slowly than earnings in the industrial and service sectors, and agriculture was especially hard hit by foreign competition. The decline in the purchasing power of industrial workers and people living on state pensions reduced demand, and the peasants, who had become accustomed to being able to sell everything they produced, were unprepared for the periodically recurring "disaster years," characterized by surplus produce or surplus meat production—for decades unheard of; they were similarly unprepared for demands regarding the quality of their produce. The lifting of all controls concerning the sale of land and the sell-off of state farms led to a gradual but steady increase in the average size of farms and—more important—to the emergence of large-scale farmers, including commercial farmers from Western Europe (largely from Holland), lured by the low price of land. New or expanded farms made use of new technology, and modernization was especially rapid in the food-processing industry, in dairies and slaughterhouses, where an increasing number of businesses met the norms of the European Union. Nevertheless, the majority of farms stood little chance of being modernized: they were too small, and their owners had neither the knowledge nor the ambition to change their way of doing things. Before 1989 the majority of people who lived in the countryside were not really peasants, but people who worked in industry or construction, where they constituted the least skilled and lowest-paid group of workers. Nevertheless, they did earn some money, and what they produced for their own use on their two or three hectares of land allowed them to make ends meet. When unemployment made itself felt in industry, it was they who were the most affected. As a result, it was in the countryside—home to one-third of the population—that discontent with the transformation and nostalgia for the days of social security and easy markets were felt most strongly.

All in all, within ten years or so after the beginning of the transformation process, the economic and social landscape underwent a pronounced change. Poland became an open country. Anyone who wished to do so could obtain a passport allowing him or her to travel abroad, something that for years had been only a dream for most people, especially the young, and every country in Europe abolished—on a reciprocal basis—all visa requirements for Poles. As a result, foreign travel increased from roughly twenty-two million trips abroad in 1990 to more than fifty-six million in 2000. Foreign exchange bureaus opened up in even the smallest towns, and hundreds of travel agencies offered excursions to the most exotic corners of the world. Young people rushed to obtain a higher education, as it was no longer a party card but a university degree that constituted a ticket to the future. The number of students grew from approximately 400,000 in the academic year 1990–91 to roughly 1.4 million in 1999–2000. International best sellers appeared in bookstores, and the Polish premieres of major foreign films took place immediately after they had opened in the United States or Britain. All of culture underwent a marked commercialization, in large part because of the appearance of private television and radio stations, which sought an audience by offering "reality programs" (such as *Big Brother*) and pop music aimed at the younger generation. The state media followed suit, reorienting their operations in terms of profitability, which could only be achieved on the basis of advertising, which in turn meant that they were obliged to broadcast the standard products of mass culture.

Alongside the old factories, many of them now shut down, ultramodern factories were constructed, hundreds of thousands of new cars, many of them imported, cruised the streets, and European supermarkets sprang up one after the other on the outskirts of large towns. Not to speak of the ubiquitous McDonald's and KFC, Shell gas stations, multiplex cinemas, and elegant boutiques and condominiums. Modern, highly specialized farms were created alongside land that was abandoned and neglected. In many towns and cities the authorities finally began to pay attention to the appearance of buildings, streets, squares, and lawns. Clean restrooms at gas stations or train stations, unheard of during the decades of communism, became something that one could take for granted.

POLITICS AND POLITICIANS

The events of 1980–89 left their mark on Polish political life, state institutions, and social behavior, which acquired characteristic features quite different from those encountered in countries with a long history of democratic rule and even somewhat different from those to be found in the other countries emerging from communism. Two such differences should be noted.

One of these was the role of trade unions, essentially the role of one of them—Solidarity. After 1989 Solidarity soon ceased to be a mass social movement, but for at least the next ten years it played a direct role in politics, had its own members of parliament, and organized a coalition of political forces. Thousands of Solidarity activists at various levels became directly involved in politics, as senators, deputies, ministers, members of regional and local councils, high state officials, factory directors, and members of supervisory boards. The best example was obviously Lech Wałęsa, who in 1990 exchanged his position as trade union chairman for that of president of Poland. Given the crisis in the ranks of the former opposition, it was under the banner of Solidarity (and its then-chairman Marian Krzaklewski) that most of the parties of the center and moderate right formed in 1997 a joint slate of electoral candidates (under the name, Solidarity Electoral Action), obtained one-third of the vote, and formed a coalition government with the party led by Mazowiecki. However, union members were to be found not only in government offices or on the floor of the parliament but also on the streets, leading demonstrations protesting against the government, even when the government happened to be made up of former Solidarity members and supporters. The experiences of 1956, 1970, and especially 1980–83 had left a long-lasting legacy, and in the struggle to defend workers' living standards or the interests of particular branch of the economy after 1989 strikes were often the preferred weapon. Moreover, these strikes maintained the customs that had arisen during the course of the earlier strikes: even in the smaller factories workers donned sashes in the national colors, covered the factory walls with national flags, and sang the national anthem. Just as though they were going to the barricades. These rituals were adopted by other trade unions, even those that had been formed after the imposition of martial law as "appendages" of the communist party or had not been established until after 1989 and were usually local in scope or represented a narrow professional group (railroad engineers or nurses, for example). Even more radical measures—such as the blockade of streets, highways, or railroad tracks—were taken by the extremist populist party, Self-Defense, whose members not only carried red-and-white banners and placards but even wore ties in the national colors. Poland was not actually ruled by trade unions, but their role in political life was considerably greater than anywhere else. Perhaps the only comparable situation would be the role played by the British Trade Union Congress, which at certain times—largely before 1926—de facto determined Labour Party policy.

Another specifically Polish feature was the role of the Catholic Church, which for decades had been the main—and often sole—counterweight to the communist party, and which since 1980, without ceasing to be anticommunist had simultaneously functioned as a mediator between the atheist regime and those members of society who were unhappy at the way they had been affected by the changes. Pope John Paul II occupied a special place as the highest moral authority for the overwhelming majority of Poles, even nonbelievers. No political group dared voice any criticism of the pope, and the only people to do so were a few extremist, anticlerical journalists. The clergy did not play a direct role in political life after 1989, but priests and bishops frequently voiced opinions not only on matters of faith or philosophy but also on public issues, sometimes urged the faithful to support this or that policy or politician, and took part in official state ceremonies regardless of whether the left or the right was in power. The number of Catholic periodicals increased, the church acquired its own television station, and some of the newly established Catholic radio stations disseminated political opinions. The largest of these, Radio Maryja, actually took the lead in forming a slate of Catholic election candidates, which obtained nearly 8 percent of the vote in the 2001 elections. The position of the church was such that public debate of issues like the teaching of religion in schools and abortion acquired particular significance. Many politicians, especially those belonging to right-wing parties, were happy to invoke the authority of the church, and even the leaders of the postcommunists tried to maintain a correct, or even positive, stance toward the church, partly because the majority of Poles declared themselves to be Catholic and partly because they wanted to distance themselves from the previous policy of combating the church.

The disintegration of the winning side in the 1989 election, and particularly the way in which divisions erupted and new parties emerged in 1990, left a powerful imprint on Polish political life. In the parliamentary elections that took place on 27 October 1991, after the term of the Sejm and Senate had been shortened, as many as twenty-nine candidate lists were registered nationwide and more than eighty were registered locally. As a result, even the largest parties—Mazowiecki's party, which campaigned under the name Democratic Union (in 1992 it renamed itself the Freedom Union), and the postcommunist Democratic Left Alliance (SLD)—received only 12 percent of the vote. Fourteen of the lists whose candidates were elected to the Sejm had fewer than ten deputies, and half of these had only one; Tymiński's party obtained just 0.5 percent of the vote. Among the exotic parties whose representatives gained election was the Polish Beer Lovers' Party, which received several times more votes than the party founded by one of the leaders and heroes of underground Solidarity, Zbigniew Bujak. This was the first election campaign in which xenophobic and anti-Semitic slogans made their appearance. Just as they had during the "war at the top" a year earlier, the post-Solidarity parties mainly fought against each other and discredited themselves in the process. Many people found it difficult to navigate their way through the large number of lists and candidates, and many were put off by the behavior of those running for office. As a result, barely 43.2 percent of the electorate bothered to go to the polls. In other words, a majority of Poles refused to take part in the elections.

The postcommunists were not the only ones happy at the fragmentation of their rivals, which helped them survive this difficult period. Wałęsa and his entourage were also happy, because the lack of a strong political party created greater opportunities for presidential action and enhanced his stature. In 1990, immediately following his election as president, Wałęsa took advantage of the fact that Mazowiecki had tendered his resignation to appoint as prime minister Jan Bielecki, a little-known politician without a strong basis of support, a liberal whose views were close to those of Balcerowicz. In this way the president ensured that he would have an influence over the government, most of whose members did not belong to any political party. In a sense this was a government of experts, but it was actually the president's government. Wałęsa intended to take similar steps following the 1991 elections, and he even considered the possibility of assuming the post of prime minister himself. In the end, however, he agreed to the formation of a government led by Jan Olszewski, a prominent opposition activist who had served as defense attorney in many political trials. During negotiations over the composition of this government Wałęsa fell out with all his more important political advisers and became increasingly dependent on a group that did not include anyone with political experience and that gradually came to be dominated by Mieczysław Wachowski, his trusted chauffeur with a murky past, whom he appointed his chief of staff. Wałęsa's forceful personality did not mesh easily with such standard features of democracy as respect for the rule of law and the principle of compromise.

Wałęsa's role increased even further when Olszewski, hoping to make his government the one to break decisively with the past, began to push a radical anticommunist line that culminated in a hastily prepared lustration campaign, designed to remove from state positions anyone who had secretly collaborated with the communist security service. The minister of internal affairs, Antoni Macierewicz, drew up a list of names that included a number of well-known activists in the former anticommunist opposition, among them the marshal of the Sejm and Wałęsa. Not surprisingly this provoked a strong counterattack. Wałęsa was supported by the Democratic Union, which opposed any attempt to settle accounts with the past, and on the night of 4–5 June 1992—exactly three years after Solidarity's electoral victory— the Olszewski government fell in an atmosphere close to hysteria. The ensuing campaign of mutual recriminations discredited all its participants, in comparison with whom the postcommunists looked like the party of reason and loyalty. While the post-Solidarity camp did manage to work together on several occasions—the 1995 presidential elections and the parliamentary elections of 1997—relations among the various groups were governed by mutual enmity.

This public quarreling only served to increase further the public's antipathy toward the former opposition. The shift in political sympathies can be seen clearly in the number of people who voted for postcommunist candidates in successive presidential elections: in 1990 Cimoszewicz received 1.5 million votes; in 1995 Aleksander Kwaśniewski received (in the first round) 6.3 million, and five years later he was elected during the first round of voting with approximately 9.5 million votes. Lech Wałęsa, who in 2000 was running for the third time, this time without the support of Solidarity, not only suffered a bitter defeat but had his political career destroyed when he received less than 1 percent of the vote. The PSL, the second party dating back to the communist era, also maintained a fairly strong position for some time. In the 1993 parliamentary elections the PSL list received 2.1 million votes, which gave it the second largest number of seats in the Sejm and made possible a coalition with the postcommunists that lasted until 1997. The success of the parties left over from the old regime by no means signified that the public had abandoned Solidarity entirely but simply that that end of the political spectrum was so fragmented that it had become ineffective. For example, in the 1993 parliamentary elections, roughly one-third of the votes cast for smaller center and right parties were "wasted," as the lists in question did not receive the necessary 5 percent of the total vote to qualify for seats in parliament. In other words, one-third of those who voted had no representative in the Sejm. The situation was highly asymmetrical: the postcommunists remained a tightly knit grouping, while the center and the left were made up of numerous parties, some of them on the decline and others on the rise. The country had neither a two-party system of the kind to be found in the United States and Great Britain and which seemed to be evolving in some West European countries nor a stable multiparty system of the kind that existed in many other countries of Western Europe.

It seems highly probable that this state of affairs resulted from the very high social cost of economic transformation, for which many people blamed politicians from the former anticommunist opposition. The discontent of a large proportion of society, including those social groups—such as workers from the largest industrial enterprises and the intelligentsia—that had provided Solidarity's main source of support during the years 1980–89, was directed against the promoters of shock therapy and those who advocated integration into the European Union. Because integration was also supported by the postcommunist leadership, who had quickly adapted to the free market and democratic rules of the game, this discontent was essentially directed against the entire establishment. It was in this context that chauvinist and anti-Semitic slogans made their appearance, and radical populist parties (such as Andrzej Lepper's Self-Defense) and nationalist organizations (such as the League of Polish Families, associated with Radio Maryja) gained supporters. A large proportion of the population simply turned its back on public life, and with the exception of presidential elections, in which about 60 percent of the electorate voted, turnout for elections never exceeded 50 percent.

Around 1993–94 one could detect emerging nostalgia for the communist era, which was identified in retrospect with the prosperity of the early years of Edward Gierek's rule. For example, his son, Adam Gierek, who had never been active in political life, ran in the 2001 elections to the Senate (on the SLD list) and received more votes than any other candidate. Attitude toward the past became one of the major political dividing lines, one that was even visible among young people who had no direct experience of communism. Radical anticommunists demanded that former communist party activists be banned from holding public office, that the property they had acquired in 1989–90 be expropriated, that all secret collaborators of the communist security service be exposed, and that all those directly responsible for criminal acts, as well as those politically responsible, be punished. They even argued that the entire process of transformation was an operation precisely planned by the KGB, and that the postcommunists remained dependent on Moscow. Some of their views—the demand that those who had violated human rights be called to account, for example—were shared by most people, but democratic legal procedures made it difficult to prosecute cases that frequently had occurred in the distant past, and some prosecutors and judges were unwilling to deal with them. As a result, the trial concerning the deaths of forty people during the 1970 strikes, in which the chief defendant was General Jaruzelski, opened in 1990 despite the length of time that had elapsed, but no verdict was ever handed down. Another case that outraged some members of the public was the acquittal of members of a special police unit, who in December 1981 had killed nine striking miners in the Wujek coal mine. Not until 1999 was the Institute of National Remembrance created as a repository for all the archives of the former security apparatus and as a research institute that would document the system of communist terror and identify those guilty of crimes. Nevertheless, both the postcommunists and populists such as Lepper tried to circumscribe its field of activity. The past became the subject of innumerable disputes and debates not only among politicians, lawyers, and historians, but among society as a whole and even within individual families. These polemics became an integral component of the social landscape, but the same was true of all the countries of East-Central Europe that underwent similar changes after 1989. Even stable democracies are familiar with debates about the past: the French have differing opinions about their revolution of 1789, and many Americans are still arguing over whether it is appropriate to fly the Confederate flag over pubic buildings. It was only in 1989 that it became possible to engage in free debate, unfettered by censorship, about any aspect of the past—for example, about Polish-Jewish or Polish-Ukrainian relations—although such debates were marked, of course, by political views. The debate about the communist part was essentially a fragment of this broader discussion.

Regardless of its specific characteristics, Polish political life developed within democratic norms and did not diverge in any significant fashion from the path taken by its closest postcommunist neighbors. The situation in Hungary was most similar to that in Poland: there the postcommunist social-democratic party twice (1994, 2002) won parliamentary elections, and the country also had a number of populist and nationalist political parties. It may well be that the success of Polish nationalists was part of a broader phenomenon to be found all across Europe, including Western Europe, at the end of the 1990s, when politicians such Jorg Haider in Austria and Jean-Marie Le Pen in France gained considerable public support.

When the twentieth century opened, Poland did not exist on the map of the world; when the century reached its end, Poland found itself living through yet another period of profound transformation. The first such period of transformation began in 1918 with the rebirth of the independent state, which despite numerous internal conflicts, shortcomings, and illegalities, embarked on a process of gradual modernization. Its development was violently interrupted by the outbreak of World War II and the invasion of its neighbors, Nazi Germany and the Soviet Union. This war inflicted extraordinary losses in the form of the murder of virtually the entire Jewish community, the death of several million Poles, and the total devastation of the country. The end of the war did not, however, bring a return to the *status quo ante*. It brought subordination to a foreign power that not only restricted Poland's sovereignty but also imposed a political system that was antidemocratic and on occasion criminal, as well economically inefficient. The fact that this system was imposed from outside was obvious from the very begin-

ning; its inefficiency became evident over time. When it collapsed in 1989—
partly as a result of massive and organized opposition by a large part of
Polish society and partly because of its own inefficiency and the imperial
center's loss of control—Poland joined the ranks of democratic states, and
its economy began, with difficulty, to function according to the principles of
the free market. The road through the twentieth century was a difficult one,
demanding from the Poles and the other nationalities living alongside them
the willpower and determination to struggle against adversity, both internal
and external. Most of all, the century was marked by the trauma of Nazi and
Soviet occupation and by the decades of subjugation to a dictatorial state,
whose founders and subsequent rulers promised much but essentially led
the country down the by-ways of modernity and far from democracy. After
such experiences, probably all Poles hope that the twenty-first century will
deal with them more leniently. Of course, it partly depends on them
whether or not these hopes are fulfilled.

Appendix: Table of Senior State Officials

Presidents of the Republic

Ignacy Mościcki (July 11, 1926–September 30, 1939)
Władysław Raczkiewicz (September 30, 1939–June 6, 1947; dead)

Premiers

Felicjan Sławoj-Składkowski (May 15, 1936–September 30, 1939)
Władysław Sikorski (September 30, 1939–July 4, 1943; dead)
Stanisław Mikołajczyk (July 14, 1943–November 24, 1944)
Tomasz Arciszewski (November 29, 1944–July 2, 1947)

Commanders in Chief

Edward Rydz-Śmigły (May 13, 1935–November 9, 1939)
Władysław Sikorski (November 9, 1939–July 4, 1943; dead)
Kazimierz Sosnkowski (September 8, 1943–September 30, 1944)
Tadeusz "Bór" Komorowski (September 30, 1944–September 24, 1946)

Ministers of Foreign Affairs

August Zaleski (September 30, 1939–August 28, 1941)
Edward Raczyński (August 28, 1941–July 14, 1943)
Tadeusz Romer (July 14, 1943–November 24, 1944)
Adam Tarnowski (November 29, 1944–July 2, 1947)

POLISH PEOPLE'S REPUBLIC, 1944–1989

First (or General) Secretaries of the Communist Party

Władysław Gomułka (November 23, 1943–September 3, 1948)
Bolesław Bierut (September 3, 1948–December 21, 1948), then president of
the Central Committee (December 21, 1948–March 16, 1954), then first
secretary (March 17, 1954–March 12, 1956; dead)

Edward Ochab (March 20, 1956–October 21, 1956)

Władysław Gomułka (October 21, 1956–December 20, 1970)

Edward Gierek (December 20, 1970–September 6, 1980)

Stanisław Kania (September 6, 1980–October 18, 1981)

Wojciech Jaruzelski (October 18, 1981–July 29, 1989)

Mieczysław F. Rakowski (July 29, 1989–January 27, 1990; self-dissolution of
the party)

Presidents

Bolesław Bierut as president of National People's Council (January 1, 1944–
February 4, 1947), then President of the Republic (February 5, 1947–
November 20, 1952)

Presidents of the People's State Council

Aleksander Zawadzki (November 20, 1952–August 7, 1964)

Edward Ochab (August 12, 1964–April 11, 1968)

Marian Spychalski (April 11, 1968–December 23, 1970)

Józef Cyrankiewicz (December 23, 1970–March 28, 1972)

Henryk Jabłoński (March 28, 1972–November 6, 1985)

Wojciech Jaruzelski (November 6, 1985–July 19, 1989)

Premiers

Edward Osóbka-Morawski as president of the Polish Committee of National
Liberation (July 21, 1944–December 31, 1944), then premier of the Provisional Government (December 31, 1944–June 28, 1945), then premier
of the Provisional Government of National Unity (June 28, 1945–
February 5, 1947)

Józef Cyrankiewicz (February 6, 1947–November 20, 1952)

Bolesław Bierut (November 21, 1952–March 18, 1954)

Józef Cyrankiewicz (March 18, 1954–December 23, 1970)

Piotr Jaroszewicz (December 23, 1970–February 18, 1980)

Edward Babiuch (February 18, 1980–August 24, 1980)

Józef Pińkowski (September 5, 1980–February 11, 1981)

Wojciech Jaruzelski (February 11, 1981–November 6, 1985)

Zbigniew Messner (November 6, 1985–September 19, 1988)

Mieczysław F. Rakowski (September 27, 1988–August 1, 1989)

Czesław Kiszczak (August 2, 1989–August 29, 1989)

Ministers of National Defense

Michał Żymierski (July 21, 1944–November 6, 1949)
Konstantin Rokossowski (November 6, 1949–November 11, 1956)
Marian Spychalski (November 13, 1956–April 11, 1968)
Wojciech Jaruzelski (April 11, 1968–November 22, 1983)
Florian Siwicki (November 22, 1983–July 6, 1990)

Ministers of Foreign Affairs

Edward Osóbka-Morawski (July 21, 1944–May 2, 1945)
Wincenty Rzymowski (May 2, 1945–February 5, 1947)
Zygmunt Modzelewski (February 6, 1947–March 20, 1950)
Stanisław Skrzeszewski (March 20, 1950–April 27, 1956)
Adam Rapacki (April 27, 1956–December 22, 1968)
Stefan Jędrychowski (December 22, 1968–December 22, 1971)
Stefan Olszowski (December 22, 1971–December 2, 1976)
Emil Wojtaszek (December 2, 1976–August 24, 1980)
Józef Czyrek (August 24, 1980–July 21, 1982)
Stefan Olszowski (July 21, 1982–November 6, 1985)
Marian Orzechowski (November 12, 1985–June 17, 1988)
Tadeusz Olechowski (June 17, 1988–August 1, 1989)

REPUBLIC OF POLAND, 1989–2002

Presidents

Wojciech Jaruzelski (July 19, 1989–December 22, 1990; until December 31,
    1989 as President of Polish People's Republic)
Lech Wałęsa (December 22, 1990–December 21, 1995)
Aleksander Kwaśniewski (December 21, 1995–reelected October 8, 2000 +)

Premiers

Tadeusz Mazowiecki (August 24, 1989–January 4, 1991; until December 31,
    1989 as Premier of the Government of the Polish People's Republic)
Jan Krzysztof Bielecki (January 4, 1991–December 6, 1991)
Jan Olszewski (December 6, 1991–June 5, 1992)
Waldemar Pawlak (June 5, 1992–July 10, 1992)
Hanna Suchocka (July 10, 1992–October 26, 1993; the first women in this
    post)

Waldemar Pawlak (October 16, 1993–March 4, 1995)

Józef Oleksy (March 4, 1995–February 7, 1996)

Włodzimierz Cimoszewicz (February 7, 1996–October 31, 1997)

Jerzy Buzek (October 31, 1997–October 10, 2001)

Leszek Miller (October 10, 2001 +)

Ministers of National Defense

Florian Siwicki (September 12, 1989–July 6, 1990)

Piotr Kołodziejczyk (July 6, 1990–December 23, 1991)

Jan Parys (December 23, 1991–May 23, 1992)

Janusz Onyszkiewicz (July 11, 1992–October 26, 1993)

Piotr Kołodziejczyk (November 10, 1993–November 10, 1994)

Zbigniew Okoński (March 4, 1995–December 22, 1995)

Stanisław Dobrzański (January 5, 1996–October 31, 1997)

Janusz Onyszkiewicz (October 31, 1997–June 16, 2000)

Bronisław Komorowski (June 16, 2000–October 10, 2001)

Jerzy Szmajdziński (October 26, 2001 +)

Ministers of Foreign Affairs

Krzysztof Skubiszewski (September 12, 1989–October 26, 1993)

Andrzej Olechowski (November 10, 1993–March 4, 1995)

Władysław Bartoszewski (March 4, 1995–December 22, 1995)

Dariusz Rosati (December 29, 1995–October 31, 1997)

Bronisław Geremek (October 31, 1997–June 30, 2000)

Władysław Bartoszewski (June 30, 2000–October 10, 2001)

Włodzimierz Cimoszewicz (October 26, 2001 +)

Biographical Notes

ANDERS, WŁADYSŁAW (1892–1970)—army officer, politician. 1914–17, cavalry officer in the Russian Army. Joined the Polish Army in 1918, graduated from the Military Academy in Paris, appointed general in 1934. Wounded in the September Campaign, imprisoned in the Soviet Union 1939–41; 1941–42, commander of the Polish Army in the USSR (known as Anders's Army), which was evacuated to the Middle East and became the Second Polish Army Corps. In 1944 he led the corps in battles in Italy (including the battle of Monte Cassino). After the war he remained in exile; 1946–54, commander in chief of the government-in-exile and political leader; member of the Council of Three and president of the National Treasury, one of the most prestigious émigré institutions.

ARCISZEWSKI, TOMASZ (1877–1955)—politician. Joined the Polish Socialist Party in 1896. During 1918–39 a PPS leader and opponent of Jozef Piłsudski. 1939–44, an organizer of the underground PPS-WRN. In 1944 parachuted into England, appointed deputy to President Raczkiewicz. 1944–47, prime minister of the government-in-exile; after 1947 in opposition to the government.

BERLING, ZYGMUNT (1896–1980)—army officer. During World War I fought with the Legions; in 1918 joined the Polish Army, rising through the ranks to become colonel. Arrested by the NKVD in September 193. Advocated cooperation with the Soviet Union. 1941–42, served in Anders's Army and remained in the USSR when it was evacuated to Iran. May 1943, appointed general and commander of Polish forces attached to the Red Army; May 1944, ousted from his command. 1945–47, worked in the Academy of the General Staff of the Soviet Army; in 1953 transferred to a civilian administrative position.

BERMAN, JAKUB (1901–84)—politician. Joined the communist party in 1928. Spent the period 1939–44 in the USSR; a member of the Central Bureau of Polish Communists. 1944–56, a member of the PPR and PZPR Politburo, responsible for security issues and ideology. Expelled from the PZPR in 1957.

BIERUT, BOLESŁAW (1892–1956)—politician. Joined the PPS-Left in 1912, the KPP in 1918. Studied at the International Lenin School in Moscow; 1930–32, Comintern emissary to several countries, including Bulgaria and Austria. 1933–38, imprisoned in Poland. Spent the period 1939–43 in the eastern provinces under Soviet occupation. 1943, became a member of the top leadership of the underground PPR. 1944–56, a member of the PPR and PZPR Politburo; 1944–47, chairman of the Presidium of the KRN; 1947–52, president of Poland; 1952–54, prime minister. In 1948 became the "Polish Stalin," the dictatorial leader of the communist party. Died in Moscow immediately after the Twentieth Congress of the CPSU.

CHRZANOWSKI, WIESŁAW (1923–)—lawyer, politician. Active in the wartime underground. 1945–48, president of the Christian Youth Union; 1948–55, imprisoned. In 1956 began working on Cardinal Wyszyński's staff. 1980–81, Solidarity adviser; 1981–84, member of the Primate's Social Council. In 1989 cofounded the Christian-National Union; subsequently held a number of prominent positions, including that of Sejm marshal, 1991–93.

CYRANKIEWICZ, JÓZEF (1911–89)—politician. PPS activist; 1939, co-organizer of PPS-WRN. Imprisoned in Auschwitz and Mauthausen concentration camps. 1945–48, a leader of the procommunist faction of the PPS; 1948–70, member of the PZPR Politburo; 1947–52 and 1954–70, prime minister. Sidelined after the strikes of December 1970.

GEREMEK, BRONISŁAW (1932–)—historian, politician. Specialist in medieval history. 1978, became active in the democratic opposition. Solidarity activist; interned after the imposition of martial law. 1983, became one of Wałęsa's key advisers; took part in the Round Table negotiations; 1989–90, chaired the parliamentary caucus of the Citizens' Committee. One of the most important leaders of the post-Solidarity center-left parties (Democratic Union, Freedom Union); minister of foreign affairs, 1997–2000.

GIEDROYC, JERZY (1906–2000)—politician, publisher. 1929–39, government employee and also publisher and editor of several conservative political periodicals. Lived abroad after 1939; served in the Polish Army during the war. 1942, began publishing and editing periodicals for the armed forces. 1947, founded in Paris the Instytut Literacki publishing house and the monthly journal *Kultura*, which he edited until the end of his life. He advocated the gradual transformation of the communist system into democracy and emphasized the need to cooperate with neighboring nations—Ukraine, Belarus, and Lithuania. *Kultura* became one of the most important Polish political publications; distributed within Poland after 1956, it was influential among opposition circles. After 1989 he decided to remain abroad and not once visited Poland.

GIEREK, EDWARD (1913–2001)—worker, politician. 1926–45, worked as a miner in France, Poland, and Belgium. Joined the communist party in 1931; 1948, returned permanently to Poland. PZPR activist; 1954–80, Central Committee member; 1956 and 1959–80, member of the Politburo. December 1970, became PZPR first secretary and introduced a program of modernization based on foreign loans. Dismissed in September 1980 after a wave of strikes; expelled from the PZPR in 1981. Interned after the imposition of martial law.

GLEMP, JÓZEF (1929–)—priest. Ordained 1956. 1967–79, a member of Cardinal Wyszyński's staff. 1979–81, Bishop of Warmia; succeeded Wyszyński as archbishop and Polish primate; 1983, ordained cardinal. Took part in negotiations with the government; 1981–89, mediated on numerous occasions between the PZPR and Solidarity.

GOMUŁKA, WŁADYSŁAW (1905–82)—politician. Joined the KPP in 1926; active in the communist trade unions; studied at the International Lenin School in Moscow; imprisoned several times in Poland. Spent the period 1939–41 in the eastern provinces, and from 1942 on on German-occupied territory. A member of the PPR's top decision-making bodies; 1944–48, general secretary of the PPR Central Committee; 1945–49, deputy prime minister and minister for the Reclaimed Territories; demoted in 1948; 1951, expelled from the PZPR, arrested and held in detention until December 1954. Returning to the PZPR leadership in 1956, he gained control of a society in turmoil, partly by launching the slogan of Polish sovereignty within the communist camp; wielded power in authoritarian fashion. Ousted from the leadership after the strikes of December 1970.

JANKOWSKI, JAN STANISŁAW (1882–1953)—politician. Cofounder of the National Workers' Union (1906); served in the Legions. During the period 1918–39 was active in center-right politics; appointed to several ministerial positions. 1939, joined the underground; 1943–45, served as government delegate to the homeland. Arrested by the NKVD, he was tried and sentenced in Moscow; died in prison in the USSR.

JAROSZEWICZ, PIOTR (1909–92)—teacher, politician. A teacher before World War II. 1940, was deported to the Soviet Union; 1943, joined the Polish Army in the Soviet Union. 1946–50, served as deputy minister of defense. From 1950 on occupied a succession of senior positions in the state administration; 1970–80, prime minister; 1981, expelled from the PZPR. Murdered, together with his wife, by unknown perpetrators.

JARUZELSKI, WOJCIECH (1923–)—army officer, politician. Deported to the Soviet Union in 1940. Joined the Polish Army in 1943; graduated from the Academy of the General Staff of the Polish Army; appointed general in 1956. 1960–65, served as chief of the armed forces' Main Political Board; 1965–68, chief of the General Staff; 1968, appointed minister of defense. 1964–89, a member of the PZPR Central committee; 1970–89, a member of the Politburo; 1981–89, first secretary of the PZPR; 1981–85, prime minister; 1985–89, chairman of the Council of State; 1989–90, president. Following the imposition of martial law (1981) wielded dictatorial power.

KISIELEWSKI, STEFAN (1911–91)—writer, politician. One of the leading independent journalists and writers of the postwar period; a regular contributor to the Catholic weekly, *Tygodnik Powszechny*. 1957–65, Sejm deputy representing the Catholic Znak group. The author of several novels dealing with political events in communist Poland; in 1968 publicly slandered by Gomułka and physically assaulted by "unknown perpetrators."

KOŁAKOWSKI, LESZEK (1927–)—philosopher. After a period of fascination with Marxism he became one of the leading revisionist philosophers. Expelled from the PZPR in 1966, he parted company with Marxism; 1970, emigrated to England. Published numerous philosophical works, including *Main Currents of Marxism,* translated into many languages. Frequently took part in political debates within the émigré community and the democratic opposition in Poland.

KUROŃ, JACEK (1934–)—politician. A leading Marxist-revisionist; in 1964 expelled from the PZPR and imprisoned. Leader of a group of young people who initiated the student strikes of 1968. One of the main organizers of the Workers' Defense Committee (1976); Solidarity activist; arrested after the imposition of martial law. Subsequently an adviser to Wałęsa, participant in the Round Table negotiations, and a minister in the Mazowiecki government. 1989–2000, a Sejm deputy.

MACIEREWICZ, ANTONI (1948–)—politician. Cofounder of KOR, publisher of illegal right-wing periodical, *Głos;* Solidarity activist, imprisoned 1981–82. In 1983 began to espouse radical anticommunist line and to oppose Wałęsa. 1989, a cofounder of Christian-National Union; subsequently joined other right-wing parties; minister of internal affairs in 1992; Sejm deputy 1991–93 and since 1997.

MACKIEWICZ, STANISŁAW (1886–1966)—writer, politician. A conservative and supporter of Piłsudski; publisher of one of the best political dailies in Poland. Went into exile in 1939. Was a member of the National Council and opposed to the conciliatory policy toward the Soviet Union. Prime minister of the government-in-exile 1954–55; returned to Poland in 1956. Subsequently harassed for his contacts with the émigré community.

MAZOWIECKI, TADEUSZ (1927–)—writer, politician. During the 1950s was active in the Catholic PAX association; in 1956 joined the independent Club of Catholic Intelligentsia and became editor of the monthly, *Więź.* Sejm deputy, 1961–72. 1977, became active in the democratic opposition; August 1980, acted as adviser to Gdańsk strike committee; 1981, appointed editor of Solidarity's official weekly; interned after the imposition of martial law. In 1983 became close adviser to Wałęsa; took part in Round Table negotiations. In August 1989 was appointed prime minister of coalition government. 1991–2000, Sejm deputy; leader of the centrist Democratic Union (subsequently, Freedom Union).

MAZUR, FRANCISZEK (1895–1975)—politician. Joined the communist movement in 1919. Spent the period 1917–30 in the Soviet Union; imprisoned after returning to Poland. Spent the first two years of the war in Soviet-occupied territory; 1941, moved to the Soviet Union. From 1945 on a member of the PPR and PZPR Central Committee; 1948–56, a member of the

Politburo. An *eminence grise* of the PZPR leadership, his responsibilities included policy toward the church. Sidelined after 1956.

MICHNIK, ADAM (1946–)—writer, politician. A leader of the younger generation of revisionists; arrested in 1968, cofounder of the democratic opposition, active in KOR, editor of the independent journal, *Krytyka.* 1980–81, active in Solidarity; imprisoned after the imposition of martial law; one of Wałęsa's closest advisers; participated in the Round Table negotiations. Sejm deputy, 1989–91. Founder (1989) and editor in chief of *Gazeta Wyborcza,* the largest-circulation daily in Poland. One of the most influential journalists in Poland; advocates establishing good relations with the postcommunists.

MIKOŁAJCZYK, STANISŁAW (1901–66)—politician. Joined the peasant movement in 1922; 1933–39, in the leadership of the Peasant Party. In 1939 went into exile. 1941–43, served as deputy prime minister, and 1943–44, as prime minister of the government-in-exile. In 1944 tried to reach an agreement with the Soviet Union. Took part in the Moscow talks of 1945. Condemned by most émigré groups, he accepted the post of deputy prime minister in the interim government dominated by the communists. President of the Polish Peasant Party and leader of the legal anticommunist opposition, under threat of arrest he fled in 1947 to the United States. Subsequently active in Polish and international émigré organizations.

MIŁOSZ, CZESŁAW (1911–)—poet. One of the leading poets of the younger generation and a radio journalist during the 1930s. After the war, entered the Polish diplomatic service; 1951, defected to the West. Author of *The Captive Mind,* a much-translated series of essays dealing with the response of intellectuals to communism, as well as many philosophical essays. 1961–78, professor at the University of California, Berkeley. Was awarded the Nobel Prize for Literature in 1980; extremely influential among opposition circles in Poland.

MINC, HILARY (1905–74)—politician, economist. Joined the communist movement in 1922. In 1939 moved to the Soviet Union, where he became one of the main organizers of the Union of Polish Patriots. In 1944 assumed de facto control of Poland's economic policy. During 1944–56 was member of the PPR and PZPR Politburo; during the period 1948–54 was one of the most influential persons in Poland, author of the six-year plan and the architect of rapid industrialization and collectivization of agriculture. Retired in 1956.

MOCZAR, MIECZYSŁAW (1913–86)—politician. Associated with the communist movement before the war. Recruited by Soviet intelligence in 1940; 1942, joined the PPR underground and commanded communist partisan units. 1944–81, was a member of PPR and PZPR Central Committee; member of the Politburo 1968–71 and 1980–81. During 1945–48 helped establish, and served in, the security apparatus; sidelined in 1948. Returned to prominence in 1956, served as deputy minister and minister of internal affairs, and president of the influential veterans' organization. Favored introducing nationalist elements into PZPR ideology and removing from the leadership party members of Jewish origin; leader of an informal group known as the Partisans. During 1964–71 was one of the most influential people in Poland.

MOCZULSKI, LESZEK (1930–)—politician, writer. In 1956 began associating with a group of former Piłsudski supporters. One of the founders of the opposition Movement in Defense of Human and Civil Rights (1977) and founder of the illegal Confederation for an Independent Poland (1979). 1980–86, imprisoned. One of the few opposition activists who did not become involved in Solidarity. 1991–97, Sejm deputy, but his party played no significant role in national politics.

OCHAB, EDWARD (1906–89)—politician. Joined the communist movement in 1929; was imprisoned in Poland. When war broke out, made his way to Soviet-occupied territory and then to the Soviet Union. 1944–68, a member of the PPR and PZPR Central Committee; 1948, became a member of the Politburo. One of Bierut's closest associates; after the death of the latter (1956) held position of first secretary for six months and then resigned in favor of Gomułka. 1968, resigned all his positions in protest against the anti-Semitic campaign waged by the authorities.

OKULICKI, LEOPOLD (1898–1946)—army officer. Served in the Legions, joined the Polish Army in 1918, and helped establish the Home Army in 1939. Arrested by the NKVD in 1941, he subsequently served in Anders's Army. In 1944 was smuggled into Poland, where he took part in the Warsaw uprising; after the uprising was crushed he evaded capture and became commander of the AK, which he disbanded in January 1945. Arrested by the NKVD, sentenced after a trial in Moscow, died in prison in the Soviet Union.

PIASECKI, BOLESŁAW (1915–79)—politician. Before the war, founder and leader of an extreme right-wing nationalist party, the National-Radical Camp. Joined the underground resistance in 1939; organized a political party, Confederation of the Nation. Arrested by the NKVD in 1944, he decided to collaborate with the communists, who agreed to let him form a Catholic association, PAX, and to publish a number of periodicals. Author of the notion that there is no fundamental contradiction between Catholicism and communism, in 1955 his writings were condemned by the Vatican. In 1964 he joined forces with nationalistic groups in the PZPR.

POPIEŁUSZKO, JERZY (1947–84)—priest. Chaplain to the Warsaw health service, in 1980 he helped striking workers; chaplain to Solidarity. After the imposition of martial law, he celebrated a monthly mass for the homeland; initiated the pilgrimages of factory workers to the monastery at Jasna Góra (Poland's major shrine). Fiercely attacked by government propaganda and harassed by the Security Service, in October 1984 he was brutally murdered by SB officials.

RACZKIEWICZ, WŁADYSŁAW (1885–1947)—politician. A leading Polish activist during the Russian Revolution of 1917. During interwar period held several prominent positions (minister, provincial administrator) and served as a senator and as chairman of the World Polish Congress. Emerged as compromise candidate to replace President Mościcki after the latter's forced resignation in 1939. Opposed the moderate line toward the Soviet Union advocated by Sikorski and Mikołajczyk. Remained in exile after the war. Shortly before his death reneged on agreement regarding his successor, which led to a long-lasting rift in the émigré community.

RAKOWSKI, MIECZYSŁAW (1926–)—politician, journalist. In 1949 began working in the PZPR Central Committee apparatus. Cofounder (1957), and until 1982 editor in chief, of the weekly *Polityka*, considered the mouthpiece of "party liberals." 1964–90, a member of the Central Committee. During the 1980s occupied a number of prominent positions; a close associate of General Jaruzelski; 1998–89, prime minister; the last first secretary of the PZPR. Since 1990 has devoted himself to journalism.

ROKOSSOWSKI, KONSTANTY (1886–1968)—army officer. Of Polish-Russian origin. Joined the Red Army in 1918. Imprisoned during 1937–40. During the period 1941–45 was one of the highest-ranking military commanders in the Soviet Union; appointed marshal in 1944. 1945–49, commanded Soviet troops stationed in Poland; 1949, appointed Polish minister of defense; 1950–56, was a member of the PZPR Politburo and one of the most influential persons in Poland. 1956, was dismissed from his post and returned to the Soviet Union.

ROWECKI, STEFAN (1895–1944)—army officer. 1914–17, fought in the Legions. In 1918 joined the Polish Army, serving as line officer and theoretician. In 1939 was the main organizer of the military underground; in June 1940 appointed commander of the Home Army. Arrested by the Gestapo in June 1943 and incarcerated in Sachsenhausen concentration camp, where he was murdered in August 1944.

SIKORSKI, WŁADYSŁAW (1881–1943)—army officer, politician. In 1908 began to play an active role in the independence movement; 1914–17, a member of the Supreme National Committee. In 1918 joined the Polish Army; commanded the Fifth Army in the war of 1920. During the years 1920–26 occupied a number of high-ranking positions, both military (including that of chief of the General Staff) and civilian (including that of prime minister). Fell out with Piłsudski after the coup of May 1926 and forced to resign from all positions. A frequent visitor to France, he grew closer to centrist opposition politicians and helped found the Labor Party (1937). 1939, went into exile; was appointed prime minister and commander in chief of the government-in-exile; advocated close cooperation with Great Britain and the United States and conciliatory approach to the Soviet Union. July 1943, died in a plane crash over Gibraltar, the cause of which remains unknown to this day.

SPYCHALSKI, MARIAN (1906–80)—architect, politician, army officer. Joined the communist movement in 1931 and became active in the underground PPR in 1942, helping to organize its military organization, the People's Guard. 1945–49, deputy minister of defense and member of the PPR and PZPR Politburo. Arrested in 1950 and charged with "rightist-nationalist deviation" (like Gomułka); released in March 1956. 1956–68, minister of defense; 1959–71, member of the Politburo. Ousted from all posts following the strikes of December 1970.

STOMMA, STANISŁAW (1908–)—politician, writer. Since 1946 one of Poland's leading Catholic politicians; author of what became known as neorealism, involving circumspect opposition political activity within the communist system. 1957–76, Sejm deputy, and the only one to abstain from voting in 1976 for the changes to the constitution (concerning the leading role of the PZPR and friendship with the Soviet Union). 1981–85, chaired the Primate's Social Council; founded (1984) the independent Club of Political Thought. Participated in the Round Table negotiations; 1989–91, senator.

TUROWICZ, JERZY (1912–2001)—journalist, politician. Before the war, was active in Catholic youth organizations. During 1945–53 and from 1956 until his death, editor in chief of the weekly *Tygodnik Powszechny*, the most important independent Catholic publication. Endorsed the notion of neorealism. Associated with the democratic opposition, and considered a major political and moral authority; took part in the 1989 Round Table negotiations.

WAŁĘSA, LECH (1943–)—worker, politician. In 1961, began working as electrician in a number of factories; 1967, began working at the Gdańsk Shipyard. Took part in the strike of December 1970; was detained and persuaded to collaborate (briefly) with the Security Service. 1978, helped organize the clandestine Free Trade Unions; August 1980, chaired the Inter-Factory Strike Committee. Cofounder and first chairman of Solidarity. Interned after the imposition of martial law; released in November 1982, he headed the then-illegal Solidarity. An advocate of reaching a compromise with the communists, he was awarded the Nobel Peace Prize in 1983, and in 1987 established the Citizens' Committee, made up of leading independent intellectuals and Solidarity activists. In August 1988 began discussions with the authorities; cochairman of the Round Table negotiations. August 1989, initiated the formation of a coalition government headed by a representative of Solidarity. During 1990–95 served as president; defeated in the elections of 1995. One of the most important symbols of the overthrow of communism.

WOJTYŁA, KAROL; JOHN PAUL II (1920–)—priest. Ordained in 1946, a philosopher and poet, seminary lecturer and professor at the Catholic University in Lublin. Ordained as bishop in 1958, and as archbishop of Kraków in 1964; 1969, appointed vice-chairman of the Polish Conference of Bishops; took an active part in the deliberations of the Second Vatican Council. His election as pope in October 1978 had an enormous impact on Poles, strengthening and broadening tendencies to resist the communist system, a process that was especially evident during his pilgrimages to Poland (1979, 1983, 1987).

WYSZYŃSKI, STEFAN (1901–81)—priest. Ordained in 1924. Alongside his activity in the ministry he was also active on social issues (including work in Christian trade unions). Chaplain to the AK during the war. In 1946 ordained as bishop of Lublin, in 1948 as archbishop of Warsaw and Polish primate; ordained cardinal in 1953. Advocated seeking a compromise with the communist authorities, coauthor of the agreement of 1950; interned 1953–56. After 1956, adopted a cautious policy, placing most emphasis on broad pastoral programs (such as the Great Novena of the Millennium) and trying to avoid conflicts with the authorities. Thanks to this, the church became both independent and exceptionally strong. During 1976–80 he encouraged some opposition activists; in August 1980 he called on striking workers to display moderation and subsequently issued the same call to Solidarity while simultaneously demanding that the authorities observe international treaties and human rights. Until 1978 he was one of Poland's most highly respected moral authorities (subsequently overshadowed by Pope John Paul II), referred to as the Primate of the Millennium.

ZALESKI, AUGUST (1883–1972)—diplomat, politician. During the years 1914–18 he was close to Piłsudski and headed the Polish lobby in London. Joined the diplomatic service in 1918; 1926–31, minister of foreign affairs and senator. Went into exile in 1939; 1939–41, minister of foreign affairs in the government-in-exile; resigned, refusing to sign the agreement with the Soviet Union; in 1947 Raczkiewicz named him his successor, and he took over as president on the death of the former, which gave rise to a long-standing conflict in the émigré community. Refused to consider a compromise and held office for twenty-five years; the conflict was resolved only after his death.

ŻYMIERSKI, MICHAŁ (1890–1989)—army officer. Began to play an active role in the independence movement in 1909. Fought in the Legions and joined the Polish Army in 1918; attained the rank of general in 1926. After the coup of May 1926 was ousted from all his posts, arrested, and in 1927 demoted and discharged from the army and sentenced to five years' imprisonment on charges of embezzlement during his tenure as head of the administration of the Polish Army. Spent the years 1932–38 in France, where he established contact with Soviet military intelligence; after the outbreak of war he attempted to become involved in the military underground, but it was not until 1943 that he became adviser to, and in January 1944 commander of, the communist military organization. Appointed minister of defense in July 1944; a clandestine PPR member, he was made a marshal in 1945; sidelined in 1949, imprisoned 1953–55. After 1956 he did not return to the army, but held a succession of secondary, titular positions.

Bibliography of English-Language Work on Recent Polish History

In this bibliography, I have tried to include all work that offers a more detailed look at topics in Polish history since 1939. Three kinds of works are omitted: first, general surveys of the era; second, memoirs (though these often provide the best look at certain events); and third, novels (about some of which the same could be said). I have also made an effort to include representative works by every historian currently working in Britain and North America on this era.

—Padraic Kenney

THEMATIC WORKS

Checinski, Michael. *Poland: Communism, Nationalism, Anti-Semitism.* New York: Karz-Cohl, 1982.

Curry, Jane Leftwich, and Luba Fajfer, eds. *Poland's Permanent Revolution: People vs. Elites, 1956–1990.* Washington, D.C.: American University Press, 1996.

Hoffman, Eva. *Shtetl: The Life and Death of a Small Town and the World of Polish Jews.* Boston: Houghton Mifflin, 1997.

Karski, Jan. *The Great Powers and Poland, 1919–1945.* Lanham, Md.: University Press of America, 1985.

Landau, Zbigniew, and Jerzy Tomaszewski. *The Polish Economy in the Twentieth Century.* Trans. Wojciech Roszkowski. New York: St. Martin's Press, 1985.

Legters, Lyman H., ed. *Eastern Europe. Transformation and Revolution, 1945–1991. Documents and Analyses.* Lexington, Mass.: D. C. Heath, 1992.

Michta, Andrew. *Red Eagle: The Army in Polish Politics, 1944–1988.* Stanford, Calif.: Hoover Institution Press, 1990.

Polonsky, Antony. *Politics in Independent Poland, 1921–1939: The Crisis of Constitutional Government.* Oxford: Clarendon Press, 1972.

Ryback, Timothy W. *Rock Around the Bloc: A History of Rock Music in Eastern Europe and the Soviet Union.* New York: Oxford University Press, 1990.

Shelton, Anita. "The Poles and the Search for a National Homeland." In *Eastern European Nationalism in the Twentieth Century,* ed. Peter Sugar. Lanham, Md.: American University Press, 1995, 243–71.

Steinlauf, Michael C. *Bondage of the Dead: Poland and the Memory of the Holocaust.* Syracuse: Syracuse University Press, 1997.

Stokes, Gale, ed. *From Stalinism to Pluralism: A Documentary History of Eastern Europe since 1945.* 2d ed. New York: Oxford University Press, 1996.

Szajkowski, Bogdan. *Next to God—Poland: Politics and Religion in Contemporary Poland.* London: Frances Pinter, 1983.

Wedel, Janine. *The Private Poland: An Anthropologist's Look at Everyday Life.* New York: Facts on File, 1986.

———, ed. *The Unplanned Society: Poland During and After Communism.* New York: Columbia University Press, 1990.

de Weydenthal, Jan B. *The Communists of Poland: An Historical Outline.* Rev. ed. Stanford, Calif.: Hoover Institution Press, 1986.

Wróbel, Piotr. *Historical Dictionary of Poland, 1945–1996.* Westport, Conn.: Greenwood Press, 1998.

CHAPTER 1: WORLD WAR II

Cienciala, Anna M. "The Activities of Polish Communists as a Source for Stalin's Policy Toward Poland in World War II." *International History Review* 7, no. 1 (1985): 129–45.

Dobroszycki, Lucjan. *Reptile Journalism: The Official Polish-Language Press under the Nazis, 1939–1945.* New Haven: Yale University Press, 1994.

Engel, David. *Facing A Holocaust: The Polish Government-in-Exile and the Jews, 1943–1945.* Chapel Hill: University of North Carolina Press, 1993.

Engel, David. *In the Shadow of Auschwitz: The Polish Government-in-Exile and the Jews, 1939–1942.* Chapel Hill: University of North Carolina Press, 1987.

Garlinski, Józef. *Fighting Auschwitz: The Resistance Movement in the Concentration Camp.* London: Julian Friedmann, 1975.

———. *Poland in the Second World War.* New York: Hippocrene, 1985.

Gross, Jan T. *Neighbors: The Destruction of the Jewish Community in Jed-wabne, Poland.* Princeton: Princeton University Press, 2001.

———. *Polish Society under German Occupation: The General-gouverne-ment, 1939–1944.* Princeton: Princeton University Press, 1979.

———. *Revolution from Abroad. The Soviet Conquest of Poland's Western Ukraine and Western Belorussia.* Princeton: Princeton University Press, 1988.

Gutman, Yisrael. *The Jews of Warsaw, 1939–1943: Ghetto, Underground, Re-volt.* Trans. Ina Friedman. Bloomington: Indiana University Press, 1982.

Jolluck, Katherine R. *Exile and Identity: Polish Women in the Soviet Union During World War II.* Pittsburgh: University of Pittsburgh Press, 2002.

Korbonski, Stefan. *The Polish Underground State: A Guide to the Under-ground, 1939–1944.* Boulder, Colo.: East European Monographs, 1978.

Krakowski, Shmuel. *The War of the Doomed: Jewish Armed Resistance in Po-land, 1942–1944.* Trans. Orah Blaustein. New York: Holmes and Meier, 1984.

Lukas, Richard C. *The Forgotten Holocaust: The Poles under German Occu-pation, 1939–1944.* Louisville: University Press of Kentucky, 1986.

Paul, Allen. *Katyn: The Untold Story of Stalin's Polish Massacre.* New York: Charles Scribner's Sons, 1991.

Peszke, Michael Alfred. *Battle for Warsaw, 1939–1944.* Boulder, Colo.: East European Monographs, 1995.

Polonsky, Antony, ed. *The Great Powers and the Polish Question, 1941–1945.* London: London School of Economics and Political Science, 1976; dis-tributed by Orbis Books.

———, ed. *Polin Thirteen: Focusing on the Holocaust and Its Aftermath.* Stud-ies in Polish Jewry, vol. 13. London: Littman Library of Jewish Civili-zation, 2000.

Prazmowska, Anita. *Britain and Poland, 1939–1943: The Betrayed Ally.* Cam-bridge: Cambridge University Press, 1995.

Sword, Keith. *Deportation and Exile: Poles in the Soviet Union, 1939–48.* New York: St. Martin's Press, 1994.

———, ed. *The Soviet Takeover of the Polish Eastern Provinces, 1939–41.* New York: St. Martin's Press, 1991.

Terry, Sarah Meiklejohn. *Poland's Place in Europe: General Sikorski and the Origins of the Oder-Neisse Line, 1939–1943*. Princeton: Princeton University Press, 1983.

Zamoyski, Adam. *The Forgotten Few: The Polish Air Force in the Second World War*. New York: Hippocrene, 1996.

Zawodny, Janusz K. *Death In The Forest: The Story of the Katyn Forest Massacre*. Notre Dame: University of Notre Dame Press, 1962.

CHAPTER 2: "TWO POLANDS"

Ciechanowski, Jan M. *The Warsaw Rising of 1944*. New York: Cambridge University Press, 1974.

Cienciala, Anna M. "The Diplomatic Background of the Warsaw Rising of 1944: The Players and the Stakes." *Polish Review*, 39, no. 4 (1994): 393–413.

Coutovidis, John, and Jaime Reynolds. *Poland, 1939–1947*. New York: Holmes and Meier, 1986.

Dziewanowski, M. K. *The Communist Party of Poland: An Outline of History*. 2d ed. Cambridge: Harvard University Press, 1976.

Hanson, Joanna K.M. *The Civilian Population and the Warsaw Uprising of 1944*. Cambridge: Cambridge University Press, 1982.

Naimark, Norman, and Leonid Gibianskii, eds. *The Establishment of Communist Regimes in Eastern Europe, 1944–1949*. Boulder, Colo.: Westview Press, 1997.

Polonsky, Antony, and Boleslaw Drukier, eds. *The Beginnings of Communist Rule in Poland, December 1943–June 1945*. London: Routledge, 1980.

Schatz, Jaff. *The Generation: The Rise and Fall of the Jewish Communists in Poland*. Berkeley and Los Angeles: University of California Press, 1991.

CHAPTER 3: "A NEW REALITY"

Bromke, Adam. *Poland's Politics: Idealism vs. Realism*. Cambridge: Harvard University Press, 1967.

Grzymala-Busse, Anna. "The Organizational Strategies of Communist Parties in East Central Europe, 1945–1989." *East European Politics and Societies* 15, no. 2 (2001): 421–53.

Kenney, Padraic. *Rebuilding Poland: Workers and Communists, 1945–1950*. Ithaca: Cornell University Press, 1997.

Kersten, Krystyna. *The Establishment of Communist Rule in Poland, 1943–1947*. Berkeley and Los Angeles: University of California Press, 1991.

Snyder, Timothy. "To Resolve the Ukrainian Problem Once and for All": The Ethnic Cleansing of Ukrainians in Poland, 1943–1947." *Journal of Cold War Studies* 1, no. 2 (spring 1999): 86–120.

Ther, Philipp, and Ana Siljak, eds. *Redrawing Nations: Ethnic Cleansing in East-Central Europe, 1944–1948*. Lanham, Md.: Rowman and Littlefield, 2001.

CHAPTER 4: BUILDING THE FOUNDATIONS

Anderson, Sheldon R. *A Cold War in the Soviet Bloc: Polish-East German Relations, 1945–1962*. Boulder, Colo.: Westview Press, 2001.

Connelly, John. *Captive University: The Sovietization of German, Czech and Polish Higher Education, 1945–1956*. Chapel Hill: University of North Carolina Press, 2001.

Crowley, David. "Warsaw's Shops, Stalinism and the Thaw." In *Style and Socialism: Modernity and Material Culture in Postwar Eastern Europe*, ed. Susan E. Reid and David Crowley. Oxford: Berg, 2000.

Gluchowski, L. W., ed. "Poland, 1956: Khrushchev, Gomulka, and the 'Polish October.'" *Cold War International History Project Bulletin* 5 (spring 1995): 1, 38–49.

Granville, Johanna. "Satellites or Prime Movers? Polish and Hungarian Reactions to the 1956 Events: New Archival Evidence." *East European Quarterly* 35, no. 4 (winter 2001): 435–71.

Hubner, Piotr. "The Last Flight of Pegasus: The Story of the Polish Academy of Science and Letters and the Warsaw Scientific Society, 1945–1952." *East European Politics and Societies* 13, no. 1 (winter 1999): 71–116.

Kemp-Welch, A., ed. *Stalinism in Poland 1944–1956*. New York: St. Martin's Press, 1999.

Korbonski, Andrzej. *Politics of Socialist Agriculture in Poland, 1945–1960*. New York: Columbia University Press, 1965.

Lebow, Katherine A. "Public Works, Private Lives: Youth Brigades in Nowa Huta in the 1950s." *Contemporary European History* 10, no. 2 (2001): 199–219.

Lewis, Flora A. *A Case History of Hope: The Story of Poland's Peaceful Revolution*. New York: Doubleday, 1958.

Syrop, Konrad. *Spring in October: The Story of the Polish Revolution in October 1956*. London: Weidenfeld and Nicolson, 1958.

Toranska, Teresa. *Them: Stalin's Polish Puppets*. Trans. Agnieszka Kolakowska. New York: Harper and Row, 1987.

Zinner, Paul, ed. *National Communism and Popular Revolt in Eastern Europe.* New York: Columbia University Press, 1956.

CHAPTER 5: REAL SOCIALISM: THE FIRM HAND

Bethell, Nicholas W. *Gomulka, His Poland, and His Communism.* Harlow: Longmans, 1969.

Diskin, Hanna. *The Seeds of Triumph: Church and State in Gomulka's Poland.* Budapest: Central European University Press, 2001.

Hiscocks, Richard. *Poland: Bridge for an Abyss? An Interpretation of Developments in Post-War Poland,* Oxford: Oxford University Press, 1963.

Kostrzewa, Robert, ed. *Between East and West: Writings from Kultura.* New York: Hill and Wang, 1990.

CHAPTER 6: REAL SOCIALISM: LA BELLE ÉPOQUE

Bernhard, Michael H. *The Origins of Democratization in Poland: Workers, Intellectuals and Oppositional Politics, 1976–1980.* New York: Columbia University Press, 1993.

Kenney, Padraic. "The Gender of Resistance in Communist Poland." *American Historical Review,* 104, no. 2 (April 1999): 399–425.

Lane, David, and George Kolankiewicz. *Social Groups in Polish Society.* New York: Columbia University Press, 1973.

Lepak, Keith John. *Prelude to Solidarity: Poland and the Politics of the Gierek Regime.* New York: Columbia University Press, 1988.

Lipski, Jan Jozef. *KOR: The Workers' Defense Committee in Poland, 1976–1981.* Berkeley and Los Angeles: University of California Press, 1985.

Raina, Peter, ed. *Political Opposition in Poland, 1954–1977.* London: Poets and Painters Press, 1978.

Simon, Maurice D., and Roger F. Kanet, eds. *Background to Crisis: Policy and Politics in Gierek's Poland.* Boulder, Colo.: Westview Press, 1981.

Taras, Ray. *Ideology in a Socialist State: Poland, 1956–1983,* Cambridge: Cambridge University Press, 1984.

Tokes, Rudolf F., ed. *Opposition in Eastern Europe.* Baltimore: Johns Hopkins University Press, 1979.

CHAPTER 7: THE LONG MARCH; PROLOGUE

Ascherson, Neal. *The Polish August: The Self-Limiting Revolution.* Harmondsworth, UK: Penguin, 1981.

Ash, Timothy Garton. *The Polish Revolution: Solidarity.* New York: Random House, 1984.

Bernhard, Michael, and Henryk Szlajfer, eds. *From the Polish Underground: Selections from Krytyka, 1978–1993.* Trans. Maria Chmielewska-Szlajfer. University Park: Pennsylvania State University Press, 1995.

Boyes, Roger. *The Naked President: A Political Life of Lech Walesa.* London: Secker and Warburg, 1994.

Brumberg, Abraham, ed. *Poland: Genesis of a Revolution.* New York: Random House, 1983.

Cirtautas, Arista Maria. *The Polish Solidarity Movement: Revolution, Democracy and Natural Rights.* New York: Routledge, 1997.

Curry, Jane Leftwich. *Dissent in Eastern Europe.* New York: Praeger Press, 1983.

de Weydenthal, Jan B., Bruce D. Porter, and Kevin Devlin. *The Polish Drama, 1980–1982.* Lexington, Mass.: Lexington Books, 1983.

Ekiert, Grzegorz. *The State Against Society: Political Crises and Their Aftermath in East Central Europe.* Princeton: Princeton University Press, 1996.

Goodwyn, Lawrence. *Breaking the Barrier: The Rise of Solidarity in Poland.* New York: Oxford University Press, 1991.

Kemp-Welch, A., ed. and trans. *The Birth of Solidarity: The Gdansk Negotiations, 1980.* New York: St. Martin's Press, 1983.

Kennedy, Michael D. *Professionals, Power, and Solidarity in Poland: A Critical Sociology of Soviet-Type Society.* New York: Cambridge University Press, 1991.

Kubik, Jan. *The Power of Symbols Against the Symbols of Power: The Rise of Solidarity and the Fall of State Socialism in Poland.* University Park: Pennsylvania State University Press, 1994.

Laba, Roman. *The Roots of Solidarity: A Political Sociology of Poland's Working Class Democratization.* Princeton: Princeton University Press, 1991.

Mason, David S. *Public Opinion and Political Change in Poland, 1980–1982.* Cambridge: Cambridge University Press, 1985.

Osa, Maryjane. "Creating Solidarity: The Religious Foundations of the Polish Social Movement." *Eastern European Politics and Societies* 11, no. 2 (1997): 339.

Ost, David. *Solidarity and the Politics of Anti-Politics: Opposition and Reform in Poland Since 1968.* Philadelphia: Temple University Press, 1990.

Staniszkis, Jadwiga. *Poland's Self-Limiting Revolution.* Princeton: Princeton University Press, 1984.

Touraine, Alain, Francois Dubet, Michel Wiewiorka, and Jan Strzelecki. *Solidarity: The Analysis of a Social Movement. Poland, 1980–81.* Trans. David Denby. Cambridge: Cambridge University Press, 1983.

de Weydenthal, J. B., ed. *August 1980. The Strikes in Poland,* Munich: Radio Free Europe, 1980.

CHAPTER 8: THE LONG MARCH: WAR AND PEACE

Byrne, Malcolm, ed. "New Evidence on the Polish Crisis, 1980–81." *Cold War International History Project Bulletin* 11 (winter 1998): 3–133.

Coughlan, Elizabeth P. "Polish Peculiarities? Military Loyalty During the 1980–1981 Solidarity Crisis." *Carl Beck Papers in Russian and East European Studies,* 1401. Pittsburgh: Center for Russian and East European Studies, University of Pittsburgh, 2000.

Curry, Jane Leftwich, trans. and ed. *The Black Book of Polish Censorship.* New York: Random House, 1984.

Flam, Helena. *Mosaic of Fear: Poland and East Germany Before 1989.* Boulder, Colo.: East European Monographs, 1998.

Garton Ash, Timothy. *The Magic Lantern: The Revolution of '89 Witnessed in Warsaw, Budapest, Berlin and Prague.* New York: Random House, 1990.

Glenn, John K., III. *Framing Democracy: Civil Society and Civic Movements in Eastern Europe.* Stanford: Stanford University Press, 2001.

Gross, Jan. "Poland: From Civil Society to Political Nation." In *Eastern Europe In Revolution,* ed. Ivo Banac. Ithaca: Cornell University Press, 1992.

Grzymala-Busse, Anna. *Redeeming the Communist Past: The Regeneration of Communist Parties in East Central Europe.* Cambridge: Cambridge University Press, 2002.

Hahn, Werner G. *Democracy in a Communist Party: Poland's Experience since 1980.* New York: Columbia University Press, 1987.

Hann, C. M. *A Village Without Solidarity: Polish Peasants in Years of Crisis.* New Haven: Yale University Press, 1985.

Hicks, Barbara. *Environmental Politics in Poland: A Social Movement Between Regime and Opposition.* New York: Columbia University Press, 1996.

Holc, Janine P. "Solidarity and the Polish State: Competing Discursive Strategies on the Road to Power." *East European Politics and Societies* 6, no. 2 (spring 1992): 121–40.

Kennedy, Michael, and Brian Porter, eds. *Negotiating Radical Change: Understanding and Extending the Lessons of the Polish Round Table Talks.* Ann Arbor: University of Michigan, 2000.

Kenney, Padraic. *A Carnival of Revolution: Central Europe, 1989.* Princeton: Princeton University Press, 2002.

Korbonski, Andrzej. "East Central Europe on the Eve of the Changeover: The Case of Poland." *Communist and Post-Communist Studies* 32, no. 2 (June 1999): 139–53.

Kurczewski, Jacek. *The Resurrection of Rights in Poland.* Oxford: Clarendon Press, 1993.

Lewis, Paul G. *Political Authority and Party Secretaries in Poland, 1975–1986.* New York: Cambridge University Press, 1989.

Lopinski, Maciej, Marcin Moskit, and Mariusz Wilk. *Konspira: Solidarity Underground.* Berkeley and Los Angeles: University of California Press, 1990.

MacEachin, Douglas J. *U.S. Intelligence and the Polish Crisis: 1980–1981.* Washington, D.C.: Center for the Study of Intelligence, 2000.

Machcewicz, Pawel. "Poland, 1986–1989: From 'Cooptation' to 'Negotiated Revolution.'" *Cold War International History Project Bulletin* 12/13 (fall/winter 2001): 93–130.

Matynia, Elzbieta. "Furnishing Democracy at the End of the Century: The Polish Round Table and Others." *East European Politics and Societies* 15, no. 2 (spring 2001): 454–71.

Michnik, Adam. *Letters from Prison and Other Essays.* Ed. and trans. Maya Latynski. Berkeley and Los Angeles: University of California Press, 1985.

Rachwald, Arthur R. *In Search Of Poland: The Superpowers' Response to Solidarity, 1980–1989.* Stanford: Hoover Institution Press, 1990.

Tittenbrun, Jacek. *The Collapse of 'Real Socialism' in Poland.* London: Janus, 1993.

EPILOGUE: POSTCOMMUNISM

Ekiert, Grzegorz, and Jan Kubik. *Rebellious Civil Society: Popular Protest and Democratic Consolidation in Poland, 1989–1993.* Ann Arbor: University of Michigan Press, 1999.

Michnik, Adam. *Letters from Freedom: Post-Cold War Realities and Perspec-*

tives. Ed. Irena Gruzinska Gross. Berkeley and Los Angeles: University of California Press, 1998.

Millard, Frances. *Polish Politics and Society.* New York: Routledge, 1999.

Rosenberg, Tina. *The Haunted Land: Facing Europe's Ghosts After Communism.* New York: Random House, 1995.

Slay, Ben. *The Polish Economy: Crisis, Reform, and Transformation.* Princeton: Princeton University Press, 1994.

Wydra, Harald. *Continuities in Poland's Permanent Transition.* New York: St. Martin's Press, 2000.

Index

JN
6760
.P33

DATE DUE

APR - 8 2010		